BERENSON'S
ITALIAN PICTURES
OF THE RENAISSANCE

PHAIDON

RAPHAEL: *Fresco: The School of Athens*. Detail. Rome, Vatican, Stanza della Segnatura. *1509–11. Cf. Plate 1185.*

ITALIAN PICTURES
OF THE
RENAISSANCE

A LIST OF THE PRINCIPAL ARTISTS
AND THEIR WORKS
WITH AN INDEX OF PLACES

BY

BERNARD BERENSON

CENTRAL ITALIAN AND
NORTH ITALIAN SCHOOLS
IN THREE VOLUMES

VOLUME I

TEXT

PHAIDON

LISTS OF WORKS BY ITALIAN RENAISSANCE PAINTERS FIRST PUBLISHED IN
1897 (CENTRAL ITALIAN PAINTERS) AND 1907 (NORTH ITALIAN PAINTERS)
REVISED EDITION 1932
ALL RIGHTS RESERVED

NEWLY REVISED AND ILLUSTRATED 1968
ADDITIONAL AND REVISED MATERIAL © PHAIDON PRESS LTD · LONDON 1968

PHAIDON PUBLISHERS INC · NEW YORK
DISTRIBUTORS IN THE UNITED STATES: FREDERICK A. PRAEGER INC
111 FOURTH AVENUE · NEW YORK · N.Y. 10003
LIBRARY OF CONGRESS CATALOG CARD NUMBER: 68-18905

SBN for complete set of three volumes: 7148 1324 9

SBN for this volume: 7148 1354 0

MADE IN GREAT BRITAIN
TEXT PRINTED BY R. & R. CLARK LTD · EDINBURGH
ILLUSTRATIONS PRINTED BY LONSDALE & BARTHOLOMEW LTD · LEICESTER

THIS VOLUME

HAS BEEN PRODUCED

IN COLLABORATION WITH

THE SAMUEL H · KRESS FOUNDATION

AS A TRIBUTE TO

BERNARD BERENSON

AND IN APPRECIATION OF

MORE THAN A QUARTER CENTURY

OF FRIENDSHIP AND CO-OPERATION

IN THE FIELD OF RENAISSANCE PAINTING

BETWEEN BERNARD BERENSON AND

SAMUEL H · KRESS

CONTENTS

VOLUME II

PLATES

THE ROMANESQUE AND EARLY GOTHIC PERIODS

1–495

THE LATE GOTHIC PERIOD

496–618

THE TRANSITION FROM GOTHIC TO RENAISSANCE IN CENTRAL ITALY

619–687

THE EARLY RENAISSANCE

688–994

VOLUME III

PLATES

THE EARLY AND HIGH RENAISSANCE

995–1988

PREFACE

T HAT in spite of serious difficulties Bernard Berenson's Lists of Central and North Italian Renaissance Pictures should be ready to appear in this fully revised and illustrated edition is more than I ever dared to expect. B.B. himself, when in his 88th year the agreement between him and the Phaidon Press was signed, never envisaged the possibility of *seeing* the task completed: all he hoped for, was to get out the first volumes. And he did in fact manage to revise the whole of the Venetian group and part of the Florentine one. For the Central and North Italians all we had, to carry on the work after his death, were additions and corrections made by him for over twenty years and the possibility of including a number of pictures left out in the editions of 1932 and 1936 because of their being in the trade. Now, in accordance with the new system adopted by B.B., they have been quoted either under the name of the former owner or as 'homeless'.

My own contribution to the revision has been very small, consisting only of some assistance and advice given to Carla Alessandri during her preparatory work. Then Luisa Vertova took over and has carried through the whole revision with scrupulous accuracy. As I anticipate alarm and criticism for any change in Berenson's attributions, I want to make it clear that she also had my full approval to make further corrections whenever she felt that B.B., were he still there to decide, would have readily accepted a correction due to further study or to the discovery of new documents and dates. Both Luisa Vertova and I knew B.B.'s system of working based on trial, error and correction of error too well not to know that he would not have wanted his Lists to be fossilized. There was nothing he hated more than scholastic pedantry; and as such he would have regarded the rigid preservation of an error.

I am happy to use this occasion for expressing my gratitude to Luisa Vertova for her indefatigable and loving dedication to the task and to all those who have given her assistance in procuring material and information; to the Phaidon Press for its willingness to complete the publication, adding an extra volume to those originally agreed upon, and particularly to Dr. I. Grafe for his useful cooperation; to the Kress Foundation for making this publication financially possible through another generous grant; to the staff of the Berenson Library for their helpfulness, and to Professor Murdoch, at the time its director, for the facilities extended to Luisa Vertova during her work on the revision.

San Martino a Mensola, April 1967   N ICKY M ARIANO

INTRODUCTION

A CONCORDANCE of the Berenson Lists, from the very select choice of pictures mentioned in the privately printed *Golden Urn* to the present edition, which Berenson decided upon in his eighty-eighth year, would be welcome. It would cast a revealing light on the increasing complexity of art-historical studies as well as on B.B.'s keen interest not only in major artistic personalities, but also in minor painters, remote from the great creative centres of visual art. This interest he never lost, tempered though it was by scepticism about the hypotheses of connoisseurship. In his introduction to the 1938 edition of the *Drawings* he insists on the provisional value of most attributions (see also here at p. xxv) and in later years he grew increasingly indifferent to the game of naming a father for every picture—to the very pursuit, indeed, that used to thrill him in his youth. The rise and fall of civilizations, the trend of a visual culture, the timeless quality of an artistic creation and the documentary significance of an artifact—these were the themes on which his mind preferred to linger toward the end of his life. His readers and his friends may have been led to assume a decisive shift of interest from connoisseurship to problems of broad historical import; and yet the very fact that he agreed to undertake a new edition for the Phaidon Press in full awareness that he 'might never see even the first volume of the new Lists in print' proves that he went on believing in the Lists as a stimulating instrument of research, whatever their occasional shortcomings.

The material turned over to me by Nicky Mariano in December 1963 for the compilation of the revised Lists of Northern and Central Italian Pictures of the Renaissance was a far cry from the text published by the Oxford University Press in 1932. The latter reflected Berenson's thought up to the end of the twenties, but his critical activity did not stop at that date. He was just as eager to demolish an 'Amico di Sandro' as he had been proud to create him, and never felt obliged to stick by an attribution because he had once believed in it. The changes between his first 'Indexes of Works by Italian Renaissance Painters'[1] and the Oxford edition of 1932 are evidence enough that he did not consider himself bound by what he had once stated in print. They also show that he had been bitten by an ambitious desire to cover the complete extant work of a master, including the products of his workshop and of his imitators. This expansionist tendency may have been aroused in him by the new stirring of his later interest in the general development of the arts through the ages; and it may have been prompted—on the practical level—by the facility he had by then acquired of obtaining assistance from more than one secretary. This

[1] Central Italian Painters 1897; revised and enlarged 1909, the same year when his book on Sassetta appeared; reprinted 1911. North Italian Painters 1907, reprinted 1910.

advantage proved, however, a double-edged weapon, for the typing out of notes often resulted only in confusion and inadvertent duplication.

In his first Lists Berenson intended to record the secure and typical works by a painter and his prefaces (see at pp. xix and xxi) categorically reject any claim to completeness. In the Oxford edition of 1932 the ideal of completeness was accepted, but it was seriously compromised in a subtly damaging way by the rule to omit all the picture on the market or supposedly so.

The *Pitture italiane del Rinascimento* (Milano, Hoepli, 1936) was a translation from the English text of 1932; it contained many corrections and some occasional additions, but did not constitute a new edition. This reminder is essential in view of the fact that in 1933 the famous Ferrara Exhibition took place, when many a Ferrarese problem was reconsidered. Berenson discussed at length with his friend Carlo Gamba the plausibility of artists such as 'Ercole Grandi' and 'Leonardo Scaletti'. He eventually exploded the first of these two lists and accepted Philip Pouncey's conclusions about the Strozzi Altarpiece. He had hoped to build up a fascinating artist on the assumption of the common authorship of two paintings at Faenza which constitute the whole of the Scaletti List of 1909 (see also his preface to the 1909 Lists, here reproduced on p. xx). Since no younger man ventured into the field, he himself put forward a tentative Scaletti list in the Oxford edition of 1932, capped by a defiant 'biography' of Scaletti himself. But that buoyant assurance is contradicted by all the Berenson notes and remarks on the back of the 'Scaletti' photographs—to such an extent that I have wondered whether he did not contemplate denying his own creation. For that reason I have omitted the 1932/36 Scaletti List from this edition.

In 1935 the exhibition devoted to fourteenth-century artists active in and around Rimini stirred up an unprecedented interest in that school of painting. Controversy as to the different personalities at work in the frescoed churches and monasteries of Ravenna, Rimini, Pomposa and Tolentino continued till after World War II, although by then many frescoes had been obliterated by bombing and could be studied only from photographs. I remember Berenson's scepticism when he talked about the efforts of grouping those exquisite panels and attractive frescoes under the names of definite 'masters'. He did accept the distinction between Giovanni da Rimini and Giovanni Baronzio da Rimini, but maintained that it was a hopeless task to identify personalities when they merge to such a degree into the choral style of a closely knit production. This is why, in the present edition, the lists of Francesco, Giovanni, Giuliano, Pietro and Baronzio are very short and the remaining paintings are grouped together in a single list.

The year 1938 saw the Melozzo Exhibition at Forlì, which was so useful for the better understanding of Romagnol painting of the Quattrocento. In 1939 three fundamental exhibitions took place: in Milan ('Leonardo da Vinci'), Turin ('Il Gotico e il

Rinascimento in Piemonte') and Brescia ('La Pittura Bresciana del Rinascimento')
offering stimuli for further research into the field of the Milanese followers of
Leonardo and of North Italian Renaissance painting in general. Berenson profited
from all three.

Alas! The tragedy of World War II meant the loss of a whole decade of studies. I
met Berenson for the first time while he was a prisoner in his own beautiful villa,
and I became his assistant in the autumn of 1945. My work proceeded steadily and
quietly and was mostly concerned with sorting out Berenson's photographic material
and bringing it up to date. At first there was no idea of *publishing* revised Berenson
Lists. After some years, however, the founder of the Phaidon Press, the late Bela
Horovitz, raised the possibility of preparing a new edition of the Lists with Berenson
and Nicky Mariano; and I was entrusted by Berenson with the responsibility of
assisting his literary executor Nicky Mariano in the editing of the Lists after his death.

The 'Bible' of the Berenson attributions was a copy of the Italian edition of the
Lists (1936) which soon became illegible from the many corrections. An attempt was
made to transfer them neatly on to a new copy, but before the year 1948, when I
was first sent abroad to check the post-war whereabouts of pictures known to B.B.
(whether 'listed' or not) it proved necessary to have this much-handled book typed
out. The material handed to me in 1963 by Nicky Mariano was therefore a type-
script, to be rechecked against the photographs in the Berenson Library and against
his own notes. Not a single letter sent by Berenson to curators of galleries, private
collectors, dealers or auctioneers was ever seen by me. Occasionally a collector has
informed me about such a letter being in his possession, and I have noticed in recent
sale catalogues that pictures are being sold with a Berenson attribution. Unfortunately Berenson used to write his letters in long-hand and kept no record of them.
He also warned me that he was shown more than once typed letters with his signature
forged. Both Nicky Mariano and myself were occasionally asked to acknowledge
receipt of photographs, mentioning Berenson's opinion, but like our master we kept
no copies. So I was bound to base myself mainly on what was written on notes and
photographs available to me in his Library and I can only express my regret if the
misplacement of any of them results in the loss of an important Berenson attribution.

Berenson was a keen collector of photographs of pictures in private hands or outside Italy, but he scarcely bothered to document himself on pictures located in the
Peninsula, for those he could reach without great effort. He enjoyed the journeys,
and he trusted his eyes better than the supposedly 'safe' mechanical eye of the camera
(see his own preface on p. xxi below). Venetian, Florentine, Ferrarese and Sienese
pictures of the Renaissance have crossed the Italian frontier in great number, but
the secondary artists of other schools are still largely represented in their original
provinces: the art historian must go to Gualdo Tadino to form his opinion of the
work of Matteo da Gualdo. Unfortunately I was unable to travel extensively for the

compilation of these revised Lists nor was it always possible to elicit an answer from the local priests or authorities. In some cases, however, I was kindly informed that the painting I was looking for, although invisible, still existed behind a huge modern canvas[1] or inside an elaborate gilt shrine.[2] In other cases, paintings believed to have been destroyed suddenly turned up. For instance: I was generously helped with information at the Milanese Soprintendenza by Dr Franco Mazzini, who assured me (against the opinion of many who insisted that 'it had never existed') that he well remembered a chapel at Garegnano and its fresco by Bergognone listed in Berenson and how disappointed he had been to discover that the urban expansion of Milan had obliterated the fresco, the chapel (which was the remains of an old Parish church) and even the street. So I marked the item as 'Destroyed', to save the student of Bergognone a useless journey to Garegnano. Recently, that very fresco—which had been detached, and further mutilated with the exclusion of the Donor's hands, to make it look complete—was sold at auction in Milan. The catalogue gave no provenance and I could never have guessed its identity, had it not been reproduced in *Rassegna d'Arte* in 1903.

Many complications arose from the fact that so many paintings mentioned in the Lists of 1932/36 were not documented by a photograph in the relevant folder. Sometimes a reproduction unearthed in the literature would reveal a work which had also entered another list. At other times I would stumble on a missing photograph in a different folder, where Berenson had put it either for comparison or because he had decided to attribute the work to another master. Many times a new photograph showing a picture in a cleaned state and at a new address bore a Berenson attribution which contradicted the last edition of the Lists; but the compiler would not be aware of this contradiction, because the range of subjects painted by Renaissance artists is limited and the names of the author and of the place were different.

The cases of double listing discovered by me have been so many, that I had to draw two conclusions: (*a*) the number of Old Master Paintings still extant in the world today is more limited than a reader of art historical literature might be led to believe; (*b*) more cases must be lurking in the present edition unnoticed, because many listed pictures are still not recorded by a photograph in the Berenson Library and because the time limits imposed on me for doing this work did not allow me to check every picture listed. When I hit upon a double listing, I was usually able to gather which of the two attributions was intended to enter the revised Lists; however, I found cases of double listing concerning even the 1957 and 1963 editions, and in those cases, I have simply recorded both. Future historians of art will surely be fascinated

---

[1] see for instance under Spanzotti, Turin, S. Domenico.
[2] see for instance under Lorenzo d'Alessandro, Caldarola. In this case I was able to obtain—with some difficulty—a reproduction of the concealed treasure and the reader should appreciate that the poor quality of Pl. 959 is largely compensated by its rarity.

by these 'double attributions'. In fact, some photographs in the Berenson Library, annotated on the back by Berenson at intervals of many years, in a handwriting that grew larger and looser, throw a revealing light on the kind of 'shots' made by patriarchs of art history, not unlike the notes made by Cavalcaselle and now kept at the Marciana in Venice. One analyses the loosening of B.B.'s handwriting and the overlapping layers of writing, watching a palimpsest of criticism and self-criticism until the back of a photograph keeps one's attention riveted more than the front.

In this post-war edition of the Berenson Lists the wise rule was adopted to record all Berenson attributions to a master, regardless of whether the painting was or was not in a permanent collection, mentioning sold pictures under their previous ownership. What was I to do with some old notes of pictures in dispersed collections which could not be identified through any photograph or reproduction? Berenson changed so many of his attributions since the late nineteenth century, old uncheckable notes were so constantly the source of double listing, and it is so unusual for any decent Old Master to disappear entirely without leaving some trace, that it seemed wiser not to weigh down a List with items omitted from the previous editions. Such notes, however, are available to scholars in the Berenson Archives.

The 1957 edition of *Venetian Pictures of the Renaissance* added 68 new Lists to the 80 old ones. In the next two volumes, devoted to the Florentine School (1963), 24 new Lists were added to the 77 old ones. The original decision to cover all the rest of Italy with only two more volumes obliged me to keep the new Lists to a minimum: they do not fill in all the gaps in the regional schools and Berenson himself would have added more than 50 new Lists, against 200 old ones (in 1909 he added 23 names to the 44 Central Italian artists of 1897 and they became 105 in 1932; while the North Italian masters grew from 74 in 1907 to over 90 in 1932). I have confined the new lists to artists on which Berenson had focused his attention in recent years and whose folder of photographs gave no rise to uncertainties of interpretation. For instance: it seemed wiser to let scholars look up Berenson's article on Cola di Petrucciolo da Orvieto ('A Sienese little master in New York and elsewhere' in *Art in America*, February 1918) since he had made no progress on that master and had not included him in his Oxford edition. On the other hand, Carli's investigation into the Pisan school had interested him—possibly in connection with the post-war renewal of the museum in Pisa—and it was easy enough to include that set of artists so fully documented in his *fototeca*. The folder of Vitale da Bologna contained the most beautiful photographs of panels which only recently found permanent abode in a museum and presented no problem for a compiler; whereas other Bolognese artists, in spite of the Bolognese exhibition of 1950 and of the old articles by E. S. Vavalà, did not appear to have been studied in much detail. Any publication on Altobello Meloni had been carefully followed, but no attention seemed to have been given to Gianfrancesco Bembo. Of Gertrude Coor's articles on Sienese painting he had a high opinion and this may have influenced his switch from the once so popular Segna to the school of Duccio or Ugolino di Nerio as regards several panels, including the S. Thomas in his own collection. (Nobody who had not worked with him can imagine how ready he was to accept a more plausible or convincing solution to a problem of attribution; and he was particularly willing to reconsider the authorship of panels in his own collection; I shall never forget the rare occasions when he took a friend personally through his house and stopped questioningly in front of this or that panel as though he were looking at it for the first time.) The List of Trecento Sienese Unidentified Pictures had grown so large as to become meaningless; I therefore split it into the three groups of Followers of Duccio, of Simone and of the Lorenzetti. I did not dare to keep the denomination 'Veronese' which Berenson used in the sense of 'Northern Italian Gothic' for listing 'Lombard' followers of Pisanello (1932/36). Lately he had been using the word Veronese in its proper Italian meaning circumscribed to Verona (see the Poldi Pezzoli Madonna, n. 586, by 'Veronese' follower of Gentile da Fabriano) and I wanted to avoid duplicity of meaning. The list of 'Milanese Trecento (mostly influenced by Giovanni da Milano)' had been abolished at some date before 1945 and the photographs of the frescoes at Lentate, Mocchirolo, S. Lorenzo in Milan, Vezzolano and Viboldone, had been filed as Northern Giotteschi together with many other photographs; to them had been added quite recently photographs of pictures dropped from the list of 'Giotto's anonymous contemporaries' in 1963 because they were not Florentine (Brussels 628, Frick Triptych, Paduan frescoes, Pavia 171). Meanwhile the material of 'Umbrian' Giotteschi had been accumulating also. The addition of these 'Anonymous' lists would have taken up much space and was pointless without many illustrations.

Shortage of space (which was partly responsible for the omission of the Scaletti list, mentioned above) imposed a minimum of new lists as well as very selective lists of unidentified pictures. The 1932/36 list of 'Ferrarese-Bolognese between 1450 and 1525' consisted of five items all tentatively attributed to 'not listed' artists (Niccolò Pisano, Benedetto Coda, Girolamo Marchesi, Niccolò dell'Abate); but a Berenson list of those artists was not clear enough to be included in this edition, and a reader interested in them is referred to the last edition. The present list of Ferrarese-Bolognese is simply the outcome of the exploded 'Ercole Grandi': several pictures ascribed to 'Grandi' were transferred to Garofalo, Costa or their workshop, others Berenson grouped around the London 'Madonna of the Monkey' or the Ferrara 'Assumption of S. Mary of Egypt', or he somehow qualified them according to some influence, and this information I have passed on to the reader. Shortage of space prompted the omission of two further lists, both concerning Leonardo da Vinci. In the case of Leonardo's Spanish followers, Fernando Llanos and Fernando Yañez de la Almedina, the publisher thought they could hardly be considered Italian. In the Berenson Library considerable space is devoted to Spanish art and literature. Berenson

listed the Fernandos of Valencia but had also folders of Pedro Campana, Masip, etc.;
and Pedro Berruguete is mentioned in Melozzo's List. However, I found no changes
or additions to the Llanos/Yañez list of 1932/36, only the bibliographical reference to
Ars Hispaniae, vol. XII, 1954, and to Chandler Post's 'History of Spanish Painting',
vol. XI, Harvard, 1953. As for the Milanese Followers of Leonardo, I had no guidance
for a revised list. Much material had been united with the material of Leonardo
himself, as 'versions, copies, imitations', and what was left in the folder boiled down
to the few pictures attributed to Melzi. In the recent edition of the 'Florentine
School' (Phaidon Press, London, 1963, pp. 107/8) two Tuscan copies were mentioned
at random for the sake of recording some lost originals (Plates 1205, 1208) and the
appendix of Leonardo's Milanese Followers was omitted, with the idea that it
belonged to the volume of the 'North Italian Pictures of the Renaissance'. Then it
was decided to group Northern and Central Italy together; this fact, the fact that
the old Berenson was more interested in the master than in the followers, and the
third fact that the *Rassegna Vinciana* covers the subject admirably for any scholar
wishing to keep up to date, seemed good enough reasons for not attempting a full-
blown inventory of derivations from and replicas after Leonardo. Those in which
Berenson recognized or guessed the hand of a specific imitator are mentioned in the
appropriate list.

In Berenson's own words, the sign (?) meant 'various shades of doubt'. Although
question marks abound in the 1932 Lists, I found even more on the photographs
and I remember his readiness to suspend judgement in several cases. For instance, he
was perfectly alive to the problem of the 'Monogrammist' or Pseudo-Civerchio,
although he did not live to read the latest literature on the subject. In 1932 he listed
the Lampugnani Circumcision as a joint work of Zenale and Civerchio and assumed
that Civerchio carried out several altarpieces on Zenale's design. He went back to
his old attribution to Zenale of the Poldi Pezzoli and Bagatti Valsecchi Saints (partly
executed by Civerchio?) but did not study consistently or afresh the more Leonardesque pictures that can be grouped round the Entombment of 1509 at S. Giovanni
Evangelista in Brescia or round the Cernuschi Circumcision in Lausanne. Was
Zenale their author? Was it Civerchio? In 1519 Zenale was elected architect of the
Duomo of Milan and Berenson believed that even earlier his main interests lay in
that direction. The predella to Civerchio's signed altarpiece of 1504 in Brescia is very
Leonardesque and could be connected with the smaller pictures of the Pseudo-
Civerchio group; but larger works, such as the above-mentioned Entombment of
1509 are not easy to fit in the progression of signed and certain altarpieces of an artist
like Civerchio, whom Berenson considered related to the 'Brescian' and not to the
'Milanese' school (i.e. not touched by the influences of Mantegna and Bramante,
which preceded in Milan the irresistible ascendancy of Leonardo). Although the
photographic material was available, I could not find enough elements to be sure of

Berenson's opinion about most of the paintings concerned. The Cernuschi 'Adoration of the Child' listed as Civerchio under Cape Town, was also marked Zenale, and had also been studied in connection with the Piazza and with Boltraffio. Many pictures were not included in the 1932/36 lists only because they were not, or were believed not to be, in permanent collections; those included at that date are distinguished in this edition with a (Pseudo?).

An even trickier problem was presented by the confusion between Girolamo da Cremona and Liberale da Verona, born out of their close co-operation on the Piccolomini miniatures. Berenson himself, when first ascribing the Viterbo altarpiece to Girolamo da Cremona (*Study and Criticism of Italian Art*, 2nd series, p. 97, London, 1902), pointed out how the swirling draperies, the colour, the types, the composition, were all 'singularly like Liberale'. He suggested the other attribution as a mere hypothesis, on the grounds that Liberale's later work shows a more slovenly line. The new findings about the dates of Girolamo's miniatures establish him as a painter of stiff stocky figures throughout his known activity and Berenson, reconsidering the problem, might well have come to the conclusion that the weight of probabilities was in favour of ascribing to Liberale the Viterbo altarpiece and the panels by the same hand (see Berenson in *Rassegna d'Arte*, March 1907, 'Una nuova pittura di Girolamo da Cremona'). The matter became further complicated by the connections with Francesco di Giorgio, also recognized by Berenson (see *Gazette des Beaux-Arts*, 1917, p. 456). This interplay of influences affects even a fragmentary panel in Berenson's own collection; but unfortunately I never discussed this problem with him and I was unable to obtain clear information from other sources about Berenson's latest thought on the subject. Therefore, as an exceptional measure, I have mentioned the disputed panels under two or three names.

Ever since the publication of the 1932/36 edition, it was the rule, at I Tatti, (1) to rectify an entry when a signature or a safe documentary evidence was discovered and to omit pictures when cleaning proved them to be utter wrecks; (2) to add panels which proved to be missing or companion pieces of listed works and to cancel items listed with a question mark, when a more convincing attribution had been put forward in the meantime. Many corrections of the first kind were due to information provided by curators of galleries; of the second sort, to the studies made by a friend of Berenson's, Federico Zeri. His lists—in the Berenson style—of Carlo da Camerino or Giovanni Antonio da Pesaro, should be kept in mind by students who want to have a more complete panorama of Marchigian transitional artists.

The biographical notices at the head of each list have occasionally been enlarged by me with documentary information, but I have maintained the integrity of Berenson's stylistic observations.

I never happened to work with Berenson on a problem of sculpture, although I remember well his enjoyment of the exhibition of Sienese pigmented sculpture (see

E. Carli's catalogue 'La Scultura Lignea Senese', 1951). I have checked the lists of sculptures by Vecchietta, Francesco di Giorgio and Neroccio against that book and against the book of Berenson's close and esteemed friend John Pope-Hennessy (*Italian Renaissance Sculpture*, London, 1958). The Francia list is not concerned with activities of that artist outside the field of painting and the one item of sculpture in the 1932 list of Amico Aspertini (the Bust of Beroaldo in San Martino at Bologna) was dropped because it had been added in the mistaken belief that it was a documented work and not because of any personal attribution of Berenson's. I found no evidence that he studied the sculptural activity of painters outside Siena. Stained-glass windows were listed under Benvenuto di Giovanni, Simone Martini, Francesco Del Cossa and I remember Berenson's excitement when the large circular window of the Duomo in Siena was restored and this new item was added in the Duccio list. While the attributions concerning stained-glass compositions remained valid, the attempt to assign maiolica ware to Timoteo Viti, following a suggestion by A. Venturi, proved fallacious: the vaguely listed 'maiolica plates' in Bologna, London, Paris and Venice were dropped from Viti's list, because they correspond to the known sets by Niccolò Pellipario da Casteldurante.

Needless to say, more than once I lost hope of disentangling the morass of contradictions and puzzles that had been accumulating over the years. More than once I wished to be relieved of the responsibility of such a new edition. Oddly enough, encouragement to persevere came from those experienced scholars who were better aware of the inevitability of mistakes. Their lesson of humility and Berenson's keen desire to provide new generations of students with a useful instrument of research, as well as Nicky Mariano's unfailing friendship, drove me on. I regret that these posthumous lists had still to be published in the Berenson style, without comments or explanations on my part, and I am thankful for the chance I was given to explain something in this introduction. Many a picture supposedly 'discovered yesterday' was in fact known to Berenson ages ago. Unfortunately sale and exhibition catalogues have become less and less informative about provenance and this new habit was a great handicap for my kind of work. On the other hand, I did not wish to deprive the revised lists of a few items I was convinced Berenson would have included, simply on the grounds that I had no evidence that he knew them. In such cases I have added the picture with an asterisk. I would also have added more homeless pictures of good quality, marking them, if needed, with an asterisk, but for the difficulty of illustrating them. These additions with an asterisk are, as the reader will notice, very rare: but they are there to prove that the conception of the 'Berenson' list has not been abandoned.

Florence, Spring 1967   LUISA VERTOVA

THE CENTRAL ITALIAN PAINTERS
OF THE RENAISSANCE

NOTE TO INDEX OF WORKS—LONDON 1897

The following lists make no claim to absolute completeness, but no genuine work by the painters mentioned, found in the better known public or private collections, has been omitted. With the exception of three or four pictures, which he knows only in the photographs, the author has seen and carefully studied every picture indicated, and is alone responsible for the attributions, although he is happy to acknowledge his indebtedness to the writings of Signor Cavalcaselle, of the late Giovanni Morelli, of Signor Gustavo Frizzoni and of Dr J. P. Richter.

Public galleries are mentioned first, then private collections, and churches last. The principal public gallery is always understood after the simple mention of a city or town. Thus, Paris means Paris, Louvre, London means London, National Gallery, etc.

An interrogation point after the title of a picture indicates that its attribution to the given painter is doubtful. Distinctly early or late works are marked E. or L.

It need scarcely be said that the attributions here given are not based on official catalogues, and are often at variance with them.

These lists are far from complete. The author hopes to revise them every few years, keeping them up to date with his further travel and researches.

PREFACE TO SECOND EDITION—LONDON 1909

Twelve years and more have passed since this book first went to the press. At that time the painters of Central Italy still lay under the hard ban of Academic judgment, and Messrs. Crowe and Cavalcaselle's sawdusty appreciations. It is different now. Book after book has appeared on Sienese art, not only in English but in German and French. Even Umbrian painting is being studied for its own wild-herb taste, and not merely in its Florentine phases, as in Signorelli and Perugino.

I venture, therefore, in this edition, to insert lists of works by painters not mentioned in the first. They would have frightened the student, even if I had then been prepared to publish them. I was not. Of some I knew enough to feel sure that much more must be ascertained before one had anything like an adequate notion of their character and activity. Of others I had not even heard. Most of them, it is true, had been treated by Crowe and Cavalcaselle, but so briefly or so vaguely as to attract no interest.

To take them in alphabetical order: Allegretto Nuzi was known by half a dozen works, and his derivation from Bernardo Daddi, which has since been noticed by several students independently, had not occurred to anyone. Andrea de Licio had never been heard of, and his painted fairy tales at Atri were unknown. Antoniazzo was a mere name. Mr Everett has repaired the fault in the *American Journal of Archeology*. Bartolo di Fredi, neglected as all the Sienese after the Lorenzetti, is still almost unknown and quite unappreciated. He was probably the most creative and determining personality in Sienese painting, between Lippo Memmi and Sassetta. Bartolomeo della Gatta is still a shadowy figure. So is Caporali, who may turn out a more charming Bonfigli. Cozzarelli had not been properly distinguished from his master and model, Matteo di Giovanni. Fei, Giovanni di Paolo, Sassetta, and Vanni were as remote as Kunchinjunga. Mr F. M. Perkins has resuscitated Vanni in the *Burlington Magazine*, and there also I printed something on Sassetta. At Fei and Giovanni di Paolo—the whimsical, absurd, frequently incredible, but always entertaining Giovanni di Paolo—Mr Perkins and I have tinkered away together. Giovanni Francesco da Rimini—an Umbrian, despite his birth—was a discovery of Dr Ricci, and the student can look him up in the files of the Milanese *Rassegna d'Arte*. Girolamo di Benvenuto was and remains annoyingly like his father and master, Benvenuto di Giovanni. Girolamo di Giovanni da Camerino I have sketched in the *Rassegna*. Lorenzo Salimbeni I had hoped to know better, but he remains the author of the Urbino frescoes and little else. Matteo da Gualdo used to be mixed up with Girolamo di Giovanni da Camerino. His outlines are not yet fixed. I am inclined to believe that toward the end of his career he refined and grew exquisite under Benozzo's influence. Matteo da Viterbo was rediscovered by Eugène Müntz, and deserves a place with the Lorenzetti. Mezzastris was confused with his fellow-pupil Niccolò da Foligno. Nelli was and remains an idiot, but as I mention him in my text, I had better insert a list of his paintings. Finally, I wish I had more to say about Scaletti of Faenza. He is one of the most fascinating artists of the Quattrocento, a lovechild of Ercole Roberti and Botticelli. I propose him as a splendid subject of research for younger men.

Apart from names of fellow-students already mentioned, I recall especially two to whom I am seriously indebted, Prof. B. Felicangeli of Camerino and Rome, for communications published and unpublished regarding Boccatis; and my countryman, the well-known critic, Mr F. Mason Perkins, for hints and monitions about Sienese as well as Umbrian painting.

Other students may have anticipated the publication of this or that result at which I have arrived in the course of the last twenty years. I am delighted that they have, for it proves that our studies have a scientific basis. But I pray these colleagues to forgive me if I have not taken the time and the trouble to keep a double entry of our agreements.

Bryn Mawr, Pa., Dec., 1908   B. B.

THE NORTH ITALIAN PAINTERS
OF THE RENAISSANCE

London 1907 (reprinted 1910)

PREFACE

I do not flatter myself that the appended lists of North Italian painters comprise any-thing like their entire works. Indeed I know of many scores that have not been in-cluded because I have not seen them, and can therefore guarantee neither their authenticity nor their presence in the places indicated. On the authority of the last edition of a well-known manual, I spent a morning looking for a picture in a remotely situated church, only to find that the church had been demolished years ago. A morning is a very precious thing, and I do not choose to be responsible for its loss to a fellow-student. On the other hand, scores of pictures that I have seen I omit, because no one knows where they may have wandered to by tomorrow. I have, however, inserted, on the inspection of photographs, some few pictures in public places and relatively permanent private collections, without having seen the originals. But in this I have used extreme caution, for only the other day I had a sharp reminder of its need. In the excellent Braun photograph of the Czartoryski portrait of a curled and perfumed minion there seemed to be clearly recognizable the hand of Sebastiano del Piombo, in a very Raphaelesque phase, it is true, yet Sebastiano. A glance at the original sufficed to dispel the error. The work is Raphael's.

The lists will be found sprinkled with interrogation points. These do not all have the same meaning, and as the resources of typography can indicate doubt, but not the shade of doubt, the student must be left to discover for himself the various reasons for uncertainty. In the larger number of cases it means that I arrived at no satisfactory conclusion regarding the picture in question. One could have omitted it. It seemed more courageous and helpful to include it, and thereby to put the student on what I hoped was at least the right track. Some of the interrogation points mean that a long time has passed since I have seen a picture, and that I do not know what I should think of it now, or that I do not know whether it is still to be found where I saw it.

Of course I have received much help from other writers and from friends. In the first place, from Morelli. He knew his Milanese even better than other schools. It has happened again and again that my own researches have compelled me to return to his conclusions after having departed from them. Bernardino de' Conti is a case in point. Fifteen years of tossing backward and forward over this incredibly unequal painter have brought me back to the problem as Morelli left it. To Dr Frizzoni my indebtedness is scarcely less. I owe acknowledgment to the various books or articles of Count Malaguzzi Valeri, of Dr W. von Seidlitz and of Mr Herbert Cook on Milanese art; of Count Carlo Gamba and Dr J. P. Richter on the Veronese; of Prof. Adolfo Venturi and Dr Corrado Ricci on the school of Ferrara-Bologna.

I am grateful for assistance in word and deed to my friends Don Guido Cagnola, Dr Frizzoni, Cav. Luigi Cavenaghi and Signor Aldo Noseda at Milan, and to Count A. Baudi de Vesme at Turin. Count Vesme, with a generosity of which I have never found the parallel, put at my disposal his notes and photographs concerning Defendente, which made it easy for me to see most of the pictures, and along with them the romantically picturesque villages where they are guarded. Which admonishes me to make my last confession. I have at times mentioned an unimportant picture because it is to be seen in delightful surroundings after a journey through beautiful country; and I have not always directed the pilgrim of beauty to repeat my experiences in Lombard market-towns where every sense is offended. To be obliged to linger in them between infrequent and uncertain trains is little short of imprisonment. They should be approached (if at all) in a motor-car, which furnishes a ready escape; and that I was enabled to see many of them in this least disagreeable fashion is due to my dear friends Lucien Henraux and Carlo Placci. I thank them for other trips as well, trips through Italian hill country, when all the days carried to the evening the buoyancy of morning.

Settignano, February 1907   B. B.

PREFACE TO THE EDITION OF 1932

THE Lists comprising this book differ from those originally appended to the four volumes of my *Renaissance Painters*, not only by bringing all the schools together under one alphabetical order, not only by including many more artists and a great many more pictures than I knew thirty-five years ago, but in being inspired by a different principle.

The Lists in previous editions, although revised from time to time, were all based on the conviction that the hand of the artist never faltered, even if his head did occasionally nod. The execution, on this theory, tended to weigh more than the creative mental effort. The question of questions was whether a painting was autograph. If it was not, it did not count, unless indeed it betrayed the hand of another painter, in which case it was included in that painter's work. An artistic personality thus shrank to a composite of those pictures only where hand and mind were one.

Would that hand and mind were always one! that the artist himself never worked with the makeshift of an inferior self, or with the help of apprentices!

This former exclusiveness was perhaps a necessary and salutary discipline. It enabled one to reach the heart of an artistic personality before starting to put out to its limits; it made one so familiar with his ways that one became able to recognize him even in his uninspired moments.

But now, fortified with this experience of the artist at his highest, one may well afford to relax from the earlier severity, and include every work that shows the distinct trace of his creative purpose, whether largely or only in small part by his own hand, whether done in his studio on his indications, or whether mere copies of lost works.

Indeed, it now seems that to confine interest to what looks like perfect achievement is dandiacal aestheticism. One who dedicates his whole life to art, and not merely his week-ends, holidays and leisure moments, cannot remain satisfied with such an adolescent attitude. Mature interest leads one at least as much to the mind of the artist as to his hand. An artistic personality includes not only all that the artist did in his best moments, but all that his mind conceived in the terms of his art, in whatever shape it has been recorded, no matter how inadequate, nor how unsatisfactory.

It might indeed seem that long experience has brought me back to the old days when everything that looked like Leonardo or Raphael produced the appropriate sentiment in the soul of the beholder. 'What then,' it may be asked, 'has been the use of all this business about renaming pictures, distinguishing originals from copies, and masters from pupils, if now we are invited to get once more our Raphael or Leonardo thrill from inferior works? What has become of the touchstone of

Quality, if we admit that the hand of a great artist can falter, and if we insist on tracing his genius through the works of his assistants and followers, and value even the humble achievements of copyists whose hands never vibrated with the master's touch? We are once again in the old uncharted regions where no compass pointing to quality any longer guides us, and where the only clue is the familiar one of the conception, the idea, the suggestion, that led us into so many bogs. The naive sight-seer and the connoisseur join hands!'

True! But though they acclaim together 'the Master', it is with a difference. The plain sightseer can undoubtedly be deeply stirred by a work of art, but it is nearly always the literary, the romantic, the associative ideas that move him. The connois-seur who has learnt to distinguish between the poetry suggested by the picture and its specific qualities as painting, is affected in another way.

In my writings on Renaissance Painters I attempted to distinguish between the Illustrative and the Decorative elements in pictures, and it may be that I over-emphasized the latter, for I have been amused and sometimes distressed to find many subsequent writers dwelling only on the decorative elements in art, which, vitalizing as they are, do their noblest service only when they convey great human ideals.

The instructed lover of art, who has learnt to distinguish the individual touch of the artist he is studying, can perceive the creative intention even in his less happy achievements, but he does not stop at the mere thought, the suggestions given by the illustration; in his disciplined imagination he re-creates the design as a whole in the exact decorative terms of the artist. And who shall say that the pleasures of a trained imagination thus stimulated are not genuine aesthetic pleasures?

In the Lists now published I have therefore been led to include not only pictures which the artists painted with more or less assistance, but such as were turned out in their studios from their designs, and even copies as well, providing they faithfully transcribe lost works. To distinguish such works from absolutely autograph pictures, I have adopted a series of signs which I enclose in brackets after the subject of the picture. These I must explain.

EXPLANATIONS

A question-mark does not mean that I expect the picture necessarily to turn out to be by the painter in whose list it is included. The intention is rather to provoke a discussion which might not arise if the picture were relegated to the limbo of anonymity, and to point out, as far as I can, the most fruitful line of inquiry.

It would have been easy to omit the pictures I have attributed with a question-mark, casting them out from the garden like worthless weeds, and my reputation would perhaps gain in certain circles had I done so. But it seems more generous to expose one's self to the risk of disparagement than to fail to call attention to the most likely affiliations of uncertain pictures. Abstention is safe, but sterile. Care must be taken, of course, to reject without mercy those attributions which are merely happy thoughts or bright guesses, and to admit only such as, even if not entirely satisfactory, are based on the fullest information, and on the truest idea of the artist available at the moment.

Even unquestioned attributions are not trademarks, although collectors and dealers would like them to be. They are stepping-stones rather than goals. None of my lists give me complete satisfaction. More and more work will be required for two or even three generations before this task will be adequately accomplished. And when it is, let us hope our successors will show their gratitude by using the material gathered by their forerunners as a foundation for their finished structure. Should their edifice prove impermanent, our ghosts may have the satisfaction of knowing that foundations at times outlast what is built upon them. To justify my attributions would not be possible in this volume, for it would require a running commentary on each of the lists, and long essays on certain items.

So much for actual attributions, questioned or unquestioned. For pictures in which the hand of assistants is traceable I have used the letters *p*. (in part by the artist) or *g.p.* (in great part). During the period with which we are concerned, no considerable work was likely to be carried through without assistance. It was seldom that a painter much in demand could indulge himself in executing with his own hand the minor parts of a picture, such as the walls or columns of buildings, furniture, obscurer bits of drapery and so on, but it is only when the more manifest parts of a picture betray another hand that I use a sign to indicate it.

For pictures done on a master's indications in his studio the letters *st*. (studio) are used, and for copies of lost works *c*. (copy).

It remains to explain the ominous letter *r*., which means ruined, repainted, or restored. This unhappy sign might indeed be placed after almost every old picture, for no work four or five, and still less six or seven centuries old, is likely to have escaped unhurt. Even the few painters who used an impeccable technique, almost as hard as enamel, could not hinder the fading of colours, the 'mellowing', as we call it, of time. Indeed, thus 'mellowed', they please our taste, as colourless sculpture, unknown in antiquity, pleases it. The pictures as they left the Old Masters' hands would horrify most people with their bright tints. But we seldom see them thus; for time and the over-zealous restorer have usually combined to reduce them in pitch. From the filling-in of cracks and of bare spots from which the paint has flaked off, to the making over of the whole picture according to the restorer's taste and fancy, there are many gradations. I have indicated with the letter *r*. only those restorations which actually change the character of the work in colour, types, or drawing. Even in these, a good deal of the original design persists, something of the structure of the figures and of the distribution of the masses betrays the original creation. Thorwaldsen worked his will and wreaked his taste upon the Aeginetan Marbles, but the archaic Greek artist triumphs over the conventionalizing hand. And in my depressing flock of Restored Pictures the old Masters contrive still to make their genius felt.

As to the sources upon which I have based my views of the influences that formed the painters, I need scarcely say that we have next to no information in the matter, and little reliable tradition, so that the influences given in these lists are derived almost entirely from observed resemblances between the works of a given painter and those of his predecessors. Personal contact is not necessarily implied. A man may owe almost everything to another, without ever having seen him.

Certain influences are so widespread that one wearies of repeating them. Such are Giotto and Simone Martini and the Lorenzetti in the Trecento; the Antique in the fifteenth and sixteenth centuries, not only in architecture and sculpture, but in painting as well; Donatello, who is behind so much Florentine and nearly all north Italian painting; Mantegna in all the schools of the north, and still more his brother-in-law, Giovanni Bellini, from whose influence no Venetian working between 1470 and 1520 is free; while Leonardo, Michelangelo and Raphael, in obvious as well as subtle ways, affected all their younger contemporaries.

ABBREVIATIONS

(see pp. xxivf. under Explanations)

c.: copy.
d.: dated (i.e. the date appears on the picture
 itself; wherever a date is given without
 this prefix, it is drawn from documents
 or other sources).
fr.: fragment.
g.p.: in great part autograph.
p.: partly autograph.
r.: ruined, restored, repainted.
st.: studio work.
st.v.: studio version.
u.: unfinished.
E.: early.
L.: late.
Sd.: signed.
* Additions (see p. xvii)

NOTE

A number after the name of a town means that the picture is in the
principal public gallery of that town, e.g. Berlin (Staatliche
Museen), Paris (Louvre), London (National Gallery), Perugia
(Pinacoteca), etc. Where honours are even between public
collections, as between the Ashmolean and Christ Church at
Oxford, or the Pitti and the Uffizi in Florence, both are mentioned.

Plate numbers in brackets refer to the illustrated Phaidon edition of
Bernard Berenson's *Italian Painters of the Renaissance*.

ALBERTINO DA LODI see PIAZZA

ALENI, Tommaso, called Il FADINO

Cremona. Active first decade sixteenth century. Partner of Galeazzo Campi and Luca della Corna.

Cremona. 168. Madonna adoring the Christ Child with SS. John Baptist, Anthony Abbot and music-making Angel (from S. Domenico). Sd and d. 1515. *Plate* 1638.

168A (dep. Brera 466). Madonna and Child enthroned with S. Anthony of Padua and S. Francis recommending a monk. Sd and d. 1500. *Plate* 1637.

169. Bust of blessing Redeemer. (?)

DUOMO, SAGRESTIA DEI CANONICI. Organ-shutters: Angel and Virgin of Annunciation. *Plates* 1642–43.

S. ABBONDIO, SANTUARIETTO DI LORETO, ALTAR R. Assumption (with Galeazzo Campi).

S. MARIA MADDALENA, CHOIR. Predella to polyptych by Galeazzo Campi: Life of S. Mary Magdalen.

S. SIGISMONDO, CLOISTER. Fresco: S. Jerome surrounded by monks. *Plate* 1644.

— — BETWEEN ARCHES. Frescoes: Busts in medallions.

— REFECTORY. Fresco: Last Supper (after Leonardo). 1508. *Plate* 1641.

Lille. 198. Madonna adoring Child, and Saint. (?) *Plate* 1639.

London. BENSON COLLECTION (EX). Madonna and Child. Sd. *Plate* 1640.

Milan. BRERA, DEPOT. Detached fresco from Convent of S. Maria di Valverde at Cremona: Adoration of the Christ Child.

Zagreb. Pietà. (?)

ALLEGRETTO see NUZI

ALTICHIERO DA ZEVIO

Verona, ca 1330–95. Founder of the school of Verona. Developed under the influence of Giotto's work and conceivably of personal contact with Andrea Orcagna of Florence. Worked in partnership with the Veronese Jacopo degli Avanzi or Avanzo.

Padua. LIVIANO, FIRST FLOOR, SALA DEI GIGANTI. Fresco: Portrait of Petrarch. *Plate* 226.

BASILICA DEL SANTO (S. ANTONIO), R. TRANSEPT, CAPPELLA DI S. FELICE (FORMERLY

CAPPELLA DI S. JACOPO). Frescoes (with Avanzo). Completed 1379.

— VAULT. Frescoes: Symbols of Evangelists, Church Fathers and Prophets.

— SPANDRELS: Frescoes: Roundels with Saints and Annunciation.

— CENTRE WALL. Frescoes: Crucifixion; on left, lunette with Pietà, and Angel and Virgin of Annunciation in spandrels above; on right, lunette with Resurrection. *Plate 218.*

— L. AND R. WALL, LUNETTES (FROM L. TO R.). Frescoes: (1) Hermogenes sends Philetus to discuss with S. James, who is preaching in temple, S. James converts Philetus, Hermogenes seeks the help of the Devil; (2) Hermogenes is lifted by Devils, then converted and baptized by S. James; (3) S. James is taken outside the town and then beheaded; (4) An Angel leads the boat with the body of S. James to Compostella and the heathen Queen Lupa grants permission to bury it in her land; (5) S. James's disciples are imprisoned (r.); (6) They are freed by an Angel and their pursuers precipitated into a ravine; (7) the wild bulls sent by Queen Lupa become meek at the sign of the cross and carry the Saint's body straight into the Queen's palace; (8) Conversion of Queen Lupa and Announcement that the palace is to become a sanctuary. *Plates 220, 221.*

— L. WALL, LOWER REGISTER. Frescoes: Ramirus king of Oviedo has a dream of S. James; the King announces his dream to his Councillors; S. James appears over the wall of the town during the battle of Clavigio and secures the victory of the Christians.

— R. WALL, LOWER REGISTER. Frescoes: SS. Catherine and James present to the Madonna and Child enthroned the donor of the chapel, Bonifacio de' Lupi di Sorogna, and his wife.

EREMITANI (SS. FILIPPO E GIACOMO), CAPPELLA DOTTO (R. OF CHOIR). Frescoes in tympanum above tomb of Diamante Dotto: Angel and Virgin of Annunciation, Coronation of Virgin with two kneeling warriors. Not before 1370. (Destroyed 1944.) *Plate 219.*

— SACRISTY. Detached fresco in roundel: Madonna and Child (fr.).

ORATORIO DI S. GIORGIO, VAULT. Frescoes: Evangelists, Church Fathers and Prophets (r.).

— ENTRANCE WALL. Frescoes: over door, Annunciation; below, Adoration of Shepherds, Adoration of Magi; further below, Flight into Egypt, Circumcision. *Plate 224.*

— ALTAR WALL. Frescoes: Coronation of Virgin, Crucifixion.

— L. WALL. Frescoes: above, S. George killing the dragon, Conversion of King Sevius, Madonna and Child worshipped by members of the Lupi family; below, S. George drinks poison, is tortured on the wheel, is beheaded. *Plate 223.*

— R. WALL. Frescoes: above, S. Catherine refuses to give up her Christian faith, argues with the Philosophers, is tortured on the wheels; below, S. Lucy answers Pascasius, stands fast against the oxen, is tortured with the fire and with the boiling oil and beheaded, S. Lucy's body worshipped by crowds. [*Plate* 322.] *Plate* 222.

Frescoed decoration (g.p.). 1377–84.

SALA DELLA RAGIONE. Fresco by west door: A trial (?)

Verona. S. ANASTASIA, CAPPELLA CAVALLI (SECOND R. OF CHOIR). Frescoes: Saints recommend members of the Cavalli family to the Madonna and Child enthroned; S. Eligius healing a horse. After 1390. *Plate* 225.

ALTOBELLO MELONE

Cremonese, active first quarter sixteenth century. Influenced by Giorgione, close to Romanino.

Algiers. MUSÉE. Predella panel to Picenardi Triptych: Finding of True Cross (see Oxford). *Plate* 1669.

Bergamo. 366. Madonna suckling Child and Infant S. John. E.

368. So-called Portrait of Cesare Borgia.

Brescia. CONTESSA PAOLINA FENAROLI BETTONI (EX). Side-panels (to New Haven Madonna?): SS. John Evangelist and Peter (or Joseph).

Columbia (Mo.). UNIVERSITY OF MISSOURI, 61.77. (KRESS STUDY COLLECTION. K 1097). Centre panel of Picenardi Triptych: Madonna and Child (see Oxford). *Plate* 1667.

Cremona. 1280. Madonna and Child with S. Stephen (fr.). L. (?)

Way to Calvary (after Ercole da Ferrara). E.

DUOMO, CHOIR, L. Frescoes: Flight into Egypt and Massacre of Innocents. 1516/7. *Plates* 1672, 1673.

— CHOIR, R. Frescoes above the arches: Last Supper; Washing of Feet and Agony in the Garden; Betrayal of Christ and Christ before Caiphas. Sd. 1517/8. *Plate* 1674.

London. 753. Christ on the way to Emmaus (from S. Bartolomeo at Cremona).

SEBASTIAN ISEPP (EX). Christ carrying Cross.

PHILIP POUNCEY. Madonna and Child with Infant S. John.

Milan. BRERA. 805. Entombment.

ARCIVESCOVADO. Lamentation. (Also listed as Fogolino?)

New York. FRED MOND (EX). Madonna suckling Child and Infant S. John.

Oxford. ASHMOLEAN MUSEUM. 273-4. Side-panels of Picenardi Triptych: Tobias and the Angel, S. Helena (central panel in Columbia; predella panels at Algiers and Paris). *Plates* 1666, 1668.

Philadelphia (Pa.). J. G. JOHNSON COLLECTION. 232. Madonna and Child.

Rome. OPERE RECUPERATE. Portrait of lady (formerly Trivulzio). *Plate* 1670.

Sands Point (Port Washington, L.I.). MRS HANNAH D. RABINOWITZ. Centre panel of polyptych: Madonna and Child enthroned (companion to Brescia?). *Plate* 1665.

Stockholm. D. L. TELANDER (EX). Venus and Cupid. *Plate 1671.*
Verona. 180. Side-panel of triptych: S. Jerome.
Homeless. Resurrection (repr. *Proporzioni* 1950, tav. CLXXVI, fig. 23).
    Predella panel to Picenardi triptych: S. Helena's journey (see Oxford). (Repr.
      Paragone, Sept. 1957, fig. 22.)
    Bust of fat man (repr. *Paragone*, Sept. 1955, fig. 13).

ALUNNO see NICCOLÒ DA FOLIGNO

AMBROGIO DA FOSSANO see BERGOGNONE

AMBROGIO DE PREDIS see DE PREDIS

AMBROSI, Pietro di Giovanni

Siena, ca 1409–60. Registered as painter 1428. Assistant and close follower of Sassetta.

Altenburg. 84. Left panel of polyptych: S. Augustine. *Plate 569.*
Amsterdam. ERNST PROEHL. S. Vittore worshipped by donor. (?)
Asciano. MUSEO D'ARTE SACRA. Triptych: Nativity, S. Augustine, S. Galganus. ca
    1455. *Plates 560, 565, 566, 567.*
Assisi. S. MARIA DEGLI ANGELI, CAPPELLA DELLA PORZIUNCOLA. Fresco: S. Bernardino.(?)
Basle. Inv. 1348. Predella panel: Miraculous birth of S. Nicholas. ca 1435. *Plate 561.*
Berlin. 1097. Predella panel: Embarkation of S. Helena (after Ambrogio Lorenzetti).
Brooklyn (New York). 34.99 (Loan of Mrs J. MacDonald). Central panel of triptych:
    Madonna and Child. *Plate 570.*
Brunswick (Maine). BOWDOIN COLLEGE MUSEUM OF FINE ARTS. 1961.100.7. KRESS
    STUDY COLLECTION. K 1235. S. Bernardino.
Esztergom. 55.185. Assumption.
    55.186. Head of Virgin. *Plate 568.*
Florence. ACTON COLLECTION. Madonna embracing the Child.
    MUSEO HORNE. 73, 74. Two cut-down panels (from frame of polyptych?): S.
    Apollonia, S. Ursula.
London. HENRY HARRIS (EX). Two panels of polyptych: SS. Bartholomew and
    Anthony Abbot.
Lucignano (Val di Chiana). MUSEO CIVICO. S. Bernardino trampling on mitres. Sd
    and d. 1448. *Plate 572.*
Oxford. ASHMOLEAN MUSEUM. 329. Annunciation.

Paganico (Grosseto). S. MICHELE. S. Blaise blessing.

Paris. MUSÉE JACQUEMART-ANDRÉ. 908. Banner: front, Crucifixion with Flagellants; back, S. Catherine crowned by Angels and surrounded by Virtues, with Flagellants below. Sd and d. 1444. *Plate 571.*

MARTIN LE ROY COLLECTION (EX). Madonna and Child enthroned with four female Saints, many Angels and God the Father at top.

Parma. PALAZZO DELLA CONGREGAZIONE DI CARITÀ S. FILIPPO NERI, PINACOTECA STUARD. 9. Predella panel: Christ enters Jerusalem.

Princeton (N.J.). 62.69. S. Paul and the Church Fathers worship the Crucifix. (?)

Rome. VATICAN, PINACOTECA. 235, 236. Two predella panels: Trial and martyrdom of S. Victorinus.

FASSINI COLLECTION (EX). S. Bernardino. (?)

San Diego (Cal.). FINE ARTS GALLERY. S. Francis receiving Stigmata.

Siena. 203. S. Bernardino standing on the world. After 1444.

ARICHIVIO DI STATO. Book-cover (Libro degli Edifizi e Muraglie de' Cassari): Mason at work. d. 1440.

OSSERVANZA, THIRD CHAPEL R. S. Bernardino. Sd and d. 1444.

Terni. BIBLIOTECA. Banner: Madonna of Mercy and three Saints (r.).

Venice. CONTE VITTORIO CINI. Inv. 6501. 'Loeser' Christ on Cross. *Plate 563.*

Homeless. Portable altarpiece: Madonna and Child enthroned with SS. John Baptist, Anthony Abbot, Bernardino and Bartholomew; in wings, two female Saints, SS. Peter and Paul; in pinnacles, Crucifixion, Angel and Virgin of Annunciation.* (repr. *Paragone*, 1963, n. 165, plate 44).

Centre panel of portable altarpiece: Madonna and Child with S. John Baptist, S. Paul, two female Saints, two Angels; Crucifixion above. *Plate 562.*

ANDREA DI BARTOLO

Sienese. Documented from 1389, died 1428. Pupil and close follower of his father, Bartolo di Fredi; influenced by Spinello Aretino.

Altenburg. 58. Portable altarpiece: Madonna and Child enthroned with SS. John Baptist and James; in wings, S. Helena, S. Anthony Abbot; in pinnacles, Crucifixion, Angel and Virgin of Annunciation.

66. Panel from pilaster of altarpiece: S. Catherine (companion to Berlin (Burlet), Oslo, Oxford, Homeless)·

Amiens. 421. Panel of polyptych: S. Anthony Abbot.

Angers. MUSÉE. Portable altarpiece: Crucifixion; in wings, SS. Catherine, Sebastian and Donor, Two Bishop Saints; in pinnacles, Annunciation.

Baltimore (Md). WALTERS ART GALLERY. 717. Madonna and Child enthroned with four Angels and four Evangelists; above, Angel and Virgin of Annunciation in roundels.

Baltimore (contd.). 741. Predella panel: Resurrection (companion to Lugano, New York and Stockholm).

    37.1018. Massacre of Innocents. *Plate* 429.

Berlin. 1095. Portable altarpiece: Madonna and Child enthroned with two Angels, SS. Catherine and John Baptist and kneeling Nun; in wings, two Deacon Martyrs, SS. Catherine and Francis; in pinnacles, Crucifixion, Angel and Virgin of Annunciation. E.(?)

    DE BURLET COLLECTION (EX). Panel from pilaster of polyptych: S. Benedict (see Altenburg).*

Bologna. 169. Predella panel: Last Supper.

    233. Coronation of Virgin.

    DEP. FROM MUSEO DI S. STEFANO. Madonna of Humility (variant at Detroit), S. James, S. Catherine (r.).

Brooklyn (New York). 34.839. Portable altarpiece: Madonna and Child; in wings, S. Anthony Abbot, Apostle; in pinnacles, blessing Redeemer, Angel and Virgin of Annunciation.(r.)

Brussels. STOCLET COLLECTION. Madonna of Humility and two Prophets in roundels above.

— (EX). Deposition. (?)

— (EX). Right panel of polyptych: S. Michael and the dragon.

    JACQUES STOCLET. Triptych: Crucifixion; Nativity, Circumcision, Last Supper, Way to Calvary, Sacrifice of Isaac, Stigmata of S. Francis, Apostle worshipping the cross, S. Marina rearing the Child outside the monastery.

Budapest. 17. Predella panel: Crucifixion. *Plate* 427.

Buonconvento (Senese). PIEVE, MUSEO. Fragmentary polyptych: Annunciation, S. Anthony Abbot, S. Mary Magdalen. Sd.

Cambridge (Mass.). 1917.195. Deposition; on back, 'Woman, behold Thy Son'. (?)

Detroit (Mich.). 22.12. Madonna of Humility (variant at Bologna).

    29.320. Blessing Redeemer (pinnacle to Princeton Madonna?).

Dublin. 1089. The parents of S. Galganus come to his hermitage with friends and a bride for him but cannot induce him to return home (companion to Pisa). *Plate* 426.

Englewood (N.J.). PLATT COLLECTION (EX). Portable altarpiece: Madonna and Child with two Angels, SS. James, Mary Magdalen, Catherine and Peter; in pinnacle, blessing Redeemer.

Esztergom. 55.148. Panel of polyptych: S. Joachim leaving the city.

Florence. ACTON COLLECTION. Two pinnacles: Evangelists.

Greenville (S.C.). BOB JONES UNIVERSITY GALLERY, GIFT OF R. LEHMAN. Madonna of Humility.

Konopist. 21209. Portable altarpiece: Trinity, SS. Stephen, John Baptist, Catherine and female Saint; in pinnacles, blessing Redeemer, Angel and Virgin of Annunciation.

La Rochelle. 139. Crucifixion. (?)

Le Havre. 12. Panel from upper register of polyptych: Bust of bishop.

Lincoln (Nebr.). UNIVERSITY OF NEBRASKA. U-359, 360-K. (KRESS STUDY COLLECTION. K 1176, K 1177). Panels of polyptych: Half-length SS. Bartholomew and Paul; half-length SS. John Evangelist and Peter.

London. VICTORIA AND ALBERT MUSEUM. 376-1876. Panel from right pilaster of altarpiece; S. Stephen (companion to Philadelphia).

W. S. M. BURNS (EX). Two panels: S. Apollonia, S. Agatha. *Plate 430.*

Lugano. THYSSEN COLLECTION. Predella panel: Way to Calvary (companion to Baltimore, New York and Stockholm).

Milan. BRERA. 479. Pinnacle: Blessing Redeemer.

484. Polyptych: Coronation of Virgin; SS. Catherine, Augustine, Peter and Paul.

Montalcino (Senese). MUSEO CIVICO. Small Pietà.

Montefollonico. S. SIGISMONDO, SECOND ALTAR L. Madonna and Child with bird (r.).

Montreal. 1099. Madonna of Humility and two Angels. *Plate 422.*

Munich. KAULBACH COLLECTION (EX). Predella panel: Presentation of the Virgin.

New Haven (Conn.). 1943.248. Madonna and Child with fourteen Saints; Angel and Virgin of Annunciation in roundels above.

New York. 12.6. Predella panel: Crucifixion (companion to Baltimore, Lugano and Stockholm).

26.2871-2. Two marriage salvers with games and hunting scenes. (?)

ROBERT LEHMAN COLLECTION. S. Lawrence on the gridiron between SS. Stephen and Augustine.

Oslo. MUSEUM. Panel from pilaster of polyptych: S. Blaise. (See Altenburg.)*

Oxford. ASHMOLEAN MUSEUM. 41. Panel from pilaster of polyptych: S. Lucy. (See Altenburg.)

Perugia. GALLERIA NAZIONALE, VAN MARLE COLLECTION (EX). Side-panels of polyptych (companions to Princeton): S. Dorothy, S. Anthony Abbot.

Philadelphia (Pa.). J. G. JOHNSON COLLECTION. 96, 97. Two panels from right pilaster of altarpiece; S. Thomas Aquinas, S. Anthony Abbot (companions to London).

Pisa. B.P. III, 45, 41, 46, 28, 43. The Archangel Michael stops Galganus' horse while he is riding to Civitella; S. Michael guides the horse to the hill where Galganus is to build his hermitage (Montesiepi); Galganus cuts down trees to build his cell; whilst Galganus is on a pilgrimage in Rome, envious monks, unable to remove his sword planted in the rock as a cross, destroy his cell, but one dies on the spot while the other is attacked by a wolf; funeral of S. Galganus (companions to Dublin). *Plate 425.*

Princeton (N.J.). 62.52. 'Platt' Madonna and Child (companion to Perugia and ? Detroit).

62.53. 'Platt' SS. Anthony Abbot and Ansanus (from pilaster of polyptych).

Richmond (Va). MUSEUM OF ART. Madonna della Cintola with Messer Palamedes and his son Matteo as donors. Sd. *Plate 423.*

Rome. PROF. ODOARDO RUFFINI. Predella: Betrayal of Christ, Way to Calvary,

Deposition, Resurrection, Descent into Limbo.

PRINCIPE FABRIZIO MASSIMO (EX). Two pinnacles from Tuscania polyptych: S. Matthew, S. John Evangelist.

Siena. 63. Bust of S. Michael.

133. Portable altarpiece: Nativity; in wings, SS. James, Dominic, Catherine and Mary Magdalen; in pinnacles, Resurrection, Angel and Virgin of Annunciation.

153. Portable altarpiece: SS. Dorothy and Mary Magdalen kneeling before a lost crucifix; in wings, S. Jerome and mourning Virgin, mourning S. John Evangelist and S. Augustine with kneeling Nun; in pinnacles, Angel and Virgin of Annunciation.

155. Four pinnacles: S. Paul, S. John Baptist, S. John Evangelist, S. Peter.

219. Triptych: Madonna and Child enthroned; S. Philip; S. James. ca 1400–10.

220. Polyptych: Madonna and Child with two Angels; SS. Stephen, John Evangelist, Dorothy and Jerome. L.

PALAZZO PUBBLICO, SALA DEI PILASTRI. Painted casket with the four Patron Saints of Siena: Savinus, Crescentius, Victor and Ansanus. 1373. *Plate* 424.

S. PIETRO OVILE. Madonna and Child.

(Environs). OSSERVANZA, FOURTH ALTAR L. Four side-panels from lower and four from upper register of polyptych for Convent of S. Petronilla: full-length SS. John Baptist, Francis, Peter and John Evangelist; knee-length SS. James, Catherine of Siena, Lawrence and Paul. d. 1413.

Stockholm. 4463. Predella panel: Deposition (companion to Baltimore, Lugano and New York).

Toledo (Ohio). 52.103. Predella panel: Crucifixion.

Tuscania (Viterbo). DUOMO. Fragmentary polyptych: Madonna and Child with donor; SS. Francis, Peter, Paul and Louis of Toulouse; in pinnacles, two Evangelists (companions to Rome, Massimo; central pinnacle missing); in predella, Last Supper, Betrayal of Christ, Way to Calvary, Crucifixion, Deposition, Entombment, Resurrection (deposited with Soprintendenza, Rome). L.

Urbino. GALLERIA NAZIONALE DELLE MARCHE. S. Michael, S. John Baptist.

Venice. CA' D'ORO. Coronation of Virgin (fr.).

Vienna. LANCKORONSKI COLLECTION. Predella panel: Nativity.

S. Augustine writing at his desk (fr.).

Washington (D.C.). 131 (KRESS COLLECTION K 23). Portable altarpiece: front, Madonna of Humility and blessing Redeemer above; back, Crucifixion.

152, 153, 154 (KRESS COLLECTON K 84, 85, 86). Panels of polyptych: Presentation of Virgin, Birth of Virgin, SS. Joachim and Anne before the Temple (g.p.).

Worcester (Mass.). 1940.31. Two panels from polyptych: S. Lucy, S. Catherine.

Homeless. Leaf of diptych: Madonna of Humility and two adoring Angels. Sd. *Plate* 421.

Madonna of Humility and many music-making Angels (repr. *Dedalo* XI, 1930/1, p. 345).

Madonna of Humility suckling the Child (repr. *Dedalo* XI, 1930/1, p. 346).
Madonna of Humility and two small Angels (repr. *Dedalo* XI, 1930/1, p. 347).
Seated S. Michael (repr. *Dedalo* XI, 1930/1, p. 348).
Crucifixion (repr. *Dedalo* XI, 1930/1, p. 349).
Two panels from pilasters of polyptych: S. Margaret, S. Cecilia (companions to Altenburg, Berlin, Oslo and Oxford).* *Plates* 431–432.
Mourning Virgin and S. John Evangelist. *Plate* 428.

ANDREA DA BOLOGNA

Dated works 1368 and 1372. Began, no doubt, in Bologna. Must have been long enough in the Marches to become close follower of Allegretto Nuzi.

Assisi. S. FRANCESCO, LOWER CHURCH, CAPPELLA DI S. CATERINA. Frescoes: Scenes from Life of S. Catherine; two groups of Saints, in one of which is a portrait of Cardinal Albornoz kneeling before Pope Clement. 1368. *Plates* 255–256.

— CAPPELLA DI S. LORENZO (NOW PASSAGE BETWEEN FIRST AND SECOND CHAPEL R.), VAULT. Fresco: Christ in Glory.

— WALLS. Frescoes: Martyrdom of S. Lawrence; Agony in the Garden and Betrayal of Christ; other fragments.

Corridonia (Macerata) (former Mont'olmo, called Pàusola 1851–1931). S. AGOSTINO. Madonna of Humility suckling the Child. Sd and d. 1372. *Plate* 252.

Fermo. 12. Polyptych: Madonna and Child enthroned, with Crucifixion above; left—Zacharias in the temple, Meeting at the Golden Gate, Birth of Baptist, Naming of Baptist, Baptism of Christ, SS. Francis and Anthony Abbot recommend Nuns to the Virgin; right—Two visions of S. John Evangelist and three Stories of Bishop Saint. Sd and d. 1368. *Plate* 254.

Offida (Ascoli Piceno). S. MARIA DELLA ROCCA, CRYPT, L. APSE. Frescoes: Crucifixion, Coronation of Virgin, Scenes from Life of S. Lucy (st.).

— — CENTRAL APSE. Frescoes: Madonna and Child with Angels, Saints, Mystic Marriage of S. Catherine (st.).

— — R. APSE. Frescoes: Scenes from Life of S. Catherine (st.). *Plate* 253.

Pàusola (Macerata). See Corridonia.

ANDREA DE LITIO see DELITIO

Sienese. Recorded from 1470 (lost works in Spedale della Scala, Siena) to 1512. Probably pupil of Vecchietta; influenced by contemporary Sienese.

Cambridge. FITZWILLIAM MUSEUM. 561. Madonna and Child with SS. Peter and Jerome.

Casciano in Vescovado (Murlo, Senese). CAPPELLA DI S. MARIA ASSUNTA IN PIAN-TASALA. Fresco: Madonna and Child enthroned with two Angels, SS. Sigismund, Nicholas, Roch and Sebastian; Dead Christ, mourning Virgin and Evangelist in roundels below (r.). Sd and d. 1514.*

Casole (Colle Val d'Elsa). COLLEGIATA. Madonna and Child with SS. Bernardino, Peter, Sebastian, Louis of Toulouse; in lunette, Massacre of Innocents; in predella, S. Bernardino rescues drowning boy Carinus; Calling of the Sons of Zebedee, Crucifixion, Martyrdom of S. Sebastian, Beheading of S. Sigismund. Sd and d. 1498. *Plate 839.*

Castel Del Piano (Siena). MADONNA DELLE GRAZIE. Madonna and Child with SS. John Baptist, John Evangelist and four Angels. E. (Not visible because object of special worship.)

Cincinnati (Ohio). 1920.75. Madonna and Child enthroned with SS. Catherine and Jerome, two Angels and Evangelist Luke. Sd and d. 1504.

Englewood (N.J.). PLATT COLLECTION (EX). Two fragments of altarpiece: SS. Augustine and John Baptist; SS. Blaise and Sebastian.

Esztergom. 55.171/2. Panels from altarpiece, cut into ovals: S. Francis, S. John Evangelist.*

Montecchio (Senese). S. ANDREA. Madonna and Child with SS. Jerome and John Evangelist.

Montepertuso (Senese). S. MICHELE. Triptych: Assumption of Virgin, a Martyr, S. Louis of Toulouse. E. (?)

Murlo (Senese). PIEVE DI S. FORTUNATO. Madonna and Child enthroned (fr., companion to Englewood).*

Pacina. S. MARIA MADDALENA. Madonna of the Rosary. Sd and d. 1505.

Paganico (Grosseto). S. MICHELE, L. WALL. Madonna crowned by two Angels, SS. Michael, Gregory, Sebastian and John Baptist.

Paris. LÉON BONNAT (EX). Mass of S. Gregory with SS. John Baptist and Jerome; Annunciation above. E. *Plate 838.*

Petroio (Senese). S. ANDREA. Fresco: Crucifixion.

Sarteano (Val di Chiana). S. MARTINO. Madonna and Child with SS. Roch and Sebastian; in pilasters of frame, small SS. Peter, John Baptist, Anthony Abbot, SS. Paul, Francis and Bernardino; in predella, Dead Christ, four busts of Saints. kneeling donors.

Siena. 290. Madonna and Child with four music-making Angels. E. (?)
298. Madonna and Child with SS. Catherine, Augustine, Sebastian and Monica (from Convent of S. Chiara at Radicondoli).

365. Nativity and Saints (from S. Maria Maddalena). *Plate* 840.

368. Crucifixion with SS. Benedict and Scholastica. d. 1502.

S. MARIA ASSUNTA (DUOMO). MUSEO DELL'OPERA. Predella: Fortitude and Prudence. L. (?)

S. MUSTIOLA ALLA ROSA, APSE. Madonna and Child with SS. Crispin and Crispinian (for the Compagnia dei Ciabattini). d. 1510. *Plate* 841.

Venice. BARONE RAIMONDO FRANCHETTI (EX). Madonna and Child with SS. Jerome and Catherine, and Man of Sorrows with two Angels below.

Homeless. Madonna and Child with S. John Baptist and Peter. (*Dedalo* XI, p. 746). Assumption and six Saints (r.). (*Dedalo* XI, p. 747).

ANDREA (SABBATINI) DA SALERNO

1480?–1530. *Follower of Cesare da Sesto, strongly influenced by Perugino and Raphael.*

Banzi (Lucania). CHIESA ABBAZIALE. Three panels of polyptych: Madonna suckling the Child, S. Peter, S. John Baptist.

Bonn. LANDES MUSEUM. Two panels from S. Alessio, Rome: S. Boniface, S. Alexis.

Budapest. 156. Dormitio.

Cava dei Tirreni (Salerno). ABBAZIA DELLA TRINITÀ, MUSEO. Panels of polyptych: Baptism of Christ; Madonna and Child in Glory; S. Peter, S. Paul; S. Benedict, S. Gregory (the last two, cut at bottom).

— CAPPELLA MORTUARIA. Frescoes: S. Benedict and his Monks; Last Judgement.

Compton Wynyates (Warwicks.). MARQUESS OF NORTHAMPTON. Madonna and Child with four Saints and donor. Sd and d. 1522.

London. FARRER COLLECTION (EX). Nativity. *Plate* 1509.

BRIDGEWATER HOUSE, EARL OF ELLESMERE. 79, 80, 80A. S. Jerome, S. Catherine, S. Rosalia. (?). Destroyed 1941.

Mertoun (Scotland). DUKE OF SUTHERLAND. 314. Small Nativity.

Montecassino. ABBAZIA, PINACOTECA. Madonna and Child with S. Catherine of Alexandria, S. Scholastica and Infant S. John.

S. Benedict receives Maurus and Placidus (r.).

Three Scenes from Life of S. Benedict: he performs a miracle, blesses Placidus, gives Maurus and Placidus the Benedictine rule (the other three scenes are by a follower). 1529–30. *Plate* 1515.

— CAPPELLA DI S. BERTARIO (EX). Frescoed lunette: Madonna and Child with two Angels. Discovered 1938. Destroyed 1944.

Montserrat (Barcelona). ABBEY. S. Bertarius surrounded by Martyrs and Abbot Squarcialupi (from church of Montecassino).* ca 1514–16.

Naples. 319. S. Nicholas enthroned with the three girls without dowry on his right and the three youths raised to life on his left (from Montecassino). ca 1517–18. *Plate* 1514.

320, 321. S. Paul and Carthusian Saint in niches.

Naples (contd.). 322, 323. Predella panels: S. Benedict welcomes Maurus and Placidus, Maurus and Placidus receive the Benedictine habit.

    325. Holy Family.

    326. S. Benedict reading (fr.).

    327. Adoration of Magi; Allegory of Religion in lunette above (from Duomo at Salerno).

    328. Polyptych: Madonna and Child, S. Leonard, S. Donatus; in upper register, Crucifixion, S. Veneranda, S. Apollonia; in predella, Last Supper (st.). d. 1521.

    337. Predella panel: S. Francis and the wolf of Gubbio.

    84027. S. Benedict enthroned with SS. Maurus and Placidus and the Fathers of the Church. 1525 (from Chapter Hall of Montecassino).

    — DEPOT. Adoration of Magi and donor (st.).

    — — (FROM S. TERESA AGLI STUDI). Descent from the Cross. L.

    GORO COLLECTION. Nativity (from Solofra; replaced there by copy).

    S. DOMENICO MAGGIORE. S. Catherine.

    S. GENNARO DEI POVERI, COURT. Frescoes: Vault: Eternal and grotteschi; lunettes; coats of arms. Walls: Six scenes from Life of S. Gennaro (r.).

    GIROLAMINI, QUADRERIA. Adoration of Magi.

    S. RESTITUTA, CHOIR, L. Predella: Female Saint before judges and other scenes. (?)

    SS. SEVERINO E SOSIO. Polyptych: below, Madonna, full-length SS. John Baptist and Catherine; above, Crucifixion, half-length SS. Benedict and Scholastica. *Plate* 1513.

Nocera Inferiore (Salerno). S. ANTONIO, HIGH ALTAR. Marriage of S. Catherine. Sd and d. 1519.

Ravello. DUOMO, SACRISTY. Ecstasy of S. Mary Magdalen.

    S. Sebastian.

Richmond (Surrey). COOK COLLECTION (EX). 80. Baptism of Christ.

Rossie Priory (Inchture, Perths.). LORD KINNAIRD. Visitation.

Salerno. MUSEO PROVINCIALE. Panels from Buccino polyptych: Madonna of Mercy, S. Anthony Abbot with donor, S. Augustine, S. Michael. 1512. *Plates* 1510–12.

    Pietà (from Duomo).

    S. GIORGIO. Madonna and Child between S. Catherine and a Bishop, two more Saints and a kneeling nun; in lunette, Noli me tangere (r.). Sd and d. 1523.

Solofra. COLLEGIATA. See Naples, Goro Collection.

Trapani. FARDELLI COLLECTION. 89. S. Gennaro reading.

Vallo di Lucania (Salerno). S. MARIA DELLE GRAZIE, CHAPEL R. Polyptych: Madonna and Child, S. Anthony of Padua, S. Pantalone; in upper register, Crucifixion and SS. Dominic and Gennaro; in predella, Christ and the twelve Apostles. doc. 1530.

Washington (D.C.). WASHINGTON CATHEDRAL (KRESS COLLECTION K 1008). Tondo: Madonna and Child with book.

Zagreb. 48. Pietà.

ANGUISSOLA, Sofonisba

Cremona. 1528–1625. Pupil of Bernardino Campi. In 1559 moved to Madrid and returned to Italy as an old woman.

Aix-en-Provence. 404. Miniature: Seated woman.

Althorp (Northampton). EARL SPENCER. Self-portrait at the harpsichord with old woman looking on. Sd and d. 1561. *Plate 1973.*

Baltimore (Md.). WALTERS ART GALLERY. 1016. Boy with sword, gloves and dog (versions at Richmond and Reims). *Plate 1976.*

Bergamo. 605. Holy Family (after Glasgow 125 by follower of Parmigianino). Inscription 'Sophonisba Anguissola adolescens, p. 1559' added later. (See Milan, Cavalieri.)

Berlin. 1705. Seated woman. Sd and d. 1557.

Brescia. 117. Portrait of man (Ippolito Chizzola?).

137. Dominican Monk (inscribed 'Sophonisba Angussola Virgo coram Amilcare patre pinxit MDLVI'). Sd and d. 1556.

Burghley House. MARQUESS OF EXETER. 323. Bearded old man seated at table, with left hand on open book. Sd. *Plate 1972.*

Corsham Court (Wilts.). METHUEN COLLECTION. Three children with dog.

Cremona. 202. Bust of lady.

Florence. UFFIZI. Self-portrait. E. Sd.

Genoa. NIGRO COLLECTION. Game of chess.

Goodwood (Chichester). DUKE OF RICHMOND. 4. Self-portrait playing on clavichord with oldish man on left (c. of Althorp).

Graz. Inv. 7. Portrait of young woman. (?)

Keir (Scotland). LT. COL. WILLIAM STIRLING. Self-portrait at the easel. *Plate 1967.*

Milan. BRERA. 762. Pietà. E.

767. Self-portrait. Sd.

POLDI PEZZOLI. 634. Portrait of a lady (her sister?).

CAVALIERI COLLECTION. Holy Family with Infant S. John and S. Francis (version at Bergamo). Sd. *Plate 1969.*

Naples. 358. Self-portrait at the spinet. E.

New York. H. G. SPERLING (EX). Oval: Self-portrait in the mirror.

O. BERBERYAN. Young woman sewing (formerly Mather Collection).

Nivaagaard. HAGE COLLECTION. 1. Amilcare Anguissola with his daughter Minerva and his son Asdrubale.

2. Portrait of old woman. *Plate 1975.*

Oberlin (Ohio). 61.84. ALLEN MEMORIAL ART MUSEUM, KRESS COLLECTION. K 1213. Roundel: a boy and a girl of the Attavanti family.

Palermo. 422. (Inv. 333). Madonna and Child from S. Martino alle Scale. (?)

Paris. FRITS LUGT. 'Ashburnham' medallion: Self-portrait. Sd and d. 1558. *Plate 1974.*

Poznań. NATIONAL MUSEUM. Inv. Mo 39. The three sisters and the governess of the artist. Sd and d. 1555. *Plate 1968*.

Rheims. 1572. Boy with dog (copy of Baltimore).

Richmond (Surrey). COOK COLLECTION. 172. Boy with dog (replica of Baltimore). 173. Young monk.

Rome. GALLERIA BORGHESE. 118. Small portrait of her sister Lucia. Sd and d. MDVLI.
  GALLERIA DORIA PAMPHILI. 148. Portrait of young woman. (?)
    373. Husband and wife.
  PRINCIPE COLONNA. Small self-portrait. Sd and d. 1558.
  GALLERIA SPADA. 304. Portrait of a lady. E. (?)
  (Environs). MENTANA. F. ZERI. Don Giulio Clovio seated at table. *Plate 1970*.
    Self-portrait (signed replica of Keir).

Siena. 497. Bernardino Campi painting a portrait of the artist.

Southampton. ART GALLERY. Portrait of a young nun (her sister Elena?).

Terzo d'Aquileja. CALLIGARIS COLLECTION (EX). Portrait of a Dominican astronomer. Sd and d. 155(5?). *Plate 1971*.

Vienna. 109. Self-portrait. Sd and d. 1554.

ANTONIAZZO ROMANO

Documented 1461 to 1510. Started under Umbrian followers of Angelico and Benozzo. Strongly influenced by Melozzo da Forlì as well as by Perugino, and slightly by Botticelli and Ghirlandajo.

Altenburg. 112. Madonna and Child.
    126, 127, 128, 129. Four panels of polyptych: Angel and Virgin of Annunciation, full-length SS. Peter and John Baptist. (st.).

Aquila. MARCHESE DRAGONETTI DE TORRES (EX). Triptych: Madonna and Child enthroned with female donor; SS. John Baptist and Mary Magdalen.

Baltimore (Md.). WALTERS ART GALLERY. 640. Full-length S. Francis. (?)
    685. Madonna adoring Child on parapet and Infant S. John.
  MUSEUM OF ART, JACOB EPSTEIN COLLECTION. Madonna and Child standing on parapet. (?)

Bayonne. 132. Miniature: Bust of Christ on altar adored by two prelates.

Berlin. S.4. Predella panel: Herod's Banquet and Beheading of Baptist in background. (?)
    I. 163. See Cassel.

Cambridge (Mass.). FOGG ART MUSEUM. 1924.23. Tabernacle: Madonna and Child with Infant S. John; God Father above, and two Angels.
    1928. 174. Panel of triptych: Full-length S. Fabian (Pope).

Campagnano (Roma). See Viterbo.

Capua. DUOMO, CAPPELLA CAETANI. Madonna and Child with SS. Stephen and Lucy. Sd and d. 1489.

Cassel. 481. (FORMERLY BERLIN I, 163). Two fragments of altarpiece joined together: Four Angels, S. Cosmas (companion to Zagreb).

Castelnuovo di Porto (Lazio). S. MARIA ASSUNTA, CAPPELLA PAGNINI. Triptych: Christ blessing Virgin, SS. Sebastian and John Baptist. Sd and d. 1501.

Civita Castellana. S. PIETRO, SECOND ALTAR R. Adoration of the Child.

Detroit (Mich.). 22.11. Madonna holding Child on parapet.
26.111. The Virgin and a female Saint recommend a kneeling worshipper to Christ in Glory (p.).

Dublin. 827. Virgin healing Pope Leo's hand (r.).

Englewood (N.J.). D. F. PLATT COLLECTION (EX). Full-length S. Francis.

Fermo. 19. 'Mater Amabilis' (p.).

Florence. UFFIZI. 3274. Portable altarpiece: Madonna and Child with God the Father above; on inside wings, SS. Peter and Paul, Angel and Virgin of Annunciation; on outside wings, SS. Sebastian and Anthony Abbot (g.p.). d. 1485.
CONTINI BONACOSSI COLLECTION. 'Barberini' Nativity with two Saints.

Fondi. S. PIETRO, R. TRANSEPT. 'Caetani' Triptych: Madonna and Child enthroned with donor; SS. Peter and Paul. Sd. *Plate* 1089.

Genazzano (Roma). CONVENTO DI S. PIO. Madonna and Child standing on parapet (r.).

Houston (Texas). MUSEUM OF FINE ARTS, EDITH AND PERCY STRAUSS BEQUEST. 21. Madonna and Child standing on parapet, with small donor.

Karlsruhe. 406, 407. Two panels of polyptych: SS. John Evangelist and John Baptist.

Lewes (Surrey). E. P. WARREN (EX). Madonna adoring the Child.

Lewisburg (Pa.). BUCKNELL UNIVERSITY. BL.K 16 (KRESS STUDY COLLECTION K 318). Pinnacle: S. Francis adoring Crucifix.

Lille. 992 (Inv. 796). Madonna adoring Child on parapet, with Infant S. John (version of Baltimore).

Lisieux. MUSÉE (COLLECTION CAMPANA). Madonna and Child with SS. John Baptist and John Evangelist (from S. Francesca Romana, Rome; st. ?).

London. COURTAULD INSTITUTE GALLERIES, GAMBIER PARRY COLLECTION. Triptych: Half-length Madonna and blessing Child with Infant S. John; full-length SS. Peter and Paul.

Los Angeles (Cal.). MUSEUM OF ART, N. SIMON FOUNDATION. 'Benson' Madonna holding Child on parapet and two Cherubim. E. *Plate* 1064.

Lugano. THYSSEN COLLECTION (EX). Madonna holding Child on parapet (st. v. of Los Angeles).

Lyons. 29 (COLLECTION CAMPANA). Version of Giotto's 'Navicella' with nuns (from S. Francesca Romana, Rome). Inscription and date 1461 overpainted.

Madrid. 577. Detached fresco: Madonna and blessing Child with two Angels. (fr.).
577A. Portable altarpiece: Head of Christ; inside wings, SS. Peter and John Baptist; outside wings, SS. Colomba and John Evangelist.

Montefalco. S. FRANCESCO (MUSEO), L. WALL. SS. Vincent, Illuminata and Nicholas of Tolentino.

Montefortino (Marches). MUSEO CIVICO. 4. Bust of S. Catherine. (?)

Naples. CAPPELLA PONTANIANA. Fresco: Madonna and Child enthroned with SS. John Baptist and Evangelist; above, putti worshipping Cross.

    S. FRANCESCO DELLE MONACHE (MADONNA DELLA ROTONDA) (DESTROYED). Madonna and Child enthroned. Not traced.

New York. 06.1214. Predella panel: Nativity.

    30.95.290. Tabernacle: Madonna and blessing Child.

    41.190.9 Madonna suckling the Child.

Parcieux. LA GRANGE BLANCHE, HENRI CHALANDON (EX). Profile bust of Blessed Michele and Worshippers. d. 1484.

Paris. 1134A. Madonna and Child enthroned (face painted over). Sd and d. 1494.

Perugia. 109. Tabernacle: Madonna and Child blessing.

Poggio Nativo (Sabina). SS. ANNUNZIATA. Triptych: blessing Christ, SS. Sebastian and Michael.

Providence (R.I.). SCHOOL OF DESIGN (EX). Madonna and Child on parapet, with Infant S. John (version of Baltimore).

Rieti. MUSEO CIVICO. Centre panel of triptych: Madonna suckling the Child and small donor. Sd and d. 1464. *Plate* 1087.

    Two left panels of triptych: S. Francis receiving stigmata; S. Anthony of Padua with lily and book.

    Detached fresco: S. Margaret (r.).

    DUOMO, CAPPELLA DI S. IGNAZIO. Fresco: Madonna and Child enthroned with Magdalen and Saintly Monk.

    SEMINARIO, SOFFIT OF ARCHWAY. Fresco: dead Christ, S. Paul and S. Bernardino da Feltre (r.).

Rome. GALLERIA NAZIONALE, PALAZZO BARBERINI. 2371. Madonna and Child enthroned with SS. Paul and Francis. Sd (formerly dated 1488?).

    6820. S. Sebastian and two donors.

    OPERE RECUPERATE. Nativity with Saints.

    COLLEGIO DEGLI SCOZZESI. Madonna and Child.

    CONVENTO DI TOR DE' SPECCHI. (See S. Francesca Romana.)

    PIO SODALIZIO DEI PICENI. Madonna and Child enthroned (from S. Salvatore in Lauro). d. 1494.

    S. AMBROGIO ALLA MASSIMA. Mourning over dead Christ.

    S. CROCE IN GERUSALEMME, APSE. Fresco: Christ in Glory and Invention of the True Cross (on Melozzo's indications).

    S. FRANCESCA ROMANA (TOR DE' SPECCHI), OLD CHAPEL. Frescoes:

    — ALTAR WALL. Madonna and Child enthroned with SS. Benedict and S. Francesca Romana accompanied by an Angel; on either side, two scenes from her Life.

    — WINDOW WALL. Upper register: S. Francesca Romana gives the speech to a dumb girl, replaces the wine given to the poor, multiplies the wheat, heals a youth; lower register: heals a girl affected by palsy, raises a dead child to life, heals a broken head, raises to life a youth beaten to death.

— WALL OPPOSITE ALTAR. Upper register; Visions of the Virgin's mantle, of the Communion received from S. Peter, of the Christ Child in her arms, of Christ taking her hand; lower register: Healing of a wounded youth, Ecstasy of S. Francesca Romana in the vineyard, Healing of a sick man, The luminous globe over the Saint's head when she received holy Communion.

— ENTRANCE WALL. Upper register: S. Francesca Romana multiplies the bread for her nuns, raises to life a drowned man, makes a vine produce grapes in January; lower register: Death of S. Francesca Romana, Burial of the Saint, Vision of Hell.

Frescoed decoration (p.; r.). d. 1468.

S. GIOVANNI LATERANO, TABERNACOLO DELLA CONFESSIONE. Frescoes: Christ on Cross with mourning Virgin, Evangelist, SS. James, Paul, Peter and Andrew. (?)

— BALDACCHINO PAPALE. Frescoes: Madonna and Child enthroned with two Angels and donor, SS. Lawrence, Baptist, Evangelist and Stephen; Coronation of Virgin, Annunciation; SS. Catherine and Anthony Abbot (p.).

— R. NAVE. Fresco: Madonna and Child enthroned.

SS. GIOVANNI E PAOLO. Madonna in Glory and SS. Jerome, Paul, Baptist and Evangelist.

S. MARIA DEL BUON AIUTO. Madonna embracing the Child.

S. MARIA DELLA CONSOLAZIONE. Madonna and Child holding globe. E.

S. MARIA SOPRA MINERVA, FOURTH ALTAR R. Annunciation with Dominican Cardinal Juan de Torquemada recommending three poor girls to the Virgin (altarpiece of the Confraternity of the Annunziata founded in 1460 for helping girls without dowry). *Plate* 1094.

— SEPULCHRE OF BISHOP COCA. Fresco: Christ as Judge with two music-making Angels and Juan Diaz de Coca (on Melozzo's indications). 1477.

— CAMERA DI S. CATERINA DA SIENA. Frescoes: Crucifixion, Annunciation, Dead Christ, S. Jerome, S. John Baptist, S. Peter and three Saints, SS. Lucy and Apollonia. 1482.

S. NICOLA IN CARCERE, R. NAVE. Detached fresco: Madonna and blessing Child in niche (r.).

PANTHEON. Fresco: Madonna and Child with SS. Francis and John Baptist (r.). Fresco: Annunciation.

S. PAOLO FUORI LE MURA, ANTICAMERA DELLA SAGRESTIA, R. WALL. Fresco: Madonna and Child on feigned ground of golden mosaic (fr. of lunette).

— — OPPOSITE ENTRANCE. Fresco: Bust of Christ.

— — OVER INNER DOOR. Fresco: S. Paul.

— PINACOTECA (SACRISTY). Madonna enthroned adoring Child in her lap, with SS. Benedict, Paul, Peter and Justina.

Rome. S. PAOLO FUORI LE MURA (contd.). Four panels of polyptych: SS. Benedict, Paul, Peter and Justina in arches of portico.

S. PIETRO IN MONTORIO, THIRD CHAPEL L. Frescoes: Madonna and Child with S. Anne and donor; David and Solomon; God the Father.

S. SABA, OVER APSE. Fresco: Annunciation. d. 1464.

— ALONG TOP OF WALLS. Frescoed frieze: Piccolomini arms, emblems, busts of Prophets and Angels in medallions.

S. SABINA, CONVENT. Dominican Saint with Redeemer and worshipper. *Plate* 1092.

SS. VITO E MODESTO, L. WALL. Fresco: upper register: Madonna and Child with SS. Crescentia and Modestus; lower register: SS. Sebastian, Margaret and Modestus. d. 1483.

VATICAN, PINACOTECA. 279. Madonna and Child adored by Members of the *Rota*, with SS. Peter and Paul.

— LIBRARY OF SIXTUS IV. Frescoes on Melozzo's designs. 1480–1.

— MUSEO PETRIANO. Fragments of fresco: Madonna and Child, S. Peter. (?)

Subiaco. S. FRANCESCO, HIGH ALTAR. Triptych (with later additions above and below): Madonna and Child, S. Francis, S. Anthony of Padua. Sd and d. 1467. *Plate* 1088.

Tivoli. DUOMO, SECOND ALTAR R. S. Vincent Ferrer with Angels and donors. (?)

— PASSAGE TO SACRISTY. Fresco: S. Anthony Abbot.

S. GIOVANNI EVANGELISTA. Frescoes: in vault, Evangelists and Church-Fathers in couples; in soffit of arch, busts of Sibyls; on walls, Assumption; Birth and Naming of Baptist. *Plates* 1090, 1091.

S. MARIA MAGGIORE, CHAPEL L. OF CHOIR. S. Anthony of Padua. E.

Valencia. MUSEO DE PINTURAS. Madonna and Child.

Velletri. CATTEDRALE, MUSEO CAPITOLARE. Madonna and Child behind parapet. d. 1483.

Madonna and Child.

Venice. CA' D'ORO. Predella panel: S. Jerome healing the lion.

Viterbo. MUSEO CIVICO (from Campagnano, S. Maria al Prato). Madonna and Child seated on cushion (p.). Fr. of altarpiece Sd and d. 1497.

Virgin in prayer (p.).

Worcester (Mass.). ART MUSEUM (EX). Madonna adoring Child and Infant S. John (st. version of Baltimore, with landscape).

Zagarolo (Lazio). S. LORENZO. Triptych of Pier Francesco Colonna: blessing Christ, SS. Peter and Paul. d. 1490.

Zagreb. 88, 89. Two fragments of altarpiece: S. Damian, four Angels (companions to Cassel).

Homeless. Madonna and Infant S. John adoring the Child. Sd and d. 1465. *Plate* 1093. Madonna and Child in the lap of S. Anne.* (Repr. *Paragone*, March 1967.)

ANTONIO DA FABRIANO

Marchigian. Active 1451 to 1489. Pupil perhaps of the Salimbeni, developed under the influence of the Vivarini and possibly of some German Master.

Arcevia (Ancona). S. MEDARDO. Angel and Virgin of Annunciation, in pilasters of altarpiece by Signorelli. *Plate 956.*

Baltimore (Md.). WALTERS ART GALLERY. 439. S. Jerome in his study (from the Fornari Collection in Fabriano). Sd and d. 1451. *Plate 784.*

Budapest. COUNT JULIUS ANDRASSY (EX). Madonna and Child enthroned with two Angels, S. Donnino and S. Peter Martyr. d. 145(7?)9.

Cerreto d'Esi (Fabriano). PARISH CHURCH. Side-panels of polyptych: S. Mary Magdalen, S. Francis; in pinnacles, Angel and Virgin of Annunciation. Stolen. *Plate 788.*

Fabriano. 13. Death of Virgin. *Plate 786.*

    35. Detached fresco: Madonna and Child enthroned, with S. Anthony Abbot and S. James recommending donor.

    Detached fresco from Casa Bigonzetti Baravelli: Madonna and Child with SS. Christopher, Michael, Andrew (r.). d. 1457.*

    S. LUCIA (VULGO S. DOMENICO), FORMER REFECTORY. Frescoes: Christ on Cross, with Dominican Saints and monks; S. Lucy and S. Catherine of Siena standing in niches. Formerly d. 1480.

    — FORMER CONVENT, UPPER HALL (LIBRARY). Fresco: Redeemer. After 1472 (date on beam in ceiling).

Genga (Fabriano). S. CLEMENTE, CHOIR. Triptych: Madonna and Child with Angels, S. Clement, S. John Baptist; in predella, half-length Apostles. Sd and d. 1474. *Plates 789-90.*

    S. Jerome and donor. E.

    — CANONICA. Standard: front, Madonna and Child enthroned and God the Father blessing in pinnacle; back, S. Clement enthroned with Flagellants and donor.

Gualdo Tadino. 6. Triptych from SS. Annunziata: S. Anne teaching little Mary; S. Joachim; S. Joseph, ca 1457.

Matelica. 26. Painted Crucifix. Sd and d. 1452. *Plate 785.*

Richmond (Va.). MUSEUM OF FINE ARTS. Left panel of polyptych: S. Clement blessing. *Plate 787.*

ANTONIO DA VITERBO (the Elder)

Not to be confused with Antonio da Viterbo the Younger (il Pastura). Active middle of the fifteenth century. Developed under influence of Gentile da Fabriano's work in Rome, then of Benozzo Gozzoli; close to Bartolomeo di Tommaso da Foligno.

Capena. s. MICHELE, R. NAVE. Triptych: Christ enthroned; S. Peter, S. Paul; outside, Annunciation. Sd and d. 1451. *Plates 619–621.*

Rome. MUSEO DEL FORO ROMANO (EX-ABBAZIA BENEDETTINA DI S. FRANCESCA ROMANA). Frescoes: Crucifixion in lunette; Entombment in lunette; Redeemer in roundel. *Plates 622–624.*

    s. PAOLO FUORI LE MURA, BAPTISTERY. Frescoes in soffits of arches: Evangelists, Church Fathers; in roundels, God the Father, S. Peter, S. Paul, S. Benedict. ca 1460/65.

ANTONIO DA VITERBO THE YOUNGER see PASTURA

ARALDI

Jossaphat de Araldis. Painter documented in Parma 1519 and 1520. Influenced by Venetian school of painting and by North European engravings.

Parma. 203. S. Sebastian. Sd. *Plate 1315.*

ARCANGELO DI COLA DA CAMERINO

Marchigian. Mentioned 1416 at Città di Castello, 1420–1422 in Florence, 1428 at Camerino. Follower of Gentile da Fabriano, influenced somewhat by Lorenzo di Niccolò and a great deal more by Fra Angelico.

Bergen. BILLEDGALLERI. Madonna and Child holding jasmin. E. *Plate 675.*

Bibbiena. ss. IPPOLITO E DONATO. Madonna and Child enthroned with six Angels.

Camerino. PINACOTECA. Madonna and Child enthroned with two Angels.

Modena. 519. Predella: S. Catherine at the wheel, Deposition, Funeral of S. Zanobi, S. Andrew tied to the Cross, S. John Evangelist in cauldron of boiling oil. (?)

Monastero dell'Isola (Cessapalombo, Macerata). PARISH CHURCH. Triptych: Christ on Cross with mourning Virgin, S. John Evangelist and two Angels; S. John Baptist and Bishop Saint; SS. Venantius and Peter. Sd and d. 1425. Destroyed 1889.

Munich. WALTER SCHNACKENBERG (EX). Madonna of Humility.

New Haven (Conn.). 1937.10. Madonna and Child enthroned with four Angels. (fr.).

New York. MISS HELEN C. FRICK. Diptych: Madonna and Child enthroned with six Angels; Crucifixion. Sd. *Plates 671–672.*

Osimo. s. MARCO, FIRST ALTAR L. Fresco: Madonna and Child enthroned with SS. Dominic and Peter Martyr.

Philadelphia (Pa.). J. G. JOHNSON COLLECTION. 124/5/6/7. Four predella panels: Visitation, Nativity, Adoration of Magi, Flight into Egypt. *Plate 674.*

Rotterdam. BOYMANS-VAN BEUNINGEN MUSEUM. Inv. 2555. Madonna and Child enthroned with two Angels.

Venice. CONTE VITTORIO CINI. Inv. 6177. Predella panel: Martyrdom of S. Lawrence. *Plate 677.*

Inv. 1304. Portable altarpiece: Madonna and Child enthroned; S. Francis receiving Stigmata, SS. Anthony Abbot and Bartholomew; Crucifixion, S. Christopher. *Plate 673.*

ASPERTINI, Amico

Bologna. 1474/5–1552. Pupil of Ercole Roberti da Ferrara, follower and assistant of Costa and Francia; went to Rome 1500–1503; influenced by Signorelli, Pinturicchio and Raphael.

Baltimore (Md.). WALTERS ART GALLERY. 441. Bust of woman reading. *Plate 1727.*

Bergamo. 313. Cassone panel: Battle scene. E. (?)

Berlin-Ost. 118. Adoration of Shepherds. Sd. *Plate 1713.*

Bologna. GALLERIA DAVIA BARGELLINI. Bust of fat man.

PINACOTECA. Inv. 558. 'Gesuati' Nativity with SS. George, Francis, John Baptist, Jerome, Eustace, Sebastian and two donors ('Pala del Tirocinio'). Sd. ca 1504. *Plate 1714.*

Inv. 561. Adoration of Magi.

— DEPOT. Detached frescoes: Madonna and Child; Holy Family.

RICOVERO DI MENDICITÀ (MISERICORDIA). Madonna suckling the Child.

S. GIACOMO MAGGIORE, CAPPELLA BENTIVOGLIO. Frescoed lunettes. Right wall— medallion with Madonna, six Apostles and Angels; Left wall—six Apostles, round circular window.

— ORATORIO DI S. CECILIA. Frescoes on walls: (5) Beheading of Valerian and his brother Tiburtius; (6) Funeral of the Martyrs; (3), (4), (7), (8) assisting L. Costa—see there; see also Francia. 1504/06. *Plate 1719.*

S. MARTINO MAGGIORE, CAPPELLA MARESCOTTI (FIRST L.). Monochrome fresco on front of altar: Entombment (r.).

— FIFTH CHAPEL R. Madonna and Child with SS. Lucy, Petronius, Nicholas and three girls without dowry.

S. PETRONIO, FIFTH CHAPEL R. Pietà. d. 1519.

Bordeaux. 102. Adoration of Magi. L. (?)

Carpi. FORESTI COLLECTION. Madonna and Child (fr., companion to Rome).

Dublin. JAMES A. MURNAGHAN. Madonna and Child with two Saints.

Florence. UFFIZI. 3808. Adoration of the Child.

CASA STROZZI. Predella: Meeting at Golden Gate, Birth of Virgin, Presentation, Marriage of Virgin. *Plates 1716–1717.*

VILLA LANDAU-FINALY (EX). Fragments of cassone: Hunters; nymph by altar.

Frankfurt a/M. 840. Bust of young man. *Plate 1725.*

Gazzada (Varese). FONDAZIONE CAGNOLA. Crucifixion.

Hanover. Inv. 301. Predella panel: Disputation of Augustine. d. 1523.

Harrow. STOGDON COLLECTION (EX). Bust of youth with flat cap.

Holkham (Norfolk). EARL OF LEICESTER. Holy Family with female Saint. *Plate* 1728.

London. BRITISH MUSEUM. MS. 29. Albani Book of Hours: f. 19 v. Nativity. Sd.
    Plate 1718.

    J. F. MINKEN (EX). Bust of lady.

Lucca. III, 2. Madonna and Child in Glory and SS. George, Joseph, John Evangelist
    and Sebastian. 1508–9.

    S. FREDIANO, ENTRANCE WALL. Fresco: Madonna on pedestal surrounded by SS.
    John Baptist, Agatha, Martha and Sebastian (r.). 1508–9.

    — CAPPELLA DI S. AGOSTINO (SECOND L.), VAULT. Frescoes: God the Father,
    Prophets (Isaiah, Jeremiah, Ezechiel, Elijah), Sibyls (Libyca, Delphica, Cumana,
    Tiburtina) and Angels.

    — — L. WALL. Frescoes: in lunette, Deposition; below, S. Ambrose baptizes
    S. Augustine, the Volto Santo carried in procession from the sea into Lucca.
    Plate 1721.

    — — R. WALL. Frescoes: in lunette, Approval of the Rule of S. Augustine; below,
    S. Frediano changes the course of the river Serchio, Nativity. *Plates* 1722–1723.

    — — END WALL. Fresco in lunette: Last Judgement (lost).

    — — SOFFIT OF ENTRANCE ARCH. Frescoes: Grotteschi framing four Scenes from
    Life of Christ (Last Supper, Washing of Feet, Agony in the Garden, Flagella-
    tion), and five roundels (Angels, busts of SS. Rita, Cassio, Fausta, Richard).
    Plate 1720.

    — — ENTRANCE PIERS. Frescoes: SS. Peter, Simon, James; SS. Paul, Andrew, John.
    Frescoed decoration commissioned by Priore Pasquino Cenami. ca 1508–9.

    COLLEGIO DI S. FREDIANO. Frescoed lunette: Madonna and Child enthroned with
    female martyr and S. James (r.). (?)

Madrid. 519. Male portrait. (?)

    524/5. Fronts of cassone: Rape of the Sabine Women; Continence of Scipio
    (companions to Vienna, Lanckoronski). E. (?)

Mellerstain (Berwicks.). EARL OF HADDINGTON. Portrait of Anna Maria Donna
    Biavati.

    Portrait of young man. *Plate* 1724.

Munich. 1059. Bust of young man. (?)

New York. FRIEDSAM COLLECTION (EX; also EX METROPOLITAN MUSEUM 32.100.73).
    So-called Taddeo Taddei.

Paris. SAINT-NICOLAS-DES-CHAMPS. Madonna and Child with Saints. *Plate* 1729.

Philadelphia (Pa.). J. G. JOHNSON COLLECTION. 247. Predella panel: Death of S.
    Bernard.

Piediluco (between Terni and Rieti). S. FRANCESCO, APSE. Frescoed vault: Christ
    and two Angels, S. Louis of Toulouse, S. Bernardino, S. Anthony of Padua,
    S. Bonaventura.

Rome. GALLERIA NAZIONALE (PALAZZO BARBERINI). S. Joseph (fr., companion to
  Carpi).

  PALAZZO SPADA. 131. S. Christopher; on back, monochrome S. Luke.

Vienna. 85. Profile of woman.

  LANCKORONSKI COLLECTION. End panels of cassone: Youth sitting among ruins;
  Perseus with the Gorgon's head (companions to Madrid). E. (?)

Washington (D.C.). 414. (KRESS COLLECTION. K 529.) S. Sebastian.

Homeless. Predella: Adoration of Shepherds, Adoration of Magi. E. *Plate* 1715.
  Portrait of old woman. *Plate* 1726.
  Amazonomachia. *Plate* 1712.

BADILE, Antonio

Verona. 1518–60. Pupil of Caroto; influenced by Torbido, Brusasorci and Titian.

Lovere. 102. Portrait of notary Lazise of Verona.

Mazzurega (Verona). S. BARTOLOMEO. Pietà. Sd and d. 1545.
  Madonna and Child with Infant S. John, SS. Francis, Valeria, Anthony Abbot
  and kneeling donor as S. Bartholomew (r.). Sd and d. 1556.

Padua. 636. Madonna and Holy Children in Glory and below, SS. Scholastica,
  Benedict, Prosdocimus, Justina. 1552. *Plate* 1916.

Turin. GALLERIA SABAUDA. 567. Circumcision. E. *Plate* 1913.

Verona. 244. Madonna and Child with SS. Andrew, Peter, John Evangelist (known
  as 'Madonna di Piazza dei Signori'). Sd and d. 1544. *Plate* 1914.

  246. Raising of Lazarus (from S. Eufemia; variant at S. Bernardino).

  380. Madonna and Child with SS. Mary Magdalen and Dionysius; Eternal
  above. E. (?)

  S. BERNARDINO, CAPPELLA AVANZI (R. OF CHOIR). Raising of Lazarus (other pictures
  by Caroto, F. Morone and N. Giolfino). d. 1546. *Plate* 1915.

  SS. NAZARO E CELSO, SECOND ALTAR L. Madonna and Child appearing to SS. John
  Baptist, Anthony Abbot, Benedict, Blaise and a page. Sd and d. 154(4?) 3?).

BALDASSARRE D'ESTE or DA REGGIO

*Illegitimate son of Niccolò III d'Este, born at Reggio Emilia before 1441, died at Ferrara
1504. Recorded 1461 at the Sforza Court in Milan, from 1469 at the Este Court in Ferrara.
Painter and medallist. Praised as a portraitist.*

Ferrara. PALAZZO SCHIFANOIA, SALA DEI MESI. Several portrait heads in lower frescoes
  (see full description of these under 'Ferrarese before 1510'). *Plate* 731.

  PINACOTECA. Fragmentary fresco detached from Oratorio della Concezione: S.
  Francis receiving stigmata, and female donor. Sd.*

Milan. CASTELLO, TRIVULZIO COLLECTION. Profile of Borso d'Este. ca 1470.
Venice. CONTE VITTORIO CINI. Inv. 6159. Profile portrait of (?)Tito Strozzi. Sd and
  d. 1493. *Plate 730.*
Washington (D.C.). 542. (KRESS COLLECTION. K 1245). Profile portrait of Francesco
  Gonzaga as a boy. *Plate 729.*

BALDUCCI, Matteo

Umbro-Sienese. Documented 1509–55. Pupil of Pacchiarotto; assistant and imitator of Pinturicchio; influenced by Fungai.

Altenburg. 116–123. Decorative panels from coffered ceiling, with Busts of Pru-
  dence, Charity, Justice and Temperance, Busts of Philosophers in medallions,
  Grotteschi, Putti.
Balcarres (Fife, Scotland). EARL OF CRAWFORD AND BALCARRES. Tondo: Diana and
  Actaeon.
Bergamo. 520. Tondo: Vulcan at his forge.
  548. Octagonal panel: Flight of Clelia.
Bourges. MUSÉE. Madonna and Child with Infant S. John.
Cambridge. FITZWILLIAM MUSEUM, MARLAY 30. Tondo: Trajan and the Widow.
Cetona (Val di Chiana). S. FRANCESCO, CAPPELLA DI S. EGIDIO. Madonna and Child
  with SS. Lawrence and Francis; in predella, roundels with Saints (r.).
Châalis (Ermenonville). MUSÉE JACQUEMART-ANDRÉ. 20. Tondo: Winter (com-
  panion to Rome, Vitetti).
Compton Wynyates. MARQUESS OF NORTHAMPTON. Predella panel: Crucifixion.
  Plate 1149.
Dresden. 38. Bust of S. Crispinus.
  40. Predella panel: S. Roch fed by the dog.
Florence. BERENSON COLLECTION. Tondo: Childhood and Old Age.
  LOESER COLLECTION (EX). Apollo and Muse. *Plate 1152.*
Gubbio. PALAZZO DEI CONSOLI, PINACOTECA. 35. Triumph of Bacchus. *Plates* 1151, 1153.
Lucardo (Certaldo). SS. MARTINO E GIUSTO. Madonna and Child with SS. John
  Baptist and Sigismund.
Oxford. CHRIST CHURCH. 56. S. Christopher. (?)
Paris. 1571, 1572. Judgement of Solomon; Judgement of Daniel.
Princeton (N.J.). F. JEWETT MATHER COLLECTION. Expulsion from Eden.
Richmond (Surrey). COOK COLLECTION. 564. Profile of young woman. (?)
Rome. PALAZZO SPADA. Nativity.
  CONTE VITETTI: Three tondi: Spring, Summer and Autumn (companions to
  Châalis).
Siena. 346. Angel (fr.).
  359. Madonna and Child with SS. Bernardino and Catherine.

364, 398. SS. Jerome and Mary Magdalen in niche; SS. Agnes and Francis in niche.

377, 379, 381, 393. Hexagonal panels: Faith, Charity, Fortitude and Justice.

382. Madonna and Child with SS. Jerome and Bartholomew. E. (?)

386. Nativity (on Pinturicchio's cartoon). *Plate* 1148.

391. Madonna and Child with SS. Jerome and Anthony of Padua.

406. Predella to S. Spirito Assumption: S. Francis receiving Stigmata, Pietà, S. Catherine of Siena receiving Stigmata. E. *Plate* 1147.

407. Nativity (from Campansi).

CASA DI RIPOSO (MADONNA DI CAMPANSI), CLOISTER. Fresco: Assumption (Saints below only; Madonna by Fungai; Eternal, Angels and Prophets above, by Pietro di Domenico).

S. CATERINA DELLA NOTTE (BY SPEDALE DELLA SCALA), SACRISTY. Bierheads: S. Catherine of Siena receiving Stigmata; S. Catherine of Siena and four Flagellants; Risen Christ.

S. MARIA ASSUNTA (DUOMO), LIBRERIA PICCOLOMINI. Frescoes: Mythological and allegorical scenes on ceiling; shields over windows; monochrome decorations on pilasters (under direct inspiration of Pinturicchio). *Plate* 1146.

— MUSEO DELL'OPERA. Panel of polyptych: S. Anthony of Padua.

S. SPIRITO, FIRST ALTAR L. Madonna of Assumption, with S. Francis and S. Catherine of Siena; in lunette, Eternal (predella in Pinacoteca 406). E. *Plate* 1147.

Tulsa (Oklahoma). PHILBROOK ART CENTER. 3363. KRESS COLLECTION. K 1154. Madonna and Child with Infant S. John (?).

Versailles. JAMES H. HYDE. Predella panel: 'Holford' Adoration of Magi. *Plate* 1150.

BARNA DA SIENA

Sienese. According to Vasari died 1381 (*misprint for* 1351?). *Followed tradition of Simone Martini.*

Altenburg. 42. Side-panel of polyptych, companion to Palermo and Pisa: S. John Baptist enthroned. E. (?)

Amsterdam. OTTO LANZ (EX). Left wing of diptych: Madonna of Humility; Angel of Annunciation in roundel above. (?)

Asciano. MUSEO D'ARTE SACRA. Centre panel of polyptych: Madonna and Child with donor. E. *Plate* 331.

Baltimore (Md.). WALTERS ART GALLERY. 737. Crucifixion. (?)

Berlin. 1071A. Centre panel of portable altarpiece: Madonna and Child enthroned with SS. Francis, James, Lawrence (?) and Benedict; dead Christ, mourning Magdalen and S. John Evangelist in three roundels above. (?)

1142. Left wing of diptych, companion to Oxford: Annunciation with kneeling Dominican; below, six half-length Saints. (?) *Plate* 336.

R. VON KAUFMANN (EX). Crucifixion.

Boston (Mass.). 15.1145. Mystic Marriage of S. Catherine and S. Anne and Virgin playing with Infant Jesus; below, S. Margaret defeats the dragon, Reconciliation of two Knights, S. Michael kills the Devil (ex voto of Arrigo di Neri Arrighetti). (?) *Plate* 327.

Florence. BERENSON COLLECTION. Portable altarpiece: Madonna of Humility (r.).
MUSEO HORNE. 55, 56. Diptych: Madonna and Child; dead Christ. (?)

Frankfurt a/M. CONSUL HARRY FULD (EX). Christ carrying the Cross; Christ on the Cross; in each pinnacle, a half-length angel. *Plates* 328-329.

New York. BLUMENTHAL COLLECTION (EX). Right panel of polyptych: Full-length S. Paul. (?)

FRICK COLLECTION. Christ carrying Cross and Dominican donor. *Plate* 330.

ROBERT LEHMAN COLLECTION. Side-panels of polyptych, companions to Siena 85, 86, 93, 94: S. Peter, S. Mary Magdalen (st.). (?)

Oxford. ASHMOLEAN MUSEUM. 47. Right wing of diptych, companion to Berlin 1142: Crucifixion and Mourning over dead Christ. (?) *Plate* 337.

Palermo. CHIARAMONTE BORDONARO COLLECTION. 83, 84. Side-panels of polyptych, companions to Altenburg and Pisa: S. Peter enthroned, S. Paul enthroned (p. or r.). E. (?)

Philadelphia (Pa.). J. G. JOHNSON COLLECTION. 95. Predella panel: in seven roundels, dead Christ, mourning Virgin and S. John Evangelist, S. Andrew, S. Anthony Abbot, S. Raphael, S. Lawrence.

Pisa. (B.P. III, 24). Side-panel of polyptych, companion to Altenburg and Palermo: S. Andrew enthroned. E. (?)

Rome. VATICAN, PINACOTECA. 156. Portable altarpiece: Crucifixion; below, six Saints.

Saint-Lô. 78. Death and Assumption of Virgin (entirely repainted by Benozzo or his pupils).

San Gimignano. COLLEGIATA, R. WALL. Frescoes: six lunettes—from right to left, Annunciation, Nativity, Adoration of Magi, Circumcision, Massacre of Innocents, Flight into Egypt; middle register, from left to right in 4 bays— Jesus disputing with the Doctors, Baptism, Calling of S. Peter, Marriage at Cana, Transfiguration, Raising of Lazarus, Entry into Jerusalem, Crowds welcome Jesus; lower register, from right to left, in 4 bays—Last Supper, Judas gets the money of his betrayal, Agony in the Garden, Betrayal of Christ, Jesus before Caiphas, Flagellation, Crowning with Thorns, Way to Calvary; 5th bay, below lunette with Massacre of Innocents—large Crucifixion occupying middle and lower register; 6th bay, below lunette with Flight into Egypt —fragments of four Scenes destroyed in sixteenth century—Resurrection, Descent of the Holy Ghost, Descent into Limbo, Deposition (with Giovanni da Asciano). [*Plate* 265.] *Plates* 332-335.

— R. NAVE, LUNETTES OVER ARCHES, OPPOSITE R. WALL. Frescoes: Six Prophets (with Giovanni da Asciano).

ORATORIO DI S. GIOVANNI (BAPTISTERY), VAULT. Fresco: Prophet (s.).

S. PIETRO, R. WALL. Fresco: Madonna leading Jesus by the hand, SS. John Baptist and Paul.

Siena. 85, 86, 93, 94. Four panels of polyptych, companions to New York, Lehman: SS. John Baptist, Catherine, Paul, John Evangelist, with Prophets and Angels in roundels above (st.). (?)

BARNABA DA MODENA

Modenese active in Piedmont, called 'civis and habitator' of Genoa in 1362 (therefore resident there at least since 1352), mentioned in Pisa 1379/80, last recorded in Genoa 1383. Pupil of some almost pure Byzantine; influenced perhaps by Riminese.

Alba (Cuneo). S. GIOVANNI BATTISTA, FIRST ALTAR R. Madonna suckling the Child and two Angels. Sd and d. 1377.

DI GIACOMO BERGUI COLLECTION. Madonna suckling the Child.

Algiers. MUSÉE DES BEAUX-ARTS. Baptism of Christ, in frame for relics. *Plate 276.*

Altenburg. 149. Predella panel: Annunciation. *Plate 278.*

Berlin. 1171. Madonna and Child. Sd and d. 1369. (Destroyed 1945.) *Plate 271.*

Biella. ADOLFO FILA COLLECTION. Noli me tangere.

Bologna. COLLEZIONI COMUNALI (formerly Museo Civico 209, 210). Nativity, Flight into Egypt. *Plate 272.*

Boston (Mass.). 15.951. Madonna and Child.

Claremont (Cal.). POMONA COLLEGE. 61.1.4 (KRESS STUDY COLLECTION. K 495). Madonna and Child; below, dead Christ with mourning Virgin and Evangelist, S. Anthony Abbot and S. Catherine (st.).

Finale Pia (Savona). SANTUARIO, HIGH ALTAR. Madonna and Child with Angels.

Frankfurt a/M. 807. Madonna and Child, scratching His left foot. Sd and d. 1367.

Genoa. 1739. Triptych: Madonna and Child; S. Catherine with female donor; S. Nicholas with male donor; above, Crucifixion, bust of S. Catherine of Siena, bust of female Saint. Sd (but with Niccolò da Voltri). *Plate 280.*

SS. COSMAE DAMIANO. Madonna and Child. Sd and d. 1383.

(SAMPIERDARENA) S. BARTOLOMEO DEL FOSSATO. Polyptych: S. Bartholomew enthroned, worshipped by Lanfranco Sacco da Pavia; on two registers, either side, eight scenes of his life [from top left: S. Bartholomew exorcizes the daughter of Polymius; christens her; forces the Devil to enter an idol; is flagellated; is crucified before Astyages; is flayed; carrying his skin on his shoulders, goes and preaches to the Armenian priests; is beheaded]; in pinnacles, from left—Madonna and Child, S. John Baptist, Christ on Cross with mourning Virgin, S. John Evangelist, and Bishop Lanfranco Sacco and the Vallombrosan Abbot Fra Matteo da Perugia in two roundels below, a monk, another monk. ca 1377–81.

Indianapolis (Ind.). JOHN HERRON ART MUSEUM. 24.5. Crucifixion.

Lavagnola (Savona). S. DALMAZZO. Polyptych: Madonna suckling the Child; SS. Michael, Dalmasius, Peter and Paul; in pinnacles, Crucifixion and half-length SS. Ambrose, Martin, Bartholomew and James. Sd and d. 1376.

London. 1437. Descent of the Holy Ghost.

2927. Coronation of Virgin, Trinity with Symbols of Evangelists, Madonna and Child with male and female donors, Crucifixion, the twelve Apostles. Sd and d. 1374. *Plate 273.*

VICTORIA AND ALBERT MUSEUM. 781–1894. Processional banner: on front, Crucifixion; on back, SS. Anthony Abbot and Eligius with donors.

COURTAULD INSTITUTE GALLERIES, LEE OF FAREHAM COLLECTION. Madonna and Child. Sd. *Plate 275.*

Milan. CRESPI MORBIO COLLECTION. Madonna and Child scratching His left foot, worshipped by a Dominican monk. Sd.

Modena. 3. Portable altarpiece: Madonna and Child with SS. John Baptist and Catherine; above, Crucifixion, in spandrels, Angel and Virgin of Annunciation. Sd. *Plate 277.*

Murcia. CATHEDRAL. FORMER CHAPEL OF NUESTRA SEÑORA DE GRACIA. Polyptych: Lower register: Madonna suckling the Child; on either side, Annunciation, Exaltation of the Cross, Saint recommending Don Juan Manuel, Saint recommending his daughter Dona Juana (Queen of Henry II of Castile), four more Saints. Upper register: S. Lucy enthroned; on either side, eight scenes from her life. Pinnacles: Crucifixion and four busts of Saints. Sd (illegible date).

New York. M. HURD COLLECTION. (EX) Coronation of Virgin. Sd.

Pisa. Inv. 36. Central panel of polyptych from Convent of S. Giovanni de' Fieri: Madonna and Child enthroned with eight Angels (called 'Madonna dei Mercanti'). Sd. ca 1380. *Plate 279.*

Inv. 37. Madonna suckling the Child with four Angels; Annunciation in two roundels above (from S. Francesco). Sd.

(ENVIRONS). RIPOLI, PIEVE DI S. MARIA, OVER SACRISTY DOOR. Madonna and Child with Saints.

Rome. PINACOTECA CAPITOLINA. 347. Ascension.

SCHIFF COLLECTION. Madonna and Child scratching His left foot. Sd.

Saltwood Castle (Kent). SIR KENNETH CLARK. Small Nativity.

San Remo. SANTUARIO DI N. SIGNORA DELLA COSTA. Fragment of Madonna enthroned and Child scratching left foot, two Angels holding cloth, cut-down S. James (?) and other Saint (st.; renaissance addition of parapet and book).

Santiago de Chile. CARLOS CRUZ COLLECTION. S. Catherine enthroned worshipped by Flagellants.

Tortona. S. MATTEO. Madonna and Child.

Turin. GALLERIA SABAUDA. 21. Madonna and Child holding scroll. Sd and d. 1370.

MUSEO CIVICO. Inv. 403. Madonna and Child scratching His left foot. Sd and d. 137..

CONTE E. BALBO BERTONE. Madonna and Child. Sd and d. 136..

Vaduz. LIECHTENSTEINSCHE SAMMLUNG. G. 868/1, 868/2. Nativity, Flight into Egypt.

Ventimiglia. CAPPELLA DI S. SECONDO. Madonna and Child with two Angels.
Homeless. Madonna and Child. *Plate 274.*

BARONZIO see RIMINI, GIOVANNI BARONZIO DA

BARTOLO DI FREDI

Sienese. First recorded in 1353, as partner of Andrea Vanni. Died 1410. Follower of Lippo Memmi and the Lorenzetti; strongly influenced by Barna.

Albury (Herts.). PATMORE LODGE, MRS. R. CRITCHLEY. Adoration of Magi.
Altenburg. 50. Predella: Crucifixion and Saints. E.
Béziers. 269. Adoration of Shepherds (r.). 1370–80.
Bolsena. S. CRISTINA, CHAPEL R. OF CHOIR. L. WALL. Fresco: Christ, worshipped by
    two flying Angels, showing His wounds to S. Christina.
Castiglione d'Orcia. S. SIMEONE. Madonna of Mercy.
Cusona (Siena). S. BIAGIO, SAGRESTIA. Central panel of triptych: Madonna della
    Rosa. Sd. *Plate 404.*
Dijon. MUSÉE, MACIET BEQUEST. Journey of the Magi (top to New York, Lehman).
Englewood (N.J.). D. F. PLATT (EX). Left panel of polyptych: S. John Baptist.*
Florence. GALLERIA CORSI. 18. Centre panel of polyptych: Madonna and Child
    enthroned and two Prophets in spandrels.*
    43. Side panel of polyptych: S. Anthony Abbot.*
Frankfurt a/M. 1006. Head of Virgin (fr.). E.
Grosseto. MUSEO DIOCESANO DI ARTE SACRA. Crucifixion.
Kansas City (Mo.). 50.13. Panel of polyptych: S. Peter; above, two Angels and three
    Heads of Saints (companion to Quimper).
London. 3896. Panel of polyptych: S. Anthony Abbot.
    COURTAULD INSTITUTE GALLERIES, LEE OF FAREHAM COLLECTION. Madonna of
        Humility suckling the Child (replica of Lippo Memmi, Berlin 1072). E.
    SIR KENNETH MUIR MACKENZIE (EX). Deposition. E.
Los Angeles (Cal.). L.2100.44–1072, 1073. Two pinnacles of Coronation polyptych:
    Angel and Virgin of Annunciation (see Montalcino and Siena). 1388.
Lucignano (Val di Chiana). MUSEO CIVICO. Triptych: Madonna and Child enthroned
    with SS. John Baptist and John Evangelist. Sd.
    S. FRANCESCO. R. WALL. Frescoes: Triumph of Death.
    — L. TRANSEPT. Frescoes: S. Francis receiving Stigmata; middle row: S. Christo-
        pher crossing the stream with Jesus on his shoulder; Madonna and Child
        enthroned with Angels; S. George slaying the dragon; lower row (partly
        destroyed): Adoration of Magi. *Plate 406.*
    — SECOND ALTAR L. Fresco: Fragment of Assumption. (?)
Mödling (Austria). BURG LIECHTENSTEIN (EX). Madonna and Child with Angels.

Montalcino. MUSEO CIVICO. Central panel of triptych: Coronation of the Virgin. Sd and d. 1388 (see Siena, Pinacoteca and Los Angeles).

Fragments of polyptych: centre panel, Deposition; side panels, Baptism, Tobias and the Angel, Filippo Ciardelli (S. Filippino) healing the sick, Levitation of Filippo Ciardelli; from pilasters, SS. Francis, Peter, Paul, Leonard. Sd and d. 1382. *Plates 411–412.*

MUSEO DIOCESANO D'ARTE SACRA (SEMINARIO). Madonna and Child (fr.).

S. AGOSTINO, CHOIR. Frescoes: vault: The four Evangelists in medallions; walls: Scenes from life of S. Augustine, Crucifixion, Saints.

— WINDOW: design of stained glass.

New Haven (Conn.). 1943.247. Pinnacle: Virgin of Annunciation.

New York. 41.100.14. Panel of polyptych: S. Lucy.

ROBERT LEHMAN. Adoration of Magi (fr., upper part at Dijon).

Paganico (Grosseto). S. MICHELE, CHOIR. Frescoes: vault: The four Evangelists; soffit of entrance arch: six female Saints; central wall: Annunciation; left wall: Nativity above and Story of S. Michael below; right wall: Adoration of Magi above and S. Michael below (p.).

— OVER NORTH ENTRANCE. Fresco: Madonna and Child with S. Michael and S. John Baptist (r.).

Palermo. CHIARAMONTE BORDONARO COLLECTION. 71. Head of S. Mark.

Parcieux. LA GRANGE BLANCHE, HENRI CHALANDON (EX). S. Michael with a Bishop Saint and a Monk Saint.

Paris. 1151. Circumcision.

SAINT-LOUIS-EN-L'ISLE, SECOND CHAPEL L. Two panels of polyptych: Full-length SS. Peter and Paul.

Perugia. 88. Triptych from S. Simone del Carmine: Madonna and Child, Saints Catherine, Mary Magdalen, Anthony Abbot, the Prophet Elijah.

Pienza. MUSEO DIOCESANO. Madonna of Mercy. Sd and d. 1364. *Plate 407.*

Poggibonsi. S. LUCCHESE, L. WALL. Fresco: S. Nicholas and the three Maidens.

— R. WALL. Fresco: Martyrdom of S. Andrew (below frescoed triptych by Fei), Charity (r.).

Quimper. MUSÉE. Side-panel of polyptych: S. Paul; two Angels in spandrels; six heads of Angels in modern framework (companion to Kansas City).*

Rodez. 210. The three Maries at the Tomb, Resurrection, Noli me tangere. (?)

Rome. VATICAN, PINACOTECA 153. Predella panel: Joachim and the Angel.

St.-Jean-Cap-Ferrat (Antibes). MUSÉE ÎLE-DE-FRANCE. Assumption.*

San Gimignano. 31. Fresco: Seven female heads (fr.).

S. AGOSTINO, R. APSE. Frescoes: Life of the Virgin [Birth of Virgin, Virgin in Temple, Presentation, Marriage, Death] (r.). 1363. *Plate 408.*

— R. WALL. Fresco: Pietà and Symbols of Passion.

COLLEGIATA DI S. MARIA ASSUNTA (DUOMO), L. NAVE. Frescoes: Scenes from the Old Testament [from left, lunettes: Creation of the World, Creation of Man, Adam in the Garden of Eden, Creation of Eve, The forbidden Tree—The

Fall of man (destroyed); middle row: Expulsion from Paradise; Murder of
Abel, Building of the Ark, the Animals entering the Ark, the end of the
Deluge, Drunkenness of Noah, Departure of Abraham and Lot from the land
of the Chaldeans, Abraham and Lot leave each other in the land of Canaan,
Dream of Joseph, Joseph in the well—other four frescoes destroyed; lower
row: Arrest of Joseph's Brothers, Joseph makes himself known to his
Brothers, Moses changes the rod into a snake, The Crossing of the Red Sea,
Pharaoh and his drowned Army, Moses on Mount Sinai, God allows the Devil
to tempt Job, the Devil kills Job's cattle, Death of the children of Job, Job's
thanksgiving to God, Job comforted by friends—other three frescoes
destroyed]. Sd and d. 1367. *Plate 405.*

Siena. 97/99–102, 106. Fragments of triptych from the Cappella delle Carceri at
Montalcino (see Montalcino, Museo Civico): left panel: The dying Virgin
taking leave of the Apostles, Marriage of the Virgin; right panel: Death of
the Virgin, the Virgin's return to Her parents; pinnacle: Assumption;
predella panels: Joachim in the Temple, Lamentation over the Dead Christ,
Birth of the Virgin; S. Macarius with two lions, S. Anthony Abbot; two
pilasters with rows of Saints running up the sides: SS. Gherard, Augustine,
Blaise, Christopher, Michael, Stephen, Bartholomew, John Evangelist; SS.
Benedict, Philip, Lucy, Catherine, Nicholas, Matthew, John Baptist, Louis of
Toulouse. 1388. *Plate 413.*

98. Two predella panels: A deacon Saint baptizing a prisoner; Martyrdom of
the deacon Saint with hot bricks.

103. Predella: S. Peter visiting a sick nun; Herod's Banquet and Beheading of
S. John; Adoration of Magi; S. John Evangelist on Patmos; S. Lucy standing
fast against the oxen.

104. Adoration of Magi. *Plate 409.*

580. Coronation from Cappuccine di S. Egidio (p.).

PALAZZO PUBBLICO, GROUND FLOOR, FIRST HALL L. Frescoes on vault: Christ and
four Evangelists, Virgin of Annunciation, Saints (r.).

Torrita (Val di Chiana). SS. FLORA E LUCILLA, SECOND ALTAR R. Triptych: Nativity;
Bishop Saint and S. Anthony Abbot. *Plate 410.*

BARTOLOMEO DELLA GATTA

*Don Pietro Dei, called Bartolomeo della Gatta. Born Florence 1448, took the Camaldolese
habit and lived in Arezzo from 1470 to his death in 1502. Formed under influence of Piero
della Francesca, Francesco di Giorgio, Verrocchio and Signorelli.*

Arezzo. PINACOTECA. 36. S. Roch imploring the Virgin. d. 1479. *Plate 942.*

37. S. Roch imploring Christ to save Arezzo from the plague. *Plate 941.*

— DEP. FROM S. BERNARDO. Detached fresco from lunette: Vision of S. Bernard.

Arezzo (contd.). BADIA (SS. FLORA E LUCILLA), ENTRANCE WALL. Fr. of fresco: S. Lawrence. d. 1476.

DUOMO, SACRISTY. Detached Fresco: S. Jerome in the Wilderness.

S. PIERO PICCOLO, SACRISTY. Blessed Jacopo Filippo da Faenza (r.). 1486. (?)

Cambridge. FITZWILLIAM MUSEUM, MARLAY BEQUEST 72. S. Julian. (?)

Castiglion Fiorentino. PINACOTECA. S. Francis receiving Stigmata. 1487. *Plate* 944.

Organ-shutter: S. Michael blessing Lorenza Visconti and her baby.

S. Julian.

COLLEGIATA DI S. GIULIANO, THIRD ALTAR R. Madonna and Child enthroned with SS. Julian, Peter, Paul and Michael; fragmentary predella with Stories of S. Julian. d. 1486. *Plates* 943, 945.

Cortona. S. DOMENICO. Fresco: S. Roch.

— NEAR L. APSE. Assumption of Virgin (SS. Benedict and Scholastica kneeling in foreground are by later hand). *Plate* 946.

Florence. MUSEO HORNE. 24. S. Roch (from Serviti, Arezzo).

ACTON COLLECTION. Predella panel: Miracle of S. Roch.

Rome. VATICAN, CAPPELLA SISTINA. Fresco: Last days of Moses (women and children near Moses, Angels indicating the Promised Land) (with Signorelli). 1482. (?) *Plate* 941.

San Sepolcro. SAN GIOVANNI EVANGELISTA (DUOMO), R. NAVE. Frescoed niche: Crucifixion with SS. Francis, Clare, John Evangelist, James and Benedict; in embrasure, S. Bonaventura and S. Sebastian.

Urbino. ARCHIVIO CAPITOLARE DEL DUOMO. Graduale D, n. 6, f. 41: Martyrdom of S. Agatha in initial O (miniature).

BARTOLOMEO DI (MAESTRO) GENTILE DA URBINO

Marchigian, ca 1470–1534. Pupil of Giovanni Santi, influenced by Timoteo Viti and Perugino.

Budapest. 1224 (85). Madonna and Child with SS. Catherine and Peter Martyr. d. 1488.

1035. Madonna and Child with S. Catherine and another female Saint. Sd and d. 1504. *Plate* 1015.

Cambridge (Mass.). FOGG ART MUSEUM, WINTHROP BEQUEST. Young lady, with ring on parapet.

Ginestreto (Pesaro). PIEVE VECCHIA. Madonna and Child with four Saints.

Lille. 24. Madonna and Child enthroned. Sd and d. 1497. *Plate* 1014.

Monteciccardo (Pesaro). S. SEBASTIANO, HIGH ALTAR. Madonna and Child enthroned with SS. Francis, Peter, Catherine and Sebastian. Sd and d. 1508.

Montefiore Conca (Forlì). S. PAOLO. Madonna of Mercy with SS. John Evangelist, Paul, Francis and Sebastian.

Urbino. GALLERIA NAZIONALE DELLE MARCHE. Martyrdom of S. Sebastian, and donors (on design by Giovanni Santi).

BARTOLOMEO DI TOMMASO DA FOLIGNO

Mentioned in Ancona (as citizen) in 1425, in Fano 1434/37 (lost works), in Foligno 1437, in Ancona 1439, in Rome 1451/52 (lost works), in Foligno 1444 to 1455. May have studied paintings by Giovanni del Ponte and Masaccio. Influenced by Gothic painters in the Marches such as the Salimbeni and later by Sassetta.

Baltimore (Md.). WALTERS ART GALLERY. 712. Predella panel: Dead Christ, mourning Virgin and John Evangelist in roundels.
456. Predella panel: Funeral and canonization of S. Francis (companion to Venice). E. *Plate 626.*
Foligno. PINACOTECA. Fresco from S. Caterina with three votive pictures: S. Barbara is dragged by her father to her martyrdom while God's hand changes into grasshoppers the sheep of the shepherd who betrayed her hiding place, and worshipping nuns below; Madonna of Loreto with two Angels worshipped by Suor Onofria; S. Anthony of Padua preaching and kneeling donor below. Sd and d. 1449.
S. NICCOLÒ, SACRISTY. Fresco: Christ on Cross, worshipped by kneeling monk.
S. SALVATORE. Fragments of polyptych: Madonna and Child enthroned with six Angels and Rinaldo Trinci as donor; S. John Baptist; the Blessed Pietro Crisci; two pinnacles with S. Bartholomew and S. Ursula, 1437. *Plate 629.*
(Environs). RASIGLIA, S. MARIA DELLE GRAZIE. Fresco: Madonna of Loreto, S. Lucy, S. Michael and two knights. (?)
London. LADY ROBERTSON. Wings of portable altarpiece: Christ on the way to Emmaus, Descent of the Holy Ghost.
Milan. BRERA. 193. Centre panel of polyptych from S. Giacomo at Pergola: Madonna and Child enthroned with Angels. E.
Moulins. 81. Predella panel: Christ on the way to Calvary (companion to Rome, Vatican and Homeless).
New York. 58.87.1, 58.87.2. 'Martin Le Roy' predella panels: Betrayal of Christ, Lamentation and Entombment. *Plate 628.*
Rome. VATICAN, PINACOTECA. 266, 267. Two predella panels: Agony in the Garden, Betrayal of Christ (companions to Moulins and Homeless). *Plate 627.*
Rospigliosi Triptych (from Collegiata di S. Venanzio, at Camerino, Marches): Coronation of the Virgin; Nativity; Adoration of Magi; Angel and Virgin of Annunciation in roundels above. *Plate 625.*
Terni. S. FRANCESCO, CAPPELLA PARADISI. Frescoes: centre wall: Christ the Judge in Mandorla with Virgin, S. John Baptist, Angels, Evangelists and Prophets; below: S. Peter watching the gate of Heaven and the Elect. Left wall: the

Souls taken to Heaven and Descent of Christ into Limbo; below, the souls in Purgatory. Right wall: Hell. Soffit of arch: six busts of Prophets. Prophets in spandrels. Formerly dated (1453?). *Plate 631.*

Vaduz. LIECHTENSTEINSCHE SAMMLUNG. G. 866. Madonna and Child with Saints.

Venice. CONTE VITTORIO CINI. Inv. 103. Left panel of predella: S. Francis renouncing his inheritance (companion to Baltimore). E.

Inv. 7005. Triptych (from S. Maria Maddalena, Foligno?): Madonna and Child enthroned with five Angels; SS. John Baptist and Mary Magdalen with Angel above; SS. Christopher and Dominic with Angel above. (1451?).

Homeless. Predella panel: Entombment (companion to Moulins and Rome, Vatican). *Plate 630.*

BAZZI see SODOMA

BECCAFUMI

Domenico (Mecuccio, Mecherino, Mecarino) da Siena. 1486–1551. Pupil of Pacchiarotto, influenced by Sodoma, Fra Bartolomeo and Raphael. Always active in Siena except for journeys to Rome (ca 1510–12, 1519, 1541–43) and to Genoa–Pisa.

Allentown (Pa.). MUSEUM OF ART. 60-25-KB (KRESS COLLECTION. K 559) 'Platt' Nativity.

Ancona. S. DOMENICO, SACRISTY. Moses and Jehova; Moses with the Tables of the Law.

Argiano (Montalcino Senese). S. PANCRAZIO. Madonna and Child with two Saints.

Bayonne. 957, 958. Sophonisba, Cleopatra (companions to London, Wallace) E.

Belgrade. WHITE PALACE. 'Benson' Flight of Clelia. *Plate 1587.*

Berlin. 2075. Martyrdom of S. Lucy. (Destroyed 1945.) *Plate 1579.*

WESENDONCK COLLECTION (EX). Marcus Curtius.

Birmingham. BARBER INSTITUTE. 'Lettiera' from Palazzo Petrucci: Reclining nymph.

Boston (Mass.). 50.861/2. Predella panels from S. Spirito altarpiece: S. Dominic burns the books; Martyrdom of S. Sigismund and of his family (see Siena, Chigi Saracini). Before 1528.

Cambridge. FITZWILLIAM MUSEUM. 1112. Portrait of youth. (?)

Cassel. HABICH COLLECTION (EX). Holy Family with S. Catherine of Siena and Infant S. John. E.

Chatsworth. TRUSTEES OF THE CHATSWORTH SETTLEMENT. 32. Book-cover: The Magistrati del Concistoro offer the keys of Siena to the Madonna delle Grazie during the siege of 1526. *Plate 1584.*

Dublin. 840. Predella panel: Risen Christ baptizing.

Englewood (N.J.). D. F. PLATT COLLECTION (EX). S. Anthony Abbot reading (fr., r.). (?)

Florence. PITTI. 359. Tondo: Holy Family with Infant S. John.

UFFIZI. 780. Tondo: Holy Family with Infant S. John.

1731. Self-portrait.

— GABINETTO DISEGNI. Monochrome sketches: 19109—David; 19108—two heads of Putti; 19111—Transfiguration; 19110, 19196—Madonna and Child.

MUSEO BARDINI. 1246. Cassone panel: Hercules' Choice.

MUSEO HORNE. 79. Cassone panel: Story of Deucalion and Pyrrha.

3235. Putti holding up Medallion with Drunkenness of Noah.

6532. Tondo: Holy Family with Infant S. John.

MUSEO STIBBERT. Predella panel: Miracle of S. Anthony of Padua and the mule.

LOESER COLLECTION (EX). Sketch for S. Francis's Vision of Perdono di Assisi.

CONTESSE MARTELLI. Cassone panels: Feast of Lupercalia, Temple of Vesta.* *Plate* 1577.

TORRIGIANI COLLECTION (EX). Tondo: Holy Family with Infant S. John.

Greenville (Ala.). BOB JONES UNIVERSITY. 36. Mystic Marriage of S. Catherine of Siena and other Saints (c.; other c. in Rome, Doria Pamphili).

Hamburg. WEBER COLLECTION (EX). See Cassel.

Henfield (Sussex). LADY SALMOND. 'Cowper' Holy Family with S. Catherine of Siena and Infant S. John.

Leghorn. GIULIO TORTOLINI (EX). Tondo: Holy Family with Infant S. John (copy of Siena, Bargagli Petrucci?).

Leicester. CITY ART GALLERY. 42.1965. Tondo: Holy Family with Infant S. John.

Leningrad. 21. Marriage of S. Catherine and eight other Saints.

Liverpool. WALKER ART GALLERY. 'Loeser' predella panel: Baptist preaching to the Multitudes.

London. 1430. Cassone panel: Story of Esther.

6368, 6369. Tanaquil, Marcia (companions to Rome, Doria Pamphili). *Plate* 1576.

VICTORIA AND ALBERT MUSEUM. C.A.I. 165. Tondo: Charity surrounded by children playing with dog and hobbyhorses.

1562.1904. Battle scene (imitating Leonardo). E.

WALLACE COLLECTION. 525. Judith (companion to Bayonne). E.

A. SCHARF (EX). Predella panel to S. Spirito altarpiece: S. Bernardino preaching (see Siena, Chigi Saracini). 1528. *Plate* 1585.

Lucca. Inv. 60. Cassone panel: Continence of Scipio.

Mells (Somerset). EARL OF OXFORD AND ASQUITH. Predella panels: Presentation of Virgin, Visitation, Adoration of Magi (companions to Siena, S. Spirito).

Montalcino Senese. S. PIETRO. Holy Family with S. Catherine (st.).

Munich. 1073. Tondo: Holy Family with Infant S. John.

Paris. R.F. 1966—1, 2, 3. Three predella panels (companions to Siena, S. Bernardino): S. Francis receiving Stigmata, S. Anthony of Padua and the mule, S. Bernardino preaching in Piazza del Campo). 1537.

PAUL BOURGET (EX). Holy Family.

Pesaro. 47. Holy Family.

Pisa. DUOMO, CHOIR. Moses breaks the Tables of the Law; Moses and the Children of Korah; Evangelists in Niches. 1537–39. *Plate* 1589.

Rome. GALLERIA NAZIONALE (PALAZZO BARBERINI). Inv. 2410. Madonna suckling Child with Infant S. John.

GALLERIA DORIA PAMPHILI. 166. S. Jerome in the Wilderness.

— PRIVATE APARTMENTS. Cornelia (companion to London 6368, 6369).

Tondo: Mystic Marriage of S. Catherine and other Saints (c.; see Greenville).

MARCHESE VISCONTI VENOSTA (EX). Tondo: Madonna and Child with Infant S. John.

CAV. LATTANZIO MARRI MIGNANELLI (EX). Holy Family with Infant S. John. *Plate* 1578.

CONTE LEONARDO VITETTI. Madonna and Child with two Saints.*

S. MARIA MAGGIORE, SALA DEL CAPITOLO DELLA CAPPELLA BORGHESE. Madonna and Child with SS. Anthony of Padua and Catherine of Siena. L.

Sarasota (Florida). RINGLING MUSEUM. Judgement of Paris.

Sarteano (Val di Chiana). S. MARTINO, NORTH WALL. Annunciation. 1546.

Siena. 344. Baptism of Christ (from Monteoliveto Maggiore).

384. Triptych: Trinity, SS. John Baptist and Cosmas, SS. John Evangelist and Damian (from Cappella del Manto, Spedale di S. Maria della Scala). 1513.

405. Birth of Virgin (from S. Paolo). ca 1543.

411, 412, 415, 416, 430. Cartoon for marble intarsias in Duomo.

417–419. Predella to n. 420: S. Catherine of Siena receiving the Lily and the Dominican Habit, receiving Communion from an Angel, Mystic Marriage of S. Catherine of Siena.

420. Altarpiece from destroyed Monastery of Monteoliveto a Porta Tufi: S. Catherine of Siena receiving Stigmata, with S. Benedict and S. Jerome at sides and Madonna and Child with Angels above.

423. Lucifer's Fall (from Spedale di S. Maria della Scala).

427. Christ in Limbo (from S. Francesco).

429. Cartoon: Shield upheld by Putti.

ARCHIVIO DI STATO. Book-cover: Mystic Marriages of SS. Catherine of Alexandria and Catherine of Siena (Biccherna). 1548. (?)

BARGAGLI PETRUCCI COLLECTION (EX). Holy Family with Infant S. John. (See Leghorn.)

CASA DI RIPOSO IN CAMPANSI, FIRST FLOOR PASSAGE. Fresco: Madonna and Child with SS. Anne, Ursula and Mary Magdalen. E.

COMPAGNIA DI S. ANTONIO ABATE (ARCICONFRATERNITA DELLA MISERICORDIA), SALA DEL CONSIGLIO. Bierheads: Madonna and Child; S. Anthony Abbot reading; Dead Christ; S. Anthony Abbot. 1540.

GUARINI DEL TAIA COLLECTION. Rape of Europa.

PALAZZO PUBBLICO, SALA DEL CONCISTORO. Frescoed ceiling: Allegories of Concordia, Iustitia, Amor Patriae, Virtutes Politicae and Roman Stories. 1529–36.

PALAZZO BINDI SERGARDI. Frescoed ceiling: Scenes from Roman History. *Plates* 1581–82.

PALAZZO CHIGI SARACINI. Altarpiece from S. Spirito: Mystic Marriage of S. Catherine of Siena and SS. Peter, Sigismund, Francis, Bernardino, Catherine of Alexandria and Paul (predella panels in Boston, London, Tulsa?). Before 1528. *Plate* 1583.

Sketch of Putti holding up medallion.

Bust of S. Bernardino.

Madonna and Child.

Lucretia stabbing herself.

S. BERNARDINO, ORATORIO SUPERIORE. Frescoes: Marriage of Virgin, Death of the Virgin (see also Pacchia and Sodoma). 1518.

Altarpiece: Madonna and Child with six Saints and Angels (companion to Paris). 1537.

S. DOMENICO, CAPPELLA DI S. CATERINA, FLOOR. Marble intarsia on design of the artist: Orpheus.

S. MARIA ASSUNTA (DUOMO), CHOIR. Frescoes in apse: Paradise, Apostles (r.). 1544.

— PIERS. Bronze statues: Eight Angels. 1548–1550. *Plate* 1590.

— FLOOR BELOW CUPOLA. Marble intarsias on design of the artist: in hexagonal sections—Elijah's Assumption, Elijah's Pact with Ahab, Ahab's Sacrifice, Elijah's Wrath, Death of false Prophets of Baal, Death of Ahab whose blood is licked by dogs, Sacrifice of Elijah; in lozenges at six corners—Elijah orders Ardias to lead Ahab to him, Ardias brings Ahab to Elijah, Elijah fed by deer, Elijah consecrates Jehu King of Israel, Elijah begs bread from the widow, Elijah raises to life the Widow's Son (extensively restored by Alessandro Franchi). 1519 onwards.

— FLOOR BEFORE HIGH ALTAR AND IN CHOIR. Marble intarsias on his design: Moses striking the Rock (1525); The Golden Calf (1531); Sacrifice of Isaac (1546). *Plate* 1591.

— MUSEO DELL'OPERA. S. Paul enthroned, with his conversion and martyrdom in background. *Plate* 1575.

Christ carrying Cross.

S. MARIA DEL CARMINE, SECOND ALTAR R. S. Michael defeats Satan. Before 1535. *Plate* 1588.

S. MARTINO, THIRD ALTAR L. Nativity. ca 1523. *Plate* 1580.

S. SPIRITO, THIRD CHAPEL R. Coronation of Virgin, with SS. Mary Magdalen, Catherine, Gregory and Anthony of Padua (for Nuns of Ognissanti; predella panels at Mells). ca 1540.

SPEDALE DI S. MARIA DELLA SCALA, CAPPELLA DEL MANTO. Remains of frescoes: ornamented border along vault; Meeting of Joachim and Anne in lunette. 1512–14.

SPEDALETTO DI MONNAGNESE (NOW SCUOLE PROFESSIONALI FEMMINILI). UPPER FLOOR. Fresco: S. Christopher.

Strasbourg. 258. Portrait bust of Girolamo da Coragnola.
Tulsa (Oklahoma). PHILBROOK ART CENTER. 3365, 3367 (KRESS COLLECTION. K 1203, K
1232). Two predella panels from S. Spirito altarpiece: S. Catherine receiving the
crown of Thorns; Baptism of Christ (see Siena, Chigi Saracini). Before 1528.
Vaduz. LIECHTENSTEINSCHE SAMMLUNGEN. 948. Temptations of a saintly monk.
Venice. SEMINARIO. 70. Penelope.
Washington (D.C.). 529 (KRESS COLLECTION. K 1194). Holy Family with Angels.
Homeless. S. Catherine receiving Stigmata. *Plate 1586.*

BENAGLIO, Francesco

Verona. ca 1432–before 1492. Close follower of Mantegna.

Bergamo. 163. Profile of S. Bernardino. (?)
Philadelphia (Pa.). J. G. JOHNSON COLLECTION. 215. Madonna and Child.
Rochester (N.Y.). MEMORIAL ART GALLERY. 'Chalandon' Madonna and Child.
Rome. MUSEO DI PALAZZO VENEZIA, VAN MARLE GIFT. Triptych: Madonna and Child
enthroned; SS. Peter Martyr and Jerome; SS. Anthony of Padua and
Catherine (r.). Sd and d. 1480.
Venice. ACCADEMIA. 617. Madonna and Child with Saints and Angels. L. (?)
Verona. 350. 'Madonna del Ventaglio.'*
    S. BERNARDINO, CHOIR. Triptych: Madonna and Child worshipped by S. Bernar-
dino; SS. Peter, Paul and Francis; SS. Anthony of Padua, Louis of Toulouse and
Jerome (after Mantegna's S. Zeno Triptych in Verona). Sd. 1462. *Plate 1297.*
Washington (D.C.). 640 (WIDENER COLLECTION). Madonna and Child.
    1130 (KRESS COLLECTION. K 1555). S. Jerome. Sd. *Plate 1300.*
Homeless. Madonna and Child. *Plate 1298.*

BENEDETTO DI BINDO

*Sienese. Died in Perugia 1417. Partner of Gualtieri di Giovanni and Niccolò di Naldo in
works for the Sienese Cathedral 1409–12.*

Perugia. S. DOMENICO, CAPPELLA DI S. CATERINA O S. PIETRO MARTIRE (FIFTH L.).
Frescoes: Annunciation; S. Catherine disputes with Doctors, converts Faus-
tina and Porphyrius; S. Peter Martyr preaching and the miracle of the cloud,
Assassination of S. Peter Martyr; Fortitude; S. Taddeus. 1415–17.
Siena. S. MARIA ASSUNTA (DUOMO), SACRISTY, CAPPELLA DEGLI ARLIQUI (L. CHAPEL).
Frescoes: on left wall, the Madonna appearing over a town in distress (frs., r.);
on right wall, Gregory the Great in procession to stop the plague in Rome and
the Archangel Michael on Castel S. Angelo (frs., r.). 1411. (?)

— MUSEO DELL'OPERA. 21. Bottom panels of dismembered cupboards for relics
  from the Cappella degli Arliqui: Four Angels, three Prophets and David, SS.
  Peter, John Evangelist, James and Andrew. 1412/13.

  63/90. Doors of dismembered cupboards for relics from the Cappella degli
  Arliqui): outside—eight (of the original 32) busts of Angels inside—eight
  stories of the True Cross [The Jews decide not to reveal the place where the
  True Cross is buried; Judas before S. Helena; S. Helena commands that Judas
  should be lowered into a well; Judas reveals the place, which is dug up;
  Raising of the Youth by the True Cross; The True Cross presented to S.
  Helena; Emperor Heraclius warned by the Angel; Penitence of Emperor
  Heraclius] (with Giovanni del Bindino). 1412/13. *Plate 487.*

BENVENUTO DI GIOVANNI DEL GUASTA

*Siena, 1436–151(8?). Pupil of Vecchietta, influenced by Francesco di Giorgio, Girolamo
da Cremona and slightly by Benozzo Gozzoli. In his late work, difficult to distinguish from
his son and partner Girolamo.*

Acquapendente. DUOMO. Lunette to Cambridge Madonna and Saints: Dead Christ
  upheld by Angels (from S. Agostino; with his son Girolamo). L.
Aix-en-Provence. 495. See Paris, Musées Nationaux.
Altenburg. 88. Portable altarpiece: Madonna and Child with two Saints.
Asciano (Senese). SS. FABIANO E SEBASTIANO, BEHIND HIGH ALTAR. Fresco: Assump-
  tion with S. Thomas receiving Girdle, S. Sebastian and S. Agatha; above,
  Dove of the Holy Ghost, Angel and Virgin of Annunciation in roundels.
Baltimore (Md.). WALTERS ART GALLERY. 743. Nativity; below, Busts of SS. Francis,
  Jerome and Bernardino. L.

  1033. Madonna and Child with SS. Bernardino of Siena and Anthony of Padua.
  (Between Benvenuto di Giovanni and Fungai.) *Plate 922.*
Berlin. ALFRED SOMMERGUTH (EX). Madonna and Angels adoring the Child.
Blois. See Paris, Musées Nationaux.
Bolsena. S. CRISTINA, CAPPELLA DEL ROSARIO. Predella to polyptych by Sano di
  Pietro: four Scenes from Life of S. George and three roundels with Dead
  Christ, mourning Virgin and Evangelist. E.
Boston (Mass.). 56.512. Predella panel: Expulsion of Adam and Eve. *Plate 845.*
Cambridge (Mass.). FOGG ART MUSEUM. 1920.14. Madonna and Child (fr., r.).*

  1927.206. Madonna and Child enthroned with SS. Augustine, Nicholas of
  Tolentino, Monica, John Evangelist, Angels and Cherubim (lunette at Acqua-
  pendente; from S. Agostino at Acquapendente; with his son Girolamo). L.
Capesthorne Hall (Chelford, Cheshire). SIR WALTER BROMLEY DAVENPORT (EX).
  Predella panel: S. James rescuing a pilgrim unjustly condemned to death at
  Toulouse (see Paris and Siena, S. Domenico). *Plate 847.*

Chiusi. DUOMO. Madonna and Child with SS. Andrew, James and Angels (st.).

Detroit (Mich.). 24.95. Madonna and Child with two Angels.

40.128. Front of cassone: Apollo and the Muses (r.).

Englewood (N.J.). D. F. PLATT (EX). Nativity.

Florence. MUSEO BARDINI. Detached fresco: S. Benedict in Glory.

BERENSON COLLECTION. Predella panel: Dead Christ upheld by Angels. *Plate* 846.

Göttingen. 201. Diptych: Adoration of Shepherds.

Grosseto. DUOMO, R. WINDOW. Stained Glass on his design: Angel and Virgin of Annunciation, Prophets, Virtues, Saints (partly r. or replaced). *Plates* 849– 850.

Hanover. 262. Madonna and Child with SS. Bernardino and Catherine of Siena (between Benvenuto di Giovanni and Pacchiarotto).

Kansas City (Mo.). 45.54 1-2. Two roundels from frame of altarpiece: Blessing Redeemer, S. Dominic (companions to New Haven and New York).

Karlsruhe. 408. Madonna and Child on parapet. (?)

London. 909. Triptych: Madonna and Child with Angels; S. Peter; S. Nicholas. d. 1479.

2482. Madonna and Child.

WALLACE COLLECTION. 543. Penitent S. Jerome.

Los Angeles. 1953.44. Predella panel: S. Jerome in Wilderness.

Lyons. MUSÉE. Side-panel of triptych: SS. John Baptist and Michael. d. 1451.

Malibu (Cal.). J. PAUL GETTY MUSEUM. A.54.P-10. Nativity; below, in roundels, S. John Baptist, Dead Christ, praying Benedictine.

Minneapolis (Minn.). INSTITUTE OF ARTS, VANDERLIP BEQUEST (EX). Madonna and Child with Goldfinch (with his son Girolamo).

Montalcino (Senese). MUSEO CIVICO. Redeemer with S. Michael, S. Egidius and Eternal with Angels above (r.).

Madonna and Child with SS. Peter, Paul and Eternal above (fr., r.).

Montepertuso (Senese). S. MICHELE ARCANGELO. Triptych: Madonna and Child enthroned with Angels; SS. Lucy and Augustine; SS. Catherine and Michael; in pinnacles, blessing Redeemer, SS. Ansanus (?) and Lawrence; in pilasters, eight small Saints; in predella, Life of Virgin, S. Sebastian and female Saint in niches at corners. Sd and d. 1475.

Moulins. 84. Madonna and Child.

New Haven (Conn.). 1871.64. Madonna and Child with two Angels. [*Plate* 273.]

1946.316. Roundel from frame of altarpiece: S. Peter Martyr (companion to Kansas City and New York).

New York. 10.148. Assumption with SS. Thomas, Francis and Anthony of Padua. Sd and d. 1498. *Plate* 852.

R. LEHMAN. Roundel from frame of altarpiece; S. Bernardino (companion to Kansas City and New Haven).

'Piccolomini' Madonna and Child.

Paris. MUSÉES NATIONAUX, COLLECTION CAMPANA. 217, 218 (dep. Aix-en-Provence and Blois). Predella panels: Massacre of Innocents and Martyrdom of S. Fabianus (see Siena, S. Domenico and Capesthorne Hall).

DOLLFUS (EX). Madonna and Child with two Angels.

Perugia. 78. Predella: in roundels, Dead Christ, mourning Virgin and Evangelist; portrait of donor.

Raleigh (N.C.). MUSEUM OF ART. GL.60.17.31 (KRESS COLLECTION. K 1833). Predella panel: Vision of S. John Gualbert.

Rome. S. PAOLO FUORI LE MURA, PINACOTECA. Madonna and blessing Child.*

Sarteano. See Siena 648, 649.

Siena. 395. Madonna and Child. L.

    434. Ascension with Saints. Sd and d. 1491.

    581. Detached fresco from Casa di Riposo in Campansi: Noli me Tangere. L.

    648, 649: Side-panels of polyptych, cut into ovals, from Sarteano: S. Bernardino, S. Anthony of Padua.

  ARCHIVIO DI STATO. Book-covers:

    Gabella: The Camerlingo pays citizens in time of peace and Condottieri in time of war. d. 1468.

    Gabella: Allegory of Good Government. d. 1474.

    Triumphal Entry of Alfonso Duque of Calabria at the head of the Sienese army in the besieged Colle Val d'Elsa. d. 1479.

  BATTISTERO, L. OF APSE. Frescoed lunette: Three miracles of S. Anthony of Padua (assisting Vecchietta ?). 1453. (?)

  PALAZZO SALIMBENI (MONTE DE' PASCHI). Fresco: Madonna of Mercy. d. 1481.

  S. DOMENICO, L. TRANSEPT, SECOND CHAPEL, L. WALL. Madonna and Child with SS. James, Fabianus, Sebastian, John Evangelist and Angels; in lunette, Pietà (for predella see Capesthorne and Paris). 1483.

  S. MARIA ASSUNTA (DUOMO), L. TRANSEPT, FLOOR. Marble intarsia on his design: Expulsion of Herod. (See also Matteo di Giovanni, Domenico di Bartolo, Beccafumi). 1484.

  — L. NAVE, FLOOR. Marble intarsia on his design: Sibilla Tiburtina (See also Cozzarelli, Matteo di Giovanni, Neroccio.) 1483.

  S. SEBASTIANO IN VALLE PIATTA, SACRISTY. Madonna and Child with SS. James and Jerome.

  SOCIETÀ ESECUTORI PIE DISPOSIZIONI, GALLERIA. Lunette: S. Catherine of Siena bringing Pope Gregory back from Avignon. 1501–2. *Plate 851.*

  SPEDALE DI S. MARIA DELLA SCALA. Ruined frescoes: S. Andrew; Two figures by a stone coffer.

  (Environs). MONISTERO DI S. EUGENIO, R. WALL. Fresco: Resurrection and busts of Saints below.

  — — L. WALL. Fresco: Crucifixion and Busts of Saints below.

  — OSSERVANZA, MUSEO. Antiphonary: Adoration of Magi in initial O.

Sinalunga (Val di Chiana). S. BERNARDINO, L. CHAPEL. Annunciation. Sd and d. 1470. *Plate 844*.

    S. LUCIA, SECOND ALTAR L. Madonna and Child with SS. Sebastian, Martin and Angels; predella (g.p.). Sd and d. 1509.

    MADONNA DELLE NEVI, HIGH ALTAR. Madonna and Child (on lines of ruined Ducciesque painting).

Torrita (Val di Chiana). SS. FLORA E LUCILLA, THIRD ALTAR R. Madonna and Child with Evangelist and S. Andrew; in lunette, Trinity and two Angels (with Girolamo di Benvenuto). Sd and d. 1497.

Viterbo. S. LORENZO (DUOMO), SALA CAPITOLARE. Madonna and Child.

Volterra. PINACOTECA. Nativity (r.). Sd and d. 147(0?).

    Predella: Birth, Presentation, Marriage and Assumption of Virgin. *Plate 843*.

    S. GIROLAMO. Annunciation with SS. Michael and Catherine, and donor. Sd and d. 1466. *Plate 842*.

Washington (D.C.). 10. (MELLON COLLECTION). Adoration of Magi.

    429, 1131–1134 (KRESS COLLECTION. K 545, 1647A–D). Predella of Passion: Agony in the Garden, Way to Calvary, Crucifixion, Descent into Limbo, Resurrection.

    599 (WIDENER COLLECTION). Madonna and Child with SS. Bernardino and Jerome.

Homeless. Predella panel: Stoning of S. Stephen. *Plate 848*.

BERGOGNONE

Ambrogio da Fossano (dicto Brecognono, bergognono), first registered among Milanese painters in 1481, died 1523. Pupil of Foppa; influenced by Zenale, and, toward the end, slightly by Leonardo, and vaguely throughout his career by the Franco-Flemings.

Amsterdam. 579–D1. Madonna and Child (formerly Oldenburg). [*Plate 362*.]

Arcore (Monza). VITTADINI COLLECTION (EX). Madonna suckling the Child. *Plate 1479*.

    Full-length S. Anthony Abbot in landscape.

Arona. SS. GRATINIANO E FELINO. Madonna and Child enthroned with Angels and SS. Jerome, Gregory, Ambrose, Augustine who recommends donor (Gerolamo Calagrani?), Felinus, Gratinianus, Carpoforus and Fidelis. E. *Plate 1469*.

Athens (Ga.). UNIVERSITY. R-9 (KRESS COLLECTION. K 1011). Madonna and blessing Child.

Basle. 1347. Predella panel (to S. Ambrogio altarpiece?): Miracle of the bees at birth of S. Ambrose (companion to Bergamo 288 and Turin).

Bergamo. 288. Predella panel (to S. Ambrogio altarpiece in Certosa di Pavia?): S. Ambrose and Emperor Theodosius (companion to Basle and Turin).

289. Madonna suckling the Child. E.

290. S. John Evangelist.

291. S. Paul.

292. Madonna offering Fruit to Child.

331. S. Jerome.

332, 335. Half-length SS. Agatha and Lucy.

333, 336. Panels of polyptych: SS. Louis of France and Quirinus.

334. Pietà.

337. Head of S. Ambrose. (?)

542, 543. Arched panels of polyptych: Full-length SS. John Evangelist and Martha.

S. SPIRITO, SECOND ALTAR R. Polyptych: Descent of Holy Ghost; at sides full-length SS. John Baptist and Ambrose, half-length SS. Jerome and Francis; at top, Annunciation and blessing God the Father. d. 1508.

Berlin. 51. Madonna and Child enthroned with two Angels. (Destroyed 1945.)

52. Madonna and Child enthroned with Angels, SS. John Baptist and Ambrose. Sd. L. (Destroyed 1945.)

Bridgeport (Conn.). MUSEUM OF ART, SCIENCE AND INDUSTRY (KRESS STUDY COLLECTION. K 578). Madonna and Child with penitent S. Jerome in background. E.

Budapest. 65 (112). Mourning over dead Christ.

4212 (PÁLFFY 10). Right panel of polyptych: Knee-length SS. Roch and Louis of Toulouse.

Busto Arsizio. ARCH. PAOLO CANDIANI. Madonna and Child enthroned with SS. Jerome, Peter, Lawrence, Anthony, Paul, John Baptist and kneeling Cardinal; in background Scenes from Life of two Saints.

Cologne. 525, 526. Panels of polyptych: S. John Baptist, S. Agnes.

Florence. BERENSON COLLECTION. Adoration of the Child (r.).

Madonna suckling the Child; in background, Flight into Egypt and Massacre of Innocents.

PROF. ROBERTO LONGHI. Madonna and Child with Rosary.

Garegnano (Milan). OLD PARISH CHURCH (EX). Detached fresco: Madonna and Child with blessing donor (fr.).

Gazzada (Varese). FONDAZIONE CAGNOLA. Dead Christ upheld by Angels and worshipped by monk.

Isolabella (Lago Maggiore). PALAZZO BORROMEO. 3. Conversion of S. Paul.

41, 48. Madonna enthroned, suckling the Child; Redeemer seated in mandorla, blessing (central panels, below and above, of polyptych in Certosa di Pavia; companions to Certosa Evangelists and Fathers of Church). doc. 1492–94.

45. Madonna and Child against hedge of roses. L.

49. Small Madonna and Child.

Lodi. INCORONATA, CAPPELLA DI S. PAOLO. Four panels from entrance to choir: Annunciation, Visitation, Adoration of Magi, Circumcision. Soon after lost fresco of choir, documented 1498–1500. *Plate 1472.*

London. 298. Madonna and Child enthroned with S. Catherine of Alexandria and S. Catherine of Siena.

779, 780. Fragments of altarpiece: Male donors, female donors.

1077, 1077A, 1077B. Triptych: Madonna and Child enthroned with Angels playing Music; Christ carrying Cross; Agony in Garden. 1501.

BUCKINGHAM PALACE, ROYAL COLLECTION. Heads of SS. Stephen and Lawrence.

COURTAULD INSTITUTE GALLERIES, LEE OF FAREHAM COLLECTION. 70. Christ on Cross with mourning Virgin and Evangelist.

Melegnano (Milan). PARISH CHURCH. Baptism (p.). Sd and d. 1506. *Plate* 1475.

Milan. AMBROSIANA. Two panels of polyptych: Half-length SS. Elizabeth and Francis, half-length SS. Peter Martyr and Christopher. L.

Madonna and Child enthroned with SS. Jerome, Augustine, Gregory, Ambrose, three Virgin Saints, a Bishop Saint and donor (Girolamo Calagrani?). E.

BRERA. 22–25. Four detached frescoes from S. Satiro: SS. Mary Magdalen, Martha and Catherine; SS. Barbara, Roch and Clare; SS. Martin, Apollonia and Agnes; Madonna and Child with Angels. 1495. *Plate* 1473.

257. Madonna in Glory with Holy Children and S. Roch below. Sd. *Plate* 1480.

258. Penitent S. Jerome between S. Ambrose and S. Catherine; in lunette, Pietà (g.p.).

259. Madonna and Child blessing monk and S. Clare. L.

260. Christ at Column.

308. Assumption and Saints; in lunette, Coronation of Virgin (g.p.). Sd and d. 1522.

721. 'Ecce Homo.'

783. Madonna and sleeping Child in landscape (p.).

CASTELLO. 310. Head of Man (fr.).

341. Penitent S. Jerome.

447. Predella panel to S. Benedetto altarpiece in Certosa di Pavia: S. Benedict giving alms (companion to Nantes). 1490.

448. S. Roch.

1118. Lunette: Dead Christ and Angels.

POLDI PEZZOLI. 474. S. Catherine.

640. Madonna and Child with two Angels.

654. Madonna suckling the Child. (?)

CRESPI COLLECTION (EX). Nativity with two Angels. *Plate* 1476.

FRIZZONI COLLECTION (EX). Head of martyr and two Angels.

DUCA GALLARATI SCOTTI. Side panels of polyptych: SS. Roch and Sebastian. E.

Top panel of polyptych: God the Father.

S. Anthony Abbot.

S. Paul.

Madonna and blessing Child, with Flight into Egypt in background.

ALDO NOSEDA (EX). Head of S. Catherine.

RASINI COLLECTION. Risen Christ.

s. AMBROGIO, MUSEO. Detached fresco: Christ among the Doctors.

s. CELSO. Baptism of Christ. Not traced.

s. EUSTORGIO, CAPPELLA BRIVIO (FIRST R.): Triptych: Madonna and Child, SS. James
    and Augustine; in predella, small SS. John Baptist, Sebastian. Catherine and
    another Saint. L.

— SACRISTY. Penitent S. Jerome. Not traced.

s. MARIA PRESSO S. CELSO, L. TRANSEPT. Madonna with SS. Roch, John Baptist, two
    Angels and donor adoring the Child (g.p.). Sd. L.

s. MARIA DELLA PASSIONE, R. TRANSEPT. Christ and the Apostles. L.

— CANONICA. Detached fresco: Madonna and Child.

— SAGRESTIA. Frescoes: twenty-four lunettes with busts of Saints and Canons of
    the Lateran Order; below (formerly covered by seventeenth-century cup-
    boards) full-length Saints in simulated portico (p.).

s. PIETRO IN GESSATE, FIFTH CHAPEL R. Detached fresco: Funeral of S. Martin and
    his Assumption into Heaven (r.).

s. SIMPLICIANO, VAULT OF APSE. Fresco: Coronation of Virgin with Saints and
    Angels. L.

Nantes. MUSÉE 18 AND CAMPANA 396. Two predella panels to S. Benedetto altarpiece
    in Certosa di Pavia: Miracle and Temptation of S. Benedict (companions to
    Milan, Castello). 1490. [*Plate 363.*]

New York. 27.39.1. Assumption of Virgin.

SUIDA-MANNING COLLECTION. Two frs. of altarpiece: S. Peter, S. John Baptist.

Paris. 1181. Circumcision. E.

    1182, 1182A. Fragments of altarpiece: S. Peter Martyr and female donor;
    S. Augustine and male Donor. E.

Pavia. Inv. 28. Christ on Way to Golgotha and Carthusian monks (from Convent
    of Certosa). Before 1497. *Plate 1474.*

(Environs). CERTOSA, MUSEO. Three panels of polyptych: S. Augustine enthroned,
    full-length SS. Peter and Paul.

— CHURCH, SECOND CHAPEL L. Two lower panels of dismembered polyptych in
    Perugino's altarpiece: SS. Gregory and Augustine, SS. Ambrose and Jerome
    (full-length, but cut at bottom) in simulated portico (companions to Second
    Chapel right and to Isolabella). doc. 1492–94.

— — SECOND CHAPEL R. Two upper panels of dismembered polyptych in Macrino
    d'Alba's altarpiece: Evangelists seated in couples (companions to Second
    Chapel left and to Isolabella). doc. 1492–94.

— — SIXTH CHAPEL L. S. Ambrose enthroned, with SS. Gervasius, Protasius, Eustor-
    gius and Margaret of Cortona (predella at Basle, Bergamo and Turin?). 1490.

— — FIFTH CHAPEL R. S. Sixtus enthroned with SS. Lawrence, Stephen, Theodore
    and Inventius. 1491.

— — FOURTH CHAPEL R. Crucifixion. Sd and d. 1490. *Plate 1470.*

— — SEVENTH CHAPEL R., OVER DOOR. Fresco: S. Catherine.

— — FIRST CHAPEL R. Virgin and five Angels adoring the Child (r.).

Pavia. CERTOSA, CHURCH (contd.). CHOIR, L. AND R. OF HIGH ALTAR. S. Peter, S.
Paul.

── ─ L. TRANSEPT. Frescoes: in vault of apse, Coronation of Virgin with praying
Ludovico il Moro and Francesco Sforza; at spring of arches, two Angels and
twelve Saints in eight medallions; at sides of apse, SS. Peter Martyr and
Ambrose, S. George and another Saint; on side walls, six Apostles at circular
windows in lunettes, and simulated windows with monks below; over door,
Head of Christ.

── ─ R. TRANSEPT. Frescoes: in vault of apse, Giangaleazzo Visconti offers the
Church to the Madonna with his sons Filippo Maria, Giovanni Maria and
Gabriele Visconti; at spring of arches, two Angels and twelve Saints in eight
medallions; at sides of apse, SS. John Baptist and Bernard, SS. Benedict and
Saint with book; on side walls, six Apostles at circular windows in lunettes,
and simulated windows with Carthusian monks below; over door, Madonna
and Child. *Plate* 1471.

── REFECTORY, VAULT. Frescoed medallions (p.). 1509.

Philadelphia (Pa.). J. G. JOHNSON COLLECTION. 259. Panel of polyptych: Full-length
Magdalen. L.

Poznań. Inv. Mo 4. Three panels of polyptych: Madonna worshipping Child in
her lap, SS. Christopher and George. E.

Rome. VISCONTI VENOSTA COLLECTION. Madonna and blessing Child with rosary.
Plate 1478.

Soissons. 23 (CAMPANA 396). Temptation of S. Benedict (transferred to Nantes).

Turin. 134. Two predella panels (to S. Ambrogio altarpiece?): Preaching of S.
Ambrose, Ordination of S. Augustine (companions to Basle and Bergamo).
135. Madonna and Child.

── GUALINO COLLECTION. 671. Madonna and Child with Carthusian monk.

Venice. CONTE VITTORIO CINI. Inv. 2073. Four busts of Prophets.

LIDO, G. BRUINI. Flagellation.

Washington (D.C.). 781 (KRESS COLLECTION. K 1399). Risen Christ.

Williamstown (Mass.). STERLING AND FRANCINE CLARK ART INSTITUTE. Portable
altarpiece: Madonna and Child enthroned with SS. Paul and John Evangelist.

Würzburg. UNIVERSITÄT, WAGNER-MUSEUM. 94 (Inv. Z 423). Madonna and three
Angels adoring the Child.

Homeless. Madonna and Child on clouds. *Plate* 1477.

BERLINGHIERO

Active in Lucca about 1220/40.

Cleveland (Ohio). 66. 237. Portable altar: Madonna and Child, Crucifixion of S.
Andrew, Last Judgement, four Saints.

Lucca. PINACOTECA. 39. Painted Crucifix from S. Maria degli Angeli. Sd. *Plate* 1.
New York. METROPOLITAN MUSEUM. Madonna and Child.

BERNARDINO DE' CONTI

School of Milan. Active ca 1490–1522. (Pupil perhaps of Zenale; see Master of Sforza Altarpiece), imitator and at times probably assistant of Leonardo.

Augsburg. See Munich.
Bergamo. 330. Madonna suckling the Child. Sd and d. 1501.
　　339. Madonna and Child with Angel musician.
Berlin. 55. Profile bust of Cardinal. Sd and d. 1499.
　　2061. Version of Leonardo's Virgin of the Rocks (formerly Sans Souci; st. replica of Milan, Castello?). Sd and d. 1522. (Destroyed 1945.) *Plate* 1398.
　　SCHLOSSMUSEUM (EX). Young Knight of Malta (Sisto della Rovere). d. 1501.
　　KULTURMINISTERIUM (EX). Alvisius Bexutius. d. 1506.
Berlin-Ost. 214. Madonna and Child with flower.
Bologna. Inv. 185. Woman with red sleeves.
Brooklyn (N.Y.). 14.141. Profile of Catellano Trivulzio. Sd and d. 1505. *Plate* 1404.
Cambridge. FITZWILLIAM (EX). Madonna and Child with flower. *Plate* 1399.
Cedar Rapids (Ohio). COES COLLEGE MUSEUM. Profile of gentleman.
Châalis (Ermenonville). MUSÉE JACQUEMART-ANDRÉ. 380. Profile bust of woman.
Detroit (Mich.). 38.80. Gentleman of the Trivulzio Family.
Florence. UFFIZI. 1883. Profile of man.
Fonthill (Wilts.). HUGH MORRISON (EX?). Profile of lady. *Plate* 1402.
Haughton Hall (Cheshire). BROCKLEBANK COLLECTION (EX). Profile of man.
Isolabella (Lago Maggiore). PALAZZO BORROMEO. Bust of woman with coral necklace.
　　Young man holding sword.
　　Profile of man.
　　Madonna and Child.
Karlsruhe. 427. Madonna and Child in landscape. L. (?)
Locarno. S. MARIA DEL SASSO. Annunciation. *Plate* 1397.
　　Angel announcing glad Tidings to Souls in Hades.
London. H. A. PETO (EX). Portrait of lady.
　　SIR GEORGE DONALDSON (EX). Madonna and Child blessing Infant S. John and Angel.
Milan. AMBROSIANA. Madonna and Child in landscape. *Plate* 1400.
　　BRERA. 271. Variant of Leonardo's Virgin of the Rocks. Sd and d. 1522.
　　MUSEO DEL CASTELLO. 487. Variant of Leonardo's Virgin of the Rocks. L.
　　POLDI PEZZOLI. 639. Madonna suckling the Child (after Leonardo's Madonna Litta).
　　CONTE GILBERTO BORROMEO. Portrait of gentleman.

Milan (contd.). TRIVULZIO DELLA SONAGLIA COLLECTION. Full-face portrait of Gian
    Giacomo Trivulzio.
Munich. 1136 (formerly Augsburg). Madonna and Child.
Paris. 1605. Profile of lady (after Leonardo?).
    1685. Profile of Bianca Maria Sforza (see De Predis, Washington 649).
    MUSÉE JACQUEMART-ANDRÉ. 658. Profile of so-called Beatrice d'Este (see De Predis,
        Washington 1145).
    673. Profile of gentleman. Sd and d. 1500.
Philadelphia (Pa.). J. G. JOHNSON COLLECTION. 269. Male portrait. Sd.
Poitiers. MUSÉE DES AUGUSTINS. 92.1.330. Head of Baptist on the platter. (?)
Potsdam. SANS SOUCI. See Berlin n. 2061.
Rome. GALLERIA BORGHESE. 151. Bust of woman. (?)
    CONTE SUARDI. Portrait of Bianca Maria Sforza. Not traced.
    VATICAN, PINACOTECA. 446. Profile of Francesco Sforza as a boy. Sd and d. 1496.
        Plate 1394.
Saint-Amand-Montrond. HÔTEL DE VILLE. Inv. 22.2.3. Profile of Charles d'Amboise.
    Sd and d. 1500. *Plate 1401.*
San Marino (Cal.). HUNTINGTON GALLERY. Profile of middle-aged lady. *Plate 1403.*
San Remo. ADOLPHE THIEM (EX). Male portrait.
Seattle (Wash.). MUSEUM OF ART. IT.37/C.7677.1 (KRESS COLLECTION. K 1591). Profile
    of Charles d'Amboise.
Spliska (Island of Brazza or Brac). CASTLE OF CERINEO FAMILY. Madonna suckling
    the Child (after Leonardo's Madonna Litta). Sd. *Plate 1396.*
Varallo Sesia. 50. Profile of Charles d'Amboise. Sd and d. 1504.
Worcester (Mass.). 1919.80. Madonna and Child. L.
Würzburg. UNIVERSITÄT, WAGNER-MUSEUM. 95. Madonna and Child playing with
    flowers. (?)
Homeless. Madonna and Child (Version of Bergamo 330 and Munich). Sd.
    Plate 1395.

BERNARDINO DI MARIOTTO

*Umbrian. Active 1497–1566. Pupil of Fiorenzo di Lorenzo; influenced by Signorelli,
Lorenzo di Alessandro and Crivelli.*

Altenburg. 132 (135). Madonna and blessing Child, crowned by two Angels, with
    SS. Jerome and Francis.
Assisi (Environs). BASTIA, PARISH CHURCH. Madonna with SS. Anthony of Padua
    and Anthony Abbot appearing to Confraternity.
Baltimore (Md.). WALTERS ART GALLERY. 641. Madonna and Child.
Bergamo. 557. Mourning over dead Christ.

Berlin. 1478. Madonna and Child with two Saints. E. (?)

Berlin-Ost. 140. Tondo: Madonna and Child with Angels. (?)

Boston (Mass.). 46.1428. Madonna and Child (r.).

Budapest. 1232 (122). Holy Trinity with S. Sebaldus (?) and Pilgrims.

Cambridge (Mass.). FOGG ART MUSEUM. 35. Mystic Marriage of S. Catherine.

Camerino. SS. ANNUNZIATA, FIFTH NICHE L. Fresco: Baptism. (?)

Châlons-sur-Marne. INV. 462, CAT. 497. Madonna and Child. (?)

Fabriano (Environs). BASTIA, PARISH CHURCH. Madonna and Child protecting Bastia, and two Angels. Sd and d. 1498.

Foligno. PINACOTECA. Madonna and Child with two Angels.

Gualdo Tadino. PINACOTECA. Madonna in Glory.

Lille. 987. S. Francis receiving Stigmata. (?)

Matelica. 32. Coronation of Virgin.

Milan. SAIBENE COLLECTION. Five pilaster panels: SS. Sebastian, Lucy, Nicholas of Tolentino, Lawrence, Nicholas of Bari.

New York. HISTORICAL SOCIETY. 1867–25A, B. Predella panels: Nativity, Resurrection. (?)

Paris. DREYFUS COLLECTION (EX). S. Mary Magdalen.

Perugia. 155. Mystic marriage of S. Catherine with SS. Peter, Mary Magdalen, Bishop Saint and Infant S. John. *Plate 985.*

    156. Madonna and Child with SS. Benedict, Francis and Infant S. John.

    157. Coronation of Virgin.

    175. Madonna and Child with SS. Andrew and Julian.

    176. Madonna and Child with SS. Anne, Roch, Sebastian and Angels. *Plate 989.*

    201. Madonna and Child worshipped by nun. d. 1492. (?)

    501. S. Galganus and an Angel.

Philadelphia (Pa.). J. G. JOHNSON COLLECTION. 144. Dead Christ with two Angels.

Potenza Picena. MINORI OSSERVANTI. Madonna and Child with SS. Francis, Anthony of Padua, John Baptist and Angels. d. 1506.

Richmond (Surrey). COOK COLLECTION. 57. Madonna and Child with S. John Baptist.

— (EX). Two predella panels: Visitation, Circumcision (companions to Rome, Colonna). *Plate 990.*

Rome. MUSEO DI PALAZZO VENEZIA. F.N. 19212. SS. Andrew and Lawrence.

PRINCIPE COLONNA (PRIVATE APARTMENTS). Two predella panels: Adoration of Shepherds, Dispute with Doctors (companions to Richmond). *Plate 988.*

SPIRIDON COLLECTION (EX). Madonna and Child.

San Severino Marche. PINACOTECA. Annunciation. d. 1514.

    Pietà.

    Entombment.

DUOMO NUOVO, SACRISTY. Banner: 'Madonna del Soccorso'. Sd and d. 1509. *Plate 984.*

S. DOMENICO, ALTAR R. (Madonna and Child with) SS. Taziana and Eustace.

San Severino Marche. S. DOMENICO (contd.). APSE. Madonna and Child in
   Glory with SS. Severinus, Catherine of Siena, Dominic, Florentius (?) and
   Infant S. John. 1512–14. *Plate* 986.

Venice. CA' D'ORO. Resurrection.

Homeless. Predella panel: Communion of S. Colomba da Rieti. *Plate* 987.
   Resurrection (repr. *Paragone* n. 177, 1964, *Plate* 49).

BERTUCCI, Giovan Battista

*Umbro-Romagnol of Faenza, active 1503–16. May have assisted Pinturicchio. Developed
under influence of Perugino, Costa and Francia.*

Ajaccio. 182, 183. Side-panels of triptych: SS. Roch and Baptist; SS. Francis and
   Stephen. (?)

Baltimore (Md.). WALTERS ART GALLERY 479. Madonna and Child.

Berlin-Ost. 120. Madonna and Child enthroned with SS. James, John Evangelist
   and Infant Baptist.
   132. Centre panel of Mengolini polyptych (see Faenza and Graz): Adoration of
   Magi, and donor. (Destroyed 1945.) *Plate* 1031.

Budapest. 60(107). Mystic Marriage of S. Catherine.

Faenza. PINACOTECA. Madonna and Child with SS. Bernardino, John Baptist,
   Celestinus and Anthony of Padua. d. 1511.
   Polyptych: Madonna and Child with Infant S. John and five Angels; above,
   Eternal; at sides, SS. Hippolytus and Romuald, SS. Benedict and Lawrence.
   Sd and d. 1506. *Plate* 1030.
   Nativity with SS. Jerome, Bernardino, John Evangelist and Infant John.
   Adoration of Magi.
   'Noli me Tangere' and SS. Peter and Andrew.
   Head of Apostle.
   Head of S. Anthony of Padua.
   Madonna and Child with S. Paul.
   Side-panels of Mengolini polyptych from Monastery of S. Caterina: S. John
   Baptist, S. Mary Magdalen (centre-panel at Berlin, lunette at Graz). ca 1509.
   Fr. of ceiling: Madonna in painted roundel with Putti holding open anti-
   phonaries.

Ferrara. BARBI CINTI COLLECTION (EX). Left panel of polyptych: S. Sebastian (companion to London, Lord Aldenham). *Plate* 1029.

Graz. SALZER COLLECTION (formerly Wittgenstein, Vienna). Lunette of Mengolini
   polyptych: Coronation and Saints (companion to Berlin and Faenza). ca 1509.

Linlathen (Dundee, Scotland). DAVID ERSKINE (EX). Madonna adoring Child with
   Infant S. John.

London. 282. Madonna and Child in Glory with two Angels musicians (r.).
   1051. Doubting Thomas.

LORD ALDENHAM (EX). Side-panel of polyptych: S. John Evangelist (companion
   to Ferrara).
WALLACE COLLECTION. Idyll.
New Haven (Conn.). 1871.92. Madonna and Child with Infant S. John and four
   Saints.
Paris. MUSÉE JACQUEMART-ANDRÉ. 1034. Narcissus.
Rome. GALLERIA SPADA. Inv. 61. Madonna and Child with infant S. John.
   MUSEO DI PALAZZO VENEZIA. Side-panel of polyptych: SS. Paul and Augustine
   (companion to Venice).
Venice. CONTE VITTORIO CINI. Inv. 6489. Side-panel of polyptych: SS. Peter and
   Stephen (companion to Rome).
Homeless. Adoration of the Child with Infant S. John. *Plate* 1032.

BIANCHI FERRARI, Francesco

Modenese. 1457–1510. Pupil probably of Tura, and follower of Ercole Roberti.

Berlin-Ost. 1182. Madonna and Child enthroned with SS. Francis, John Baptist,
   Ambrose and Jerome. E. *Plate* 754.
Cremona. 129. Crucifixion.
Florence. R. LONGHI: Predella panel: S. Francis receiving Stigmata.
   STROZZI COLLECTION. Madonna and Child enthroned and kneeling SS. Jerome,
   John Baptist and donor Giambattista Strozzi.
Modena. 10. Crucifixion, with SS. Jerome and Francis (from S. Francesco della
   Mirandola). *Plate* 755.
   17. 'Noli me tangere.'
   53. Annunciation (left unfinished at death).
   DUOMO, SACRISTY, CEILING. Frescoes: three medallions with Madonna and Child,
   Mystic Lamb, S. Geminianus. 1507.
   S. PIETRO, SECOND ALTAR L. Madonna and Child with SS. Sebastian and Jerome and
   three music-making Angels; in predella, Scenes from Life of S. Jerome. L.
   Plates 756, 758–759.
Rome. GALLERIA NAZIONALE, PALAZZO BARBERINI. Agony in the Garden.
   JANNETTI DEL GRANDE (EX). Crucifixion with SS. Dominic and Peter Martyr.
   Plate 757.
York. 734. Madonna and Child. (?)

BOCCACCIO BOCCACCINO

Cremona, born ca 1465, died 1524/5. Employed by Ercole I of Ferrara 1497–1500; docu-
mented in Venice before 1505; journey to Rome 1512–14. Influenced by Alvise Vivarini

and other Venetians as well as by Costa, Foppa, Bramantino, and no doubt Netherlandish and German engravings.

Berlin-Ost. 1489. Madonna and Child with SS. John Baptist and Ursula (formerly deposited at Münster).

    H. WENSTENBERG COLLECTION (EX). Madonna and Child against landscape (r., fr.; companion to Cremona, Carotti and to London, Rodd?)

Birmingham. CITY ART GALLERY. P. 11'57. Sacra Conversazione with SS. John Baptist, Nicholas of Bari, Angel Raphael, female Saint and donor.

Boston (Mass.). MUSEUM OF FINE ARTS. 'Crespi' Madonna and Child. *Plate* 1659.

Bucarest. Inv. 737. Madonna and Child standing on parapet (after Bellini).

Budapest. 4240 (PÁLFFY 13). Nativity with S. Jerome. *Plate* 1663.

Cambridge. FITZWILLIAM MUSEUM (EX). Madonna and Child. (?)

Carpi. FORESTI (EX). Madonna and Child.

Combe House (Presteigne). URSULA HARRISON (EX). Madonna of the goldfinch by a window.

Copenhagen. STATENSMUSEUM. 72. Madonna and Child with apple. E.

Cremona. 160–165. Frs. of frescoes from Anterefettorio of S. Agostino: Four heads of blessed Augustinians, two heads of Angels. Formerly Sd and d. 1497.

    166. S. Jerome in the wilderness (from Incoronata). Sd. *Plate* 1652.

    167. Madonna and Child enthroned with SS. Anthony of Padua and Vincent. Sd and d. 1518. *Plate* 1662.

    S. AGATA, L. TRANSEPT. Holy Family and Magdalen (finished by Galeazzo Campi). Sd by Galeazzo Campi and d. 1518.

    S. MICHELE. Organ-shutters (inside): Angel and Virgin of Annunciation (p.).

    DUOMO, APSE. Fresco in vault: Christ in Glory with Symbols of Evangelists and SS. Imerius, Omobonus, Peter and Marcellinus. Sd and d. 1506. *Plate* 1653.

    — TRIUMPHAL ARCH. Frescoed lunette: Annunciation. 1507.

    — CENTRAL NAVE, L. WALL. Frescoes above arches: First Arch—Joachim and the Angel, Meeting at the Golden Gate, Sd and d. 1515; Second Arch—Birth of Virgin and Marriage of Virgin, Sd and d. 1514 and 1515; Third Arch—Annunciation and Visitation; Fourth Arch—Nativity and Circumcision, Sd; Eighth Arch—Disputation with Doctors. Sd and d. 1518. *Plates* 1654–8, 1664.

    — TRANSEPT. Crucifixion with kneeling Benedetto Fodri (from Palazzo Vescovile).

    G. CAROTTI. 'Mond' fragment of a Sacra Conversazione: Bust of female Saint (see Berlin, Wenstenberg).

Ferrara. 83. Dormitio Virginis. E. *Plate* 1651.

    ORATORIO DELLA CONCEZIONE. Frescoes: Adoration of Magi, Circumcision, Dormitio (begun by Boccaccio Boccaccino in 1497–1500; continued by his pupil Garofalo). (Now transferred to Pinacoteca?).

Florence. UFFIZI. 8539. 'La Zingarella.'

    MUSEO HORNE. 59. Head of Christ. E. (?)

CONTINI BONACOSSI COLLECTION. Panels of polyptych: Evangelists John and Matthew.

Hamburg. 743. Madonna and Child.

Helena (Arkansas). PHILLIPS COUNTY MUSEUM. A. 368-B. (KRESS COLLECTION. K 1056). Madonna embracing the Child. (?)

Le Mans. MAISON DE LA REINE BÉRENGÈRE. Madonna and Child. d. 1495. Not traced.

Leningrad. 5. Madonna and Child.

London. 806. Way to Calvary.

LORD RENNELL OF RODD (EX). Half-length Saint with cross and book (fr.; companion to Berlin, Wenstenberg; and Cremona, Carotti?). *Plates* 1650.

Manchester. G. BEATSON BLAIR BEQUEST. Madonna and Child with goldfinch against curtain.

Milan. BRERA. 809. Madonna and Child against curtain. L.

Modena. 432. Holy Family and Shepherd in landscape.

Munich. 693. Blessing Redeemer.

BARON VON LIPHART (EX). Madonna and Child worshipped by two Angels.

Naples. 68. Adoration of Shepherds (r.). E.

New York. 30.95.289. Madonna and Child with goldfinch (r.).

Oneonta (N.Y.). HARTWICK COLLEGE. Madonna and Child (formerly Hurd Collection).

Padua. 88 (Inv. 461). Madonna and Child with goldfinch (from Convento delle Eremite). E.

91 (Inv. 175) Madonna and Child with SS. Lucy and Catherine.

Paris. 1401A. Funeral of the Virgin.

Rome. GALLERIA DORIA PAMPHILI. 125. Madonna and Child with SS. John Baptist, Peter, Nicholas and Female Saint.

PRINCIPESSA NICOLETTA BUONCOMPAGNI LUDOVISI. Annunciation.

Sankt Gallen. BARON FRANZ. Madonna and Child. Sd and d. 149?.

Thirlestane House (Cheltenham). LORD NORTHWICK (EX). Madonna and Child with SS. Peter and Paul.

Venice. ACCADEMIA. 600. Sacra Conversazione or Mystic Marriage of S. Catherine, with SS. Peter, Lucy and John Baptist. Sd. *Plate* 1661.

CA' D'ORO. Madonna of the cherries.

MUSEO CORRER. 51. Madonna adoring the Child.

32. Madonna and Child with SS. Justina (?) and John Baptist.

PALAZZO DUCALE. Madonna and Child against curtain and landscape.

S. GIULIANO, FIRST ALTAR L. Madonna and Child with SS. Peter, Michael, John Baptist, John Evangelist. Sd.

Vicenza. 169. Madonna and Child (replica of Hamburg).

Vienna. LIECHTENSTEINSCHE SAMMLUNG (EX). Madonna and Child enthroned. Sd. *Plate* 1660.

Warsaw. NARADOWE MUSEUM. Dead Christ upheld by Angel. (?)

Homeless. Madonna and Child. *Plate* 1649.

PSEUDO-BOCCACCINO see GIOVANNI AGOSTINO DA LODI

BOCCATI

Giovanni di Piermatteo d'Antonio, called Boccati or Boccatis da Camerino (Marches). Became citizen of Perugia 1445. Documented again at Camerino 1465–70, at Orvieto 1473, at Perugia 1479/80. Possibly pupil of Lorenzo Salimbeni; influenced by Piero della Francesca and Fra Filippo Lippi.

Ajaccio. 257. Madonna and Child enthroned with eight Angels and four Putti. *Plate 769.*

Belforte sul Chienti. S. EUSTACHIO. Polyptych: Madonna and Child enthroned with Angels; full-length SS. Eustace, Peter as Pope, James and Venantius; upper register, Crucifixion, Angel and Virgin of Annunciation; knee-length SS. Guardato, Nicholas, Sebastian, Eleuterius; in pinnacles, roundels with God the Father and four Prophets; in pilasters, six small full-length Saints (Mary Magdalen, Barbara, Agatha, Lucy, Catherine, Anthony Abbot); in predella, four Scenes from Life of S. Eustace, SS. John Evangelist, Jerome, Matthew, Paul, John Baptist, Andrew and two panels with adoring Angels. Sd and d. 1468. *Plate 775.*

Budapest. 1209 (74). Altarpiece from Cappella di S. Savino dei Petrangeli at Orvieto: Madonna and Child enthroned, with SS. Giovenale, Savinus, Augustine and Jerome (head of Virgin repainted by Lorenzo da Viterbo) (companion to London?). d. 1473.

Camerino. S. MARIA IN VIA. Predella: Rescue of the body of a Saint from a boat to a church (S. James at Compostella?).

Castel Santa Maria (by Castelraimondo near Camerino). CHIESA DELL'ASSUNTA. Coronation of Virgin with eight Angels, S. Venantius and S. Sebastian. d. 1463.

Compiègne. 1, 2. Predella panels: Martyrdom of a Saint; Investiture of a Bishop. (?)

Esztergom. 55. 206. Crucifixion.

Fiordimonte (see Nemi).

Florence. BERENSON COLLECTION. Madonna and Child with Angels. [*Plate 296.*] Predella panel: Marriage of Virgin (companion to Rome, Colonna). (?)

Helsinki. ATENEUM. Adoration of Magi (r.).

London. SIR THOMAS BARLOW (EX). Two predella panels (companions to Budapest?): Banquet of Totila and S. Savinus; Death of S. Savinus. (1473?). *Plate 777.*

Nemi (Fiordimonte, Macerata). PARISH CHURCH. Three panels of polyptych joined together: Madonna and Child enthroned, with Angels; S. John Evangelist, S. Macarius of Egypt.

Oberlin (Ohio). ALLEN MEMORIAL ART MUSEUM. 61. 78 (KRESS COLLECTION. K 1298). Fragment of altarpiece: SS. John Baptist and Sebastian.

Palermo. CHIARAMONTE BORDONARO COLLECTION. 411. Madonna and sleeping Child with four Putti. *Plate 776.*

Paris. MARTIN LE ROY COLLECTION (EX). Fragment of altarpiece: Two Angels holding candlesticks.

Perugia. 147. 'Madonna dell'Orchestra.'

148. Madonna suckling the Child and four Angels.

149. Madonna of Mercy.

150. 'Madonna del Pergolato': Madonna and Child enthroned, surrounded by Angels, the four Church Fathers, S. Dominic, S. Francis, and Flagellants (two Saints left, repainted later); in predella, S. Thomas Aquinas, Betrayal of Christ, Crucifixion, Way to Calvary, S. Peter Martyr (from S. Domenico). Sd and d. 1447. *Plates 770, 771, 774.*

437. Deposition (from S. Agata) (r.). Sd and d. 1479.

Pióraco. (Environs, see Seppio.)

Ponce (Puerto Rico). MUSEO DE ARTE 62.0261 (KRESS COLLECTION. K 358). Bust of monk.

Poznań. Inv. MO 938 (ex Mielzynski Coll.). Madonna and Child with three Putti.

Princeton (N.J.). 62.55. 'Nevin' and 'Platt' Madonna and Child with two Angels.

Rome. GALLERIA COLONNA. Three predella panels (companions to Florence, Berenson): Birth of Virgin; Kneeling donors. (?)

NEVIN COLLECTION (EX). Madonna and Child enthroned with six Angels. *Plate 772.*

VATICAN, PINACOTECA. 121, 122. Two panels from upper register of polyptych: Blessed Giovanni da Prato and S. George; S. Anthony of Padua and S. Clare (companions to Turin?).

Seppio (Camerino). S. MARIA, CHAPEL BEHIND HIGH ALTAR. Centre and side-panel of triptych: 'Madonna delle Lacrime', S. Sebastian (S. Vincent, lost). d. 1466. *Plate 773.*

Tolentino. S. FRANCESCO. Detached fresco: Madonna di Loreto (r.). 1454. (?)

Turin. GALLERIA SABAUDA (GUALINO COLLECTION). 662. Crucifixion.

Venice. CA' D'ORO. Crucifixion.

CONTE VITTORIO CINI. Inv. 6312. Crucifixion.

BOLTRAFFIO, Giovanni Antonio

Milanese imitator of Leonardo. 1467–1516. Was in Bologna 1500/02.

Ajaccio. Inv. Mfa. 852.1.685. Bust of young gentleman. (?)

Bergamo. 297. Tondo: Madonna suckling the Child.

527. Blessing Redeemer.

Berlin-Ost. 207. S. Barbara (from S. Satiro). Commissioned 1502. *Plate* 1430.

    207B. Madonna and Child with book and flower. (Destroyed 1945.) *Plate* 1421.

Berne. 54. Bust of young Man.

Broomhall (Dunfermline). LORD ELGIN (EX). Youth holding arrow (st. version of Chatsworth).

Budapest. 52 (115). Madonna and Child.

    4224 (Pàlffy 14). Madonna and Child with SS. John Baptist, Sebastian and donor Bassano da Ponte. ca 1508.

Cambridge (Mass.). FOGG ART MUSEUM. 1930.193. Madonna suckling the Child (st. v. of Milan, Castello).

Chatsworth (Bakewell). TRUSTEES OF THE CHATSWORTH SETTLEMENT. 51. Bust of young woman with initials C B on her coat; on back, skull and inscription 'Insigne sum Jeronimi Casii' (possibly portrait of Costanza Bentivoglio painted for the poet Girolamo Casio). *Plates* 1425–1426.

Cleveland. WILLIAM G. MATHER COLLECTION. Bust of man with cap.

El Paso (Texas). MUSEUM OF ART. 1961-6/17 (KRESS COLLECTION. K 1183). Madonna and Child with flower and book.

Florence. UFFIZI. 2184. Narcissus.

    CONTINI BONACOSSI COLLECTION. Bust of Girolamo Casio (formerly 'Frizzoni'). *Plate* 1427.

Isolabella (Lago Maggiore). PALAZZO BORROMEO. Bust of lady in grey.

    Head of man in black.

    Head of boy crowned with ivy.

    Christ falling under Cross. L. (?)

Lille. 197. Portrait of Girl. (?)

London. 728. Madonna suckling the Child. [*Plate* 368.]

    2496. Madonna and Child with book and flower. *Plate* 1424.

    2673. Narcissus.

    3916. Profile of man with cap.

    EARL OF NORTHBROOK (EX). Bust of Salvator Mundi.

Lugano. THYSSEN COLLECTION. 'Borromeo' portrait of lady.

Messina. EUGENIA SCAGLIONE FRIZZONI (EX). Profile head of S. Sebastian. *Plate* 1428.

Milan. BRERA. 281. Male and female worshipper.

    CASTELLO. 280. Madonna suckling the Child.

      279, 281. Two panels of triptych: SS. Gervasius and Bernard recommending kneeling father and two sons; SS. Roch and Sebastian recommending kneeling mother and two daughters.

      433. Portrait of woman.

    POLDI PEZZOLI. 57. Portrait of bearded man.

      642. Madonna and Child with flower.

      660. Madonna suckling the Child. (?)

    CRESPI COLLECTION (EX). Replica of London n. 2496.

    MARIO CRESPI. 'Salvator Mundi.'

FRIZZONI (EX) Tondo: Bust of S. Sebastian.

CONTESSA TERESA SORANZO MOCENIGO (EX). Portrait of Clarice Pusterla.

S. MAURIZIO, CHOIR. Frescoes: on arch, Annunciation; in lunettes, Noli me Tangere, Visitation, Saints; along open gallery, 26 roundels with half-length Saints. 1505–10. *Plates* 1419–1420, 1422–1423.

Montreal. 7. Madonna and Child on parapet, against landscape.

Moscow. PUSHKIN MUSEUM. 2667. 'Stroganoff' youth with arrow and coat decorated with lilies (st. version of Chatsworth).

New York. 30.95.252. Profile of old woman. L.

R. M. HURD (EX). Version of Leonardo's Virgin of the Rocks, with donor (c.).

Paris. 1169. Altarpiece from Casio Chapel in Church of the Misericordia at Bologna: Madonna and Child with S. John Baptist, S. Sebastian and kneeling Marchione Casio and his son the poet Girolamo Casio. doc. 1500. *Plate* 1429.

MUSÉE JACQUEMART-ANDRÉ. 1049. Profile of youth.

Pavia. Inv. III. Bust of lady.

Philadelphia (Pa.). J. G. JOHNSON COLLECTION. 268. Portrait of youth.

Powis Castle (Shrops.). EARL OF POWIS (EX). Profile of young man; on back, profile of young woman.

Raleigh (N.C.). MUSEUM OF ART. GL.60.17.40 (KRESS COLLECTION. K 2190). 'Dreyfus' Head of girl crowned with flowers (st. version or copy?).

Rome. S. ONOFRIO. Frescoed lunette: Madonna and Child with donor.

Sands Point (Port Washington, Long Island). MRS. HANNAH D. RABINOWITZ. Madonna suckling the Child.

San Francisco (Cal.). PALACE OF THE LEGION OF HONOR. 1935.4. Profile of gentleman.

Schloss Sebenstein. PRINZ LIECHTENSTEIN (EX). 399. Bust of S. Sebastian.

Vienna. CZERNIN COLLECTION (EX?). 14. 'Salvator Mundi.'

BARON TUCHER (EX). Madonna and Child blessing Infant S. John.

Washington (D.C.). 895 (RALPH AND MARY BOOTH COLLECTION). Bust of youth with cap.

Worcester (Mass.). 1940.38. Portrait of lady.

BONAVENTURA BERLINGHIERI

Documented in Lucca 1228/74, son of Berlinghiero, but closer to Byzantine tradition than his father.

Pescia. S. FRANCESCO. Full-length S. Francis and six scenes from his life. Sd and d. 1235. *Plate* 2.

BONFIGLI, Benedetto

Perugia. Mentioned 1445, died 1496. Pupil perhaps of Boccatis; developed under the influence of Fra Angelico and Benozzo Gozzoli. Worked in partnership with Caporali.

Bayonne. 959. Predella panel: Two flagellants (companion to Chantilly and Munich).

Chantilly. 8. Predella panel: Two flagellants (companion to Bayonne and Munich).

Civitella Benazzone (Perugia). PARISH CHURCH. Banner: Madonna of Mercy.

Corciano (Perugia). S. MARIA, L. ALTAR. Banner: Madonna of Mercy (r.). d. 1472.

El Paso (Texas). MUSEUM OF ART. 1961-6-14 (KRESS COLLECTION. K 1313). Central panel of triptych: Madonna of Humility (companion to Homeless). E. *Plate 684.*

Florence. BERENSON COLLECTION. Nativity. [*Plate 299.*]

Munich. 650, 651. Two panels of polyptych: S. Francis' marriage with Poverty, S. Francis receives from a monk the yoke of obedience (companions to Bayonne and Chantilly).

New York. OTTO H. KAHN COLLECTION (EX). Madonna and Child with two Angels (r.).

Perugia. 34–40. Frescoed decoration of the Cappella dei Priori: Siege of Perugia and Invention of the Body of S. Hercolanus; the Body transferred to the church of S. Lorenzo; transferred to the church of S. Pietro; S. Louis of Toulouse is ordained; performs the miracle of the fish; another miracle of S. Louis of Toulouse; Funeral of S. Louis of Toulouse. Begun 1454 and not finished at death. *Plate 687.*

138. Annunciation and S. Luke (with Caporali). *Plate 685.*

143, 144, 145. Triptych from S. Domenico: Madonna and Child with Angels, SS. Peter and Catherine, SS. Paul and Peter Martyr (companion to Caporali, 142 etc.). 1467.

158 Madonna and Child with four Angels and SS. Thomas, Jerome, Francis and Bernardino (with Caporali).

164 Banner of S. Bernardino. d. 1465.

227 Miracle of S. Bernardino (on Perugino's design). 1473.

CARMINE. Madonna and Child with two Angels and Worshippers (r.).

S. FIORENZO. Banner: Madonna and Child in Glory, with Angels, SS Fiorenzo, Francis, Sebastian, Blessed Filippo Benizzi and predella. d. 1476. *Plate 686.*

S. FRANCESCO AL PRATO, CAPPELLA DELLA SS. CONCEZIONE. Banner: Madonna of Mercy (p.). d. 1464.

S. MARIA NUOVA, SECOND ALTAR R. Banner: Virgin, SS. Benedict, Scholastica and Blessed Paolo Bigazzini plead with Christ, who is throwing lightning bolts on Perugia. d. 1472.

S. PIETRO, L. NAVE, END WALL. Pietà with SS. Leonhard and Jerome (st.). d. 1469. (?)

Homeless. Left panel of triptych: S. Sebastian and Bishop Saint (companion to El Paso). *Plate 683.*

BONSIGNORI, Francesco

Verona. ca 1455–1519. Pupil, perhaps, of Benaglio; 1490 went to Mantua; close follower of Mantegna; influenced by Liberale, and finally by Costa.

Baltimore (Md.). WALTERS ART GALLERY. 449. Profile of warrior.
    450. Bust of prelate in black.
Florence. BARGELLO, CARRAND COLLECTION. Christ bearing Cross, and S. Veronica.
    BERENSON COLLECTION. Furniture panel: Apollo and Daphne.
London. 736. Portrait of man. Sd and d. 1487. *Plate 1313.*
Mantua. PALAZZO DUCALE (REGGIA DEI GONZAGA). Way to Golgotha. L.
    Vision of Blessed Osanna Andreasi, with Isabella d'Este (from S. Vincenzo).
    (Environs). S. MARIA DELLE GRAZIE, CAPPELLA ZIBRAMONTI. S. Sebastian.
Philadelphia (Pa.). J. G. JOHNSON COLLECTION. 171. Bust of elderly man.
    172. Bust of youthful Saviour.
Verona. 148. Madonna and sleeping Child. Sd and d. 1483.
    271. Madonna and Child enthroned with SS. Onophrius, Jerome, Christopher,
        Bishop Saint and Altobella Avogadro, widow of Donato Dal Bovo. Sd and
        d. 1484. *Plate 1309.*
    S. ANASTASIA, OVER SACRISTY DOOR. Fresco: Two Angels holding curtain.
    S. BERNARDINO, CAPPELLA DEI BANDA (SECOND R.). Madonna and Child enthroned
        with SS. Jerome and George. Sd and d. 1488. *Plate 1310.*
    SS. NAZARO E CELSO, CAPPELLA DI S. BIAGIO (L. TRANSEPT). Madonna and Child in
        Glory and SS. Blaise, Sebastian and Juliana (predella by Girolamo dei Libri).
        1514–19. *Plate 1314.*
    S. PAOLO, FIRST CHAPEL R. Madonna and Child with SS. Anthony Abbot and Mary
        Magdalen. E. *Plate 1311.*
Vicenza. S. LORENZO, FOURTH ALTAR, R. TRANSEPT. Crucifixion.
York. 732. Predella panel: Two captive kings before a judge.
Homeless. Bust of Petrus Leonius. *Plate 1312.*

BONVICINO see MORETTO

BORGOGNONE (Ambrogio da Fossano) see BERGOGNONE

BRAMANTE

Monte Asdrualdo (Urbino) 1444–1514 Rome. Architect, sculptor and painter. As painter, pupil of Piero della Francesca; ending as mere decorator.

Bergamo. PALAZZO DEL PRETORE (MUSEO DI STORIA NATURALE). Detached frescoes from façade: Philosophers seated and framed with architectural motives between windows (frs.). 1477.

Milan. BRERA. EIGHT DETACHED FRESCOES FROM CASA PANIGAROLA, ca 1480–85.

489. Heraclitus and Democritus. *Plate 1375.*

490. Man with mace.

491. Man with sword. *Plate 1376.*

492, 493, 494, 495. Busts of warriors (frs).

496. The Singer (fr.).

— FROM ABBAZIA DI CHIARAVALLE.

816. Christ at Column. ca 1490.

CASTELLO. Detached frescoes from ground floor room at Casa Fontana Silvestri: medallions with Heads, Tritons and Najads.

CASA FONTANA SILVESTRI (CORSO VENEZIA 16), FAÇADE. Frescoes: Heroes in simulated portico (lost); frieze with playing Putti and roundels. (See also Zenale and Butinone.)

Rome. VATICAN, PINACOTECA. 342. Detached fresco from Bergamo: Monochrome bust of man in roundel. *Plate 1374.*

BRAMANTINO

Bartolomeo Suardi, Milano ca 1465–1530. Possibly pupil of Butinone; influenced by Foppa and Mantegna; close follower of Bramante.

Ajaccio. Inv. Mfa 852.1.960. Predella panel: Two Deacon Saints before a King. (?)

Berlin. E. SIMON (EX). Madonna holding fruit and Child. *Plate 1378.*

GLOGOWSKY COLLECTION (EX). Madonna and Child in landscape.

Boston (Mass.). 13.2859. Madonna suckling the Child. E. *Plate 1377.*

Bucarest. Inv. 22. Mourning over the dead Christ.

Cologne. 527. Jupiter visiting Philemon and Baucis. E. *Plate 1379.*

Columbia (Mo.). UNIVERSITY OF MISSOURI. 61.71 (KRESS STUDY COLLECTION. K 377). Madonna and Child.

Florence. CONTINI BONACOSSI COLLECTION. Madonna and Child with eight Saints (from destroyed Church of S. Maria del Giardino, Milan).

Gazzada (Varese). DON GUIDO CAGNOLA (EX). Nude statue on pedestal (not finished).

Isolabella (Lago Maggiore). PALAZZO BORROMEO. S. John on Patmos.

Locarno. S. MARIA DEL SASSO, R. ALTAR. Flight into Egypt. 1522.

London. 3073. Adoration of Magi. [*Plate* 366.]

Lugano. THYSSEN COLLECTION. 50A. 'Ecce Homo.'

Mezzana Superiore (Somma Lombardo). S. STEFANO. Pietà with SS. Sebastian and Roch.

Descent of the Holy Ghost.

Milan. AMBROSIANA. Madonna and Child with two Angels, S. Michael and S. Ambrose.

Nativity. *Plate* 1380.

Head of S. John Baptist on a platter. (?)

Detached frescoed lunette from S. Sepolcro: Pietà. *Plate* 1381.

BRERA. 15. Detached fresco from Broletto Nuovo: Madonna and Child with two Angels. 1508.

17. Detached fresco from S. Maria Vetere: S. Martin and the Beggar. ca 1515.

279. Holy Family.

309. Crucifixion. L. *Plate* 1384.

722. Dead Christ (st.).

CASTELLO. Detached fresco from S. Maria del Giardino: 'Noli me Tangere' (st.).

— SALA DEL TESORO. Frescoes: three roundels—the Duke watches the weighing of the Gold; Mercury plays music to Argus; Killing of Argus.

— TRIVULZIO COLLECTION. Tapestries representing the Months. Soon after 1501. *Plates* 1385-1386.

RASINI COLLECTION. S. Sebastian.

SOLA COLLECTION. Lucretia.

WERNER COLLECTION. Pietà (from S. Barnaba).

S. MARIA DELLE GRAZIE, OVER DOOR OF OLD SACRISTY. Monochrome fresco: Madonna and Child with S. James and S. Louis of Toulouse.

— DOOR TO CLOISTER, LUNETTE. Monochrome fresco round a marble Madonna: S. Peter and S. Rose kneeling.

— CHIOSTRO GRANDE. Frescoes with Scenes from Life of S. Dominic. Destroyed 1943.

S. MARIA DELLA PASSIONE, SIXTH CHAPEL R., ALTAR. Fresco from S. Maria in Monforte: Virgin appearing to Blessed Giannetta ('Madonna di Caravaggio'). (?)

New York. 12.178.2. Madonna and Child with vase of pinks.

S. H. KRESS FOUNDATION. K 1762. Predella panels: Raising of Lazarus; Gathering of Manna.

Paris. MUSÉE JACQUEMART-ANDRÉ. 1016. Madonna and Child enthroned with SS. John Evangelist and Matthew. L.

Philadelphia (Pa). J. G. JOHNSON COLLECTION. 267. Lucretia..

Rome. GRASSI COLLECTION. S. Sebastian.

Vienna. ARTARIA COLLECTION (EX). Pietà. *Plate* 1382.

Washington (D.C.). 1619 (KRESS COLLECTION. K 1528). Predella panel: Christ appears to the Apostles.

Homeless. Pietà. *Plate* 1383.

BREA, Ludovico

Nizza, ca 1443–1523. (His brother Antonio died 1527.) Follower of local Franco-Flemish traditions. Influenced by Justus of Alemania in Genoa, by Foppa and, no doubt, by Perugino as well.

Ajaccio. Inv. Mfa 852.1.956/953/560. S. Catherine of Alexandra, S. Catherine of Siena, S. Ursula. (?)

Antibes. NOTRE DAME DE LA GARDE. Polyptych: Madonna of Rosary (st., r.). Formerly d. 1515.

Arcs. See Les Arcs.

Bar. See Le Bar.

Biot (Alpes Maritimes). PARISH CHURCH, L. OF ENTRANCE. Polyptych: Madonna of the Rosary, six Saints and Trinity.

Bonson (Alpes Maritimes). CHAPELLE DE ST. JEAN BAPTISTE. Polyptych: SS. John Baptist, Clare and Catherine; in lunettes, Pietà, Angel and Virgin of Annunciation; predella (with Antonio). d. 1517.

Briançonnet (Alpes Maritimes). PARISH CHURCH. Madonna of the Rosary; in predella, Man of Sorrow and eight Saints.

Brigue (Ventimiglia). S. MARTINO, FIFTH ALTAR R. Crucifixion and Saints.

Camporosso (Bordighera). PARISH CHURCH, SACRISTY. Polyptych: Martyrdom of S. Sebastian, S. Anthony Abbot, S. John Baptist, Crucifixion. (?)

Cimiez. See Nice.

Coursegoules. S. JEAN-BAPTISTE. Polyptych of S. John Baptist.

Diano Borello. PARISH CHURCH. Polyptych of S. Michael. Sd and d. 1516 (Antonio).

Diano Borganzo. PARISH CHURCH. Polyptych: Madonna and Child with SS. Michael, Roch, etc. Sd and d. 1518 (Antonio).

Genoa. PALAZZO BIANCO. 308, 311. Panels of dismembered polyptych from S. Bartolomeo degli Armeni: S. Peter; Crucifixion. Commissioned not later than 1481.

  298. S. Anthony Abbot enthroned. Sd and d. 1504 (Antonio).

CHIESA DELLA MADONNETTA. Annunciation. L.

S. MARIA DI CASTELLO, SECOND ALTAR R. Coronation of Virgin, All Saints; in predella, Mourning over dead Christ. Commissioned 1512. *Plate 1209.*

— FIFTH ALTAR L. Polyptych: Conversion of S. Paul, SS. Dominic and Stephen; above, half-length SS. John Baptist and Jerome; in predella, Preaching of S. Dominic, Pietà, Stoning of S. Stephen.

MARCHESA NEGROTTO CAMBIASO (from S. Maria della Consolazione). Ascension. Sd and d. 1483.

Grasse (Alpes Maritimes). CATHEDRAL. S. Honoratus enthroned, with SS. Clement and Lambert; in pilasters of frame, six small Saints (p.).

Le Bar (Alpes Maritimes). PARISH CHURCH. Polyptych: Madonna and Child with S. James and twelve other Saints.

Lérins (Alpes Maritimes). ABBAYE DE S. HONORÉ, SACRISTY. Panels of dismembered polyptych: Full-length S. John Baptist, half-length S. Peter and S. Benedict.

Les Arcs (Var). PARISH CHURCH. Polyptych: Madonna and Child, SS. John Baptist, Peter, Honoratus and Benedict; in upper register, Crucifixion and SS. Blaise, Victor, Sebastian and Margaret; in pilasters of frame, six small Saints. 1501.

Lieuche (Alpes Maritimes). PARISH CHURCH. Polyptych: Annunciation and SS. Louis of Toulouse, Anthony Abbot; in upper register, Crucifixion flanked by SS. Christopher, John Baptist, Raphael with Tobias, Sebastian, Michael and Catherine; in predella, Christ and the Apostles. d. 1499. *Plate* 1208.

Lille. 988. S. Anthony of Padua.

London. HENRY HARRIS (EX). Annunciation.

Luceram (Alpes Maritimes). PARISH CHURCH. Polyptych: S. Bernard enthroned and SS. Honoratus and Benedict; in upper register, Crucifixion and two Saints. 1500. (?)

Lower register of polyptych (for upper panels and predella, see Nice 2875/6): SS. Margaret, Lazarus Bishop of Marseilles, Mary Magdalen, Peter Martyr and Claude Bishop.

Marseilles. PARANQUE COLLECTION. Polyptych: S. Margaret flanked by SS. John Baptist, Catherine, Magdalen and Peter; in upper register, Pietà, flanked by SS. Francis, Michael, Lawrence and Dominic; in pilasters of frame, eight small Saints. Sd and d. 1494.

Monaco (Alpes Maritimes). CATHEDRAL. Polyptych: S. Nicholas enthroned, flanked by SS. Michael, Stephen, Lawrence and Mary Magdalen; in upper register, half-length S. John Baptist, Angel of Annunciation, Pietà, Virgin of Annunciation, S. Anne with Virgin and Child; in pilasters of frame, eight small Saints. Sd and d. 1500.

Pietà with Antonio Teste as donor, flanked by Agony in the Garden, Betrayal of Christ, Flagellation, Mocking of Christ, Way to Calvary, Crucifixion. d. 1505.

Montalto Ligure (Porto Maurizio). S. GIORGIO. Polyptych: S. George and the Dragon, flanked by SS. Louis of Toulouse, John Baptist, Peter, Sebastian; in upper register, Madonna and Child flanked by SS. Lucy, Michael, Bernard and Catherine; in predella, Pietà and Scenes from Life of S. John Evangelist (p.).

Moulins. 605. Circumcision.

Narbonne. 641. Assumption of Virgin. (?)

New Haven (Conn.). 1943.262/3. Two predella panels: Visitation and Christ among Doctors. *Plate* 1207.

Nice. MUSÉE MASSENA. 2875. Predella panel from Luceram polyptych: S. Margaret meets Olibrius, is arrested, scourged, unharmed by the Dragon, scorched with torches, beheaded. *Plate* 1205.

2876. Upper panels from Luceram polyptych: SS. Francis, Crépin Martyr and Saint; SS. Honoratus, Dominic, Blessed Pierre de Luxembourg, Crépinien.

— DEP. FROM PRIVATE COLLECTION? SS. Sebastian and Roch.

Nice (contd.). ARCICONFRATERNITA DELLA MISERICORDIA, SACRISTY. Madonna and
Child, SS. Cosman and Damian (in polyptych by Miralheti).
Madonna of Mercy.

S. AGOSTINO. Pietà.

(Environs). CIMIEZ, CHURCH OF FRANCISCAN MONASTERY, CHOIR. Triptych: Pietà,
S. Martin with the Beggar, S. Catherine. Sd and d. 1475. *Plate* 1198.

— — L. TRANSEPT. Crucifixion and Saints; in spandrels, two Prophets; in pilasters
of frame, six small Saints; in predella, five Scenes of the Passion. Sd and
d. 1512.

— — R. TRANSEPT. Deposition; in predella, Entombment, Resurrection, Marys at
Sepulchre, 'Noli me tangere' (with Antonio). L.

— SOSPEL, PENITENTS NOIRS. Madonna of Mercy (r.). (Sd and d. 1465?)

Ravenna. 179. Madonna adoring the Child. E. (?)

Savona. 5. Crucifixion.

DUOMO, FIRST ALTAR R. Polyptych: Assumption of Virgin, flanked by Nativity and
Marriage of S. Catherine; in upper register, half-length SS. Peter and Francis;
in predella, Pietà and nine Saints. Sd and d. 1495.

— FIRST ALTAR R. Madonna and Child with Saints.

ORATORIO DI S. MARIA DI CASTELLO. Polyptych from High Altar of Savona
Cathedral: lower register, Madonna and Child enthroned with Angels and
kneeling Cardinal Giuliano della Rovere (by Foppa); at sides, SS. John Baptist
and John Evangelist; in upper register, Fathers of the Church; at top, the four
Evangelists; in predella, Beheading of Baptist, Salome's Dance, Adoration of
Magi, S. John Evangelist at Patmos, Assumption of S. John Evangelist; in
pilasters of frame, statuettes of Saints. Signed and d. 1490 by Foppa under
Madonna; Sd and d. 1490 by Ludovico Brea under S. John Evangelist.
Plate 1197.

Taggia (Porto Maurizio). S. DOMENICO, CHOIR. Madonna of the Rosary, enthroned
between S. Dominic and female martyr, surrounded by Pope, King, Eccle-
siastics and Laymen. doc. 1513.

Two side panels of polyptych: Bishop Saint with Angel of Annunciation above
and three small Saints in pilaster of frame; Deacon Martyr with Virgin of
Annunciation above and three small Saints in pilaster of frame.

Pietà. E.

Polyptych: S. Catherine of Siena flanked by SS. Lucy and Agatha; in upper
register, S. Michael, Annunciation, S. Raphael with Tobias. doc. 1488.
Plates 1199–1201.

— HIGH ALTAR. Polyptych: Madonna of Mercy, flanked by SS. Dominic and John
Evangelist, James the Great and Peter Martyr; in upper register, half-length
SS. Thomas Aquinas, Osanna of Mantua? (lost Crucifixion?) half-length SS.
Catherine of Siena and Vincent Ferrer; in predella, Christ and Apostles.
doc. 1483/4. *Plate* 1202.

— SECOND ALTAR R. Madonna of Mercy. L.

— CAPPELLA CURLI (L. OF CHOIR). Polyptych: Baptism of Christ with kneeling Benedetto and Lazzaro Curli, flanked by SS. Peter and Paul; in upper register, at centre, Pietà surrounded by Angel and Virgin of Annunciation, S. Francis and S. Dominic, at sides, SS. Dominic, Pons, Mary Magdalen, Sebastian; in pilasters of frame, SS. Catherine of Alexandria, Peter Martyr, Vincent Ferrer and SS. Lucy, Bernard, Catherine of Siena; in predella, Christ and the Apostles. Formerly d. 1495. *Plate 1203*.

— L. NAVE. Polyptych: Annunciation, flanked by SS. Fabian and Sebastian; in upper register, half-length SS. Dominic and Pantaleo (r.). d. 1494.

Toulon (Environs). EGLISE DE SIX-FOURS. Polyptych: Madonna and Child, flanked by SS. John Baptist, Peter, Honoratus and Benedict; in upper register, Crucifixion flanked by SS. Martin, Victor, Sebastian and Margaret.

Vercelli. MUSEO BORGOGNA. SS. Catherine, Louis of Toulouse, Anthony Abbot and Leonard.

Villars-du-Var. PARISH CHURCH. Polyptych: Scenes from Life of Christ and Saints. (?)

Homeless. Madonna and Child enthroned. *Plate 1204*.

Madonna crowned by Angels and blessing Child. *Plate 1206*.

BRESCIANINO, Andrea del

Andrea Piccinelli, Sienese, active from 1507 till after 1525. Pupil probably of Pacchia; influenced by Beccafumi, Fra Bartolomeo, Raphael and Andrea del Sarto.

Ajaccio. MUSÉE FESCH. 205. Bust of woman (version of Berlin, Schweizer).

Altenburg. 166. Two fragments: Angel and Virgin of Annunciation.

Attingham Park (Shrewsbury). NATIONAL TRUST. Male portrait (variant of Philadelphia).

Baltimore (Md.). WALTERS ART GALLERY. 1678. Holy Family and young Saint (st.).*

Berlin. 230. Version of Leonardo's Madonna and Child with S. Anne. (Destroyed 1945.)

SCHWEITZER COLLECTION (EX). Bust of young woman. *Plate 1571*.

Bibbiano (Siena). S. LORENZO. Madonna and Child with SS. John Baptist and Jerome.

Bournemouth. MAJOR N. E. J. SPEARMAN. Madonna and Child (after Raphael). (?)

Brussels. M. A. DE DONCKER (EX). Portrait of young woman.

Burghley House (Stamford, Northamptonshire). MARQUESS OF EXETER. 425. Madonna and Child with SS. Michael, Jerome and Infant John.

Cambridge (Mass.). 1942.1661. Tondo: Madonna and Child with two Angels.

Cleveland (Ohio). 16.786. Crucifixion. E. (?)

Dublin. JUDGE JAMES A. MURNAGHAN. Predella panel: Resurrection. *Plate* 1567.

Englewood (N. J.). PLATT COLLECTION (EX). Madonna and Child with Infant S. John.

Florence. UFFIZI. 1622. Madonna and Child with Infant S. John, five Angels and Dominican Monk.

BERENSON COLLECTION. Portrait of lady.

LOESER COLLECTION (EX). Madonna and sleeping Child with Infant S. John. Heads of two young Saints (fr.).

S. CROCE, MUSEO DELL' OPERA. Assumption.

Gazzada (Varese). FONDAZIONE CAGNOLA. Profile of young woman (variant of Rome, Borghese and Homeless).

Glasgow. 214. Predella panel: Adoration of Magi. (?)

Graz. 195. Profile of young woman.

London. 4028. Madonna and Child with S. Paul, S. Catherine and Infant S. John.

W. J. M. ENRIGHT (EX). Madonna and Child (st.).

HENRY HARRIS (EX). Madonna and sleeping Child with Infant S. John in landscape (p.).

EARL OF YARBOROUGH (EX). 'Barberini' bust of S. Catherine.

Madrid. 505. Version of Leonardo's Madonna with S. Anne (Spanish copy of lost Brescianino?).

Montpellier. 577. Bust of young man.

Montreal. DR. S. P. RETY (EX). Bust of woman.

Munich. 1075. Holy Family.

Nantes. 63. Madonna and Child.

Naples. 144. Tondo: Madonna and Child with Infant S. John.

500. Madonna and Child with Infant S. John.

Palermo. CHIARAMONTE BORDONARO COLLECTION. 12. S. Francis receiving Stigmata.

38. Madonna and Child with Infant S. John and two young Saints.

MUSEO DIOCESANO. Madonna and Child with Infant S. John and two female Saints.

Paris. MARTIN LE ROY (EX). Reclining Venus with Cupids.

Philadelphia (Pa.). J. G. JOHNSON COLLECTION. 113. Portrait of young man (variant of Attingham Park).

114. Madonna and Child with Infant S. John, SS. Sebastian and Catherine of Siena (r.).

Richmond (Surrey). COOK COLLECTION (EX). 66. Copy of Raphael's Madonna at Berlin 248.

Rome. GALLERIA NAZIONALE, PALAZZO BARBERINI. Lady in turban and fur. *Plate* 1570.

GALLERIA BORGHESE. 88. Profile of young woman (st. version; see Gazzada and Homeless).

324. Venus and Cupids in niche. *Plate* 1574.

Siena. 408. Predella: Annunciation, Nativity, Crucifixion, Ascension.

409. Madonna and Child enthroned with SS. Jerome, Mary Magdalen, Michael, Benedict, Dominic and Catherine of Siena.

PALAZZO CHIGI SARACINI. 134. Tondo: Madonna with view from window.

    244. Portable altarpiece: Mourning Virgin, Evangelist and Magdalen round a bronze Crucifix; inside doors, S. Augustine and S. Jerome; outside doors, Grotteschi. *Plate* 1569.

PALAZZO PUBBLICO, MUSEO. Madonna and Child with two Angels.

S. MARIA ASSUNTA (DUOMO), MUSEO DELL'OPERA. 10. Baptism (p.). 1524.

SS. PIETRO E PAOLO (CONTRADA DELLA CHIOCCIOLA), HIGH ALTAR. Coronation of Virgin and seven Saints below.

UGURGERI COLLECTION (EX). Madonna and Child. *Plate* 1573.

Stockholm. R. PETRE COLLECTION (EX). Madonna and Child blessing the Infant S. John. *Plate* 1568.

Turin. GALLERIA SABAUDA. 118. Tondo: Madonna and Child with SS. Jerome and John Baptist.

    121. Tondo: Madonna and Child with four Angels.

ACCADEMIA ALBERTINA. 133. Holy Family.

Vienna. LANCKORONSKI (EX). S. Catherine of Siena.

Zurich. LANDOLTHAUS. Portrait of lady.

Homeless. Madonna and Child with SS. Catherine, Joseph? and Infant John. *Plate* 1566.

    S. Mary Magdalen. *Plate* 1572.

    Profile of lady (version of Rome, Borghese).

BRUSASORCI (BRUSASORZI), Domenico

Verona. 1516–67. Pupil of Caroto; influenced by Torbido, Titian, Parmigianino and Michelangelo.

Baltimore (Md.). WALTERS ART GALLERY. 452. Bust of man with white beard. *Plate* 1934.

    585. Portrait of gentleman. (?)

Bergamo. 609. Bust of youngish man in oval.

ALMA AND MARIA FRIZZONI (EX). Bust of prelate. Destroyed by fire. *Plate* 1935.

Florence. UFFIZI. 1870. Head of man.

Lovere. 85. S. Francis.

    89. William the Confessor. 1560.

    92. S. Jerome.

Mantua. S. BARBARA, CHOIR. Beheading of S. Barbara. 1564.

DUOMO, CAPPELLA DEL SACRAMENTO. S. Margaret in prison. 1552. *Plate* 1933.

Milan. BRERA. 110. S. Anthony Abbot and S. Paul Hermit breaking bread, and Redeemer above.

CASTELLO. 21. Male portrait. *Plate* 1937.

MME GINOULHIAC (EX). Woman playing guitar.

Nogarole Rocca (Verona). PARISH CHURCH. Risen Christ and donor. (?)

Philadelphia (Pa.). J. G. JOHNSON COLLECTION. 227. Shepherd and flock. (?). *Plate* 1936.

Princeton (N.J.). 35.35. Last Supper.

Providence (R.I.). 30.057. 'Warren' portrait of lady by window. [*Plate* 358.]

Sarasota (Fla.). RINGLING MUSEUM. Male portrait. (?)

Stuttgart. 497. Head of man. 1558. (?)

Trent. MUNICIPIO, SALA DEL CONSIGLIO. Detached frescoes from façade of Palazzo Cloz-Salvetti: Seasons, Scenes from Roman History. d. 1551. *Plates* 1930, 1931.

Venice. MUSEO CORRER. Inv. 330. Head of man.

Verona. 38. Bonucius Moscardus. 1561.

   79. Busts of two men.

   329. Portrait of musicians.

   2064. Adoration of Magi.

   PALAZZO ARCIVESCOVILE, SALONE DEI VESCOVI. Frescoed walls: above, Prelates behind balustrade; below, Landscapes. 1566. *Plates* 1944–1945.

   PALAZZO DELLA GRAN GUARDIA. Fragments of frescoes.

   PALAZZO RIDOLFI DA LISCA, CENTRAL HALL. Frescoes: Entry of Charles V and Clement VII into Bologna. *Plate* 1943.

   S. EUFEMIA, THIRD ALTAR R. Madonna and Child appearing to SS. Sebastian, Roch, Monica, Augustine and two donors.

   S. FERMO MAGGIORE, FIRST ALTAR R. Fresco: Beheading of S. Paul.

   S. GIORGIO IN BRAIDA, THIRD ALTAR L. Top panel in polyptych by G. F. Caroto (inserted under lunette): Man possessed by Devil, and two allegorical figures. *Plate* 1938.

   S. GIOVANNI IN VALLE, BEHIND HIGH ALTAR. S. John Baptist.

   S. LORENZO, HIGH ALTAR. Madonna and Child appearing to SS. Lawrence, Augustine and John Baptist. 1566.

   S. MARIA IN ORGANO, L. TRANSEPT, CHAPEL L. OF CHOIR. Frescoes: outside—Resurrection, two Sibyls, Saints; inside—Putti in vault; music-making Angels and Evangelists in lunettes; Pool of Bethesda, Raising of Lazarus, on walls.

   — CHOIR. Six landscapes set in the stalls.

   — SACRISTY. Nine landscapes set in the woodwork: Temptation of Christ, Baptism, Calling of Sons of Zebedee, the Man sick of palsy, the Good Samaritan, the Field of Wheat, the Sower, Dives in Hell, Lazarus in Heaven. *Plates* 1941–1942.

   S. MARIA DELLA SCALA, THIRD ALTAR L. S. Gregory and donor.

   — CHOIR. Fresco in Tomb of Boniface: Trumpeting Angel. After 1551.

   SS. NAZARO E CELSO, OVER THIRD ALTAR R. Fresco: Way to Golgotha. (?)

   — FOURTH ALTAR R. Frescoed lunette: Martyrdom of female Saint. (?)

   — FIFTH ALTAR L. Madonna and Child with SS. Peter, Paul, Margaret and music-making Angel; in frescoed lunette above, Christ giving Keys to S. Peter.

S. PIETRO MARTIRE. Madonna and Child appearing to SS. Peter Martyr and Zeno.

S. STEFANO, L. WALL. Christ carrying Cross and nine Saints below.

— CUPOLA. Frescoes: Ascension, Angels with Symbols of Passion.

— SACRISTY. Four half-length Veronese Bishop Saints (Giovanni, Felice, Moderato, Manio).

SS. TRINITÀ, FIRST ALTAR R. Fresco: S. Ursula and her maidens.

— FIRST ALTAR L. Fresco: Mystic Marriage of S. Catherine.

— OVER WEST DOOR. Fresco: God the Father blessing.

— UNDER NUNS' GALLERY. Fresco: Conversion of S. Paul. *Plate* 1932.

Vicenza. 63. Pietà.

Ceiling fresco from Palazzo Chericati: Apollo and Diana, Signs of Zodiac.

(Environs). VILLA DI CALDOGNO, GROUND FLOOR HALL. Frescoes: Monochrome Giants holding frieze with Putti; between them, Banquet, Concert, Game, Dance; over doors, four couples of Slaves and two female Allegories (g.p.).

Vienna. AUSPITZ COLLECTION (EX). Gentleman holding letter.

Volargne (Valpolicella). VILLA DEL BENE, LOGGIA. Frescoes: Racemes and twenty-three colossal heads of Poets Laureate; four landscapes divided by five monochrome figures in niches; scenes of Roman history over side doors; monochrome figures seated over front doors (p.).

— STAIRCASE. Frescoes: Two sacred scenes, Vine and Putti (p.).

— FIRST ROOM L. Frescoed frieze on two walls: monochrome Caryatids and landscapes with Biblical stories; over doors, monochrome male nudes crouching (p.; r. 1944). *Plates* 1939–1940.

— SECOND ROOM L. Frescoes: over doors, David and Justice in niches; monochrome female figures and landscapes with sacred scenes (p.; ruined in 1944).

BUTINONE, Bernardino, da Treviglio

Milanese school. Recorded activity 1484–1507. Developed under the influence of Foppa and the Paduans. Worked in close partnership with Zenale.

Baltimore (Md.). WALTERS ART GALLERY. 445. Madonna and Child with cat (after Foppa).

539. Bust of praying Virgin (fr.). L. (?)

Bergamo. 283. Panel from Series of Life of Christ: Circumcision. *Plate* 1348.

287. Madonna with sleeping Child. Inscribed on parapet BERNARDUS B (or P.?). (?)

Berlin. 1144. Pietà. ca 1480–84. (Destroyed 1945.) *Plate* 1344.

Chantilly. 23. Bust of Virgin.

Chicago (Ill.). 33.1003, 1004. Panels from Series of Life of Christ: Flight into Egypt, Deposition. *Plate* 1345.

Edinburgh. 1746. Panel from Series of Life of Christ: Baptism.

Florence. PROF. R. LONGHI. Two panels with half-length Apostles holding books in circular windows (from Brera Triptych?; companions to Parma and Utrecht). ca 1485.

Gazzada (Varese). FONDAZIONE CAGNOLA. Flagellation. L. (?)

Gosford House (Haddington, Scotland). EARL OF WEMYSS AND MARCH. Two panels from pilaster of altarpiece: S. Peter and Apostle in niches (companions to Montauban).

Isolabella (Lago Maggiore). PALAZZO BORROMEO. Madonna and Child enthroned with four music-making Angels, S. John Baptist and S. Justina. Sd. *Plate* 1356.
Panel from Series of Life of Christ: Marriage at Cana.
Circumcision.
Profile of young man.

Keir (Scotland). STIRLING COLLECTION. Panel from Series of Life of Christ: Baptism.

London. 3336. Panel from Series of Life of Christ: Nativity.

SIR THOMAS BARLOW (EX). S. Sebastian (fr.).

MRS J. MACDONALD. Panel from Series of Life of Christ: Adoration of Magi. *Plate* 1347.

LADY MUIR-MACKENZIE (EX). Madonna and Child.

S. G. WARBURG. Nativity.

Milan. AMBROSIANA. I, 5. Two small panels: S. Louis of Toulouse and S. Bonaventura standing on marble floor against landscape.

— FORMER REFECTORY. S. Lawrence, S. Stephen. Not traced.

BRERA. 242. Triptych from Cappella di S. Leonardo al Carmine: Madonna and Child with SS. Vincent and Bernardino (see also Florence, Parma and Utrecht). Sd and d. 1484. *Plate* 1352.

250. Madonna and Child with open book (after Foppa).

CASTELLO. 342. Portable tabernacle with thirteen Scenes from Life of Christ.

ALDO CRESPI. Two panels from Series of Life of Christ: Entombment, Resurrection.

DUCA GALLARATI SCOTTI. Madonna and Child enthroned with six Angels musicians. Wrongly inscribed 'Mantegna 1461'. *Plates* 1354–1355.

O. VENIER COLLECTION. Presentation.

PALAZZO FONTANA SILVESTRI. Frescoed Hall: full-length Apollo and Muses in architectural frames; frieze with Centaurs, racemes and medallions with heads (frs., r.) (with Zenale).

S. AMBROGIO. See Zenale.

S. MARIA DELLE GRAZIE, NAVE. Frescoes: on pillars, ten full-length Dominican Saints in niches (four left, six right); in lunettes over arches, simulated circular windows with knee-length Dominican Saints (p.). After 1482. *Plates* 1349–1351.

— CHIOSTRO GRANDE, VAULT OF PORTICO. Medallions with Saints. Destroyed.

S. PIETRO IN GESSATE, L. TRANSEPT, CAPPELLA GRIFI. Frescoes commissioned from Butinone and Zenale by Senator Ambrogio Grifi in 1489 and finished before death of donor in 1493. Signed by Butinone and Zenale (but the latter's hand is hard to distinguish in fragments now visible).

— — VAULT. At centre of umbrella-shaped ceiling, Bust of Christ; in each of the five segments, one adoring and two music-making Angels.

— — WALLS. Simulated loggia opening on a landscape with Episodes from Life of S. Ambrose [R. Wall, from top of mountain downwards: Investiture of S. Ambrose as Bishop, S. Ambrose baptizing, healing, praying for Victory of Theodosius, blessing Acolytes, acting as Judge—the tortured Man, pulled by a Cord, and a Monkey are shown in lunette above. L. Wall, from top of mountain: S. Ambrose prevents Theodosius from entering the Church, performs a miracle?, baptizes (S. Augustine?), preaches, condemns the heretic (Manes?); two peacocks in lunette above. Altar Wall: in lunette, S. Ambrose on horseback; on either side of altar, continuation of the landscape with figures].

S. MARIA DELLA VISITAZIONE IN S. SOFIA, SECOND PILLAR L. Madonna and Child. 1500. (?)

Montauban. MUSÉE INGRES. 118. Panel from pilaster of altarpiece: S. Paul in niche (companion to Gosford House).

New York. SUIDA MANNING COLLECTION. Panel from Series of Life of Christ: Christ in the House of Simon.

Paris. 1523. Madonna and Child with two music-making Angels.

MUSÉE JACQUEMART-ANDRÉ. 1013. Profile of elderly man.

Parma. 434. Half-length Apostle with book in circular window (companion to Florence and Utrecht; from Brera Triptych?).

Pavia. GALLERIA MALASPINA. 175. Panel from Series of Life of Christ: Doubting Thomas.

Rome. GALLERIA NAZIONALE, PALAZZO BARBERINI. Crucifixion.

Treviglio. S. MARTINO, CHAPEL ALTERED BY INTRODUCTION OF ORGAN. Frescoes in vault, God the Father at centre and three Angels in each section of vault; at spring of arches, music-making Putti and busts of Saints at simulated circular windows; on wall, fragments of unidentified scene. ca 1485.

— END OF R. NAVE. Polyptych commissioned from Butinone and Zenale 1485, not yet completely paid 1507. Lower register: Madonna and Child enthroned with six Angels (Angels only by Butinone), flanked by three female Saints (left panel, Zenale) and SS. John Baptist, Stephen, John Evangelist (right panel, Butinone). Upper register: S. Martin and the Beggar (Zenale), flanked by SS. Zeno, Gustav (or Mauritius?) and Peter (left panel, Zenale) and by SS. Sebastian, Anthony of Padua and Paul (right panel, Butinone). Predella: Nativity (mostly Butinone), Crucifixion (Butinone), Resurrection (mostly Zenale) separated by half-length Fathers of the Church. [*Plate 365.*] *Plates* 1353, 1357, 1358.

Turin. GUALINO COLLECTION (EX). Triptych: S. Dionysius holding his head, flanked by S. Anthony Abbot and by S. Zeno Bishop; in predella, Pietà, Flagellation and Martyrdom of S. Dionysius. E.

Utrecht. ARCHIEPISCOPAL MUSEUM. Two panels with Apostles holding books, in simulated circular frames (from Brera Triptych?, companions to Florence and Parma).

Vaduz. LIECHTENSTEINSCHE SAMMLUNG. Panel from Series of Life of Christ: Christ before Caiphas.

Homeless. Panel from Series of Life of Christ: Last Judgement (cut down). *Plate 1346.*

CALISTO DA LODI see PIAZZA

CAMERINO see BOCCATIS DA CAMERINO

CAMERINO see GIROLAMO DI GIOVANNI DA CAMERINO

CAMPI, Galeazzo

Cremona, 1477–1536. Follower of Boccaccio Boccaccino, influenced by Perugino.

Bergamo. 275. Circumcision.
   Madonna and Child with S. Anthony Abbot and four female Saints. d. 1519.
Billericay. RAMSDEN HALL, T. W. BACON. Angel of Annunciation.
Brooklyn (New York). 32.799. Bust of Saviour.
Cambridge. FITZWILLIAM MUSEUM. 908. Madonna and Child. Sd. *Plate 1645.*
Casalmaggiore. BIGNAMI COLLECTION. Raising of Lazarus (from Cremona, S. Lazzaro). Sd and d. 1515.
Cremona. 115. Madonna and Child enthroned with SS. Catherine, Christopher and Infant S. John.
   S. ABBONDIO, SANTUARIETTO DI LORETO, ALTAR R. Assumption. *Plate 1648.*
   S. AGATA, see Boccaccino.
   S. AGOSTINO, FIFTH ALTAR R. Madonna and Child.
   S. MARIA MADDALENA, CHOIR. Polyptych: Nativity, Saintly Pope, S. Mary Magdalen; in upper register, Risen Christ with two Saints, busts of SS. Peter and Paul (predella with Life of Magdalen, by Aleni). *Plate 1647.*
   S. SEBASTIANO. Madonna and Child with SS. Sebastian and Roch. Sd and d. 1518.

Milan. BRERA. 326. Madonna and Child with SS. Blaise and Anthony Abbot (from Robecco d'Oglio). Sd and d. 1517. *Plate 1646.*

BAGATTI VALSECCHI COLLECTION. Small Circumcision.

Solarolo Ranieri. PARISH CHURCH. S. Peter between S. Philip and S. Paul (st.). 1528.

Viadana. S. MARIA ASSUNTA DEL CASTELLO, CHOIR. S. Christopher. Sd and d. 1516.

Vienna. 493. Circumcision.

WITTGENSTEINSCHE SAMMLUNG. Madonna and Child (after Mazzola). Sd and d. 1511.

CAMPI, Giulio

Cremona ca 1500/2–1572. Pupil of Romanino, influenced by Parmigianino, Lotto, Titian and Dosso; later by Giulio Romano.

Alba. DUOMO, SACRISTY. S. Lawrence before the judge. Sd and d. 1566.

Bayonne. MUSÉE BONNAT. Inv. 964. Knee-length gentleman holding gloves. (?)

Brescia. 99–106. Detached frescoes: Fragments of frieze. L. *Plate 1945–a.*

Budapest. 1083. Detached fresco: Judgement of Solomon.

Chatsworth. DEVONSHIRE COLLECTION. 425. Bust of boy (r.). E.

Cleveland (Ohio). 16.794. Knee-length old man in black, holding letter and glove.

Cremona. 132. Detached fresco: Curtius (fr.).

S. ABBONDIO, HIGH ALTAR. Madonna and Child with SS. Nazzarus and Celsus. Sd and d. 1527. *Plate 1946.*

S. AGATA, CHOIR. Frescoes: S. Agatha's breasts are torn, S. Peter brings the healing ointment to S. Agatha in prison, S. Agatha is rolled over live coals, at S. Agatha's funeral an Angel puts under her head a marble slab praising her purity. Sd and d. 1537. [*Plate 394.*] *Plate 1950.*

DUOMO, R. TRANSEPT. Organ-shutters: Esther before Ahasverus, Triumph of Mardochai, Death of Ananias. d. 1567.

— CAPPELLA DEL SANTISSIMO (R. OF CHOIR). Last Supper. Sd. *Plate 1955.* Gathering of Manna.

— CAPPELLA DELLA MADONNA DEL POPOLO (L. OF CHOIR). Birth of Baptist, Preaching of Baptist, Baptism of Christ (Signed), Herod's Feast. d. 1568. *Plate 1958.*

— L. TRANSEPT. S. Michael. Sd and d. 1566.

S. MARGHERITA. Frescoes (detached and put back): right wall, Christ preaching, disputing with Doctors, Circumcision; left wall, Entry into Jerusalem (p.?), Raising of Lazarus (p. ?), Transfiguration. 1547. *Plate 1954.*

S. MICHELE, THIRD ALTAR R. Crucifixion with donor. L.

S. PIETRO AL PO, FIRST ALTAR L. Madonna and Child with SS. John Baptist and Paul.

S. SIGISMONDO, HIGH ALTAR. Madonna and Child in Glory appears to SS. Daria, Sigismund, Jerome, Chrysanthes, and to Francesco and Bianca Maria Sforza; Annunciation in roundels above. Sd and d. 1540. *Plate 1952.*

Cremona (contd.). S. SIGISMONDO, ENTRANCE WALL, LARGE LUNETTE. Fresco: Annunciation. 1557.

— VAULT OF NAVE, FIRST BAY. In octagonal centre, Descent of the Holy Ghost; in ovals, two Episodes from Bible. 1557.

— L. TRANSEPT. Frescoes: in lunette, round circular window, two Prophets; in soffit of arch, Putti with Symbols of Passion, two oblong Episodes from the Bible (Moses striking the Rock, Gathering of Manna), two niches with Church Fathers (SS. Gregory and Ambrose); ornamental friezes. 1542.

— R. TRANSEPT. Frescoes: in lunette, round circular window, two Prophets; in soffit of arch, Putti with Symbols of Passion, two oblong Episodes from the Bible (Solomon receives the Queen of Sheba, Judgement of Solomon), two niches with Church Fathers (SS. Jerome and Augustine); ornamental friezes. 1542. *Plate* 1953.

Florence. PITTI. 493. Half-length man, bearded, with large hat.

UFFIZI. 958. Man playing guitar.

1628. Portrait of Giulio Campi's father, Galeazzo Campi. Formerly dated 1535.

91959. Nativity.

Geneva. LEDERER COLLECTION. Knee-length knight crowned with laurel holding roll on parapet with left hand. (?)

Grenoble. Inv. 5. Male portrait. (?)

Hampton Court. ROYAL COLLECTIONS. 1422. Bust of man with black cap. L. *Plate* 1957.

London. 2511. Half-length portrait of man with compass before harpsichord.

EARL OF YARBOROUGH (EX). Man leaning on rock and pointing at his forehead while writing 'Hic intus est omnis beatitudo mea'.

Lugano. THYSSEN COLLECTION. Half-length bearded man with large hat. E.

Milan. AMBROSIANA. Christ in Garden.

BRERA. 97. Pietro Strozzi as pilgrim.

329. Nativity with S. Francis and two donors. *Plate* 1948.

330. Altarpiece from S. Maria delle Grazie et Soncino: Madonna and Child in Glory, with SS. Francis, Catherine and Stampa Soncino as donor. Sd and d. 1530.

POLDI PEZZOLI. 556. Allegory. Sd and d. 152(1?). *Plate* 1947.

S. MARIA DELLA PASSIONE., L. TRANSEPT. Crucifixion. Sd and d. 1665.

PALAZZO BORROMEO. 31. Nativity.

MARCHESE FOSSATI (EX). Young woman arranging flowers in vase. *Plate* 1951.

Paris. 1385. Holy Family with Infant S. John.

Philadelphia (Pa.). MUSEUM OF ART, WILSTACH COLLECTION. W.96–1–6. Lady.

Pittsburgh. CARNEGIE INSTITUTE. Bust of youth.

Poitiers. 83.3.1. Man with dog. (?)

Rome. GALLERIA NAZIONALE, PALAZZO BARBERINI. 632. Writer with dog.

GALLERIA BORGHESE. 121. Young woman as Judith. E. (?)

Soncino (Crema). S. MARIA DELLE GRAZIE. Frescoes. Sd and d. 1530 (finished later).

— VAULT OF NAVE. Simulated arbour or pergola, with roundels containing Christ, Holy Family, Martyrs, Prophets, two scrolls with dedication by Francesco Sforza and date 1530.

— VAULT OF CHOIR. Roundels with Evangelists, wreaths, ribbons. *Plate* 1949.

— VAULT OF APSE. Five sections, with simulated circular windows: four Church Fathers and Hermit Saint.

— APSE, R. WALL. Three Carmelite Saints peering out of simulated circular windows: Basilius, Octovianus, Theodoricus (on opposite wall, real window).

— CHOIR SCREEN. Four colossal Putti drawing curtains.

TRIUMPHAL ARCH. Assumption, with Apostles and donor. Sd.

— LUNETTES OF NAVE. Prophets.

Stuttgart. Inv. 396. Replica of Florence, Uffizi 1628.

Turin. GALLERIA SABAUDA. 124. Adoration of Magi.

Venice. CONTE VITTORIO CINI. Inv. 2061. Portrait of lady.

Vienna. COUNT LANCKORONSKI (EX). Half-length portrait of bearded young man.

BARON OFENHEIM (EX). Seated young gentleman.

Worcester (Mass.). 1922.195. Bust of youth with viola.

Zagreb. 'Ecce Homo'. (?)

Homeless. Bust of man with glove. *Plate* 1956.

CAPORALI, Bartolomeo

Perugia, ca 1420–ca 1505. Pupil of Benozzo Gozzoli, partner of Bonfigli, influenced by Boccatis, Piero della Francesco and later by Perugino.

Amelia. MUNICIPIO, PINACOTECA. S. Anthony Abbot enthroned (by Piermatteo d'Amelia?).

Assisi. S. FRANCESCO, MUSEO DEL SACRO CONVENTO. Ecce Homo.

Berlin. 137A. Madonna and Child enthroned with two Angels (painted in Benozzo's studio).

Budapest. 1306. Detached fresco: Madonna and Child (r.).

1307. Detached fresco: Madonna and Child (fr., r.). (?)

Deruta (Perugia). S. ANTONIO. Frescoes: Madonna of Mercy, SS. Bernardino and Francis; in vault, Evangelists.

(Environs). LA FANCIULLATA, CHAPEL, ALTAR WALL. Frescoed niche: Madonna and Child with six Angels; in embrasure, God the Father, S. James, S. Anthony; on face of arch, Annunciation, S. Sebastian and S. Bernardino (r.). d. 1459. *Plate* 678.

Florence. UFFIZI. 3250. Madonna and Child enthroned with four Angels. E.

LOESER COLLECTION (EX). Three pinnacles: God the Father, David, Isaiah.

EX-CONVENT OF S. GIORGIO ALLA COSTA (CASERMA VITTORIO VENETO). Fresco: Christ and Virgin plead with God the Father for the Faithful; in foreground, Vallombrosan monk. d. 1487.

Isola Maggiore (Lake Trasimeno). s. ANGELO. Painted Crucifix.

Leningrad. 4157, 4159. Two predella panels: SS. Francis, Herculanus, Luke and James; SS. Nicholas, Lawrence, Peter Martyr and Anthony Abbot.*

London. 1843. Predella panel: Adoration of Magi and Christ on Cross. *Plate 679.*
  2863. Madonna and Child with Angels (Madonna and Child studio of Benozzo Gozzoli, Angels only by Caporali).

Montelabbate (Perugia). s. MARIA, R. ALTAR. Fresco: Madonna and Child in Glory with SS. Anthony Abbot and Bernardino; below, SS. Sebastian and Roch plead for the Faithful; in embrasure, roundels with Christ, Prophets and Sibyls; on face of arch, God the Father, Angel and Virgin of Annunciation. d. 1488. *Plate 680.*

Montone (Perugia). s. FRANCESCO, FIRST ALTAR L. Fresco: S. Anthony in Glory with S. John Baptist, Angel Raphael and Tobias. Sd and d. 1491.
— FIRST ALTAR R. Banner against the plague: Madonna of Mercy with SS. Sebastian, Francis, Blaise, John Baptist, Gregory, Nicholas, Anthony of Padua and Bernardino. d. 1482.

Naples. 51. Madonna and Child. d. 1484.
  938. S. Jerome in his study. E.

Padua. 949. Portrait of gentleman (not in 1957 catalogue).

Passignano (Lake Trasimeno). MADONNA DELL'OLIVO. Fresco: Madonna and Child with two Angels holding curtain. E.

Périgueux. MUSÉE. Triptych: Madonna and Child, S. John Baptist and S. Sebastian (st.).

Perugia. 125. Madonna and Child with six Angels. E.
  138. Annunciation with S. Luke (with Bonfigli).
  140–141. Adoration of Magi; in predella, Baptism of Christ, Crucifixion, Miracle of S. Nicholas.
  142. Two pinnacles from S. Domenico triptych: Angel and Virgin of Annunciation (companions to 165, 167, 171, 172 below and to Bonfigli's 143, 144, 145). 1467. *Plates 681–682.*
  153, 154. Two fragments of Pala Cacciatori at Castiglion del Lago: Head of S. John Evangelist and Seraphim; Head of S. Mary Magdalen (companions to Udine). 1487.
  158. Madonna and Child enthroned with SS. Thomas, Jerome, Francis, Bernardino and four Angels; God the Father above (with Bonfigli).
  160–163. Fragments of lost Pietà for the Cappella Verde in the Duomo: Angels holding symbols of the Passion (with Bonfigli). 1477.
  165, 167, 171, 172. Panels from pilasters of S. Domenico triptych: Angels with flowers (companions to 142 above and to Bonfigli 143, 144, 145). 1467.
  166. Detached fresco from Monastery of S. Giuliana: Christ and Virgin in

Glory after Assumption and Coronation; below, half-length SS. Giuliana, Benedict and Bernard. d. 1467.

222, 228, 229. Miracles of S. Bernardino on Perugino's design. 1473.

221. Fresco: Pietà with female Saint and Magdalen.

DUOMO, MUSEO DELL'OPERA. Pietà. d. 1486.

(Environs). CIVITELLA D'ARNA, PARISH CHURCH. Madonna and Child with SS. Sebastian and John Baptist and two Angels. d. 1492.

Rocca S. Angelo or **Rocchicciola** (Perugia). S. FRANCESCO. Votive frescoes: Madonna and Child enthroned with S. Jerome, S. Anthony of Padua and donor. d. 1487.

Madonna and Child enthroned and two Angels.

Udine. GALLERIA D'ARTE ANTICA. Fragment from Pala Cacciatori at Castiglion del Lago: S. Anthony Abbot and Seraphim (companion to Perugia, 153, 154). 1487.

Zagreb. 32. Madonna and Child enthroned with S. Francis, S. Bernardino and four Angels. d. 1465.

Homeless. Half-length Madonna and Child (after Benozzo Gozzoli's Madonna of 1456 at Perugia). E. *Plate 676*.

CAROTO, Giovanni

Verona. 1488–?1566. Brother and partner of Giovanni Francesco Caroto, from whom it is hard to distinguish him.

Baltimore (Md.). DR REULING (EX). Madonna and Holy Children.

Brescia. CONTI MARTINENGO (EX). Madonna and Child. *Plate 1897*.

Budapest. 97 (153). Madonna and Child appearing to SS. James and John Evangelist. L. (?)

Pavia. 14. Madonna and Child in landscape with SS. John Baptist and Christopher (with his brother Giovanni Francesco; variant at Augusta).

Princeton (N.J.). 35.32. Bust of monk.

Verona. 239. Fragment of altarpiece once in Cappella di S. Niccolò, S. Maria in Organo, destroyed by fire: Male and female donor.

265. Madonna and Child appearing to SS. Lawrence and Jerome.

1597–8. Five frs. of polyptych: Madonna and Child, SS. Roch, Sebastian, George, Paul.

1626. Flight into Egypt. *Plate 1892*.

S. EUFEMIA, CAPPELLA DAL VERME SPOLVERINI DEGLI ANGELI (R. OF CHOIR). Frescoes: Homecoming of Tobias with his Bride and Healing of his Father; SS. Lucy and Apollonia (with his elder brother). *Plate 1891*.

S. GIORGIO IN BRAIDA (OR MAGGIORE), ENTRANCE TO CHOIR. Angel and Virgin of Annunciation. *Plates 1894-1895*.

Verona (contd.). S. MARIA MATRICOLARE (DUOMO), FOURTH CHAPEL L. Madonna and Child enthroned with SS. Martin, Stephen and donor. Sd and d. 1514. *Plate 1893.*

S. MARIA DELLA SCALA, THIRD ALTAR. S. Ambrose between SS. Paul and Joseph worshipped by Father and Son, Mother and Daughter; in lunette, Annunciation. *Plate 1898.*

S. PAOLO, HIGH ALTAR. Madonna and Child enthroned with SS. Peter and Paul. Sd and d. 1516. *Plate 1896.*

S. STEFANO, R. TRANSEPT. Madonna and Child appearing to SS. Andrew and Peter. L. *Plate 1899.*

Volargne (Valpolicella). VILLA DEL BENE, ROOM R. Frescoed frieze and simulated pictures: Holy Family (with his elder brother), Baptism of Christ, Jacob's Dream, Dives and Lazarus; over doors: Jesus and the Woman of Samaria at the Well; Jesus on the Lake of Galilee (r.).

CAROTO, Giovan Francesco

Verona, ca 1480–1546. Pupil of Liberale. Active for Visconti, Milan ca 1510, for Marchese di Monferrato ca 1515/20. Influenced by Mantegna, Bonsignori, Catena, Francia; and later by Raphael. Assisted by his younger brother Giovanni.

Amsterdam. RIJKSMUSEUM. Dido. E.

Augusta (Ga.). G. HERBERT ART INSTITUTE. 007 (KRESS COLLECTION. K 1058). Madonna and Child in a landscape with SS. Augustine and Jerome (variant by his brother at Pavia).

Baltimore (Md.). WALTERS ART GALLERY. 464. Profile of young poet.

Bergamo. 186, 1045. Predella panels: Massacre of Innocents, Birth of Virgin. Sd and d. 1527. *Plate 1885.*

200. Predella panel: Adoration of Magi (companion to Budapest).

504. Predella panel: Judgement of Solomon.

Berlin-Ost. 1434. Mourning over dead Christ (r.).

Bionde di Visegna (Verona). PARISH CHURCH. Madonna and Child with Saints. 1540.

Brussels. 633. Doubting Thomas and Baptist. E. (?)

635. Head of boy. (?)

Budapest. 1043 (180). S. Michael.

SÁNDOR LEDERER (EX). Madonna and Child. *Plate 1876.*

Predella panel (formerly Weber, Hamburg): Nativity (companion to Bergamo).

Casale Monferrato. S. DOMENICO. Fresco: Madonna and Child with Angels (fr., r.).

Dresden. 66. Madonna and Child with two Angels.

Erbizzo (Verona). PARISH CHURCH. Madonna and Child with S. James and another Apostle (p.).

Florence. UFFIZI. 3392/3. Organ-shutters: Massacre of Innocents, on back S. Joseph and two Shepherds; Flight into Egypt, on back, Circumcision (r.). *Plate* 1874.

Frankfurt a/M. 857. Madonna and Child. E. Sd. *Plate* 1878.

Leipzig. Inv. 1652. Madonna adoring Child. *Plate* 1877.

Liverpool. 2765. S. James between two Saints (p.).

London. PHILIP POUNCEY. Virgin laid on bier (st., r.; companion to Princeton). *Plate* 1882.

Mantua. PALAZZO DUCALE (REGGIA DEI GONZAGA). S. Paul between SS. Sebastian and John Baptist.

    ACCADEMIA VIRGILIANA. Fresco: Madonna and Child with donor. 1514.

    CHIESA DELLA CARITÀ, CHOIR. SS. Michael, Cosmas, Damian and Saint with banner.

Melchett Court (Romsey, Hants) (EX). 'Mond' Madonna and Child with Infant S. John.

Mezzana di Sotto (Verona). PARISH CHURCH. Mystic Marriage of S. Catherine, with S. Paul and donor with wife, son and daughter.

Milan. CRESPI MORBIO COLLECTION. 250. Madonna and Child in landscape.

    BENIGNO CRESPI (EX). Madonna and Child with youthful Baptist, S. Joseph and Holy Ghost. Sd. ca 1530. *Plate* 1884.

Modena. 250. Virgin sewing and Holy Children beside her. Sd and d. 1502. *Plate* 1875.

New York. ROBERT MINTURN (EX). 'Salvator Mundi'. E.

Oxford. ASHMOLEAN MUSEUM. 90. Crucifixion.

    CHRIST CHURCH. 77. Predella panel: Martyrdom of S. Catherine.

Paray-le-Monial. 49. S. Anastasia with Host and Dead Christ. (?)

Philadelphia (Pa.). J. G. JOHNSON COLLECTION. 223. Pietà (r.). L.

Pommersfelden. SCHLOSSMUSEUM. 280. Madonna and Child holding butterfly, with SS. Francis and Catherine.

Portland (Oregon). ART MUSEUM. 61.42. (KRESS COLLECTION. K 1117). Predella panel: Entombment.

Prague. Inv. 01394. S. John at Patmos.

Princeton (N.J.). 35.31. Madonna and Child with Infant S. John.

    35.33, 35.34. Virgin surrounded by Apostles on her death-bed, Dead Virgin carried by Apostles to her grave (st. or r.) (companion to London).

Richmond (Surrey). COOK COLLECTION. 197 (ex?). Ladies and knights in landscape. (?)

Rome. GALLERIA COLONNA. 220. Holy Family with S. Francis.

San Benedetto Po (Mantua). ABBAZIA DI POLIRONE, FIRST CHAPEL L. Vision of Faith.

Tisoi (Belluno). SS. SEVERO E BRIGIDA. Polyptych: Madonna and Child enthroned, four Saints, Eternal above.

Trent. DUOMO. Madonna and Child enthroned with blessing Eternal above, four Saints and Infant S. John. Sd.

Turin. GALLERIA SABAUDA. 136. Madonna and Child in landscape. L.

    — GUALINO COLLECTION. 690. S. Sebastian.

Turin (contd.). VINCENZO FONTANA (EX). Mourning over dead Christ. Sd and d. 1515. *Plate* 1880.

Venice. ACCADEMIA. 609. Virgin sewing. E.

Verona. 83. Herodias.

    92. Madonna and Holy Children.

    108. 'Pietà della Lacrima'.

    112. Temptation of Christ.

    114. Holy Family with Infant S. John, S. Elizabeth and Angel. Sd and d. 1531. *Plate* 1886.

    119. Madonna and Child (simplified version of Vienna, Tucher).

    130. Boy with Drawing (version of Luini).

    132. Children of Israel in Desert.

    140. Christ bearing Cross.

    142. Bust of young Benedictine monk.

    154. Fall of Lucifer.

    251. S. Catherine.

    260. Madonna and Saints adoring Christ Child, and Calvary in background.

    262, 325. Madonna and Child in Glory, with SS. Joseph and Mary Magdalen; Ecce Homo and four Saints.

    300. Washing of Feet, and Madonna with Prophet above. L.

    341. Sophonisba (version of Giampietrino at Isolabella).

    343. The three Archangels. Sd.

    566. Detached fresco: Veronica.

    762. S. Sebastian.

PALAZZO ARCIVESCOVILE. Raising of Lazarus. Sd and d. 1531. *Plate* 1889.

CASA VIGNOLA. Fresco: Madonna and Child with SS. John Baptist and Bartholomew.

PIAZZA DELL'ERBE, N. 36. Frescoes: Madonna and Child in Glory; below, nudes.

S. ANASTASIA, FOURTH ALTAR R. Madonna and Child in Glory; below, SS. Anthony Abbot and Martin with beggar. L.

S. BERNARDINO, CAPPELLA DELLA CROCE (R. OF CHOIR). Christ taking leave of his Mother (other pictures by Francesco Morone, Giolfino and Antonio Badile). L.

S. EUFEMIA, CAPPELLA DAL VERME SPOLVERINI DEGLI ANGELI (R. OF CHOIR). Frescoes: Tobias' Homecoming with his Bride and Healing of his Father; SS. Lucy and Apollonia (with his brother Giovanni). *Plate* 1891.

S. FERMO MAGGIORE, L. CHAPEL. Madonna, Child and S. Anne appearing to SS. John Baptist, Peter, Roch and Sebastian. Sd and d. 1528.

S. GIORGIO IN BRAIDA (OR MAGGIORE), THIRD CHAPEL L. Composite altarpiece: lunette with Transfiguration; side-panels with SS. Roch and Sebastian (centre panel by Recchia, 1882; between it and lunette, Man possessed by Devil, and allegories, by Domenico Brusasorci). Sd.

— FIRST CHAPEL L. S. Ursula and her Maidens. Sd and d. 1545. [*Plate* 351.]

    Predella: Agony in the Garden, Mourning over dead Christ, Resurrection. *Plates* 1888, 1890.

S. GIROLAMO. Fresco on Triumphal Arch: Annunciation. Sd and d. 1508. *Plate* 1879.

S. MARIA IN ORGANO, NAVE, R. WALL. Frescoes: Crossing of Red Sea, Moses receiving the Tables of the Law; David and Goliath, Translation of Elijah; two Olivetan Monks, SS. Michael and John (frescoes on opposite wall, by Giolfino).

— L. TRANSEPT, EAST WALL. Fresco: Angel.

Vienna. BARON TUCHER (EX). Madonna and Child with butterfly. Sd. *Plate* 1883.

Volargne (Valpolicella). VILLA DEL BENE, CENTRAL HALL. Frescoes: twelve mono-chrome Terms and Caryatids and Scenes of the Apocalypse between them; four full-length Sibyls in niches and four half-length Sibyls over doors. *Plates* 1881, 1887.

— ROOM TO R. Frescoed frieze and simulated pictures (mostly by his son Giovanni, q.v.).

CAVALLINI, Pietro

Roman school. Mentioned from 1273 to 1308; may have lived on till 1350 at least. Schooled in traditions of the Byzantine court painters.

Naples. PALAZZO ARCIVESCOVILE. Bishop Umberto di Montauro (died 1320); in pinnacle, S. Paul (g.p.). (?)

S. GENNARO (DUOMO), CAPPELLA DI S. LORENZO (SECOND L. IN CHOIR). Fresco: The Tree of Jesse (r.). *Plates* 150, 151.

S. MARIA DI DONNA REGINA. Frescoes by Cavallini and Assistants. Later than 1308.

— TRIUMPHAL ARCH OF APSE. Frescoes: Hierarchies of Angels (fr., p.).

— NAVE (L. AND R. WALL). Frescoes: Overlifesize Patriarchs, Prophets and Apostles, in pairs separated by a palmtree (p.).

— NUN'S LOFT (CORO DELLE MONACHE), CENTRAL WALL. Fresco: Last Judgement [between roof and sixteenth-century ceiling—Virgin of Apocalypse; between windows—Christ in mandorla worshipped by Virgin and Baptist, with S. Michael, Abraham, Isaac and Jacob above, Exaltation of Cross and Resurrection of Dead below; R. and L. of windows—Hosts of Angels, Rows of Prophets and Saints, Elect entering Paradise, Damned cast into Hell; bottom frieze—half-length S. Januarius with male and female Patron Saints] (p.). *Plates* 157–160.

— — (WALL L. OF APSE). Frescoes: in fifteen upper scenes, Passion of Christ [Entrance into Jerusalem? (r.), Last Supper, Washing of Feet, Agony in the Garden, Capture of Christ, Flagellation (r.), Christ dragged through the streets, Mocking and Way to Calvary, Nailing to Cross, Crucifixion, Deposition and Mourning, Resurrection and Descent into Limbo, Marys at the tomb and Noli me Tangere, Apparitions of Christ to the Apostles at Emmaus and through the closed doors, Doubting Thomas] (top row cut by sixteenth-century ceiling); in five lower scenes, Life of S. Elizabeth of Hungary [the food she takes to the poor is converted into roses, her marriage, her self-mortification, her charities, S. Elizabeth reaches Eisenach with her companions, founds a hospital and performs miracles while lying dead on the bier]; on the walled-up window, from top, Ascension, Descent of the Holy Ghost, SS. Ladislas, Stephen and Elizabeth of Hungary (st.). *Plate* 162.

—— (WALL R. OF APSE). Frescoes: Scenes from the Life of S. Catherine of Alexandria [she accuses Maxentius, Maxentius writes a decree; she is taken to prison, martyrdom of the philosophers converted by her] and from the Life of S. Agnes [she goes to school, the son of the prefect meets with her repulse, he asks his father to force her to love him, Agnes taken to a brothel, her martyrdom, the son of Emperor Constantine is healed from leprosy by intercession of S. Agnes] (top row cut by sixteenth-century ceiling; st.). *Plate* 161.

Rome. S. CECILIA, CORO DELLE MONACHE. Frescoes: Last Judgement (r.); Annunciation (r.); Esau received by the dying Isaac; Jacob's Dream. *Plates* 152–155.

S. CRISOGONO, APSE. Mosaic: Madonna and Child enthroned between SS. James and Crisogono (on Cavallini's design?).

S. GIORGIO IN VELABRO, APSE. Fresco: Christ in Glory and S. George, Virgin, S. Peter and S. Sebastian. Soon after 1295. *Plate* 148.

S. GIOVANNI LATERANO, SANCTA SANCTORUM. Frescoes: Martyrdom of SS. Peter, Paul, Stephen, Lawrence and a female Saint; Christ enthroned with SS. Peter and Paul and Pope (Boniface VIII?); Scene from Life of (S. Nicholas?) (r.).

S. MARIA IN ARACOELI, L. TRANSEPT. Frescoed lunette above Tomb of Cardinal Matteo D'Acquasparta (died 1302): Madonna and Child with S. John Evangelist (?), S. Francis and kneeling Cardinal (g.p.). *Plate* 149.

S. MARIA IN TRASTEVERE, TRIBUNA. Mosaics: Birth of Virgin, Annunciation, Nativity, Adoration of Magi, Circumcision, Dormitio Virginis, Madonna and Child with SS. Peter and Paul and kneeling Cardinal Bertoldo Stefaneschi (on Cavallini's design). *Plate* 156.

VATICAN, MUSEO DI S. PIETRO. Fragment of fresco: Two heads of Saints from demolished Basilica di S. Pietro. (?)

Valencia. 125. Coronation with SS. Peter and Paul (st.).

CAVALLINI's Immediate Followers

Capua. S. SALVATORE MINORE (CARMINIELLO). Frescoed apse: Descent of the Holy Ghost (r.).

Fiesole. MUSEO BANDINI. Triptych: Madonna and Child enthroned with Mary Magdalen, S. Francis and two Angels; Flagellation, Mocking of Christ and Crucifixion.

Florence. S. CROCE, CAPPELLA VELLUTI. Frescoes: S. Michael defeats Satan; Miracle of the Bull on Mount Gargano. (Between Cavallini and Cimabue.) *Plates* 168, 169.

Fürstenau (Michelstadt). ERBACH VON FÜRSTENAU COLLECTION. Two panels with Scenes from the Apocalypse. (Follower close to Guariento.)

Montefiascone. S. FLAVIANO. Madonna and Child, Angels and Saints in five roundels over central arch and several other frescoes on walls.

Naples. S. CHIARA, REFETTORIO (bombed 1943). Fresco: Christ enthroned with six Saints, worshipped by King Robert of Anjou and his family.

    S. DOMENICO MAGGIORE. Frescoes: S. John Evangelist in cauldron of boiling oil, Vision of the Saint, 'Noli me Tangere', Penitence of Mary Magdalen (r.). (Assistants who helped Cavallini in S. Maria di Donna Regina.)

    S. LORENZO MAGGIORE, R. TRANSEPT. Frescoes: Nativity, Dormitio Virginis.

New Haven (Conn.). 1943.238. Crucifix painted on both sides, with donor at foot of Cross. (Follower influenced by Duccio.)

Perugia. PALAZZO DEI PRIORI, SALA DEL GRAN CONSIGLIO (DEI NOTARI). Frescoes: Scenes from Old Testament. Begun 1297. *Plate 165.*

Philadelphia (Pa.). J. G. JOHNSON COLLECTION. 116. Nativity.

St.-Jean-Cap-Ferrat (Antibes). MUSÉE ÎLE-DE-FRANCE. Assumption; eight scenes of the end of the Virgin's life. *Plates 163, 164.*

Stimigliano (Val Teverina). S. MARIA IN VESCOVIO, ENTRANCE WALL. Fresco: Last Judgement (r.). *Plate 167.*

    — L. AND R. WALLS. Frescoes: Scenes from Old and New Testament (r.). *Plate 166.*

CAVAZZOLA (Paolo Morando)

Verona 1486–1522. Pupil of Domenico Morone; influenced by his fellow-pupils, and by Caroto, Giolfino and Raphael.

Bergamo. 566. Lady holding glove before parapet.

Chartres. 86. See Paris.

Chicago (Ill.). 37.1000. Mourning Evangelist (fr. of Crucifixion).

Dresden. 201. Giovanni Emilio de' Megli holding rosary. [*Plate 356.*]

Florence. UFFIZI. 911. Youthful warrior and his page.

    SERRISTORI COLLECTION. Madonna and Infant S. John. E.

Frankfurt a/M. 1192. Madonna and Angel Gabriel. d. 1519.

Gazzada (Varese). FONDAZIONE CAGNOLA. Madonna reading and Child. Sd and d. 1509.

Greenville (S.C.). BOB JONES UNIVERSITY GALLERY. 29. Replica of Verona n. 292.

Harewood House (Yorks.). EARL OF HAREWOOD (EX). Portrait of youth against myrtle-grove (r.).

London. 735. Panel of polyptych: S. Roch. Sd. 15(18?).

    777. Madonna and Child with young Baptist and Angel. Sd. *Plate 1336.*

Milan. TRIVULZIO COLLECTION. Christ carrying Cross, and donor.

    Portrait of Giulia Trivulzio. Sd and d. 1519. *Plate 1341.*

Münster i/W. DIÖZESANMUSEUM. Madonna and Child with SS. Andrew and John Evangelist (r.). 1515.

Paris. MUSÉES NATIONAUX (FROM CHARTRES). Madonna and Child with S. Francis. *Plate* 1335.

Philadelphia (Pa.). J. G. JOHNSON COLLECTION. 220. Madonna and Child in landscape. (?)

Piazzola sul Brenta. VILLA CAMERINI. Double portrait of bald man in fur coat and youth in armour.

Prague. Inv. 0464. Bust of gentleman. *Plate* 1343.

Verona. 85. Madonna and Child with Infant S. John. Sd. *Plate* 1337.

111. Madonna suckling Child. Sd. E.

143. Madonna embracing Child. E.

298. Doubting Thomas with Ascension and Descent of Holy Ghost in background (from S. Chiara). *Plate* 1338.

292, 295, 303, 308, 392, 394. Polyptych from Cappella della Croce in S. Bernardino: Flagellation, Agony in Garden (Sd), Christ helped by Simon of Cyrene on way to Calvary (Sd), Deposition (Sd and d. 1517), Busts of SS. Bernardino da Feltre, Joseph, Bonaventura and John Baptist. *Plate* 1339.

302. SS. Michael and Paul.

307. SS. Peter and Baptist.

335. Madonna and Child in Glory with Cardinal and Theological Virtues, SS. Francis and Anthony of Padua; below, SS. Elizabeth of Hungary, Bonaventura, Sigismund, Yves and female donor. d. 1522.

576. Holy Family and Angel.

— FROM BADIA CAVALENA. Madonna and Child with SS. John Baptist and Benedict.

PALAZZO N. 29 VIA DEL PARADISO. Frescoes: Augustus and the Sibyl, Sacrifice of Isaac. E.

S. BERNARDINO, CHIOSTRO. Frescoed lunette: Madonna and Child. (?)

— ENTRANCE TO CHURCH, L. Frescoes: S. Bernardino; below, Madonna and Child.

— — R. Frescoes: Christ carrying Cross; Monk (r.).

S. MARIA IN ORGANO, R. TRANSEPT. Frescoes: Angels Michael and Raphael in niches.

SS. NAZARO E CELSO, CAPPELLA DI S. BIAGIO, OVER ENTRANCE ARCH. Fresco: Annunciation and two Bishop Saints (frescoes in cupola are by Falconetto, in apse by Montagna; altarpiece is by Bonsignori with predella by Girolamo dai Libri). 1510–11. *Plate* 1333.

Vicenza. 86. Bust of man as S. Cosmas (replica of Prague).

Vienna. AUSPITZ COLLECTION (EX). Bust of young woman. *Plate* 1342.

Homeless. Madonna and Child. E. *Plate* 1334.

Man holding laurel-branch before parapet, and his dog. *Plate* 1340.

CECCARELLI, Naldo

Sienese. Pupil of Lippo Memmi, documented 1347.

Baltimore (Md.). WALTERS ART GALLERY. 1024. Christ on Cross with mourning
Virgin, S. John Evangelist and S. Mary Magdalen. (?)
   1159. Madonna and Child, standing, in frame for relics.
Budapest. 9 (42). Madonna and Child.
Cambridge. FITZWILLIAM MUSEUM. 558. Christ on Cross with mourning Virgin
and S. John Evangelist; in pinnacle, S. Stephen.
Cambridge (Mass.). FOGG ART MUSEUM, ADELE AND ARTHUR LEHMAN BEQUEST.
1965.96. SS. Blaise, Catherine and Lawrence.
Dresden. 28. Madonna and Child. E. (?)
Florence. MUSEO HORNE. 53. Madonna and Child.
Montepulciano. PINACOTECA. Madonna and Saints.
New York. OTTO H. KAHN (EX). Wing of diptych: Virgin of Annunciation.
Princeton (N.J.). 62.57. 'Platt' predella panel with arms of Spedale della Scala and
seven roundels: S. Cosmas, S. Agnes, female Saint with book, Dead Christ,
S. Catherine, S. Ursula, S. Blaise.
Radicondoli. CHIESA DEL CIMITERO. Madonna and Child.
Richmond (Surrey). COOK COLLECTION (EX). 4. Madonna and Child. Sd and d.
1347. *Plate* 320.
Siena. 115. Polyptych: Madonna and Child; SS. Anthony Abbot, Michael, John
Evangelist, Stephen; in pinnacles, Redeemer and Angels. *Plate* 319.
   S. MARTINO. Madonna suckling the Child.
Tyninghame (Prestonkirk, East Lothian). EARL OF HADDINGTON. Portable altarpiece:
Full-length Madonna and Child holding scroll; in wings, SS. Bartholomew
and Eligius (?); SS. Nicholas and Anthony Abbot; Angel and Virgin of
Annunciation. *Plate* 322.
Vaduz. LIECHTENSTEINSCHE SAMMLUNG. G 862. Dead Christ and eight roundels with
Saints in frame. Sd. *Plate* 321.

CECCO DI PIETRO

Pisan. Documented 1370–1381.

Agnano (Gubbio). PIEVE. Polyptych: Madonna and Child, SS. Jerome, Nicholas,
Benedict, Margaret; upper register, Annunciation and eight Saints; in pin-
nacles, Redeemer and Evangelists.
Copenhagen. 112. Centre panel of polyptych: Madonna and Child enthroned with
goldfinch. Sd. *Plate* 460.
Paris. MUSÉES NATIONAUX, CAMPANA 40/43 (DEP. NANTES NN. 179, 180 AND DEP.

RENNES NN. 3443, 3445) AND CAMPANA 44, 45 (LOST?). Six side-panels of polyptych, companions to Portland: S. Peter and S. Bartholomew; S. John Baptist and S. Nicholas; S. Christopher and another Saint. 1386.

Pisa. B.P. V, 16. S. Simon enthroned and six kneeling Brethren (from S. Simoncino a Porto a Mare). Sd and d. 1374. (Lost?)

94 (B.P. V, 14 and IV, 26, 31). Polyptych: Pietà with SS. Catherine and Lucy; SS. Gregory, Mary Magdalen, Margaret and Augustine. Sd and d. 1377.

95 (B.P. III, 17). Polyptych from S. Marta: Crucifixion; on either side, in two registers, SS. Barbara, Catherine, Agatha, Ursula, Mary Magdalen, Margaret, Martha, Agnes; in pinnacles, Redeemer and Evangelists; in predella, Entombment, two Stories of S. Ursula, two Stories of S. Margaret. Sd and d. 1386.

96 (Uffizi gift 1949). Centre panel of triptych from Nicosia: Madonna and Child (side-panels with Baptist and Bartholomew, lost). Sd and d. 137?.

97 (B.P. III, 29). Predella panel: Olibrius meets S. Margaret. *Plate 458.*

98 (B.P. V, 39, 45). SS. Michael, Blessed Gherardesca and another Saint; SS. Ranieri, Bona and John Baptist.

99 (B.P. III, 30). Crucifixion.

S. MARTINO, CHAPEL. Frescoes on vault: Redeemer, Evangelists, Apostles. d. 1395.

Portland (Oregon). ART MUSEUM. 61.44 (KRESS COLLECTION. K 1174). Centre panel of polyptych: Madonna and Child enthroned, blessing two donors (companion to Paris). Sd and d. 1386. *Plate 459.*

Homeless. Madonna suckling the Child (fr.). *Plate 455.*

Crucifixion. *Plate 454.*

S. Peter. *Plate 457.*

Pope with palm (companion to Two Apostles in Florence, Private Collection, repr. by E. Carli, *Pittura pisana del trecento*, 1961, fig. 145). *Plate 456.*

CESARE MAGNI

Milanese school. Active first half sixteenth century. Pupil of Bergognone and close follower of Cesare da Sesto.

Arcore. VITTADINI COLLECTION (EX). Madonna and Child.

Attingham Park (Shrops.). NATIONAL TRUST. Sacra Conversazione.

Bergamo. 301. Madonna and Child blessing Infant S. John in landscape. *Plate 1498.*

Berlin-Ost. (EX) 673. Madonna with SS. Sebastian and Roch. *Plate 1500.*

Bonn. 28. Circumcision. *Plate 1495.*

Isolabella (Lago Maggiore). PALAZZO BORROMEO. 37. Adoration of Magi. *Plate 1499.*

Milan. AMBROSIANA. Madonna and Child with flowers.

— BRIVIO COLLECTION. Madonna and Child with SS. Peter and Jerome (ex Cook). Sd and d. 1530. *Plate 1501.*

BRERA. 275. Holy Family with Infant S. John. *Plate 1496.*

CASTELLO. 311. S. Jerome.

DONNA SESSA FUMAGALLI. Coronation of Virgin. *Plate* 1497.

S. MARIA DELLE GRAZIE, FORMER REFECTORY. Copy of Leonardo's Last Supper.

Naples. 87. Copy of Leonardo's 'Virgin of the Rocks'.

89. Madonna and Child with SS. Jerome and Ambrose. L.

Palermo. CHIARAMONTE BORDONARO COLLECTION. Nativity. (?)

Rome. GERMAN EMBASSY. See Berlin.

Saronno. S. MARIA DEI MIRACOLI. Frescoes: S. Martin, S. George. Sd.

Vercelli. MUSEO BORGOGNA. Madonna and Child with rosary. E. (?)

Vigevano. S. AMBROGIO (DUOMO), FIRST ALTAR R. Crucifixion with SS. John Evangelist, Jerome, Ambrose and Bishop G. Pietra. Sd 1531.

CESARE DA SESTO

Sesto Calende, 1477–Milan 1523. Imitator of Leonardo da Vinci; strongly influenced by Raphael, and slightly by Michelangelo and Lotto.

Balcarres (Fife, Scotland). EARL OF CRAWFORD AND BALCARRES. S. John Baptist in the Wilderness. *Plate* 1505.

Elton Hall (Peterborough). SIR RICHARD PROBY, BT. Holy Family with infant S. John and Zacharias ('Madonna del Bassorilievo'; see Milan, Brera).

Glasgow. 1588. S. John Baptist in Wilderness (?). *Plate* 1504.

Leningrad. 14. Holy Family with S. Catherine (bozzetto in Rome).

Lisbon. MUSEU DE ARTE ANTIGA. Madonna and Child with Infant S. John.

Lodi. PINACOTECA. Adoration of Magi (variant of Naples). L.

London. 2485. Salome (versions attributed to Luini and Solario; see Vienna).

Milan. AMBROSIANA. Head of Redeemer. E.

BRERA. 272. 'Madonna del Bassorilievo' (st. v. of Elton Hall).

276. Madonna suckling the Child in landscape (version at Strasbourg).

754. Penitent S. Jerome.

CASTELLO. 468–73. Panels from Polyptych of S. Roch: S. Roch, S. Christopher and S. Sebastian in landscapes; Madonna and Child, SS. John Baptist and John Evangelist on clouds. 1523. *Plate* 1506.

POLDI PEZZOLI. 667. Madonna and Child with Lamb. (?)

DUCA GALLARATI SCOTTI. Baptism of Christ (landscape by Bernazzano).

MELZI D'ERIL COLLECTION (EX). Tondo: Madonna and Child with Infant S. John.

Mondello Valdese (Palermo). TORRE DELL'ADDAURA, PRINCIPE DI BELMONTE. Madonna and Child in landscape. (?)

Naples. 98. Adoration of Magi from S. Niccolò at Messina. *Plate* 1507.

Paris. 1604. Madonna and Child with S. Elizabeth, Infant S. John and S. Michael holding scales ('La Vierge aux Balances') (?). *Plate* 1502.

Richmond (Surrey). COOK COLLECTION. Penitent S. Jerome.

Rome. GALLERIA BORGHESE. 161. Female saint.*

    MISS ANDERSON. Holy Family with S. Catherine (see Leningrad). *Plate* 1503.

San Francisco (Cal.). DE YOUNG MEMORIAL MUSEUM. 61-44-15 (KRESS COLLECTION. K 1625). Madonna and Child enthroned with SS. George and John Baptist (formerly Cook; from S. Giorgio dei Genovesi at Messina). L. *Plate* 1508.

Strasbourg. MUSÉE. Madonna (Variant of Milan, Brera 276).

Vienna. 91. Salome.

CICOGNARA, Antonio

Painter and miniaturist of Cremona, recorded 1480–1500. Close follower of the Ferrarese painters Tura and Cossa.

Bergamo. ACCADEMIA CARRARA. Three Tarocchi Cards of the Colleoni set, painted for Filippo Maria Visconti or for his Court; Star, Moon, Pluto's Castle. ca 1480. *Plates* 741–742.

Cremona. PINACOTECA. Codex IV (Antiphonary 1, from Cathedral) f.3 r. Illuminated page: Isaiah in initial A, Angel and Virgin of Annunciation in roundels, ornamental border. Sd and d. 1483.

Ferrara. Inv. 64 (BERENSON GIFT). Madonna and Child in niche. Sd and d. 1480. *Plate* 744.

    PALAZZO SCHIFANOIA, SALA DEI MESI, NORTH WALL. Execution of parts of frescoes (see under Ferrarese before 1510). E. (?)

Milan. COLOGNA COLLECTION (EX). Madonna and Child enthroned between SS. Justine and Catherine. Sd and d. 1490.

New York. MORGAN LIBRARY. MS 630, nos. 11, 14, 19. Three Tarocchi Cards of the Colleoni set, painted for Filippo Maria Visconti or for his Court: Fortitude, Temperance, Sun. ca 1480. *Plate* 743.

CIVERCHIO, Vincenzo, da Crema

Crema, ca 1470–1544. Pupil of Foppa; strongly influenced by Zenale and Leonardo, and later by Romanino. [See Introduction, p. xv.]

Bergamo. 298. Madonna suckling the Child (Pseudo.)

    338. A Franciscan Saint. Sd.

    505. Tabernacle doors: outside, Annunciation; inside, S. Benedict and S. Scholastica. *Plate* 1365.

Berlin. 1826. Predella panel: Circumcision (companion to Vienna). (Pseudo.)

Birmingham (Ala.). MUSEUM OF ART. 61.111 (KRESS COLLECTION. K 1115). S. Peter in niche. (?)

Brescia. 146. Polyptych from S. Afra: S. Nicholas of Tolentino in Glory, flanked by SS. Roch and Sebastian; in lunette, Pietà. Sd and d. 1495. *Plate* 1367.

S. AFRA, UPPER CHURCH, R. WALL. Two Bishops.

S. ALESSANDRO, SECOND ALTAR R. Pietà with SS. Sebastian, Onophrius, Paul and Magdalen; in predella, Agony in the Garden, Incredulity of S. Thomas, 'Noli me tangere'. Sd and d. 1504. *Plates* 1368–1369, 1371.

S. GIOVANNI EVANGELISTA, L. TRANSEPT, CAPPELLA DEL CORPUS DOMINI. Pietà. d. 1509. (Pseudo.)

Budapest. 1142 (1352–3). Organ-shutters: outside, Death of Virgin; inside, S. John Baptist, S. Peter (r.). Sd and d. 1531.

Caiolo. PARISH CHURCH. Sculptured altarpiece. Sd and d. 1539.

Cape Town. JOSEPH ROBINSON (EX). Adoration of the Child. (Pseudo.)

Crema. PALAZZO ZURLA DE POLI. The Flood, The Acts of Mercy. Sd and d. 1540.

DUOMO, SECOND ALTAR L. SS. Sebastian, Christopher and Roch. 1519.

Cremona. CRIGNANI COLLECTION. Nativity.*

Lecco. S. GIOVANNI SOPRA LECCO. Pietà. Sd and d. 1539.

Lovere. 36. Baptism of Christ. Sd and d. 1539. *Plate* 1373.

57. Madonna and Child with SS. Lawrence and John Baptist. Sd. L. *Plate* 1372.

Milan. AMBROSIANA. See Zenale.

BRERA. 248. Nativity and S. Catherine. Sd. [*Plate* 378.]

734. Holy Family.

764. Madonna and Child with two Angels. (Pseudo.)

CASTELLO. 251. Trial and Beheading of S. Catherine.

315. Nativity (r.).

PALAZZO ARCIVESCOVILE. Tabernacle doors: Annunciation and six Saints.

POLDI PEZZOLI. See Zenale.

BAGATTI VALSECCHI. See Zenale.

S. AGOSTINO DELLE MONACHE, HIGH ALTAR. Madonna and Child.

S. AMBROGIO, MUSEO. See Zenale.

S. EUFEMIA, FIRST CHAPEL L. Fresco (now covered by modern picture): Madonna and Child with S. Catherine and donor. (?)

S. MARIA DEL CARMINE, FIRST CHAPEL R. Frescoes: on left wall, Crucifixion and Saints; on right wall, Adoration of Magi. (?)

S. PIETRO IN GESSATE, R. TRANSEPT. Madonna standing in a landscape gives a book to the Infant Jesus, who stands with two ears of wheat in His right hand (known as 'Madonna delle Grazie del Luini').

Palazzolo d'Oglio. S. FEDELE, WALL L. OF DOOR. Polyptych: Madonna and Child with Saints; predella. Sd and d. 1525.

Palermo. CHIARAMONTE BORDONARO COLLECTION. Pietà. *Plate* 1370.

Paris. 1545. See Zenale.

S. NICHOLAS-DES-CHAMPS. Baptism of Christ.*

Philadelphia. J. G. JOHNSON COLLECTION. 263. Predella panel: Circumcision.

Princeton (N.J.). 100. 'Ecce Homo' between two Angels. (?)

Rome. FINARDI COLLECTION. S. Francis. Sd.*

Travagliato. S. MARIA DI CAMPAGNA. Assumption of Virgin. Sd and d. 1517.
Turin. ACCADEMIA ALBERTINA. 142. Madonna suckling the Child (r.).
Verona. 123. Madonna suckling the Child. (?)
Vienna. MOLL COLLECTION (EX). Predella panel: Annunciation (companion to Berlin).
(Pseudo.)
Homeless. Madonna and Child with S. Francis (with Zenale). *Plate* 1363.

COLA D'AMATRICE

*Nicola di Filotesio, from Amatrice (Abruzzi), painter and architect, born 1489, documented
1509-1550, honorary citizen of Ascoli, where he was mainly active. Pupil probably of Pietro
Alamanno; formed under influence of Umbrians, Raphael, and Michelangelo.*

Ascoli Piceno. CIVICA PINACOTECA. 41. (returned to church of S. Vittore).
    42, 43, 44, 45, 46, 47. Two Sibyls, two pairs of Angels holding crosses, Abraham,
David (all on gold background, from polyptych on high altar of S. Francesco
at Ascoli; companions to Melbourne). Commissioned 1516, completed 1533.
    48. Christ on the way to Calvary (after Raphael's 'Spasimo di Sicilia' in Madrid).
Plate 1173.
    49. Christ institutes the Sacrament of Eucharist (from the Oratorio del Corpus
Domini). Sd.
    50, 52, 55. Large lunettes from S. Margherita: Christ carrying the Cross on the
way to Calvary, Crucifixion, Mourning over the dead Christ.
    51. Polyptych from Piagge: Madonna and Child enthroned with two Angel
musicians; SS. Bartholomew and Mark; in upper register, Pietà, half-length
SS. Mary Magdalen and Lucy. 1509. *Plate* 1166.
    53, 54. Mourning Virgin, mourning S. John Evangelist (frs.).
    56. Detached fresco from S. Margherita: Redeemer. Not traced.
    57. Large lunette from S. Margherita: Madonna of Mercy with SS. Francis and
Bonaventura (st.; companion to — 50, 52, 55).
    58. Madonna and Child with SS. Sebastian, Anthony of Padua, Roch and
Francis (p.).
   MUSEO VESCOVILE. 2. Polyptych from S. Maria in Caprilia: Madonna and Child
enthroned crowned by Angels; S. Augustine, S. Christina, busts of SS.
Christianzanus and Anthony Abbot; Head of Redeemer in tympanum. E.
    4, 5, 6, 7. Four panels from S. Angelo Magno: SS Leonard, Michael, Bernhard
and Benedict.
    8. Polyptych from SS. Benedetto e Cristina at Rosara near Ascoli: Madonna
and Child enthroned; S. John Baptist; S. Anthony Abbot; half-length S.
Catherine, Risen Christ, S. Lucy.
   S. AGOSTINO, L. WALL. Fresco framed in tabernacle: Christ carrying the Cross
(version of Pinacoteca 48).

SS. ANNUNZIATA, REFECTORY. Frescoed lunette: Christ on the way to Calvary. d. 1519.

S. FRANCESCO. S. Francis with four Saints, donors and Angels. (?)

— CONVENTO DEI PADRI CONVENTUALI. Detached frescoes from destroyed oratory below: Scenes from the Old Testament.*

S. PIETRO MARTIRE, R. OF ENTRANCE. Fresco: S. John Evangelist. L.

S. VITTORE. Madonna and Child with four Saints (hosts of Angels fighting the Devils over Ascoli, in background). d. 1514. *Plate* 1171.

Campli (Teramo, Abruzzi). PARISH CHURCH, L. ALTAR. Two panels: SS. Ursula, Mary Magdalen, Catherine and John Baptist; SS. Clement, Sebastian, (Joseph?) and (Clare?). *Plate* 1167.

SACRISTY. Madonna and Saints. 1501. Not traced.

Città di Castello. PALAZZO VITELLI DELLA CANNONIERA (PINACOTECA), SALA X. Frescoed frieze near ceiling: thirty-five battle scenes and military ceremonies (recording deeds of the Vitelli family?). L.

Grenoble. Inv. 1294, 1295 (cat. 477, 478). Two panels from polyptych: S. John Baptist, S. Victor. (?)

London. BLAKESLEE COLLECTION (EX). Annunciation. (?)

Melbourne (Victoria). 3078/4. Panel from polyptych of S. Francesco, Ascoli: Invention of the True Cross (companion to Ascoli 42–47). 1516–33.

Rome. PINACOTECA CAPITOLINA. 97. Dormition and Assumption of Virgin.

PRINCIPE COLONNA (PRIVATE APARTMENTS). Triptych: Madonna and Child, S. John Baptist, S. Anthony Abbot. d. 1524 (after Pietro Alamanno).

VATICAN, PINACOTECA. 372. Triptych: Assumption; SS. Benedict and Lawrence; SS. Mary Magdalen and Gertrude. Sd and d. 1515. *Plates* 1169–1170.

Tivoli. S. MARIA MAGGIORE, CHAPEL L. OF CHOIR. Four Saints, Coronation of Virgin, predella. (?)

Urbino. GALLERIA NAZIONALE DELLE MARCHE. Blessed Giacomo della Marca.

Vienna. 40. Nativity. (?)

Homeless. Mourning over dead Christ. *Plate* 1172.

'Fesch' Madonna and Child enthroned with SS. Peter, Louis of Toulouse and Francis. Sd and d. 1512. *Plate* 1168.

CORREGGIO

Antonio Allegri called Correggio. 1494 or earlier—1534. Pupil of Bianchi, and of Francia and Costa; was well acquainted with the works of Mantegna, Raphael, Leonard, and Michelangelo. Probably had personal contact with Dosso and the Venetians.

Berlin. 218. Leda (head is modern) (for Federico II Gonzaga; companion to Rome and Vienna).

Budapest. 55 (121). Madonna and Child with Infant S. John.

Chicago (Ill.). ART INSTITUTE. Madonna and Child with Infant S. John.*
Detroit (Mich.). 26.94. Marriage of S. Catherine. E. *Plate* 1790.
 28.63. The 'Crespi' Madonna and Child. E.
Dresden. 150. The 'S. Francesco' Madonna and Child. 1515.
 151. Madonna and Child with S. Sebastian. 1525.
 152. 'La Notte'. 1530.
 153. Madonna and Child with SS. George, Geminianus, Peter Martyr and John
  Baptist. L.
Florence. UFFIZI. Madonna and Child in Glory. E.
 1453. Nativity.
 1455. Rest during Flight into Egypt, with Franciscan monk. *Plate* 1796.
Frankfurt a/M. 1176. Madonna and Child with Infant S. John. 1517.
Glasgow. CITY ART GALLERY. 124. Detached fresco from S. Giovanni at Parma:
 Head of an Angel (fr.).
Hampton Court. Inv. 142. Holy Family with S. James. E.
 Inv. 392. S. Catherine reading.
Leningrad. HERMITAGE. 'Yousoupoff' Lady holding bowl of nepenthe. Sd.*
London. 10. Education of Cupid or Celestial Venus (companion to Paris 1118).
 15. 'Ecce Homo' with fainting Virgin.
 23. Madonna and Child with S. Joseph in background. *Plate* 1792.
 2512. The Magdalen. E.
 3920. Detached fresco: Head of an Angel (fr.). 1520–4.
 3921. Detached fresco: Heads of two Angels (fr.). 1520–4.
 APSLEY HOUSE. WHI585–1948. Agony in the Garden. *Plate* 1789.
 COURTAULD INSTITUTE GALLERIES, LEE OF FAREHAM COLLECTION. Pietà. E.
Los Angeles (Cal.). COUNTY MUSEUM. A.5832.46–26. Holy Family with Infant S.
 John.
Madrid. 111. 'Noli me Tangere'.
 112. Madonna and Child in Landscape with Infant S. John.
 ACADEMIA. 483. S. Jerome contemplating a skull. E.
Milan. BRERA. 427. Adoration of the Magi. E.
 788. Nativity with S. Anne adoring the Child. E. *Plate* 1788.
 CASTELLO SFORZESCO. 253. Madonna and Child with Infant S. John. E.
Modena. 129. Madonna and Child.
Munich. 934. Madonna and Child with SS. Ildefons, Jerome and Angel.
Naples. 105. Bust of S. Anthony Abbot.
 107. Madonna and Child (called 'La Zingarella').
New York. 12.211. SS. Peter, Martha, Leonard and Mary Magdalen. E.
Orléans. Inv. 1101. Holy Family with Infant S. John. (r.) E.
Paris. 1117. Marriage of S. Catherine.
 1118. Antiope or Terrestrial Venus (companion to London 10). [*Plate* 390.]
 1118A. Allegory of Virtue. *Plate* 1795.
 1118B. Allegory of Vice. *Plate* 1794.

Parma. 31. Detached fresco: 'Madonna della Scala' (fr.).

350. 'Madonna della Scodella'. Before 1530.

352. Deposition. 1520–4.

351. Madonna and Child with SS. Jerome and Mary Magdalen, and two Angels. L. [*Plate* 393.]

353. Martyrdom of SS. Placidus and Flavia. 1520–4. *Plate* 1797.

758. Detached fresco: Annunciation in lunette (r.).

Inv. 1450. Frescoed lunette detached from the Biblioteca: Coronation of the Virgin. 1520–4.

BIBLIOTECA. Sinopia of Coronation.

DUOMO. Frescoes in dome: Assumption of the Virgin. 1520–4.

S. GIOVANNI EVANGELISTA. Frescoes in dome: Vision of S. John Evangelist. 1524–30. *Plate* 1798.

— L. TRANSEPT, OVER DOOR. Frescoed lunette: S. John Evangelist writing. 1524.

CONVENTO DI S. PAOLO, VAULT. Frescoes: Diana and Putti. *Plate* 1793.

Pavia. Inv. 27. Holy Family with SS. Elizabeth and Infant S. John. E.

Philadelphia (Pa.). JOHN G. JOHNSON COLLECTION. 1173A. Madonna and Child with SS. Elizabeth and Infant S. John.

Rome. BORGHESE GALLERY. 125. Danae (for Federico II Gonzaga; companion to Berlin and Vienna).

570. Madonna and Child with Infant S. John. (c.?)

San Diego (Cal.). 42:133. Bust of the Virgin (c.).

Strasbourg. 274. Judith with the head of Holofernes. E.

Vienna. 59. Ganymede (for Federico II Gonzaga: companion to Berlin, Leda and Rome, Danae).

64. Jupiter and Io (for Federico II Gonzaga: companion to Berlin, Leda and Rome, Danae). [*Plate* 391.]

HERRMANN EISSLER (EX). Pietà. *Plate* 1791.

Washington (D.C.). 194 (KRESS COLLECTION. K 196). 'Frizzoni' Marriage of S. Catherine.

1557 (TIMKEN COLLECTION). Madonna and Child with Infant S. John.

COSSA, Francesco Del

Ferrara 1435–77. Pupil of Tura; strongly influenced by Domenico Veneziano, Castagno and Baldovinetti; and to some extent by Benozzo Gozzoli. Active in Bologna 1452–67 and again from 1472.

Berlin. 115A. Autumn. (?) [*Plate* 338].

Berlin-Ost. KÖPENICK SCHLOSS, KUNSTGEWERBEMUSEUM. Stained glass window from Bologna: Madonna and Child enthroned. 1462–67. *Plate* 733.

Bologna. Inv. 580. 'Pala del Foro dei Mercanti': Madonna and Child enthroned with S. Petronius, S. John Evangelist and Alberto de' Cattanei as donor. Sd and d. 1474. *Plate 737*.

MADONNA DEL BARACCANO, BEHIND HIGH ALTAR. Fresco: Madonna and Child enthroned (by Lippo Dalmasio?), restored by Cossa, who added landscape, two Angels holding candlesticks and kneeling Bente Bentivoglio (r.). Formerly Sd and d. 1472.

S. GIOVANNI IN MONTE, NORTH WINDOW. Stained glass Madonna and Child (other fragments at Ferrara and Longare). 1467.

S. PETRONIO, CHOIR STALLS. Intarsias: S. Ambrose, S. Petronius, 1473.

Dresden. 43. Annunciation, from Convent of Osservanza at S. Michele in Borgo, Bologna. ca 1470–72. *Plate 734*.

44. Predella panel: Nativity (st.).

Ferrara. 39. Stained glass roundel: Cherubim and Chalice (from S. Giovanni in Monte at Bologna). 1467.

PALAZZO SCHIFANOIA, SALA DEI MESI, EAST WALL. Frescoes: March and April (g.p.); the remaining scenes on the same wall were done (the best of them perhaps on Francesco del Cossa's cartoons) by his followers; the other frescoes in the same room, by artists under his or Tura's influence. See under 'Ferrarese before 1510' for full description. 1470. *Plates 731, 732, 735, 736*.

Gazzada (Varese). FONDAZIONE CAGNOLA. 45, 46. Two roundels from Griffoni polyptych: Angel and Virgin of Annunciation (p.). (See London.)

London. 597. Centre panel of Griffoni polyptych from S. Petronio, Bologna: S. Vincent Ferrer (other panels at Gazzada, Milan, Rome, Washington; see also under Ercole da Ferrara, Venice, for pilasters of frame).

Longare (Vicenza). VILLA COSTOZZA, CONTE DA SCHIO. Stained glass: Eagle and Gozzadini coat of arms (fr. from S. Giovanni al Monte, Bologna). d. 1467.

Lugano. THYSSEN COLLECTION. Two panels (formerly Gosford House): S. Monica, S. Catherine (companions to Dresden Annunciation?)

Bust of young man holding ring.

Milan. BRERA. 449. Lower side-panels of Griffoni polyptych: S. John Baptist, S. Peter. (See London.)

Paris. MUSÉE JACQUEMART-ANDRÉ. 946. Stained glass roundel: Madonna and Child. 1462–67.

Rome. VATICAN, PINACOTECA. 286. Predella to Griffoni polyptych: S. Vincent Ferrer heals a leper; raises to life the sister of the Aragonese Queen, killed by a stone while listening to the Saint preaching; rescues the son of a stonemason from a building ruined by a fire; raises to life a child killed by his mother (executed by Ercole da Ferrara). [*Plate 339*.]

Washington (D.C.). 226 (KRESS COLLECTION. K 241). Madonna adoring Child with three Angels.

338/9 (KRESS COLLECTION. K 416, 417). Upper side-panels of Griffoni polyptych: S. Florian, S. Lucy. (See London.) *Plate 738*.

793 (KRESS COLLECTION. K 1361). Roundel from top of Griffoni polyptych: Crucifixion. (See London.)

COSTA, Lorenzo

Bologna 1460—Mantua 1535. Pupil of the Ferrarese painters Francesco Del Cossa and Ercole Roberti; influenced slightly by Antonello and Giovanni Bellini; partner of Francia at Bologna, and finally court-painter at Mantua.

Amsterdam. 726 D-1. Holy Family.

Assisi. F. M. PERKINS COLLECTION. Madonna and Child with two Angels adoring the Child.

Atlanta (Georgia). ART ASSOCIATION GALLERIES. 58.38-41 (KRESS COLLECTION. K 319, a, b, c, d). Eight small Saints from pilasters of altarpiece: SS. Nicholas of Tolentino, Christopher, Julian, Vincent, Catherine, Roch, Sebastian and Lucy. E (?).

Barcelona. DON B. GRASES HERNÁNDEZ. Pietà. E.

Bayonne. Inv. 963. S. Jerome? in landscape (from pilaster or predella?).

Bergamo. 533. S. John Evangelist (fr.).

560. Cain slaying Abel (companion to London and Rome, Visconti Venosta (st.). ca 1506.

S. ALESSANDRO DELLA CROCE, SACRISTY. Christ carrying Cross.

Berlin. 112. Circumcision. Sd and d. 1502. (Destroyed 1945.) *Plate* 1634.

112A. 'S. Maria delle Rondini Altarpiece': Madonna and Child enthroned with SS. Jerome, Francis, Bernard and George. E (?). (Destroyed 1945.)

Berlin-Ost. 115. Pietà. Sd and d. 1504.

Bologna. Inv. 586. S. Petronius enthroned with SS. Francis and Dominic. Sd and d. 1502.

Inv. 552. Madonna and Child enthroned with SS. Sebastian and James. Sd and d. 1491.

Inv. 554. Madonna and Child enthroned with SS. Petronius and Tecla. d. 1496.

Inv. 585. Marriage of Virgin. Sd and d. 1505.

S. GIACOMO MAGGIORE, CAPPELLA BENTIVOGLIO, R. WALL. Madonna and Child enthroned with Giovanni II Bentivoglio, his wife, four sons and seven daughters. Sd and d. 1488. *Plate* 1626.

— — L. WALL. Frescoes: Triumph of Death, Triumph of Fame. 1490. *Plates* 1628-1629.

— — ALTAR WALL. Frescoed lunette: Vision of the Apocalypse at Patmos (restored by Cignani).

— ORATORIO DI S. CECILIA. Frescoes on walls (from altar, left): (2) S. Urban Pope converts Valerian; (9) S. Cecilia distributing Alms. *Plate* 1604.

— — (3) Baptism of Valerian; (4) Cecilia and Valerian crowned by an Angel; (7) Cecilia disputing with Prefect Almadrius; (8) Martyrdom and Beheading of Cecilia (st.; partly Aspertini and others). *Plate* 1606.

— — (1) and (10) see Francia; (5) and (6) see Aspertini.

Frescoed decoration 1504-1506.

S. GIOVANNI IN MONTE, SEVENTH CHAPEL R. 'Ghedini Altarpiece': Madonna and Child enthroned with SS. Augustine, Posidonius, John and Francis. Sd. and d. 1497. *Plate* 1630.

— APSE. Coronation of Virgin and six Saints. Sd and d. 1501.

— FAÇADE. Stained glass in circular window: S. John Evangelist at Patmos. After 1481. (?)

S. MARIA DELLA MISERICORDIA, CHOIR. Pinnacles to Bentivoglio Nativity (see Francia, Bologna Inv. 584): Risen Christ, Angel and Virgin of Annunciation (st.) (companion to Milan). 1499.

S. MARTINO MAGGIORE, FIFTH ALTAR L. Assumption (g.p.). doc. 1506.

S. PETRONIO, CAPPELLA BACIOCCHI (SEVENTH L.). Madonna and Child enthroned with SS. James, Jerome, Sebastian and George. Sd and d. 1492. *Plate* 1627.

— — Stained-glass window on design of the artist.

CONTE GIUSEPPE SCARSELLI. Venus. *Plate* 1633.

Boston (Mass.). 25.227. Bust of blond woman.

Budapest. 1257. Venus.

6103. Holy Family with SS. Jerome and Francis.

Detroit (Mich.). ALFRED J. FISHER GIFT. Male portrait.

Downton Castle (Ludlow). MAJOR KINCAID LENNOX (EX). Cardinal Bibbiena and penitent S. Jerome in background. *Plate* 1631.

Dresden. 47A. Virgin of Annunciation (fr. r.).

Dublin. 526. Holy Family.

Florence. UFFIZI. 6D. Madonna and Child enthroned with SS. Martin and Dorothy.

3282. S. Sebastian. E.

8384. Portrait of Giovanni Bentivoglio. Sd.

Graz. PALAIS ATTEMS (EX). S. Jerome in Wilderness.

Hampton Court. ROYAL COLLECTIONS. Inv. 233. Female Saint bearing Cross (p.).

Inv. 355. Lady with lap-dog.

Le Havre. 27. S. Margaret in prayer (g.p.).

Leipzig. Inv. 1384. S. Sebastian.

London. 629. Polyptych: Madonna and Child with Saints. Sd and d. 1505.

2083. Portrait of Battista Fiera.

2486. Concert. E.

3103, 3104. Fall of Manna, Miriam's rejoicing (companions to Bergamo and Rome, Visconti Venosta; st.). ca 1506.

3105. Adoration of Shepherds (p.).

R. BENSON (EX). Dead Christ upheld by Angels.

Baptism of Christ.

Lugano. THYSSEN COLLECTION. Group of singers.

Lyons. Inv. B.495. Holy Family. E.

Manchester (New Hampshire). CURRIER GALLERY OF ART. Bust of lady.

Mantua. S. ANDREA, SECOND ALTAR L. Madonna and Child enthroned with SS. Sebastian, Paul, Elizabeth, Infant John, Roch, Jerome? and Pope. Sd and d. 1525.

Memphis (Tennessee). BROOKS MEMORIAL ART GALLERY. 61.94 (KRESS COLLECTION.
   K 466). S. Paul.

Milan. BRERA. 429. Predella to Bentivoglio Nativity (see Francia, Bologna Inv. 584):
   Adoration of Magi (companion to S. Maria della Misericordia, Bologna).
   Sd and d. 1499. *Plate 1632.*

   MARCHESE BRIVIO. S. Anne teaching the Virgin to read.

Monteveglio (Bologna). ABBAZIA. Assumption (companion to Raleigh).

New York. 07.304. S. Anthony of Padua with SS. Ursula and Catherine. Sd. L.
   30.95.292. S. Lucy. (?)

   ANDREW CARNEGIE (EX). Holy Family.

Orléans. Madonna and Child. [Not traced; burnt in war?]

Paris. 1261, 1262. Court of Isabella d'Este (after 1506); Kingdom of Comus (1511–12)
   (from Studiolo d'Isabella at Mantua; see Mantegna and Perugino). [*Plate 344.*]
   Plate 1635.

   MUSÉE JACQUEMART-ANDRÉ. 1051. Communion of S. Mary of Egypt and S. Onophrius.

Philadelphia (Pa.). J. G. JOHNSON COLLECTION. 244. Madonna and Child. E.

Prague. 87. (FORMERLY TEPLITZ.) Commander Federico Gonzaga and his entourage.
   1522. *Plate 1636.*

Raleigh (N.C.). MUSEUM OF ART. GL. 60.17.36-8 (KRESS COLLECTION. K 502). Predella
   to Monteveglio altarpiece: Funeral of the Virgin. ca 1490.

Reggio Emilia. CONTI CASSOLI. S. Sebastian.

Rome. GALLERIA BORGHESE. 395. Christ at Column.

   S. NICOLA IN CARCERE, L. NAVE. Christ in Glory appears to Virgin and eight
   Apostles.

   MARCHESE ALFREDO DUSMET (EX). Annunciation.

   MARCHESE VISCONTI VENOSTA. Creation of Eve, Moses striking the Rock (companions to Bergamo and London; st.). ca 1506.

Toledo (Ohio). MUSEUM OF ART. 'Barberini' Holy Family.

Vaduz. LIECHTENSTEINSCHE SAMMLUNGEN (EX). Bust of man. E.

Venice. CONTE VITTORIO CINI. Inv. 6169. Madonna and Child. L. (?)

Worcester (Mass.). 1940.32. Adoration of Shepherds.

Homeless. Bust of Virgin Annunciate* (repr. *Pantheon*, 1961, p. 143).

COZZARELLI, Guidoccio

Siena, 1450–1516. Assistant and close follower of Matteo di Giovanni.

Altenburg. 82. Bishop Saint.

Altenburg (contd.) 83. Panel from pilaster: S. Vincent Ferrer.
   89. Predella panel: Pietà.
Amherst (Mass.). COLLEGE. 1961-76. (KRESS COLLECTION. K 168). Madonna and Child
   with two Angels.
Ancaiano (Siena). S. BARTOLOMEO. Madonna and Child with SS. Bernardino and
   Sebastian.
Assisi. SACRO CONVENTO, PERKINS DONATION. 6. Nativity with SS. Dominic and
   Catherine of Siena.
   F. M. PERKINS COLLECTION (EX?). Madonna and Child with SS. Michael and Jerome
   and two Angels (r.).
Atlanta (Ga.). ART ASSOCIATION GALLERIES (STRAUS GIFT). 'Kaufmann' Madonna and
   Child with two Angels.
Balcarres (Fife, Scotland). EARL OF CRAWFORD AND BALCARRES. Predella panel: S.
   Jerome heals the lion. (?)
Baltimore (Md.) WALTERS ART GALLERY. 498. Cavalcade (fr.).
   586. Madonna and Child with two Angels.
Boston (Mass.). 06.121. Madonna and Child with two Angels (r.).
Brooklyn (N.Y.). 49.138. Predella: SS. Bernardino, Blaise, Peter, Paul, Anthony
   Abbot, Catherine of Siena.
Budapest. 61. Heads of Angels.
Buonconvento (Siena). PIEVE DEI SS. PIETRO E PAOLO, MUSEO. Predella: Life of Virgin.
   Madonna and Child with two Angels (r.).
Cambridge. SIR SIDNEY COCKERELL (EX). Tondo: Visitation.
Columbia (S.C.). MUSEUM OF ART. 62-919 (KRESS COLLECTION. K 1743B). Panels from
   frame of altarpiece: SS. Peter, Anthony Abbot, Roch and Francis (com-
   panions to Milan, Saibene and Tulsa).
Coral Gables (Fla.). LOWE ART GALLERY. 61.22 (KRESS COLLECTION. K 1286). An-
   nunciation and Departure for Bethlehem. *Plate* 823.
Englewood (N.J.). D. F. PLATT COLLECTION (EX). Madonna and Child enthroned,
   with two Saints and kneeling Bishop (r.).
Florence. AVV. GUSTAVO RIMINI. Two panels of polyptych: S. Bernardino, S. Anthony
   of Padua.
Gazzada (Varese). FONDAZIONE CAGNOLA. Madonna and Child with two female
   Saints.
Lille. 951. Madonna and Child with SS. Jerome and John Baptist (r.) (?).
   990. Vision of S. Catherine of Siena (r.).
London. SIR THOMAS BARLOW (EX). Predella panel: Miracle of the True Cross.
   ALYS RUSSELL (EX) Predella: Dead Christ held by two Angels, the Virgin, S. John
   Evangelist, S. Peter and S. Jerome. *Plate* 830.
   WOODWARD COLLECTION (EX). Front of Cassone: Camilla engaged in battle (com-
   panion to Philadelphia, Paris and New York).
Madison (Wis.). UNIVERSITY. 61.4.11 (KRESS COLLECTION. K 1283). 'Platt' Madonna
   and Child (r.).

Milan. BRERA. 473. Madonna and Child with two Angels.

SAIBENE COLLECTION. Panel from frame of altarpiece: S. Lawrence (companion to Columbia and Tulsa).

Montefollonico (Senese). CHIESA DELL'OPERA DEL TRIANO. Madonna and Child with SS. Sebastian and Anthony Abbot.

Monte San Savino (Arezzo). S. CHIARA. Two panels of triptych: SS. Sigismund and Apollonia; SS. James and Donnino.

Montingegnoli (Senese). S. SISTO, AT SIDES OF HIGH ALTAR. Two panels: S. Bernardino, S. Sixtus.

New York. 11.126.2. Front of Cassone: Cloelia swimming the Tiber (companion to London, Paris and Philadelphia).

GEORGE A. HEARN (EX). Madonna and Child with two Angels.

R. LEHMAN. Madonna and Child.

Orléans. ORANGERIE. Madonna and Child with two Angels.

Oxford. CHRIST CHURCH. 40. Madonna and Child with two Angels (r.). (?)

Paganico (Grosseto). S. MICHELE. Madonna and Child with two Angels, SS. John Baptist, Michael, Anthony Abbot and saintly Monk. E.

Paris. MUSÉE DE CLUNY. 1705/6. Two fronts of cassone: Return of Ulysses. *Plate 822.*

TROTTI COLLECTION (EX). Front of cassone: Lucretia stabbing herself (companion to London, New York and Philadelphia).

Philadelphia (Pa.). J. G. JOHNSON COLLECTION. 111. Front of Cassone: Battle of Camilla and Aeneas (companion to London, New York and Paris).

112. Madonna and Child with SS. James and Bernardino. (r.). (?)

Pitigliano (Grosseto). SS. PIETRO E PAOLO, APSE. Madonna and Child with SS. Peter, Francis and two Angels; at bottom, S. Clare, Dead Christ with mourning Virgin and Evangelist, S. Bernardino. Sd and d. 1484.

Princeton (N.J.). 41.45. (GIFT OF MRS WARBURG.) Lunette: Madonna and Child with two Angels, S. Bernardino and S. Francis.

Rapolano (Senese). ORATORIO DI S. BARTOLOMEO. S. Anthony of Padua and four Scenes from his Life.

Rome. MARCHESE PIERO MISCIATELLI. Two heads of Angels.

VATICAN, PINACOTECA. 308. Four predella panels: Scenes from Life of S. Barbara. 1479. *Plate 821.*

Rosia (Senese). PIEVE DI S. GIOVANNI BATTISTA, HIGH ALTAR. Madonna and Child, S. Anthony Abbot and S. Sebastian (fr.).

Rotterdam. BOYMANS-VAN BEUNINGEN MUSEUM. Inv. 2556. Predella panel to Sinalunga altarpiece: Martyrdom of SS. Simon and Taddeus (ex Auspitz, Vienna). 1486. *Plate 825.*

Siena. 296. S. Sebastian. d. 1495.

297. S. Catherine surrounded by emblems of Doctors' and Apothecaries' Guild. ca 1480.

302. Detached fresco: Saint with dragon (fr.).

304. Blessed Aldobrandina Ponsia.

Siena (contd.) 367. Madonna and Child with Angels, S. Jerome and Blessed Giovanni Colombini. Sd and d. 1482.

    378. S. Francis.

    445. S. Catherine changing her heart with Christ's.

ARCHIVIO DI STATO. Book-covers:

Gabella: Presentation of Virgin with SS. John Evangelist and Nicholas. d. 1484.

Gabella: The Virgin steering the Vessel of the Sienese Republic. d. 1487.

Gabella: Camarlingo and Executors beseeching Virgin to enter Siena. d. 1489.

— Miniature: Pope in Consistory granting indulgences.

PALAZZO PUBBLICO, SALA DEI CARDINALI. Madonna and Child with Angels. d. 1484.

PIAZZA DEL CAMPO, TABERNACLE ON HOUSE n.2 (EX). Detached fresco: Madonna enthroned, crowned by Angels. *Plate 824.*

RICOVERO (MADONNA DI CAMPANSI), WOMEN'S WARD. Fresco: S. Francis receiving Stigmata.

BARZELOTTI CAMAIORI COLLECTION (FROM BELCARO). Madonna and Child with SS. Bernardino and Catherine of Siena.

CONTE GIUSEPPE PLACIDI (EX). Predella panel: Flight into Egypt.

Madonna and Child with four Angels.

SOCIETÀ ESECUTORI PIE DISPOSIZIONI, GALLERIA. 10. Dead Christ in Tomb.

    23, 24. Bier-heads: Madonna of Mercy; Christ on cross and Flagellants.

    27. Bier-head: Madonna of Mercy with S. Bernardino and three Blessed. d. 1494.

    31. Bier-head: Cross worshipped by Flagellants.

S. MARIA ASSUNTA (DUOMO), UNDER DRUM OF CUPOLA. Monochrome frescoes: Single figures of Prophets.

— L. NAVE, FLOOR. Marble intarsia from his design: Libyan Sibyl. 1483. (See also Benvenuto di Giovanni, Matteo di Giovanni, Neroccio.)

— LIBRERIA PICCOLOMINI. Miniatures:

Antiphonary 6 F, f. 3: Isaac blessing Jacob. *Plate 827.*

Antiphonary 15 Q: Assumption; Birth of S. John Baptist.

Antiphonary 26 R; f. 4: Birth of Virgin; f. 80: Procession.

FONTEGIUSTA, CIRCULAR WINDOW OVER DOOR. Stained-glass Madonna with S. Bernardino and S. Catherine of Siena (r.).

MISERICORDIA. Bier-head: Dead Christ; on back, S. Anthony Abbot.

Bier-head: S. Anthony Abbot (on front and back).

S. SEBASTIANO IN VALLE PIATTA (CONTRADA DELLA SELVA), SACRISTY. Madonna and Child with SS. Sebastian and Margaret.

— (Environs). BELCARO. Fresco: SS. Roch and Sebastian. Not traced.

— — VICOBELLO, MARCHESA CHIGI ZONDADARI BONELLI. 'Spalliera' panels: Callisto, Lucretia, Hippo.

Sinalunga (Val di Chiana). S. BERNARDINO, CHAPEL L. OF ENTRANCE. Madonna and Child with SS. Simon and Taddeus, God the Father and Angels; in pilasters, SS. Peter, Francis, Catherine of Siena, Paul, Bernardino and Apollonia (companion to Rotterdam). Sd and d. 1486.

Baptism of Christ with SS. Jerome and Augustine. *Plate 826.*

— UPSTAIRS (CLAUSURA). Lunette: Madonna and Child with two Saints and two Angels.

Stockholm. 214. Adoration of Magi (r.).

Trequanda (Val di Chiana). MADONNA DELLE NEVI. Fresco: Madonna. (?)

Tucson (Arizona). UNIVERSITY. 61.109 (KRESS COLLECTION. K 1173). Crucifixion.

Tulsa (Okla.). PHILBROOK ART CENTER 3372. (KRESS COLLECTION. K 1743A). Panels from frame of altarpiece: SS. Ursula, Christopher, Sebastian (companions to Columbia and Milan, Saibene).

Vienna. S. VON AUSPITZ (EX). 'Palmieri Nuti' Madonna enthroned and thirteen Saints.

A. FIGDOR (EX). Book-cover: Measuring the Corn. *Plate 828.*

Biccherna: The Noveschi, headed by young Pandolfo Petrucci, enter Siena (23 June 1487) under the protection of the Madonna and of S. Ediltrude. d. 1488.

Williamstown (Mass.). STERLING AND FRANCINE CLARK ART INSTITUTE. Predella panel: Calling of SS. Peter and Andrew.

Homeless. Adoration of Shepherds. *Plate 829.*

DEFENDENTE FERRARI

School of Vercelli. Born at Chivasso, pupil and collaborator of Spanzotti, influenced by Macrino d'Alba and even more by Northern art. Dated works 1501–35.

Amsterdam. 922–B1 (VOM RATH, EX-OLDENBURG N. 41). Madonna and Child with S. Anne and two music-making Angels. Sd and d. 1528. *Plate 1252.*

922–B2. Copy of Raphael's Madonna of Orléans. d. 1526.

Avigliana (Torino). S. GIOVANNI, FIRST ALTAR R. S. Ursula and her Virgins; in predella (not belonging to it), Scenes from Life of Magdalen.

— SECOND ALTAR R. Triptych: Madonna and Child enthroned; S. Crispinus; S. Crispinianus; two Saints in roundels above; three Scenes from Life of SS. Crispinus and Crispinianus in predella. d. 1535.

— FOURTH ALTAR R. Triptych: Penitent S. Jerome; S. John Baptist; S. Bernard; in predella, Beheading of Baptist, S. Jerome in the Wilderness, Vision of S. Bernard. *Plate 1246.*

— FOURTH ALTAR L. Triptych: Nativity; S. Sebastian; S. Roch; half-length SS. Francis and Saint with book; in roundel above, dead Christ with Symbols of Passion (predella is modern). Sd and d. 1511.

— FIRST ALTAR L. Triptych: (centre panel is modern); S. Lawrence; S. John Baptist with Donor; in predella, Annunciation to Joachim and Anne, Meeting at the Golden Gate, Birth of the Virgin.

— CHOIR. S. Ursula and her Virgins kneeling before the Pope.

S. Nicholas surrounded by children and S. Lucy.

SS. Sebastian and Roch. *Plate 1254.*

Avigliana. S. GIOVANNI, CHOIR (contd.). S. Christopher.
S. Anthony Abbot beaten by devils.
> MADONNA DEI LAGHI. Annunciation; side-panels (not belonging to centre) with S. Sebastian and S. Roch; in predella, Visitation, Nativity, Adoration of Magi.

Baltimore (Md.). WALTERS ART GALLERY. 711. Madonna and Child enthroned with seven Putti and S. Joseph.

Bergamo. 303, 304. Flagellation; Christ seated on Cross. *Plates* 1249, 1250.
305. Adoration of Shepherds (u.). Sd. *Plate* 1256.

Berlin-Ost. 1147. Nativity with donor. 1510. [*Plate* 380.]

Biella. EX-CONVENT OF S. GIROLAMO, CHOIR STALLS. Twenty decorative compositions. 1523.

Budapest. SÁNDOR LEDERER (EX). Predella panel: Naming of S. John Baptist. *Plate* 1245.

Buttigliera Alta (Torino). S. ANTONIO DI RANVERSO, HIGH ALTAR. Polyptych: Nativity; full-length SS. Anthony Abbot and Roch; half-length SS. Sebastian and Bernardino of Siena; in predella, Life of S. Anthony Abbot. *Plate* 1258.
Shutters to cover polyptych, painted on both sides: outside, Angel and Virgin of Annunciation, Visitation, Adoration of Magi; inside, S. Maurice, Meeting of SS. Anthony and Paul in the wilderness, S. Jerome in the wilderness, S. Christopher.

Cambridge (Mass.). FOGG ART MUSEUM. 1941.134 (GIFT OF F. WARBURG). Adoration of the Child by candlelight.

Carmagnola (Torino). COLLEGIATA, SACRISTY. Madonna and Child enthroned with SS. Maurice and Alexander.

Caselle Torinese. MUNICIPIO. Madonna and Child enthroned with SS. George (?), Christopher, Sebastian and Francis. Dated on back 1501. *Plate* 1243.

Cavour (Saluzzo). S. LORENZO, FIRST ALTAR L. Triptych: Mystic Marriage of S. Catherine (missing side-panels replaced by copies).

Chivasso (Torino). ASSUNTA, SECOND ALTAR R. Deposition (p., r.).

Ciriè (Torino). S. GIOVANNI BATTISTA (DUOMO), FIRST ALTAR L. 'Madonna del Popolo.' d. 1519 (the date was transferred into the centre of the picture when the panel was cut into an oval).
> CONFRATERNITA DEL S. SUDARIO. Assumption; Angel and Virgin of Annunciation in roundels above; Death and Burial of Virgin in predella. d. 1516.

Cuneo. MUSEO CIVICO. Circumcision; in predella, four miracles of S. Anthony of Padua (p. ?). d. 1513.
> S. MARIA DEGLI ANGELI, SAGRESTIA. Predella, Deposition and scenes from life of S. Anthony Abbot.

Denver (Col.). MUSEUM OF ART. E–IT–18–XVI–946 (KRESS COLLECTION. K 70). Christ in the house of Simon (with Spanzotti? see there).

Erlenbach. HANS CORAY (EX). Madonna suckling the Child.

Feletto Canavese (Torino). PARISH CHURCH, FIRST ALTAR R. Triptych: Adoration of the Child with SS. Agatha and Lucy (c.); SS. John Baptist and Stephen; SS. Roch and Lawrence; in predella, Man of Sorrow and Apostles. 1522.

Organ-shutters: Madonna and Child with S. Anne; Ecce Homo.

Florence. CONTINI BONACOSSI COLLECTION. Madonna suckling the Child.

Adoration of Magi (with Spanzotti?)

CHARLES LOESER (EX). Tondo: Temptation of Eve.

Ivrea. ASSUNTA (DUOMO), SACRISTIES. Adoration of the Child with S. Clare and nuns of her Order. d. 1519.

Adoration of the Child with Blessed Vermondus (Robert Veremond) recommending donor. Sd and d. 1521. *Plate 1251.*

Leinì. SS. PIETRO E PAOLO, SACRISTY. Adoration of Magi. 1514.

London. 1200, 1201. Top panels of polyptych, companions to Milan 718, 719 and Turin, Accademia Albertina: Half-length SS. Peter Martyr and Bishop, half-length SS. John Baptist and Nicholas of Tolentino (with Spanzotti?).

Madison (Wis.). UNIVERSITY OF WISCONSIN 61.4.7 (KRESS COLLECTION. K 519). Madonna and Child enthroned with four Putti, Baptist and Evangelist.

Milan. BRERA. 718, 719. Right and central panel of polyptych, companions to London 1200, 1201 and Turin, Accademia Albertina: full-length SS. Sebastian and Catherine, full-length S. Andrew with cross (with Spanzotti?).

Münster i/W. DIÖZESANMUSEUM. 20. Bust of youth.

New York. 15.56. Right panel of polyptych: Full-length SS. Lawrence and John Evangelist.

Paris. 1005B, 1005C. Birth of Baptist, Deposition (fr.).

Pavia. Inv. 96. Crucifixion (later version of Turin, Inv. 209; r.).

Philadelphia (Pa.). J. G. JOHNSON COLLECTION. 276. Madonna enthroned, suckling the Child, with SS. John Evangelist, Catherine, Anthony Abbot and Apostle (st.).

Ranverso. See Buttigliera Alta.

Rome. VATICAN, PINACOTECA. Depot 612 (formerly 165, 167). Lunettes: Isaiah, Jeremiah.

276A, 277A. Full-length Baptist (r.), kneeling S. Catherine (s.?).

PALAZZO ROSPIGLIOSI, PALLAVICINI COLLECTION. 185A. Right panel of polyptych: S. Nicholas of Tolentino.

179-184. Predella panel (formerly Genova, Medici del Vascello): Man of Sorrows and Apostles (r.).

SPIRIDON COLLECTION (EX). Pietà (p.).

Madonna of Mercy (variant of Ciriè; bought by Cambò?).

Rosazza (Biella). SS. PIETRO E GIORGIO, CHOIR. Polyptych: S. Yves and other Saints. E.

Rotterdam. D. G. VAN BEUNINGEN (EX VIENNA, AUSPITZ). Predella panel: Nativity.

Sagra di S. Michele (Val di Susa). CHURCH, HIGH ALTAR. Triptych: Madonna and Child, S. John Vincent recommending Bishop Urbano di Miolans; S. Michael; in predella, Visitation, Nativity, Adoration of Magi.

CONVENT. Madonna and Child enthroned (version of Turin, Palazzo Reale) with SS. Lawrence and Michael. ca 1525–30.

Two panels of polyptych: Half-length SS. Benedict and Scholastica (st.).

San Benigno Canavese. ASSUNTA, SACRISTY. Madonna and Child enthroned with music-making Putti and SS. Benedict, Benignus, Agapitus and Tiburtius; in predella, Baptism, Judgement, Beheading of Tiburtius. ca 1525–30. *Plate 1257.*

San Martino Alfieri (Asti). PARISH CHURCH. Polyptych: The Virgin in Glory (Immacolata); Annunciation to Joachim and Anne, Marriage of Virgin, Death of S. Joseph (?); in soffit above, Meeting at the Golden Gate, Birth of Virgin, Presentation of Virgin; in predella, Christ and Apostles (st.).

Stresa Borromeo. ISTITUTO ROSMINI. Portable triptych: Adoration of Magi (later variant of Leinì); Nativity; Pietà. Sd and d. 1523. *Plate 1253.*

Stuttgart. Inv. 760. Christ and the Doctors (later version of Spanzotti's at Turin, Inv. 213). Sd and d. 1526. *Plate 1222.*

Susa. S. GIUSTO (DUOMO), SALA CAPITOLARE. Adoration of the Child (from the Certosa di S. Maria in Banda). *Plate 1238.*

Turin. ACCADEMIA ALBERTINA. 127. Left panel of polyptych, companion to London 1200, 1201 and to Milan, 718, 719: Full-length SS. Francis and Agatha with kneeling donor (with Spanzotti?).

218. Adoration of the Child with SS. John Baptist, Dominic, Francis, James and two more Saints (st.).

GALLERIA SABAUDA. 30 bis. Left panel of triptych: SS. Jerome and John Baptist with kneeling donor.

35. Mystic Marriage of S. Catherine; in predella, five Scenes from Life of S. Catherine.

36. Triptych: Madonna enthroned suckling the Child, two Angels and two music-making putti; S. Barbara with donor; S. Michael; in predella, four Scenes from Life of S. Barbara.

38. SS. Bartholomew, Thomas, Peter and John Baptist.

41. Left panel of polyptych: half-length S. Mauritius.

52. Adoration of Magi. E. (?)

MUSEO CIVICO. Inv. 209. Crucifixion.

Inv. 210. S. Jerome praying in the wilderness. Sd.

Inv. 211. Holy Family adoring the Child (simplified version of Susa and Ivrea, r.).

Inv. 212. Nativity by night. d. 1510. *Plate 1247.*

Inv. 214. Panel of polyptych: Half-length blessing Bishop.

Inv. 215, 216. Shutters: Full-length SS. Michael and Catherine; on back, in grisaille, kneeling Magdalen and Christ as gardener.

Inv. 219, 220. Two panels of polyptych: Half-length S. Yves with newly married couple; half-length Baptist with lamb (companions to Homeless S. Jerome?). L.

Inv. 221, 222. Two panels of polyptych: Half-length S. Francis with female donor; half-length S. Catherine.

Inv. 223, 224. Two panels of polyptych: Busts of Angel and Virgin of Annunciation.

Inv. 225, 226. Tondi from polyptych: Busts of Angel and Virgin of Annunciation.

Inv. 227. Madonna suckling the Child.

Inv. 228. Predella panel: Circumcision. *Plate 1244.*

Inv. 229. Predella panel: Nativity with two Shepherds.

Inv. 230. Predella panel: Adoration of the Child.

Inv. 231. Predella panel: Nativity. (?)

Inv. 232. Predella panel: Flight into Egypt.

Inv. 233. Predella panel: Visitation (st.).

Inv. 234. Predella panel: Flight into Egypt (st.).

Inv. 235. Predella panel: Meeting at the Golden Gate (st.).

Inv. 236. Predella panel: Visitation (st.).

Inv. 237. Predella panel: Presentation of the Virgin (st.).

Inv. 238. Predella panel: S. John Evangelist in the cauldron of boiling oil.

Inv. 290. Triptych: S. Jerome in the wilderness; S. John Baptist; S. John Evangelist; half-length SS. (Nazzarus and Celsus?); in roundels above, Angel and Virgin of Annunciation; in monochrome and gold predella, Flagellation, Way to Calvary, Crucifixion, Mourning over the dead Christ, Entombment. ca 1525.

Inv. 352. Circumcision.

Inv. 354. Left panel of polyptych (ex-Gualino): full-length S. Pantaleo and kneeling donor; on back, in grisaille, SS. Roch and Sebastian.

Inv. 398. S. Jerome praying in the Wilderness. d. 1520. *Plate 1248.*

Inv. 423. Predella panel: Procession of Christ and Saints led by putto.

Inv. 486. Coronation of Virgin. ca 1525–30.

PALAZZO REALE. Madonna and Child enthroned with SS. John Baptist, Nazzarus and kneeling donor. d. 1523.

S. AGOSTINO. S. Nicholas of Tolentino in Glory.

S. GIOVANNI BATTISTA (DUOMO), SECOND ALTAR R. Polyptych: Madonna enthroned suckling the Child and two music-making Putti; left, full-length S. Ursus and half-length S. Crispinus; right, full-length S. Crispinianus and half-length S. Thebaldus; in soffit above, Annunciation, Visitation, Nativity; in predella, Agony in the Garden, Betrayal of Christ, Flagellation. 'Ecce Homo', Way to Calvary (with Spanzotti?)

Vaduz. LIECHTENSTEINSCHE SAMMLUNG. Panel of triptych: SS. Peter and Paul.

Vercelli. MUSEO BORGOGNA. Triptych: Madonna and Child with two music-making putti; SS. Francis and Bernardino; SS. Sebastian and Margaret (p.; with Girolamo Giovenone?).

Polyptych from Bianzè: Madonna and Child enthroned with two Angels; full-length Bishop Saint; full-length S. Joseph; Descent from the Cross (after Rogier van der Weyden); half-length SS. John Baptist and Lucy (g.p.). L.

Centre panel of triptych: Nativity with Shepherds.

Centre panel of polyptych: Assumption. *Plate 1242.*

Vienna. LANCKORONSKI COLLECTION. Predella panel: Christ before Pilate.
　BARON TUCHER (EX). Madonna suckling the Child (st.).
Worcester (Mass.). 1920.49. Left panel of polyptych: Full-length S. John Baptist (version of Turin, Inv. 290).
　　1920.50. Left panel of polyptych: Full-length S. Anthony of Padua.
Zagreb. 76. Right fragment of altarpiece: SS. Catherine and Peter Martyr. (?)
Homeless. Panel of polyptych: Half-length S. Jerome, reading (companion to Turin, Inv. 219, 220?). L. *Plate 1255.*

DELITIO, Andrea

Abruzzese painter of Guardiagrele (not Lecce nei Marsi), active in the last decades of the fifteenth century. Pupil perhaps of Girolamo di Giovanni da Camerino; developed under the influence of Niccolò da Foligno and Lorenzo d'Alessandro and probably of wandering North Italian and ultramontane artists.

Aquila. MUSEO NAZIONALE ABRUZZESE. 25. Detached fresco from the church of the Beata Antonia: Adoration of the Child.
　　26. Diptych from S. Maria la Nuova at Cellino Attanasio: Mystic Marriage of S. Catherine; Crucifixion. *Plates 662–663.*
　S. AMICO, ALTAR. Fragment of fresco, formerly over door in cloister: Madonna suckling the Child and two flying Angels (other four Angels, S. James and John Baptist, lost).
Atri. S. AGOSTINO, ENTRANCE WALL L. Fresco: Madonna and blessing Child, with SS. John Baptist, James and Worshipper (r.). (?)
　S. MARIA ASSUNTA (CATHEDRAL), CHOIR. Frescoes.
　— — VAULT: SS. Matthew and Jerome, Charity and Justice; SS. John Evangelist and Augustine, Faith and Hope; SS. Luke and Ambrose, Prudence and Obedience; SS. Mark and Gregory the Great, Fortitude and Temperance; ornamental heads and portrait heads in roundels of frieze. *Plates 666–667, 668.*
　— — SOFFITS: entrance arch, six knee-length female Saints in niches; right arch, busts of SS. Stephen, Anthony Abbot, Nicholas and Onophrius in niches; left arch, busts of SS. Julian, Blaise, Dominic and Sebastian in niches.
　— — WALLS: Life of Virgin (g.p.) and Saints. LEFT, FROM TOP: lunette: Expulsion of Joachim from the temple; 2nd register: Birth of Virgin, Presentation of Virgin, Virgin praying and working; 3rd register: Flight into Egypt; in spandrels of arch: Self-portrait; Busts of Duke Andrea Matteo III d'Acquaviva and attendant; 4th register: The Virgin receives the annunciation of her death; on pillar: knee-length SS. Apollonia and Reparata; on octagonal pier: SS. Gregory the Great, Sebastian, Leonard and Lawrence. *Plates 667, 669, 670.*
　— — CENTRE, FROM TOP: lunette: Annunciation to Joachim in the desert; 2nd

register: Marriage of Virgin, (window), Annunciation; 3rd register: Massacre of Innocents, Christ among Doctors (fr.), Marriage at Cana; 4th register: The dying Virgin taking leave of the Apostles (fr.), Death of Virgin (frs., cut by insertion of throne in the middle), Assumption (fr. with worshipping Bishop, canons and two Angels; above, painted over with a Christ in sepulchre).

—— RIGHT, FROM TOP: lunette: Meeting of Joachim and Anne at the Golden Gate; 2nd register: Visitation, Nativity, Adoration of Magi; 3rd register: Baptism of Christ; in spandrels of arch, Bust of young Donor, Bust of Canon; 4th register: Coronation of Virgin; on pillar, knee-length S. Barbara and female Saint; on octagonal pier: S. Vito holding two wolves by the leash, Bishop Saint holding a millstone and a (hammer?), S. Clement, S. Stephen. *Plate 666.*

Fragments of frescoes in other parts of the church.

Baltimore (Md.). WALTERS ART GALLERY. 715. Portable triptych: Madonna and Child enthroned, with Christ on Cross above; SS. Paul and female Martyr; SS. Francis and Clare. *Plate 665.*

Guardiagrele. COLLEGIATA DI S. MARIA MAGGIORE, UNDER PORTICO, BY L. DOOR. Fresco: large S. Christopher. Sd and d. 1473.

Isola del Gran Sasso. CONA (CHAPEL) DI S. SEBASTIANO. Frescoes: outside, Angel and Virgin of Annunciation; inside, Madonna and Child with SS. Sebastian and Roch.

Mutignano (Atri). PARISH CHURCH. S. Sylvester enthroned and four stories. (?)

New York. R. LEHMAN. Virgin of Annunciation (also listed Masolino).

Providence (R.I.). RHODE ISLAND SCHOOL OF DESIGN. 22.101. Predella panel: S. Benedict blessing Totila. *Plate 664.*

DEODATO ORLANDI

Lucchese. Signed works from 1288 to 1308.

Altenburg. 1. Madonna and Child enthroned and two Angels.

Berlin. 1041. Joachim and the Angel, Visitation, Birth of Baptist, Naming of Baptist, Baptist preaching to multitudes, Last Judgement. *Plate 16.*

Frankfurt. 1887. Finial of crucifix: Mourning S. John Evangelist.

Lucca. 40. Painted Crucifix. Sd and d. 1288. *Plate 14.*

New York. R. M. HURD (EX). Madonna and Child. Sd and d. 1308.

Pisa. 4. Dossal: Madonna and Child, SS. Dominic, James, Peter and Paul, Angels in spandrels. Sd and d. 1301. *Plate 15.*

5. Madonna and Child enthroned, with four Angels.

(Environs). S. PIETRO IN GRADO. Frescoes: Scenes from Life of SS. Peter and Paul. (?)

San Miniato (Valdarno). MUSEO DIOCESANO. Painted Crucifix from S. Chiara. Sd and d. 1301.

DE PREDIS, Ambrogio

Milanese, active 1472–1506 and probably later. Formed under influence of Zenale and Butinone; assistant and close follower of Leonardo.

Amsterdam. 1920. B–1. Profile of young woman.

Bergamo. 529. Bust of page. L.
    547. Profile of youth.

Bristol. 1653. Francesco Sforza as a boy. *Plate* 1408.

Cambridge (Mass.). FOGG ART MUSEUM. 1943.1331. Profile of youth aged sixteen. d. 1506.

Cracow. Inv. XII, 230. Profile of girl (r.).

Florence. UFFIZI. 1494. Profile of courtier (c.?).
    8383. Copy of portrait of Beatrice d'Este in Paris.

Hamburg. CONSUL WEBER (EX). Profile of youth.

Hanover. PROVINZIALMUSEUM (EX). Profile of man with hooked nose (deposited by Thyssen n. 173 at Wallraf Richartz Museum, Cologne).
    Profile of young man with red hat.

Kansas City (Mo.). 61–63 (KRESS COLLECTION K 1565). The Archinto portrait. (?)

Le Mans. 1029. Profile of woman (c.?).

London. 1093. Virgin of the Rocks (later version of Leonardo's at Paris, made under Leonardo's supervision).
    1661, 1662. Side-panels to the Virgin of the Rocks: Music-making Angels. *Plate* 1405.
    1665. Portrait of youth. Sd and d. 1494. *Plate* 1406.
    5752. Profile of lady (formerly Gutekunst). *Plate* 1407.

Lugano. THYSSEN COLLECTION. Portrait of Valante Balbiani.
    Profile of Rodolfo Gonzaga.

Madrid. LÁZARO COLLECTION. Youthful Christ.

Milan. AMBROSIANA. Profile of young lady.
    BIBLIOTECA TRIVULZIANA. Ill. Mss. Donato Grammatica codex 2167: miniatures on ff. 1 verso, 10 verso, 42 verso, 52 verso.
    BRERA. 790. Portrait of young man. After 1500.
    CASTELLO. 73, 92. Fragments of frescoes: Scenes of Creation. (?)
    CONTI PORRO (EX). Portrait of Gian Galeazzo Sforza.

Modena. 48. Profile of man in scalloped cap.

Monaco (Alpes-Maritimes). PRINCE DE MONACO. Profile of Lucien I Grimaldi.

New York. 91.26.5. Girl with cherries. (?) [*Plate* 367.]

Oxford. CHRIST CHURCH. 156. Copy of Beatrice d'Este, Paris.

Paris. MUSÉE JACQUEMART-ANDRÉ. 666. Profile of lady.
    BARON SCHICKLER (EX). Profile of Beatrice d'Este (copies at Florence and Oxford).

Philadelphia (Pa.). J. G. JOHNSON COLLECTION. 264. Profile of old man.
    265. Profile of young woman.

Vaprio d'Adda (Milano). VILLA LITTA MELZI. Fresco: Madonna and Child. (?)

Vienna. 69. Emperor Maximilian. Sd and d. 1502. *Plate* 1409.

Washington (D.C.). 649 (WIDENER COLLECTION). Profile of Bianca Maria Sforza (ribbon of jewel inscribed 'Merito et Tempore') (another c. after Leonardo, by Bernardino de' Conti, in Paris).

    1145 (KRESS COLLECTION K 1526). So-called Beatrice d'Este (another c. after Leonardo, by Bernardino de' Conti, in Paris, Jacquemart-André 658). (?)

DOMENICO DI BARTOLO

Siena. About 1400– *before* 1447. *Pupil probably of Taddeo di Bartolo; influenced by the earliest Florentine Naturalists.*

Bridgeport (Conn.). MUSEUM OF ART, SCIENCE AND INDUSTRY, KRESS STUDY COLLECTION. K 269. Cassone panel (companion to Philadelphia): A couple kneeling before a king (*Decameron* V, 2?). *Plate* 793.

Brooklyn (N.Y.). 34.840. Madonna of Humility. (?)

Florence. FERRONI COLLECTION (EX). Three panels: SS. Francis, Anthony of Padua and Paul. (?)

Melbourne. 2124/4. S. George and the Dragon. (?)

Paris. 1624. Panel from pilaster of altarpiece: S. Jerome reading. (?)

Perugia. 116. Polyptych from S. Giuliana: Madonna and Child with kneeling nun; SS. Benedict, John Baptist, Juliana and Bernard; in trefoils of pinnacles, blessing Redeemer, Angel and Virgin of Annunciation, SS. Peter and Paul; in predella, S. John Baptist goes into Wilderness, preaches to the Multitudes, is beheaded, preaches to Herod, Baptism of Christ. Sd and d. 1438.

Philadelphia (Pa.). J. G. JOHNSON COLLECTION. 20. Cassone panel (companion to Bridgeport): A family, a girl praying by her bed, a couple (*Decameron* V, 2?).

    102. Madonna and Child. Sd and d. 1437. *Plate* 792.

Pisa. B.P. V, 14. Blessed Ranieri. (?)

    DUOMO, R. PILLAR. Fresco: S. Jerome. (?)

Princeton (N.J.). 62.58 'Platt' Madonna and Child enthroned (fr. from central panel of altarpiece). *Plate* 791.

Siena. 164. Madonna and Child with five Angels. Sd and d. 1433.

    207. Madonna of Humility and Angels. E. (?)

    PALAZZO PUBBLICO, GROUND FLOOR, SALA DI BICCHERNA, L. WALL. Parts of Sano di Pietro's fresco of Coronation: eight heads of Saints to left, head of praying saint to right, and five heads in medallions.

    S. MARIA ASSUNTA (DUOMO), R. TRANSEPT. Intarsia of marble floor on design of the artist: Emperor Sigismund enthroned (see also Matteo di Giovanni, Benvenuto di Giovanni, Cozzarelli and Beccafumi). 1434. *Plate* 790-a.

    S. RAIMONDO AL RIFUGIO (CONSERVATORI FEMMINILI), ALTAR R. Virgin in prayer.

Siena (contd.). SPEDALE DI S. MARIA DELLA SCALA, BIBLIOTECA OR SALA DI S. PIETRO. Fresco transferred in 1610 to decorate end wall: Madonna of Mercy worshipped by Pope Eugenius IV, Cardinals and Saints (r.). Sd and d. 1445.

— PELLEGRINAIO. Frescoes: Right wall: I—Care, Education and Marriage of the Foundlings (1440); II—Feeding and Clothing of the Poor (1443); III—Care of the Sick (1443). Left wall: IV—Pope Celestinus III grants privilege of independence to the Spedale (1443); V—Blessed Agostino Novello gives the habit to the Rector of the Hospital (with Priamo della Quercia, who painted onlookers on left); VI—Enlargement of the Spedale with funds given by the Bishop (1443). [*Plate 270.*] *Plates 795, 796.*

— SALA DI S. PIO (INFERMERIA). Monochrome fresco: Blessed Sorori in prayer.

Venice. CA' D'ORO. Birth-plate: Birth of S. John Baptist (r.).

Vienna. FIGDOR COLLECTION (EX). Lid of marriage-box: Gentleman greeting a lady.

Washington (D.C.). 796 (KRESS COLLECTION. K 1388). Madonna and Child enthroned with SS. Peter and Paul. *Plate 794.*

DOSSO

Giovanni Lutero, called Dosso. Ferrarese. Documented at Mantua 1512, at Florence 1517; was possibly in Rome between 1520 and 1522; died 1542. Developed under influence of Giorgione, Titian and later Raphael. Was assisted by his brother Battista.

Allentown (Pa.). MUSEUM OF ART. 60.13.KB. KRESS COLLECTION. K 226. 'Barberini' Standard-bearer.

Amherst (Mass.). AMHERST COLLEGE. 1961.77. KRESS COLLECTION. K 1123B. S. James (fr. of altarpiece, companion to Tucson; with Battista).

Bergamo. SIGRA BICE EYNARD FRIZZONI. Roundel: Angel playing harp.
    LORENZELLI COLLECTION. Predella panel (?): Holy Family with Infant S. John.

Berlin. 161. Admiral Giovanni Moro. (?) (Destroyed 1945.)

Berlin-Ost. 264. The four Church Fathers (with Battista).

Birmingham. BARBER INSTITUTE. One of ten panels with episodes from the Aeneid, from the 'Camerino d'Alabastro' of Alfonso I d'Este in Ferrara: Aeneas landing in Africa (companion to Ottawa). ca 1520. *Plate 1741.*

Bucarest. Inv. 1. Oval fr. of Holy Family and Infant S. John (st.; possibly Battista).

Budapest. 4442. Madonna and Child with Bishop Saint and kneeling woman.

Budrio (Bologna). PINACOTECA CIVICA INZAGHI. Madonna and Child in Glory with SS. Roch and Sebastian.*

Cambridge (Mass.). FOGG ART MUSEUM. 1966.74. GIFT OF E. H. ABBOT JR. Gentleman with large hat.

Canford Manor. VISCOUNT WIMBORNE (EX). Rest on Flight with Infant S. John (st.).

Cardiff. 287. Manto and her son, founder of Mantua.*

Castle Ashby. MARQUESS OF NORTHAMPTON. Sleeping Antiope (with Battista).

Chantilly. 43. Lady in turban (c.).

Cleveland (Ohio). 16,803. Young man holding letter. L. (?)

    49.185. Holy Family and Shepherd.

Coral Gables (Fla.). LOWE ART GALLERY. 61.26 (KRESS COLLECTION. K 1529). Flight into Egypt (st.). *Plate 1757.*

Darmstadt. 94. General in armour. *Plate 1747.*

Detroit (Michigan). 30.412. Holy Family in landscape (simplified version by Battista at Parma).

Dresden. 125. S. Michael (companion to Battista Dossi's S. George). 1540. *Plate 1754.*

    126. Justice (finished after his death by Battista). 1544.

    127. Peace (st.). 1544.

    128. Coronation of Virgin and below, the four Church Fathers and S. Bernardino. 1532. Destroyed.

    129. Immaculate Conception and SS. Anselm, Ambrose, Jerome and Augustine. Destroyed.

    130, 131. Dawn, Night (st.). 1544.

    155. Portrait of scholar.

Eger (Hungary). GALERIE. Diamond-shaped panel from ceiling of 'Camerino d'Alabastro' in Este Palace in Ferrara: Fawns and nymph (companion to Modena and Venice). ca 1525.

Faenza. Two fragments of Christ among Doctors: Head of Virgin, Head of Pharisee. Dated on frame of altarpiece still in situ (First Chapel R., Duomo) 1536.

Ferrara. Inv. 178, 180. Two predella panels (see Garofalo, Ferrara n. 161): Adoration of Shepherds, Adoration of Magi. (c?). 1519.

    Inv. 186. Altarpiece from Portomaggiore: Madonna and Child enthroned, worshipped by SS. John Baptist and Jerome (with Battista).

    Inv. 187. S. John Evangelist (with Battista).

    Inv. 189–194. Polyptych from S. Andrea: Madonna and Child enthroned with Infant S. John, Andrew, John Evangelist, Jerome and six more Saints below, Glory of Angel above (p.); at sides, full-length SS. Sebastian and George, seated SS. Ambrose and Augustine (p.); at top, Risen Christ.

Florence. PITTI. 147. Nymph and Satyr. E.

    148. 'Stregoneria'. L.

    380. Bust of S. John Baptist.

    UFFIZI. 889. Portrait of warrior.

    8382. Rest on Flight.

— DEPOT. 7. Madonna and Child appearing to Baptist and Evangelist (r.; from Codigoro).

    MUSEO HORNE. 80. Allegory of Music. *Plate 1751.*

    CHARLES LOESER (EX). Youth behind parapet.(?)

    R. LONGHI. Youth with basket of flowers. *Plate 1744.*

Florence (contd.). CASA STROZZI. Christ in Garden. Possibly 1517.

Frankfurt a/M. 1509. Head of young man. (?)

Genoa. GNECCO COLLECTION. S. John Baptist.

Graz. Inv. 4. Hercules and the Pygmies. *Plate* 1752.

Hampton Court. Inv. 38. Bust of S. William.

    Inv. 46. Man with puzzle ('Carpendo Carperis Ipse').

    Inv. 151. Holy Family with S. Elizabeth.

    Inv. 883. Gentleman holding letter. *Plate* 1748.

    Inv. 906. Portrait of gentleman with left hand on his heart.

Hartford (Conn.). WADSWORTH ATHENEUM. Scene from Ariosto's *Orlando Furioso*
      (st.?).

Leningrad. 403. Sibyl.

London. 1234. Poet and Muse (fr.). *Plate* 1745.

    3924. Adoration of Magi. *Plate* 1743.

    4032. Pietà.

    5279. Bacchanal.

   PETER CORBETT. Ariadne (fr.).

   DONALDSON COLLECTION (EX). 'Rochdale' Venus in landscape (with Battista). L.
      Plate 1760.

Milan. BRERA. 431.432. Francesco d'Este as S. George; S. John Baptist. L.

    433. S. Sebastian.

   BARGELLESI COLLECTION. Nativity with Virgin drying towel by brazier.

   SAIBENE COLLECTION. Holy Family.*

    Moses striking the Rock (st.).

    Sacra Conversazione with three Holy Children (st.).

Milwaukee (Wis.). ALFRED BADER. Seated old Prophet (companion to New York
    and Tel Aviv).

Modena. 145. Judith (g.p.).

    171. Madonna and Child in Glory appears to SS. Michael and George.

    177. Alfonso d'Este (st.).

    178. Ercole d'Este (after a lost Ercole Roberti?). 1524.

    169. Court jester.

    172–176. Diamond-shaped panels with three figures each: 'Musica Corda Levat';
      'Modica Mensa Juvat'; Scene of Seduction; Lovers; Bacchus (companions to
      Eger and to Venice, Cini; from Este palace at Ferrara).

   DUOMO, SECOND ALTAR L. S. Sebastian between SS. John Baptist and Jerome;
    above, Madonna and Child between SS. Lawrence and Roch. 1522. *Plate* 1746.

   S. BIAGIO (CARMINE). Albert the Great (p.?). 1530.

Moscow. PUSHKIN MUSEUM. Landscape with S. Francis receiving Stigmata, S.
    Jerome in Wilderness, Martyrdom of S. Catherine, S. Christopher, S. George
    and the Dragon.

Naples. 593. Madonna and Child with Infant S. John (st.?).

New York. 26.83. Three Ages of Man.

CHRYSLER COLLECTION. Man holding tablet with numbers (formerly Baltimore, Walters, 1676; companion to Milwaukee and Tel Aviv).

Ottawa. NATIONAL GALLERY OF CANADA. One of ten panels with episodes from the Aeneid, from the 'Camerino d'Alabastro' of Alfonso I d'Este: Aeneas and the Cumaean Sibyl at the entrance of the Underworld (companion to Birmingham). ca 1520. *Plate* 1742.

Paris. 1554. Rest on Flight. (?)

Parma. 391. Adoration of Magi (st.).

1074. S. Michael and Assumption (from Duomo at Reggio; mostly by Battista). 1533.

Pesaro. VILLA IMPERIALE, SALA DELLE CARIATIDI. Decorative frescoes (p.). 1532–33.

Philadelphia (Pa.). J. G. JOHNSON COLLECTION. 251. Prelate pointing at drawing of maze.

Portomaggiore. MUNICIPIO. See Ferrara 186.

Providence (R.I.). 54.177. Noah entering the Ark (r.).

Rome. CAMPIDOGLIO, PINACOTECA. 1. Holy Family (finished by Battista).

GALLERIA NAZIONALE, PALAZZO BARBERINI. SS. John Evangelist and Bartholomew with two donors (from Palazzo Chigi; p.). 1527.

GALLERIA BORGHESE. 1. Apollo.

22. SS. Cosmas and Damian cure a man (from Spedale di S. Anna at Ferrara).

181. Astolfo with the head of Giant Orilla or Saul and David (c.?).

211. Madonna and Child.

215. Nativity (with Battista).

217. Circe or Melissa.

220. Nativity.

225. Gyges and Candaules.

304. Diana and Calisto (execution by Battista).

GALLERIA COLONNA. Man in armour. (?)

GALLERIA DORIA PAMPHILI. 411. Dido.

447. Girolamo Beltramoto. E. (?)

MUSEO DI CASTEL SANT'ANGELO. Bacchanal.

SENATORE CESARE SILI (EX). Penitent S. Jerome.

CONTE LEONARDO VITETTI. S. Jerome in Wilderness.

GASPARINI COLLECTION. Tournament.*

(Environs). MENTANA. F. ZERI. Forest with goats (fr.).

Rovigo. 224-226 (147, 150, 151). Madonna and Child enthroned with five Saints; SS. Benedict and Bartholomew; SS. Lucy and Agatha (mostly by Battista).

Stockholm. 2163. Portrait of man with large hat. (?)

Tel Aviv. A. ROSNER. Young seated Prophet (companion to Milwaukee and New York). *Plate* 1750.

Trent. CASTELLO DEL BUON CONSIGLIO. Frescoes. 1531–32.

— TOP OF STAIRCASE. S. Vigilius recommends Cardinal Clesius to the Virgin and Child. d. 1532.

Trent. CASTELLO DEL BUON CONSIGLIO (contd.). SALA GRANDE. Frieze with Putti playing (mostly Battista).

— BIBLIOTECA, VAULT. Twelve hexagonal sections with Poets or Philosophers.

— — WALLS. Fathers of the Church; Madonna and Child with Bishop Clesius (r.).

— ANTICHAPEL, VAULT. Putti; in 16 lunettes, Gods and Goddesses (chiefly Battista).

— STUA DELLA FAMEJA. In spandrels, simulated statues; in lunettes, Aesop's Fables (with Battista and others; found under whitewash, 1961–1964).*

— ROOM ABOVE CHAPEL. Frieze with busts of Emperors and Empresses; Astronomers; simulated statues (p.).

— CAMERA DEGLI STUCCHI. Virtues and Liberal Arts (g.p.). d. 1532.

Tucson (Arizona). ST. PHILIP'S IN THE HILLS, KRESS STUDY COLLECTION. K 1123A. Fragment of altarpiece: S. Philip (with Battista; companion to Amherst).

Turin. GUALINO COLLECTION (EX). Circe.

Tyninghame (East Lothian). EARL OF HADDINGTON. Sancta Paula.

Venice. CONTE VITTORIO CINI. 2047. Woman and warrior.

Inv. 6265. Diamond-shaped panel from Este palace at Ferrara: Anger, Sorrow and Merriment (companion to Modena and Eger). ca 1526.

A. FREZZATI (EX). Court jester (variant of Modena).

Vienna. 25. Penitent S. Jerome. E. Sd.

— DIRECTOR'S ROOM. Young man pointing to right.

9110. 'Lanckoronski' Jupiter, Mercury and Iris. *Plate* 1749.

Washington (D.C.). 361 (KRESS COLLECTION 448). Departure of the Argonauts.

481 (KRESS COLLECTION 1129). Santa Lucretia.

716 (KRESS COLLECTION 1323). Circe or the sorceress Alcina. [*Plate* 389.]

Worcester (Mass.). 1921.79. Rest on Flight (r.).

Homeless. Temptation of Christ. *Plate* 1755.

The Baptist's head brought to Herod. E. *Plate* 1740.

Holy Family with Infant S. John. *Plate* 1756.

DOSSI, Battista

Ferrarese. Went to Rome 1517, died 1548. Follower and assistant of his brother Dosso; influenced by such Flemings as Scorel. The following are a few examples of his work.

Amherst. See Dosso.

Bergamo. 260. Madonna and Child with S. George and Bishop Saint.

FRIZZONI COLLECTION (EX). Small Lunette: Putti holding Crown over Este Eagle.

Berlin-Ost. See Dosso.

Breslau. 369. Beheading of Baptist. d. 1541.

Castle Ashby. MARQUESS OF NORTHAMPTON. Sleeping Antiope (with Dosso).

Castle Howard (Yorks.). MAJOR HOWARD. Rest on Flight with Infant S. John.

Dresden. 124. S. George (companion to Dosso's S. Michael; paid to Dosso and Battista 1540; execution by Girolamo da Carpi).

126. Justice (begun by Dosso). 1544.

El Paso (Texas). MUSEUM OF ART. 1961–6/19 (KRESS COLLECTION. K 1749). The Hunt of the Calydonian Boar. (?)

Ferrara. Inv. 186. Altarpiece from Portomaggiore: Madonna and Child enthroned, worshipped by SS. Jerome and John Baptist (on Dosso's design).

Inv. 187. S. John Evangelist (with Dosso).

ESTE PALACE (EX). Tapestry on his design: Arethusa transformed into a pool (companion to Paris). 1543–45.

Hamburg. RUTH NOTTEBOHM. Stoning of S. Stephen (formerly Berlin, Gottschewski).

Hildesheim. 350. Venus.

Leipzig. FRITZ HARCK (EX). Flight into Egypt. *Plate 1758.*

London. I. O. CHANCE. 'Northwick' Adoration of Shepherds.

DONALDSON. See Dosso.

Milan. BRERA. 431, 432. Side-panels of triptych (with Dosso).

SAIBENE COLLECTION. 'Agosti Mendoza' Holy Family reading from large book.*

Modena. 170. Madonna and Child with SS. Francis and Bernardino appearing to male and female Confratelli della Neve.

179. Nativity. 1534. *Plate 1759.*

Naples. 76. Madonna and Child with kneeling Saint.

Paris. LOUVRE, SALLE DE LA COLONNADE. Two tapestries on his design: At the Fall of Phaethon, Io, transformed into a cow, is watched by Argus in the shape of Juno's peacock, the Heliades are turned into poplars, and Cycnus into a swan; four Caryatids against a riverscape (companions to Ferrara). 1543–45.

Parma. 396. Madonna and Child in landscape (simplified version of Dosso at Detroit).

1074. S. Michael and Assumption, from Duomo at Reggio (on Dosso's design). 1533/34.

Rome. CAMPIDOGLIO, PINACOTECA. 1. Holy Family (begun by Dosso).

GALLERIA BORGHESE. 184. Psyche carried to Olympus.

215. Nativity with Infant S. John and Angel (with Dosso).

245. Rest on Flight.

304. Diana and Callisto (with Dosso).

s.n. Some Tapestries for Estensi. 1544.

GALLERIA COLONNA. 145. Cassone: Mythological scene.

Rovigo. 217 (46). Baptism. (?)

224–226 (147, 150, 151). Triptych: Madonna and Child enthroned with five Saints; SS. Benedict and Bartholomew; SS. Lucy and Agatha (on Dosso's design).

Salzburg. RESIDENZ–GALERIE, CZERNIN COLLECTION. 88. Adoration of Shepherds.

Trent. CASTELLO DEL BUONCONSIGLIO. ANTI CHAPEL. Frescoes: see under Dosso. 1531–1532.

Tucson see Dosso.

Venice. CONTE VITTORIO CINI. Inv. 5988. Adoration of Magi.

    6347. 'Oldenburg' Holy Family with Infant S. John.

Wilanow. CASTLE. Madonna and Holy Children.*

Homeless. Noli me Tangere (repr. *Arte Antica e Moderna*, 1965, pl. 133A).*

    Rest on Flight (repr. *Arte Antica e Moderna*, 1965, pl. 133B).*

DUCCIO DI BUONINSEGNA

Sienese. Active 1279 to his death, not later than 1318. Heir to the finest Byzantine traditions of the eleventh and twelfth centuries.

Balcarres (Fife, Scotland). EARL OF CRAWFORD AND BALCARRES. Crucifixion from Chapel of S. Gualbert in S. Trinita, Florence. *Plate* 38.

Berlin. III, 43 (EX). Pinnacle (to Siena Maesta?): Half-length Angel. (Sold 1922, now in South Hadley.)

Berne. 873. Madonna and Child enthroned with six Angels.

Boston (Mass.). 45–880. Portable altarpiece: Crucifixion with blessing Redeemer and two Angels above; in wings, two Bishop Saints (g.p.). *Plates* 33, 35.

Brussels. JACQUES STOCLET. Madonna and Child.

    Pinnacle (to Siena Maestà?): Half-length Angel (st.; companion to Florence, Philadelphia and South Hadley).

Budapest. 6 (43). Predella panel: S. John Baptist preaching (st., r.).

Florence. UFFIZI. 'Rucellai' Madonna and Child enthroned with six Angels; in frame, thirty roundels with Saints and Prophets. Commissioned by the Laudesi di S. Maria Novella in 1285. [*Plate* 243.]

    CONTINI BONACOSSI COLLECTION. 'Tadini Buonsegni Madonna' (st.; with Ugolino di Nerio?).

    LOESER COLLECTION (EX). Two pinnacles (to Siena Maestà?): Half-length Angels (st.; see Brussels).

Hampton Court. ROYAL COLLECTIONS. 1223. Portable altarpiece: Crucifixion; Madonna and Child enthroned with four Angels and Annunciation below; Christ and Virgin enthroned with six Angels and S. Francis receiving Stigmata below (g.p.). *Plate* 30.

Langeais (Touraine). CHÂTEAU. Madonna and Child (st.).

London. 566. Portable altarpiece: Madonna and Child with four Angels; SS. Dominic and Aurea; in pinnacles, Daniel, Moses, Isaiah, David, Abraham, Jacob, Jeremiah. *Plate* 31.

    1139. Predella panel from front of Siena Maestà: Annunciation. 1308–11.

    1140, 1330. Predella panels from back of Siena Maestà: Christ healing the Blind Man, Transfiguration. 1308–11.

Massa Marittima. DUOMO. Fragment of a 'Maestà': front, Madonna and Child enthroned; back, Crucifixion flanked by cut-down Scenes of Passion [Christ before Annas, Crowning with Thorns, Way to Calvary, Agony in Garden, Descent from Cross, Entombment, Mocking of Christ, all r.] (st.; with assistance of Simone Martini?). Not finished in 1316.

New York. FRICK COLLECTION. Predella panel from back of Siena Maestà: Temptation of Christ on the mountain. 1308–11. *Plate 36.*

MR AND MRS J. D. ROCKEFELLER JR. Predella panels from back of Siena Maestà: Christ and the Woman of Samaria; Raising of Lazarus. 1308–11.

Perugia. 29. Centre panel of polyptych from S. Domenico: Madonna and Child; six Angels in spandrels.

Philadelphia (Pa.). J. G. JOHNSON COLLECTION. 88. Pinnacle (to Siena Maestà?): Half-length Angel (st.; see Brussels).

Siena. 20. Madonna and Child enthroned with four Angels and three Franciscan monks. E. *Plate 29.*

28. Polyptych: Madonna and Child, SS. Augustine, Paul, Peter, Dominic; in pinnacles, Redeemer and four Angels (Madonna only; the rest, st.).

35. Portable altarpiece: Madonna and Child enthroned with two Angels, SS. Peter and Paul and female donor; below, eight busts of Saints; above, Coronation of Virgin, Angel and Virgin of Annunciation; in wings, Nativity, Flagellation, Way to Calvary, Crucifixion, Deposition, Entombment (p., r.).

47. Polyptych: Madonna and Child; SS. Agnes, John Evangelist, John Baptist, Mary Magdalen; upper register, busts of Abraham, Isaac, Jacob, Jeremiah, Moses, David, Isaiah, Elijah, Daniel, Malachi; in pinnacles, blessing Redeemer, and four Angels (g.p., r.).

SOCIETÀ ESECUTORI DI PIE DISPOSIZIONI. Portable altarpiece: Crucifixion, Flagellation, Entombment (r.).

— SPEDALE DELLA SCALA. Crucifixion (st.).

S. MARIA ASSUNTA (DUOMO). Stained glass window: Dormition, Assumption and Coronation of Virgin; four Evangelists and four Saints. 1288.

— MUSEO DELL'OPERA. 37. 'Crevole' Madonna and Child, with two Angels (not to be confused with Madonna from Crevole by Master of Città di Castello, n. 24).

26–55. Fragments of dismembered Maestà formerly in the Duomo of Siena (1308-1311):

Middle part from front of Maestà: Madonna and Child enthroned, with twenty Angels, SS. Catherine, Paul, John Evangelist, Ansanus, Savinus, Agnes, Peter, John Baptist, Victor, Crescentius, and ten Apostles above. Sd. *Plate 32.*

Six predella panels (Infancy of Christ and Prophets) from front of Maestà: Adoration of Magi, Solomon, Circumcision, Malachi, Massacre of Innocents, Jeremiah, Flight into Egypt, Hoseas (other panels in London and Washington).

Six top panels from front of Maestà: The Virgin receives the annunciation of her imminent death, takes leave of S. John Evangelist, takes leave of the Apostles, Dormitio, Funeral, Burial of Virgin (the central panel is missing). *Plate 37.*

Siena. S. MARIA ASSUNTA (DUOMO), MUSEO DELL'OPERA (contd.). Middle part from back of Maestà; twenty-six Scenes of Passion [lower register—Christ enters Jerusalem, Washing of Feet, Last Supper, Christ talks to the Apostles, Judas' pact with the High Priests, Agony in the Garden, Betrayal of Christ, Denial of Peter, Christ before Annas, Christ before Caiphas, Beating of Christ, The Pharisees accuse Christ, Christ interrogated by Pontius Pilate; upper register—Christ before Herod, Christ white-clad before Pilate, Flagellation, Crowning with Thorns, Pilate washes his hands, Way to Calvary, Crucifixion, Deposition, Entombment, the three Maries at the Tomb, Christ's Descent into Limbo, Noli me tangere, Christ on the way to Emmaus]. [*Plates 245–248.*]

Three predella panels (The preaching of Christ) from back of Maestà: Christ disputing with the Doctors; Christ tempted in the Temple, Marriage at Cana (other panels in London, New York and Washington). [*Plate 244*].

Six top panels from back of Maestà: Christ appearing to the Apostles through closed doors; Doubting Thomas; Christ appearing on the lake of Tiberias, on Mount of Galilee, at supper before His Ascension; Descent of the Holy Ghost; (the central panel is missing). [*Plate 249.*]

South Hadley (Mass.). MOUNT HOLYOKE COLLEGE. GIFT OF MRS CAROLINE HILL. Pinnacle (to Siena Maestà?): Half-length Angel (st., see Brussels).

Washington (D.C.). 8 (MELLON COLLECTION). Predella panel from front of Siena Maestà: Isaiah, Nativity, Ezechiel. 1308–11. *Plate 34.*

252 (KRESS COLLECTION. K 283). Predella panel from back of Siena **Maestà**: Calling of the Sons of Zebedee. 1308–11. [*Plate 250.*]

DUCCIO'S Contemporary Imitators and Immediate Followers

Badia a Isola. SS. SALVATORE E CIRINO. Madonna and Child enthroned with two Angels (Master between Duccio and Cimabue). *Plate 39.*

Besançon. MUSÉE DES BEAUX-ARTS. Christ on Cross, mourning Virgin, mourning Evangelist in roundels.

Birmingham (Ala.). MUSEUM OF ART. 61.104 (KRESS COLLECTION. K 592). Fragmentary polyptych: Madonna and Child, SS. Augustine, John Baptist, Michael and Dionysius Areopagita.

Bonn. DR P. CLEMEN (EX). Deposition.

Brussels. PHILIPPE STOCLET (EX). Pinnacle: Crucifixion.

Buonconvento. PIEVE DI S. PIETRO. Madonna and Child (r.).

Castelfiorentino. COLLEGIATA DEI SS. IPPOLITO E BIAGIO, HIGH ALTAR. Madonna and Child (close to Cimabue).

Chianciano. MUSEO DI ARTE SACRA. Painted Crucifix from S. Polo in Rosso.

Fragmentary polyptych from S. Giovanni Battista: Madonna and Child, SS. Michael, John Baptist, John Evangelist and Bartholomew; pairs of Saints above (two pairs missing).

Cincinnati (Ohio). 1953.220. Leaf of diptych: Crucifixion.

Cleveland (Ohio). 62.257-8. Two pinnacles: Busts of Angels (companions to Raleigh).

Cologne. Inv. 608. Panel of polyptych (companion to following, and to Manchester and Utrecht): S. John Baptist (same hand as Badia a Isola).

— (EX). Pinnacles of polyptych (companion to above, and to Manchester and Utrecht): Redeemer and four Angels (same hand as Badia a Isola).

Esztergom. Inv. 55.134/5. Two pinnacles: Isaiah, Jeremiah.

Florence. CHARLES LOESER (EX). Madonna and Child.

Indianapolis (Ind.). JOHN HERRON ART MUSEUM. 51.98. 'Orsini Baroni' Madonna and Child (r.).

THE CLOWES FUND. 'Tratzeberg' Madonna and Child (fr.; same hand as Badia a Isola).

Leningrad. PRINCE ANDRÉ GAGARIN (EX). Crucifixion.

London. 565. Fragment of 'Maestà': Madonna and Child with six Angels (close to Master of Città di Castello, same hand as Siena 592).

Montalcino. MUSEO CIVICO. Triptych from Conservatorio di S. Caterina: Madonna and Child, S. Augustine, S. Dominic; in pinnacles, Redeemer and two Angels.

Montepulciano. MUSEO CIVICO. Madonna and Child with two Angels.

Moscow. PUSHKIN MUSEUM. 224. Madonna and Child (formerly Stchekin Collection).

New York. 20.160. Madonna and Child, with Annunciation and Nativity below (same hand as Birmingham).

R. LEHMAN COLLECTION. Diptych: Madonna and Child with nine Angels; Crucifixion.

'Goodhart' leaf of diptych: Madonna and Child worshipped by father and son (same hand as Birmingham).

Nocera Umbra. PINACOTECA. Madonna and Child (r.).

Paris. MARQUIS DE GANAY. Madonna and Child (r.).

REINACH COLLECTION. Madonna and Child enthroned with eight Angels, SS. Catherine and Lucy; five busts of Saints below and two busts of Saints above (same hand as Birmingham).

Pomarance (Volterra). S. GIOVANNI BATTISTA, L. OF ENTRANCE. Madonna of the goldfinch. d. 1329.

Raleigh (N.C.). MUSEUM OF ART. GL.60.17.2. KRESS COLLECTION. K 219. Pinnacle formerly Conte Della Gherardesca, Florence: Christ blessing (companion to Cleveland).

Rome. SCHIFF COLLECTION (EX). Madonna and Child (r.; from S. Francesco, Lucca).

San Rocco a Pilli (Siena). PARISH CHURCH. Madonna and Child.

San Sepolcro. MUSEO. Polyptych from S. Chiara: Resurrection (between Segna and Pietro Lorenzetti, close to early Taddeo di Bartolo).

Siena. 18. Madonna and Child enthroned (follower of Master di Città di Castello).

22. Two panels of polyptych: S. John Baptist with Angel above; S. Peter with Angel above (r.).

Siena (contd.). 583. Madonna and Child (r.).

592. Madonna and Child (same hand as London 565).

593. Madonna and Child (same hand as Badia a Isola).

604. Madonna and Child with four Angels and two female Saints; Annunciation above.

606. Centre panel of polyptych: Madonna and Child (Master of Chianciano).

South Hadley (Mass.). MRS SAMUEL HALE. Three cut-down panels of polyptych (companion to Cologne and Utrecht): SS. Paul, John Evangelist and Peter (same hand as Badia a Isola).

Utrecht. 4. Centre panel of Ramboux polyptych: Madonna and Child (fr.; companion to Cologne and Manchester; same hand as Badia a Isola).

Venice. CONTE VITTORIO CINI. Inv. 6314. Fragment of 'Maestà' from Argentieri Collection: Madonna and Child with four Angels (r.; same hand as Badia a Isola).

Inv. 6494. Double diptych: Madonna and Child, Crucifixion, Descent from Cross, Entombment. *Plates* 61, 63.

Washington. 1629 (KRESS COLLECTION K 2063). Madonna and Child enthroned with four Angels (close to Master of Città di Castello).

Homeless. Enthroned Madonna and Child with two Angels. *Plate* 62.

Enthroned Madonna and Child with four Angels. *Plate* 60.

Madonna and Child (see *Dedalo* XI 1930, p. 265).

ERCOLE DA FERRARA

Ercole de' Roberti or Grandi or da Ferrara. ca 1450–96. Active in Bologna 1482–86; at Venice and Mantua 1489–90; followed Alfonso d'Este to Rome in 1492. Pupil of Tura, assistant and partner of Francesco del Cossa; influenced by the Bellini, Mantegna and Antonello.

Baltimore (Md). WALTERS ART GALLERY. 476. Scene from Story of Susanna (st.; fr.; companion to Homeless).

Bergamo. 533. S. John Evangelist (fr.).

Berlin. 111. Altarpiece from S. Lazzaro at Ferrara: Madonna and Child with SS. John Evangelist, Apollonia, Catherine and Jerome (begun by Tura, executed by Ercole). (Destroyed 1945.)

112C. S. John Baptist. E. [*Plate* 340.]

112D. Madonna and Child. E.

113A. Atalanta's Race (c.).

Berlin-Ost. 112E. S. Jerome.

Bologna. Inv. 591. Deposition (S. Joseph of Arimathea, S. Francis, S. Catherine and landscape by much later hand).

Inv. 603. S. Michael (fr.).

s.n. Detached fresco from Cappella Garganelli in S. Pietro: Head of Magdalen (fr. of Crucifixion). 1482–86.

ISTITUTO DI STORIA DELL'ARTE. Portrait of Giovanni II Bentivoglio.

S. PIETRO, SACRISTY, BERENSON GIFT. Copy of Crucifixion (lower part left and right) frescoed in the Cappella Garganelli (see also Paris and Sarasota for copies of Death and Assumption of Virgin; Hanover for copies of Donors; Annunciation is entirely lost).

Chicago (Ill.). 47.90. Madonna of the cherries. L.

Dresden. 45, 46. Predella panels from High Altar of S. Giovanni in Monte at Bologna: Way to Calvary, Betrayal of Christ (companions to Liverpool). Before 1486. [*Plate* 342.]

Ferrara. Inv. 70. S. Jerome reading. E.

PALAZZO SCHIFANOIA, SALA DEI MESI. See under Cossa and Ferrarese before 1510. ca 1470.

VENDEGHINI COLLECTION. Panel (from pilaster of Cossa's Griffoni polyptych; companion to Paris, Rotterdam and Venice, Cini): S. Petronius in niche (on Cossa's design).

Florence. UFFIZI. 8542 (dep. at Museo Horne). S. Sebastian (c.).

BERENSON COLLECTION. Predella panel: Crucifixion. [*Plate* 343.]
Two panels: S. Jerome and S. John Baptist (st.).

CONTE RUCELLAI. Battle of Argonauts (fr.; st.; companion to London, Lugano, Padua, Paris).

Hanover. LANDESMUSEUM, KESTNER 16, 17. Kneeling male and female donors (copy of destroyed fresco in Cappella Garganelli at S. Pietro, Bologna).

Lewisburg (Pa.). BUCKNELL UNIVERSITY. BL.KIO (KRESS STUDY COLLECTION. K 387). Madonna and Child with pears. E. (?)

Liverpool. 2773. Predella panel from High Altar of S. Giovanni in Monte, Bologna, companion to Dresden: Pietà. Before 1486. *Plate* 750.

London. 1127. Predella panel: Last Supper (companion to 1217); see Rome, Chigi).
1217. Predella panel: Gathering of Manna. *Plate* 753.
1411. Diptych: Nativity; Dead Christ upheld by Angels, with SS. Jerome and Francis. *Plate* 752.

SIR THOMAS BARLOW. Penitent S. Jerome.

LADY HOUSTOUN BOSWALL. Jason kills the dragon before Medea (st.; companion to below and to Florence, Lugano, Padua, Paris).

CHARLES BUTLER (EX). Madonna and blessing Child. (?)

C. P. WILSON. King and Councillors (fr., st.; companion to above and below).

Lugano. THYSSEN COLLECTION. Return of the Argonauts with Medea (st.; companion to Florence, London, Padua, Paris).

Milan. BRERA. 428. Altarpiece from S. Maria in Porto at Ravenna: Madonna and Child enthroned, with SS. Anne, Elizabeth, Augustine and Blessed Pietro degli Onesti. doc. 1480–81. *Plate* 749.

BARGELLESI COLLECTION. Two fragments from a penitent S. Jerome (companions to Saibene?).

Milan (contd.). CANTO COLLECTION (EX). Madonna and blessing Child (p.). L.
   SAIBENE COLLECTION. Lion (fr. of penitent S. Jerome, companion to Bargellesi?).
Modena. 178. Lucretia, Brutus and Collatinus (st.).
New York. 30.95.299. Madonna and Child; Dead Christ upheld by Angels in
   lunette (st.).
Padua. 64 (Inv. 2293). Small roundel: S. Eustace. (?)
      67 (Inv. 424). Hercules and the Argonauts in a boat (st.; companion to
      Florence, London, Lugano, Paris).
Paris. 1677. Four men standing (c. after lost fresco of Death and Assumption of
   Virgin in Cappella Garganelli, S. Pietro, Bologna; see there).
      1677A, B. Two panels from pilasters of Griffoni polyptych, companions to
      Ferrara, Rotterdam and Venice, Cini: S. Michael and S. Apollonia in niches
      (see under Cossa, London). E.
      2684. Christ before Pilate.*
      MUSÉE DES ARTS DÉCORATIFS. Fragment of cassone: Banquet of Argonauts (st.;
      companion to Florence, London, Lugano, Padua).
Philadelphia (Pa.). 243. Bust of lady.
Richmond (Surrey). COOK COLLECTION. 119A. Brutus and Portia (companion to
   Washington).
Rome. CONTE BLUMENSTHIL. Pietà and two donors. L.
   PRINCIPE CHIGI (EX). Abraham and Melchizedek (c. of lost companion to London,
      1127, 1217). *Plate 751.*
   STROGANOFF COLLECTION (EX). Adoration of Shepherds (p.).
   VATICAN, PINACOTECA. 286. Predella to Griffoni polyptych (see under Cossa,
      London): Miracles of S. Vincent Ferrer.
Rotterdam. BOYMANS-VAN BEUNINGEN MUSEUM. 2561. Panel from pilaster of
   Griffoni polyptych, companion to Ferrara, Paris and Venice: S. Anthony
   Abbot in niche (on Cossa's design; see under Cossa, London). E.
   2562. Portrait of Pietro Cenni.
Sarasota (Fla.). RINGLING MUSEUM. Death of Virgin (copy of lost fresco in Garganelli
   Chapel, S. Pietro, Bologna; see there).
Turin. GALLERIA SABAUDA, GUALINO COLLECTION. 664. Madonna and Child. E.
Venice. CONTE VITTORIO CINI. Inv. 4053, 4054, 1218. Three panels from pilasters of
   Griffoni polyptych, once in S. Petronio at Bologna (companions to Ferrara,
   Paris and Rotterdam): SS. Jerome, Catherine, Michael in niches (see for other
   parts under Cossa, London; and for predella, Rome, Vatican). E.
Washington (D.C.). 330–331 (KRESS COLLECTION. K 408, 409). Profiles of Giovanni
   II Bentivoglio and his wife Ginevra.
   (AILSA MELLON BRUCE FUND.) Hasdrubal's wife with her two children (formerly
   Richmond, Cook). [*Plate* 341.]
Homeless. Stoning of the two Elders (fr., st.; companion to Baltimore; repr.
   R. Longhi, *Officina Ferrarese, Nuovi Ampliamenti*, 1956, p. 182, fig. 426).

EUSEBIO DA SAN GIORGIO

Active in Perugia 1492–1540. Pupil of Perugino and Pinturicchio; influenced by the young Raphael.

Assisi. S. DAMIANO. Fresco: Annunciation. d. 1507.
Fresco: S. Francis receiving Stigmata. Sd and d. 1507.

Belgrade. ROYAL PALACE (EX). Tondo: Nativity with Infant S. John.

Boston (Mass.). 52. Bust of S. Sebastian (after Raphael at Bergamo).

Budapest. 1084. Predella: Legendary subject.

Detroit (Mich.). 25.146; 27.10. Predella panels: S. Nicholas of Tolentino resuscitating the birds, saving a youth from drowning. *Plates* 1159–1160.

Dublin. 212. Madonna and Child with young monk and S. Catherine (st. replica of Philadelphia).

Lisciano Niccone (Cortona). VAL DI ROSE, PARISH CHURCH. Madonna and Child with SS. Nicholas of Bari and Romuald, and the Blessed Bucarello and Francesca Romana (g.p.).

Liverpool. 2866. Predella panel: Adoration of Magi.

London. SIR EDUARD MOUNTAIN BT. (EX?). Tondo: Holy Family.

Matelica. S. FRANCESCO, FOURTH CHAPEL R. Madonna and Child enthroned with SS. Anthony of Padua, John Evangelist, Andrew and Nicholas of Tolentino; in predella, three Scenes from Life of S. Anthony of Padua. Sd and d. 1512. *Plate* 1157.
S. GIOVANNI. Madonna and Child.

Minneapolis (Minn.). INSTITUTE OF ARTS (EX). Madonna and Child (fr.).

Naples. SS. TRINITÀ DEI PELLEGRINI. S. Sebastian.

Perugia. 279. Madonna and Child with SS. Bernardino, Thomas of Volterra, Jerome and Sebastian (on Perugino's design). d. 1500.
282. Madonna and Child enthroned with SS. Peter, Catherine, Agatha, Paul and Angels. d. 1509.
287. Adoration of Magi. d. 1505. *Plate* 1155.
343. Madonna and Child with SS. Benedict and John Baptist.
347. SS. Anthony Abbot, Francis and Bernardino. 1513.
MONASTERO DI S. AGNESE, CORO DELLE MONACHE. Frescoes: Mourning Virgin, Evangelist and Angels around sculptured Crucifix; in embrasure of arch, Eternal, S. Roch and S. Sebastian. d. 1519.
S. PIETRO, L. AISLE. Adoration of Magi. d. 1508. *Plate* 1156.

Philadelphia (Pa.). J. G. JOHNSON COLLECTION. 145. Madonna and Child with S. Catherine and young Saint (st., r.).

Rome. VATICAN, PINACOTECA. 221. Madonna and Child with Infant S. John (p.?).
SCHIFF COLLECTION (EX). Predella panel: S. Nicholas of Tolentino saving two hanged men. *Plate* 1158.

Homeless. S. Sebastian. *Plate* 1154.

EVANGELISTA DA PIAN DI MELETO

Evangelista di Maestro Andrea, born at Pian di Meleto (Marches) ca 1470—Urbino 1549.
Pupil of Giovanni Santi, influenced by Ercole Roberti and Perugino.

Altenburg. 113. Madonna and Child with S. Sebastian and adoring Shepherds. (?)
Florence. GALLERIA CORSINI. 408, 410-13, 415. The Muses Clio, Polyhymnia, Melpomene, Calliope, Terpsichore and Erato (on design by Giovanni Santi; from Palazzo Ducale, Urbino). *Plates* 1017, 1019.
Richmond (Surrey). COOK COLLECTION (EX). 49. Annunciation. (?)
Rome. S. PAOLO FUORI LE MURA, PINACOTECA. S. Sebastian between SS. Michael and Roch; inside wings, SS. Peter and Paul; outside wings, Angel and Virgin of Annunciation. L. (?)
Urbino. GALLERIA NAZIONALE DELLE MARCHE. Six Apostles in niches.
   Companion panels: Tobias and the Angel, S. Roch.
   Female martyr with flask of blood.
  DUOMO, SACRISTY. Madonna and Child enthroned with SS. Nicholas, Anthony Abbot, Mary Magdalen and another female Saint.
  S. CROCE. Fresco: S. Sebastian.

FARINATI, Paolo

Verona. 1524–1606. Pupil of Giolfino; influenced by Torbido and Brusasorci.

Amsterdam. RIJKSMUSEUM (FROM THE HAGUE). 921D. A–I. Adoration of Magi.
Arona. SS. GRATINIANO E FELINO, SECOND CHAPEL. Side-canvas to Grenoble Deposition: Three Soldiers opening Sepulchre. doc. 1573.*
  — SECOND CHAPEL R. Side-canvas to Grenoble Deposition: Maries at the Sepulchre. doc. 1573.
Belfiore d'Adige (Verona). S. VITO. Madonna and Child with SS. John Baptist and Paul. 1584.
Berlin. REICHSKANZLER PALAIS (KAISER-FRIEDRICH MUSEUM 305) (EX). Circumcision. (Destroyed 1945.)
Bonn. 237. Bust of old man.
Budapest. 83 (134). Christ carrying Cross.
   110 (175). Madonna and Child with SS. Elizabeth, Michael and Infant John.
   849. Martyrdom of S. Catherine.
Cremia (Lago di Como). S. MICHELE, HIGH ALTAR. S. Michael defeating Lucifer.
  — ALTAR L. S. Anthony Abbot.
Dijon. T.11. Marriage of S. Catherine. (?)
Dunfermline. EARL OF ELGIN (EX). A blacksmith. (?)
Florence. UFFIZI. 932. Head of S. Paul.

Frassino (PESCHIERA DEL GARDA). SANTUARIO DELLA MADONNA. Nativity with SS. Francis and Bernardino. Sd and d. 1560.

Madonna appearing to SS. Francis and Sebastian and Blessed Andrea Grego. Sd and d. 1576. *Plate* 1922.

Holy Family with S. Elizabeth and Infant S. John. d. 1586. *Plate* 1924.

SS. Francis and Anthony Abbot worshipping Eternal. Sd and d. 1560. *Plate* 1921.

Garda. S. STEFANO. S. Stephen. d. 1576.

Gotha. 508. Male portrait.

Grenoble. 481 (Inv. 18). Deposition (side-canvases at Arona). doc. 1573.

Karlsruhe 420. Vision of a monk (replica of Philadelphia, Johnson 193, by Girolamo Muziano). (?)

Lonato (Brescia). PARISH CHURCH. SS. Sebastian, James and Fabian crowned by Angels. Sd and d. 1582.

London. FARRER COLLECTION (EX). Madonna and Child.

Lovere. 81. Man of Sorrows.*

Madrid. DUQUE DE ALBA. Head of old man.

Mantua. DUOMO, CAPPELLA DEL SACRAMENTO. S. Martin and the beggar. 1552. *Plate* 1917.

Milan. BRERA. 117. Last Supper. (?)

POLDI PEZZOLI. 554. Madonna and Child. L.

BAGATTI VALSECCHI COLLECTION. S. Roch.

PALAZZO BORROMEO. 38. Portrait of ecclesiastic.

Mori (Trento). PARISH CHURCH. Madonna of the Rosary. 1604.

Negrano di Villazzano (Trento). CAPPELLA DEL PALAZZO CAZUFFI. Entombment with S. Francis. 1589.

New Haven (Conn.). 1871.100. Christ appearing to SS. Peter and Paul.

New York. HISTORICAL SOCIETY. B–39. Abraham and Hagar.

Padenghe (Brescia). SS. MARIA E EMILIANO. Madonna and Child with SS. Emiliano, Miletto, Cassiano, Ippolito, Vito and Modesto. 1582–9.

Paris. 1586. Council of Trent. (?) *Plate* 1927.

1594. Knight of Malta. (?)

1674E. Madonna and Child with S. Anne, in Glory.

Pavia. Inv. 26. Mystic Marriage of S. Catherine. *Plate* 1929.

Peschiera. MADONNA DEL FRASSINO. See Frassino.

Piacenza. S. SISTO. Martyrdom of S. Fabian.

Miracle of S. Benedict. 1599.

Pozzuolo (Mantua). PARISH CHURCH. Nativity. Sd and d. 1575.*

Prague. Inv. 0814. Magdalen adoring Cross. *Plate* 1918.

Princeton (N.J.). 35.40. Coronation of Virgin with two Portrait Busts.

35.41. Adoration of Shepherds.

Prun de Negrar (Verona). PARISH CHURCH. Conversion of S. Paul. Sd and d. 1590. *Plate* 1923.

S. Michael defeating Lucifer.

Richmond (Surrey). COOK COLLECTION (EX). 184. Two old men.

Rome. GALLERIA BORGHESE. 97. Bust of old man holding gloves. (?)

MUSEO DI PALAZZO VENEZIA. F.N.19193. Madonna and Child with Infant S. John. F.N.19194. Christ on way to Golgotha. *Plate* 1928.

Roverchiara (Verona). S. ZENO. Christ carrying the Cross and SS. Zeno and Lawrence. Sd.*

Sabbionara di Avio (Ala). S. ANTONIO. SS. Anthony, Francis and Paul Hermit.

Salò (Lago di Garda). S. BERNARDINO, CHOIR. Nativity. Sd and d. 1584.
Annunciation. Sd and d. 1584. *Plate* 1925.

San Benedetto Po (Mantua). ABBAZIA DI POLIRONE, ATRIO DELLA SAGRESTIA. Portrait of Mathilda di Canossa (by Orazio Farinati). 1587.

Siena. 636. Christ carrying the Cross. Sd and d. 1592.*

Soave (Verona). S. LORENZO, FIRST ALTAR R. 'Marogna' altarpiece: SS. Bovo, Anthony Abbot and Francis. 1595.

Stuttgart. 522 (Inv. 759). Portrait of a Venetian.

Tarmassia (Verona). PARISH CHURCH. Visitation. 1601.

Trent. CHIESA DEI FRANCESCANI. Deposition (variant of Grenoble, painted for Tommaso Cazuffi). 1589.

Trobbiolo (Volciano, Brescia). CHIESA DELLA TRINITÀ. Trinity with SS. Stephen and Anthony Abbot. 1586–8.

Vangadizza (Verona). PARISH CHURCH. Entombment. Sd.*

Venice. CA' D'ORO. Prelate with open book.

S. ZACCARIA. Crucifixion. 1568.*

Verona. 13. 'Ecce Homo.' Sd. 1562.

58. Knight of Malta.

197. Madonna and Child (fr.).

408. Banner of Capuchin convent: Trinity. 1584–87.

496. SS. Anne, Bartholomew and Jerome. Sd and d. 1568.

497. Adoration of Magi.

501. 'Ecce Homo.' d. 1593.

574. 'Fogazza' altarpiece: Madonna appearing to SS. Onophrius, Francis and Jerome, with male and female donors. Sd and d. 1592.

850. Deposition. 1556.

862. Marriage of S. Catherine. Sd and d. 1602.

Moses and the Daughters of Jethro. 1584.

— SALA GIULIARI. Small cassone: Apollo and Marsyas.

— DEP. PRETURA. Madonna and Child with SS. Francis and Anthony of Padua.

CASA DEGLI ACOLITI (PIAZZA VESCOVADO). Fresco: Pietà. 1567.

CASA NICOLIS (CORTE QUARANTA). Fresco: Coronation of Charles V. 1582.

PALAZZO DELLA GRAN GUARDIA, SALONE, L. WALL. Fresco: Victory of the Veronese over Barbarossa at Vaccaldo. 1598. *Plate* 1926.

S. ANASTASIA, L. TRANSEPT. Deposition. 1589.

Miracle of S. Hyacinth. 1595.

S. GIORGIO IN BRAIDA, CHOIR, L. WALL. Fall of Manna.

— R. WALL. Multiplication of Loaves and Fishes. Sd and d. 1603.

S. GIOVANNI IN FONTE, BEHIND HIGH ALTAR. Baptism. 1568.

MADONNA DI CAMPAGNA. Nativity. Sd and d. 1589.

S. MARIA IN ORGANO, FOURTH ALTAR R. S. Michael. Sd and d. 1596.

— CHOIR. Massacre of Innocents (1556); Feast of S. Gregory; Triumph of Constantine; Christ walking on Water (1558).

S. MARIA DEL PARADISO, HIGH ALTAR. Assumption.

SS. NAZZARO E CELSO, CHOIR. Frescoes: Vault of Apse, Eternal holding Crowns for Martyrs; SS. Nazarus and Celsus dragged before the Emperor and beheaded; Vault above altar: flying Putti; Left lunette, SS. Nazarus and Celsus destroy the idols; Right lunette, the Saints are put in jail. *Plate 1920.*

— WALLS. Four Stories of S. Celsus. 1575.

— SECOND ALTAR R. Annunciation; above, frescoed lunette with Adam and Eve. 1557. *Plate 1919.*

S. PAOLO, FIRST ALTAR R. Deposition.

— FIRST ALTAR L. Transfiguration.

— R. TRANSEPT. 'Falconi' altarpiece: Madonna in Glory appearing to SS. Nicholas, Francis and donor. Sd and d. 1588.

S. PIETRO IN MONASTERO. Annunciation. Sd and d. 1592.

S. STEFANO, L. TRANSEPT. Descent of the Holy Ghost. d. 1598.
Madonna in Glory and two Saints.

S. TOMASO, FIRST ALTAR L. Madonna in Glory appearing to SS. Albert and Jerome. d. 1569.

— THIRD ALTAR L. Madonna appearing to SS. Anthony Abbot and Onuphrius.

(Environs). CA' DI DAVID, PARISH CHURCH, SACRISTY. Descent of the Holy Ghost. d. 1603.

— SAN GIOVANNI LUPATOTO. SS. John Baptist, Roch and Elizabeth. d. 1598.

Vicenza. PALAZZO NIEVO (PREFETTURA). Christ appearing to SS. Peter, Diego and Anthony Abbot with kneeling Giannantonio Pancera. d. 1593.*

Vienna. 385. S. Sebastian.
387. S. John Baptist.
401. Marriage of S. Catherine.

Volciano. See Trobbiolo.

Worcester (Mass.). 1915.77. Bearded old man. [*Plate 357.*]

FEI, Paolo di Giovanni

Sienese. Active 1372 to 1410. Pupil of Bartolo di Fredi and Andrea Vanni.

Altenburg. 51. Madonna and Child with four Angels, S. John Baptist, S. Andrew and female donor.

Altenburg (contd.). 60, 61. Two predella panels (companions to New York, Historical Society): Adoration of Shepherds, Adoration of Magi.

Amsterdam. 432–B1. Madonna of the goldfinch.

Asciano. MUSEO D'ARTE SACRA. Side panels of polyptych (surrounding Madonna by Taddeo di Bartolo): full-length SS. Paul and John Baptist; full-length SS. Agatha and Peter; busts of the four Evangelists (from the Collegiata di S. Agata).

Assisi. F. M. PERKINS COLLECTION. Panel of polyptych: Trinity.

Atlanta (Ga.). ART ASSOCIATION GALLERIES. 58.42. (KRESS COLLECTION. K 187). Central panel of polyptych from a Roman monastery: Madonna and Child enthroned with SS. Francis and Louis and two Angels. d. MCCCXXXIII (read 1373?)

Bayeux. MUSÉE. Left panel of polyptych: Half-length S. John Baptist (companion to Frankfurt).

Bergamo. 321. Portable altarpiece: Marriage of S. Catherine and Redeemer above: in wings, SS. Peter and John Baptist, SS. Paul and John Evangelist, Angel and Virgin of Annunciation.

Boston (Mass.). GARDNER MUSEUM. SS. Mary of Egypt, Francis and Jerome.

Brussels. 629. Crucifixion.

UCCLE, VAN GELDER COLLECTION. Predella panel: Marriage of the Virgin.

Cologne. 505. Portable altarpiece: Madonna and Child enthroned with SS. John Baptist, Bartholomew, two female Saints and kneeling Dominican; in wings, SS. Peter and Paul, Angel and Virgin of Annunciation. (?)

506. Crucifixion; below, Redeemer with SS. Jerome, Francis, Catherine and another female Saint.

SCHNÜTGEN MUSEUM (EX). Centre panel of portable altarpiece: Madonna and Child enthroned with two Angels, four Saints and reclining Eve.

Englewood (N.J.). PLATT COLLECTION (EX). Madonna of Humility suckling the Child.

Florence. BERENSON COLLECTION. Portable altarpiece: Madonna and Child enthroned with three Angels and four Saints; in pinnacle, Crucifixion; in wings, SS. Anthony Abbot and female Saint, SS. Catherine and James, Angel and Virgin of Annunciation.

Frankfurt a/M. 1002. Right panel of polyptych: Half-length S. Catherine (companion to Bayeux).

CARL VON WEINBERG. Full-length S. Catherine (from S. Gimignano).

Gotha. MUSEUM (EX). Panel of polyptych: Half-length S. Lawrence.

Memphis (Tenn.). BROOKS MEMORIAL ART GALLERY. 61.188. (KRESS COLLECTION. K 38.) Christ on the Road to Calvary.

Modena. 4. Madonna and Child.

Münster i/W. DIÖZESANMUSEUM. 35. Bust of S. Mary Magdalen.

Naples. 273. Wings of portable altarpiece: SS. John Evangelist and Louis of Toulouse, SS. John Baptist and Francis, Angel and Virgin of Annunciation.

DUOMO, CAPPELLA MINUTOLI. Portable altarpiece: Crucifixion with Trinity above;

in wings, SS. James and (Margaret?), medallion with Prophet, Angel of Annunciation; S. John Baptist and Bishop Saint, medallion with Prophet, Virgin of Annunciation. Inscribed as a gift of Cardinale Minutoli in 1412.

New York. 41.190.13. Madonna suckling the Child.

HISTORICAL SOCIETY. B–8. Predella panel: Crucifixion (companion to Altenburg).

BLUMENTHAL COLLECTION (EX). S. Stephen.

ROBERT LEHMAN. Madonna and Child enthroned with Angels and SS. John Evangelist, Peter, Paul, John Baptist, Agnes, Catherine, Lucy and another Saint, reclining Eve below and Angel and Virgin of Annunciation in roundels above.

Diptych: Madonna and Child with two Angels and SS. John Baptist and James, Crucifixion, Angel and Virgin of Annunciation in pinnacles.

EMMET JOHN HUGHES. 'Meinhard' Marriage of S. Catherine, with two Angels, S. Bartholomew and female donor.

Palermo. CHIARAMONTE BORDONARO COLLECTION. 214. Crucifixion.

218. Madonna and Child with Saints.

Parma. CONGREGAZIONE DI CARITÀ (PINACOTECA STUARD). 3. S. John Baptist.

Poggibonsi. S. LUCCHESE, RIGHT WALL. Frescoed triptych: Madonna and Child, S. Christopher, S. Anthony Abbot; in pinnacles, Redeemer, Angel and Virgin of Annunciation (fresco by Bartolo di Fredi below). E. (?)

Richmond (Surrey). COOK COLLECTION. 5. Left panel of triptych: Group of kneeling female Saints.

Rome. CONTE L. VITETTI. Portable altarpiece: Madonna and Child with two Angels and SS. Peter, Bartholomew, Evangelist and Andrew; Christ on Cross above; in wings, SS. Michael and Augustine, SS. Mary Magdalen and Catherine and two Evangelists in roundels above. *Plate* 417.

VATICAN, PINACOTECA. 220. Portable altarpiece: Crucifixion; in wings, four Saints, Angel and Virgin of Annunciation.

268. Predella panel: Adoration of the Shepherds.

Rotterdam. BOYMANS-VAN BEUNINGEN MUSEUM. 2543. Portable altarpiece: Madonna and Child enthroned with five Angels; Crucifixion above; in wings, SS. Francis, Anthony Abbot, Lucy and Catherine; SS. Michael, Christopher and two other Saints; in pinnacles, Crucifixion, Angel and Virgin of Annunciation.

San Diego (Cal.). FINE ARTS GALLERY. Two panels of portable altarpiece: SS. John Baptist and Anthony Abbot; SS. Francis and Ansanus; on back, monochrome S. Christopher and S. Anthony Abbot.

Siena. 96. Predella panel: a knightly Saint taken to prison by two soldiers, and bystanders. (?)

116. Birth of the Virgin flanked by SS. James and Catherine, SS. Bartholomew and Elizabeth of Hungary; in pinnacles, Redeemer, Angel and Virgin of Annunciation, two Seraphim. *Plate* 416.

126. Side-panels of polyptych: S. James, S. John Baptist, S. Vitale.

137. Portable altarpiece: Mystic Marriage of S. Catherine and two Angels, SS.

Lucy, James and Bartholomew; in wings, S. Francis and John Baptist, SS. Anthony Abbot and John Evangelist.

141. Madonna and Child enthroned with two Angels, S. Catherine and S. John Baptist.

146. Diptych: Madonna and Child enthroned with two Angels, S. Catherine and S. Agnes; Crucifixion; in pinnacles, Angel and Virgin of Annunciation.

154. Portable altarpiece: Madonna and Child with two Angels; SS. Dominic and Catherine, SS. Christopher and Bartholomew; Angel and Virgin of Annunciation. E. (?)

222. Centre panel of portable altarpiece: Madonna and Child enthroned with SS. Mary Magdalen, John Evangelist, Catherine of Alexandria and Thomas.

300. Polyptych from S. Andreino alle Serre di Rapolano: Madonna and Child enthroned; SS. Andrew and John Baptist, S. Francis and Prophet Daniel; in pillars, SS. Agnes, Margaret, Catherine, Nicholas, Bartholomew, James. Sd. *Plate* 415.

585. Madonna and Child enthroned with SS. John Baptist, Anthony Abbot, Peter and Catherine. (?)

S. MARIA DELLA SCALA (SS. ANNUNZIATA), CAPPELLA DEI MALATI, HIGH ALTAR. Madonna and Child with seven Angels. *Plate* 419.

S. BERNARDINO FUORI PORTA CAMOLLIA. Polyptych: Madonna and Child, eight kneeling Saints; in pinnacles, Redeemer, four heads of Angels.

S. MARIA ASSUNTA (DUOMO), FOURTH ALTAR L. Madonna suckling the Child.

Washington (D.C.). 1623 (KRESS COLLECTION. K 1547). 'Chigi-Zondadori' Assumption, with Angel and Virgin of the Annunciation above. [*Plate* 267.]

1361 (KRESS COLLECTION. K 2045). Presentation of the Virgin. *Plate* 418.

Homeless. Right panel of polyptych: Half-length S. Lawrence. *Plate* 420.

FERRARESE before 1510

Albi (Tarn). CATHEDRAL. Frescoes in vault and chapels: Christ in Glory, Coronation of Virgin, Wise and Foolish Virgins, Patriarchs, Saints and Prophets.

Athens (Ga.). UNIVERSITY OF GEORGIA. R-7 (KRESS COLLECTION. 1834). Ecce Homo.

Bologna. 281. Predella panel (companion to Pesaro): Death of Jacopo del Cassero. (School of Cossa.)

592. Madonna and Child with SS. John Baptist and Anthony. (School of Cossa.)

804. Madonna and Child enthroned. (Follower of Tura.) *Plate* 747.

DEP. FROM S. GIOVANNI IN MONTE. Madonna and Child with two Angels. d. 1493. (School of Cossa.)

S. PETRONIO, FIFTH CHAPEL L. (CAPPELLA VASELLI), ALTAR. Martyrdom of S. Sebastian, and donor Donato Vaselli.

— — WALLS. Annunciation; Apostles in niches.

— SIXTH CHAPEL R., ALTAR. S. Jerome.

Boston (Mass.). 17.198. Desco: front, Solomon meeting the Queen of Sheba; back, Cupid with cornucopia (c. of a lost Domenico Veneziano by ? early Cossa).

Budapest. 1143, 1144 (99, 100). Two music-making Angels. (Close to Cossa.)

Cambridge. FITZWILLIAM MUSEUM. 1652. 'Dreyfus' Nativity. (Close to Ercole Roberti.)

Claremont (Cal.). POMONA COLLEGE (KRESS STUDY COLLECTION. K 1218). Ecce Homo in portico.

Edinburgh. 1535. Madonna and Child with Angels.

Ferrara. Inv. 65. Full-length S. Jerome reading. (Follower of Tura and Cossa, possibly Spanish.)

PALAZZO SCHIFANOIA, SALA DEI MESI. Frescoes by Cossa (q.v.), and other Ferrarese artists.

— EAST WALL:

March (top register—Triumph of Minerva; middle register—zodiacal sign of Aries, Negro Giant, seated woman, Youth holding arrow and ring; lower register—Duke Borso d'Este performs Justice, Departure for the Hunt). *Plate 732.*

April (top register—Triumph of Venus; middle register—zodiacal sign of Taurus or Bull, Woman and Child, Nude with key, Nude with snake and arrow; lower register—Duke Borso d'Este surrounded by Courtiers and talking to his Fool, Races on foot, on horses and on donkeys).

May (top register—Triumph of Apollo; middle register—zodiacal sign of Gemini or Twins, Man with rod and kneeling Boy, Musician, Archer; lower register—Peasants pruning and mowing).

— NORTH WALL.

June (top register—Triumph of Mercury; middle register—zodiacal sign of Cancer or Crab, young Woman with tiara and rod; lower register—Duke Borso d'Este receives a message, the Hunters' Return).

July (top register—Triumph of Jupiter; middle register—zodiacal sign of Leo or Lion, eastern Priest, kneeling Archer, a Savage; lower register, Duke Borso d'Este receives a petition, leaves on horseback with falcon). *Plate 748.*

August (top register—Triumph of Ceres; middle register—zodiacal sign of Virgo, Woman with pomegranate and ears of wheat, Asian Writer, Old Man praying; lower register—Cavalcade of Duke Borso d'Este, the Duke receives an Ambassador).

September (top register—Triumph of Lust: middle register—zodiacal sign of Libra or Scales, Man with trumpet and lance, Man kneeling, Naked Man imploring an Archer; lower register—Duke Borso d'Este receives a Venetian Nobleman, the Duke goes hunting).

School of Cossa (see also under latter). 1470.

Florence. CASA STROZZI. Two allegorical figures. (Close to Tura.)

The Hague. N.K. 1577. 'Lanz' Annunciation. (School of Cossa.)

London. FORBES COLLECTION (EX). Cassone panel (companion to Paris): Punishment of the Elders. (Close to Zoppo.) *Plate* 740.

Lyons. AYNARD COLLECTION (EX). Cassone panels: Battle, Knight pursuing a girl, Departure of a ship. (Close to Ercole Roberti.)

Madison (Wis.). UNIVERSITY (KRESS STUDY COLLECTION. K 334). S. Justina and donor.

Mainz. GEMÄLDEGALERIE. Inv. 230, 231. Two roundels: Allegory and Triumph of Chastity. (School of Ercole Roberti.)

Memphis (Ala.). BROOKS MEMORIAL ART GALLERY. 61.199 (KRESS COLLECTION. K 1231). S. Sebastian in niche. (Close to Maineri.)

Modena. 49. Portrait of young man. d. on back 1494. (Close to Bianchi Ferrari.)

Munich. W.A.F. 255. Madonna and Child with SS. Anthony of Padua, Bernardino of Siena, Benedict and Augustine. (Follower of Tura and Cossa.)

   8709. Portrait of Uberto de' Sacrati with wife and son. *Plate* 745.

New York. R. LEHMAN COLLECTION. Profile portraits of Gozzadini and his wife.

Nonantola (Modena). ABBAZIA, L. WALL. Ascension (r.).

— R. WALL. Frescoes: Annunciation and Saints.

Paris. VAN MOPPES COLLECTION (EX). Cassone panel (companion to London): Susanna and the Elders, Susanna's Trial. (Close to Zoppo.) *Plate* 739.

Perugia. VAN MARLE COLLECTION (EX). Architectural landscape with boats and figures (fr.). (Close to Cossa.)

Pesaro. 77, 78 (13, 14). Predella panels (companions to Bologna 281): S. Francis and the death of the Knight of Celano; S. Francis receiving Stigmata. (School of Cossa.)

Rotterdam. BOYMANS-VAN BEUNINGEN MUSEUM. 2548. Adoration of Magi. (Possibly Galassi.)

San Diego (Cal.). 47.39. Christ on the way to Calvary. (Close to Ercole Roberti.)

Strasbourg. 219. Madonna and Child. (Between Ercole Roberti and Zoppo.)

Vaduz. LIECHTENSTEINSCHE SAMMLUNG. Two small ovals: Angel and Virgin of Annunciation. (School of Ercole Roberti.) Not traced.

Venice. MUSEO CORRER. Inv. 53. Profile portrait of youth (initialled on parapet A.F.P., inscribed on architrave IO. BAT. FUSSA. P.). (Close to Cossa.)

   CONTE VITTORIO CINI. Inv. 2059. 'Stroganoff' Baptist in the Wilderness. (School of Zoppo.)

      Inv. 6736. Portable altarpiece: Madonna suckling the Child on throne with peacock and dove, and kneeling S. Margaret; in lunette, Dead Christ.

Washington (D.C.). 1141 (KRESS COLLECTION K 1725). Bust of woman with white bonnet. (Close to Ercole Roberti.)

Homeless. Madonna and Child enthroned with two Angels (assistant of Cossa who worked at Schifanoia, in Triumph of Mercury). *Plate* 746.

FERRARESE–BOLOGNESE, Unidentified, 1450–1525

[*See Introduction*, p. XIV.]

Assisi. PERKINS COLLECTION. Madonna adoring Child on parapet (same hand as London 'Madonna of the Monkey').

Bergamo. 540. Bust of Magdalen (between Costa and Garofalo).

Budapest. 69. S. John Evangelist.

Chicago (Ill.). RYERSON COLLECTION (EX). Madonna and Child (same hand as London 'Madonna of the Monkey').

Ferrara. 43. Assumption of S. Mary of Egypt. *Plate* 1615.

MASSARI ZAVAGLIA COLLECTION. Lunette to London 1119: Pietà. 1494–1500. *Plate* 1623.

Liverpool. 2778. Madonna suckling the Child (same hand as London 'Madonna of the Monkey').

London. 1119. The Strozzi altarpiece, from the Oratorio della Concezione in S. Francesco at Ferrara: Madonna and Child enthroned with SS. William and John Baptist; on reliefs, Judgement of Solomon, Sacrifice of Isaac, two Heads of Prophets, Fall of Man, Nativity, Circumcision, Massacre of Innocents, Flight into Egypt, Christ disputing with the Doctors (cut at sides; companion to Ferrara lunette; between Maineri and Costa, possibly by both). Commissioned 1494 but finished around 1500. *Plate* 1625.

3102. 'Madonna of the Monkey' with SS. Nicholas of Tolentino and S. Catherine of Siena (close to early Garofalo). *Plate* 1772.

New Haven (Conn.). 1943.261. Christ on Cross with mourning Virgin and S. John Evangelist; Redeemer in tympanum. (Same hand as Ferrara 'Assumption of S. Mary of Egypt'.) *Plate* 1616.

Nîmes. 443. Madonna and Child with female Martyr (between Costa and Garofalo).

Rome. GALLERIA DORIA PAMPHILI. 487. Holy Family (same hand as London 'Madonna of the Monkey').

Venice. CONTE VITTORIO CINI. Inv. 6270. S. Michael (close to Giovanni Agostino da Lodi).

ISOLA DI S. GIORGIO MAGGIORE, FONDAZIONE GIORGIO CINI. 'Cook' Annunciation.

Homeless. S. Francis receiving Stigmata (same hand as Ferrara 'Assumption of S. Mary of Egypt'). *Plate* 1615-a.

Circumcision (same hand as London 'Madonna of the Monkey'). *Plate* 1773.

FERRARI see DEFENDENTE FERRARI

FERRARI see GAUDENZIO FERRARI

FIORENZO DI LORENZO

Perugia, ca 1440–February 1522. Pupil of Umbrian followers of Benozzo Gozzoli; strongly influenced by young Perugino.

Aix-en-Provence. 389. S. Sebastian and a family of donors.

Baltimore (Md.). WALTERS ART GALLERY. 1089. S. Jerome in wilderness (r., c.?).

Bergamo. 539. S. Jerome in penitence (g.p.).

Bettona (Perugia). PALAZZO DEL PODESTÀ, PINACOTECA. Detached fresco: S. Michael. E.

Boston (Mass.). MUSEUM OF FINE ARTS, 20.431. Madonna and Child with S. Jerome. *Plate* 1066.

    47.232. Detached fresco: S. Sebastian (r.). (?)

Copenhagen. THORWALDSEN MUSEUM. 4. Wings of portable triptych: S. John Baptist, S. Eligius holding hammer.

Deruta (Perugia). S. FRANCESCO. Fresco: Eternal, SS. Roch and Romano and view of Deruta. d. 1478.

Edinburgh. 1745. S. Francis receiving Stigmata.

Frankfurt a/M. 1078. Madonna and Child enthroned with SS. Christopher and Sebastian. *Plate* 1067.

Fratticciola Selvatica (between Perugia and Gubbio). ORATORIO DI S. MARIA DELLE GRAZIE, CHAPEL L. OF ENTRANCE. Votive frescoes: Left wall, Madonna and Child, Christ on Cross, Christ in Tomb; Right wall, S. Michael, S. Leonard and Bishop Saint (all r.). E.

Greenville (S.C.). BOB JONES UNIVERSITY GALLERY. 20. Christ on Cross (st.).

Hanover. 100. Side-panel of polyptych: Full-length S. Peter. L. (?)

London. 1103. Triptych: Madonna and Child enthroned with four Angels, SS. Francis and Bernardino recommending donor; S. John Baptist; S. Bartholomew. E.

    SIR RONALD STORRS (EX). S. Jerome in wilderness.

Montelabbate (between Perugia and Sansepolcro). S. MARIA, L. WALL. Frescoed niche: Crucifixion with SS. Sebastian and Roch; in tympanum, Resurrection; in spandrels, two roundels with SS. Blaise and Christopher; in embrasure of arch, three roundels with Eternal, Angel and Virgin of Annunciation, and full-length SS. Anthony Abbot and Bernardino (g.p.). 1491–92.

New Haven (Conn.). 1971.68. S. Jerome in Penitence. E.

Perugia. 177. Detached fresco from S. Giorgio dei Tessitori (companion to 434, 435): Mystic Marriage of S. Catherine, and S. Nicholas. d. 1498.

    178–9. Altarpiece from Choir of Nuns at Monteluce: Adoration of Shepherds; in predella, SS. Michael, Louis of Toulouse, Bernardino, Francis, Clare, Anthony of Padua, Jerome. E. [*Plate* 300.]

    208-219. Polyptych for Silvestrini di S. Maria Nuova: Madonna and Child with two Angels; SS. Benedict and Peter; S. John Evangelist and Blessed Paulinus;

in pilasters, Angel and Virgin of Annunciation, SS. John Baptist and Sebastian, two blessed Monks; in pinnacles, Eternal, S. Ambrose?, S. Jerome, S. Augustine, S. Gregory Martyr. 1487–93.

230. Triptych of Justice: Madonna and Child enthroned with two Angels, kneeling flagellant and prior; SS. Mustiola and Andrew; SS. Peter and Francis; in predella, knee-length SS. Bernardino and John Baptist, Confratello della Giustizia, Dead Christ in Sepulchre with mourning Virgin and Evangelist, Confratello della Giustizia, SS. Jerome and Sebastian. *Plate* 1074.

231. S. Sebastian and donor.

235. Altarpiece with central niche for missing sculpture: above, Madonna and Child in garland and two Angels; below, SS. Peter and Paul. Sd and d. 1487. *Plate* 1076.

236. Madonna and Child with Angels in wreath (after Mantegna).

237. Franciscan Saints in roundels.

432. Detached fresco from Collegio della Mercanzia: Madonna of Mercy. Formerly Sd and d. 1476. *Plate* 1075.

434, 435. Detached frescoes from S. Giorgio dei Tessitori (companions to 177): Nativity; SS. John Baptist, Francis and Sebastian (frs.). d. 1498.

464. Detached fresco from Chiesa Nuova: Madonna and Child with Angels, in lunette.

S. MARIA DI MONTELUCE, ROOM BEHIND APSE. Detached fresco: Crucifixion with mourning Virgin, Evangelist, Francis and Clare. 1491.

CONTE SALVADORI (EX). Salvator Mundi. (?)

Rome. GALLERIA DORIA PAMPHILI. 131. Madonna holding Child on parapet (st.).

PALAZZO SPADA. S. Sebastian. *Plate* 1069.

PALAZZO VENEZIA. P.V. 1812. Portable altarpiece: Nativity, Annunciation. (?)

STEPANOV COLLECTION (EX). Madonna and Child.

VATICAN, PINACOTECA. 282. Tondo: Christ on Cross.

FOPPA (Vincenzo da Brescia)

Founder of the Milanese School, Vincencius Brixiensis was born in Brescia between 1427 and 1430. Studied probably at Padua in school of Squarcione; influenced by Giovanni Bellini, and later by Mantegna and Bramante. First recorded at Pavia 1458, made citizen of Pavia 1468. Worked in Genoa 1461, 1471–74, 1488–90. After 1490 went back to Brescia and died there between May 1515 and October 1516.

Allington Castle. LORD CONWAY (EX). Madonna and Child with two Angels musicians.

Dead Christ with Symbols of Passion.

Baltimore (Md.). WALTERS ART GALLERY. 706. Full-length SS. Agnes and Catherine.

Basle. SARASIN VARNERY COLLECTION (EX). Knee-length SS. Bartholomew and Gregory.

Bergamo. 279. S. Jerome in the wilderness. Sd.

284. Crucifixion. Sd and d. 1456. *Plate* 1192.

Berlin. I. 133. Pietà from Milan, S. Pietro in Gessate. Sd. (Destroyed 1945.)

1368. Madonna and Child with apple.

Bernay (Eure). MUSÉE (CAMPANA COLLECTION). Predella panel: S. Ambrose expelling the Arians (st.).

Brescia. 124. 'Pala dei Mercanti': Madonna and Child enthroned with SS. Faustinus and Giovita. d. 1496.

129. 'Orzinuovi' banner: front, Madonna and Child with SS. Bernardino and Catherine; back, S. Sebastian between SS. Roch and George. doc. 1514.

AVEROLDI COLLECTION (EX). See Milan, G. Langhi.

S. MARIA DEL CARMINE, CAPPELLA AVEROLDI, VAULT. Frescoes: Evangelists and Church Fathers (p.) 1475.

CHIESA DELLA PURITÀ DI MARIA VERGINE. Madonna suckling the Child (variant of Philadelphia).*

(Environs) CHIESANUOVA, PARISH CHURCH. Centre panel of triptych: Nativity (companion to Geneva).

Budapest. 1071–82. Detached frescoes: twelve medallions with Solomon, David and Prophets (st.).

1372. Fresco: S. Jerome penitent (st.).

Cambridge (Mass.). FOGG ART MUSEUM. 1939.100. 'Crespi' Madonna suckling the Child.

Châalis (Ermenonville). MUSÉE JACQUEMART-ANDRÉ. 19. Bishop Saint. (?)

Crema. STRAMEZZI COLLECTION. 'Vittadini' Annunciation with S. Jerome.

Denver (Col.). MUSEUM OF ART. E-IT-18-XV-931 (KRESS COLLECTION. K 493). S. Christopher.

Detroit (Mich.). L. P. FISCHER COLLECTION. Adoration of the Child with kneeling monk. Sd.

Florence. BERENSON COLLECTION. Madonna and Angels. E.

Madonna suckling the Child. [*Plate* 361.]

Predella panel: Martyrdom of S. Sebastian. L.

CONTINI BONACOSSI COLLECTION. 'Frizzoni' Madonna and Child with Angel.

VENTURA COLLECTION (EX). Dead Christ in Tomb between Virgin, S. John Evangelist, S. Nicholas of Tolentino and S. Nicholas of Bari. ca 1480.

Geneva. DURAND MATTHIESEN COLLECTION. Side-panels of triptych: S. John Baptist and S. Apollonia (companions to Brescia, Chiesanuova).

Isolabella (Lago Maggiore). PALAZZO BORROMEO. Two panels: Angel and Virgin of Annunciation. L.

London. 729. Adoration of Magi. L. [*Plate* 360.] *Plate* 1195.

WALLACE COLLECTION. 538. Detached fresco from Banco Mediceo in Milan: The young Cicero. ca 1462–64. *Plate* 1191.

GEORGE FARROW (EX). S. Jerome.

Louisville (Kentucky). J. B. SPEED ART MUSEUM. 'Chalandon' S. John Baptist.

Milan. BRERA. 19. Detached fresco from S. Maria di Brera: Madonna and Child with SS. John Baptist and John Evangelist. d. 1485. *Plate* 1193.

20, 21. Detached frescoes from S. Maria di Brera: Martyrdom of S. Sebastian; Pietà. ca. 1485.

307. Polyptych from S. Maria delle Grazie at Bergamo: Madonna and Child enthroned with four Angels; at sides, SS. Jerome, Alexandre, Vincent and Anthony; upper register, SS. Clare and Bonaventura, S. Francis receiving Stigmata, SS. Louis of Toulouse and Bernardino of Siena; at top, Redeemer; in predella, two Angels with Symbols of Passion, Annunciation, Visitation, Nativity, Flight into Egypt. *Plate* 1194.

CASTELLO. I. Martyrdom of S. Sebastian.

45, 48, 52. Three detached frescoes from S. Maria del Giardino: S. John Baptist; S. Joachim?; S. Francis receiving Stigmata.

305. Madonna and blessing Child.

— COLLEZIONE TRIVULZIO. Madonna embracing Child.

—— Two panels of polyptych: S. Augustine and S. Theodore.

POLDI PEZZOLI. 641. Profile of Francesco Brivio. (?)

643. Madonna and Child.

BERNASCONI COLLECTION (EX). Madonna del Latte and Infant S. John.

ALDO CRESPI. Madonna and Child, with four Angels.

GERLI COLLECTION. Circumcision.

G. LANGHI (EX). 'Averoldi' Madonna and Child.

RASINI COLLECTION. S. Stephen and S. John Baptist.

S. EUSTORGIO, CAPPELLA PORTINARI. Frescoes. ca 1464–68.

—— VAULT. Angels; Four Church Fathers in pendentifs; eight half-length Apostles in simulated circular windows.

—— LARGE LUNETTES: Over entrance, Assumption; left, S. Peter Martyr heals a youth and assassination of S. Peter Martyr; over Altar, Annunciation; right, S. Peter Martyr preaching in the square stops the clouds to protect his audience from the sun, and S. Peter Martyr defeats the Devil with the Host.

Minneapolis (Minn.). INSTITUTE OF ARTS. 66.37.1–2. Two panels of polyptych: S. Sirus, S. Paul.*

Monza. DUOMO, SACRISTY. Four panels of polyptych: Small Crucifixion; Beheading of S. John Baptist, SS. Stephen and John Baptist, SS. Peter and Paul (st.).

New Orleans (La.). I. DELGADO MUSEUM OF ART. 61.70 (KRESS COLLECTION. K. 1220). S. Paul. L.

New York. 30.95.293. Madonna and Child against hedge of roses.

Paris. CHÉRAMY COLLECTION (EX). 'Ecce Homo' (r.).

Pavia. Inv. 21. 'Pala Bottigella': Madonna and Child with SS. Matthew, John Baptist, Stephen, Jerome, Blessed Dominic of Cataluna and Blessed Sibillina of Pavia recommending Giovanni Matteo Bottigella and his wife Bianca Visconti (g.p.). 1480–86.

Philadelphia (Pa.). J. G. JOHNSON COLLECTION. 257. Madonna suckling the Child.

Princeton (N.J.). 62–59. Madonna and Child enthroned with two Angels and donor.

Raleigh (N.C.). MUSEUM OF ART. GL.60.17.22 (KRESS COLLECTION. K 1092). Madonna and Child.

Savona. 28. 'Pala Fornari': Madonna and Child enthroned with Manfredo Fornari as donor; at sides, S. John and S. Jerome; upper register, busts of SS. Augustine and Anthony of Padua; in tympanum, Dead Christ and Cherubim; in pilasters, six small Saints; in predella, Christ and the Apostles. d. 1489.

    ORATORIO DI S. MARIA DI CASTELLO. Polyptych from High Altar of Savona Cathedral: Madonna and Child enthroned with Angels and Cardinal Giuliano della Rovere as donor; at sides, SS. John Baptist and John Evangelist; in upper register, the four Church Fathers; at top, the four Evangelists; in pilasters of frame, statuettes of Saints; in predella, Beheading of Baptist, Salome's Dance, Adoration of Magi, S. John Evangelist at Patmos, S. John Evangelist's Assumption. Sd and d. 1490 by Foppa under Madonna, Sd and d. 1490 by Ludovico Brea under S. John Evangelist. *Plates* 1196, 1197.

Venice. CONTE VITTORIO CINI. Inv. 2063. Madonna and Child enthroned with SS. Faustinus, Giovita and Infant S. John.

Vienna. BARON OFENHEIM (EX). Two panels: S. John Baptist and S. Dominic.

Washington (D.C.). 1142, 1624. (KRESS COLLECTION 1559, 1560). Two panels of altarpiece: S. Anthony of Padua, S. Bernardino of Siena (ex Cook).

Worcester (Mass.). 1924.13. Holy Family with Infant S. John. L.

Homeless. Top panel of polyptych. Dead Christ upheld by Angel (repr. *Arte Lombarda*, 1963, 2, p. 113).*

FRANCESCO DI GENTILE DA FABRIANO

Marchigian. Active 1460 to end of century. Pupil of Antonio da Fabriano. Influenced by the Vivarini, the Bellini, Crivelli, Justus van Ghent, Melozzo, Pinturicchio etc.

Arcevia (Ancona). S. MEDARDO. Six Saints in pilasters framing Signorelli's Baptism. *Plate* 956.

Assisi. F. M. PERKINS COLLECTION. Triptych: Madonna and Child with two Angels; Christ at column, S. John Baptist.

    Processional standard: Pietà; back, S. Sebastian and flagellants.

Baltimore. WALTERS ART GALLERY. 566. 'Ecce Homo.' (?)

    713. Madonna and Child with Infant S. John and Angel. (?)

Beffi (Aquila). MADONNA DEL PONTE. Triptych: Madonna and Child enthroned with two Angels; Nativity; Dormition and Coronation. E. (?)

Bergamo. ING. PESENTI. 'Leatham' Bust of Youth (r.). Sd.

Bracciano. CASTELLO. Visitation. Sd.

Derby. A. W. PUGIN (EX). Fragments of polyptych: Madonna and Child enthroned with Angels; SS. Jerome and Giovanni da Prato; SS. Clement and Sebastian; kneeling donor; three predella panels with Nativity, Crucifixion, Resurrection. d. 1462.* *Plates 972–975.*

Florence. BERENSON COLLECTION. Annunciation (r.).

Gotha. 492 (EX). Male portrait. (?)

Kilburn (London). S. AUGUSTINE. Trinity.

Lille. 1078. Bust of Christ.

1092. Small S. Sebastian.

Matelica. 36. Triptych: Crucifixion; Nativity, and S. Adrian on horseback above; Adoration of Magi, and Flaying of S. Bartholomew above.

37. Crucifixion; in predella, two groups of flagellants and eight stories of the true Cross (g.p.).

S. FRANCESCO, FOURTH CHAPEL R. Triptych: Madonna and Child enthroned with two Angels; S. Francis, S. Bernardino; in pilasters, Angel and Virgin of Annunciation and four small Saints; in predella, two kneeling donors and four Scenes from Life of S. Bernardino. *Plate 971.*

Melchett Court (Romsey, Hants.). LORD MELCHETT (EX). 'Mond' Man of Sorrows. *Plate 982.*

Milan. BRERA. 481, 482. Processional standard: Madonna in Glory and blessing Christ in pinnacle; back, S. Sebastian with SS. Anthony Abbot and Dominic, and Baptist in pinnacle. *Plates 979–980.*

Nevers. 25. Panel from pilaster of altarpiece: Baptist in niche.

Paris. MUSÉES NATIONAUX, CAMPANA 270 (DEP. VALENCIENNES). Panel of polyptych: S. Nicholas of Tolentino.

Perugia. 879. (BERENSON GIFT). Processional standard: Annunciation with blessing God the Father in pinnacle; Madonna and Child enthroned with Angels, and Dead Christ in pinnacle.

Philadelphia (Pa.). J. G. JOHNSON COLLECTION. 129. Madonna and Child with pomegranate (r.).

Rome. GALLERIA NAZIONALE. Two Angels. *Plates 976–977.*

MUSEO DI PALAZZO VENEZIA. Bust of S. John Baptist (fr.).

VATICAN, PINACOTECA. 263. Madonna of the butterfly (r.). Sd.

Valenciennes. (See Paris.)

Washington (D.C.). DUMBARTON OAKS. Ecce Homo. Sd. *Plate 981.*

Zagreb. 39. Ecce Homo and donor.

Homeless. Right panel of triptych: S. Bernardino. *Plate 978.*

Siena 1439–1501. Architect, sculptor, painter and miniaturist. Pupil of Vecchietta; partner of Neroccio until 1475, then active for about ten years at Urbino; influenced by Pollajuolo, Girolamo da Cremona and possibly also Botticelli. [See introduction, p. XVII.]

Amiens. 281. See Paris, Campana 276.

Atlanta (Ga.). ART ASSOCIATION GALLERIES. 61.25 (KRESS COLLECTION. K 1564). Predella panel: Nativity.

Baltimore (Md.). WALTERS ART GALLERY. 1034. Madonna and Child blessing (fr., r., p.).

Boston (Mass.). 41.921. Madonna and Child with SS. Jerome, Anthony of Padua?, and two Angels.

　EDWARD WHEELWRIGHT. Front of cassone: Helen of Troy holding bow and Ugurgieri coat of arms; Judgement of Paris and Rape of Helen; Paris holding Bartolini-Salimbeni coat of arms.

Brussels. HENRI WAUTERS. A girl speaks to her lover from a window (companion to Florence, Berenson and New York). (Liberale? Girolamo de Cremona?)

Chiusi. S. SECONDIANO (DUOMO), SALA CAPITOLARE. Antiphonary B, f. 3. Nativity in initial N. ca 1458–61. *Plate 876.*

Coral Gables (Fla.). LOWE ART GALLERY. 61.25 (KRESS COLLECTION. K. 1370). 'Platt' Madonna and Child with two Angels (g.p.; from Monistero di S. Eugenio near Siena).

Duino. PRINZ VON THURN UND TAXIS. Madonna and Child with SS. Jerome, Anthony Abbot and two Angels. E.

Florence. BARGELLO, CARRAND. Scipio Africanus on pedestal in landscape (background by Master of Griselda; companion to Pacchiarotto at Baltimore, Neroccio at Washington, Master of Griselda on Signorelli's design at Budapest, Milan, Richmond and Washington). *Plate 906.*

　STIBBERT MUSEUM. 4098, 12922. Two cassone panels: Mythological hunting scenes. (?)

　BERENSON COLLECTION. Scene outside a temple or palace (fr.). [*Plate 274.*]

　　Fragment with youths (companion to Brussels and New York) (Liberale? Girolamo da Cremona?)

Kansas City (Mo.). 41.9. Cassone panel: Story of Tobias.

Lockinge House (Wantage, Berks.). THOMAS LOYD. Triumph of Chastity (g.p.).

London. 1682. S. Dorothy leading Christ Child. E.

Los Angeles (Cal.). ART MUSEUM. Detached fresco: 'Fidelitas'. *Plate 884.*

Malibu (Cal.). J. PAUL GETTY MUSEUM. A57–P–2. Cassone panel: Love bound. *Plate 885.*

Melbourne. NATIONAL GALLERY OF VICTORIA, FELTON BEQUEST. Profile of lady.

New York. 20.182. Triumph of Diana (fr. of cassone).

　41.100.2. Nativity (fr.; companion to Washington).

43.98.8. Fragment with chess players (companion to Brussels and Florence, Berenson). (Liberale, Girolamo da Cremona?)

PAUL SACHS (EX). Madonna and Child (p.)

Paris. 1640A. Front of cassone: Rape of Europa.

MUSÉES NATIONAUX, CAMPANA 276 (DEP. AMIENS). Madonna and Child against Landscape.

Portland (Oregon). ART MUSEUM. 61.36 (KRESS COLLECTION. K 530). Front of cassone: Meeting of Dido and Aeneas.

Port Washington (N.Y.). S. R. GUGGENHEIM (EX). Madonna and Child with SS. Jerome and Bernardino. *Plate 892.*

Richmond (Surrey). COOK COLLECTION 8 (EX). Front of cassone: Triumph of Chastity (p.).

Rome. CASTELLI MIGNANELLI COLLECTION. Madonna suckling the Child.

Siena. 274–6. Joseph and Potiphar's Wife; Susanna and the Elders; Joseph sold by his Brothers (r.). E.

277. Annunciation.

288. Madonna and Child with Angel.

291. Madonna and Child with SS. Peter and Paul.

293. Madonna and Child with SS. James and Jerome.

306. Virgin of Annunciation (from Osservanza).

428. Stripping of Christ (execution by Pietro di Domenico).

437. Nativity with SS. Bernardino and Thomas Aquinas (from Monastery of S. Benedetto fuori Porta Tufi). Sd. 1475/6.

440. Coronation for Monteoliveto Maggiore. 1471/2. *Plate 883.*

ARCHIVIO DI STATO. Book-cover: The Madonna of the Earthquake. d. 1467. *Plate 890.*

CONTE PICCOLOMINI. Madonna suckling Child, with SS. Bernardino and Catherine of Siena (st.).

S. DOMENICO, LAST ALTAR R. Nativity (Pietà in lunette, by Matteo di Giovanni; predella by Fungai). [*Plate 275.*]

(Environs). OSSERVANZA, MUSEO. Codex 3, Treatise 'De Animalibus' by Albert the Great: f. 1—Allegory of Chastity and three Labours of Hercules in ornamented border. 1463. *Plate 879–882.*

Fr. Alfon. Ordinis S. Augustini 'Super Primum Sententiarum Commentum': Allegory of Theology. 1466.

Washington (D.C.). 799. (KRESS COLLECTION. K 1356). Eternal and Angels (oval fr., companion to New York).

SCULPTURES

Berlin. I. 1574. Terracotta relief: Mythological scene. Destroyed.

v. 60. Bronze medallion: S. Jerome.

Dresden. ALBERTINUM. Bronze statuette: Aesculapius.

London. BRITISH MUSEUM, ROBINSON BEQUEST. Bronze medal: front—Profile of Federico da Montefeltro; reverse—Nude rider slaying a lion-headed, serpent-tailed dragon (S. George?).

    VICTORIA AND ALBERT MUSEUM. 251–1876. Replica of lost Allegory of Discord (alias Lycurgus and Maenads).

Paris. LOUVRE. Wooden statue: S. Christopher. E.

Perugia. 746. Bronze relief: Flagellation with Virgin and Evangelist in foreground.

Siena. DUOMO, HIGH ALTAR. Bronze statues: Angels carrying Candlesticks. 1497.

— Bronze Putti. 1489–90.

    PINACOTECA. Wooden statue: S. John Baptist (for Compagnia di S. Giovanni Battista della Morte, Siena). (Formerly at Fogliano.) 1464. *Plate 888.*

    PALAZZO CHIGI SARACINI. Marble replica of lost Allegory of Discord.

Vaduz. LIECHTENSTEINSCHE SAMMLUNGEN. Bronze medallion: S. Anthony Abbot.

Venice. S. MARIA DEL CARMELO. Bronze relief from Oratorio della Croce, Urbino: Mourning over dead Christ. ca 1475–77.

Washington (D.C.). A.293.16B (KRESS COLLECTION). Bronze relief: Judgement of Paris.

    A.165.2C (KRESS COLLECTION). Bronze relief: S. Jerome in wilderness.

    A.400.123B (KRESS COLLECTION). Bronze medallion: S. Sebastian.

    A.401.124B (KRESS COLLECTION). Bronze medallion: S. John Baptist.

FRANCESCO DAI LIBRI (IL VECCHIO)

Verona, ca 1451–after 1502 and before 1514. Son of Stefano 'scriptor a Libris' 'aminiator' and father of Girolamo dai Libri, painter. [Since the signature 'Franciscus Veronensis' on the Missal for Cardinal Domenico Della Rovere in the Morgan Library MS. 306 was proved to refer to a Francesco di Bettino and not to a Francesco di Stefano, the tentative attribution to our artist of other miniatures or pretty predella panels had to be dropped as well as the assumption of Mantegna's influence. This reduces the List to little more than Gerola's 'Maestro del Cespo dei Garofani'—a name adopted by Berenson himself on the back of his photographs.]

Baltimore (Md.). WALTERS ART GALLERY. 497. Madonna embracing the Child.

Detroit (Mich.). INSTITUTE OF ARTS. Madonna and Child with open book.

Lovere. 25. S. Anthony of Padua.

Mizzole (Verona). S. FENZO (EX). Madonna and Child with SS. John Baptist, Fidenzio, Zeno, Catherine; in lunette, Christ in Sepulchre; in predella, Penitent S. Jerome, Nativity, S. Francis receiving Stigmata.

Quinzano (Verona). S. ROCCO. Triptych: Nativity with S. Roch; S. Sebastian; S. Alexander.

Triptych: Madonna and Child; S. Sebastian; S. Roch (st.). d. 1500.

Venice. CESARE LAURENTI (EX). Altarpiece from S. Pietro Incariano: Pietà with SS.

Peter (or Joseph?) and Jerome; in predella, S. Francis receiving Stigmata, Dead Christ in Sepulchre, S. Jerome in the wilderness.

Verona. 134. Blessed Lorenzo Giustiniani blessing a kneeling acolyte.

152. Madonna and Child enthroned between vases with pinks.

344, 345, 399, 400. Panels of polyptych from S. Clemente: SS. Bartholomew, Roch, Bernardino and Francis. E. (?)

360. Altarpiece from S. Silvestro: Madonna and Child with music-making Angels, S. Sylvester Pope and S. Benedict Bishop; in lunette, Crucifixion; in predella, Pietà and Symbols of Passion, S. Catherine, S. Lucy. d. 1487.

368. Triptych from S. Cecilia: S. Cecilia, S. Tiburtius and S. Valerian. *Plate* 1287.

369. Triptych from S. Giacomo alla Pigna: Madonna and Child, S. Peter, S. James (st.).

372. Triptych from S. Maria Consolatrice: Madonna and Child with donor; S. Maria Consolatrice; S. Catherine of Alexandria; in predella, the four Church Fathers, and three Scenes from Life of S. Maria Consolatrice. *Plate* 1285.

385. Triptych from S. Giacomo alla Pigna: Madonna and Child; S. Blaise; S. Sebastian.

696. Altarpiece from S. Matteo: Holy Family with S. Catherine and S. John Baptist.

S. ANASTASIA, CAPPELLA LAVAGNOLI (FIRST L. OF CHOIR). Frescoes: on left wall, from top: Miraculous Draught of Fishes, Crucifixion, Christ preaching on the shore of Lake Galilee; on right wall, S. John Evangelist in Patmos. L. (?)

S. ELENA. Triptych: Pietà; S. Helena; S. Catherine. d. 1490.

S. LORENZO. Fresco around a carved Christ: Symbols of the Passion. (?)

S. MARIA MATRICOLARE (DUOMO). FIRST AND SECOND CHAPELS LEFT. Ornamental frescoes. (?)

— BIBLIOTECA CAPITOLARE. Triptych: S. John Evangelist, S. James (Madonna by other hand).

SS. NAZARO E CELSO, SACRISTY. Triptych: Dead Christ with Symbols of the Passion; S. Benedict; S. Albert. *Plate* 1286.

Homeless. Madonna and Child with SS. Roch, Dominic, female Martyr, Sebastian and donor. *Plate* 1288.

Mystic Marriage of S. Catherine and Angels. *Plate* 1290.

Madonna and Child. *Plate* 1289.

FRANCESCO NAPOLITANO

Close follower of Leonardo, active around 1500; possibly pupil of Ambrogio De Predis.

Amsterdam. 1709—DI (VOM RATH BEQUEST). Madonna and Child with goldfinch.

Cambridge. FITZWILLIAM, MARLAY BEQUEST 51. Two wings of portable altarpiece: SS. Roch and Sebastian, Angel and Virgin of Annunciation above.

Cambridge (Mass.). FOGG ART MUSEUM. 1923.37. Madonna and Child (later version of New York).

Cleveland (Ohio). 16.779. Madonna and Child.

Milan. BRERA. 278. Madonna and Child. *Plate* 1517.

Naples. CERTOSA DI S. MARTINO. Epiphany with young Charles V as a King. (?)

New York. HISTORICAL SOCIETY. 508. Madonna and Child. E.

Rotterdam. BOYMANS-VAN BEUNINGEN MUSEUM. Inv. 2546. 'Auspitz' Martyrdom of S. Sebastian. (?)

Stockholm. 2636. Madonna and Child enthroned with two Angels. *Plate* 1518.

Zurich. KUNSTHAUS (on loan from Gottfried Keller Stiftung). 397. Madonna and Child enthroned with SS. John Baptist and Sebastian. Sd. *Plate* 1519.

397A. Madonna and Child. Sd. *Plate* 1516.

FRANCESCO DA RIMINI see RIMINI

FRANCESCO DA TOLENTINO

Umbro-Marchigian. Active ca 1500–35. Pupil perhaps of Agapiti; influenced by Antonio Solario and the Umbrian Painters.

Cori (Latina). S. OLIVA, APSE. Frescoes: vault, Coronation of Virgin; below, Landscape with Saints; on pilasters, two female Saints (r.). 1507. (?)

Liveri di Nola. SANTUARIO DI S. MARIA A PARETE, THIRD ALTAR R. Adoration of Magi. Sd and d. 1525.

Polyptych: Madonna and Child with Infant S. John; S. Barbara, S. Anthony Abbot; Crucifixion in lunette; predella. Sd and d. 1530 or 1531. *Plates* 1163–1165.

Naples. S. MARIA DI DONNA REGINA. Fresco: Martyrdom of S. Ursula and her Maidens. (?)

S. MARIA NUOVA, REFECTORY. Large frescoed lunette: Adoration of Magi with Coronation of Virgin above, Franciscans at sides; below, Annunciation, Nativity. *Plate* 1162.

Rome. S. GREGORIO, CHAPEL R. OF CHOIR. Predella: S. Michael in central medallion with seven knee-length Saints and Apostles on either side. L.

Tolentino. DUOMO, CAPPELLA DI S. CATERVO. Frescoes: in vault, Evangelists; End wall, Madonna and Child with SS. Catervo and Sebastian; Left wall, Adoration of Magi; Right wall, Crucifixion. *Plate* 1161.

FRANCESCO DI VANNUCCIO

Sienese, active in the second half of the fourteenth century. Close to Bartolo di Fredi.

Berlin. 1062B. Front: Madonna and Child with SS. Francis and Catherine (?) and kneeling monk (r.); back: Christ on Cross with mourning Mary and John, kneeling Bishop Saint and monk. Sd and d. MCCCLXX. *Plate 385.*

    R. VON KAUFMANN 84 (ex). Reliquary. *Plate 382.*

Cambridge. GIRTON COLLEGE. Diptych: Annunciation with two donors; Assumption. *Plate 383.*

Greenville (S.C.). BOB JONES UNIVERSITY MUSEUM. Painted Crucifix. *Plate 386.*

The Hague. MUSEUM MEERMAN VAN WESTREENEN. Madonna and Child with SS. Lawrence and Andrew.

London. WALLACE COLLECTION. 550. Left wing of triptych: Madonna and Child with Cherubs; below, SS. Peter and John Baptist.

Montepulciano. MUSEO CIVICO. 16. Small reliquary: Madonna and Child; below, SS. John Baptist, Paulinus of Nola and Louis of Toulouse.

Munich. KAULBACH COLLECTION (EX). Christ on Cross with mourning Mary and John, kneeling S. Francis and S. (?) Galganus. *Plate 384.*

New York. MISS HELEN FRICK. S. Catherine.

Perugia. VAN MARLE COLLECTION (EX). Predella panel: Dead Christ in Sepulchre; on either side, S. Catherine disputing with the philosophers, S. Catherine unharmed by the wheels.

Philadelphia (Pa.). J. G. JOHNSON COLLECTION. 94. Christ on Cross with mourning Mary and John and two Angels. (Sd and d. r.).

Siena. 183. Portable altarpiece: Madonna and Child with three Angels and SS. Bartholomew, Catherine, Elizabeth of Hungary, John Baptist; in wings, SS. Anthony and Augustine, SS. Francis and Clare.

    S. DOMENICO. Madonna del Rosario. (?)

    S. GIOVANNI DELLA STAFFA (ALSO CALLED S. GIOVANNINO IN PANTANETO). Madonna and Child (fr.). (?)

FRANCIA, Francesco

Bologna, ca 1450–1517. Began as jeweller. Pupil perhaps of Francesco del Cossa, influenced by Ercole Roberti da Ferrara. Partner of Costa.

Berea (Ky.). BEREA COLLEGE. 140.10 (KRESS COLLECTION. K 356). Madonna and Child with Infant S. John.

Bergamo. 267. Christ carrying Cross.

Berlin. 122. Madonna and Child in Glory, with SS. Giminianus, Bernard, Dorothy, Catherine, Jerome and Louis of Toulouse. Sd and d. 1504. (Destroyed 1945.)
    125. Holy Family ('Madonna Bianchini'). Sd. E. *Plate 1592.*

Berlin–Ost. 121. Lunette: Pietà with female Saint. *Plate* 1608.

Besançon. Inv. 896. 1.12. Roundel from predella: Dead Christ.

Bologna. PINACOTECA. Madonna and Child with S. Francis (stolen March 1920).

    Inv. 551 (373). Crucifixion with S. Jerome and S. Francis (p.). Sd.

    Inv. 570. (82) Predella: Nativity, Madonna suckling the Child and Infant S. John, S. Augustine pointing at crucified Christ. ca 1507.

    Inv. 571 (372). 'Madonna Scappi': Madonna and Child with SS. Paul, Francis and Infant John. Probably 1490–92.

    Inv. 573 (83). Dead Christ upheld by Angels.

    Inv. 575 (371). Annunciation and SS. John Evangelist, Francis, Bernardino and George. Sd and d. 1500. *Plate* 1603.

    Inv. 583 (78). 'Pala Felicini' also called 'Madonna del Gioiello': Madonna and Child with SS. John Baptist, Monica, Augustine, Francis, Procolo and Sebastian, and Bartolomeo Felicini as donor. Sd and d. 1494. *Plate* 1598.

    Inv. 584 (81). Centre panel of altarpiece from S. Maria della Misericordia commissioned by Anton Galeazzo Bentivoglio: Adoration of Child with S. Augustine and donor. (See also Costa at Bologna, Misericordia and at Milan.) d. 1499. *Plate* 1599.

    Inv. 586. Two *nielli*: Crucifixion, Resurrection.

    Inv. 587 (79). Annunciation; at sides, SS. John Baptist and Jerome. ca 1508.

    Inv. 589 (80). Madonna and Child with SS. Augustine, George, John Baptist, Stephen and Angel holding lily (from Manzuoli Chapel in Maria della Misericordia). E.

COLLEZIONI COMUNALI. Christ on Cross with SS. John Evangelist and Jerome. Sd. E.

PALAZZO COMUNALE, SALA DE'ERCOLE. Fresco: Madonna del Terremoto. d. 1505. *Plate* 1591-a.

PALAZZO HERCOLANI (EX). The Eternal. d. 1514.

S. GIACOMO MAGGIORE, CAPPELLA BENTIVOGLIO, ALTAR. Madonna and Child with SS. George, Augustine, Florian, John Evangelist, Sebastian, two adoring and two music-making Angels; Pietà in lunette. Sd. 1499.

— ORATORIO DI S. CECILIA. Frescoes: Marriage of S. Cecilia and Valerian (first, left of Altar); Burial of S. Cecilia (first, right of Altar; p.). 1504/06. (See also Aspertini and Costa.) *Plates* 1605, 1607.

S. MARIA DELLA MISERICORDIA, SECOND CHAPEL R. Stained glass window: Madonna and Saints adoring the Child (on design by the artist). 1499.

— SIXTH CHAPEL R. Stained glass window: S. John Baptist (on design of the artist).

— SIXTH CHAPEL L. Baptism. Not traced.

S. MARTINO MAGGIORE, FIRST CHAPEL L. Madonna and Child with SS. Roch, Bernardino, Anthony Abbot, Sebastian and two Angels; above, Dead Christ upheld by Angels; in predella, Christ carrying Cross. Sd. After 1506.

SS. VITALE E AGRICOLA, FIRST CHAPEL L. Angels and landscape round a Madonna and Child by Sano di Pietro. L. *Plate* 1614.

Boston (Mass.). GARDNER MUSEUM. Madonna and blessing Child. L.

Brescia. 140. Madonna and Child with Infant S. John in landscape.

s. giovanni evangelista, battistero, r. wall. Trinity and four Angels.

Budapest. 48 (75). Madonna and Child with Infant S. John (st.).

61 (72). Madonna and blessing Child on parapet, with two Angels (st.).

4244 (pálffy 37). Holy Family.

4259 (pálffy 38). Predella panel: Crucifixion (g.p.). L.

Carshalton (Surrey). rev. courbould. Madonna and Child with S. Petronius.

Cesena. madonna del monte, third chapel r. Circumcision (Pietà in lunette is by Girolamo Marchesi). Sd. L.

Châalis (Ermenonville). musée jacquemart-andré. 389. Madonna and Child.

Chantilly. 17. Annunciation and Albert the Great. (1503?)

Columbia (S.C.). museum of art. 54–402/12 (kress collection. k 165). Madonna and Child with goldfinch. L.

Dresden. 48. Baptism. Sd and d. 1509.

49. Adoration of Magi. *Plate* 1611.

49a. Lucretia (g.p.).

Dublin. 120. Lucretia (g.p.; other versions, Dresden and New York). *Plate* 1613.

Ferrara. duomo, sixth altar l. Coronation of Virgin and Saints (p.). Sd. L.

Florence. uffizi. 1444. Portrait of Evangelista Scappi.

8398. Madonna and Child enthroned with SS. Francis and Anthony of Padua kneeling (p.).

contini bonacossi collection. 'Frizzoni' S. Francis. *Plate* 1600.

Forlì. 98. Adoration of Shepherds. L.

Glasgow. 146. Predella panel: Nativity (companion to Lisbon). E. *Plate* 1594.

Hampton Court. Inv. 456. Baptism. Sd. E.

Inv. 1097. Knee-length S. Sebastian (g.p.).

Leipzig. Inv. 1649. Madonna and Child standing on parapet. Sd and d. 1517. *Plate* 1609.

Leningrad. 65. Pietà.

68. Madonna and blessing Child; in background Ascension and Resurrection (st.). Sd. L.

69. 'Pala Calcina': Madonna and Child with SS. Lawrence, Jerome and two music-making Angels (g.p.). Sd and d. 1500.

Lisbon. gulbenkian foundation. Predella panel: Baptism (companion to Glasgow). E. *Plate* 1597.

London. 179, 180. S. Anne, the Virgin and Child with SS. Sebastian, Paul, Lawrence, Romuald and Infant John; in lunette, Pietà and two Angels (from Cappella di S. Anna in S. Frediano, Lucca). Sd. After 1510.

638. Madonna and blessing Child with two Saints.

2487. The Poet Bartolomeo Bianchini (see Berlin). ca 1490.

2671. Pietà.

3927. Madonna of the cherries (replica of Taymouth Castle).

benson collection (ex). 57. Madonna and Child with S. Francis.

London (contd.). EARL OF NORTHBROOK (EX). Holy Family with S. Francis (st.). Sd and d. 1512.

Long Island (N.Y.). ROSLYN, CLARENCE MACKAY (EX). Madonna and Child with Angel and Infant S. John.

Los Angeles (Cal.). COUNTY MUSEUM 'Salomon' Madonna and Child with SS. Jerome and Francis. L.

Lucca. S. FREDIANO, R. TRANSEPT. Coronation of Virgin with SS. Anselmus and Augustine, an Augustinian Monk, David and Solomon; in predella, Abbot Helsinius is saved from shipwreck and celebrates Mass before a picture of the Immaculate Conception; A Franciscan defending the Immaculate Conception among flames; Miracle of the sword; Miracle of the Child fallen from the terrace (g.p.). Sd. L.

Luton Hoo (Beds.). WERNHER COLLECTION. 12. Madonna and Child with SS. Nicholas and Cecilia (st.).

Madrid. DUQUE FERNÁN NÚÑEZ. S. Sebastian.

Milan. BRERA. 319. Portrait of Poet Girolamo Casio (fr. r.). ca 1486?
448. Annunciation.
POLDI PEZZOLI. 601. S. Anthony of Padua.

Munich. 994. Madonna adoring Child in rose garden. Sd. [*Plate* 346.]
1052. Madonna and Child with two Angels. E.

New Haven (Conn.). 1959.15.10. 'Gambaro Madonna.' Sd and d. 1495. *Plate* 1596.

New York. 14.40.638. Federigo Gonzaga as a boy. 1510.
41.100.3. Madonna and Child with S. Francis and another Saint.
65.220.1. S. Roch (from Bologna, S. Rocco). d. 1502. *Plate* 1602.
MORGAN LIBRARY. Madonna and Child behind parapet, with S. Dominic and S. Barbara. L.
MRS LANGBOURNE WILLIAMS. The 'Crespi' S. Barbara. Sd.
MRS BORCHARD (EX). Predella panel: Pietà.
R. LEHMAN COLLECTION. Madonna with S. Francis and another Saint.
STANLEY MORTIMER (EX). Madonna and Child with S. Francis. L. *Plate* 1612.

Oldenburg. 63 (ex). Bust of Virgin in prayer (fr.).

Paris. 1435. Nativity.
1436. Crucifixion with S. Job (p.). Sd.
MARCEL COTTREAU (EX). Madonna and blessing Child behind parapet (version of New York, Stanley Mortimer).
HEUGEL COLLECTION (EX). Portrait of Bernardino Vanni. E. *Plate* 1593.

Parma. 123. Mourning over dead Christ. Sd. L.
130. Madonna and Child with SS. Benedict, Justina, Scholastica, Placidus, Benedict and Infant S. John (g.p.). Sd and d. 1515.
359. Madonna and Child with Infant S. John (p.). L.

Philadelphia (Pa.). ACADEMY OF FINE ARTS. 422. Head of Virgin (fr., st.). L.
J. G. JOHNSON COLLECTION. 1282. Madonna and Child (st.). L.

Raleigh (N.C.). MUSEUM OF ART. GL. 60.17.39 (KRESS COLLECTION. K 2158). Madonna and Child with two Angels. Sd.

Rome. CAMPIDOGLIO, PINACOTECA. 19. Circumcision (st.; S. Jerome, portrait and other figures, much later).

GALLERIA NAZIONALE, PALAZZO BARBERINI. 712. S. George and the Dragon. E.

GALLERIA BORGHESE. 57. S. Francis.

61. Madonna and Child in rose garden.

65. Votive picture: S. Stephen in prayer. Sd. E.

San Giovanni in Persiceto (Bologna). PALAZZO MUNICIPALE. S. John Baptist.

San Marino (Cal.). HUNTINGTON GALLERY. Madonna and Child with SS. Francis and Anthony of Padua (st.). Sd.

São Paulo (Brazil). 12. Madonna and Child with Infant S. John (st.). L.

Taymouth Castle. MARQUESS OF BREADALBANE (EX). Madonna of the cherries (replica in National Gallery, London). *Plate* 1601.

Toronto. FRANK P. WOOD. Madonna and Child with S. Francis.

Turin. ACCADEMIA ALBERTINA. 132. S. John Baptist. *Plate* 1595.

GALLERIA SABAUDA. 155. Pietà with S. Anthony of Padua. Sd and d. 1515.

Venice. CONTE VITTORIO CINI. Inv. 6466. Bust of S. George (fr.; st.).

Vercelli. MUSEO BORGOGNA. Madonna and Child with S. Anthony Abbot (p.). L.

Verona. 155. Madonna and Child with SS. Francis, Anthony Abbot and Angel behind parapet (g.p.). Sd.

Vienna. 47. Madonna and Child with SS. Catherine, Francis and Infant S. John. Sd.

AKADEMIE. 505. Madonna and Child enthroned with S. Petronius (the S. Luke by later hand). 1513.

Wallington (Northumberland). SIR GEORGE TREVELYAN. Madonna and Child. *Plate* 1610.

Washington (D.C.). 1143 (KRESS COLLECTION. K. 1531). Bishop Altobello Averoldo. L.

Wellesley (Mass.). COLLEGE, NORTON SIMON FOUNDATION LOAN. 'Beckwith Spencer' Marriage of S. Catherine (st.).

Worcester (Mass.). 1916.11. Madonna and Child with Infant S. John (p.). L.

York. 735. Lucretia (g.p.; variants at Dresden and Dublin).

FUNGAI, Bernardino

Born at Fungaia near Siena 1460, died in Siena 1516. Assistant to Benvenuto di Giovanni (1482); influenced by Francesco di Giorgio and Pietro di Domenico, as well as by Perugino, Signorelli, Pinturicchio and other Umbrians.

Altenburg. 130. Blessing Eternal (fr. of Nativity).*

Amsterdam. OTTO LANZ (EX). Coronation of Virgin with Saints and Angels. *Plate* 927.

Assisi. F. M. PERKINS COLLECTION. Bust of Christ (?).

Baltimore (Md.). WALTERS ART GALLERY. 1033. Madonna and Child with S.

Bernardino and S. Anthony of Padua (between Fungai and Benvenuto di Giovanni).

Bergamo. 319. Madonna and Child with two Angels.

Budapest. 4209 (PÁLFFY 8). Madonna and Child holding periwinkle.

Cambridge (Mass.). FOGG ART MUSEUM, KINGSLEY PORTER BEQUEST. Madonna and Child holding flowers.

Chambéry. 425. Holy Family and S. Francis.

Chiusi. S. SECONDIANO (DUOMO), L. NAVE. Nativity with SS. Vincent and Jerome; in predella, Martyrdom and Beheading of S. Vincent, Adoration of Magi, S. Jerome and the lion; S. Jerome in wilderness; in pilasters, Angel and Virgin of Annunciation, SS. Stephen, Sebastian, Catherine of Alexandria and Catherine of Siena. *Plate 933.*

Cologne. 507. Madonna and Child with two Saints.

Columbia (Mo.). UNIVERSITY OF MISSOURI. 61.74 (KRESS COLLECTION. K 378). Right panel of triptych: S. Louis of France.

Columbus (Ohio). HOWALD COLLECTION. Madonna and Child with bird.

Coral Gables (Fla.). UNIVERSITY OF MIAMI, LOWE ART GALLERY. 61. 23 (KRESS COLLECTION. K 1341). Tondo: Adoration of the Child with SS. Mary Magdalen, John Baptist and Jerome; in background, S. Christopher, and S. Francis receiving Stigmata.

Florence. UFFIZI. 3335. Miniature: Nun taking the habit.

   BERENSON COLLECTION. Predella: Marriage of Virgin, Dead Christ with Angels, Annunciation (damaged 1944).

   LOESER COLLECTION (EX). A Sibyl (companion to Pszczyna).

Gazzada (Varese). FONDAZIONE CAGNOLA. A Sibyl. (?)

Gotha. 488. Predella panel: Marriage of Virgin.

Hartford (Conn.). WADSWORTH ATHENEUM. 1962.445. 'Lehman' Nativity.

Houston (Texas). 44–560. EDITH A. AND PERCY S. STRAUS COLLECTION. Front of cassone: Rescue of Hippo. *Plates 935, 937.*

Leningrad. 1892, 1893. Two cassone panels: Story of Scipio (companions to London, Woodward and Homeless).

London. 1331. Tondo: Madonna and Child; in background, Nativity and Journey of Magi.

   2764. Madonna and Child with SS. Peter and Paul (property of Victoria and Albert Museum).

   HENRY HARRIS (EX). Oriental hero. (?)

   S. MAYNARD (EX). Predella panel: Ecstasy of S. Catherine of Siena.

   W. H. WOODWARD (EX). Two end-panels of cassone (companions to Leningrad and to Homeless): Story of Scipio. *Plates 934, 936.*

Maidenhead. SIR THOMAS MERTON. Predella panel: S. Clement thrown into the sea (companion to York).

Montenero. CHIESA DELLA MADONNA. Madonna and Child enthroned, crowned by Angels, with SS. John Baptist and Stephen. *Plate 938.*

New Haven (Conn.). 1943. 257A, B. Angel and Virgin of Annunciation.

New Orleans (La.). DELGADO MUSEUM. 61.68 (KRESS COLLECTION. K 248). Predella panel: S. Lucy standing fast against the oxen.

New York. 26.109. Nativity (r.).

    41.100.38. Madonna and Child with two Angels (c. of 'Ourousoff' Madonna).

    PERCY S. STRAUS (EX). 'Ourousoff' Madonna adoring Child and two Angels. *Plate 929.*

Pszczyna. CASTLE. Inv. 6076. A Sibyl (st.; companion to Florence, Loeser).*

Richmond (Va.). MUSEUM OF ART. Madonna and Child with SS. Anselm and Sebastian.

Siena. 305. Madonna of Humility (r.).

    363. Madonna suckling the Child, with S. Jerome and Angel (r.).

    374. Madonna and Child with SS. Mary Magdalen and Anthony Abbot (r.).

    385. Madonna and Child.

    431. Altarpiece from Carmine: Coronation of Virgin and SS. Jerome, Sebastian, Anthony of Padua and Nicholas. Sd and d. 1512. *Plate 940.*

    441. Assumption of Virgin, and SS. Francis and Bernardino. L.

    ARCHIVIO DI STATO. Book-cover: Sacrifice of Isaac. d. 1485.

    CASA DI RIPOSO (MADONNA DI CAMPANSI), CLOISTER. Madonna in fresco of Assumption (with Balducci and Pietro di Domenico).

    ISTITUTO DEI SORDOMUTI (EX-CONVENT OF S. MARGHERITA), FORMER REFECTORY. Frescoes: Last Supper; in lunettes, Agony in Garden, Crucifixion, Betrayal of Christ. L.

    PALAZZO SALIMBENI (MONTE DE' PASCHI). Frescoes: SS. Catherine and Bernardino of Siena, SS. Lucy and Anthony of Padua, Emblems of Siena.

    S. DOMENICO, SIXTH ALTAR R. Predella under Francesco di Giorgio's Nativity: Christ appears to S. Catherine of Siena, Martyrdom of S. Sebastian, Massacre of Innocents, Preaching of S. Dominic, Communion of Mary Magdalen (with 'Noli me Tangere' in background). [*Plate 275.*] *Plate 939.*

    FONTEGIUSTA, THIRD ALTAR R. Coronation of Virgin and SS. John Baptist, Louis of France, Jerome and Roch.

    S. GIROLAMO, CLOISTER. Frescoed niche: Assumption. 1487.

    S. MARIA DEI SERVI, HIGH ALTAR. Coronation of Virgin, with twelve Saints and Angels. 1498–1501.

    — SECOND CHAPEL L. S. Mary Magdalen and Infant S. John, S. Joseph and Christ-child.

    SANTUARIO CATERINIANO, ORATORIO DELLA CUCINA. S. Catherine receiving Stigmata; in predella, S. Catherine receiving Communion; receiving the Dominican habit (side-panels added 1524 by another hand; top panels added 1564 by Riccio). 1497. *Plate 930.*

    (Environs). LE GROTTE, ABOVE HIGH ALTAR. Monochrome fresco: Assumption.

    — MONISTERO DI S. EUGENIO (EX). Dead Christ upheld by Angels. Sd. *Plate 931.*

Strasbourg. 228A, B. Predella panels: Scenes from Life of S. Mark.

Toulon. 182. Madonna and Child with two Angels.

Turin. GUALINO COLLECTION (EX). Madonna and Child with two Cherubim.

Venice. ACCADEMIA. 57. Madonna and Child enthroned with SS. Peter, Paul and two Angels (st.). Sd?

Washington (D.C.). HOWARD UNIVERSITY. 61.152-3-P (KRESS STUDY COLLECTION. K 1163). Four half-length Saints from predella: Apollonia, Dominic, James, Donatus.

York. 804. Predella panel (companion to Maidenhead): S. Clement striking water from the rock. *Plate 932.*

Homeless. Scipio on a pedestal among the Roman Senators. (*Dedalo*, XI, p. 756; companion to Leningrad and London, Woodward.)

Madonna and Child (r.). (*Dedalo*, XI, p. 757.) *Plate 928.*

Madonna and Child (r.). (*Dedalo*, XI, p. 761.)

Tondo: Madonna and Child with two Angels and Infant S. John. (*Dedalo*, XI, p. 760.)

GAROFALO

Benvenuto Tisi, called Garofalo. Ferrara ca 1481–1559. Pupil of Panetti; influenced by Dosso, slightly by Palma Vecchio, and a great deal by Raphael.

Alnwick Castle (Northumberland). DUKE OF NORTHUMBERLAND. Christ healing the possessed at the Lake of Galilee.

— (EX). Woman adorning herself.

Amsterdam. 947. Holy Family and S. Anne, S. Joachim and Infant S. John. L.

947A-1. Half-length Madonna and Child seated on steps.

OTTO LANZ (EX). Madonna and Child with goldfinch. E.

Argenta. PALAZZO MUNICIPALE. Madonna and Child enthroned between Job and Lazarus. 1513 (dep. Pinacoteca, Ferrara).

Ariccia. PALAZZO CHIGI (EX). Holy Family of the Grapes.

Atlanta (Ga.). ART ASSOCIATION GALLERIES. 58.44 (KRESS COLLECTION. K 1750). Predella panel: Adoration of Magi. E.

Baltimore (Md.). WALTERS ART GALLERY. 1077. Predella panel to Ferrara Inv. 161: Circumcision (versions at Berlin, Englewood, Liverpool, Paris).

Bari. MUSEO. Christ carrying the Cross.

— DEP. FROM GALLERIA NAZIONALE, ROMA: 'Chigi' Ascension.

Basle. DR. TOBIAS CHRIST (EX). Nativity (st. v. of Ferrara Inv. 160).

Bergamo. 272. Half-length Madonna and Child before parapet.

510. Half-length Madonna and Child against curtain and landscape (r.).

536. Holy Family.

Berlin. 3/65. 'Northwick' Stoning of S. Stephen. Sd and d. 153(0?).

R. VON KAUFMANN (EX). Circumcision (version of Baltimore).

EUGEN SCHWEITZER (EX). Predella panel: Christ and the Woman of Samaria.

Berlin-Ost. 243. Penitent S. Jerome. d. 1524.

Birmingham. CITY ART GALLERY. Agony in the Garden. d. 1524.

Birmingham (Ala.). MUSEUM OF ART. 61.94 (KRESS COLLECTION. K 214). Baptism of Christ, with kneeling nun.

Bologna. Inv. 635. Holy Family with SS. Elizabeth and Infant John.

MUSEO DAVIA BARGELLINI. Madonna suckling the Child in landscape.

S. SALVATORE, FIRST ALTAR L. S. John Baptist taking leave of his father. Sd and d. 1542. *Plate* 1787.

MOLINARI PRADELLI COLLECTION. Holy Family and S. Anne.

Bonn. 80 (ex). 'Wesendonck' Madonna and Child with Infant S. John.

Boughton House. DUKE OF BUCCLEUCH. Holy Family with S. Catherine.

Bowood (Calne, Wilts.). MARQUESS OF LANSDOWNE. Mythological scene.

Breslau. 131. Annunciation.

Brunswick (Maine). BOWDOIN COLLEGE MUSEUM OF FINE ARTS. 1961.190.5 (KRESS STUDY COLLECTION. K 1227). 'Kaufmann' Presentation of Virgin.

Brussels. FIEVEZ COLLECTION (EX). Predella panel: Circumcision (replica of Naples).

Budapest. 165 (162). Christ and the Woman taken in Adultery (st.). L.

Busto Arsizio. ARCH. PAOLO CANDIANI. Christ on Cross, SS. Peter and Andrew, and Bernardino Barbadigo as donor (from S. Pietro at Ferrara). 1544.

Cambridge. MARLAY COLLECTION (EX). Nativity. E.

Canford Manor (Ashby St. Ledgers). VISCOUNT WIMBORNE (EX). Two tondi from S. Bernardo at Ferrara: Angel and Virgin of Annunciation.

Canterbury. CATHEDRAL. Detached fresco from Foresteria of Certosa at Ferrara, companion to Montecassino: S. Christopher. 1525.

Castellarano (Reggio Emilia). S. VALENTINO. Madonna and Child with SS. Eleucadius and Stephen. d. 1517. *Plate* 1775.

Chicago (Ill.). MARTIN A. RYERSON (EX). Madonna and Child against curtain and landscape.

Codigoro. S. MARTINO (destroyed). (See FLORENCE, UFFIZI.)

Columbus (Ohio). GALLERY, SCHUMACHER COLLECTION. Madonna and Child. E.

Coral Gables (Fla.). LOWE ART GALLERY. 61.7 (KRESS COLLECTION. K 60). Madonna and Child in Glory.

Cracow. Inv. XII. 205. Adoration of Magi. E.

Crespino (Rovigo). SS. MARTINO AND SEVERO. Madonna and Child enthroned with S. Francis and Mary Magdalen (p.). d. 1525.

Dallas (Texas). MUSEUM. 1939.2 (KRESS COLLECTION. K 1032). Predella panel: Madonna and Child with S. Jerome. L.

Detroit (Mich.). 31.23. 'Northbrook' Holy Family and S. Anne.

Dresden. 132. Poseidon and Athene. d. 1512.

133. Madonna adoring Child. d. 1517.

134. Madonna and Child with SS. Peter, George and Bernard. Sd and d. 1530.

135. Venus and Mars before Troy.

136. Holy Family.

Dresden (contd.). 137. Madonna and Child with SS. Geminianus, Cecilia, Anthony of Padua and Bernardinus.

    138. Bacchanal. L.

    139. Diana and Endymion (st.).

    140. Christ in Temple (st.).

    141. Marriage of S. Catherine (st.). 1537.

El Paso (Texas). MUSEUM OF ART. 1961–6/18 (KRESS COLLECTION. K 2143). Circumcision. L.

Englewood (N.J.). PLATT COLLECTION (EX). Circumcision (unfinished version of Baltimore).

Escorial. PHILIP II BEDROOM. Madonna and Child with SS. Roch and Sebastian.

Ferrara. Inv. 74. Roundel from S. Francesco altarpiece: Return from Egypt (st.; see Inv. 161). 1519.

    Inv. 76. Lunette from S. Francesco altarpiece: Flight into Egypt (st.; see Inv. 161). 1519. *Plate* 1776.

    Inv. 123–126. Detached fresco from refectory of Minori Osservanti at S. Spirito: Last Supper; in three lunettes, Noah, David, Moses (monochrome). 1544.

    Inv. 143. Detached fresco from refectory of Augustinians at S. Andrea: Allegory of the Old and New Testament. 1524.

    Inv. 147. 'Madonna del Libro' (or 'del Riposo') and Leonello dal Pero as donor (from S. Francesco). d. 1525.

    Inv. 148. Madonna and Child in Glory and SS. Jerome, Francis, with donors of the Suxena Family. d. 1514.

    Inv. 151. Nativity from S. Francesco. d. 1513.

    Inv. 152. Invention of the True Cross. 1536.

    Inv. 153. Raising of Lazarus. Sd and d. 1534. *Plate* 1786.

    Inv. 154. Adoration of Magi. d. 1537.

    Inv. 155. 'Madonna del Pilastro' with SS. John Baptist, Jerome, other two Saints and Ludovica Trotti as donor. doc. 1523.

    Inv. 156. Adoration of Magi and S. Bartholomew (p.). d. 1549.

    Inv. 159. Agony in the Garden.

    Inv. 160. Nativity. E.

    Inv. 161. Massacre of Innocents from S. Francesco (companion to Inv. 74, 76, to Baltimore and to Dosso, Ferrara). 1519.

    Inv. 173. Predella panel from Nuzzarelli Chapel in S. Andrea: Mass of S. Nicholas of Tolentino (companion to New York).*

    Inv. 174–177. Four monochrome predella panels: Vision of the Emperor Constantine, S. Sylvester shows him the picture of SS. Peter and Paul, Miracle of the Bull, Pope Silvester baptizing the Emperor. *Plate* 1781.

    Inv. 225. Detached fresco from Oratorio della Concezione: Circumcision (finishing cycle of frescoes begun by Boccaccino). ca 1510.

    PALAZZO DI LUDOVICO IL MORO, AULA COSTABILIANA (SALA DEL TESORO). Frescoes: in lunettes, monochrome scenes with Myth of Eros and Anteros; in ceiling, dodecagonal frame with simulated cameos, monochrome frieze, and people with musical instruments looking down from balcony (p.). *Plate* 1779.

— SALA DELLE SIBILLE E DEI PROFETI. Frescoes: in lunettes, Monochrome Sibyls and Prophets; in vault, Moses looking down from balcony and Monochrome Scenes and decorations (st.; damaged by war).

— SALA DI GIUSEPPE. Frescoed ceiling: Monochrome Scenes from Life of Joseph.

PALAZZO (TROTTI) DEL SEMINARIO, SALETTA DELLE ALLEGORIE. Frescoes: Figures praying and Allegories. 1517–19.

— SALETTA DI DAVID E GIUDITTA. Frescoes: Monochrome friezes with Putti, heads and Satyrs, David, Judith; in centre of ceiling, hexagonal frame and people looking down from balcony. 1517-19. *Plate* 1778.

DUOMO, ENTRANCE WALL. Two detached frescoes from suppressed Church of S. Peter: SS. Peter and Paul.

— CAPPELLA DEL SACRAMENTO (L. OF CHOIR), L. WALL. Madonna and Child ('Vergine Liberatrice'). d. 1532.

— THIRD ALTAR L. Madonna and Child with SS. Silvester, Jerome, John Baptist, Maurelius, Archangel and female Saint. Sd and d. 1524.

— SACRISTY. Annunciation (still there?)

— CORO D'INVERNO. Two canvases from S. Silvestro: S. Peter, S. Paul (st.). Destroyed 1944.

S. FRANCESCO, FIRST CHAPEL L. Frescoes: Right and left of Altar, Two kneeling Members of Massa family; right wall, Betrayal of Christ flanked by monochrome Zaccarias and Jeremiah. Sd and d. 1524.

— CHAPEL R. Frescoes: Nativity and Rest on Flight.

S. MONICA, OVER DOOR. Fresco very much repainted. (?)

Florence. UFFIZI. 1365. Annunciation. L.

— DEPOT FROM CODIGORO. Madonna and Child with S. Martin and S. Rosalia. E.

PITTI. 5. Bust of S. James pointing at Betrayal of Christ (variant of same figure in Dosso's polyptych at Ferrara, Inv. 189/194).

6034. Augustus and the Sibyl (st. version of London, Graham).

Fondra (Bergamo). PARISH CHURCH, FIRST ALTAR R. Annunciation. Sd and d. 1541.

Frankfurt a/M. 976. Holy Family. *Plate* 1780.

Glasgow. 155. Vision of S. Augustine.

167, 171. S. Barbara, S. Catherine.

Hampton Court. ROYAL COLLECTION. Madonna and Child with SS. Anne and Joachim. Sd and d. 1533. *Plate* 1785.

Innsbruck. 531. Madonna and Child with S. John Baptist, S. Francis and female Martyr.

Knole (Kent). LORD SACKVILLE. Judith with the Head of Holofernes.

Leningrad. 59. Adoration of Shepherds. Sd.

1848. Marriage of Cana. Sd and d. 1531. *Plate* 1783.

— FROM GATCHINA. Sacrifices according to the Old and the New Testaments. Miracle of Loaves and Fishes.

Liverpool. 2777. Circumcision (variant of Paris, Louvre 1550).

2778. Madonna suckling the Child. E.

London. 81. Vision of S. Augustine. *Plate* 1784.

170. Holy Family and Saints.

642. Agony in the Garden.

671. Madonna and Child enthroned and Saints. d. 1517.

3118. Bust of S. Catherine. (?)

3928. Sacrifice to Ceres. d. 1526.

WILLIAM GRAHAM (EX). Augustus and the Sibyl. d. 1537.

COL. T. MORGAN GREVILLE GAVIN (EX). Bust of S.? George. E.

E. JOLL. Holy Family with S. Elizabeth and Infant S. John. E.

E. MACLACLAN. Nativity (variant of Ferrara 160).

W. MARTIN. Self-portrait as King David.

C. FAIRFAX MURRAY (EX). Christ and the Woman of Samaria.

GORDON RICHARDSON (formerly Earl Fitzwilliam). Adoration of Shepherds (earlier version of Leningrad). *Plate* 1782.

Los Angeles (Cal.). A.57.37. 47–1. S. James worshipped by a nun.

Milan. BRERA. 438. Deposition. Sd and d. 1527.

439. Crucifixion with young donor.

440. Annunciation. Sd and d. 1550.

442. Madonna and Child.

BARGELLESI COLLECTION. 'Haversham' Circumcision. d. 1537.

Modena. 169. Madonna and Child with S. John Baptist, S. Lucy and old Contardo d'Este as S. Pellegrino. Sd and d. 1532.

Montecassino. ABBAZIA, GIFT SCACCIA SCARAFONI 1957. Detached fresco from Foresteria of Certosa at Ferrara, companion to Canterbury: 'Costabili' Holy Family. d. 1525.

Montpellier. (126) Inv. 825.1.97. Martyrdom of S. Sebastian (st.).

Munich. 1080 Pietà. d. 1530.

1081. Madonna and Child with S. Michael and John Baptist.

1082. Madonna and Child (from Nymphenburg).

Nantes. MUSÉE. Holy Family in landscape (st.).

Naples. 71. Madonna and Child with S. Jerome. (?)

74. Adoration of Magi (p.).

80. S. Sebastian. (?)

ARCHIVIO. Inv. 83963. Predella panel: Circumcision (replica of Brussels).

New Orleans (La.). DELGADO MUSEUM OF ART. 61.78 (KRESS COLLECTION. K 1111). S. Jerome in the Wilderness.

New York. 17.190.23/24. Two predella panels (companions to Ferrara Inv. 173): S. Nicholas of Tolentino reviving the birds, bringing a child back to life.

Padua. 103 (Inv. 458). Sacra Conversazione with SS. Joachim, Elizabeth and Infant S. John (later version at Windsor).

Palermo. Inv. 76 Madonna and Child with Infant S. John.

Paris. 1550. Predella panel: Circumcision (see Baltimore). *Plate* 1777.

    1553. Madonna and sleeping Child.

    1554. Adoration of the Child with Symbols of Passion.

Parma. 366. Nativity (r.).

    369. Madonna and Child in Glory (r.).

Poznań. Inv. Mo 15. Jupiter and Io. E.

Rome. CAMPIDOGLIO, PINACOTECA. 2. Holy Family with SS. Elizabeth, Zacharias and Infant John; on back, sketch of Circumcision.

    4. Holy Family and S. Jerome (st.).

    5. Annunciation. d. 1528.

    6. Coronation of S. Catherine (p.).

    7. Nativity.

    18. Madonna in Glory and Meeting of SS. Francis and Anthony of Padua below.

    20. Madonna and Child with Infant S. John (deposited at Palazzo dei Conservatori).

    174. S. Lucy (st.) (dep. Palazzo Conservatori).

    192. Madonna and Child and four Church Fathers (dep. Palazzo dei Conservatori).

    194. Marriage of S. Catherine (dep. Palazzo Conservatori).

    197. Madonna and Child with Infant S. John.

  GALLERIA NAZIONALE (PALAZZO BARBERINI). Inv. 1266. Nativity.

  Picus transformed into a bird.

  Story of the Vestal Claudia.

  S. Cecily crowned by an Angel.

  S. Anthony Abbot between S. Anthony of Padua and S. Cecily (formerly Chigi). d. 1523.

  S. Sebastian.

 — DEPOT. See S. Paolo fuori le Mura.

  GALLERIA BORGHESE. 204. Marriage at Cana (p.). L.

    205. Deposition. L.

    208. Madonna suckling the Child with S. Joseph, Infant S. John and S. Anthony of Padua. (st.).

    210. Madonna and Child. E.

    213. Madonna and Child with SS. Peter and Paul (g.p.).

    216. Martyrdom of S. Catherine (st.).

    221. Christ and the Woman of Samaria (g.p.).

    224. Nativity.

    236. Calling of S. Peter.

    237. Flagellation.

    239. Adoration of Magi (st.). d. 1543.

    240. Madonna del Mappamondo, with SS. Michael, Zacharias, Anne and Joseph.

    242. Madonna and Child with Saints (st.).

Rome. GALLERIA BORGHESE (contd.). 244. 'Noli me tangere' (st.).

247. Conversion of S. Paul. 1545.

409. Holy Family.

GALLERIA DORIA PAMPHILI. 139. Holy Family with SS. Joachim and Anne.

144. Holy Family in Glory with SS. Zacharias, Elizabeth and Infant John, appearing to SS. Francis and Bernardino.

161. Visitation (st.).

MUSEO DI PALAZZO VENEZIA. P.V.5179. S. Jerome in the Wilderness.

PALAZZO ROSPIGLIOSI, PALLAVICINI COLLECTION. 490. S. James the More (version of Florence, Pitti).

S. PAOLO FUORI LE MURA, PINACOTECA. Adoration of Magi (g.p.). L.

Agony in the Garden (g.p.). L. (?) (dep. at Palazzo Barberini).

VATICAN, PINACOTECA. 355. Augustus and the Sibyl. d. 1544.

330. Mystic Marriage of S. Catherine (r.).

358. Holy Family with S. Catherine.

Southam (Glos.). EARL OF ELLENBOROUGH (EX). S. Luke painting the Virgin. E.

Strasbourg. 253. (EX). Nativity. E.

Syon House (Middlesex). DUKE OF NORTHUMBERLAND. S. John Baptist.

Tours. 735. S. Sebastian (st.). Not traced, possibly identical with Montpellier.

Turin. GALLERIA SABAUDA. 153. Christ disputing with Doctors.

154. Roundels in frame of Mazzolino's altarpiece: Redeemer, Head of Baptist, Heads of Martyrs, S. Francis, S. Catherine (st.).

Vaduz. LIECHTENSTEINSCHE SAMMLUNG. G 172. S. Christopher. L.

— (EX). Madonna and Child with Infant S. John.

Valcesura (Ferrara). S. MARGHERITA. Madonna and Child blessing donors, between S. Sebastian and S. Margaret.*

Venice. ACCADEMIA. 56. Madonna and Child in Glory and SS. John Baptist, Augustine, Peter and Paul. Sd and d. 1518.

CONTE V. CINI. Inv. 1330, 1331. S. Catherine and female martyr in roundels (st.).

Vienna. 647. S. Roch in landscape.

LANCKORONSKI COLLECTION. Mars, Venus and Cupid.

Warsaw. NARODOWE MUSEUM. 'Potocki' Madonna and Child in Glory.

Homeless. Nativity with Shepherd (variant of Cambridge). E. *Plate* 1774.

GAUDENZIO FERRARI

School of Vercelli. Born at Valduggia ca 1480, died at Milan 1546. Probably pupil of Macrino d'Alba; strongly influenced by Bramantino, scarcely less by Perugino and Leonardo, and slightly by Correggio.

Amsterdam. 922 D–I. Madonna and Child with two Putti. (?)

Arcore, see Paris.

Arona (Novara). S. MARIA, CAPPELLA BORROMEO. Polyptych: Nativity; in lunette above, God the Father and Angels; at sides, SS. Ambrose and George; SS. Martin and Jerome; SS. Catherine and Barbara; SS. Gaudentius and Peter Martyr with donor; in predella, Christ and Apostles. Sd and d. 1511.

Bellagio (Lago di Como). Environs. See San Giovanni.

Bergamo. 293–6. Predella panels to Marriage of S. Catherine, Novara, Duomo: dancing and music-making Putti. ca 1525–30.

    343. Centre panel of triptych (companion to Merate and to Milan, Borromeo): Madonna and Child in a meadow, with columbines in foreground (from Monastery of S. Chiara, Milan). L.

  S. ALESSANDRO DELLA CROCE, SACRISTY. 12–15. Four panels of polyptych: S. Jerome and three Dominican Saints.

Berlin. 213. Annunciation.

  EUGEN SCHWEITZER (EX). Two monochrome predella panels: Music-making Putti standing in niches (companions to Detroit, Varallo and Vercelli). L.

  Two monochrome predella panels: Putti seated on grass, playing the flute and the triangle.

Besançon. Inv. 896.1.141/2. Two predella panels: each with a worshipping Angel. L.

Biella. PARISI COLLECTION. Crucifixion.

Budapest. 4684 (124A). 'Crespi' Pietà.

Busto Arsizio (Milan). S. MARIA DI PIAZZA, L. WALL. Polyptych: Assumption, Eternal blessing, SS. John Baptist, Jerome, Michael and Francis; in predella, Life of Virgin (g.p.). Sd and d. 1541.

Canobbio (Lago Maggiore). S. MARIA DELLA PIETÀ. Christ on the Way to Calvary; in predella, two pairs of worshipping Angels. L.

Casale Monferrato. S. EVASIO (DUOMO). SACRISTY. Baptism (oval fr.). 1534.

Castle Ashby (Northampton). MARQUESS OF NORTHAMPTON. Madonna and Child enthroned, with birds pecking apples in foreground (old copy of Milan, Brera 277).

Como. DUOMO, THIRD CHAPEL R. (CAPPELLA DI S. ABBONDIO), R. OF ALTAR. Outside right cover to S. Abbondio carved altarpiece: Flight into Egypt (inside by Luini). L. *Plate* 1274.

  Prophet (over Luini's picture).

  — THIRD CHAPEL L. (CAPPELLA DI S. GIUSEPPE), L. OF ALTAR. Outside left cover to S. Abbondio carved altarpiece: Marriage of the Virgin (inside by Luini). L.

Detroit (Mich.). 52.29A, B. Two monochrome predella panels with music-making Putto in niche (companions to Berlin, Varallo and Vercelli). L.

Eltville. GRÄFIN VON FRANCKEN SIERSTORPFF. Adoration of the Child with S. Andrew.

Florence. CONTINI BONACOSSI COLLECTION. Birth of Virgin.

Frankfurt a/M. 1790. Adoration of the Child with two music-making Angels (r.). E.

Greenville (S.C.). BOB JONES UNIVERSITY. Fall of S. Paul (st. ?).L.

Isolabella. PALAZZO BORROMEO. Madonna and Child.

    10. S. Sebastian.

    12. Holy Family with S. Joachim.

    14. S. Roch.

    16. Predella panel, companion to Bergamo and Merate: Monochrome Putti with crown (from Monastery of S. Chiara, Milan). L.

Leipzig. MUSEUM. Old copy of Milan, Brera 277.

London. 1465, 3925. Panels of polyptych: Risen Christ, S. Andrew (p.; companions to Maggianico). L.

    3068. 'Layard' Annunciation. E.

    J. C. PRESTON (EX). Side-panel of polyptych: SS. Catherine of Alexandria and Apollonia.*

Maggianico (Lecco). S. ANDREA, R. ALTAR. Three panels of polyptych: S. Ambrose, S. Bonaventura, S. Anthony Abbot (p.; companions to London). L.

Merate. MARCHESE PRINETTI. Side-panel of triptych, companion to Bergamo and Milan: Dominican nun (from Monastery of S. Chiara, Milano). L.

Milan. BRERA. 26-38. Detached frescoes from S. Maria della Pace: Presentation of the Virgin; Expulsion of Joachim; Annunciation to S. Anne; Two women discuss S. Anne's pregnancy; lunette with Consecration of Mary (tondo), Angel and Virgin of Annunciation (corners); Adoration of Magi (in three parts); lunette with Assumption of Mary (tondo) and music-making Putti (corners); Visitation with penitent Jerome in background; spandrel with music-making Putto. 1545.

    277. Cut-down centre panel of triptych: Madonna and Child (old copies at Castle Ashby, and Leipzig; side-panels at Moscow).

    321. Martyrdom of S. Catherine (from the suppressed church of S. Angelo). L.

    CASTELLO SFORZESCO. 307: Monochrome predella: Christ and Apostles.

    POLDI PEZZOLI. 650. Madonna and Child enthroned with SS. Dominic, Peter Martyr, Catherine and Martha. ca 1520.

    S. AMBROGIO, CAPPELLA DELLO STRECCHIONE (FIRST R.). Frescoes: Mourning over the dead Christ; Adoring Angels; Saints in niches. L.

    — CAPPELLA DI S. BARTOLOMEO (SECOND R.). Madonna and Child with SS. Bartholomew and John Baptist.

    S. GIORGIO AL PALAZZO, FIRST ALTAR R. S. Jerome and donor.

    S. MARIA PRESSO S. CELSO, DEAMBULATORIO, FOURTH BAY R. Baptism.

    S. MARIA DELLE GRAZIE, CAPPELLA DI S. CORONA (FOURTH R.). Frescoes: vault, eight Angels with Symbols of Passion; centre wall, by window, two Angels; right wall, Flagellation and 'Ecce Homo'; left wall, Crucifixion. d. 1542.

    S. MARIA DELLA PASSIONE, L. TRANSEPT. Last Supper (with G. B. della Cerva). doc. 1544.

Morbegno (Sondrio). S. ANTONIO, LUNETTE OVER DOOR. Fresco: Nativity.

    ASSUNTA E S. LORENZO, L. WALL BY DOOR. Birth of Virgin. doc. 1520-26.

Moscow. PUSHKIN MUSEUM. 148, 150. Two panels of polyptych, companions to Milan, Brera 277: S. Cecilia with kneeling monk; S. Margaret.

Notre Dame (Indiana). UNIVERSITY GALLERY, 61.47.8–9 (KRESS COLLECTION. K 1210, 1211). Two monochrome predella panels with kneeling Angels.

Novara. MUSEO DEL BROLETTO. 216, 217. Predella panels: Two pairs of kneeling Angels.

    S. GAUDENZIO, SECOND ALTAR L. Polyptych: Madonna and Child enthroned with two curtain-raising Angels and SS. Gaudentius, Ambrose, and two Martyrs; Nativity; Angel and Virgin of Annunciation; SS. Peter and John Baptist; SS. Paul and Bishop Saint; in predella, the four Church Fathers and Scenes from Life of S. Gaudentius. doc. 1514–16, and 1521 (last payment).

    S. MARIA ASSUNTA (DUOMO), SECOND ALTAR R. Mystic Marriage of S. Catherine with SS. Gaudentius, Joseph and Agapitus; in predella, Pietà (side panels of predella at Bergamo). ca 1525–30.

Pallanza (Lago Maggiore). (Environs). MADONNA DI CAMPAGNA, CUPOLA. Frescoes.

Paris. 1285. S. Paul in his study. Sd and d. 1543.

    GENTILI COLLECTION (FORMERLY VITTADINI, ARCORE) EX. Centre panel of polyptych: Madonna and Child enthroned, worshipped by two Angels.

Roccapietra (Valsesia). S. MARTINO, HIGH ALTAR. Four panels of polyptych: SS. Ambrose and Gaudentius; SS. Martin and John Baptist; Angel and Virgin of Annunciation.

    MADONNA DI LORETO. (See Varallo, Environs.)

Rome. PRINCIPE ODESCALCHI. 'Balbi di Piovera' Holy Family.

San Giovanni (Lago di Como). S. GIOVANNI BATTISTA, R. OF CHOIR. Risen Christ worshipped by Saint and donors.

Sarasota (Fla.). RINGLING MUSEUM OF ART. 'Holford' Nativity with kneeling Cardinal.

Saronno. S. MARIA DEI MIRACOLI, CUPOLA. Fresco: Concert of Angels. 1534–36. *Plate 1273.*

Turin. GALLERIA SABAUDA. 43, 44, 47, 48. Panels of dismembered polyptych (for the Congregazione di S. Anna at Vercelli?): Meeting of Joachim and Anne; God the Father blessing among Cherubs; S. Anne and the Virgin with Jesus and two music-making Angels; Expulsion of Joachim. (1508?). *Plate 1265.*

    46. Right panel of polyptych: S. Peter and donor.

    49. Madonna and Child with SS. Martin and Mauritius and music-making Putto. L.

    50. Crucifixion, from Casale Monferrato. *Plate 1270.*

    51. Mourning over the dead Christ. L.

    MUSEO CIVICO. Inv. 424. Three monochrome predella panels (formerly Panshanger): Christ and Apostles.

    Sketch of Crucifixion.*

Valduggia (Valsesia). ORATORIO DI S. ROCCO. Frescoes: SS. Crispinus, Crispinianus, Helen with the Cross, George on horseback. 1516.

    ORATORIO DI S. GIORGIO. Fresco: Nativity with S. Barbara (r.).

Varallo Sesia. 70–73. Frs. of frescoes from S. Maria delle Grazie: Heads of man with red cap, of friar, of youth, of Peter Martyr. E.

Varallo Sesia (contd.). 74. Angel of Annunciation (from Sacro Monte; r.). E. (?)
75–78. Church Fathers from predella of Gattinara polyptych.
79. Monochrome predella: Martyrdom of S. Catherine.
80, 81. Two monochrome predella panels: Standing putto with harp; standing
putto with double-bass (companions to Berlin, Detroit and Vercelli).
83. Lunette from Oratorio di S. Francesco al Sacro Monte: S. Francis receiving
Stigmata (sc.).
S. GAUDENZIO (COLLEGIATA), APSE. Polyptych: Mystic Marriage of S. Catherine;
above, Pietà; at sides, S. John Baptist, S. Mark, S. Gaudentius, S. Peter. ca
1516–20.
S. MARIA DELLE GRAZIE, WALL BETWEEN NAVE AND CHOIR. Frescoes: in tympanum,
God the Father blessing with two Putti; upper register, Annunciation,
Nativity, Adoration of Magi, Flight into Egypt, Baptism of Christ, Raising
of Lazarus, Entry into Jerusalem, Last Supper; centre of middle and lower
registers, Crucifixion, flanked by: Washing of Feet, Agony in the Garden,
Betrayal, Capture, Christ before Pilate, Flagellation, Pilate washes his hands,
Way to Calvary, Nailing on the Cross, Deposition, Descent into Limbo,
Resurrection; in spandrels, two tondi with S. Francis and S. Bernardino.
Sd and d. 1513. [*Plate* 374.] *Plates* 1266–1268.
— L. CHAPEL (CAPPELLA DI S. MARGHERITA). Frescoes: left wall, Circumcision;
right wall, Christ and the Doctors. Formerly d. 1507.
— EX-CONVENTO DEI MINORI OSSERVANTI, CLOISTER. Fresco: Pietà. E.
(Environs). MADONNA DI LORETO, LUNETTE OVER PORTAL. Fresco: Adoration of the
Child with two Angels. ca 1520.
(Environs). SACRO MONTE, CHAPELS ALONG THE ROAD LEADING UP TO THE CHURCH.
Frescoes and painted statuary.
— V CAPPELLA. Fresco: Adoration of Magi (r.).
— XXXVIII CAPPELLA. Fresco: Crucifixion. 1523. *Plate* 1269.
— XL CAPPELLA. Fresco: Pietà (r.).
Vercelli. MUSEO BORGOGNA. Madonna and Child with SS. Agnes, John Baptist,
Nicholas of Tolentino, Joseph, Anthony Abbot, Catherine and three Putti
(g.p.).
Detached fresco from the Spedale di S. Rocco: S. Roch. ca 1530.
Monochrome predella panels: Christ on the way to Calvary, Circumcision.
Two predella panels: Monochrome music-making Putti (companions to Berlin,
Detroit and Varallo; st.).
Detached fresco: Last Supper. L.
Three sketches: Worshipping of the Golden Calf, The Brazen Serpent, Banquet.
S. CRISTOFORO, HIGH ALTAR. 'Madonna del Melarancio' (Madonna and Child
with SS. Christopher, John Baptist, Joseph, Nicholas, Bernard?, seven Putti
and kneeling donor). 1529–30.
— CAPPELLA DELL'ASSUNTA (L. OF CHOIR). Fresco over altar: Assumption. d.
1534.

— — L. WALL: Frescoes: Birth of Virgin, Marriage of Virgin, Adoration of the
Shepherds, S. Theresa and Bishop Saint with two female donors, Adoration
of Magi (with assistance from B. Lanino). 1532–34. *Plates* 1271–1272.

— CAPPELLA DELLA MADDALENA (R. OF CHOIR). Fresco over altar: Crucifixion.
1530–32.

— — R. WALL. Frescoes: Preaching of Christ, Christ in the House of Simon,
S. Mary Magdalen landing at Marseilles, Assumption of S. Mary Magdalen
(with assistance from B. Lanino). 1530–32.

GENGA, Girolamo

*Urbino. 1476–1551. Pupil of Signorelli; influenced by Timoteo Viti, Raphael and Sodoma.
Active mainly as architect during the last twenty years of his life.*

Bergamo. 322. Predella panel from Cesena altarpiece (companion to Columbia and
Milan): S. Augustine baptizing three Catechumens. 1513–18.

Berlin-Ost. I, 317. Dispute about Original Sin. 1515.

Columbia (S.C.). MUSEUM OF ART. 54–402/13 (KRESS COLLECTION. K 113). Predella
panel from Cesena altarpiece (companion to Bergamo and Milan): S. Augustine giving his habit to three catechumens. 1513–18. *Plate* 1842.

Florence. PITTI. 369. Male portrait. (?)

UFFIZI. 1535. Martyrdom of S. Sebastian.

MUSEO DEL BARGELLO, CARRAND COLLECTION. Faenza tile: Martyrdom of S.
Sebastian (on Genga's design).

Gradara (Pesaro). CASTELLO. Fresco: Battle scene.

Lisbon. 266. Madonna and Child. L.

London. SIR HENRY HAWORTH (EX). Madonna suckling Child and Infant S. John in
landscape. E. *Plate* 1841.

Milan. BRERA. 512. Altarpiece from S. Agostino, Cesena: Madonna with Holy
Children, six Saints, four Fathers of the Church, three singing Putti in foreground and Eternal with Putti scattering jasmin blossoms above (predella
panels at Bergamo and Columbia). 1513–18. *Plate* 1844.

Nantes. 66. (275). Madonna with Holy Children and SS. Joseph and Zacharias in
landscape.

Pesaro. VILLA IMPERIALE. Frescoed ceiling: Francesco Maria della Rovere and his
troops on simulated tapestry held by Putti. 1530. *Plate* 1846.

Rome. GALLERIA BORGHESE. 443. Madonna and Child with Infant S. John.

S. CATERINA DA SIENA, ORATORIO. Resurrection. Sd. *Plate* 1845.

VATICAN, PINACOTECA. 347. Madonna and Child in Glory, and SS. John Baptist,
Lawrence, Jerome and monk. (?)

Siena. 333, 334. Two detached frescoes from Palazzo Petrucci: Freeing of prisoners;

Flight of Aeneas from Troy (companions to Signorelli and Pinturicchio in
London). 1509–10. *Plates 1847–1848.*

433. Tondo: Madonna and Child with Infant S. John and S. Anthony of Padua.

503. Madonna and Child with Infant S. John.

S. MARIA ASSUNTA (DUOMO). MUSEO DELL'OPERA. 16. Transfiguration. 1510. *Plate*
1843.

Strasbourg. 242. Rape of the Sabine Women (from Palazzo Petrucci in Siena).

GENTILE DA FABRIANO

*Marchigian. 1370(?)–1427. Continued tradition of Allegretto Nuzi and was subjected to
Franco-Flemish influence.*

Berlin. 1130. Madonna and Child with S. Nicholas, S. Catherine and donor (from
S. Niccolò, Fabriano). Sd. E. *Plate 528.*

Crenna di Gallarate. CARMINATI COLLECTION. S. Francis receiving Stigmata (from
Seminario of Fabriano).

Florence. UFFIZI. 887. Side-panels of 'Quaratesi' polyptych: SS. Mary Magdalen,
Nicholas, John Baptist, George; in pinnacles, Angel and Virgin of Annunciation, SS. Francis and Dominic (see Hampton Court). 1425. *Plate 533.*

8364. Adoration of Magi; in pinnacles, Christ as Judge, Angel and Virgin of
Annunciation; in frame, Ezechiel, Micah, Moses, David, Baruch and Isaiah;
in predella, Nativity, Flight into Egypt (central panel, Paris). Sd and d. 1423.
[*Plate 291, 292.*] *Plate 530.*

BERENSON COLLECTION. Head of Virgin (fr.).

Two panels from frame of (Valle Romita?) polyptych: S. Peter, S. Paul. E.

LOESER COLLECTION (EX). Bust of hermit Saint.

Hampton Court. ROYAL COLLECTIONS. 1230. Centre panel of 'Quaratesi' polyptych:
Madonna and Child enthroned with six Angels in pinnacle, blessing Christ
(companion to Florence, Uffizi; Rome, Vatican and Washington). 1425. *Plate*
533.

Milan. BRERA. 497. Polyptych from Valle Romita: Coronation; SS. Jerome, Francis,
Dominic, Mary Magdalen; upper register, S. John Baptist in the wilderness,
Assassination of S. Peter Martyr, S. Thomas Aquinas in his study, S. Francis
receiving Stigmata (see Florence, Berenson). Sd. E. *Plate 529.*

New Haven (Conn.). 1871.66. Madonna and Child. Sd.

New York. 30.95.262. Madonna and Child with music-making Angels.

FRICK COLLECTION. Madonna and Child enthroned with SS. Lawrence and Julian.
Plate 532.

Orvieto. CATHEDRAL, L. WALL. Fresco: Madonna and Child (r.). ca 1425.

Paris. 1278. Predella panel: Circumcision (see Florence, Uffizi). 1425.

HEUGEL COLLECTION. Coronation. *Plate 531.*

Perugia. 129. Madonna and Child with music-making Angels.

Pisa. B.P. V, 26. Madonna of Humility.

Rome. VATICAN, PINACOTECA. 247, 248, 249, 250. Four predella panels from 'Quaratesi' polyptych: Birth of S. Nicholas, S. Nicholas and the three Maidens without dowry, S. Nicholas helps the seafarers, S. Nicholas raises three youths back to life. (See Hampton Court). 1525. *Plate 533*.

— — DEPOT. S. Anthony of Padua (st.).

— — MUSEO SACRO. Fragment of fresco: Head of Charlemagne.

Tulsa (Okla.). PHILBROOK ART CENTER. 3358 (KRESS COLLECTION. K 535). Madonna and Child with two Angels (st.).

Velletri. CATTEDRALE, MUSEO CAPITOLARE. Madonna and Child with two Angels. 1426/7.

Washington (D.C.). 366 (KRESS COLLECTION K 472). 'Goldman' Madonna and Child. [*Plate 293*.]

379 (KRESS COLLECTION K 486). Predella panel from 'Quaratesi' polyptych: Worshippers at tomb of S. Nicholas of Bari. (See Hampton Court.) 1525. *Plate 533*.

GERA, Jacopo di Michele called

Pisan, mentioned 1371–95. Close to Giovanni di Nicola, later influenced by Luca di Tommè. His surviving works probably date from 1365 to 1385.

Calci (Pisa). PIEVE. Centre panel of polyptych. Madonna and Child with goldfinch.

Montenero (Livorno). SANTUARIO. Madonna and Child.

Palermo. MUSEO DIOCESANO. Triptych from Chiesa dell'Annunciata: S. Anne with Virgin and Child on her lap; S. John Evangelist; S. James. Sd.

GALLERIA NAZIONALE. Two side-panels of polyptych: Full-length SS. George and Agatha.

Pisa. 102. Madonna and Child flanked by SS. Francis and Anthony Abbot (from Convent of S. Matteo). Sd. *Plate 462*.

103. Madonna and Child flanked by SS. Mary Magdalen and Margaret (from Convent of S. Nicola). Sd. *Plate 463*.

San Miniato (Valdarno). MUSEO DIOCESANO. Processional standard from Parish Church of Marti: front, Crucifixion; back, Flagellation.

Siena. 221. Wings of diptych: SS. Paul and John Baptist, SS. Peter and Daniel, Angel and Virgin of Annunciation.

Volterra. PINACOTECA. Madonna and Child flanked by SS. Lucy and Catherine. *Plate 461*.

PALAZZO DEI PRIORI. Mystic Marriage of S. Catherine and S. Lucy.

GETTO DI JACOPO DA PISA

Pisan, active second half fourteenth century.

Pisa. 104. S. Dominic surrounded by SS. Augustine, Bartholomew, Hilarion, John Baptist and John Evangelist; above, Annunciation and Blessing Redeemer. Sd and d. 1391. *Plate 453.*

GHISSI, Francescuzzo

Marchigian pupil and close follower of Allegretto Nuzi. Active 1359–95 (?).

Ascoli Piceno. S. AGOSTINO, SECOND ALTAR R. Madonna of Humility and two Angels.

Fabriano. S. DOMENICO, LAST CHAPEL R. Madonna of Humility. Sd and d. 1359.

Fermo. 15. Madonna of Humility.

Montegiorgio (Ascoli Piceno). S. SALVATORE. Madonna of Humility and Angel. Sd and d. 1374. *Plate 217.*

Rome. VATICAN, PINACOTECA. 192. Madonna of Humility suckling the Child. *Plate 216.*

GIACOMO DI MINO see PELLICCIAJO

GIACOMO DEL PISANO

Assistant to Giovanni di Paolo, executed several of his late works. Also influenced by Verrocchio, through some imitator.

Asciano. MUSEO D'ARTE SACRA. Centre panel of polyptych from Abbey of S. Galgano (companion to Siena 199, 201): Assumption (on Giovanni di Paolo's design). ca 1470–75.

Baltimore (Md.). WALTERS ART GALLERY. 554. Polyptych: Madonna and Child enthroned with six Angels and kneeling monk; S. Nicholas; S. Galganus; in pinnacles, Redeemer, Angel and Virgin of Annunciation; in pilasters, four Saints (partly on Giovanni di Paolo's design).

Dublin. 1202. Triptych: Madonna and Child enthroned with two Angels; penitent Magdalen; S. Peter. Sd. *Plate 618.*

London. F. F. MADAN COLLECTION (EX). 'Platt' Madonna embracing the Child. KERR LAWSON COLLECTION (EX). Half-length S. Catherine of Siena.

Luxembourg. MUSÉE D'HISTOIRE ET D'ART. Triptych: Madonna and Child enthroned with three Angels; SS. Agnes and Peter; SS. Paul and Nicholas.

Madison (Wis.). UNIVERSITY. 61.48 (KRESS COLLECTION. K 1053). Madonna embracing the Child and two Angels against hedge of roses.

Poggioferro (Grosseto). PARISH CHURCH. Centre panel of polyptych from Cotone: Madonna and Child enthroned with four Angels (face r.).

Richmond (Va.). VIRGINIA MUSEUM OF ART. Madonna and Child with two Angels. *Plate 616.*

San Diego (Cal.). FINE ARTS GALLERY. Madonna adoring the Child and two Angels against a hedge of roses. *Plate 617.*

Siena. 199, 201. Side-panels of S. Galgano polyptych (companions to Asciano): S. Mary Magdalen, S. Galganus; SS. Benedict and Bernard. ca 1470–75.

   324. Polyptych from S. Silvestro at Staggia: Madonna della Cintola (on Giovanni di Paolo's design); S. Bernardino, John Baptist, Michael, Fabian; in predella, Dead Christ, mourning Mary Magdalen, Virgin, S. John Evangelist, S. Anthony Abbot and two donors. Formerly Sd by Giovanni di Paolo and d. 1475.

   575. Madonna and Child enthroned with S. Galganus, Moses, King David, Bishop Saint (Savinus?), SS. Stephen, Peter, John Baptist, Bartholomew, Paul, Lawrence and twelve Angels; in spandrels, Annunciation; in pilasters, ten little Saints (a second Annunciation in added lunette).

Trequanda (Val di Chiana). PREPOSITURA, R. WALL. Triptych: Madonna and Child enthroned with four Angels and kneeling S. Bernardino; S. Sebastian; S. Fabian; in pilasters, S. Gregory the Great, S. Augustine, S. Francis, S. Sebastian.

Tucson (Ariz.). UNIVERSITY OF ARIZONA. 62.152 (KRESS STUDY COLLECTION. K 440). Madonna and Child holding bird, with two Angels.

GIAMPIETRINO

Milanese imitator of Leonardo. Active first decades of sixteenth century.

Amsterdam. 1785–B1. Madonna and Child by a window.

Barcelona. D. B. GRASES HERNÁNDEZ. 'Ecce Homo.'

Bergamo. 345. Penitent Magdalen (replica of New York, Bishop Tarak).

Berlin. 205. Half-length penitent Magdalen.

   215. Half-length S. Catherine between wheels.

   SCHWEITZER COLLECTION (EX). Half-length penitent Magdalen.

Blaschkow (Bohemia). GASTON VON MALLMAN (EX). Madonna and Child (replica of London, Hallam Murray).

Budapest. 47 (108). Madonna and Child with SS. Michael and Jerome. *Plate 1520.*

   49. Madonna of the cherries. *Plate 1521.*

Burgos. CATHEDRAL, CAPILLA DEL CONDESTABILE. Half-length penitent Magdalen.

Cambridge (Mass.). FOGG ART MUSEUM. 1927.201. Holy Family and Angel.

Chantilly. 28. Head of girl.

Charlton Park (Malmesbury). EARL OF SUFFOLK (EX). Madonna suckling the Child.

Chesterfield. G. LOCKER-LAMPSON (EX). (EX SIR GEORGE DONALDSON). Magdalen by open sarcophagus.

Esztergom. 55.276. Madonna and Child (versions at Lucerne, Minneapolis and Richmond).

Florence. UFFIZI. 8544. Half-length S. Catherine.

   MUSEO HORNE. 69. Half-length penitent Magdalen (replica of New York, Bishop Tarak).

Gazzada (Varese). FONDAZIONE CAGNOLA. Holy Family.

Gosford House. EARL OF WEMYSS AND MARCH. Half-length penitent Magdalen (replica of New York, Bishop Tarak).

Hampton Court. Inv. 412. S. Catherine.

Isolabella (Lago Maggiore). PALAZZO BORROMEO. (Some pictures may be in Milan.) Dido.

   Sophonisba.

   Penitent Magdalen.

   S. Michael.

   S. Mary Magdalen.

   Mourning Virgin and S. John Evangelist (with Marco d'Oggiono).

   Abundance with cornucopia. *Plate 1528.*

Keir (Scotland). STIRLING COLLECTION (EX). Magdalen.

Le Havre. 19. Madonna embracing the Child (replica of Lucerne).

Lewisburg (Pa.). BUCKNELL UNIVERSITY BL.K.12 (KRESS STUDY COLLECTION. K 347). Cleopatra.

London. 3097. Christ carrying the Cross.

   3930. Salome with the head of the Baptist. L.

   COURTAULD INSTITUTE GALLERIES. GAMBIER PARRY COLLECTION. Madonna and Child with S. Jerome.

   Madonna and Child with lily (version of Marco d'Oggiono at Le Mans).

   BENSON COLLECTION (EX). (See Seattle.)

   DORCHESTER HOUSE, CAPT. HOLFORD (EX). Holy Family with Infant S. John.

   MR. HALLAM MURRAY (EX). Madonna and Child (replicas at Blaschkow and Milan, Castello). *Plate 1522.*

   HUMPHREY WARD (EX). Madonna and Child.

   (Environs). SYON HOUSE, DUKE OF NORTHUMBERLAND. Madonna suckling the Child (replica of Charlton Park).

Lucerne. SCHLOSS MEGGENHORN, MATHILDE FREY-BAUMANN. Madonna embracing the Child.

Lugano. MUSEO DI BELLE ARTI. 'Cook' Nativity. *Plate 1525.*

Madison (Wis.). UNIVERSITY OF WISCONSIN. 61.4.6 (KRESS COLLECTION. K 346). Lucretia.

Milan. AMBROSIANA. S. John Evangelist holding cup.

   Half-length penitent Magdalen.

Madonna and Child with female Saint.
Madonna and Child.
'Ecce Homo.'
— FROM S. SEPOLCRO. Holy Family with S. Roch and three Putti.
BRERA. 261. Madonna and Child with lamb (unfinished).
262. Penitent Magdalen seated among rocks, holding Crucifix and book.
263. Half-length Magdalen with arms crossed over breast.
CASTELLO. 304. Madonna and Child (replica of London, Hallam Murray).
306. Magdalen.
POLDI PEZZOLI. 648. Madonna and Child; on back, Geometry.
BAGATTI VALSECCHI COLLECTION. Polyptych: Madonna and Child, and four Saints.
Christ enthroned.
ALDO CRESPI. Madonna suckling the Child and Infant S. John. *Plate* 1526.
VONWILLER COLLECTION. Egeria. *Plate* 1523.
Minneapolis (Minn.). INSTITUTE OF ART (EX). Madonna and Child (formerly Platt and Carpenter Collections; see Richmond).
Munich. VON NEMES COLLECTION (EX). Madonna of the cherries.
Salome with the Head of the Baptist.
Nancy. Inv. 28 (80). Bust of blessing Christ.
Inv. 942 (93). 'Ecce Homo.'
Naples. 99. Madonna and Child with SS. John Baptist and Jerome.
Nervi. HEIRS OF MARCHESE FRANCESCO SPINOLA. Madonna and Child with SS. Joseph and Stephen.
Neuwied. SCHLOSS SEGENHAUS, PRINZ WIED. Leda (after Leonardo). [*Plate* 369.]
New York. MRS LANGBOURNE WILLIAMS. Madonna and Child.
R. M. HURD (EX). 'Holford' Madonna and Child with Infant S. John. *Plate* 1527.
BISHOP JOHN TARAK. Magdalen with book.
Oberlin (Ohio). ALLEN MEMORIAL ART MUSEUM. 61.81. (KRESS COLLECTION. K 1238). Cleopatra (variant of Paris).
Paris. 1686. Cleopatra (formerly Aynard). *Plate* 1529.
MARQUIS DE GANAY. Magdalen reading a book.
HIS DE LA SALLE COLLECTION (EX). Head of girl.
SALOMON REINACH (EX). 'Ecce Homo.'
Pavia. S. MARINO, HIGH ALTAR. Madonna and Child with SS. John Baptist and Jerome; in background, reliefs of Judith and Judgement of Solomon. Dated on frame 1521. *Plate* 1524.
Perugia. VAN MARLE (EX). Magdalen with book and Angel.
Philadelphia (Pa.). J. G. JOHNSON COLLECTION. 271. Madonna and Child with Infant S. John.
Ponce (Puerto Rico). MUSEO DE ARTE. 62.0263 (KRESS COLLECTION. K 1159). S. John Baptist.
Portland (Oregon). ART MUSEUM. 61.38 (KRESS COLLECTION. K 1021). Magdalen opening vase of ointment.

Richmond (Surrey). COOK COLLECTION. III. Madonna embracing the Child (versions at Esztergom and Minneapolis). *Plate 1525.*

Rome. CASTEL SANT'ANGELO, LASCITO MENOTTI. Christ carrying the Cross. Mocking of Christ.

ALBERTINI COLLECTION. Penitent Magdalen.

PALAZZO ROSPIGLIOSI, PALLAVICINI COLLECTION. Madonna suckling the Child (see version by Oggiono, Borghese n. 456).

VILLA ALBANI. Madonna and Child with lily.

VISCONTI VENOSTA COLLECTION. S. Roch.

Magdalen.

Profile of Cardinal Ascanio Sforza. (?)

LORD RENNELL (EX). Madonna and blessing Child.

Rovigo. 78. Christ and Veronica (c.).

109. 'Ecce Homo.'

Seattle (Washington). ART MUSEUM. IT.37/G. 3478.1 (KRESS COLLECTION. K 1064). Madonna of Humility with Infant S. John by a window (with Marco d'Oggiono.

Stuttgart. Inv. 724 (504). Madonna and Child with S. Jerome.

Sundorne Castle (Shrewsbury). DOWAGER LADY BURGHLEY (EX). Madonna and Child. (1907, not checked.)

Turin. ACCADEMIA ALBERTINA. 221. Version of Leonardo's Virgin of the Rocks.

240. Mocking of Christ. L.

GALLERIA SABAUDA. 138. Christ carrying the Cross (version at Rome, Castel S. Angelo).

140. SS. Catherine and Peter Martyr.

MUSEO CIVICO. Inv. 174. Magdalen reading by a rock.

Valencia. 661. Madonna and Child.

Waco (Texas). BAYLOR UNIVERSITY. 551A (KRESS COLLECTION. K 1216). Bust of suffering Christ.

Washington (D.C.). HOWARD UNIVERSITY. 61.154.P (KRESS COLLECTION. K 1230). Magdalen holding vase of ointment.

GIOLFINO, Niccolò

Verona, 1476–1555. Son of a sculptor, trained in Liberale's shop until 1492, taught Paolo Farinati. Fresco painter, cartographer, decorator of cassoni.

Altenburg. 190, 191 (100, 101). Two scenes from Roman history.

Bergamo. ACCADEMIA CARRARA. 606. Madonna and Child in landscape. *Plate 1904.*

Berlin. 284. Lucretia (version of a Bramantino in Casa Sola Busca at Milan). (Destroyed 1945.)

Berlin-Ost. 1176. Madonna and Child in Glory with Hope, Faith and Charity, below, SS. James, John Evangelist and donor. *Plate 1906.*

Bloomington (Ind.). INDIANA UNIVERSITY (KRESS STUDY COLLECTION. K 1199). Cassone panel: Deucalion and Pyrrha after the Flood.

Cambridge. FITZWILLIAM MUSEUM. 208, 210. Furniture panels: Two scenes from myth of Atalanta.

Cambridge (Mass.). FOGG ART MUSEUM. 1943.1841. Furniture panels: Sacrifice of Iphigenia.

Florence. BERENSON COLLECTION. Two furniture panels: Myth of Phaethon.

MUSEO HORNE. 6552, 6553. Two furniture panels: Myth of Phaethon.

Genoa. PALAZZO ROSSO N. i 57: Profile of man in fur (after earlier portrait—by Pisanello?).

Lavagno. S. BRIZIO. Madonna and Child in Glory, and below Tobias and Angel with three Saints.*

London. BENSON COLLECTION (EX). Three cassone panels: Darius Hystaspes (?) crowned outside walled city; Death of Smerdis (?); a woman and general talking over severed head.

Lovere. 22. Cassone panel: Vestal Tuccia proving her innocence. (?)

Meggenhorn (Switzerland). FRAU BAUMANN. Cassone front: Three scenes of dying youth. *Plates* 1901, 1903.

Oberlin (Ohio). 61.82 (KRESS COLLECTION. K 593). Lucretia stabbing herself.

Philadelphia (Pa.). J. G. JOHNSON COLLECTION. 217, 218. Two cassone panels: Triumph and Drunkenness of Silenus.

Princeton (N.J.). 35.28. Predella panel: Bishop Saint, S. George? and Deacon Martyr in landscape.

35.29. Predella: Circumcision. (?)

35.30. Cassone panel: Chiomara and the Centurion.

Rome. GALLERIA NAZIONALE (PALAZZO BARBERINI). F.N.19201. Madonna suckling Child.

MUSEO DI PALAZZO VENEZIA. 19195. Scenes from life of S. Julian. *Plate* 1905.

Vercelli. MUSEO BORGOGNA. Madonna and Child with Infant S. John in landscape. (?)

Verona. 189. Furniture panel: Achilles at Scyros (st.).

240. Madonna and Child.

249. 'Caliari' altarpiece from S. Matteo Concortine: Madonna and Child in glory appearing to SS. John Evangelist, Jerome and to kneeling Don Girolamo de' Caliari.

546–550, 562–3. Detached frescoes from Teatine Monastery of S. Niccolò: Astronomy holding armillary sphere, War holding sword, Arithmetic counting on her fingers, Music with psalter, Poetry with swan, Pharmacopoeia with ointments, Geography with globe. *Plates* 1900, 1902.

751, 752. Two cassone panels with Triumphs (st.).

1577. Two predella panels: Trial and Martyrdom of S. Agatha.

— DEP. FROM S. STEFANO. Madonna and Child with SS. John, Jerome, Francis, Maurus, Simplicius and Placidia.*

Verona (contd.). CASE MAZZANTI (PIAZZA DELLE ERBE 26–30). Frescoed façade (with
A. Cavalli). ca 1532–37. (?)

CASA PARMA LAVEZZOLA (VIA S. PIERO INCARNARIO 2). Frescoed façade: Allegory
of Time (r.). 1542.

S. ANASTASIA, FOURTH CHAPEL L. Descent of the Holy Ghost; in predella, Life of
S. Dominic. Sd and d. 1518.

— SECOND ALTAR L. Christ in Glory with seven Angels holding Symbols of
Passion; below, S. Erasmus, S. George, Martyrdom of S. Erasmus in background and two donors (Giovanni and Bonsignorio?) of the Faella family in
foreground. Sd and d. 1520. *Plate* 1907.

S. BERNARDINO, FIRST CHAPEL R. Frescoes: Vault; Risen Christ, S. Francis and two
Franciscan Blessed; at sides, music-making Putti, four Prophets and twelve
Apostles; Walls: Scenes from Life of SS. Francis and John Evangelist. ca
1522. *Plates* 1856–a, 1908–1909.

— CAPPELLA DELLA CROCE (R. OF CHOIR). Lunette: Resurrection.
Betrayal of Christ; Christ before Pilate; Christ laid on the Cross (other pictures
by F. Morone and G. F. Caroto).

— CLOISTER. Fresco: Heads of three monks. Not traced.

S. MARIA MATRICOLARE (DUOMO), SECOND ALTAR R. Lunette and side-panels to
Liberale's Adoration of Magi: above, Entombment, at sides, SS. Sebastian
and Bartholomew, SS. Roch and Anthony Abbot.

S. MARIA IN ORGANO, R. WALL OF NAVE. Frescoes: Creation and Expulsion from
Paradise; Flood; Sacrifice of Isaac; Joseph sold by his Brothers; three roundels
in spandrels, with S. John Baptist, S. Peter and S. Paul.

— R. TRANSEPT, CAPPELLA DEL SACRAMENTO. Frescoes: outside—large lunette with
Ascension; Prophets; Angel and Virgin of Annunciation in niches; inside—
Fall of Manna, Jewish Passover, Saints, Instruments of Passion. *Plates* 1910–12.

S. MARIA DELLA SCALA, THIRD ALTAR L. Fresco: Madonna of Mercy and medallions.

— FIFTH ALTAR L. Descent of the Holy Ghost. Falsely Sd and d. 1486.

Vicenza. 142. Madonna and Child.

Vienna. AKADEMIE, GIFT HONIGSCHMIED. Three music-making Angels.

GIOVANNETTI see MATTEO DA VITERBO

GIOVANNI AGOSTINO DA LODI (Pseudo-Boccaccino)

*Lombard active first decades of sixteenth century. Possibly pupil of Bramantino, influenced
by Leonardo, Solario, Alvise Vivarini.*

Allentown (Pa.). ART MUSEUM. 61.41.KG (KRESS COLLECTION. K 1291). Adoration of
Shepherds.

Altenburg. 161. Predella panel: Baptist preaching and baptizing the multitudes.

Baltimore (Md.). WALTERS ART GALLERY. 545. Madonna and Child with window on left. (?)

Berlin. 1550. Organ-shutter: front, Angel of Annunciation; back, seated Evangelist. *Plates* 1447–48.

Berlin-Ost. 1424. Madonna and S. Joseph worshipping Jesus, who plays with S. Lucy.

Brescia. 114. Bust of S. Jerome (replica of Cremona).

Bribano (Belluno). ORATORIO DI S. NICCOLÒ. Triptych: Madonna and Child; S. Roch; S. Sylvester.

Cleveland (Ohio). 16.781. Predella panel: Adoration of Shepherds. E.

Cremona. 87. Bust of S. Jerome.

El Paso (Texas). MUSEUM OF ART 1961–6/16ab (KRESS COLLECTION. K 8, 9). Panels of triptych: S. John Evangelist; S. Matthew with the Angel.

Gazzada (Varese). CAGNOLA FOUNDATION. Madonna and Child with Angel holding a bowl of fruit. *Plate* 1444.

Genoa. VIEZZOLI COLLECTION. Young man. *Plate* 1445.

London. WILLIAM GRAHAM COLLECTION (EX). Adoration of Magi. *Plate* 1453.

Lugano. THYSSEN COLLECTION. Satyr playing to a nymph, with Apollo and Daphne in background. *Plate* 1451.

The story of Syrinx. *Plate* 1452.

Milan. BRERA. 317. Adoration of Magi.

318. Baptism of Christ.

789. Busts of SS. Peter and John Evangelist. Sd. E. *Plate* 1443.

797. Madonna and Child with Angel offering an orange.

AMBROSIANA, DONO BRIVIO. Assumption.

MUSEO DEL CASTELLO. 357. S. John Evangelist blessing the poisoned cup (r.).

DEL MAJNO COLLECTION. Bust of young girl.

PRINCIPE DI MOLFETTA. A female martyr.

Modena. 262. Madonna embracing the Child and S. Sebastian. *Plate* 1450.

Naples. 95. Madonna and Child in landscape and busts of two donors. *Plate* 1449.

Nashville (Tennessee). PEABODY COLLEGE. A-61-10-5. (KRESS COLLECTION. K 1217). Madonna and Child.

New York. 58.182. Male portrait.

Pavia. DUOMO, FIRST CHAPEL L. IN CHOIR. Holy Family. (?)

Poznań. Inv. MO 28. Entombment.

Rome. ALBERTINI COLLECTION. Madonna and Child.

Treviso. MUSEO CIVICO. Christ in Emmaus. Not traced.

Turin. GALLERIA SABAUDA. 137. Marriage of S. Catherine (r. or c.).

FONTANA COLLECTION (EX). Holy Family.

Venice. ACCADEMIA. 598. The three ages of man (busts of youth, middle-aged man and old man).

599. Washing of feet. d. 1500. *Plate* 1446.

605. Madonna and Child with Simon and S. Jerome.

Venice (contd.). CA' D'ORO. Pietà with S. Jerome and donor.

S. STEFANO, SACRISTY. Marriage of S. Catherine and donor.
Full-length S. John Baptist and Jerome.

CONTE V. CINI. Inv. 6270. See Ferrarese-Bolognese.

(Environs). S. LAZZARO DEGLI ARMENI. Madonna and Child with donor.

— S. PIETRO MARTIRE A MURANO, CHAPEL R. OF CHOIR. Madonna and Child enthroned with SS. John Baptist, George and two Bishop Saints.

Verona. 89. Left panel of altarpiece: SS. Mary Magdalen and Martha.

Vienna. AKADEMIE. 153A. Busts of three Apostles.

530. Predella panel: Christ taking leave of His Mother. (?)

GIOVANNI DA MONTERUBBIANO see PAGANI

GIOVANNI DI NICOLA DA PISA

Pisan. Documented 1326–60. Pupil of Lippo Memmi; possibly father of Gualtieri di Giovanni.

Assisi. SACRO CONVENTO DI S. FRANCESCO, F. M. PERKINS DONATION. 42. Left panel of polyptych: S. James.*

London. HENRY HARRIS (EX). Madonna and Child holding bird and ears of wheat. (?)

New York. ROERICH MUSEUM (EX). Centre panel of polyptych: Madonna and Child.*

Palermo. GALLERIA NAZIONALE. Madonna of Humility suckling the Child (r.).

Pisa. 65 (B.P. IV, 33). Polyptych from S. Marta: Half-length Madonna and Child; SS. Bona, John Baptist, Mary Magdalen, Bartholomew; in pinnacles, blessing Redeemer and four busts of Saints. Sd and d. 13(50?). *Plate 323.*

66 (DEP. FROM S. VITO). Madonna and Child blessing a donor.

67 (B.P. III, 10/12/13/14). Fragments of polyptych: Half-length Madonna and Child; SS. Peter, John Baptist, Bartholomew (p.).

S. MARTINO. Frescoes: Annunciation, Visitation, Birth of Virgin, Nativity, Adoration of Magi, Circumcision (p.?, r.).

SEMINARIO VESCOVILE. Two pinnacles: Angel and Virgin of Annunciation. *Plate 326.*

Soiana (Pisa). PARISH CHURCH. Madonna and Child (r.). (?)

Venice. CA' D'ORO. Madonna of Humility. *Plate 325.*

Williamstown (Mass.). WILLIAMS COLLEGE, MUSEUM OF ART. 60.13 (KRESS COLLECTION. K 4). Centre panel of polyptych: Madonna of Humility suckling the Child and six Angels in spandrels. (?)

Homeless. Madonna and Child.* *Plate 324.*

GIOVANNI DI PAOLO

Siena. 1399–1482. Pupil probably of Paolo di Giovanni Fei; close follower of Sassetta. This 'Greco' of the Quattrocento must have been in touch with contemporary Byzantine painting.

Altenburg. 76. Small Madonna with carnations on frame. Sd.

    77. Centre panel of predella to Pecci polyptych from S. Domenico at Siena (companion to Baltimore, Castelnuovo Berardenga and Siena): Crucifixion. 1426.

    78. Crucifixion.

    79. Book-cover: 'Noli me tangere'.

Asciano. MUSEO D'ARTE SACRA. Centre panel of polyptych: Assumption (p.; with Giacomo del Pisano). ca 1470–75.

Assisi. SACRO CONVENTO DI S. FRANCESCO. PERKINS DONATION. 23. S. James (fr.).

    25. S. Bernardino.

Bagnoregio. S. AGOSTINO. Left and right panel from polyptych of Castiglion Fiorentino: S. Catherine and kneeling Bishop; S. Monica with Augustinian nuns. 1457.

Baltimore (Md.). WALTERS ART GALLERY. 489A, B, C, D. Four predella panels to Pecci polyptych from S. Domenico at Siena (companions to Altenburg, Castelnuovo Berardenga and Siena): Raising of Lazarus, Way to Golgotha, Deposition, Entombment. 1426. *Plate 590.*

    554. Polyptych (see Giacomo del Pisano).

    727. Crucifixion.

    1029. Front of cassone: Story of Camilla (r.).

Baschi (Orvieto). PARISH CHURCH. Triptych: Madonna and Child enthroned crowned by two Angels and Christ above; SS. James and Nicholas; Angel and Virgin of Annunciation.

Basle. ROBERT VON HIRSCH. Centre panel of Branchini polyptych from S. Domenico at Siena: Madonna and Child enthroned with Cherubim. Sd and d. 1427.

Berlin. 1112B. Predella panel: Christ on the Cross with Virgin and Evangelist.

    1112C. Predella panel (companion to Cleveland, New York 41.100.4, Rome, Vatican 132 and to Washington): Crucifixion.

    2170, 2171. Two predella panels (companions to Houston and New Haven): S. Clare receives from S. Francis the Franciscan habit; S. Clare rescues seafarers.

    SCHLOSSMUSEUM. Predella panel: S. Jerome appearing to S. Augustine (companion to Paris). L.

    K 9224. Book-cover: Triumph of Death. d. 1437.

Besançon. MUSÉE. S. Augustine enthroned (st.).

Boston (Mass.). 36.772. Madonna of Humility.

    GARDNER MUSEUM. Predella panel (companion to Cambridge, Fogg 1943.112, New York Linsky, Oxford): Christ disputing with the Doctors.

Brussels. ADOLPHE STOCLET. Madonna of Humility against landscape (fr., r.).

    MLLE MICHÈLE STOCLET. Two panels from 'Pizzicaiuoli' altarpiece (see Siena 211): Scenes from Life of S. Catherine of Siena (Mystic marriage; S. Catherine's Vision of Christ). 1447/9. *Plate* 610.

Budapest. 21 (49). Pinnacle (companion to Cologne, Seattle and Siena 195): The Evangelist Matthew. L.

Cambridge. FITZWILLIAM MUSEUM. 1758. S. Bartholomew.

    2323. Funeral of the Virgin; S. Bartholomew; female Saint (companion to El Paso).

    MARLAY BEQUEST. MS. 2988. Illuminated page: Two Scenes from life of female Saint. E. (?)

Cambridge (Mass.). FOGG ART MUSEUM. 1921.13. Panel of polyptych: S. Catherine of Siena.

    1938.131. Bust of S. Augustine (fr.; companion to New York, Lehman and Homeless). *Plate* 600.

    1943.112. Predella panel: Nativity (companion to Boston, to New York, Linsky and to Oxford).

Castelnuovo Berardenga. PREPOSITURA. Centre panel of Pecci polyptych from S. Domenico at Siena: Madonna del Rosario and Angels (companion to Altenburg, Baltimore and Siena). Sd and d. 1426. *Plate* 591.

Castiglione d'Orcia. S. SIMEONE. Madonna suckling the Child with two Angels; Crucifixion above.

Castiglion Fiorentino. PINACOTECA (GIÀ COLLEGIATA). Two panels from polyptych: Madonna and Child; S. Catherine of Alexandria. Sd and d. 1457.

Chalon-sur-Saône. (See Paris, Musées Nationaux.)

Chantilly. 9. Five dancing Angels (fr.).

Cherbourg. 166. (See Paris, Musées Nationaux.)

Chicago (Ill.). 33.1010/5. Six panels (from reliquary doors?): S. John Baptist entering the Wilderness; Meeting with Christ; S. John Baptist in prison; Salome kneeling before Herod; Beheading of S. John Baptist; Salome presenting Herod with the severed head (companions to Muenster, New York Lehman, Tours). *Plate* 602.

Chiusure (near Monteoliveto di Siena). CANONICA DI GROSSENANO. Two panels: S. Michael; S. Bernardino.

Cleveland (Ohio). 42.536. Predella panel (companion to Berlin, New York 41.100.4, Rome 132 and Washington): Adoration of Magi (after Gentile da Fabriano).

    Two panels from 'Pizzicaiuoli' altarpiece (see Siena 211): SS. Dominic, Augustine and Francis invest S. Catherine with the Dominican scapular; S. Catherine and the Beggars.

Colle Val d'Elsa. S. PIETRO, CONSERVATORIO FEMMINILE. Circumcision.

Cologne. WALLRAF-RICHARTZ MUSEUM (EX). Pinnacle (companion to Budapest, Seattle and Siena 195): The Evangelist John. L.

Compiègne. 3660. Predella panel: Pope giving investiture to Bishop.

Detroit (Mich.). 66.15. Panel from 'Pizzicaiuoli' altarpiece (see Siena 211): S. Catherine dictating to Blessed Raimondo da Capua. 1447–49. *Plate* 608.

LILLIAN HENKEL HAASS COLLECTION. Madonna and Child.

Dublin. 1768. Painted Crucifix. *Plate* 603.

El Paso (Texas). MUSEUM OF ART, 1961–6/8 (KRESS COLLECTION. K 500). Predella panel: Assumption, S. John Evangelist, S. Victor (companion to Cambridge 2323).

Englewood (N.J.). DAN FELLOWS PLATT COLLECTION (EX). Portable altarpiece: Madonna and Child with SS. Catherine and Margaret.

Esztergom. 55.181. Predella panel (companion to Florence, Bargello): S. Ansanus baptizing.

55.183. Nativity.

Florence. UFFIZI. 3255. Panels of polyptych (companions to New York and Rome, Vatican): Madonna and Child enthroned; SS. Dominic, Peter, Paul and Thomas Aquinas. Sd and d. 1445.

MUSEO DEL BARGELLO, CARRAND COLLECTION 6. Predella panel (companion to Esztergom): Beheading of S. Ansanus.

16. Salver: Judgement of Paris.

BERENSON COLLECTION. Madonna of Humility.

The Hague. KRÖLLER COLLECTION. Predella panel from Fondi polyptych (companion to Siena nn. 174–176): Adoration of Magi. 1436.

Hanover. KESTNER MUSEUM. 11, 186. Diptych: Madonna and Child; SS. John Baptist and Bernardinus (g.p.).

Houston (Texas). MUSEUM OF ART, STRAUSS GIFT. 18. Predella panel (companion to Berlin 2170, 2171 and New Haven): S. Clare saves a child mauled by a wolf. *Plate* 607.

53–3. ROBERT LEE BLAFFER MEMORIAL COLLECTION (formerly Paris, Kelekian). Two left panels of polyptych: S. Ursula, S. John Baptist (companions to New York 88.3.111 and Siena). *Plate* 592.

Istia d'Ombrone (Grosseto). S. SALVATORE. Madonna and blessing Child.

Kansas City (Mo.). 61–58 (KRESS COLLECTION. K 432). Portable altarpiece: Madonna and Child with SS. Jerome and Augustine and Angels; above, SS. Anthony Abbot and John Baptist, SS. Mary Magdalen and Bernardino, Angel and Virgin of Annunciation.

London. 3402. SS. Fabian and Sebastian worshipped by Brethren of the Misericordia (st.).

5451/4. Four oblong Scenes from Life of Baptist (Birth and Naming, S. John Baptist goes into the wilderness, Baptism of Christ; the Baptist's head presented to Herod).

BRITISH MUSEUM, YATES THOMPSON, DANTE CODEX. Miniatures of Paradise. *Plates* 595–597.

HENRY HARRIS (EX). Panel from frame of polyptych: S. John Baptist.

J. POPE-HENNESSY. Miniature: Saint.

Lugano. THYSSEN COLLECTION. 153. Madonna of Humility and two Angels (p.).
Panel from 'Pizzicaiuoli' altarpiece (see Siena 211): S. Catherine before the Pope
at Avignon. 1447–49.

Minneapolis (Minn.). VANDERLIP BEQUEST. Panel from 'Pizzicaiuoli' altarpiece (see
Siena 211): Death of S. Catherine of Siena. 1447–49.

Modena. 18. Nativity.

Montalcino (Senese). MUSEO CIVICO. Madonna and Child crowned by two Angels.

Montenero sull'Amiata. S. LUCIA. Madonna and Child crowned by two Angels (r.).

Montepulciano. S. AGOSTINO, SECOND ALTAR R. S. Nicholas of Tolentino. Sd and
d. 1456.

Münster i/W. LANDESMUSEUM. 355, 356. Two panels (companions to Chicago,
New York Lehman and Tours): Naming of S. John Baptist; Baptist before
Herod.

New Haven (Conn.). 1871.59. Predella panel: S. Clare blessing the three loaves of
bread before Pope Innocent IV (companion to Berlin and Houston).

    1871.62. Predella panel: Martyrdom of a Bishop.

    1943.255. Madonna and Child with SS. Jerome and Bartholomew.

New York. 88.3.111. Right panels of polyptych: SS. Matthew and Francis (companion to Houston and Siena).

    06.1046. Predella panel (companion to Florence, Uffizi and R. Lehman):
Paradise. 1445.

    32.100.76. Fragmentary polyptych: Madonna and Child enthroned with four
Angels; SS. Monica (?), Augustine, John Baptist and Nicholas of Tolentino.
Sd and d. 1454. *Plate* 615.

    32.100.83A, B, C, D. Four panels from pilasters of polyptych: SS. Catherine,
Barbara, Agatha and Dorothy.

    32.100.95. Panel from 'Pizzicaiuoli' altarpiece (see Siena 211): Communion
of S. Catherine of Siena. 1447–49.

    41.100.4. Predella panel (companion to Berlin, Cleveland, Rome Vatican 132,
Washington 334): Circumcision.

    41.190.16. Madonna and Child with two Angels and small donor. E.

    MISS HELEN FRICK. Nativity.

    ROBERT LEHMAN COLLECTION. Centre panel of polyptych: Coronation of Virgin.

    Panel from reliquary doors: front, Zacharias and the Angel; back, Angel of
Annunciation (companion to Chicago, Muenster and Tours).

    Predella panel: Expulsion from Paradise (companion to Uffizi and to Metro-
politan Museum). 1445. *Plate* 601.

    Predella panel: Raising of Tabitha (or miracle of S. Paul).

    Panels from the 'Pizzicaiuoli' altarpiece (see Siena 211): S. Catherine of Siena
prays for the recovery of her mother, S. Catherine of Siena receiving stigmata, Blessed Ambrogio Sansedoni and Blessed Andrea Gallerani. 1447–49.
Plate 609.

    S. Ambrose (fr., companion to Cambridge, Fogg and Homeless). *Plate* 598.

S. Nicholas of Tolentino.

Madonna and Child with SS. Agnes and Jerome (r.).

JACK LINSKY. Predella panel (companion to Boston, Gardner Museum, Cambridge, Fogg and Oxford, Ashmolean): Adoration of Magi.

A. SACHS COLLECTION (EX?). S. John Baptist.

Oxford. ASHMOLEAN MUSEUM. 179. Predella panel (companion to Boston, Gardner Museum, Cambridge, Fogg and New York, Linsky): Baptism of Christ.

CHRIST CHURCH. 30. Predella panel: Crucifixion. L.

Palermo. CHIARAMONTE BORDONARO COLLECTION (EX). Five upper panels of polyptych: half-length Redeemer and four Evangelists.

Paris. 1695A. Predella panel: S. Gregory the Great staying the plague at Castel Sant'Angelo (r., companion to Berlin). L.

MUSÉES NATIONAUX, CAMPANA 34 (DEP. CHALON-SUR-SAÔNE). Right panel of polyptych: S. Clement and Virgin of Annunciation above.

— CAMPANA 361 (DEP. CHERBOURG). Triptych: Nativity. SS. Galganus and Ansanus; in pinnacles, God the Father, Angel and Virgin of Annunciation.

HEUGEL COLLECTION (EX). Back of a reliquary: Franciscan monk kneeling before a vision.

MARTIN LE ROY COLLECTION (EX). Predella panel: Martyrdom of S. John Evangelist.

Parma. 432. Predella panel: Christ and Saints. L. *Plate* 614.

Philadelphia (Pa.). MUSEUM OF ART. 45.25.121/2. Two roundels from altarpiece: S. Lawrence, S. Stephen.

— J. G. JOHNSON COLLECTION. 105. Predella panel (companion to Rome, Vatican): Way to Golgotha. E.

723. Predella panel (to Montepulciano?): S. Nicholas of Tolentino rescues seafarers (companion to Vienna).

Pienza. ASSUNTA (DUOMO), R. NAVE. Madonna and Child enthroned with SS. Bernardino, Anthony Abbot, Francis and Clare; in lunette, Pietà; in predella, three roundels with Dead Christ, mourning Virgin and S. John Evangelist (g.p.). Sd and d. 1463.

MUSEO DIOCESANO. Miniatures. 1462.

Rome. GALLERIA DORIA PAMPHILI. 132, 134. Two predella panels: Birth and Marriage of Virgin. E.

PALAZZO CHIGI (EX). Two predella panels: Levitation of a Franciscan Saint; Franciscan care of the poor.

VATICAN, PINACOTECA. 123, 125. Full-length S. Michael, Madonna and Child.

124, 129. Two predella panels (companions to Philadelphia): Mourning over the dead Christ, Agony in the Garden. E.

126, 127. Two panels from pilasters of altarpiece: Evangelists (see Florence, Uffizi).

130. Predella panel (companion to Siena, Opera del Duomo): Clothing of S. Anthony of Padua.

131. Book cover: Annunciation. 1445.

Rome. VATICAN, PINACOTECA (contd.). 132. Predella panel (companion to Berlin, Cleveland, New York 41.100.4 and Washington): Nativity (after Gentile da Fabriano).

Saint Louis (Mo.). 56.41. Predella panel: Lecture of S. Thomas Aquinas.

Seattle (Wash.). MUSEUM OF ART. IT 37/G.4393.I. KRESS COLLECTION. K 1094. Pinnacle (companion to Budapest, Cologne and Siena 195): The Evangelist Luke. L.

Siena. 172. Last Judgement. *Plate 612.*

    173. Triptych: S. Nicholas enthroned and SS. Bernardino, Francis, Clare and Louis of Toulouse; in roundels, SS. Paul and Jerome. Sd and d. 1453.

    174, 175, 176. Predella panels to Fondi polyptych: Presentation of Virgin, Crucifixion, Flight into Egypt (companions to Hague). 1436. *Plate 594.*

    178. Portable altarpiece: Madonna and Child with Angels, SS. Nicholas, Lucy, Augustine, Catherine; in pinnacles, Dead Christ, Angel and Virgin of Annunciation.

    179. Portable altarpiece: Madonna and Child with two Angels; S. Catherine and S. Ansanus.

    180. S. Jerome in his study.

    186, 187, 188, 189. SS. Gregory, Sebastian, Paul and Francis.

    190, 192. Two pilasters from altarpiece: SS. Peter, Dominic, Ursula and Catherine of Siena; SS. Catherine, Bernardino, Francis and Evangelist.

    191. Polyptych; Madonna and Child; SS. Nicholas and Galganus, SS. Clare and Ursula; in pinnacles, blessing Redeemer, Last Communion of Magdalen, S. Francis receiving Stigmata. Sd and d. 1445.

    195. Pinnacle (companion to Budapest, Cologne and Seattle): The Evangelist Mark. L.

    193, 197. Left panels of Pecci polyptych from S. Domenico at Siena (companions to Altenburg, Baltimore and Castelnuovo Berardenga): S. John Baptist, S. Dominic. 1426.

    198. Predella to polyptych for Abbey of S. Galgano (companion to following): S. Benedict promulgating his rule; Communion of Magdalen; Virgin taking leave of the Apostles and Dormitio; Miracle of the sword of S. Galganus at Montesiepi, Vision of S. Bernard. Emblems of Abbey of S. Galgano. ca 1470/5.

    199, 201. Side panels of polyptych for Abbey of S. Galgano (companions to above): SS. Benedict, Mary Magdalen, Galganus and Bernard (executed by Giacomo del Pisano). ca 1470–75.

    200. Crucifixion. Sd and d. 1440. *Plate 604.*

    206. Madonna and Child against landscape. E.

    208. Pinnacle: Redeemer (companion to 195?).

    211. Centre panel of 'Pizzicaiuoli' altarpiece for S. Maria della Scala (companion to Brussels, Cleveland, Detroit, Lugano, Minneapolis, New York and Utrecht): Circumcision, 1447–49.

212. Christus Patiens, Christus Triumphans. E. *Plate* 589.

213. S. James. E.

214. Kneeling Bishop.

215. S. Andrew. E.

324. Polyptych from S. Silvestro at Staggia: Madonna della Cintola (design only; executed by Giacomo del Pisano). Formerly Sd and d. 1475.

575. 'Maestà' with SS. David, Ambrose, Bartholomew, Paul, Lawrence, Moses, Thomas, John Baptist, Peter, Stephen and twelve Angels etc. (see Giacomo del Pisano).

— DEP. FROM VIA DELLE TERME, TABERNACLE. Madonna and Child (fr. of centre panel of polytypch, companion to Houston and New York). *Plate* 593.

ARCHIVIO DI STATO. Book-covers.

Biccherna: Pope Eugenius IV crowning Sigismund as Emperor. 1433. (?)

Biccherna: S. Jerome and the lion. d. 1436.

Gabella: S. Peter Alexandrinus enthroned with Angels. d. 1440.

Madonna of Mercy (from Spedale di S. Maria della Scala, Libro Vitale). 1458.

BIBLIOTECA COMUNALE, GRADUALE H, I, 2. Miniatures: f. 5, Christ appearing to a supplicant in initial F; f. 9, A pilgrim in initial R; f. 91, Praying Monk in initial D.

— ANTIPHONAL FROM LECCETO, G, I, 8. Twenty-seven Miniatures. *Plate* 613.

PALAZZO PUBBLICO, GROUND FLOOR. Fresco: wolf, forest, etc.

S. ANDREA, HIGH ALTAR. Coronation of Virgin, with SS. Peter and Andrew, Sd and d. 1445.

SS. GIOVANNINO E GENNARO. Mourning Virgin and Evangelist (frs., cut around edges).

S. MARIA ASSUNTA (DUOMO), MUSEO DELL'OPERA. 18. S. Jerome with book; Redeemer above (st.). L.

60. Predella panel (companion to Rome, Vatican 130): S. Francis appearing to his Brethren at Arles.

S. MARIA DEI SERVI, L. TRANSEPT. Madonna of Mercy. Sd and d. 143(6?).

S. PIETRO OVILE, FIRST ALTAR L. Painted Crucifix.

S. STEFANO, HIGH ALTAR. Predella to Andrea Vanni's polyptych: Nurture of S. Stephen, Stoning of S. Stephen, Miracles at his Tomb, Crucifixion, Story of S. Bernardino, S. Bernardino inspired by S. Augustine, Vision of S. Bernardino. *Plate* 398.

CONFRATERNITA DELLA MADONNA SOTTO LE VOLTE (SPEDALE DELLA SCALA), SACRISTY. Monochrome fresco on pillar: S. John Baptist (r.).

(Environs). S. LEONARDO AL LAGO, FORMER REFECTORY. Monochrome fresco: Crucifixion and busts of Saints in frieze (fr.).

South Hadley (Mass.). MOUNT HOLYOKE COLLEGE, GIFT OF CAROLINE R. HILL. Fragment of altarpiece: Head of Virgin and Angel holding crown.

Stockholm. DR. W. A. GREEN (EX). Madonna and Child with SS. Bartholomew and James.

Tours. CHÂTEAU DE VILLANDRY, MME CARVALLO. Panel from reliquary doors (companion to Chicago, Münster and New York): S. John Baptist preaching (fr., r.).

MUSÉE, LINET BEQUEST. Madonna and Child. *Plate* 606.

Upton House (Banbury, Oxon.). NATIONAL TRUST. Predella panel: Presentation of Virgin (companion to Rome, Doria?). E.

Utrecht. 14, 15/16A. Two panels from pilasters and one from predella of 'Pizzicaiuoli' altarpiece (see Siena 211): S. Galganus, Franciscan Martyr, Crucifixion. 1447–49. *Plate* 605.

Vienna. AKADEMIE. 1177. Predella panel (to Montepulciano?): S. Nicholas of Tolentino appearing over the walls of a city hit by the plague (companion to Philadelphia). *Plate* 611.

LANCKORONSKI COLLECTION. Christ on Cross with Virgin and Evangelist.

LEDERER COLLECTION (EX). Head of Angel (fr.).

Washington (D.C.). 13 (MELLON COLLECTION). Adoration of Magi.

334 (KRESS COLLECTION. K 412). Predella panel (companion to Cleveland, Berlin, New York 41.100.4 and Rome, Vatican 132): Annunciation.

Homeless. S. Gregory (fr.; companion to Cambridge, and to New York, Lehman). *Plate* 599.

Panel from pilaster of altarpiece: S. Christopher (repr. in *Festschrift für Kurt Bauch*, 1957, frontispiece).

GIOVANNI DI PIETRO DA NAPOLI

Possibly a pupil of Andrea Vanni in Naples. Active in Pisa, with Martino di Bartolomeo, in the first decade of the fifteenth century.

New Haven (Conn.). 1871.70. Deposition.

Pisa. 48 (B.P. V, 37). Fresco transferred on canvas, from Church of Dominican nuns: Christ on Cross with mourning Virgin and S. John Evangelist, S. Francis and two donors. Sd and d. 1405. *Plate* 448.

49 (B.P. V, 16). Polyptych from Spedale di S. Chiara: Madonna and Child enthroned; SS. Augustine and John Baptist, with Evangelist in roundel above; SS. John Evangelist and Clare, with Evangelist in roundel above (original pinnacles—Trinity, Annunciation—and predella, lost). Documented as by G. di P. da Napoli assisted by Martino di Bartolomeo, 1402. *Plate* 446.

51 (B.P. V, 17). Altarpiece from Convent of S. Caterina: Mystic Marriage of S. Catherine and kneeling donor (with Martino di Bartolomeo). d. 1404. *Plate* 447.

52 (B.P. IV, 15). Triptych from monastery of S. Domenico: Madonna and Child enthroned; SS. Mary Magdalen, Dominic, John Evangelist and Scholastica; in roundels, S. John Baptist and S. Stephen.

GIOVANNI DA PISA

Pisan follower of Taddeo di Bartolo, active in Genoa 1401–21.

Rome. CARDINAL ZELADA (EX). Polyptych: Madonna enthroned, SS. Agatha and Stephen, SS. Francis and (Cristina?); two roundels with Prophets; in pinnacles, Crucifixion, Angel and Virgin of Annunciation; in pilasters of frame, six Saints; in predella, five Stories from the Life of S. Stephen. Sd. *Plate 484.*

San Simeon (Cal.). HEARST MEMORIAL. Triptych: Madonna and Child, S. John Baptist, S. Anthony Abbot; in pinnacles, Crucifixion, Angel and Virgin of Annunciation; in pilasters of frame, six Saints. Sd and d. 1423. *Plate 481.*

GIOVANNI DA RIMINI see RIMINI

GIOVANNI FRANCESCO DA RIMINI

Born at Rimini, ca 1425, died at Bologna before 1470. Documented in Padua 1442, 1444. May have been pupil of Girolamo di Giovanni da Camerino; influenced by Benozzo Gozzoli and Bonfigli.

Atlanta (Ga.). ART ASSOCIATION GALLERIES. 58.43 (KRESS COLLECTION. K 1580). Adoration of the Child with S. Helena and Infant S. John (formerly Corsi Collection, Florence). *Plate 632.*

Autun. 49, 50. Predella panels: Nativity; Flagellation and Crucifixion of a Saint.

Baltimore (Md.). WALTERS ART GALLERY. 488. Madonna and Child.

Bologna. 255. Adoration of the Child with Infant S. John and two Angels.
   S. DOMENICO, L. CHAPEL. Madonna and Child enthroned (r.). Sd and d. 1459.

Brooklyn (New York). 34.835. Tondo: Blessing God the Father and four Angels. *Plate 636.*

Cologne. ERZBISCHÖFLICHES DIÖZESANMUSEUM. Inv. M.4. Predella panel: Funeral of Virgin.

Florence. ACCADEMIA. 3461. S. Vincent Ferrer and three Scenes from his Life. (?)
   CHARLES LOESER COLLECTION (EX). Panel from pilaster of polyptych: S. Anthony of Padua (companion to Venice, Cini).

Hanover. LANDESGALERIE. 108. Predella panel: Pietà and two donors.

Konopist. CASTLE. 21193. Christ with Saints and female donor. (?)

Le Mans. 11. Adoration of the Child with Infant S. John.

Liverpool. 2781. Madonna and Child with two Angels.

London. 2118. Madonna and Child and two heads of Angels. Sd and d. 1461. *Plate 634.*

Paris. 1659. Predella panel: S. Nicholas and the girls without dowry.

Perugia. 126–127–128. Triptych from S. Francesco al Prato: Madonna and Child enthroned, S. Jerome, S. Francis. *Plate* 633.

Pesaro. 79. Predella panel: S. Dominic fed by the Angels. *Plate* 637.

Richmond (Surrey). COOK COLLECTION 10 (EX). Tondo: God the Father sends the Dove (fr. of Annunciation).

Rome. VATICAN, PINACOTECA. 309. Predella panel: Miracle of S. James at Domingo della Calzada.

Spoleto. ARCIVESCOVADO. Triptych from S. Eufemia: Assumption, Bishop Saint, S. Lucy; in predella, S. Lucy helps the poor, is accused, stands fast against the oxen, Dead Christ in Tomb, two Angels (with Matteo da Gualdo). *Plate* 638.
   PINACOTECA. 31. Detached fresco: Madonna and Child with two Angels.

Urbino. 31. Detached fresco: Madonna and Child with two Angels (r.).
   104. Head of Dominican monk (fr.).

Venice. CONTE VITTORIO CINI. Inv. 6131/2. Two panels from pilaster of altarpiece: S. Thomas Aquinas, S. Francis (companions to Florence, Loeser).

Homeless. Madonna and Child with two Angels. *Plate* 635.

GIOVENONE, Girolamo

School of Vercelli. First documented work 1513. Died 1555. Fellow-pupil and follower of Gaudenzio Ferrari. Father-in-law of Lanino.

Avignon (formerly). Replica of Spanzotti's Christ and the Doctors, Turin Inv. 213. Sd and d. 1513.

Baltimore (Md.). WALTERS GALLERY. 567. Copy of Raphael's Madonna d'Orléans.

Bergamo. 342. Triptych: Madonna and Child, four Saints, donor and wife. Sd and d. 1527. *Plate* 1261.

Biella. ISTITUTO QUINTINO SELLA. Mourning over the dead Christ.

Boston (Mass.). 22.636. Madonna and Child in landscape, with Infant S. John (variant at Mortara).

Gattinara (Biella). MADONNA DEL ROSARIO, HIGH ALTAR. Triptych: Madonna and Child enthroned; S. John Evangelist; S. Mary Magdalen; monochrome predella with Apostles.

Geneva. MUSÉE ARIANA. 236. Right panel of polyptych: Full-length S. Roch and Blessed Amadeus.

Grignasco (Valsesia). ASSUNTA, PILLAR R. OF CHOIR. The family of the Virgin. (?)

London. 1295. Madonna and Child enthroned with two music-making putti, two Saints and two donors. ca 1510–15.

Madison (Wis.). UNIVERSITY OF WISCONSIN. 61.4.4 (KRESS COLLECTION. K 221). Nativity. E.

Milan. CASTELLO SFORZESCO. 399, 400. Side-panels of polyptych: SS. George, Apollonia and donor; SS. Lucy, Rosa and donor.

Mortara. s. LORENZO. Madonna and Child in landscape with SS. Roch and Sebastian.

Nashville (Conn.). PEABODY COLLEGE FOR TEACHERS. A–61–10–7 (KRESS COLLECTION. K 1627). 'Cook' Madonna and Child with S. Apollonia and another female Saint. Sd. ca 1520-25.

Pavia. Inv. 16. The Church Fathers. (?)

Richmond (Surrey). COOK COLLECTION. 65. Copy of Raphael's Madonna d'Orleans.

Rivoli (Turin). MUNICIPIO. Madonna and Child enthroned with SS. Joseph and Julius.

Santhià (Vercelli). s. AGATA, FIRST CHAPEL L. Polyptych: Madonna and Child enthroned, S. Roch, S. Michael, S. John Baptist, S. Sebastian; upper register: S. Lucy, S. Lawrence, S. Agatha, Bishop Saint, S. Catherine. d. 1531.

Trieste. BIBLIOTECA. Portrait of a lady.

Trino Vercellese. CONVENTO DI SUORE DOMENICANE. Triptych: Madonna suckling the Child; S. Dominic with donor; S. Lawrence (?) with donor's wife.

Turin. GALLERIA SABAUDA. 39. Madonna and Child enthroned with SS. Abbondius and Dominic recommending the widow of Domenico Buronzo and her children Pietro and Girolamo. Sd and d. 1514. *Plate* 1260.

    40. Madonna and Child enthroned with SS. Mary Magdalen, Catherine, Eusebius and Peter Martyr.

  MUSEO CIVICO. Inv. 208. S. Jerome praying in the wilderness.

    Inv. 467. Adoration of the Child with a Bishop Saint (after Defendente). E.

Vercelli. MUSEO BORGOGNA. Adoration of the Child; in roundels above, Angel and Virgin of Annunciation; in predella, Man of Sorrows, S. Roch and S. Sebastian. Sd. E. *Plate* 1259.

  Adoration of the Child with SS. Eusebius and Bernardino (r.). E.

  Madonna and Child enthroned with SS. John Baptist and Maurice (r.). Sd and d. 1513. (?)

  Four panels of polyptych: S. John Baptist with kneeling monk; S. Catherine; S. Rosa ?; S. Christopher carrying Jesus. *Plate* 1262.

  Triptych composed of panels not belonging together: Adoration of the Child; S. Michael; penitent S. Jerome.

  Crucifixion, with Renaissance architecture in background. E.

  Crucifixion. L. (?)

PALAZZO ARCIVESCOVILE. Adoration of Magi.

s. CRISTOFORO, SACRISTY. Adoration of the Child with SS. Joseph, Peter Martyr, Anthony Abbot and Anthony of Padua. L. *Plate* 1263.

s. FRANCESCO, FIRST CHAPEL R. S. Ambrose. doc. 1527–35. *Plate* 1264.

s. GIULIANO, R. NAVE. Frescoes: Christ with Cross, S. Francis receiving Stigmata, S. Catherine, Bishop Saint, S. Sebastian.

— L. NAVE. Frescoes: S. Anthony Abbot, S. Augustine, S. Roch.

Siena. 1470–1524. Son and pupil of Benvenuto di Giovanni, from whose worst his best is not easily distinguished. Works marked 'E' almost certainly done in Benvenuto's studio, and perhaps on his cartoons.

Assisi. F. M. PERKINS COLLECTION. Agony in the Garden.

Baltimore (Md.). WALTERS ART GALLERY. 721, 732. Panels of polyptych: S. Lucy, S. Anthony Abbot.

Berlin. 1071. Predella panel: Assumption with S. Catherine of Siena (companion to Cambridge and Denver).

   A. VON BECKERATH (EX). Lunette: Dead Christ upheld by Angels.*

   R. VON KAUFMANN (EX). Madonna and Child with S. Jerome and female martyr.

Buonconvento (Senese). PIEVE DEI SS. PIETRO E PAOLO, PINACOTECA. Annunciation, with SS. Francis and Anthony Abbot.

Cambridge (Mass.). FOGG ART MUSEUM. 1941.132. Madonna and Child with two Angels.

   1947.25. Predella panel: S. Catherine of Siena exorcizing the Devil (companion to Berlin and Denver).

Cetona (Val di Chiana). S. FRANCESCO (CLAUSURA). Madonna and Child enthroned (fr., r.).

Denver (Col.). MUSEUM OF ART. E–IT–18–XV–942 (KRESS COLLECTION. K 1295). Predella panel: S. Catherine of Siena exorcizing a woman possessed by the Devil (companion to Berlin and Cambridge). *Plate 857.*

   E–IT–18–XV–943 (KRESS COLLECTION K 222). Front of Gherardesca marriage salver: Venus and Cupid (r.; companion to Rome, Castel S. Angelo).

Detroit (Mich.). ROBERT GRAHAM. Predella panel: Pope Liberius tracing the foundations of S. Maria Maggiore (see Siena 414).

Dresden. 33. Madonna and Child with SS. Jerome and John Baptist.

Dublin. 839. Madonna and Child with SS. Mary Magdalen and Jerome (r.).

Englewood (N.J.). PLATT COLLECTION (EX). Predella panel: Dead Christ upheld by Angels. L.

Florence. MUSEO BARDINI. Madonna and Child with SS. Jerome and Bernardino. (?)

MUSEO HORNE. 33. Venus and Cupid in Landscape.

   BERENSON COLLECTION. Predella panel: Vision of the Roman Patrician (see Siena 414). *Plate 854.*

   R. LONGHI. Predella panel: Virgin covering with snow the site of the church to be built for her (see Siena 414).

Frankfurt a/M. 776. Way to Calvary, Crucifixion, Deposition.

Gallarate. CARMINATI COLLECTION. Madonna and Child with SS. Jerome and Bernardino; in lunette, Dead Christ. E.

Ginestreto (Siena). S. DONATO. Madonna and Child with SS. Jerome and Bernardino.

Grosseto. MUSEO D'ARTE SACRA. Madonna and Child with SS. Jerome and Bernardino.

Hartford (Conn.). 1953.236. Madonna and Child with SS. Michael and Catherine (r.). CHARLES C. CUNNINGHAM. Madonna and Child.

Lewisburg (Pa.). BUCKNELL UNIVERSITY. BL. K 5. (KRESS STUDY COLLECTION. K 1744A). Panels from pilasters of altarpiece: SS. Augustine, Jerome and Albert the Great (companions to New Orleans).

Liège. MUSÉE. Mystic Marriage of S. Catherine, and two Angels, S. John Baptist, S. Anthony of Padua.

London. ANTHONY POST. Augustus (companion to Fungai, London, ex Harris). W. MOSTYN-OWEN. 'Filangeri' Nativity.

Malibu (Cal.). J. PAUL GETTY MUSEUM. G-29. Adoration of Shepherds.

Montalcino. MUSEO CIVICO. Nativity.
Side-panels of altarpiece: S. Anthony of Padua, S. Leonard.
MUSEO DIOCESANO. Assumption with S. Thomas receiving the girdle, between S. Francis and S. Anthony of Padua. ?1498. *Plate 853.*

Montepulciano. MUSEO CIVICO. Nativity. E.

New Haven (Conn.). 1871.65. Marriage salver: Love bound by maiden. E.
1943.256. Madonna and Child with two Angels, SS. Leonard and Jerome. E.
1943.259. Nativity.

New Orleans (La.). DELGADO MUSEUM OF ART. 61.69 (KRESS COLLECTION. K 1744B). Panels from pilaster of altarpiece: SS. John Baptist, Margaret and Blessed Ambrose Sansedoni (companions to Lewisburg).

New York. R. LEHMAN COLLECTION. Madonna and Child with SS. Bernardino and Michael. L.
MRS. E. A. GOODHART (HEIRS?). Nativity with six Saints.
RICHARD HURD (EX). Madonna and Child with SS. Peter and Paul.

Palermo. CHIARAMONTE BORDONARO COLLECTION. 66. Madonna and Child with SS. Jerome and Angels.
74. Madonna and Child with SS. Jerome and John Baptist.

Paray-le-Monial. 190. Predella: S. Francis receiving Stigmata, Last Communion of S. Mary Magdalen.

Paris. 1668. Marriage salver: Judgement of Paris. L. *Plate 859.*
DOLLFUSS COLLECTION (EX). Madonna and Child with two Angels.

Rome. GALLERIA NAZIONALE, PALAZZO BARBERINI. 705. Crucifixion with SS. Jerome and Francis.
MUSEO DI CASTEL S. ANGELO. Back of Gherardesca marriage salver: Cupid with bow and arrow (companion to Denver).

Saturnia (Maremma). PARISH CHURCH, L. CHAPEL. Madonna and Child with SS. Mary Magdalen and Sebastian. E.

Siena. 342. Nativity.
369. Pietà.
370. Four Saints.

Siena (contd.). 372. Birth of Virgin.

    373. Dead Christ upheld by Angels.

    380. Madonna and Child.

    414. Altarpiece from Cappella Sozzini in San Domenico: Madonna and Child enthroned with SS. Dominic, Jerome, S. Catherine of Siena, S. Catherine of Alexandria and Angels carrying snowballs (predella panels with Legend of Madonna of the Snow at Detroit, Florence and Homeless; lunette is by Matteo di Giovanni and belonged to Placidi triptych). Sd. and d. 1508. *Plate* 856.

    PALAZZO CHIGI SARACINI. Nativity with Infant S. John and Putti above.

    — (EX). Vestal Tuccia, Vestal carrying fire, Cleopatra. L. *Plate* 860.

    CHIESA DI FONTEGIUSTA, OVER HIGH ALTAR. Frescoed lunette, Assumption. 1515.

    SS. GHERARDO E LUDOVICO (NEAR S. FRANCESCO), CLOISTER. Fresco: Christ on Cross and kneeling Cardinal.

    S. MARIA DEL CARMINE, FIRST ALTAR R. Frescoes at sides of Assumption: S. Lawrence; Hermit Saint.

    SANTUARIO CATERINIANO, ORATORIO DELLA CAMERA, ALTAR. S. Catherine receiving stigmata.

    (Environs). OSSERVANZA, THIRD CHAPEL R. S. Elizabeth of Hungary and kneeling female pilgrim. (?)

    — — MUSEO. Detached fresco: Resurrection of the Dead.

Torrita (Val di Chiana). MADONNA DELLE NEVI. END WALL. Frescoes: Annunciation; at sides, in superimposed niches, SS. Sebastian and Costantius Bishop, SS. Roch and Flora; in niche over altar, Assumption (version of Benvenuto di Giovanni at New York); in embrasure, Eternal, Saints and Prophets (r.). E.

Tulsa (Okla.). PHILBROOK ART CENTER. 3369 (KRESS COLLECTION. K 1287). Nativity with S. Jerome.

Venice. CA' D'ORO. Marriage salver: Hercules's Choice. E. *Plate* 858.

    CONTE VITTORIO CINI. Inv. 6324. Madonna and Child enthroned with SS. Bartholomew and Blaise.

Washington (D.C.). 446. (KRESS COLLECTION. K 1078). 'Benson' Portrait of lady.

York. 731. Madonna and Child with SS. Francis and Bernardino.

Homeless. Predella panel: Vision of Pope Liberius (see Siena 414). *Plate* 855. Nativity (repr. *Dedalo*, XI, p. 646).

GIROLAMO DA CARPI

Ferrara. 1501–56. Pupil of Garofalo; close follower of Dosso, whom he seems to have assisted; strongly influenced by Raphael and Parmigianino.

Berlin. PRINZ HEINRICH VON PREUSSEN (EX). Adoration of Magi.*

Bologna. S. MARTINO MAGGIORE, FIRST ALTAR R. Adoration of Magi. 1530–1.

    S. SALVATORE. Mystic Marriage of S. Catherine, with SS. Sebastian and Roch.

Dresden. 124. S. George and the Princess.

    142. Opportunity and Patience. 1541. *Plate 1818.*

    143. Venus drawn by swans.

    144. Judith. *Plate 1817.*

    145. Rape of Ganymede.

Ferrara. Inv. 60. Detached fresco: S. Catherine.

    CASTELLO. Three frescoes here transferred from elsewhere: Vintage, Triumph of Ariadne, Triumph of Bacchus.

    PALAZZO ARCIVESCOVILE, PASSAGE FROM SEMINARIO TO DUOMO. Full-length portrait (c.).

    S. FRANCESCO, NAVE AND TRANSEPTS. Frescoed frieze: Racemes, Putti and half-length Saints.

    S. PAOLO, R. TRANSEPT. Penitent S. Jerome.

Florence. PITTI. 36. Archbishop Bartolini Salimbeni de' Medici. *Plate 1811.*

    311. Portrait of Alfonso d'Este (c. of Titian at Metropolitan Museum, New York).

Glasgow. 1587. Holy Family with S. Catherine. *Plate 1816.*

London. MRS GRONAU. S. Luke and the Virgin (companion to below). *Plate 1814.*

    MR AND MRS J. GERE. Nativity (companion to above). *Plate 1815.*

Modena. 164. Bust of gentleman of Este family. (?)

    188. Adoration of Magi. *Plate 1812.*

Pesaro. VILLA IMPERIALE. Frescoes: Coronation and Procession of Charles V and other scenes (with Dosso).

Rome. GALLERIA DORIA PAMPHILI. 280. Holy Family and Infant S. John in landscape. (?)

Rovigo. S. FRANCESCO. Descent of the Holy Ghost; predella panel: S. Francis receiving Stigmata (rest of predella, as well as Eternal and Annunciation in lunette and medallions, lost).

Washington (D.C.). 475 (KRESS COLLECTION. K 1113). Assumption of Virgin and Giulia Muzzarella as donor. *Plate 1813.*

GIROLAMO DA CREMONA

Active 1467–83. Chiefly miniaturist. Developed under influence of Mantegna, Liberale and slightly of Vecchietta and his followers. [See Introduction, p. XVI.]

Berlin. 1655. S. Peter heals a cripple (companion to Cambridge). (Girolamo or Liberale?)

    SCHWEITZER COLLECTION (EX). Miniature: Crucifixion. *Plate 871.*

Brussels. HENRI WAUTERS. A girl speaks to her lover from a window (companion to Florence, Berenson and New York). (Girolamo, Liberale or Francesco di Giorgio?)

Cambridge. FITZWILLIAM. P.D. 21–1961. S. Peter refuses Poppaea's alms (companion to Berlin). (Girolamo or Liberale?) *Plate 867.*

Chiusi. S. SECONDIANO (DUOMO), SALA CAPITOLARE. Antifonario M, f. 4: Coronation of Virgin. 1472.

Florence. BARGELLO. Breviario 68 (from S. Maria Nuova): Miniatures. ca 1474.
  Folio 79 recto—Resurrection, Marys at Tomb.
  Folio 87 verso—Ascension.
  Folio 116 verso—Annunciation. *Plate 874.*
  Folio 125 recto—Birth of Virgin. *Plate 873.*
          —Adoration of Magi.
  BIBLIOTECA NAZIONALE, Magl. II, III, 27. 'Raimundi Lulii Opera Chemica.'
    Miniatures.
  BERENSON COLLECTION. Fragment with youths (companion to Brussels and New
    York). (Girolamo, Liberale or Francesco di Giorgio?)
  SERRISTORI COLLECTION. Nativity (Girolamo or Liberale?)
Le Havre. 50. Rape of Helen (Girolamo or Liberale?)
London. VICTORIA AND ALBERT MUSEUM. 817–1894. Miniature: S. Catherine before
    Maxentius. Sd. *Plate 870.*
  DAVID M. CURRIE. Illuminated Initial B.
Mantua. BIBLIOTECA. Missal of Barbara of Brandenburg: Miniatures. 1462–66.
  Folio 1—Crucifixion.
  Folio 26—Nativity (close to Belbello). *Plate 869.*
  Folio 38—Initial I as flagstaff.
  Folio 420—Ascension and roundels with Saints (close to Belbello).
  Folio 509—SS. Peter and Andrew.
  Folio 601—S. Andrew.
  Folio 605—S. Thomas.
  Folio 612—Conversion of S. Paul.
  Folio 633—SS. James and Philip.
  Folio 635—Finding of True Cross.
  Folio 637—Martyrdom of Saint.
  Folio 650—Birth of Baptist.
  Folio 656—SS. Peter and Paul.
  Folio 661—Visitation.
  Folio 673—S. James the More.
  Folio 695—Birth of Virgin.
  Folio 703—S. Matthew.
  Folio 706—S. George.
  Folio 708—S. Francis.
  Folio 714—SS. Simon and Judas.
  Folio 717—All Souls.
  Folio 720—Bishop Saint.
  Folio 724—S. Catherine.
New Haven (Conn.). 1871.71. Nativity.
New York. 43.98.8. Fragment with chess players (companion to Brussels and
    Florence, Berenson). (Girolamo, Liberale or Francesco di Giorgio?)
  49.7.8. Miniature: Deposition.

MORGAN LIBRARY. 'De Civitate Dei': Frontispiece. 1475.

Rome. S. FRANCESCA ROMANA, SACRISTY. Madonna and Child with four Angels, S. Benedict (?) and S. Francesca Romana. (Girolamo or Liberale?) *Plate 866.*

Siena. 309. Annunciation. *Plate 875.*

DUOMO, LIBRERIA PICCOLOMINI. Miniatures (N.B.: the codices having been differently numbered at different times, we give their full titles and only the numbers actually inscribed on them; they are listed in chronological order):

CODEX I (also 12, 10, 28): 'Graduale a Festo Sancti Petri Usque Ad Assumptionem Beate Virginis Marie et in Dedicatione Sancti Johannis et Sancti Clementis' (see also Liberale). 1472 (not 1468).

    f. 49—Assumption.

    f. 64—Birth of Virgin. *Plate 872.*

    —S. Augustine.

CODEX 26 (also 17, 2): 'Graduale Commune Sanctorum'. Probably 1473.

    f. 2—Two Apostles holding Olive Branches.

    f. 4—Four Apostles.

    f. 23—Young Martyr looking up (on Liberale's design).

    f. 46—An Apostle.

    f. 49—Three young Martyrs (one of them female).

    f. 52—Two Deacon Martyrs.

CODEX 27 (Milanesi XVIII): 'Graduale in Dedicatione Ecclesie'. 1473.

    f. 2—Distribution of alms.

    f. 34—Two Hermits (on Liberale's design).

    f. 42—Three Virgin Martyrs round a column (on Liberale's design).

    f. 75—Consecration of a Church.

CODEX 29 (also 18, 3): 'Graduale a Dominica Prima Adventus Usque Ad Festum Sancti Sylvestri' (see also Liberale). 1473.

    f. 2—David in Prayer.

    f. 45—S. John Baptist preaching.

    f. 51—Joseph and Mary on the Way to Bethlehem.

    f. 58—Nativity (on Liberale's design). *Plate 878.*

    f. 70—Adoration of the Shepherds. *Plate 877.*

    f. 76—Stoning of S. Stephen.

    f. 83—S. John at Patmos.

    f. 89—Massacre of Innocents.

    f. 97—Death of S. Peter Martyr.

    f. 110—Pope Sylvester baptizing Emperor Constantine.

CODEX (Milanesi VII): 'Graduale A Resurrectione Domini Nostri Usque Ad Corpus Christi' (payments January–May 1473).

    f. 20—Resurrection and four Scenes in roundels of frame.

    f. 36—Jesus reveals His Nature to His Disciples (on Liberale's design).

    f. 40v.—'Ego Sum Pastor Bonus' (on Liberale's design).

Siena. DUOMO, LIBRERIA PICCOLOMINI. CODEX (Milanesi VII) (contd.): f. 44v.—Jesus and the Pharisees ('Flebitis Vos, Mundus autem gaudebit') (on Liberale's design).

f. 55—'Exivi a Patre' (on Liberale's design).

f. 66—Ascension.

f. 71—Ecstasy of the Apostles at the appearance of their Lord.

f. 100—Descent of the Holy Ghost.

f. 127—The Holy Trinity (on Liberale's design).

f. 132—Corpus Domini.

CODEX 31 (also 19, 4): 'Graduale A Circumcisione Domini Usque Ad Dominicam V Post Epiphaniam' (with Liberale). Paid to Liberale July 1473?

f. 2r—Circumcision.

f. 7v—Adoration of Magi.

f. 13r—Jesus disputing in the Temple.

f. 19r—Marriage at Cana.

f. 26—Healing of the Leper.

CODEX 28 (also 21, 6): 'Graduale A Dominica III Quadragesimae Usque Ad Dominicam Passionis' (with Liberale). Payments August 1473.

f. 2—Jesus frees a Man possessed by the Devil.

f. 39—Multiplication of Breads.

f. 74—Jesus chased from the Temple.

CODEX 30 (also 22, 7): 'Graduale A Dominica Palmarum Usque Ad Missam Sabati Sancti (on Liberale's design). 1473.

f. 2—Jesus entering Jerusalem (paid to Liberale December 1473).

f. 15—Feast in the House of Simon.

f. 22—Jesus before Pontius Pilate.

f. 28—Jesus on the Way to Golgotha.

f. 37—Jesus washing the feet of the Apostles.

f. 76—Pietà.

CODEX 21 (ALSO 10, L): 'Antiphonarium A Vigilia Ascensionis Usque Ad Corpus Domini.' (partly on Liberale's design?). ca 1474.

f. 3—Ascension.

f. 32—Descent of the Holy Ghost.

f. 81—The Holy Trinity.

f. 107—The Christian Sacrifice of the Mass.

f. 114—The Sacrifices to God in pagan times.

CODEX 32 (also IA): 'Antiphonarium A Sabbato I De Adventu Ad Vesperos Vigiliae Nativitatis.' Finished by Liberale in 1473 or 1474.

f. 4—God speaks to a Prophet.

f. 41—Jesus weeps over Jerusalem.

f. 69—God speaks to a Prophet.

f. 133—'Canite Tubam.' [*Plate 353.*]

CODEX 16 (Milanesi XIV): 'Antiphonarium A Cathedra Petri Usque Ad Annuntiationem.' Begun by Liberale in September 1475 and possibly on his design.

f. 7v.—Calling of SS. Peter and Paul.

f. 33v.—Annunciation.

Vienna. LANCKORONSKI COLLECTION (EX). Angel rescuing a woman from the Devil.(?)

Viterbo. DUOMO. Redeemer with SS. John Evangelist, Leonard, Benedict (?), and John Baptist and Bishop Settala. d. 1472. (Girolamo or Liberale?) *Plate 868.*

GIROLAMO DI GIOVANNI DA CAMERINO

Active middle decades of fifteenth century. Pupil probably of Boccatis da Camerino; developed first under the shadow of the Vivarini, later of Crivelli; registered among painters in Padua 1450; influenced by various Umbrian followers of Benozzo and Piero della Francesca.

Balcarres (Fife). EARL OF CRAWFORD AND BALCARRES. Madonna and Child (st.).

Brno. Up. 11088. Christ on Cross, with Virgin, John Evangelist, Angels and donor.

Camerino. PINACOTECA. 4. Banner from Tedico: Madonna of Mercy, with SS. Venantius and Sebastian. Sd and d. 1463.

    6. Annunciation and donors (Giulio Cesare da Varano and his daughter, the blessed Camilla?); in lunette, Pietà with two Franciscan Saints, Angels, Symbols of Passion and self-portrait (from Spermento). *Plate 782.*

    22. Detached fresco from S. Agostino: Madonna and Child with SS. Jerome, John Baptist, Augustine, Venantius, two more fragmentary Saints and donor Melchiorre Bandini (died 1473).

    24. Detached fresco from S. Agostino: Madonna and Child with SS. Anthony of Padua, Anthony Abbot and two small Donors. d. 1449.

    s.n. Detached fresco from S. Francesco: Madonna and Child with SS. Francis, John Baptist, Anthony Abbot, Venantius and Donor. d. 1462.

    SS. ANNUNZIATA, THIRD NICHE R. Frescoes: Angel and Madonna and Madonna and Child (fr.); Temperance, Prudence. Not traced.

    DUOMO, SECOND SACRISTY. Triptych: Christ on Cross with mourning Virgin, Evangelist and Magdalen; S. Michael; S. John Baptist.

    (Environs). ACQUACANINA, S. MARGHERITA. Fresco: Christ on Cross, SS. Margaret, Christopher, Nicholas and Sebastian (r.). L.

    — BOLOGNOLA, VILLA MALVEZZI, CAPPELLA. Frescoes: Madonna and Child enthroned with Angels. Vault: 'Ecce Homo', SS. Nicholas of Tolentino, Anthony Abbot and Catherine; S. Sebastian and Madonna of Mercy (r.). L.

    — S. MARIA DI RAGGIANO. Fresco: Crucifixion (fr.).

Englewood (N.J.). PLATT COLLECTION (EX). Madonna of Mercy. (?)

Fiordimonte (Macerata). CASTELLO, CAPPELLA. Fresco: Crucifixion and SS. Savinus, Helena, Bartholomew and Bishop Saint.

Florence. MUSEO BARDINI. SS. Peter and Blaise.

Milan. BRERA. 796. Madonna and Child with SS. John Baptist and Francis.

    811. Polyptych from Gualdo Tadino: Madonna and Child enthroned with six Angels; above, Crucifixion; on either side, full-length SS. Nicholas, Catherine, Apollonia and Nicholas of Tolentino; half-length SS. Sebastian, Peter, Lawrence and Jerome. [*Plate 295.*] *Plate 779.*

    ACHILLE CHIESA (EX). Madonna and Child (r.).

Montesanmartino (Macerata). S. MARIA DEL POZZO, SACRISTY. Fragmentary polyptych: Madonna and Child enthroned with four Angels; above, Angel and Virgin of Annunciation in roundels, Crucifixion; on either side, full-length SS. Thomas and Ciprianus; half-length S. Michael with S. Peter in pinnacle; S. Martin and the Beggar with S. Paul in pinnacle. Sd and d. 1473. *Plate 783.*

Paris. MUSÉES NATIONAUX, CAMPANA 275 (DEP. TOURS 185). S. John Baptist in archway, with kneeling donor. *Plate 781.*

Piòraco (Camerino). CHIESA DEL CROCIFISSO. Fresco: Christ on Cross.

Rome. MUSEO DI PALAZZO VENEZIA, WURTZ BEQUEST. Madonna and Child with Angels and kneeling Bishop Saint, S. John Baptist, S. Nicholas, S. Michael (from S. Michele di Bolognola near Camerino).

    DEL PERO COLLECTION (EX). Pinnacles: Angel and Virgin of Annunciation. *Plate 778.*

San Pellegrino (Gubbio). S. PELLEGRINO. Polyptych: Madonna and Child enthroned with Angels; SS. Michael and John Evangelist, SS. James and Pellegrino; in pinnacles, SS. John Baptist, Peter, God the Father, SS. Paul and Jerome (r.).

Sarnano (Macerata). S. MARIA DI PIAZZA. Standard: Crucifixion; back, Annunciation. *Plate 780.*

Serrapetrona (Macerata). (Environs). CASTEL SAN VENANZIO, PARISH CHURCH. Christ on Cross with mourning Virgin, Evangelist and Magdalen (r.).

Tours. 185. (See Paris, Musées Nationaux.)

Urbino. GALLERIA NAZIONALE DELLE MARCHE. Top panel of polyptych: Crucifixion.

Venice. CONTE VITTORIO CINI. Inv. 6498. Madonna and Child enthroned with four Angels.

GIROLAMO DAI LIBRI

Verona. 1474–1555. Son of Francesco dai Libri, pupil of Domenico Morone; influenced by Mantegna, Montagna, Savoldo, Luini, Perugino and Raphael.

Bennebroek (Haarlem). DE HARTEKAMP, FRAU VON PANNWITZ. Predella: S. Lorenzo Giustiniani saying Mass, giving Communion to a woman, freeing a woman possessed by Devils, Funeral of S. Lorenzo Giustiniani. *Plates 1320–1321.*

Bergamo. 552. S. John Evangelist reading.

Berlin-Ost. 30. Madonna and Child enthroned in landscape with SS. Bartholomew and Zeno and Angels.

    SCHWEITZER COLLECTION (EX). Miniature: Allegorical figure of Music in initial O.

Budapest. 1153 (135). S. John Baptist and donor; in background, Baptism of Christ and Baptist preaching.

Cleveland (Ohio). 55.281. Miniature: Nativity. *Plate 1319.*

Esztergom. 55.195. Madonna and sleeping Child.

London. 748. Madonna and blessing Child with S. Anne and three Angels. Sd.

    VICTORIA AND ALBERT MUSEUM. C.A.I. 98. Beheading of S. Catherine. (?)

    MRS MARK HAMBOURG (EX?). Christ in Galilee. *Plate 1324.*

    LORD DE SAUMAREZ (EX). Madonna and Child. E. *Plate 1316.*

Malcesine (Lago di Garda). PARISH CHURCH, FIRST ALTAR R. Deposition. E. *Plate 1317.*

Marcellise (Verona). PARISH CHURCH. Organ-shutters from S. Maria in Organo at Verona: outside, SS. John Evangelist and Benedict, SS. Mary Magdalen and Catherine; inside, Daniel and Isaiah, Nativity. Commissioned from Girolamo dai Libri and Francesco Morone in November 1515, completed Easter 1516.

Melchett Court (Romsey, Hants). LORD MELCHETT (EX). Two 'Mond' panels: S. Peter, S. John Evangelist.

Montecassino. BIBLIOTECA. Miniatures in Filelfo's *Office of the Madonna.*

Monteforte d'Alpone (Verona). MENSA VESCOVILE. Christ and the Woman of Samaria.

New York. 20.92. Madonna and Child holding pink, with SS. Catherine, Leonard, Augustine, Apollonia and three music-making Angels.

Venice. ACCADEMIA. 703. Madonna suckling Child and two music-making Angels. E.

Verona. 115. S. Sebastian.

    138. Madonna and Child.

    252. 'Maffei' altarpiece from S. Giacomo alla Pigna: Madonna and Child with SS. Roch and Sebastian.

    253. Baptism of Christ.

    290. 'Presepio dei Conigli' from S. Maria in Organo: Nativity with SS. John Baptist and Jerome and rabbits in foreground. *Plate 1318.*

    333. 'Madonna della Quercia' appearing to SS. Peter and Andrew. [*Plate 352.*]

    339. 'Madonna dell'Ombrello': Madonna and Child enthroned with S. Joseph, Tobias and the Angel. Sd and d. 1530. *Plate 1323.*

Miniatures:

    311. Resurrection in the letter D.

    313. Mass.

    316. Entry into Jerusalem and Way to Calvary.

    317, 318. Initials.

    323. Cardinal holding church, Olivetan abbot.

PIAZZA DELLE ERBE, N. 23. Fresco: Madonna and Child enthroned with SS. Joseph, John Baptist, Putti and four Evangelists above. (r.)

S. ANASTASIA, R. TRANSEPT. 'Centrego altarpiece': Madonna and Child with SS. Thomas, Augustine, Cosimo Centrego and his Wife. 1512.

S. GIORGIO IN BRAIDA, FOURTH ALTAR L. Madonna and Child with two Bishop Saints and three Angels. Sd and d. 1526.

Verona (contd.). SS. NAZARO E CELSO, CAPELLA DI S. BIAGIO (L. TRANSEPT). Predella to Bonsignori's altarpiece: S. Blaise heals a Boy, Martyrdom of S. Sebastian, Beheading of S. Juliana. 1525.

    S. PAOLO, THIRD ALTAR R. Madonna and Child with S. Anne, Joseph, Joachim and two members of Baughi family. L. *Plate 1322*.

    S. TOMASO CANTUARIENSE, FOURTH ALTAR R. S. Roch between SS. Sebastian and Job.

Wolfenbüttel. HERZOG AUGUST BIBLIOTHEK, COD. 277-4 EXTR.: Miniatures f. 1 v. —Apollo and Muses; f. 23 r.—Apollo and Daphne.

GIULIANO DA RIMINI see RIMINI

GIULIANO DI SIMONE DA LUCCA

Active late fourteenth century. Close to Martino di Bartolomeo.

Castiglione Garfagnana. S. MICHELE. Centre panel of polyptych: Madonna del Latte; Blessing Saviour in trefoil above. Sd and d. 1389. *Plate 378*.

Leghorn. LARDEREL COLLECTION (EX). Madonna and Child enthroned, S. James, S. Michael, two female Saints and Eve at feet of throne. *Plate 380*.

Paris. 1621. Madonna del Latte with four music-making Angels, SS. Mary Magdalen, Nicholas, Dorothy and Peter, and Eve at her feet. *Plate 381*.

Parma. 443. Madonna enthroned with four adoring Angels, SS. Catherine, John Baptist, Francis and a Virgin Martyr, and Eve below the throne; above, Christ on Cross with mourning Mary and John. *Plate 379*.

GIULIO ROMANO

Giulio Pippi. Rome ca 1499. From October 1524 Court painter and architect at Mantua. Died there 1546. Pupil and assistant of Raphael; influenced by Michelangelo.

Budapest. 125. Diana and Endymion (st.).

Detroit (Mich.). 66.41. Allegory with Phoenix, Apollo, Phaethon, Harpy, Giant, Satyr and Nymph. (?)

Dresden. 103. 'Madonna del Catino'.

Florence. UFFIZI. 1810. Self-portrait.

    2147. Madonna and Child with book and flowers.

    CHARLES LOESER (EX). Predella panel: Birth of Infant.

Geneva. ERICH LEDERER. Alexander the Great. 1537.

Genoa. S. STEFANO. Stoning of S. Stephen. ca 1523. *Plate 1852*.

Hampton Court. 76. Lady receiving visitors. (?)

Hanover. LANDESGALERIE. 289. Portrait of lady. (?)

Madrid. 323. 'Noli me tangere'.

Mantua. PALAZZO DUCALE (REGGIA DEI GONZAGA). Decorative frescoes (executed chiefly by Assistants). 1537–8.

    PALAZZO DEL TÈ. Frescoes: Story of Cupid and Psyche; Fall of Giants and other subjects (g.p.). 1532–4. *Plates* 1855, 1856.

Moscow. PUSHKIN MUSEUM. Woman at mirror. [*Plate* 321.]

Munich. 1300. Bust of an ecclesiastic. (?)

Naples. 'Madonna del Gatto'. *Plate* 1849.

Paris. 1418. Nativity from Chapel of Isabella Boschetti in S. Andrea at Mantua. 1531. *Plate* 1854.

    1419. Madonna and Holy Children.

    1420. Triumph of Titus and Vespasian.

    1421. The Forge of Vulcan.

    1422. Male Portrait.

    1422A–D. Cartoons for Tapestries.

    1438. Circumcision. L.

    1498. See Raphael.

Parma. 371. Deesis with SS. Paul and Catherine (p.).

Rome. GALLERIA NAZIONALE, PALAZZO BARBERINI. Madonna and Child. E.

    GALLERIA BORGHESE. 373. Head of Madonna (c.?).

    374. Madonna and Holy Children.

    PALAZZO ZUCCARI, FIRST FLOOR, DINING ROOM. Detached frescoes from Villa Lante: Historical and decorative subjects.

    VILLA ALBANI. Frescoes: Olympic Contests. *Plate* 1851.

    FARNESINA. See Raphael.

    ARACOELI, SACRISTY. Madonna and Child with SS. Elizabeth and Infant John.

    S. MARIA DELL'ANIMA. Holy Family with SS. James, Mark and Infant John. *Plate* 1850.

    S. PRASSEDE, SACRISTY. Flagellation.

    VATICAN, PINACOTECA. 'Madonna di Monte Luce' (with Penni). 1525.

    — SALA DI COSTANTINO. Frescoes: Battle of Ponte Molle; Constantine addressing his troops. 1524. *Plate* 1853.

Saltwood Castle (Kent). SIR KENNETH CLARK. 'Cook' S. Catherine (version of Parma).

Strasbourg. 259. 'Fornarina'.

Verona. S. MARIA IN ORGANO, CHOIR. Frescoes: Life of the Virgin (executed by Torbido on design of Giulio Romano).

Vienna. 31. S. Margaret.

    35. Symbols of four Evangelists.

GIUNTA PISANO

Pisan painter, documented 1229–54.

Assisi. S. MARIA DEGLI ANGELI. Painted Crucifix. Sd.

Bologna. S. DOMENICO. Painted Crucifix. Sd. *Plate* 7.

Brussels. STOCLET COLLECTION. Dead Christ in Tomb. *Plate 6.*
Northampton (Mass.). SMITH COLLEGE. 24.18.1. Portable Cross (painted both sides).
Pisa. MUSEO NAZIONALE DI S. MATTEO. Painted Crucifix from S. Ranierino. Sd.

GIUSTO DE' MENABUOI

Born in Florence 1320/30. Active in Milan 1363, 1367, in Padua since the end of that decade. Became Paduan citizen before 1375. Died in Padua after 1387 and before 1393. Influenced by Altichieri and Avanzo, Veronese painters active in Padua.

Athens (Georgia). UNIVERSITY OF GEORGIA. R. 3, 4, 5 (KRESS STUDY COLLECTION. K 1122, K 231 a and b, K 179). Side panels of Terzaghi polyptych (left to right): SS. Anthony Abbot, Thomas Aquinas, John Baptist, Catherine of Alexandria, Paul, Augustine (see Rome). 1363.

London. 701. Portable Triptych: Coronation of Virgin; wings, outside—Expulsion of Joachim from the Temple, Joachim and the Angel, Meeting of Joachim and Anne at the Golden Gate, Birth and Presentation and Marriage of Virgin; wings, inside—Angel and Virgin of Annunciation, Nativity, Crucifixion. Sd and d. 1367. *Plate 227.*

Montecassino. ABBAZIA. Reliquary: Madonna and Child; inside wings, four seated Saints; outside wings, four standing Saints.

New York. TOLENTINO COLLECTION (EX). Six roundels with busts of Saints (see Rome). 1363.

Padua. BAPTISTERY, VAULT. Frescoes: Paradise; in circular frieze around it, Stories from the Old Testament [Creation of the World, Creation of Adam and Eve, Fall of Man, Expulsion from Eden, Sacrifices of Cain and Abel, Death of Abel, Curse of Cain, Lamech and Enoch, Assumption of Enoch, God tells Noah to build the Ark, the Flood, Noah sacrifices to God in gratitude at the end of the Flood, Noah's drunkenness, the Tower of Babel, Abraham and the three Angels, Lot and his daughters, Sacrifice of Isaac, old Isaac sends Esau hunting, gives Jacob his blessing, Esau's return, Jacob's ladder, the first altar, Laban's and Jacob's flocks, Jacob wrestling with the Angel, Reconciliation of Jacob and Esau, Joseph sold by his brothers, Joseph's dream, Joseph Viceroy of Egypt].

— SPANDRELS. Frescoes: the four Evangelists seated above their Symbols and flanked by two Prophets.

— NORTH WALL (R. OF APSE). Frescoes: upper register—Annunciation to Zacharias, Birth of Baptist, Naming of Baptist; middle register—the Baptist preaching to the Multitudes, Baptism of Christ, the Baptist in prison (below window), Miracles of Jesus Christ; lower register, Herod's feast, Beheading of Baptist, Salome offers the Baptist's head to Herodias, Raising of Lazarus.

— EAST WALL (OPPOSITE APSE). Frescoes: upper register—Presentation of Virgin, Annunciation, Visitation; middle register—sepulchral monument of Fina Buzzacarina: in lunette, S. John Baptist recommends Fina Buzzacarina to the

Madonna and the other Saints; in embrasures of arch, three Franciscan Saints
and three female Saints and Angels; in face of arch, Angels adoring the Holy
Ghost; in pinnacles of monument, busts of blessing Redeemer and of Angels;
left and right of monument, Massacre of Innocents, Christ and the Doctors;
lower register—Christ entering Jerusalem, Last Supper. *Plates* 231-232, 234, 236.

— SOUTH WALL (L. OF APSE). Frescoes: upper register—Nativity, Adoration of
Magi, Circumcision; middle register—Miraculous draught of fishes, Calling
of Matthew, Marriage at Cana; lower register—Agony in the Garden,
Betrayal of Christ, Christ before Caiaphas.

— WEST WALL (OVER APSE). Frescoes: between windows—Crucifixion; left—
Flight into Egypt, Transfiguration; right—Descent into Limbo, Maries at the
tomb; below left arch—frescoed lunette: Pilate washing his hands and Denial
of Peter; below right arch—frescoed lunette: Ascension.

— APSE, VAULT. Fresco: Descent of the Holy Ghost.

— — SPANDRELS. Frescoes: The four Horsemen of the Apocalypse on the white,
the red, the pale, the black, horse.

— — CENTRAL LUNETTE. Fresco: God the Father in a mandorla, amid the 24 old
Men, the mystic Lamb in His lap.

— — L. LUNETTE. Fresco: S. John Evangelist's vision of Christ, of the seven candlesticks and of the seven churches.

— — R. LUNETTE. Fresco in three sections: the Lamb opens the book of prophecies;
eclipse and earthquake; the Angels calling at the four corners of the earth.

— — L. WALL. Frescoes: upper register—Call of the first, second and third trumpets; fires on earth, wreckages at sea, poisoned waters; middle register—the
Dragon with seven heads and the Woman who has given birth to a boy;
S. Michael and his Angels fight the Dragon and his Devils, the Woman,
dressed in sun, standing on the moon, crowned with stars, is given the great
eagle wings and the earth swallows up the river issued from the Dragon's
neck; lower register—Babylon riding the Beast; ten Kings fight the Lamb.

— — ALTAR WALL. Frescoes: upper register—Call of the fourth and fifth trumpet;
the earth throws up smoke and locusts as big as horses; middle register—the
Leopard with seven heads rising from the sea; the Lamb on Mount Sion
surrounded by the pure; lower register—the Fall of Babylon; Christ with
three crowns on a white horse leads a victorious host. *Plates* 229, 230.

— — R. WALL. Frescoes: upper register—Call of the sixth trumpet and the destruction of mankind by the heavenly hosts; the seventh Angel with a book;
middle register—three Angels herald the Last Judgement; the Angels reaping
the world; lower register—the Dragon is chained and the new Jerusalem is
founded; the marriage of the mystic Lamb.

— — SOFFIT OF ENTRANCE ARCH. Fresco: the seven Angels of the Apocalypse with
the seven cups of the Divine Wrath.

— — HIGH ALTAR. Polyptych: Madonna and Child enthroned; on superimposed
rows, either side, twelve Scenes from Life of Baptist; in pinnacles, Baptism of

Christ and Saints; in predella, Pietà and Saints; Carraresi and Buzzacarini coats of arms. *Plates* 228, 230.

The whole decoration commissioned by Fina Buzzacarina, wife of Francesco Novello da Carrara, Lord of Padua. 1376.

BASILICA DEL SANTO (S. ANTONIO), CAPPELLA DEL BEATO LUCA BELLUDI (FORMERLY DEI SS. GIACOMO E FILIPPO). Frescoes: In soffit of entrance arch and in all free spaces, roundels with Ancestors of Virgin.

— VAULT. Frescoes: Evangelists in roundels.

— L. WALL. Frescoes: in lunette, Miracles of S. Philip; below, Crucifixion of S. Philip.

— R. WALL. Frescoes: in lunette, Preaching of S. James; below, S. James rescues a pilgrim; S. James frees a merchant unjustly imprisoned in a tower.

— ENTRANCE WALL. Frescoes: in lunette, Martyrdom of S. James; in roundels, Jacob, S. Joseph; below, S. John Baptist, S. John Evangelist.

— APSE, VAULT AND LUNETTES. Frescoes: three roundels with Pantocrator, S. Philip holding incense-burner, S. James holding chalice; by circular window three more roundels with Holy Ghost, Isaiah and Jeremiah, and Annunciation; in left lunette, S. Philip disputing in Asia; in right lunette, S. James receiving communion from Christ.

— — CENTRAL WALL. Frescoes: above sarcophagus of Blessed Belludi: Madonna and Child enthroned between two Angels, being presented Fina Buzzacarina by SS. Francis and Louis of Toulouse, and her husband Francesco Novello da Carrara, Lord of Padua, by S. Anthony of Padua and Blessed Luca Belludi; in roundels above, two Ancestors of the Virgin, Amon and Josiah.

— — BETWEEN CENTRAL WALL AND L. WINDOW. Fresco: S. Philip recommends (to the Madonna) the donor's wife, Margherita Capodivacca, and her children. Above and below, Manasseh, Obed.

— — BETWEEN CENTRAL WALL AND R. WINDOW. Fresco: S. James recommends (to the Madonna) the donors Naimerio and Manfredino de' Conti. Above and below, Booz, Jeconiah.

— — BEYOND L. WINDOW. Convex corner fresco: Blessed Belludi has a vision of S. Anthony prophesying the end of Ezzelino's tyranny (view of Padua in background).

— — BEYOND R. WINDOW. Corner fresco: Blessed Belludi intercedes with Christ for the poor gathered round his tomb.

Frescoed decoration 1382/83.

— PASSAGE TO CLOISTERS, R. WALL, TOMB OF NICCOLÒ AND BOLZANELLO DA VIGONZA. Frescoes: in lunette, Coronation of Virgin and two kneeling donors recommended by Saints; in soffit of arch, eight busts of Saints; on face of arch, Blessing Redeemer, Angel and Virgin of Annunciation. 1380. *Plate* 233.

CAPPELLA DEGLI SCROVEGNI, APSE. Fragments of frescoes: Two Madonnas suckling the Child in niches. *Plate* 235.

EREMITANI, CAPPELLA CORTELLIERI O DEL SACRO CUORE (FORMERLY DI S. AGOSTINO,

FIRST R.), ALTAR WALL. Frescoes: S. Augustine enthroned and donor Tebaldo Cortellieri (lost).

— — L. WALL. Frescoes: from top—Theologia; Isaiah, Moses, Paul, Gregory, Ambrose, Jerome; the seven Cardinal and Theological Virtues; Magister Albertus de Padua, Beatus Johannes Bononiensis, Averroes (frs., r.).

— — R. WALL. Frescoes: from top—Philosophia; Socrates, Plato, Aristotle, Livy, Seneca; the Liberal Arts; Priscianus, Cicero, Pythagoras, Euclid, Jubal, Ptolemy (frs., r.).

— — SOFFIT OF ENTRANCE ARCH. Fresco: Saints (frs., r.).

Frescoed decoration. 1370.

— CAPPELLA SANGUINACCI (L. OF CHOIR), R. WALL. Fresco: Madonna and Child enthroned with three Saints and kneeling donor (Enrico Spisser?) (r.). 137(6?).

S. BENEDETTO VECCHIO, L. NAVE, CAPPELLA DI S. LUDOVICO, ENTRANCE ARCH. Frescoed soffit: motives from the Apocalypse. 1382 (rest of decoration finished after his death). Destroyed 1944.

Rome. SCHIFF-GIORGIONI COLLECTION. Centre panel of polyptych: Madonna and Child enthroned (companion to Athens, New York and Homeless). Sd and d. 1363.

Homeless. Top panels of 'Terzaghi' polyptych: Half-length S. Ambrose (repr. *Paragone*, March 1957, fig. 4); Half-length S. Cecilia (repr. *Arte Veneta*, 1947, fig. 2) (see Rome). 1363.

GRANDI see ERCOLE DA FERRARA

GREGORIO DI CECCO DI LUCA

Sienese. Adopted son and pupil of Taddeo di Bartolo. Documented 1389–1423.

Bettona (Perugia). S. MARIA MAGGIORE. Assumption.

Boston (Mass.). 22.403. Annunciation, with Crucifixion above.

London. 1317. Predella panel: Marriage of Virgin (r., companion to Rome and Siena). *Plate 483.*

Rome. VATICAN, PINACOTECA. 187. Predella panel: Birth of Virgin (companion to London and Siena). *Plate 482.*

Siena. OPERA DEL DUOMO. 25. Predella panel: Crucifixion (companion to London and Rome).

49. Polyptych from Tolomei altar of Visitation in the Duomo: Madonna of Humility suckling the Child, with six music-making Angels; SS. Augustine and John Baptist; SS. Peter and Paul; four Evangelists in trefoils; in pinnacles, Virgin of Assumption, busts of S. Blaise and S. Ansanus (fr.). Sd and d. 1423. *Plate 480.*

GUALTIERI DI GIOVANNI DA PISA
(Master of the Life of the Virgin)

Author of frescoes in middle chapel of sacristy, Siena cathedral, identified with Gualtieri di Giovanni da Pisa, born in Pisa 1375/80, mentioned in Pisa 1400, active in the cathedral of Siena since 1409 and mentioned in Siena up to 1445.

Berlin. 1069. Predella panel: S. Margaret meets Olibrius. *Plate 495.*

Notre Dame (Indiana). UNIVERSITY ART GALLERY. 61.47.3 (KRESS COLLECTION. K 114). Madonna and Child (from Assisi, Convento delle sepolte vive). (?) *Plate 493.*

Philadelphia (Pa.). FLEISCHER MEMORIAL. Madonna and Child enthroned, worshipped by kneeling monk. *Plate 492.*

Siena. 140. Triptych from S. Marta: Madonna and Child enthroned; S. Andrew; S. Onophrius. *Plate 490.*

    S. MARIA ASSUNTA (DUOMO), SACRISTY, MIDDLE CHAPEL, L. WALL. Frescoes: in lunette, Birth of Virgin; below, Marriage of Virgin (r.). 1411. *Plates 488, 491.*

    — — R. WALL. Frescoes: in lunette, Presentation of Virgin; below, Visitation (r.). 1411. *Plates 489, 494.*

    — L. CHAPEL (DEGLI ARLIQUI), ENTRANCE WALL. Frescoes: from top, Prophet, S. Margaret seated with cross and book, S. Agnes.

    S. MARIA DEL CARMINE. FIRST ALTAR R. Fresco: Madonna della cintola, with S. Lucy and another female Saint (the figure of the Virgin is lost).

    S. MARTA (ORFANOTROFIO), CLOISTER. Frescoes: Life of Hermits.

    SPEDALE DI S. MARIA DELLA SCALA, PELLEGRINARIO, VAULT. Frescoes: Saints and Prophets. 1439.

Zagreb. 14 (28). Predella panel: S. Anthony Abbot tempted by the golden porringer.

GUARIENTO DI ARPO

Paduan, recorded 1338–70. Derives his art from Byzantine Venetians, influenced by Giotto.

Arezzo. PINACOTECA, DONO CARLO ANGELI. Armed Angel ('Principatus' from Carraresi Chapel; see Padua, Museo).

Bassano del Grappa. MUSEO CIVICO. Painted Crucifix with female donor (from S. Francesco). Sd. E. *Plate 237.*

    S. FRANCESCO. Painted Crucifix (formerly Duomo; r.). L.*

Berlin-Ost. 2059. Madonna and Child enthroned with Angels and donor (r.).

Bolzano. S. DOMENICO, FORMER CAPPELLA DI S. NICCOLÒ. Fragmentary frescoes: Scenes from Life of S. Augustine, S. George and the Princess; Angels; in soffit of entrance arch, six Prophets (partly discovered and restored 1935; destroyed 1944).

Cambridge (Mass.). FOGG ART MUSEUM. 1928.114. Cross painted on front and back.

> 1962.279 (KINGSLEY PORTER BEQUEST). Armed Angel ('Principatus' from Carraresi Chapel, see Padua, Museo).

Catajo (Padua). CASTELLO. Angel weighing Soul (from Carraresi Chapel; see Padua, Museo).

Ferrara. PINACOTECA. Left wing of diptych: Crucifixion (companion to Raleigh).

Innsbruck. LANDESMUSEUM FERDINANDEUM. Detached fresco from S. Agostino at Padua: male head in profile (fr., companion to Padua, Eremitani).

— EX. Triptych: Crucifixion; small Saints at sides.

London. COURTAULD INSTITUTE GALLERIES, LEE OF FAREHAM COLLECTION. Madonna and Child enthroned. *Plate 241.*

New York. 88.3.86. Madonna and Child.

> TOLENTINO COLLECTION (EX). Madonna and Child enthroned with Symbols of Evangelists.

Padua. ACCADEMIA DI SCIENZE, LETTERE ED ARTI, SALA (FORMER CAPPELLA DEL CAPITANIO IN THE CARRARESI PALACE). Frescoes (g.p.). After 1345 and before 1365.

— R. WALL. Upper register: Noah blessed by God and found drunken by his Sons (mutilated by window); Gomorra set on fire by the Angels and Lot's Wife transformed into a statue of salt, Sacrifice of Isaac; (window) Jacob receives news of Joseph's death (fr.) and Joseph sold by his Brothers. Lower register: Pharaoh's guard stops the Mother of Moses (window); Ezekiel sees the Chariot of Fire; Sadrac, Mesac and Abednego are thrown into the fiery furnace and rescued by an Angel (window); Judith and Holofernes.

— L. WALL. Two detached frescoes: God speaks to Adam and Eve; Joseph speaks to Pharao. *Plate 249.*

MUSEO BOTTACCIN. Hexagonal panel: Redeemer; two lunette-shaped panels: Busts of Cherubim (from Carraresi Chapel, see Museo Civico).

MUSEO CIVICO. Inv. 1984–2010. Twenty-seven fragments from Ceiling of Carraresi Chapel (now Accademia; companions to Arezzo, Cambridge, Catajo, Padua Museo Bottaccin, Pavia). After 1345 and before 1365:

> Inv. 1986. Circular panel: Madonna and Child.
>
> Inv. 1987. Circular panel: Evangelist Matthew.
>
> Inv. 1990/91, 1993/4, 2008/9. Six panels with an Angel holding captive a Devil ('Potestates').
>
> Inv. 1984, 1988, 1995. Three panels with an Angel fully armed ('Principatus').
>
> Inv. 2000/2/3/5. Four panels with an Angel weighing a Soul (Archangels? 'Dominationes'?). *Plate 243.*
>
> Inv. 1998/99, 2010. Three panels with an Angel holding a Soul (Angels? Archangels?).
>
> Inv. 1996/97, 2004. Three panels with an Angel succouring Beggars or Ship-wrecks ('Virtutes').

Padua. MUSEO CIVICO (contd.). Inv. 1985, 1989, 1992, 2001, 2006/07. Panel with ten Angels seated holding Lily and Globe (Thrones?); five panels with an Angel seated, holding Sceptre and Globe ('Dominationes'?). *Plate 242.*

SS. FILIPPO E GIACOMO (EREMITANI), CHOIR. Frescoed decoration (g.p.).

— — VAULT. Church Fathers in medallions. Destroyed 1944.

— — L. WALL. From top: Evangelist Mark and John; S. Philip saved by snake from sacrificing to Mars, replaces idol with Cross; S. Augustine ordains African Bishops and S. Philip nailed on the Cross; Vision of young S. Augustine and S. Augustine consecrated as Bishop. *Plate 250.*

— — R. WALL. From top: Evangelists Mark and Luke; S. James praying and baptizing; S. James thrown from Temple and Siege of Jerusalem; William of Aquitaine hands the rule to the Augustinian monks and Alexander II joins the Augustinians with the Eremitani. Destroyed 1944.

— — SOFFIT OF ENTRANCE ARCH, INNER SIDE OF PIERS. Busts of Saints; full-length Saints. Partly destroyed 1944.

— — DADO. Monochrome Allegories of Seven Planets and Seven Ages of Man (Moon or Infancy, Mercury or Childhood, Venus or Adolescence, Mars or Virility, Sun or Maturity, Jupiter or Middle Age, Saturn or Old Age. The last three destroyed. *Plate 245.*

— — APSE. Vault in five sections: Christ as Judge and Apostles enthroned. Between windows: the Blessed and the Damned; window embrasures: small Scenes from Old Testament. Monochrome dado: Christ on Way to Calvary, 'Ecce Homo', Risen Christ, Christ in Limbo, Christ in Tomb with mourning Virgin and Evangelist. Soffit of arch: Saints. Largely destroyed 1944. *Plates 246–247, 248, 251.*

— — FROM S. AGOSTINO. Three fragments of fresco formerly decorating Carraresi Tomb at S. Agostino: Coronation of Virgin, two donors (Ubertino and Jacopino da Carrara?); companions to Innsbruck.

— SECOND CHAPEL R. Frescoes: soffit of entrance arch, six half-length female Saints in mandorlas; on walls, frs. of Annunciation? of scenes from Life of S. Francis? (r.).

— ENTRANCE WALL. Painted Crucifix with SS. James, Philip. Augustine and Trinity (st.).

Pavia. MUSEO MALASPINA. Bust of Cherub (from Carraresi Chapel; see Padua, Museo).

Raleigh (N.C.). MUSEUM OF ART. GL.60.17.17 (KRESS COLLECTION. K 1091). Right wing of diptych: Madonna and Child in Glory and four small Saints below (companion to Ferrara).

South Hadley (Mass.). MOUNT HOLYOKE COLLEGE FOR GIRLS. Tondo: Christus Triumphans.

Venice. MUSEO CORRER. Inv. 1890. S. Michael (r., st.).

PALAZZO DUCALE. Detached fragments of burnt fresco covered by Tintoretto's Paradise: Coronation of Virgin (r.). 1365–68.

CONTE VITTORIO CINI. Inv. 7009. Panel from polyptych: Ascension.

SS. GIOVANNI E PAOLO, CHOIR, L. WALL. Fragmentary fresco: Angel, Virtue (r.). (?)

Vienna. CZERNIN COLLECTION. 22. Polyptych: Coronation of Virgin; on either side, Nativity, Adoration of Magi, Circumcision, Washing of Feet, Betrayal of Christ, Flagellation, Deposition, Descent into Limbo, 'Noli me tangere', Descent of the Holy Ghost, Ascension of Christ, Last Judgement; in pinnacles, S. Justina, S. Francis, Angel of Annunciation, Presentation of Virgin, S. Martin and the Beggar, Crucifixion, S. Nicholas, Birth of Virgin, Virgin of Annunciation, Bishop Saint, S. Catherine; in frame, two roundels with Busts of Angels, six roundels with Busts of Saints. d. 1344. *Plate 238.*

Homeless. Angel weighing soul (from Ceiling of Carraresi Chapel; see Padua, Museo). Repr. *Belvedere* III, 1923, Heft 9, *Plate 41.*

Nativity. *Plate 240.*

Madonna and Child enthroned. *Plate 239.*

Angel with shield and spear. *Plate 244.*

GUIDO DA SIENA

Founder of the Sienese school, still all but Byzantine. Was active in the latter part of the thirteenth century.

Altenburg. 6, 7, 8. Side-panels of Badia Ardenga altarpiece: Adoration of Magi, Flight into Egypt, Flagellation (see Siena, Palazzo Pubblico).

Arezzo. 2. Madonna and Child enthroned (s.).

Cambridge (Mass.). FOGG ART MUSEUM. 1920.20. S. Dominic.

1923.15. Nativity.

Florence. ACCADEMIA. 435. Madonna and Child enthroned.

Grosseto. MUSEO D'ARTE SACRA. Last Judgement.

London. COURTAULD INSTITUTE GALLERIES, LEE OF FAREHAM COLLECTION. Pediment: Coronation of Virgin with Brandifoglio coats of arms.

New Haven (Conn.). 1871.2. Crucifixion.

Paris. STRÖLIN COLLECTION. Side-panels of Badia Ardenga altarpiece: Nativity, Circumcision (see Siena, Palazzo Pubblico). *Plate 20.*

Princeton (N.J.). 144. Side-panel of Badia Ardenga altarpiece: Annunciation (see Siena, Palazzo Pubblico).

62.48. Madonna and Child (formerly Platt, Englewood).

Siena. 4. Shutters: S. Francis receiving Stigmata; S. Clare repulsing the Saracens with a pyx; Martyrdom of S. Bartholomew; Martyrdom of S. Catherine. *Plate 18.*

5. The Gallerani shutters: inside—S. Francis receiving Stigmata; S. Dominic praying for the recovery of Reginald, who is given a Dominican habit by the Virgin; the Blessed Andrea Gallerani feeding the poor; the Blessed Andrea

Gallerani in prayer; outside—the Blessed Andrea Gallerani (died 1251) receiving pilgrims (st.).

6. Madonna and Child with SS. Peter, Paul, John Evangelist and Andrew (st.; cut at sides).

7. Dossal from S. Francesco at Colle Val d'Elsa (cut at sides): Madonna and Child and SS. Francis, John Baptist, John Evangelist and Mary Magdalen. d. 1271. *Plate 19*.

8. Lenten hanging (?): Raising of Lazarus, Transfiguration and Entry into Jerusalem. *Plate 22*.

9–13. Five side-panels of altarpiece from Badia Ardenga: Massacre of Innocents, Betrayal, Crucifixion, Deposition, Entombment (see Palazzo Pubblico, Siena).

15. S. Peter enthroned and six Stories on either side (Annunciation, Nativity, Calling of Peter and Andrew, the Angel leads S. Peter out of Prison, Fall of Simon Magus, Martyrdom of S. Peter) (st.).

16. Madonna and Child (st.). Formerly d. 1262.

587. Madonna and Child enthroned. L.

PALAZZO PUBBLICO, SALA DEL MAPPAMONDO. Altarpiece from Badia Ardenga: Madonna and Child enthroned (heads and hands repainted by Ugolino di Nerio); in pinnacle, blessing Christ and two Angels; in spandrels, six Angels (scenes from Life of Virgin, now at Altenburg, Paris, Princeton, Siena 9–13, Utrecht, may have been on either side). Sd and d. 12(21); variously read 1261/71/81. *Plate 21*.

S. MARIA ASSUNTA (DUOMO). 'Madonna del Voto' (fragment of dossal). After 1260. (?)

S. MARIA DEL CARMINE. Madonna and Child. (?)

Utrecht. ARCHIEPISCOPAL MUSEUM. 5. Side-panel of altarpiece from Badia Ardenga (see Siena, Palazzo Pubblico): Christ mounting the Cross (r.).

JACOPO DI MINO see PELLICCIAJO

JACOPO DA SANSEVERINO see SALIMBENI

LANINO, Bernardino

School of Vercelli, ca 1511–81/2. Pupil and follower of Gaudenzio Ferrari. Son-in-law of Girolamo Giovenone.

Auckland (New Zealand). ART GALLERY. Two panels of polyptych: young warrior Martyrs (Mauritius and Alexander?).

Berlin-Ost. 1412. Visitation and donor.

Biella. S. SEBASTIANO, R. OF CHOIR. Assumption; in predella, Life of Virgin. Sd and
    d. 1543. *Plate 1275.*

    S. STEFANO NUOVO (DUOMO), SACRISTY. Madonna and Child enthroned with SS.
    John Baptist, Roch, Sebastian and John Evangelist and donor.

Bloomington (Ind.). INDIANA UNIVERSITY. L.62.165 (KRESS STUDY COLLECTION.
    K 1126). Madonna and Child (version of Naples).

Borgosesia (Vercelli). SS. PIETRO E PAOLO, THIRD ALTAR L. Madonna and Child with
    five Putti and SS. Gaudentius, Peter, Catherine, Apollonia, Paul and John
    Baptist; in predella, SS. Peter and Paul, S. Peter walking on the water,
    S. Paul expelled from Damascus. Sd and d. 1539.

Bracciano (Roma). CASTELLO. Christ in Glory with six Angels (fr., r.).

Busto Arsizio (Milano). S. MARIA IN PIAZZA. Annunciation, Nativity, Adoration
    of Magi, Angels.

    — ALTAR L. OF CHOIR. Baptism (here deposited from Milan, Brera). Sd and d.
    1554.

Campiglia Cervo (Biella). SS. GIUSEPPE E BERNARDINO. Polyptych: Madonna and
    Child enthroned, with Pietà above; right and left, eight Saints; in tympanum,
    God the Father; in predella, monochrome Angels, Church Fathers and
    Apostles.

Casale Monferrato. CONFRATERNITA DI GESÙ. Circumcision; in lunette, Angels. Sd
    and d. 1554.*

Cossato (Novara). ASSUNTA, CHOIR. Assumption (r.). Sd.

Crevacuore (Biella). S. SEBASTIANO. Deposition (replica of Vercelli, S. Giuliano).

Florence. BARGELLO. Carrand 35. The Redeemer.

Gattinara (Biella). S. PIETRO, CHOIR. Frs. of polyptych: Madonna and Child, SS.
    James, Peter, John Baptist, John Evangelist; predella with busts of Saints (now
    in Museo at Vercelli?).

Isolabella (Lago Maggiore). PALAZZO BORROMEO. The Redeemer.

Legnano. S. MAGNO, CHOIR. Frescoes: S. Magnus, The Redeemer, S. Sebastian,
    S. Roch, Life of Virgin (right wall—Circumcision, Massacre of Innocents,
    Flight into Egypt, Christ and the Doctors; left wall—Marriage of Virgin,
    Visitation, Nativity, Adoration of Magi). doc. 1560–64.

Lessona (Biella). S. LORENZO. Madonna and Child enthroned with SS. George,
    Lawrence, John Baptist and Eusebius. Sd and d. 1568.

London. 700. Holy Family with SS. Paul, Gregory and Mary Magdalen. Sd and
    d. 1543.

Milan. BRERA. 84, 85, 86. Frs. of frescoes from S. Marta: S. Martha, S. Mary Mag-
    dalen, three music-making Putti. *Plate 1240.*

    266. S. Francis. ca 1545.

    322. Baptism. Sd and d. 1554 (deposited at Busto Arsizio).

    323. Holy Family with S. Martha, male Saint and donor.

    POLDI PEZZOLI. 647. Madonna and Child (r.). Wrongly signed Calisto Piazza.

Milan. POLDI PEZZOLI (contd.). 651. Madonna suckling the Child and two Angels.

S. AMBROGIO, CAPPELLA DI S. GIORGIO (SEVENTH BAY R.). Frescoes: Left wall—in lunette, Trial by fire; below, Beheading of S. George. Right wall—in lunette, Judgement; below, S. George killing the dragon. Entrance arch—Putti with garlands and Creation of Eve. Entrance piers—S. John Evangelist, S. John Baptist. Sd. ca 1545–50. *Plate 1276.*

— SPLAY OF R. DOOR. Frescoes: Christ carrying Cross and three Maries (not traced).

S. NAZZARO MAGGIORE, CAPPELLA DI S. CATERINA (L. TRANSEPT). Frescoes: Martyrdom of S. Catherine and four scenes of her life; above, God the Father and Angels. doc. 1546–48 (with Della Cerva).

— R. TRANSEPT. Last Supper (after Gaudenzio Ferrari's at S. Maria della Passione).

Mortara. S. CROCE. Adoration of Magi. Sd and d. 1553.

Naples. MUSEO FILANGIERI. 1466. Madonna and Child.

Novara. S. MARIA ASSUNTA (DUOMO), SAGRESTIA INFERIORE. Detached frescoes from the Cappella di S. Giuseppe del Vecchio Duomo: Massacre of Innocents, Marriage of Virgin, Annunciation, Visitation, Adoration of Magi, Flight into Egypt, four heads of Saints.

— THIRD ALTAR R. Christ on Cross and Saints. 1550–60.

Occimiano (Monferrato). SS. LORENZO E GIORGIO. Madonna and Child enthroned with SS. Catherine and Ursula, each recommending four women and two children. d. 1580.

Raleigh (N.C.). NORTH CAROLINA MUSEUM OF ART. GL.60.17.45 (KRESS COLLECTION. K. 1570). Madonna and Child enthroned with six Dominican Saints and eight donors. Sd and d. 1552. *Plate 1279.*

Romagnano (Valsesia). S. SILANO, CHOIR. Descent of the Holy Ghost (wrongly inscribed on back 1517). (1542?)

Rome. PINACOTECA CAPITOLINA, GALLERIA CINI. Inv. 252. Portrait of Cassiano dal Pozzo. Sd.* *Plate 1281.*

(Environs.) MENTANA. F. ZERI. Esther before Ahasverus.

Sarasota (Fla.). RINGLING MUSEUM OF ART. 42. Nativity with S. Andrew (after Gaudenzio, ibidem).

Saronno. S. MARIA DEI MIRACOLI. Frescoes in spandrels of cupola: Adam's family; Cain's birth; Abel with his flock and Cain at the plough; Sacrifices of Abel and Cain; Abel's death; God appears to Cain.

Senigallia. CONTE MASTAI FERRETTI (EX). Resurrection. Sd and d. 1567.

Turin. ACCADEMIA ALBERTINA. 189, 191. Heads of children. (Not traced.)

252. S. Clare.

254. S. Francis.

GALLERIA SABAUDA. 42. Deposition. Sd and d. 1558. *Plate 1278.*

57. Madonna and Child with Infant S. John.

60. Holy Family with S. Jerome.

62. Madonna and Child with SS. John Baptist, Augustine, Lucy and James. Sd and d. 1564. *Plate 1280.*

65. Madonna and Child with SS. Anthony Abbot, Sebastian, Roch and John Baptist. Sd. Commissioned 1534. *Plate 1283.*

Valduggia (Valsesia). S. GIORGIO, BEHIND HIGH ALTAR. Polyptych: Madonna and Child enthroned with four Angels and four Saints; S. George; S. John Baptist; half-length SS. Peter, Paul, Stephen and Bishop Saint; tympanum with God the Father blessing; in predella, the four Church Fathers and the twelve Apostles. Sd and d. 1564.

Varallo Sesia. PINACOTECA. Detached fresco: Descent of the Holy Ghost.

Vercelli. MUSEO BORGOGNA. 'Madonna del Cane.' Sd and d. 1563. *Plate 1284.*

Annunciation.

Banner: Madonna and Child with S. Anne and Penitents recommended by SS. Michael and Peter Martyr.

Eight detached frescoes from S. Caterina: Putti with scrolls; Three scenes from Life of S. Catherine.

Detached frescoes from S. Francesco: eight spandrels with music-making Angels; lunettes with Sibyls; Annunciation; four Putti.

PALAZZO ARCIVESCOVILE. Madonna and Child enthroned with two flying putti, S. John Baptist recommending a Knight of Malta, S. Michael. Sd and d. 1576.*

S. ANDREA, SALA CAPITOLARE. Fragments of fresco: lunette with three music-making Putti; Madonna and Child in Glory.

S. BERNARDINO, APSE. Fresco: Crucifixion (st.). 1577.

S. CRISTOFORO, CAPPELLA DELL'ASSUNTA (L. OF CHOIR). Frescoes: Adoration of Shepherds and parts in frescoes by Gaudenzio Ferrari. E. *Plates 1271-72.*

S. GIULIANO, ALTAR R. OF HIGH ALTAR. Deposition. Sd and d. 1547. *Plate 1277.*

— HIGH ALTAR. Adoration of Magi (r.). *Plate 1282.*

S. PAOLO, APSE. 'Madonna della Grazia.' Sd and d. 1568.

— SECOND ALTAR L. Adoration of the Child with S. Ambrose. doc. 1565.*

LIBERALE DA VERONA

Verona, 1445(?)–1526. Recorded in and around Siena 1466 to 1476, in Venice 1487. Pupil of Vincenzo di Stefano; influenced by Girolamo da Cremona, Mantegna, Bellini and in his dotage, by Raphael. [See Introduction, p. XVI.]

Altenburg. 54. Madonna and Child.*

Amsterdam. OTTO LANZ (EX). Predella panel: Flight into Egypt.

Berlin. 46A. S. Sebastian. (Destroyed, 1945.)

1655. S. Peter heals a cripple (companion to Cambridge). (Liberale or Girolamo da Cremona?)

Berlin-Ost. 1183. Madonna and Child enthroned, with S. Lawrence, S. Christopher and two Olivetan Saints. Sd and d. 1489. *Plate 1858.*

EUGEN SCHWEITZER (EX). 'Frizzoni' Madonna and Child (after Mantegna).

Boston (Mass.). GARDNER MUSEUM. Nativity.

Brno. A.137. Bust of S. Sebastian.

Brussels. HENRY WAUTERS. A girl speaks to her lover from a window (companion to Florence, Berenson and New York). (Liberale, Girolamo da Cremona or Francesco di Giorgio?)

Budapest. 1028 (96) AND 1145. Madonnas adoring the sleeping Child (versions in Columbus, Florence, Milan, Verona, Vicenza).

    PÉTERI COLLECTION (EX). Madonna and Child. E.* *Plate* 864.

Cambridge. FITZWILLIAM MUSEUM. P.D.21–1961. S. Peter refuses Poppaea's alms (companion to Berlin). (Liberale or Girolamo da Cremona?) *Plate* 867.

Cannes. MUSÉE DE LA CASTRE. Christ at Column.*

Chiusi. S. SECONDIANO (DUOMO), SALA CAPITOLARE. Miniatures. 1466/69.

    Codex A—f.4 recto: God speaks to a Prophet.

    Codex Q—f.1 recto: Communion of the Apostles.

        f.51 verso: Resurrection.

        f.101 verso: Ascension. *Plate* 862.

    Codex R—f.1 recto: Descent of the Holy Ghost.

        f.21 recto: Christ preaching to monks.

        f.25 recto: Priest giving Communion.

    Codex Y—f.1 verso: Washing of Feet.

        f.22 recto: Two monks singing.

        f.70 verso: Death rising from Sepulchre.

Columbus (Ohio). GALLERY OF FINE ARTS, SCHUMACHER COLLECTION. Madonna adoring the sleeping Child (see Budapest).

Cracow. MNIC N.1.57501. Virgin and Child in the lap of S. Anne.* *Plate* 1859.

Florence. BERENSON COLLECTION. Onlookers (fr., companion to New York and to Brussels).

    ENRICO COSTA (EX). Virgin adoring sleeping Child (see Budapest).

    CHARLES LOESER (EX). S. Sebastian.

    PROF. ROBERTO LONGHI. Christ at Column.

    MARCHESE TORRIGIANI (EX). Mourning over dead Christ.

    SERRISTORI COLLECTION. Nativity (Liberale or Girolamo da Cremona?).

Gargagnano (Valpolicella). VILLA SEREGO ALIGHIERI. Madonna and Child.

Grenoble. Inv. 1768. Madonna and Child with Angel.

Le Havre. 50 (COLL. CAMPANA 234). Cassone panel: Rape of Helen of Troy. (Liberale or Girolamo da Cremona?)

Leipzig. Inv. 1165. Madonna adoring sleeping Child (see Budapest).

London. 1134. Madonna and Child with Angels.

    1336. Dido's Death.

    PHILIP POUNCEY. Dead Christ in Sepulchre upheld by Angels. *Plate* 1865.

Lovere. ACCADEMIA TADINI. Madonna and Child with Infant S. John and Angels.*

Milan. BRERA. 177. S. Sebastian with Venice in background.

    GUSTAVO FRIZZONI (EX). Small Madonna with book.

AVV. BARNABÒ. 'Noseda' Madonna with sleeping Child. Sd Caroto and d. 1507.

ALDO NOSEDA (EX). Predella: Madonna and eight Saints.

CRESPI (EX). Madonna adoring the sleeping Child.

Munich. 7821. Pietà.

New York. 43.98.8. Chess-players (fr.; companion to Florence, Berenson and to Brussels). (Girolamo da Cremona, Liberale or Francesco di Giorgio?)

Philadelphia (Pa.). J. G. JOHNSON COLLECTION. 216. S. John in Patmos.

Princeton (N.J.). 35-25, 35-26. Panels from triptych formerly Monga Collection Verona: S. Sebastian, Blessed Augustinian.

35-27. Holy Family with Angel Gabriel and Saint holding pincers (r.). T.

Rome. MUSEO DI PALAZZO VENEZIA. Adoration of the Child (r., st.).

S. FRANCESCA ROMANA. Madonna and Child between S. Benedict and S. Francesca Romana. (Liberale or Girolamo da Cremona?) *Plate* 866.

ILO NUNES. 'Noseda' Madonna and Child with two singing Angels by window.

Saint Louis (Mich.). CITY ART MUSEUM. 321.51. S. Sebastian (st. v. of Berlin).

Siena. BIBLIOTECA COMUNALE. Messale Romano X, II, 3.

f.180—Illuminated page: Crucifixion and the four Evangelists in roundels. 1471.

DUOMO, LIBRERIA PICCOLOMINI. Miniatures. (N.B. The codices having been differently numbered at different times, we give their full titles and only the numbers actually inscribed on them; they are listed in chronological order):

Codex 3 (also 16, 24, 9): Graduale a I Dominica usque ad XVI Dominicam post Pentecostem (16 parables and stories of Christ, finished 1468).

f.1 recto: 'Thou beholdest the mote in thy brother's eye but considerest not the beam in thine own eye'. *Plate* 861.

f.6 recto: The Good Shepherd.

f.10 verso: 'When thou makest a feast, call the poor, the maimed, the lame, the blind'.

f.16 recto: The miraculous draught of fishes.

f.21 verso: The Master instructs His Disciples not to quarrel with one's brother.

f.27 recto: Multiplication of loaves and fishes.

f.33 recto: 'Beware of false Prophets'.

f.38 recto: The parable of the bad steward.

f.43 verso: Christ weeps over Jerusalem.

f.48 verso: The Pharisee and the Publican.

f.54 verso: The healing of the dumb man.

f.60 recto: The good Samaritan.

f.67 verso: The healed leper kisses Christ's foot.

f.73 recto: Jesus speaks to the Apostles: 'respicite volatilia coeli'.

f.77 verso: Jesus raises the son of the widow of Naim.

f.82 verso: Jesus heals the man sick of dropsy.

Codex 2 (also 17, 20, 5): Graduale a Dominica Septuagesimae usque ad Dominicam Tertiam Quadragesimae. Finished 1470.

Siena. DUOMO, LIBRERIA PICCOLOMINI. Codex 2 (contd.).

 f.1 recto: The parable of the labourers of the vineyard. Sd. *Plate* 863.

 f.9 verso: The parable of the sower.

 f.16 verso: Christ heals the man born blind.

 f.29 recto: The ashes.

 f.36 verso: L'Aquilone.

 f.45 verso: Christ tempted by the Devil.

 f.96 recto: Scribes and Pharisees ask Jesus for a sign.

Codex 4 (also 18, 20, 10): Graduale a Dominica XVII usque ad Dominicam XXIII post Pentecostem. (Five miniatures in frames by Francesco Rosselli, preceding the four by Pellegrino di Mariano.) 1470.

 f.18 recto: The barren fig tree.

 f.56 verso: 'Render unto Caesar what is Caesar's'.

 f.62 recto: Jesus heals the woman who suffered from an issue of blood.

 f.73 verso: The Sacrament of Confession.

 f.80 recto: S. Gregory's vision of S. Michael over Castel S. Angelo.

Codex 1 (also 12, 10, 28): Graduale A Festo Sancti Petri Usque ad Assumptionem Beatae Virginis Marie et in Decollatione Sancti Johannis et Sancti Clementis. (Seven miniatures by Liberale, three by Girolamo da Cremona). 1472–73.

 f.2 recto: Liberation of S. Peter.

 f.12 verso: Visitation.

 f.40 recto: S. Lawrence with two Angels.

 f.76 recto: S. Matthew and the Angel. [*Plate* 354.]

 f.80 verso: S. Michael slaying the Devil.

 f.94 verso: Virgin Mary and all Saints.

 f.101 verso: S. Martin and the Beggar.

Codex (Milanesi VII): Graduale a Resurrectione Domini Nostri usque ad Corpus Christi. Payments January to May 1473. (See under Girolamo da Cremona.)

Codex 26 (also 17, 2): Graduale commune Sanctorum. Probably 1473.

 f.23 verso: Young martyr looking up (coloured by Girolamo da Cremona).

Codex 27 (Milanesi XVII): Graduale in Dedicatione Ecclesie. ca 1473.

 f.34 recto: Two hermits (finished by Girolamo).

 f.42 recto: Three Virgin Martyrs (finished by Girolamo).

Codex 28 (also 21, 6): Graduale a Dominica Tertia Quadragesimae usque ad Dominicam Passionis (coloured by Girolamo da Cremona). 1473.

 f.2 recto: Jesus exorcizes a man possessed by the Devil.

 f.21 verso: Ornamental border with putto and dragon.

 f.39 recto: Multiplication of loaves.

 f.74 verso: Christ stoned by the people.

 f.94 verso: Ornamental border with harpies.

Codex 29 (also 18, 3): Graduale a Dominica Prima Adventus usque ad Festum Sancti Sylvestri (see also Girolamo da Cremona). 1473.

f.11 recto: S. John Baptist questioned by a Levite and a Pharisee.

f.58 recto: Nativity. *Plate 878.*

f.64 recto: Adoration of the Shepherds.

f.103 verso: Presentation in Temple.

Codex 30 (also 22 1, 7): Graduale a Dominica Palmarum usque ad Missam Sabati Sancti (coloured by Girolamo da Cremona). 1473.

f.2 recto: Jesus entering Jerusalem (paid to Liberale December 1473).

f.15 verso: Feast in the House of Simon.

f.22 verso: Jesus before Pontius Pilate.

f.28 recto: Way to Golgotha.

f.37 recto: Washing of Feet.

f.76 verso: Pietà.

Codex 31 (also 19 1, 4): Graduale a Circumcisione Domini usque ad Dominicam V post Epiphaniam (Payments July 1473; see under Girolamo da Cremona).

Codex 32 (also marked 1A): Antiphonarium a Sabbato Primo de Adventu usque ad Vesperos Vigiliae Nativitatis (begun by Girolamo da Cremona, finished by Liberale in 1473 or 1474).

f.4 verso: God speaks to a Prophet.

f.41 verso: Jesus weeps over Jerusalem.

f.69 recto: God speaks to a Prophet.

f.133 recto: 'Canite Tubam'. [*Plate 353.*]

Codex 21 (also 10, L): Antiphonarium A Vigilia Ascensionis Usque ad Corpus Domini. ca 1474. (See under Girolamo da Cremona.)

Codex 16 (Milanesi XIV): Antiphonarium a Cathedra Petri. 1475. (See under Girolamo da Cremona.)

Sommacampagna. ZENO FORLATI. Madonna and Child with SS. Sebastian and Roch.*

Stockholm. UNIVERSITY GALLERY. 60. Madonna and Child with four Angels. *Plate 1864.*

Turin. GALLERIA SABAUDA, RACCOLTA GUALINO 668. Madonna and Child with S. Catherine.

Venice. S. LIO, ABOVE SIDE DOOR. Dead Christ mourned by four Angels. Probably 1487.

Verona. 176. Right shutter, from S. Maria della Scala: front, Adoration of Magi; back, S. Peter (left shutter, lost). *Plate 1866.*

204. Adoration of the Child with S. Jerome (from monastery of S. Fermo).

275. Holy Family.

315. Miniature: Descent of the Holy Ghost. *Plate 1857.*

377. Deposition (from S. Tommaso Cantuariense).

430. Nativity.

625. S. Jerome between SS. Francis and Paul (from Cappella di S. Girolamo in S. Maria della Vittoria). L.

723. Madonna of the goldfinch with two Angels.

798. Bust of S. Sebastian (fr.?).

Verona (contd.). 838. Cassone: Triumph of Chastity and Love.

    865. Madonna and sleeping Child (r.; see Budapest; replica of Boschi S. Marco, Verona Environs).

    1584. Sleeping Christ Child (fr.).

    s.n. Sacrifice of Isaac with Francesco Miniscalchi and his sister as donors. *Plate 1860.*

    — Miniatures: 309—Nativity; 310—Olivetans praying in letter A; 315—Descent of Holy Ghost; 321—Adoration of Magi; 1660—S. John Evangelist.*

    PALAZZO ARCIVESCOVILE. Predella: Birth of Virgin, Adoration of Magi, Death of Virgin. *Plate 1861.*

    PIAZZA DELLE ERBE N. 27. Fresco: The Eternal surrounded by Angels and Fall of Man (r.).

    S. ANASTASIA, CAPPELLA BONAVERI (THIRD ALTAR R.). Frescoes: in lunette, Mourning over dead Christ; above, Angels [on pilasters, found under whitewash in 1966, SS. Peter, Paul, Peter Martyr, Dominic, Lucy and another Saint*]. *Plate 1863.*

    — — (NEARBY). Ecstasy of S. Mary Magdalen with S. Catherine and S. Toscana.

    S. FERMO MAGGIORE, CHOIR, L. CHAPEL. S. Anthony of Padua surrounded by SS. Bernard, Catherine, Nicholas and another female Saint.

    S. LORENZO, L. NAVE. Entombment. Not traced.

    S. MARIA MATRICOLARE (DUOMO), CAPPELLA DEI CALCASOLI (SECOND R.). Adoration of Magi (Lunette and side-panels added by Giolfino 1524). *Plate 1862.*

    — BIBLIOTECA CAPITOLARE. Madonna suckling the Child.*

    S. MARIA DEL PARADISO, FOURTH ALTAR R. S. Metrone flanked by SS. Dominic and Anthony of Padua.

    S. TOSCANA, ALTAR R. Triptych: S. Toscana between SS. Peter and John Baptist; in predella, Life of S. Toscana.

    CONVENTO DELLE STIGMATE. Madonna and blessing Child, standing on parapet.

    MARCHESE DI CANOSSA. Madonna della Rosa. L.

    Environs. BOSCHI S. MARCO. Madonna and sleeping Child (see Budapest).

Vicenza. 143. Madonna and sleeping Child (see Budapest).

Viterbo. DUOMO. Blessing Christ with SS. John Evangelist, Leonard, Benedict and John Baptist, and Bishop as donor. d. 1472. (Liberale or Girolamo da Cremona?) *Plate 868.*

Homeless. Madonna and Child with SS. Jerome, Anthony of Padua and four Angels. *Plate 865.*

LIPPO DALMASIO

Filippo di Tommaso or del Maso de' Scannabecchi; also known as Lippo delle Madonne. Bolognese, recorded at Pistoia ca 1384 and later, died in Bologna after 1410.

Bologna. PINACOTECA. Centre panel of portable altarpiece: Coronation of Virgin with blessing Redeemer above. Sd and d. 1394. *Plate 284.*

Madonna suckling the Child. Sd. *Plate 287.*

PII ISTITUTI EDUCATIVI. Triptych from the Collegio di S. Croce: Madonna and Child enthroned with two Angels; SS. John Baptist and Augustine with S. Petronius holding the city of Bologna in quatrefoil above; SS. Peter and Paul with Saint in quatrefoil above. Sd.

COLLEGIO DI SPAGNA, SACRISTY. Fresco: Madonna of Humility suckling the Child. Sd.

S. DOMENICO, MUSEO. 'Madonna del Velluto.'

S. ISAIA, SACRISTY. Fresco: Madonna and Child with two Angels.

S. MARIA DELLA MISERICORDIA, SECOND CHAPEL R. Fresco: Madonna suckling the Child. Sd and d. 1397.

S. PETRONIO, PILLAR NEAR THIRD CHAPEL L. Fresco: Christ enthroned.

S. PROCOLO, PORTAL. Frescoed lunette: Madonna and Child with S. Benedict and S. Sixtus Pope.

Florence. PROF. R. LONGHI. Pinnacle: Angel of Annunciation (fr.).

Lawrence (Kansas). UNIVERSITY GALLERY. 54.116. Madonna and Child.

London. 752. Madonna of Humility. Sd.

Milan. DUCA VISCONTI DI MODRONE. Deposition. (?)

Norton Hall (Glos.). SIR WALTER POLLEN. Madonna and Child enthroned (r.). Sd and d. 1409. *Plate 285.*

Pistoia. MUSEO. Detached fresco: Madonna suckling the Child and four Angels. d. 1407. *Plate 286.*

S. DOMENICO, CONVENT. Detached fresco from church: Madonna suckling the Child with Angels carrying pavilion (Casa di Loreto) above, S. Dominic recommending male donor and S. Catherine recommending female donor. E. (?)

LORENZETTI, Ambrogio

Sienese, active 1319–1348. Pupil of his elder brother Pietro, influenced by the works of Giovanni Pisano and Giotto.

Asciano (Senese). CASA BARGAGLI, GRANARY. Frescoes: medallions with the four Seasons.

MUSEO D'ARTE SACRA. The Badia a Rofeno triptych (an assembled altarpiece in a Renaissance frame): S. Michael slaying the dragon; full-length SS. Bartholomew and Bernard; Madonna and Child (former centre panel of polyptych inserted in a large triangular pinnacle); Busts of Evangelist and of Bishop Saint in two smaller triangular pinnacles (g.p. and r.).

Boston (Mass.). 39.536. 'Platt' Madonna and Child (from S. Eugenio, Siena).

Brussels. JACQUES STOCLET. Madonna and Child (r.).

Budapest. 22 (44). Cut-down panel: Enthroned Madonna and Child holding scroll.

Cambridge (Mass.). FOGG ART MUSEUM. 1939.113. Portable Crucifixion. 1953.203. Pinnacle: S. Agnes.

El Paso (Texas). MUSEUM OF ART. 1961–6/4 (KRESS COLLECTION. K 1354). Madonna and Child.

Florence. UFFIZI. 8346. Circumcision. d. 1342. *Plate 96.*

8348, 8349. Two panels from S. Procolo: S. Nicholas throws the gold to the girls without dowry and is consecrated; S. Nicholas delivers a child possessed by the Devil and performs the miracle of the corn. ca 1332. [*Plate 262.*]

9411, 8731, 8732. Reconstructed triptych from S. Procolo: 'Berenson' Madonna and Child, with Saviour in pinnacle; SS. Nicholas of Bari and Proculus, with Evangelist and Baptist in pinnacles. Formerly signed and dated 1332. *Plate 95.*

MUSEO ARCIVESCOVILE (SEMINARIO MAGGIORE, CESTELLO). Madonna and Child enthroned, from Vico l'Abate, S. Angelo. d. 1319.

Frankfurt a/M. 1005. Portable altarpiece: Crucifixion, flanked by SS. John Baptist, Bartholomew and two female Saints; below, Nativity and Announcement to the Shepherds (st.).

London. 1147, 3071, 3072. Fragments of frescoes: Heads of four nuns; Head of Annunciate Virgin; Head of S. Catherine.

Lucerne. ABEGG STOCKAR. 'Ourousoff' Holy Family.

Massa Marittima. PALAZZO COMUNALE. 'Maestà': Madonna and Child enthroned with Angels, Saints and the three Theological Virtues. *Plate 94.*

Milan. BRERA. 968. 'Cagnola' Madonna and Child.

Minneapolis (Minn.). 35.7.95. S. Catherine.

Montenero sull'Amiata. S. LUCIA. Painted Crucifix (r.).

New York. 41.190.26. Madonna and Child with goldfinch (from Pompana).

Roccalbegna (Grosseto). PARISH CHURCH. Madonna and Child holding flowers, and portions of haloes and martyr's palm to the sides (fr. of centre panel); two side-panels with SS. Peter and Paul on seats with lion heads. E. *Plate 92.*

San Galgano (Siena). ORATORIO DI MONTESIEPI. Frescoes. Ceiling: four medallions with Prophets. Lunette: Maestà [Madonna and Child enthroned with Angels carrying flowers, SS. John Baptist, Paul, Peter, John Evangelist, Benedict, Francis and nine other Saints, and Eve reclining at her feet]. Below: Annunciation. Right and left lunette: worshipping Saints and Angels and S. Galgano presenting to S. Michael the rock pierced by his sword (r.).

Siena. 52, 53. Two panels of polyptych from Convent of S. Marta: S. Paul with Lion of S. Marc in pinnacle, S. John Baptist with Angel of S. Matthew in pinnacle.

65. Portable Madonna and Child surrounded by six Angels, SS. Dorothy, Catherine and the kneeling Doctors of the Church. [*Plate 258.*]

70. Townscape (fr.).

71. Landscape (fr.).

77. The S. Petronilla polyptych: Half-length Madonna and Child, SS. Dorothy and Mary Magdalen; full-length Baptist and Evangelist; Lamentation over the dead Christ.

88. Annunciation ('Madonna dei Donzelli'). Sd and d. 1344. [*Plate* 259.]

90, 314. Side-panels to Sant'Angelo in Colle Madonna by Pietro Lorenzetti: SS. Peter and Paul (st.). E.

92. Allegory of Fall and Redemption (r.; very close to both Ambrogio and Pietro). *Plate* 91.

598. Painted Crucifix from S. Maria del Carmine. *Plate* 90.

605. Madonna and Child with goldfinch (from Pieve di Rapolano). E.

ARCHIVIO DI STATO. Gabella cover: Good Government. 1344.

PALAZZO PUBBLICO, SALA DELLA PACE. Frescoes: Allegory of Bad Government; Allegory of Good Government. 1338/40. [*Plate* 261.] *Plates* 97, 98.

— LOGGIA. Fresco: Madonna and Child blessing globe, with Cardinal Virtues below (fr., r.). 1340.

Fresco: S. Augustine with donor, Evangelist, S. Catherine.

S. MARIA ASSUNTA (DUOMO), MUSEO DELL'OPERA. 52. Four panels of polyptych: SS. Catherine, Romuald, Francis and Mary Magdalen; in trefoils of pinnacles, SS. Andrew, Peter, Paul and John Baptist.

S. AGOSTINO, CAPPELLA PICCOLOMINI, LUNETTE. Fresco: Madonna and Child in Glory worshipped by SS. Agatha, Augustine, Bartholomew, Michael, Anthony Abbot, Apollonia, Clare and Catherine. 1348? [*Plate* 264.]

— COLLEGIO CONVITTO TOLOMEI. Frescoes right of entrance: Heads of Saints in medallions.

S. FRANCESCO, THIRD CHAPEL L. OF CHOIR. Frescoes transferred from the Chapter House: Ordination of S. Louis of Toulouse; Franciscan Martyrdom at Ceuta (r.). *Plate* 93.

— EX-CONVENT, REFECTORY. See under Seminario.

S. PIETRO ALLE SCALE, CANONICA. Madonna and Child (p.).

Full-length SS. Peter and Paul (p.).

Full-length SS. Michael and Lucy (p.).

SEMINARIO, CAPPELLA. Madonna suckling the Child.

Vico l'Abate. See Florence, Seminario Maggiore.

LORENZETTI, Pietro

Sienese. Active 1305–1348. *Probably pupil of Duccio, influenced by Simone Martini and Giovanni Pisano.*

Altenburg. 47, 48. Diptych: Madonna and Child (r.); 'Ecce Homo'. Sd.

Arezzo. PIEVE, HIGH ALTAR. Polyptych: Madonna and Child; SS. Donatus, John Evangelist, John Baptist and Matthew with Angels above; upper row: Annunciation and SS. John, Paul, Vincent, Lucas, James, James the Less, Marcellinus, Augustine; in pinnacles, Virgin in Glory and four female Saints. Sd and d. 1320. *Plate* 79.

Assisi. S. FRANCESCO, LOWER CHURCH, CAPPELLA ORSINI. Fresco: Madonna and Child with SS. Francis and John Evangelist; on parapet, Orsini coats of arms, Christ on the Cross, bust of donor. E. [*Plate 260.*]

— CEILING AND WALLS OF L. TRANSEPT. Frescoes: Christ enters Jerusalem, Washing of Feet, Last Supper, Betrayal, Flagellation, Way to Calvary, Crucifixion, Deposition, Entombment, Christ in Limbo, Resurrection, S. Francis receiving Stigmata, busts of SS. Rufinus, Catherine, Clare, Margaret (g.p.). E. [*Plate 263.*] *Plate* 80.

— APSE OF L. TRANSEPT. Frescoed triptych: Madonna and Child, S. Francis and S. John Baptist.

— R. TRANSEPT. Fresco: Five Franciscans worshipping the Madonna by Cimabue above.

SACRO CONVENTO, F. M. PERKINS DONATION. Madonna and Child with pomegranate (st.; companion to Bridgeport).

Panel of polyptych: S. Margaret (companion to New York).

Predella panel: Funeral of a Saint.

Baltimore (Md.). WALTERS ART GALLERY. 731. Portable altarpiece: Madonna and Child with two Angels, two female Saints and SS. Ansanus and Dofanus.

Berlin. 1077, 1077A. The Blessed Humility cures a nun of nasal haemorrhage, Miracle of the ice in August (see Florence, Uffizi 8347).

Bridgeport (Conn.). MUSEUM OF ART, SCIENCE AND INDUSTRY (KRESS STUDY COLLECTION. K 1224A, B). Two right panels of polyptych from Città di Castello: S. Andrew, S. Anthony Abbot (companions to Assisi, Perkins; st.).

Cambridge (Mass.). FOGG ART MUSEUM. 1943.119. Christ on the Cross with the Virgin, the Evangelist, SS. Francis and Clare. E.

Campriano (Murlo). PARISH CHURCH. Madonna and Child.

Castiglion del Bosco (Buonconvento). S. MICHELE ARCANGELO. Frescoes behind the high altar: Annunciation; left, SS. Anthony Abbot, John Baptist, Stephen; right, SS. Michael, Bartholomew and Francis. d. 1345.

Castiglione d'Orcia. PIEVE. Madonna and Child. E. *Plate* 76.

S. MARIA MADDALENA. Madonna and Child (r.). E.

Cortona. MUSEO DIOCESANO, SALA II. Madonna and Child with four Angels. Sd. E.

— SALA I (CHIESA SUPERIORE, OVER ALTAR). Painted Cross (from S. Marco).

— STAIRS. Cut-out Crucifix.

Dijon. G.I. Portable altarpiece: Madonna and Child with four Angels, two female Saints, S. Peter and Baptist; Crucifixion, S. Christopher, Annunciation (st.).

Florence. UFFIZI. 445. Madonna and Child surrounded by Angels (from S. Francesco, Pistoia). Sd and d. 1340 (read 1320 ?).

8347. Blessed Humility and Scenes of her Life [The Saint argues with her husband Ugolotto for separation and the higher life; A physician recommends Ugolotto the celibate state; Ugolotto is clothed in the religious habit; the Saint is miraculously helped to read in the refectory of S. Perpetua; She is miraculously helped over the walls of S. Perpetua and across the river Lamone;

She heals the foot of a Vallombrosan monk; S. John Divine invites her to leave Faenza and her arrival at the gates of Florence; She collects bricks for her church of S. Giovanni Evangelista; She raises a child to life outside Porta San Gallo; two nuns to whom the Saint is dictating observe the Holy Ghost by her ear; Burial of the Saint] (see Berlin for two missing Scenes). Commissioned 1311; d. 1316, read 1341. *Plates 87–88*.

 6129-6131. Three pinnacles from altarpiece of the Blessed Humility: SS. Mark, Luke and John Evangelist.

 6120-6126. Seven roundels from predella to altarpiece of the Blessed Humility: Dead Christ, Mourning Virgin, Mourning Evangelist, SS. Peter, Paul, Benedict and John Gualbert.

MUSEO HORNE. 47, 48, 49. Panels of polyptych: SS. Catherine, Margaret and Benedict (companions to Le Mans and Montichiello). *Plate 78*.

PALAZZO VECCHIO, LOESER BEQUEST. Madonna and Child.

S. LUCIA DEI MAGNOLI. S. Lucy (r.).

BERENSON COLLECTION. Reliquary panel: Madonna and Child worshipped by a Dominican (companion to Homeless). *Plate 85*.

SERRISTORI COLLECTION. Madonna and Child. E.

Frankfurt a/M. 995. Triptych: Crucifixion, Madonna and Child with kneeling Deacon; Calling and Assassination of S. Matthew; S. John Evangelist's Vision at Patmos and Ascension; in spandrels, tympanums and pinnacles, Prophets, Saints, Angels and Virgin of Annunciation.

Le Mans. 10. Panel of polyptych: S. Agatha (companion to Florence, Horne and Montichiello).

 286, 287. Wings of portable altarpiece: S. Catherine and Angel of Annunciation above; S. Augustine and Virgin of Annunciation above (st.)

London. 1113. Predella panel to Nativity altarpiece, Opera del Duomo, Siena: S. Savinus before a Judge. 1342.

Lucerne. ABEGG STOCKAR COLLECTION. S. Leonard.

Milan. POLDI PEZZOLI. 593. Madonna and Child with SS. Agnes, Catherine and six Angels; in pinnacle, Redeemer.

Montichiello (Pienza). PIEVE DEI SS. LEONARDO E CRISTOFORO. ALTAR R. Centre panel of polyptych: Madonna and Child, companion to Florence, Horne and Le Mans (temporarily dep. Soprintendenza, Siena). *Plate 77*.

Münster i/W. SEMINAR. Small 'Pietà'.

 334. Madonna and Child with Angels and SS. Peter, Paul, Baptist, Evangelist (r.).

New Haven (Conn.). YALE UNIVERSITY, RABINOWITZ GIFT. Panel of Carmine polyptych: SS. Andrew and James with Prophet above (companion to Rome and Siena). 1329.

 1942. 323. Mourning Virgin (from a painted cross?). (?)

New York. 13.212. Panel of polyptych: S. Catherine of Alexandria (companion to Assisi).

Philadelphia (Pa.). J. G. JOHNSON COLLECTION. 91. Madonna and Child worshipped by a monk (companion to Vienna).

Rome. VATICAN, PINACOTECA. 163, 166. Two panels of Carmine polyptych: SS. Peter and John Baptist (companions to New Haven and Siena). 1329.

168. Christ before Pilate.

SEN. R. BASTIANELLI. Panel of polyptych: blessing S. James with book.

Saltwood Castle (Kent). SIR KENNETH CLARK. Madonna and Child.

Sant'Angelo in Colle (Montalcino). S. MICHELE ARCANGELO. Centre panel of triptych: Madonna and Child (side-panels by Ambrogio at Siena, 90, 314)(r.). E.

Sant'Ansano in Dofana (Siena). CAPPELLINA DEL MARTIRIO. See Siena, Pinacoteca.

Seattle (Wash.). ART MUSEUM. IT.37/L.8873.1 (KRESS COLLECTION K 277). Triptych: Madonna and Child, SS. Peter and Paul; in pinnacles, Blessing Saviour and two Saints.

Siena. 50. Polyptych from S. Giusto: SS. Julia, Peter, Paul and Augustine; Annunciation and eight small Saints (g.p.).

62, 64. Two panels of Carmine polyptych: SS. Taddeus and Bartholomew with Prophet above; SS. Thomas and James with Prophet above (see below). 1329.

68. Christ on Cross with mourning Virgin and S. John Evangelist (st.).

75. Apostle.

79, 81, 82. Panels of polyptych from S. Cecilia a Crèvole: SS. Bartholomew, Cecilia and John Baptist; in pinnacles, SS. Agnes, Catherine and Clare. d. 1332.

83, 84 AND S.N. Predella to Carmine polyptych: Pope Honorius III approves the Carmelite Order, the Pope allows the white habit, Dream of Sebach, father of the Prophet Elijah, Carmelite Hermits by Elias' well, S. Albert hands the Carmelite rule to S. Brocardus (see below). 1329. *Plate 83.*

92. Allegory of Fall and Redemption (r.; very close to both Ambrogio and Pietro). *Plate 91.*

147. Crucifixion (st.).

161. Madonna and Child (c.).

578, 579. SS. Agnes and Catherine. E.

FROM SANT'ANSANO IN DOFANA. 'La Maestà del Martirio' (*alias* centre panel of Carmine polyptych): Madonna and Child with four Angels, S. Nicholas and the Prophet Elijah (other parts at New Haven, Rome, Siena 62, 64, 83, 84). Sd and d. 1329. *Plate 82.*

S. DOMENICO, PILLAR OF THE OLD CHAPEL BY THE CAMPANILE. Fresco: S. John Baptist recommends a warrior to the Madonna (fr.). *Plate 86.*

S. FRANCESCO, FIRST CHAPEL L. OF CHOIR. Fresco (detached from Chapter House?): Crucifixion.

— SALA DEL CAPITOLO: Fresco: resurrected Christ (fr., r.).

S. MARIA ASSUNTA (DUOMO), MUSEO DELL'OPERA. 50. Birth of the Virgin (from Cappella di S. Savino; see London). Sd and d. 1342. *Plate 89.*

S. MARIA DEI SERVI, SECOND CHAPEL L. OF CHOIR. Frescoes: Herod's Feast, Assumption of S. John Evangelist, Saints (r.).

— SECOND CHAPEL R. OF CHOIR. Frescoes: S. Agnes, Massacre of Innocents. *Plate* 81.

— OVER DOOR OF FIRST CHAPEL R. Fresco: Last Judgement (r., fr.).

Vienna. OUROUSOFF (EX). Two Angels in spandrels (companion to Philadelphia).

Washington (D.C.). 546. (WARBURG GIFT). Triptych: Madonna and Child, SS. Catherine and Mary Magdalen; in pinnacles, Blessing Saviour and two Angels. Sd and d. 13 (21?).

Homeless. Christ worshipped by a Dominican, in frame of relics (companion to Florence, Berenson Collection). *Plate* 84.

LORENZETTI, Ambrogio and Pietro, Close Imitators

Florence. BERENSON COLLECTION. Polyptych: Madonna and Child, SS. Francis, Baptist, Nicholas and Magdalen; in pinnacles, Redeemer, SS. James, Paul, Peter, Louis of Toulouse.

MUSEO HORNE. 57. Christ on Cross with mourning Virgin and Evangelist.

Genoa. NOSTRA SIGNORA DELLA CONSOLAZIONE. Painted Crucifix from S. Agostino (close to Pietro). ca 1350.

S. MARIA DI CASTELLO. Madonna and Child (close to Pietro).

London. BROCKLEBANK COLLECTION (EX). Madonna and Child with two female Saints (r.).

Montefalco. S. AGOSTINO. Fresco: Coronation of Virgin with reclining Eve and two donors in frieze.

New Haven (Conn.). 1871.11. S. Martin and the beggar (companion to Paris; possibly fr. of side-panel to A. Lorenzetti, Siena 65; also close to Lippo Vanni).

Oxford. EXETER COLLEGE. Upper panels of polyptych: Four Apostles (r.) (close to Pietro).

Paris. 1562A. S. Nicholas and the three maidens without dowry (companion to New Haven; possibly fr. of side-panel to A. Lorenzetti, Siena 65; also close to Lippo Vanni).

LEON SUZOR. Adoration of Magi (companion to Zürich).

Raleigh. NORTH CAROLINA MUSEUM OF ART. GL.60.17.8 (KRESS COLLECTION. K 539). Centre piece of right wing of diptych: Crucifixion (companion to Rome).

Rome. VATICAN, PINACOTECA. 29. Crucifixion.

170. Left wing of diptych: Madonna and Child with two Angels, flanked by SS. Agnes, Lucy, Catherine, Magdalen, Margaret, Dorothy, Clare and Agatha; above, Angel and Virgin of Annunciation (companion to Raleigh; also listed 'Follower of Giotto').

Siena. 89, 91. Cut-down panels of polyptych: S. Anthony Abbot, S. Massimino.

S. PIETRO ALLE SCALE. Blessing Redeemer (close to Pietro).

Tulsa (Oklahoma). PHILBROOK ART CENTER. 3344. (KRESS COLLECTION. K 27). Christ on Cross with mourning Virgin and John Evangelist; Evangelist in roundel above.

Zürich. TOPIC MIMARA (EX). Circumcision (companion to Paris; possibly 'Ugolino Lorenzetti').

Homeless. Two panels of polyptych: Bust of hermit Saint, bust of Apostle (repr. *Dedalo*, XI p. 271).

'LORENZETTI, UGOLINO' see UGOLINO

LORENZO D'ALESSANDRO

San Severino Marche, mentioned from 1462, died 1503. Pupil of either Girolamo di Giovanni da Camerino or Matteo da Gualdo; strongly influenced by Niccolò da Foligno and to a lesser degree by Crivelli.

Baltimore (Md.). WALTERS ART GALLERY. 496, 496A. Processional standard: Crucifixion; back, S. Michael worshipped by Flagellants. *Plate* 960.

Caldarola (Tolentino). S. MARIA DEL MONTE. Madonna holding a ribbon which encircles two tables supported by SS. Francis of Assisi, Anthony of Padua, Martin of Tours, Gregory of Spoleto, Flagellants and two lay Gentlemen; on left table, the castle of Caldarola, a bowl full of coins, a box inscribed 'conserva'; on right table, two similar boxes and kneeling Women and Flagellants; eight Saints kneeling in sky and on rocks above. (This Madonna of the Brotherhood which ran a bank as well as a hospital is always concealed behind Baroque ornaments on the high altar.) Sd and d. 1491. *Plate* 959.

Cleveland (Ohio). 16.800. Madonna and Child enthroned with SS. Anthony Abbot, Sebastian, Mark and Severinus. [*Plate* 294.]

Corridonia (Macerata) (former Mont'Olmo, called Pàusola 1851–1931). SS. PIETRO, PAOLO E DONATO, CANONICA (NOW PINACOTECA). Triptych: Madonna and Child S. John Baptist, S. Mary Magdalen; above, Dead Christ, two busts of Saints. Sd and d. 1481. *Plate* 958.

Dijon. 82, 83. Panels from pilaster of altarpiece: S. Bernardino, S. Agatha (companions to Le Havre).

Florence. UFFIZI. 3142. Lunette: Pietà.

Gàgliole (San Severino). CERQUETA. Frescoed Tabernacle: Madonna and sleeping Child; in embrasure, full-length SS. Anthony Abbot and Sebastian (r.).

Le Havre. 35. Panels from pilaster of altarpiece: S. Francis, S. Clare (companions to Dijon).

London. 249. Mystic Marriage of S. Catherine, with SS. Dominic and Augustine and donor. Sd.

Matelica. MUSEO PIERSANTI. The Virgin seated in the lap of S. Anne, S. Sebastian and S. Roch; above, Dead Christ between S. Michael and S. Dominic.

OSPEDALE CIVILE, CAPPELLA. Fresco: Madonna di Loreto. E. (?)

Pàusola. See Corridonia.

Pergola (Pesaro). CAPPELLA DEL PALAZZOLO. Frescoed lunette: Ascension with
Prophets holding scrolls above; on either side, S. Agapitus and S. Secundus. E.

Pollenza (Macerata). SS. FRANCESCO E ANTONIO DA PADOVA, APSE. S. Anthony of
Padua worshipping the Virgin. Sd and d. 1496. *Plate 962.*

Rome. GALLERIA NAZIONALE (PALAZZO BARBERINI). Madonna of Humility suckling
the Child, worshipped by SS. Francis, Sebastian and two putti.

VATICAN, PINACOTECA. 241. Fragment of a Virgin seated in the lap of S. Anne.

BORIS CRISTOFF. Pietà. d. 14(91?).

San Severino Marche. 15. Madonna and Child enthroned with Angels, S. John
Baptist and S. Severinus.

S. LORENZO IN DOLIOLO, CHOIR. Nativity with donor; above, Madonna and Child. E.

— (Environs). LA MAESTÀ. Votive frescoes: S. Sebastian and Madonna adoring the
Child in her lap; S. Sebastian; Madonna and Child in the lap of S. Anne;
Christ on Cross; Madonna and Child.

Sarnano (Macerata). S. MARIA DI PIAZZA. Frescoed niche: Madonna adoring the
Child, and music-making Angels; in soffit, Christ holding crown, Angels,
S. John Baptist and donor, Bishop Saint; around the niche, God the Father,
Angel and Virgin of Annunciation, SS. Sebastian and Roch. Sd and d. 1483.
Plate 961.

Serrapetrona (Macerata). PARISH CHURCH. Polyptych: Madonna and Child, full-
length SS. Sebastian, Francis, Peter, James; above, dead Christ upheld by
Angels, SS. Bonaventura, John Baptist, Michael, Catherine; in predella,
twelve Apostles, and SS. Catherine, Apollonia, Nicholas and Lucy. Formerly
dated 1494. *Plate 963.*

Treia (Macerata). ACCADEMIA GEORGICA. Madonna and Child.

Urbino. GALLERIA NAZIONALE DELLE MARCHE. Baptism (after lost Giovanni Bellini of
ca 1480).

Zagreb. 31–33. Predella: Christ between SS. Peter and Paul, and ten Apostles.

Homeless. Madonna and Child. ca 1480. *Plate 957.*

LORENZO DI PIETRO see VECCHIETTA

LORENZO DA SANSEVERINO THE ELDER see SALIMBENI

LORENZO DA VITERBO

*Lorenzo di Jacopo di Pietro Paulo. ca 1444 (?)–1472 (?). Developed under the influence of
Benozzo Gozzoli.*

Bayeux. MUSÉE. 170. Predella panel: Adoration of Magi. *Plate 1086.*

Budapest. 1094. Christ on Cross, with mourning Virgin and Evangelist.

Rome. GALLERIA NAZIONALE, PALAZZO BARBERINI. Altarpiece from S. Michele at Cerveteri: Madonna and Child enthroned, with SS. Michael and Peter. Sd and d. 1472. *Plate* 1085.

S. MARIA MAGGIORE, UPPER SACRISTY, VAULT. Frescoes: Evangelists (r.) (?)

Viterbo. S. MARIA DELLA VERITÀ, CAPPELLA MAZZATOSTA. Frescoes, badly damaged by 1944 bombardment.

— — VAULT. Frescoes: Evangelists, Church Fathers, Prophets and Doctors (four figures in each quart of vault). *Plate* 1084.

— — SOFFIT OF ARCH. Frescoes: Eight Saints.

— — R. WALL. Frescoes: Presentation of Virgin; below, Marriage of Virgin (among onlookers, self-portrait, portraits of Nardo Mazzatosta and of historian Niccolò della Tuccia). Sd and d. 1469. [*Plate* 297].

— — ALTAR WALL. Fresco: Assumption of Virgin. *Plate* 1083.

— — R. WALL. Frescoes: Annunciation; below, Nativity.

LUCA DI TOMMÈ

Sienese. Active between 1356 *and* 1399. *Pupil probably of 'Ugolino Lorenzetti' or possibly of Lippo Vanni; follower of the Lorenzetti.*

Balcarres (Fife, Scotland). EARL OF CRAWFORD AND BALCARRES. Four predella panels from polyptych 51, Siena: Christ introduces S. Thomas to the messenger of the Indian King on a boat to Caesarea; the King of India offers S. Thomas a banquet and a dog brings in the hand that slapped the Saint; S. Thomas in prison converts the brother of the King, is liberated and baptizes the King; S. Thomas is killed, after his prayers destroy the pagan idol (companions to Rome, Vatican 195). (With Tegliacci.) 1362. *Plates* 366–367.

Basle. ROBERT VON HIRSCH. Predella panel: Adoration of Magi (companion to San Francisco).

Budapest. 28. Predella panel: Last Communion of Mary Magdalen (companion to Hautecombe, to Rome, Vatican 221, to Siena 112 and to Homeless). E. (?)*

Buonconvento. PIEVE A PIANA. Madonna suckling the Child and two Angels (fr. of central panel) (r.).

Cambridge. FITZWILLIAM. 563. Madonna and Child enthroned with four Angels. E.

Càscina (Pontedera). S. GIOVANNI DEI CAVALIERI GEROSOLIMITANI. Polyptych: Annunciation, S. Francis, S. Nicholas of Bari and two other Saints; Prophets in spandrels and roundels above.

Detroit (Michigan). 29.319. Christ carrying the Cross.

Florence. MUSEO BARDINI. Panel of polyptych: S. John Baptist. *Plate* 372.

Foligno. S. NICCOLÒ, SACRISTY. Madonna and Child with four Angels.

Hautecombe (Savoie). ABBAYE. Predella panel: Assumption of Mary Magdalen (see Budapest). E. (?)*

Kew Gardens (Surrey). A. WELKER. Centre panel of polyptych: Madonna and Child; in pinnacle, blessing Redeemer.

Konopist. CASTLE. 21198. Portable altarpiece: Deposition, with Dead Christ and Symbols of Passion above; in wings, S. Peter, S. Andrew, Angel and Virgin of Annunciation.

Los Angeles (Cal.). A.2531.31-1 (KRESS COLLECTION. K 69). Madonna and Child enthroned with SS. Paul and Nicholas.

Lucignano (Val di Chiana). MUSEO CIVICO. Polyptych: Madonna and Child, SS. John Baptist, Michael, Catherine and Peter; in pinnacles, Christ with two Angels, Angel and Virgin of Annunciation, two Saints (st.).

Mercatello sul Metauro. S. FRANCESCO. Triptych: Madonna and Child; S. Anthony Abbot (S. Francis is by Bacci Venuti).

Montalcino (Senese). MUSEO CIVICO. Centre panel of polyptych: Madonna with Child caressing her cheek.

Montepulciano. MUSEO CIVICO. Crucifixion from S. Francesco.
Upper row of Angels in Spinello Aretino Coronation.

Nashville (Tenn.). GEORGE PEABODY COLLEGE (KRESS STUDY COLLECTION. K 1014). Pinnacle: Crucifixion.

New Haven (Conn.). 1871.12. Assumption. *Plate* 368.
1943.245. Madonna and Child with two Angels, SS. Ansanus and Galganus (st.).
1943.246. Predella: Crucifixion, Madonna, S. John Evangelist, S. Dominic and S. Francis.

New York. 41.100.34. Centre panel of polyptych: Madonna enthroned and blessing Child.
JESSE I. STRAUS COLLECTION (EX). Crucifix painted on both sides: front—finials with resurrected Christ, mourning Mary and John, S. Francis; back—S. Michael, S. Peter, S. Paul and S. Louis of Toulouse.

Perugia. GALLERIA NAZIONALE. Polyptych from Spoleto: Madonna and Child enthroned; SS. Paul, Peter, Apollinaris and John Baptist; in pinnacles, Redeemer and four Saints.

Pieve a Piana. See Buonconvento.

Pisa. B.P. V, 5. Crucifixion. Sd and d. 1366. *Plate* 369.

Polesden Lacey (Surrey). NATIONAL TRUST. Madonna and Child with SS. John Baptist and Catherine and three Angels (formerly Leningrad, A. Gagarin).

Ponce (Puerto Rico). MUSEO DE ARTE. 64.0270. (KRESS COLLECTION. M 4.) Madonna and Child holding scroll.

Princeton (N.J.). 1. Madonna and Child with goldfinch, and Prophets in spandrels.

Raleigh (North Carolina). MUSEUM OF ART. GL.60.17.5. (KRESS COLLECTION. K 1741). Pinnacle: Blessing Christ.

Rapolano (Senese). CHIESA DELLA FRATERNITA. Centre panel of polyptych: Madonna and Child.

Rieti. 7, 12, 21. Polyptych: Madonna and Child, SS. Peter, Paul, Dominic and Peter Martyr, two Prophets in spandrels. Sd and d. 1370. *Plate* 373.

Rome. VATICAN, PINACOTECA. 195. Predella panel from Siena polyptych 51: Crucifixion (companion to Balcarres). (With Tegliacci.) 1362.

    221. Predella panel: Raising of Lazarus (companion to Budapest, Siena 112 and Homeless). E. (?)

San Diego (Cal.). ART GALLERY, LENT BY THE PUTNAM FOUNDATION. Portable altarpiece: Crucifixion with Trinity, and Resurrection in pinnacle; in wings, Nativity, Adoration of Magi, Mocking of Christ, Deposition, and Angel and Virgin of Annunciation above.*

San Francisco (Cal.). DE YOUNG MEMORIAL MUSEUM. 61.44.3. (KRESS COLLECTION. K 34). Predella panel: Crucifixion (companion to Basle).

Siena. 51. Polyptych: Madonna and Child enthroned with six Angels; SS. John Baptist, Thomas, Benedict and Stephen. Sd by Luca di Tomè and Tegliacci and d. 1362. *Plate 365.*

    109. Polyptych: Madonna and Child with S. Anne; SS. Catherine, John Baptist, Anthony Abbot and female Saint; in pinnacles, S. Andrew and four Evangelists. Sd and d. 1367. *Plate 364.*

    112. Predella panel: Christ in the house of Simon (companion to Budapest, Rome 221 and Homeless). E. (?)

    113. S. James in roundel. (?)

    123, 124, 138, 139. Pinnacles: three Prophets and S. Catherine.

    184. Mystic Marriage of S. Catherine, with Baptist and two Angels; in pinnacle, reading S. Joseph. E. (?)

    586. Polyptych from Munisterino alle Tolfe: Madonna and Child; SS. John Baptist and Gregory; SS. Francis and Augustine; in pinnacles, Redeemer and four Saints (r.). Sd.

    594. Triptych from S. Biagio di Filetta: Mystic Marriage of S. Catherine, S. Bartholomew and S. Blaise (r.).

    CHIESA DELLA CONTRADA DEL BRUCO. Madonna and Child with goldfinch.

    PALAZZO PUBBLICO, SALA DEI PILASTRI. Annunciation, with blessing Redeemer above.

    S. SPIRITO, THIRD CHAPEL L. Painted Crucifix.

    (Environs). GRANCIA A CUNA. Frescoes: Adoration of Magi, Circumcision.

Sovicille (Senese). VILLA BUDINI GATTAI, CAPPELLA DEI SS. FILIPPO E GIACOMO ALLE SEGALAIE. Panels of polyptych: Madonna and Child, SS. James and Andrew, Annunciation (r.).

Torri (Senese). ABBAZIA, S. MUSTIOLA. Madonna and Child. *Plate 371.*

Vienna. LANCKORONSKI COLLECTION. Panels of polyptych: full-length SS. John Baptist and John Evangelist (r.).

    DR. G. ARENZ (EX). Virgin of Annunciation.

Homeless. Panel of polyptych: S. Stephen. *Plate 370.*

    Predella panel: Crucifixion (Sopr. Firenze 55234: companion to Budapest, Rome 221 and Siena 112). E. (?) (fig. 11 in *Paragone*, 1958, no. 105).

    Angel and Virgin of Annunciation (figs. 4 a, b in *Paragone*, 1958, no. 105).

LUINI, Bernardino

Milanese school. Died before July 1532. Probably pupil of Bergognone; influenced by Bramantino and Leonardo.

Baltimore (Md.). MUSEUM OF ART, JACOBS COLLECTION. 38.227. Marriage of S. Catherine.

Bergamo. 302. Nativity (p., see Garscube).
509. Madonna and Child with Infant S. John. E.

Berlin. 217. Madonna and Child with apple.
219. Nativity (st. version of Garscube).
FRIEDRICH LIPPMANN (EX). Bust of young Saviour blessing.

Berlin-Ost. 219A-I. Detached frescoes from Casa Rabia: A—Venus, Europa and Hymenaeus; B—Europa and her friends gather flowers; C and D—Nymphs gathering flowers; E—Europa crowning the Bull with flowers; F—Europa sits on the Bull; G—Europa rides on the Bull at sea; H—Naiads and Tritons; I—Europa crossing the sea and a Nymph seated on the shore (see also Milan Castello, Paris and Washington). *Plates* 1484, 1486.

Bobbio. S. MARIA ASSUNTA (DUOMO). Eleven panels of dismembered polyptych: Assumption, Group of Apostles, SS. John Baptist, Peter, Michael, Paul, Gregory, Ambrose, Jerome, Augustine, and music-making Angel.

Boston (Mass.). 21.2287. Salome with the Head of the Baptist (variants at Florence, Isolabella, Paris, Vienna).

Brooklyn (N.Y.). 32.382. Octagonal fragment: Christ carrying the Cross.

Brussels. MUSÉE SOMZÉE. S. Sebastian. Sd and d. 1527.

Budapest. 51 (106). Madonna and Child with S. Elizabeth and Infant S. John.
58(110). Madonna and Child with SS. Catherine and Barbara.
51.2962. Studio version of Messina.

Busto Arsizio. S. MARIA DI PIAZZA. Detached frescoes (see Brera, nn. 52-55).

Cambridge (Mass.). FOGG ART MUSEUM. 1930.194. Madonna and Child with Infant S. John.

Cernusco Montevecchia. CONTE LURANI. Detached fresco from Cappella di S. Antonio, S. Maria della Pace: Annunciation, SS. John Baptist and Catherine.

Chantilly. 24. Infant Christ.
25, 26. Detached frescoes from Villa Pelucca near Monza: Child gathering grapes, Bust of young woman (see Milan, Brera).

Chiaravalle (Milan). ABBAZIA, R. TRANSEPT AT TOP OF STAIRS. Fresco: Madonna and Child with two Angels in landscape. doc. 1512.

Chicago (Illinois). LAKE FOREST, J. R. THOMPSON (EX). Madonna and standing Child.

Cincinnati (Ohio). 1927.404. Madonna and Child with S. Catherine. L.

Cleveland (Ohio). 16812. Madonna and Child.

Como. DUOMO. FOURTH CHAPEL R. Madonna and Child with SS. Jerome, Dominic,

Anthony of Padua and Augustine, and donor Girolamo Raimondi; in predella, S. Peter, Penitence of S. Jerome in the Wilderness, S. John Baptist, Funeral of S. Jerome at the Monastery, S. Paul. Sd.

— THIRD CHAPEL R. (CAPPELLA DI S. ABBONDIO). L. OF ALTAR. Inside right cover to S. Abbondio carved altarpiece: Adoration of Magi (outside by Gaudenzio Ferrari). After 1514.

   Prophet (painted over by Gaudenzio).

— THIRD CHAPEL L. (CAPPELLA DI S. GIUSEPPE), R. OF ALTAR. Inside left cover to S. Abbondio carved altarpiece: Adoration of Shepherds (outside by Gaudenzio Ferrari). After 1514.

Copenhagen. 406. Bust of S. Catherine. L.

Corsham Court (Wilts.). LORD METHUEN. Vanity and Modesty.

Detroit (Mich.). 26.110. SS. Sebastian and George.

   HIGBIE COLLECTION (EX). Modesty and Vanity (see Corsham Court, Locko Park, Paris, and San Diego).

Dijon. CA. 30. Madonna and Child standing on her knees.

Dudley Castle (Stafford). EARL OF DUDLEY (EX). Madonna and Holy Children in landscape (g.p.).

Elton Hall (Peterborough). SIR RICHARD PROBY, BT. Child with puzzle.

Englewood (N.J.). PLATT COLLECTION (EX). Detached fresco from Villa Pelucca: Kneeling Angel (see Milan, Brera).

Florence. UFFIZI. 1454. Salome with the Head of the Baptist.

   MUSEO STIBBERT. Roman Charity (c.).

   CONTINI BONACOSSI COLLECTION. Panel of polyptych: S. Sebastian in niche (companion to Isolabella). E.

Garscube (Dunbartons.). SIR GEORGE CAMPBELL (ON LOAN, GLASGOW GALLERY). Virgin and S. Joseph adoring Christ Child and Flight into Egypt in background (variants at Bergamo, Berlin, Isolabella, Milan Yucker Collection, Oakly Park).

Gerenzano (Saronno). BEATA VERGINE DEL SOCCORSO. Fresco behind altar: Madonna and Child with SS. Christopher, Roch, Sebastian, Anthony Abbot and kneeling donor. Sd and d. 1507.*

Hampton Court. Inv. 127. 'Flora.'

Houston (Texas). MUSEUM OF FINE ARTS. 61.67 (KRESS COLLECTION. K 1764). Pietà.

Isolabella (Lago Maggiore). PALAZZO BORROMEO. Nativity (st.; see Garscube).

   Panels of polyptych: SS. Peter, Martha, Bishop in niches (companions to Florence, Contini Bonacossi). E.

   Salome with the Head of the Baptist (see Boston).

   Susanna and the Elders.

   Madonna and Child with Tobias, the Angel and donor.

   Detached fresco from Villa Pelucca: Bust of girl in profile (see Milan, Brera).

Legnano (Milan). S. MAGNO, HIGH ALTAR. Polyptych: Madonna and Child enthroned with five Angel-Musicians and Cherubs; SS. Magnus, Ambrose, John Baptist and Peter; above, God the Father blessing, Angels holding banners;

in predella, Pietà, four Evangelists, Crucifixion, Deposition, Resurrection, Appearance to Disciples. 1523.

Leningrad. 71. Madonna and Child.

247. S. Sebastian (the head is a portrait).

259. Crucifixion with SS. Paul and Francis.

Locko Park. DRURY LOWE COLLECTION (EX). 89, 93. Modesty and Vanity (see Corsham Court, Detroit, Paris and San Diego).

London. 18. Christ and the Pharisees.

3090. Madonna and Child (st.).

3935. Madonna and Child with Infant S. John.

3936. S. Catherine of Alexandria (g.p.).

APSLEY HOUSE (DUKE OF WELLINGTON). Joseph and Potiphar's Wife.

COURTAULD INSTITUTE GALLERIES, LEE OF FAREHAM COLLECTION. Madonna and Child enthroned with S. Antonino Arcivescovo and a beggar, S. John Baptist recommending female donor. d. 1526.

WALLACE COLLECTION. 8. Madonna and Child.

10. Madonna and Child with flower.

526, 537. Detached frescoes from Villa Pelucca: Child under grape vine; Head of girl (see Milan, Brera).

DOWDESWELL (EX). Bust of female Martyr crowned with laurel and holding book (st. v. at Port Washington).

LADY (MALCOLM) ROBERTSON. 'Ellesmere' Head of woman.

Los Angeles (Cal.). MUSEUM OF ART, GIFT NORTON SIMON. Two left side-panels from 'Torriani' polyptych: S. Alexander and S. Catherine in niches.

Predella from 'Torriani' polyptych at Mendrisio: Meeting of SS. Sisinius, Martyrius and Alexander; Ordination of the three Saints; The three Saints disputing by the Altar of Saturn; the three Saints dragged by their feet; Assassination of SS. Sisinius, Martyrius and Alexander. *Plate 1491.*

Lugano. CASA GUIDI. (See Lugano, Environs, Dino di Sonvico.)

S. MARIA DEGLI ANGELI, END WALL. Fresco: Crucifixion; in background Agony in the Garden, Crowning with Thorns, Way to Calvary, Entombment, Doubting Thomas, Ascension; in spandrels below, monochrome Prophets (Isaiah, Simeon, Hosea, Jeremiah David, Zacharias); on piers, S. Sebastian and S. Roch. d. 1529.

— FIRST CHAPEL R. Frescoed lunette once over door of Sacristy: Madonna and Child with Infant S. John and Angel. d. 1530.

— R. WALL. Three fragments of detached fresco from refectory: Last Supper.

(Environs). DINO DI SONVICO, S. NAZZARO. Detached fresco from Church of Franciscans at Lugano: Christ on Cross with mourning Magdalen and Evangelist and two Angels with Symbols of Passion.

Luino (Lago Maggiore). S. PIETRO, CHOIR, R. WALL. Fresco: Adoration of Magi. (?)

Madrid. 242. Holy Family with Holy Children embracing each other.

ENCARNACIÓN. Nativity (old c. of Oakley Park).

Maggianico (Lago di Como). S. ANDREA. Eight panels of dismembered polyptych: lower register, Madonna and Child, S. Andrew, S. Sebastian; upper register, S. Anthony Abbot, S. Catherine, Angel and Virgin of Annunciation, God the Father blessing. ca 1515.

Mendrisio. S. SISINIO (EX). 'Torriani' polyptych: see Los Angeles, Philadelphia, Turin and Whitby.

Messina. EUGENIA SCAGLIONE FRIZZONI (EX). Madonna and Child with Infant S. John (destroyed; copies at Budapest 2962/51 and at Karlsruhe).

Milan. AMBROSIANA. Madonna suckling the Child (g.p.).

Holy Family with S. Joachim and S. Anne.

Youthful Christ blessing.

Infant Baptist with Lamb.

Cartoon: Healing of Tobias.

Detached fresco from Oratorio di S. Corona: Crowning with Thorns. doc. 1521–22.

BRERA. 289. Madonna del Roseto.

291. Madonna and Child standing on her lap (dep. at Museo del Castello).

387. Drunkenness of Noah (from Sacristy of S. Barnaba).

— DETACHED FRESCOES FROM S. MARIA DELLA PURIFICAZIONE (*vulgo* DELLE VETERE):

18. Madonna and Child enthroned and the Abbess Cusani as S. Catherine of Siena (deposited at the Museo della Tecnica).

39, 40. S. Antonino Arcivescovo, S. Thomas Aquinas.

41, 42. Kneeling Angels (Museo della Tecnica).

43, 44. Angels with incense-burners.

45. Elijah and the Angel (Museo della Tecnica).

46. Risen Christ and Angels (Museo della Tecnica).

47. Bust of S. Ursula.

48. S. Roch (Museo della Tecnica).

49. S. Sebastian.

50. Madonna suckling the Child and Infant S. John (Museo della Tecnica).

— DETACHED FRESCOES FROM S. MARTA (1516–22):51. Two roundels with male profiles (Museo della Tecnica).

52. Monochrome Magdalen in niche (dep. Busto Arsizio, S. Maria di Piazza).

53. Monochrome Lazarus in niche (dep. Busto Arsizio, S. Maria di Piazza).

54. Monochrome S. Marcella in niche (dep. Busto Arsizio, S. Maria di Piazza).

55. Monochrome S. Marta in niche (deposited at Busto Arsizio, S. Maria di Piazza).

69. Redeemer (deposited Museo della Tecnica).

— DETACHED FRESCO FROM S. MARIA DI BRERA (1521): 66, 67. Madonna and Child with SS. Anthony Abbot and Barbara; God the Father (two frs. of same fresco; deposited at Museo della Tecnica). Sd. and d. 1521.

— DETACHED FRESCO FROM S. MICHELE ALLA CHIUSA (ca 1518–20): 63. Madonna and Child with Infant S. John and Lamb.

— DETACHED FRESCOES FROM S. MARIA DELLA PACE, CAPPELLA DI S. ANTONIO: 293. Madonna and Child with S. Marta, S. John Evangelist and kneeling nun.

— — CAPPELLA DI S. GIUSEPPE (1518–20): s.n. Vault with eight sections, and twelve lunettes: Archangels, Angels playing Music, Cherubim.

s.n. Entrance arch: Busts of SS. Luke, David, Solomon, Isaiah; Expulsion of Joachim from the Temple.

64, 297. Angels.

294. Meeting at the Golden Gate (st.).

295. Annunciation to S. Anne (st.).

296. S. Joseph's Dream (st.). *Plate* 1483.

298. Birth of Virgin (st.).

299. Presentation of Virgin (p.).

300. Education of Virgin.

301. Dedication of Virgin to the Temple.

302. Designation of Joseph as Mary's Husband.

303. Marriage of Virgin.

304. Companions of Joseph.

305. Visitation.

— DETACHED FRESCOES FROM VILLA PELUCCA NEAR MONZA (1520–23) (see also Chantilly, Englewood, Isolabella, London Wallace Collection, Paris Louvre, Milan Cicogna).

— — CAPPELLA: 288. Angels carrying S. Catherine to Mount Sinai. *Plate* 1488.

735. God the Father.

736. Kneeling Angel (companion to Englewood and Milan, Cicogna).

— — MAIN HALL: 748. Forge of Vulcan (once over mantelpiece).

70. Israelites leaving Egypt.

737. Moses on Mount Sinai.

738. Moses striking the Rock.

739. Passover (st.).

740, 741. Crossing of the Red Sea.

742. Miriam rejoicing (p.).

743. Offering for Ark of Covenant (p.).

744. Gathering of manna. *Plate* 1489.

745. Plague of Egypt (g.p.).

— — ROOM OF ADONIS: 73. Sacrifices to Pan (from over mantelpiece).

72. Galloping rider.

74. Myrrha changed into a tree.

76. Birth of Adonis.

— — GABINETTO: 71. A game.

75. Bust of young woman (other busts of girls at Chantilly, Isolabella, London Wallace Collection, Pavia 68).

16, 746, 747. Putti under vines (other Putti at Chantilly, London Wallace Collection, Paris Louvre).

Milan BRERA, DETACHED FRESCOES FROM VILLA PELUCCA NEAR MONZA, GABINETTO (contd.). 749. Bathing girls. *Plate* 1485.

750. Girl and youth (fr. of game).

— 61. Fresco transferred on canvas: Madonna and Child with S. Anne (deposited Museo della Scienza).

CASTELLO. Detached frescoes from Casa Rabia: Head of a youth, Head of a woman, old man (frs.; two fragments with Palaces and Temples, destroyed 1943; see also Berlin, Milan Noseda, Paris, Washington).

Detached frescoes from Casa della Tela: roundels in lunettes with portraits of the Sforza Family (Muzio Attendolo, Francesco Sforza and Bianca Maria Visconti, Galeazzo Maria Sforza and Bona di Savoia, Gian Galeazzo Sforza and Isabella d'Aragona, Ludovico il Moro and Beatrice d'Este, Maximilian I and Bianca Maria Sforza, Cardinal Ascanio Sforza, Maximilian Sforza, Francesco II Sforza (p.). 1522–26.

Detached fresco from portico of Palazzo Landriani: Monochrome Hercules and Atlas.

POLDI PEZZOLI. 652. S. Jerome in the Wilderness.

659. Diptych: Mourning Virgin; Christ carrying the Cross.

663. Marriage of S. Catherine.

664. Raising of Cross. (?)

MUSEO DELLA SCIENZA E DELLA TECNICA LEONARDO DA VINCI (Monastero di S. Vittore). Detached frescoes deposited from Brera (see there).

S. AMBROGIO, FIRST CHAPEL L. (BATTISTERO). Fresco: Risen Christ with two Angels. E.

— MUSEO. Detached frescoes: Madonna and Child with lemon tree (fr.).
Christ carrying the Cross, three Maries.

— CAPPELLA DI S. GIOVANNI (THIRD R.). Madonna dell'Aiuto with SS. Jerome and Roch (st.).

S. GIORGIO AL PALAZZO, CAPPELLA DEL SS. SACRAMENTO. Frescoed vault, Crucifixion (in three sections); over altar—Mourning over Dead Christ, and Mocking of Christ in lunette above; left—Flagellation; right—'Ecce Homo'. 1516. *Plates* 1481–1482.

S. MARIA DEL CARMINE, SECOND CHAPEL L. Fresco: Madonna and Child with SS. Roch and Sebastian (g.p.).

— R. TRANSEPT. Mourning over Dead Christ with SS. Ambrose and Augustine; Resurrection in tympanum above and Story of the True Cross in predella (called 'Madonna della Passione'). (?)

S. MAURIZIO, WALL DIVIDING THE NUNS FROM THE FAITHFUL, SIDE OF ALTAR. Frescoes: upper register—Martyrdom of S. Mauritius, Assumption (r.), S. Sigismund of Burgundy offers the church to S. Mauritius; lower register, left of altar— in lunette, SS. Placidus, Benedict and John Baptist with Alessandro Benti-voglio; below, S. Cecilia, S. Ursula and putto holding candle round grate; lower register, right of altar—in lunette, SS. Scholastica, Agnes and Catherine with Ippolita Sforza Bentivoglio; below, S. Apollonia, S. Lucy and Putto holding candles round image of the Blood of the Redeemer. *Plate 1493.*

— — SIDE OF NUNS. Frescoes: upper register—Betrayal of Christ, Mocking of Christ, S. Martin and the Beggar, Way to Calvary (lunette), Nailing to the Cross (lunette), Entombment (lunette), Resurrection, Noli me Tangere; Lower register, left of altar—Blood of Redeemer flanked by SS. Lucy and Agnes and two Angels with Virgin Martyr in roundel below; on pilaster, S. Sebastian and roundel with Bust of S. Francis; Lower register, right of altar—on pilaster, S. Roch and roundel with bust of Peter Martyr; SS. Catherine and Agatha with three Angels round grate, Salome with the Head of Baptist in medallion (st.).

Frescoed decoration, 1522–24.

— CAPPELLA BESOZZI O DI S. CATERINA (THIRD R.). Frescoes: in vault, God the Father and six Angels with Symbols of Passion; wall behind altar, Christ at Column between SS. Catherine and Lawrence with donor Francesco Besozzi and in simulated windows above, mourning Virgin and Evangelist, Denial of S. Peter; side walls, Martyrdom of the wheel, Beheading of S. Catherine; spandrels above entrance arch, Two Sibyls (Erythrea, Agrippina). d. 1530.

CONTE CICOGNA. Fr. of fresco from Villa Pelucca; Adoring Angel (see Brera 288).

ALDO CRESPI. Madonna and Child with book. E.

BENIGNO CRESPI (EX). S. Jerome in the Wilderness.

CONTE PAOLO GERLI. 'Mond' Venus.

LITTA MODIGNANI COLLECTION. Madonna and Child.

ALDO NOSEDA (EX). Fragment of fresco from Casa Rabia: Head of girl in profile.

YUCKER COLLECTION. 'Stroganoff' Nativity. (See Garscube.)

Monza. DUOMO, PILLAR L. OF CHOIR. Fresco: S. Gerardo dei Tintori.

Morimondo. S. MARIA, PORCH OF CHAPTER HOUSE. Fresco: Madonna and Child enthroned with SS. Bernard, Benedict and Infant S. John; below, monochrome Cardinal Virtues (r.; st.?). d. 1515.

Muncie (Indiana). BALL STATE TEACHERS COLLEGE. Young lady.

Naples. 92. Madonna and Child (p.).

MUSEO FILANGIERI (EX). 1489. Madonna and Child with Suor Alessandra Bentivoglio (lost).

New Orleans (La.). I. DELGADO MUSEUM OF ART. 61.77 (KRESS COLLECTION. K 1087). 'Benson' Nativity (variants at Bergamo, Isolabella).

New York. J. P. LABEY (EX). Man writing at his desk.

MRS RUSH H. KRESS. K 584. 'Northbrook' Madonna and Child with Infant S. John.

Nivaagaard (Copenhagen). HAGE COLLECTION. 34. Madonna and Child.

Oakly Park (Shrops.). EARL OF PLYMOUTH. Nativity (See Garscube.).

Orford (Suffolk). S. BARTHOLOMEW, GIFT OF DR S. MAYNARD. Banner: Holy Family with S. John Baptist and donor. d. MDXXVX. (?)

Ottawa. 3454. Holy Children with lamb.

Paderno Dugnano. S. MARIA NASCENTE. Organ shutters from S. Eustorgio in Milan: Sacrifice of Isaac, Conversion of S. Paul. 1524.*

Paris. 1353. Holy Family.

    1354. Madonna and sleeping Child with Angels.

    1355. Salome.

    1357, 1358. Two fragments of fresco from Villa Pelucca: Putti under vines. (See Milan, Brera.)

    1359-61. Detached frescoes from Oratorio di Greco Milanese: Nativity, Adoration of Magi, Blessing Christ. [*Plate* 371.]

    1363-65. Detached frescoes from Oratorio di Greco Milanese: Annunciation, Pietà, Curius Dentatus (st.).

    1862. Detached fresco from Casa Rabia: Silence (see Milan, Castello.)

    — ARCONATI VISCONTI BEQUEST. 2. Madonna picking iris while Jesus is held by little Angel ('Madonna di Menaggio').

    BARONNE ÉDOUARD DE ROTHSCHILD. Bust of youth.

      Madonna and Child with Infant S. John in landscape (several copies known). *Plate* 1490.

    BARON EDMOND ROTHSCHILD. 'Sciarra' Modesty and Vanity (see Corsham, Detroit, Locko Park and San Diego).

Pavia. Inv. 115 (n. 68). Detached fresco from Pelucca: Bust of girl (see Milan, Brera 75).

    (Environs). CERTOSA, SAGRESTIA DEL LAVABO. Fresco here transferred from Portico: Madonna and Child in landscape. After 1514.

    — PORTICO, R. AND L. of PORTAL. Frescoes: S. Christopher and S. Sebastian in niches. After 1514.

    — MUSEO. Panels of polyptych: S. Martin, S. Ambrose.

Philadelphia (Pa.). ACADEMY OF FINE ARTS. Madonna in landscape.

    MUSEUM OF ART, J. G. JOHNSON COLLECTION. 275. Left panel of 'Torriani' polyptych: S. Anne (see Mendrisio). 1524 or later.

Ponte Valtellina. S. MAURIZIO, OVER ENTRANCE. Frescoed lunette: Madonna and Child with S. Mauritius on horseback and two Putti.

Port Washington (N.Y.). SOLOMON GUGGENHEIM (EX). Bust of poetess (st. v. of London, Dowdeswell).

Richmond (Surrey). COOK COLLECTION. Madonna with music-making Angel, and S. George offering the Child the palm of martyrdom and the dragon's head (g.p.).

Rome. COLONNA. Madonna and Child with S. Elizabeth and Infant S. John (r.).

San Diego (Cal.). 36.23. Modesty and Vanity (see Corsham, Detroit, Locko Park, Paris).

    46.73. Bust of Salome (c. of Muncie; fr.).

Sarasota (Fla.). RINGLING MUSEUM. Madonna of the dragonfly with SS. Roch and Sebastian (formerly Weimar).

Saronno. S. MARIA. DEI MIRACOLI. Frescoes. 1525/32.

    — ANTICAPPELLA. Left wall: Marriage of Virgin; Right wall, Christ in Temple.

— CAPPELLA. Vault: Angels (sinopie—see also Cesare Magni and Gaudenzio
Ferrari):

— — Left wall: in lunette, S. Luke and S. Jerome; in spandrels, Sibilla Persica,
Sibilla Libyca; Circumcision; below, monochrome figures of Peace and three
Virtues. Sd and d. 1525. *Plate* 1494.

— — Right wall: in lunette, S. John and S. Augustine; in spandrels, Sibilla
Delphica, Sibilla Chimica; Adoration of Magi; below, four monochrome
Virtues.

— — Two lunettes on the other two walls: S. Matthew and S. Ambrose; S. Mark
and S. Gregory.

— CHOIR OF APSE. SS. Catherine and Apollonia and two Angels. 1527–32.

— ENTRANCE TO ANTECHAPEL. SS. Anthony Abbot, Christopher, Roch, Sebastian.
1531–32.

— PORCH. Nativity.

Taplow Court (Bucks.). LORD DESBOROUGH (EX). Holy Family with SS. Elizabeth
and Infant S. John.

Turin. DI ROVASENDA COLLECTION. Central panel of 'Torriani' polyptych: Madonna
and Child enthroned with SS. Sisinius and Martyrius (see Mendrisio). 1524
or after. *Plate* 1492.

Utrera (Seville). S. MARIA DE LA MESA. Madonna and Child enthroned with SS.
Sebastian and Roch.

Vaduz. LIECHTENSTEINSCHE SAMMLUNG. G 847. Madonna and Child with Infant S.
John.

Vienna. 82. Christ carrying the Cross.

86. Salome.

87. S. Jerome in the Wilderness.

HARRACH COLLECTION. 312. S. Jerome in the Wilderness.

Warwick Castle. EARL OF WARWICK. Fr. of fresco from S. Maria della Pobbia near
Monza: Head.

Washington (D.C.). 37. (MELLON COLLECTION.) Portrait of lady.

231 (KRESS COLLECTION. K 249). Venus.

263 (KRESS COLLECTION. K 297). Madonna and Child with pink.

720–28 (KRESS COLLECTION. K 1314–22). Nine detached frescoes from Casa Rabia,
with Legend of Cephalus and Procris (Procris' Prayer to Diana, Cephalus
hiding the Jewels, Cephalus and Pan at the Temple, Cephalus at the Hunt,
Procris pierced by Cephalus' Javelin. The Illusion of Cephalus, the Despair of
Cephalus, Misfortunes of Cephalus, Procris and the Unicorn) (see Milan,
Brera). *Plate* 1487.

1608. (KRESS COLLECTION. K 2159.) Bust of Magdalen.

NATIONAL COLLECTION OF FINE ARTS. 1906.9.10. HARRIET LANE JOHNSTON BEQUEST.
Madonna and running Child.

Whitby (Yorks.). MARQUESS OF NORMANBY. Left panel of 'Torriani' polyptych: S.
Sisinius in niche (see Mendrisio). 1524 or later.

LUTERI see DOSSO

MACRINO D'ALBA

School of Vercelli (Piedmont). Documented works 1494–1508. Died before 1528. Developed under the influence of Ercole Roberti, Foppa and Leonardo; seems to have been acquainted with Tuscan painting, notably Botticelli's, Signorelli's and Ghirlandajo's.

Alba. PALAZZO COMUNALE, SALA DEL CONSIGLIO. Madonna and Child enthroned with S. Francis, S. Thomas Aquinas and two female donors. Sd and d. 1501. *Plate* 1239.

    S. GIOVANNI BATTISTA, THIRD ALTAR R. Adoration of the Child with SS. Joseph, Anthony of Padua, Augustine and Jerome. Sd and d. 1508.

Antwerp. MUSÉE MAYER VAN DEN BERGH. 216. Central panel of triptych: Madonna crowned by Angels, suckling the Child, with three putti at her feet. (?)

Baltimore (Md.). WALTERS ART GALLERY. 570. SS. Sebastian and Francis in landscape. (?)

    689, 690. Fragments of altarpiece: S. Sebastian, S. Anthony Abbot. (?)

Boston (Mass.). CABOT LODGE COLLECTION. Madonna enthroned, adoring the sleeping Child in her lap, with SS. Michael, Bernardino of Siena, Clare, Stephen and two flying Angels (from S. Chiara, Monferrato). Sd and d. 1507.

Crea (Casale Monferrato). SANTUARIO DI S. MARIA ASSUNTA, APSE. Madonna and Child enthroned with SS. James, John Baptist, Augustine and Jerome. Sd and d. 1503.

    — MUSEO. Male and female heads (Marquess of Monferrato and his bride?) from pilasters of altarpiece above.

Cuneo. CASSA DI RISPARMIO. Side panels of triptych: SS. John Baptist and Mary Magdalen, SS. John Evangelist and Michael.

El Paso (Texas). MUSEUM OF ART. 1961–6/15 (KRESS COLLECTION. K 1776). Adoration of Shepherds (variant of Alba, S. Giovanni, d. 1508).

Frankfurt a/M. 837. Triptych from S. Francesco d'Alba: Madonna and Child enthroned; S. Joachim and the Angels; Meeting of Joachim and Anne. Sd. L.

Isolabella (Lago Maggiore). PALAZZO BORROMEO. Profile of red-haired man.

Milan. BORROMEO. 35. Bishop Andrea de' Novelli. *Plate* 1234.

    SENATORE BORLETTI. Madonna suckling the Child.*

Neviglie (Alba). PARISH CHURCH. Mystic marriage of S. Catherine, with SS. Vincent, John Baptist, Francis, Jerome and Mary Magdalen (on loan at Galleria Sabauda, Turin).

Newbattle Abbey (Dalkeith, Scotland). MARQUESS OF LOTHIAN (EX). Half-length Baptist.

New York. HISTORICAL SOCIETY. B-22. Nativity with SS. John Baptist, Jerome and George; Donor and Colosseum in background. Sd and d. 1505. *Plate* 1232.

MORGAN LIBRARY. Knight of Malta. Sd and d. 1499. *Plate* 1235.

MRS BORCHARD (EX). Madonna suckling the Child.*

Pavia (Environs). CERTOSA, SECOND ALTAR R. Polyptych: upper register, Resurrection (side-panels by Bergognone); lower register, Madonna and Child enthroned, S. Ugone, S. Anselm. Sd and d. 1496.

Rome. PINACOTECA CAPITOLINA. 104. Madonna and Child enthroned with S. Martin and S. Nicholas.

San Martino Alfieri (Asti). CASTELLO. Nativity.

Strasbourg. Inv. 117. Madonna suckling the Child (st.v. of Milan, Borletti). d. 1510.*

Tortona. PALAZZO VESCOVILE. Triptych from the Abbazia di Lucedio by Trino Vercellese: Madonna and Child enthroned with four Angels; S. Agostino di Gasothez di Traù recommending the kneeling Annibale Paleologo of Monferrato; S. John Baptist. Sd and d. 1499.

Turin. GALLERIA SABAUDA. 23. S. Francis receiving Stigmata. Formerly Sd and d. 1506. *Plate* 1236.

24, 25. Left and right panel of polyptych: full-length SS. James and John Baptist against landscape.

26. Altarpiece from Certosa d'Asti: Madonna and Child in Glory with six Angels and SS. John Baptist, James, Bishop Ugo and penitent Jerome. Sd and d. 1498. *Plate* 1231.

29. Right panel of triptych: SS. Ambrose and Gregory the Great.

31, 33. Lower panels of polyptych (companions to below): full-length SS. Paul and Louis of Toulouse, full-length SS. Peter and Bonaventura. Sd. and d. 1506.

32, 34. Upper panels of polyptych (companions to above): half-length SS. Anthony of Padua, Catherine and John Evangelist; half-length SS. Lawrence, Dorothy and John Baptist. 1506.

MUSEO CIVICO. Inv. 428. Triptych (formerly Philadelphia, Wilstach): Madonna and Child enthroned; SS. James and John Evangelist with male donor; SS. John Baptist and Dominic with female donor. Sd and d. 1494. *Plate* 1230.

Homeless. Pietà. *Plate* 1229.

Madonna suckling the Child, and two Angels.* *Plate* 1233.

MAGNI see CESARE MAGNI

MAINERI, Gian Francesco

Parma. Active 1489–1504. Pupil of Ercole Roberti da Ferrara. Eclectic imitator of many of his North Italian contemporaries.

Allington Castle. LORD CONWAY (EX). Madonna and Child between SS. Cosmas and Damian, with SS. Eustace and George in background. *Plate* 1621.

Berlin. 1632. Holy Family of the Veil; in background, statues of Adam and Eve and Phoenix burning on altar.

Bologna. Inv. 564. Head of Alessandro Faruffino (fr. of altarpiece formerly in S. Maria degli Angeli at Ferrara, with S. Catherine of Siena worshipped by A. Faruffino and his wife Caterina Machiavelli).

Bucarest. Inv. 23, 24. Allegories of Good and Bad Omen.

Canford Manor (Ashby St. Ledgers). VISCOUNT WIMBORNE (EX). 'Costabili' Madonna and Child with S. Joseph and Joseph of Arimathea.

Copenhagen. 413. Christ carrying the Cross (after Solario).

Ferrara. TADDEI COLLECTION. Christ carrying the Cross.

Florence. UFFIZI. 3348. Christ carrying the Cross (after Solario).
 (Environs). QUINTO, PROF. S. P. CARTER (EX?). Christ carrying the Cross.

Gotha. 504. Madonna adoring the Child.

Leningrad. 1969. Christ carrying the Cross (after Solario).

London. 1119. The 'Strozzi' Altarpiece. (See under Ferrarese-Bolognese 1450–1525.)
 COURTAULD INSTITUTE GALLERIES, LEE OF FAREHAM COLLECTION. Dead Christ with mourning Virgin and Evangelist and Veronica below.

Luton Hoo (Beds.). SIR HAROLD WERNHER. 13. Holy Family of the veil, with statues of Adam and Eve in background.

Madrid. 244. Holy Family of the veil, with S. Francis receiving stigmata in background.

Milan. BRERA. 819. Head of Baptist on the platter (after Solario). Sd. *Plate* 1617.
 DR GRIECO. 'Cook' Flagellation with kneeling Dominican. *Plate* 1622.
 LURATI COLLECTION. Adoration of Shepherds.
 TRECCANI COLLECTION. Holy Family with statues of Adam and Eve in background and loving doves on altar. *Plate* 1619.

Modena. 175. Christ carrying the Cross (after Solario). *Plate* 1618.

Paris. RICHTEMBERGER (EX). Marriage of S. Catherine.

Richmond (Surrey). COOK COLLECTION. Nativity. (?)

Rome. GALLERIA DORIA PAMPHILI. 164. Christ carrying the Cross (after Solario).

Rotterdam. MUSEUM BOYMANS-VAN BEUNINGEN. Inv. 2554. 'Auspitz' Nativity.

Turin. ACCADEMIA ALBERTINA. 164. Madonna and Child. Sd. *Plate* 1620.

Vicenza. 345. Christ carrying the Cross (after Solario).

Zagreb. Madonna with donor kissing Child's hand (copying Montagna except donor).

Homeless. Adoration of Shepherds. *Plate* 1624.
 Holy Family. (*L'Arte*, 1907, p. 149.)

MANTEGNA, Andrea

Isola di Cartura 1431–Mantua 1506. Paduan School. Brought up in workshop of his adoptive father, Squarcione. Influenced by his future father-in-law, Jacopo Bellini, and even more powerfully by Donatello, and Pizzolo, as whose assistant he may have started. Uccello, Castagno, and possibly Fra Filippo Lippi may have had a certain effect upon him. (Works followed by an E were probably painted before 1470; by an L, after 1490).

Bergamo. 157. Resurrection (c.).
170. Madonna embracing Child.
Berlin. 9. Bust of Cardinal Ludovico Mezzarota. 1459.
27. Madonna and Child seated on parapet, Putti in frame (c. of Tulsa Madonna).
29. Circumcision.
S 5. Madonna embracing sleeping Child. L.
Bologna. PINACOTECA. Christ in Limbo (c.).
Boston (Mass.). GARDNER MUSEUM. Sacra Conversazione (g.p.; signature added later).
MUSEUM OF FINE ARTS. 33.682. Madonna and Child (c.).
Carpi. FORESTI COLLECTION (EX). Two panels with Tritons and Satyrs (st.). *Plate 711.*
Castle Ashby (Northants.). MARQUESS OF NORTHAMPTON. Adoration of Magi. L.
Plate 710.
Cincinnati (Ohio). 1927.406. Monochrome: Esther and Mordecai. L.
Cleveland (Ohio). 51.394. Miniature: Entombment.
Copenhagen. 416. Dead Christ and two Angels. Sd.
Correggio (Reggio Emilia). CONGREGAZIONE DI CARITÀ. Bust of Christ. d. 1493.
Dresden. 51. Holy Family with SS. Elizabeth and Infant John. L.
Dublin. 442. Monochrome: Judith. L. [*Plate 334.*]
Ferrara. AVV. MARIO BALDI. Fragment from upper part of Death of Virgin: Christ taking her Soul to Heaven (companion to Madrid).
Florence. UFFIZI. 375. Portrait of Cardinal Carlo de'Medici.
910. Triptych: Adoration of Magi, Circumcision, Ascension. [*Plate 333.*]
1384. 'Madonna of the Quarries.'
(Environs). VILLA DI PRATOLINO. PRINCE PAUL OF YUGOSLAVIA. Head of S. Simeon(fr.).
Frankfurt a/M. 1046. Bust of S. Mark. E. Sd. *Plate 702.*
Gosford House (East Lothian). EARL OF WEMYSS AND MARCH. Madonna and Child enthroned (contemporary c.).
Hampton Court. ORANGERY. 873–881. Nine cartoons: Triumph of Caesar (r.). 1484–92. *Plates 708–709.*
Klagenfurt. HISTORISCHES MUSEUM. 19, 20. Cassone, stuccoed and painted: Story of Trajan and the widow (g.p.; for marriage of Paola Gonzaga and Count of Gorizia, 1477?).
London. 274. Madonna and Child with SS. Mary Magdalen and John Baptist. Sd. ca 1500.
902. Triumph of Scipio, for F. Cornaro. 1504–6.

London (contd.). 639, 1106, 1381. Three panels on his design: 'Noli me tangere', Resurrection, Maries at Tomb.

    1125. Monochrome: Tuccia and Sophonisba (p.). L.

    1145. Monochrome: Samson and Delilah. L.

    1417. Agony in the Garden. Sd. E. [*Plate* 330.]

    3091. Madonna embracing Child, and four busts of Saints (after Mantegna).

    5641. 'Imperator Mundi.' L.

Madrid. 248. Death of Virgin (fr.; companion to Ferrara). E.

Mantua. PALAZZO DUCALE. Detached fresco from Palazzo Biondi at Mantua: 'Occasio' and 'Penitentia' (st.).

   — CAMERA DEGLI SPOSI. Frescoed decoration: vault—figures and putti looking down from circular opening, monochrome medallions of Roman Emperors held by Putti, monochrome scenes in triangular sections over lunettes; walls— Marchese Ludovico Gonzaga and his wife Barbara di Brandeburgo surrounded by children and courtiers; Marchese Ludovico meets his son Cardinal Francesco. Sd and d. 1474. [*Plate* 332.] Plate 706.

   S. ANDREA, FAÇADE. Frescoes: Ascension, SS. Andrew, Longinus (r.).

   — FIRST CHAPEL L., CUPOLA. Frescoes: Evangelists, Garlands and Coat of Arms (on his design). L.

— — Madonna and Child with SS. Elizabeth and Infant John. L.

— — Baptism of Christ (st.). L.

Milan. BRERA. 163. S. Bernardino and Angels (st.). d. 146(9?).

    198. Madonna and Child with Cherubim, for Eleonora d'Aragona. 1485.

    199. Dead Christ. L.

    200. Polyptych from S. Giustina at Padua: S. Luke writing, flanked by SS. Scholastica, Prosdocimus, Benedict, Christina; upper register, half-length SS, Sebastian, Jerome, mourning Virgin, dead Christ, mourning Evangelist, Augustine, Stephen. Formerly Sd and d. 1453.

   CASTELLO, TRIVULZIO COLLECTION. Altarpiece from S. Maria in Organo at Verona: Madonna and Child in Glory and SS. John Baptist, Gregory, Benedict, Jerome. Sd and d. 1497.

   POLDI PEZZOLI. 609. Profile of S. Bernardino (close follower).

    625. Madonna embracing Child.

    627. Profile bust of man (close follower).

Montreal (Canada). MUSEUM OF FINE ARTS. 103, 104. Two monochrome panels: Judith, Dido (st.).

Munich. PRINT ROOM. L 709. Mucius Scaevola. L.

Naples. 60. Bust of young Cardinal Francesco Gonzaga. ca 1462.

    61. S. Eufemia. Sd and d. 1454. *Plate* 703.

New York. 14.40.643. Holy Family and Saint. L.

    32.100.97. Madonna and Child with Cherubim. E.

    32.130.2. Adoration of Shepherds. E.

    49.7.11. Portrait in miniature.

Padua. 63 (Inv. 404). Detached fresco from Scuola dei SS. Marco e Sebastiano: Squatting archer (fr., st.). 1481.

BASILICA DEL SANTO, MUSEO ANTONIANO. Frescoed lunette: SS. Anthony of Padua and Bernardino kneeling (r.). Sd and d. 1452. *Plate 701.*

EREMITANI, CAPPELLA OVETARI. Part of frescoed decoration commissioned 1448 from Antonio Vivarini, Giovanni d'Alemagna, Niccolò Pizzolo and Mantegna: Left wall—Calling of SS. James and Andrew (g.p.), S. James preaching subdues Devils sent by Hermogenes (g.p.), Baptism of Hermogenes, S. James before Herod Agrippa, S. James heals a blind man on the way to his martyrdom, Beheading of S. James (finished by 1457); Altar wall—Assumption (g.p., ca 1454–57); Right wall—Martyrdom of S. Christopher (other frescoes signed by Ansuino da Forlì and Bono da Ferrara). Destroyed 1944 except for Assumption and Martyrdom of S. Christopher. [*Plate 331.*] *Plate 704.*

Paris. 1373. Predella panel to S. Zeno Triptych in Verona: Crucifixion (companion to Tours). 1459.

1373A. S. Sebastian.

1374. *Vierge de la Victoire* with kneeling Francesco Gonzaga. 1496.

1375, 1376. Parnassus; Allegory of Vice and Virtue (from Studiolo d'Isabella d'Este in Ducal Palace at Mantua). L. *Plate 707.*

CABINET DES DESSINS. Monochrome: Judgement of Solomon. L.

MUSÉE JACQUEMART-ANDRÉ. 1020. Madonna and Child with SS. Jerome and Louis.

1041. Madonna and Child with three Saints (st. or r.). L.

1045. 'Ecce Homo' (st.). L.

LIONEL DE ROTHSCHILD. S. Bernardino. (?)

Princeton (N.J.). 35.53. Madonna and Child (close follower).

San Diego (Cal.). 46.65. Madonna in prayer. Sd. (c.) (?)

São Paulo (Brazil). 15. S. Jerome in wilderness. [*Plate 335.*]

Taynuilt (Argyl.). SIR STEPHEN COURTAULD. Christ in Limbo (after M's design).

Tours. 259, 260. Predella panels to S. Zeno Triptych in Verona: Agony in the Garden, Resurrection (companions to Paris). 1459.

Tulsa (Okla.). PHILBROOK ART CENTER. 3370 (KRESS COLLECTION. K 1653). 'Butler' Madonna and Child.

Turin. GALLERIA SABAUDA. Madonna and Child with five Saints and Infant S. John (r. or st.). L.

UNIVERSITY LIBRARY. Valerius Maximus (Historia Augusta): Medallions of Roman Emperors. (?)

Venice. ACCADEMIA. 588. S. George.

CA' D'ORO. S. Sebastian. L. *Plate 712.*

S. MARIA DEI FRARI. Frescoed frame of Monument of Federico Cornaro: Putti and two medallions with Roman heads (g.p.). E.

Verona. 87. Holy Family and female Saint (st. variant of Dresden). L.

163. Christ carrying Cross (c. or r.). L.

2166. Madonna and Child with S. Juliana (c.).

Verona (contd.). s. ZENO, CHOIR. Triptych: Madonna and Child enthroned with Angels; SS. Peter, Paul, John Evangelist, Augustine; SS. Benedict, Lawrence, Zeno, John Baptist (predella panels in Paris and Tours). 1459. *Plate 705.*

Vienna. 81. S. Sebastian. Sd in Greek. E.

    81A, B. Monochrome panels: Sacrifice of Isaac; David and Goliath.

    AKADEMIE. 1084. Madonna and Child enthroned with Saint and Angels (Flemish copy?).

Washington (D.C.). 32 (MELLON COLLECTION). Penitent S. Jerome. E.

    289 (KRESS COLLECTION. K 325). Monochrome: Judith.

    377 (KRESS COLLECTION. K 483). Madonna suckling Child. L. (?)

    600 (WIDENER COLLECTION). Bust of condottiere. Sd and d. 1455 (c.).

    638 (WIDENER COLLECTION). Judith.

    1088 (KRESS COLLECTION. K 1709). Profile of man.

    1146 (KRESS COLLECTION. K 1563). 'Cook' Infant Saviour blessing.

MARCO D'OGGIONO

Oggiono (Como) ca 1475–ca 1530. Milanese imitator of Leonardo; possibly pupil of Butinone.

Auckland. ART GALLERY. Madonna suckling the Child (formerly Fonthill).

Bergamo. 961. Right panel of triptych: full-length S. Roch (companion to Milan, Poldi Pezzoli).

    s. ALESSANDRO (DUOMO). Head of Christ.

Berlin-Ost. 210A. S. Sebastian.

    1608. S. John Baptist and kneeling Ecclesiastic.

    EUGEN SCHWEITZER (EX). Predella panel: Betrayal of Christ.

Besate (Milano). PARISH CHURCH, CAPPELLA BERTOGLI. Madonna and Child with S. Bernardino of Siena, Francis and Jerome. doc. 1524.

Blois. MUSÉE. 'Crespi' double triptych: Madonna and Child with music-making Angels and SS. John Baptist and Peter recommending donors; Bishop Saint between S. Gualbert? and S. Clare. Sd. *Plates 1410–1412.*

Burghley House (Northants.). MARQUESS OF EXETER. 501. Madonna and Child.

Capesthorne Hall (Shrops.). BROMLEY-DAVENPORT COLLECTION (EX). Madonna della Violetta.

    Angels.

Chantilly. 29. S. Barbara.

Florence. BARON VON HADELN (EX). Holy Family reading.

Greenville (S.C.). BOB JONES UNIVERSITY GALLERY. 34. (R. Lehman gift). Tondo: Madonna and Child with Infant S. John, called 'Madonna del Lago'.

Hampton Court. Inv. 391. Holy Children embracing (variant of London, Mond).

Isolabella (Lago Maggiore). PALAZZO BORROMEO. Mourning Virgin and Evangelist (with Giampietrino).

Le Mans. M. HERVÉ-MATHÉ (EX). Madonna and Child holding lily (version by Giampietrino at London, Courtauld Institute).

London. 1149. Madonna and Child.

BURLINGTON HOUSE. Copy of Leonardo's Last Supper.

BENSON COLLECTION (EX). Madonna of Humility suckling the Child and worshipped by S. John Baptist.

MOND COLLECTION (EX). Holy Children embracing.

Mezzana Superiore (Somma Lombardo). S. STEFANO. Triptych: Assumption, S. John Baptist and S. Stephen; in predella, Beheading of Baptist, Visitation, Pietà, Nativity, Stoning of S. Stephen, four small Saints in niches.

Milan. AMBROSIANA. Triptych from refectory of Canons of S. Sepolcro: Madonna and Child, S. John Baptist, S. John Evangelist.

Madonna and Child.

BRERA. 77-82. Detached frescoes from S. Maria della Pace: lunette with Fall of Man; S. Christopher; two fragments from Dormition; lunette with Marriage at Cana; fragment of Man pouring water. *Plate* 1416.

269, 270. Two panels from Convent of Minori Osservanti at Maleo near Lodi: S. Anthony of Padua and female worshipper; S. Francis of Paola and female worshipper.

311. Panel from polyptych of S. Maria della Pace: S. Paul.

312. Assumption from S. Maria della Pace.

313. The Angels Michael, Raphael and Gabriel defeat Satan. Sd. *Plate* 1418.

320. Madonna and Child with S. John Baptist, S. Paul and Angel making music.(?)

CASTELLO. 278. Madonna embracing the Child. (?)

343. Madonna embracing the Child. (?)

POLDI PEZZOLI. 644. Left panel of triptych: S. Sebastian (companion to Bergamo).

PALAZZO ARCIVESCOVILE. S. Catherine and another female Saint.

MELZI D'ERIL COLLECTION. S. Roch.

S. Martin and the beggar.

VONWILLER COLLECTION. 'Bonomi Cereda' Madonna embracing the Child.

LURATI COLLECTION (EX). Christ seated in landscape upheld by S. John Evangelist; on the rock by His side a chalice with Symbols of Passion; in sky Angel with scroll inscribed 'Ecce Passionis mysteria'.

S. EUFEMIA, THIRD CHAPEL L. Madonna and Child with SS. John Baptist, Euphemia, Catherine, Bishop Saint and Angels.

S. MARIA DELLE GRAZIE, OLD SACRISTY. S. John Baptist worshipped by Conte Gasparo Vimercati. *Plate* 1417.

— REFETTORIO. Copy of Leonardo's Last Supper.

New York. S. H. KRESS FOUNDATION (EX). K 581. S. Mary Magdalen. (?)

Nîmes. 464. Madonna and Child.

Oggiono (Lago di Como). S. EUFEMIA, L. WALL. Assumption and SS. Nicholas of Tolentino, Francis, Sebastian, Roch, Ambrose, female Martyr, Apollonia, Stephen.

Oggiono (Lago di Como). S. EUFEMIA (contd.).

THIRD ALTAR R. Fresco: Madonna and Child with three female Saints.

Oslo. HARRY FETT. Madonna and Child.

Palermo. CHIARAMONTE BORDONARO COLLECTION. S. Jerome.

Paris. 1382. Holy Family with Zacharias, S. Elizabeth, Infant S. John and three Shepherds in background.

1383A. Madonna suckling the Child (replica at Princeton).

1603. Copy of Leonardo's Last Supper.

Princeton (N.J.). 1034. Madonna suckling the Child (replica of Paris).

Rome. GALLERIA BORGHESE. 435. Bust of Christ blessing globe.

456. Madonna suckling the Child.

VISCONTI VENOSTA COLLECTION. S. Catherine recommending a donor to the Virgin.

San Remo. GARBARINO COLLECTION. Lady as S. Catherine.

San Simeon (Cal.). HEARST MEMORIAL. Two panels of polyptych: S. Stephen, S. Bonaventura. *Plates* 1413, 1415.

Seattle (Wash.). MUSEUM OF ART IT.37/G.3478.I (KRESS COLLECTION. K 1064). Madonna and Child with Infant S. John (with Giampietrino).

Strasbourg. 263. Visitation.

Turin. ING. GALLO. Assumption of Magdalen.

Verona. DEPOT. Madonna and Child with Infant S. John. (?)

Vienna. LEDERER COLLECTION (EX). Bust of half-naked woman pointing at shell. [*Plate* 370.]

Warsaw. Inv. 211641. Madonna and Child.

Homeless. Madonna seated in landscape with the Holy Children. *Plate* 1414.

MARGARITO (Margaritone d'Arezzo)

Tuscan, active in the second half of the thirteenth century.

Arezzo. PINACOTECA. S. Francis. Sd.

Castiglion Fiorentino. S. FRANCESCO. S. Francis. Sd.

Cortona. S. FRANCESCO. S. Francis. Sd.

Ganghereto (Valdarno). PARISH CHURCH. S. Francis. Sd. *Plate* 8.

London. 564. Dossal from S. Margherita at Arezzo: Madonna and Child; at sides, Nativity, S. John Evangelist in the cauldron of boiling oil, S. John Evangelist raising Drusiana, S. Benedict pricked by thorns, Beheading of S. Catherine, S. Nicholas and the Devil's vase, S. Nicholas frees the three prisoners, S. Margaret unharmed by the dragon. Sd. *Plates* 11–13.

Montelungo (Arezzo). S. MARIA. Madonna and Child with Archangel Gabriel and three small Saints in the background. Sd.

Montepulciano. MUSEO CIVICO. S. Francis. Sd.

Monte San Savino. S. MARIA DELLE VERTIGHE. Madonna and Child and two stories on either side; two shutters, each with three Saints (p.). Sd and d. 12(8?)3.

Rome. VATICAN, PINACOTECA. S. Francis. Sd.

Siena. 2. S. Francis (r.). Sd.

Washington (D.C.). 807 (KRESS COLLECTION. K 1347). Madonna and Child with four small Saints in background. Sd. *Plate 9.*

Zurich. KUNSTHAUS. S. Francis. Sd. *Plate 10.*

MARTINI see FRANCESCO DI GIORGIO MARTINI

MARTINI see SIMONE MARTINI

MARTINO DI BARTOLOMEO DA SIENA

Son of a goldsmith; first registered as a painter in Siena 1389; active in and around Pisa as partner of Giovanni di Pietro da Napoli 1398–1405; died 1434/5. Pupil of Jacopo di Mino del Pelliciajo; influenced by Andrea Vanni and Taddeo di Bartolo.

Altenburg. 53. Portable altarpiece: Madonna and Child with SS. Bartholomew, Andreas, two female Saints and two Angels; in wings, SS. Christopher, James, Angel and Virgin of Annunciation.*

148. Predella panel: Crucifixion.

Asciano (Senese). MUSEO DI ARTE SACRA. Centre panel of altarpiece: Annunciation; blessing Redeemer above.

Bagnoregio. S. AGOSTINO, FIRST ALTAR L. Two panels of polyptych: S. Augustine with donor; S. Bonaventura; in pinnacles, Angel and Virgin of Annunciation.*

Bayonne. 4. Madonna of Humility; blessing Redeemer above.

Berlin. 1107. Predella panels: Two scenes from Life of S. Catherine of Siena.

Brooklyn (N.Y.). 32.782. Madonna and Child with SS. Peter, Anthony Abbot and two female Saints (r.).

Budapest. 45(8). Portable altarpiece: Madonna and Child with SS. Bartholomew and Catherine, and blessing Redeemer above; in wings, S. James, S. Anthony Abbot, Angel and Virgin of Annunciation (r.).

Cambridge. FITZWILLIAM MUSEUM. 553. Two pinnacles: Angel and Virgin of Annunciation.

Cambridge (Mass.). FOGG ART MUSEUM, GEORGE NAUMBURG BEQUEST. 1958.33. Madonna of Humility.

Campagnatico (between Siena and Grosseto). S. MARIA. Frescoed Tabernacle: Scenes from Life of Virgin. (?)

Càscina (Pontedera). S. GIOVANNI DEI CAVALIERI GEROSOLIMITANI. Frescoes: Crucifixion, with God the Father at top; below, two lost scenes, Birth of Baptist,

Baptist and Christ in Wilderness (fr.), Baptism of Christ; frescoes on bottom register are lost, excepting Beheading of Baptist and Baptist's head brought to Herod.

— LEFT WALL. Frescoes: monochrome Scenes from Old Testament; Saints in niches below.

Frescoes Sd and d. 1398.

Columbus (Ohio). GALLERY OF FINE ARTS, HOWALD COLLECTION. Right panel of polyptych: Knee-length S. Ursula.

El Paso (Tex.). MUSEUM OF ART. 1961–6/6 (KRESS COLLECTION. K 110). Predella panel: Crucifixion.

Florence. BARGELLO, CARRAND 9. Madonna and Child with four Saints and two Angels; dead Christ above.

Frankfurt a/M. 988–994. Seven scenes from Life of S. Stephen. *Plates 441–444*.

London. HENRY HARRIS (EX). Predella panel: Death of S. Benedict.

Los Angeles. COUNTY MUSEUM OF ART. Coronation of Virgin. *Plate 439*.

Milan. TULLIO FOSSATI BELLANI (FORMERLY BONICHI, ASCIANO). Madonna and Child. Sd and d. 1408. *Plate 437*.

New Haven (Conn.). 1942.322. Pinnacle: Blessing Redeemer.

New York. 30.95.263/6. Four panels of polyptych from Orvieto: SS. Anthony Abbot, Stephen, James and Galganus; in pinnacles, Angel and Virgin of Annunciation, Baptist and Bishop.

Perugia. VAN MARLE COLLECTION (EX). Top panel of polyptych: Christ enthroned. *Plate 435*.

Philadelphia (Pa.). MUSEUM OF ART. 45.25.120 a, b, c, d. Predella panels: Scenes from lives of Saints. *Plate 440*.

Pisa. B.P.V, 16 (Vigni 49). Polyptych from Spedale di S. Chiara: Madonna and Child enthroned; SS. Augustine and John Baptist, with Evangelist in roundel above; SS. John Evangelist and Clare, with Evangelist in roundel above (original pinnacles—Trinity, Annunciation—and predella, lost). Documented as by Giovanni di Pietro da Napoli assisted by Martino di Bartolomeo (his, the Madonna). 1402. *Plate 446*.

B.P.V, 17 (Vigni 51). Altarpiece from Convent of S. Caterina: Mystic Marriage of S. Catherine and kneeling donor (with Giovanni di Pietro da Napoli, who did most of it). d. 1404. *Plate 447*.

B.P.V, 18 (Vigni 50). Polyptych with half-length figures from Spedale dei Trovatelli: Madonna and Child; SS. Anthony Abbot, Bartholomew, John Baptist and Lucy; in pinnacles, Redeemer and four Saints (p.?). Sd and d. 1403. *Plate 445*.

Poughkeepsie (New York). VASSAR COLLEGE. Madonna and Child enthroned with four small kneeling Donors.

Rome. VATICAN, PINACOTECA. 164. Predella panel: S. Benedict teaching.

226, 230. Two square predella panels repainted in sixteenth century: S. Anthony Abbot in prayer, Death of S. Anthony Abbot. (?)

MARCHESE MISCIATELLI. 'Ecce Homo.'

Sassari (Sardinia). MUSEO. Triptych: SS. Nicholas, Anthony Abbot and Lawrence.

Settimo (Pisa). S. BENEDETTO, HIGH ALTAR. Small Madonna and Child; five Saints in predella.

— FIRST ALTAR R. Madonna and Child. E.

Siena. 58. Polyptych: Madonna and Child; SS. Augustine and Francis, SS. Clare and John Baptist; in pinnacles, Crucifixion, S. Peter and S. Paul. (?)

105. Annunciation. E.

120. Four panels of polyptych: SS. James, Mary Magdalen, Catherine and Ansanus, with busts of Saints in pinnacles.

160. Polyptych: Madonna and Child; SS. John Evangelist, Lawrence, Ansanus and Augustine.

303. S. John Baptist, with Virgin of Annunciation above (r.).

322. S. Michael, with Angel of Annunciation above (r.).

PALAZZO PUBBLICO, FIRST FLOOR, SALA DEI PRIORI O DI BALIA, VAULT. Frescoes: sixteen Virtues (Peace, Mercy, Justice, Fortitude, Faith, Hope, Circumspection, Intelligence, Prudence, Temperance, Humility, Chastity, Meekness—Charity and two more Virtues are lost), one figure in each quart of vault (frescoes on walls are by Spinello Aretino). Commissioned 1407, paid 1408.

— SALA DEI PILASTRI. Triptych: S. Mary Magdalen, between S. Stephen and S. Anthony Abbot; in pinnacles, Madonna and two Angels. Formerly Sd and d. 1408. *Plate 433.*

S. ANSANO, ANTICA COMPAGNIA DI (via Sallustio Bandini, Università). Frescoed lunette over door: Madonna and Child with four Saints (r.).

S. FRANCESCO, R. WALL. Frescoed lunette: Visitation (r.).

S. MARTA, CORO DELLE MONACHE. Fresco: Burial of S. Martha (?)

SOCIETÀ ESECUTORI DI PIE DISPOSIZIONI, GALLERIA. 17. Tabernacle: S. Eustace, with Madonna and Child above.

SPEDALE DI S. MARIA DELLA SCALA, LAST ROOM TOWARDS VIA DEL CAPITANO. Frescoes: Trinity with SS. Philip, Lawrence and female donor; full-length Christ; full-length John Baptist.

— ORATORIO DELLA MADONNA SOTTO LE VOLTE O DEI DISCIPLINATI, SACRISTY. Monochrome fresco: Last Judgement (r.).

Homeless. Side-panels of polyptych: S. John Baptist, S. Mary Magdalen, with Angel and Virgin of Annunciation above. *Plates 434, 436.*

Madonna and Child. *Plate 438.*

MARTINO DA LODI see PIAZZA

MASSONE (MAZONE, MASONE), Giovanni

Piedmontese painter and woodcarver active in Genoa and Savona. Mentioned 1453–1510. Influenced by Foppa and local Ligurian painters.

Alençon. 155. Polyptych. (See Paris Musées Nationaux.)

Genoa. PALAZZO BIANCO (DEP. FROM S. GIULIANO D'ALBARO). Crucifixion.

    S. MARIA DI CASTELLO. Polyptych: lower register, Annunciation and SS. James, John Baptist, Peter Martyr, Sebastian; upper register, Crucifixion and SS. Benedict? and Roch; in predella, Marriage of Virgin, Visitation, Nativity, Epiphany, Flight into Egypt. Circumcision. Probably ca 1463. *Plate 1212.*

Liverpool. 2788. S. Mark enthroned with SS. Paul, Catherine, John Baptist and Justina. *Plate 1211.*

Paris. 1384. Three panels of polyptych: Nativity; S. Francis recommending Pope Sixtus IV, S. Anthony of Padua recommending Cardinal Giulio della Rovere, later Pope Julius II (from S. Francesco, Savona; see there). Sd and d. 1490. *Plates 1214, 1215.*

    MUSÉES NATIONAUX N. 4. Christ appearing to S. Mary Magdalen and to other Saints. d. 1477.

Pontremoli (Massa Carrara). SS. ANNUNZIATA. Polyptych: Madonna and Child, Four Evangelists, Crucifixion, Annunciation and predella. (?)

Quarona (Vercelli). S. GIOVANNI. Polyptych: Madonna and Child enthroned; above, S. John Baptist; on either side, eight full-length Saints; at top, Angel and Virgin of Annunciation; in predella, Saints. (?)

Savona. 18. Polyptych: lower row, S. Ambrose, Annunciation, S. Jerome; upper row, S. Bernardino?, Crucifixion, S. Anthony of Padua. 1493?

    23. Polyptych: lower register, S. Bernardino with donor, Nativity, S. Bonaventura; upper register, S. Francis, Crucifixion, S. Dominic. Sd. ca 1490–95. *Plate 1210.*

    s.n. Crucifixion (possibly from upper register of Della Rovere polyptych, see Paris). *Plate 1213.*

Taggia. S. DOMENICO, FIRST ALTAR R. Side-panels of polyptych joined together: S. Erasmus and S. Vincent; Angel and Virgin of Annunciation; two pilasters with six small Saints (Dominic, Scholastica, Nicholas, Francis, Benedict, Blaise).

MASTER OF THE BAPTIST'S DOSSAL

Sienese active in the second quarter of the thirteenth century. (His dossal is certainly the finest in colour and one of the finest in every other respect of all remaining pre-cimabuesque and pre-duccesque Tuscan paintings.)

Siena. 14. Dossal from Monastery of S. Petronilla: S. John Baptist enthroned; on either side twelve Scenes from His Life (Left—Annunciation to Zacharias, Visitation, Birth of Baptist, S. Elizabeth presenting the Infant S. John to the Virgin and Child, An Angel carrying the Infant S. John into the Wilderness, S. John Baptist having a Vision of Christ; Right—S. John Baptist and two Disciples meeting Jesus in the Wilderness, Baptism of Christ, Beheading of Baptist, Baptist's Head brought to Herod, Baptist in Limbo, Christ and the Virgin receiving S. John Baptist in Heaven). *Plate* 17.

MASTER OF CITTÀ DI CASTELLO

Sienese active first half fourteenth century. Close follower of Duccio di Buoninsegna and Ugolino di Neri. See also under Duccio's imitators.

Città di Castello. 72. 'Maestà': Madonna and Child enthroned with six Angels and donor. *Plate* 59.

Copenhagen. 835 (ON LOAN FROM NY CARLSBERG GLYPTOTEK). Centre-panel of polyptych: Madonna and Child, and Angels in spandrels. *Plate* 56.

Detroit (Mich.). 24.96. Madonna and Child holding scroll.

New Haven (Conn.). 1943.242, 243. Side-panels of polyptych: S. Peter, S. John Baptist (companions to Vienna). *Plate* 55.

Siena. 29–32. Side-panels of polyptych from Pieve di S. Cecilia at Crevole, companions to Opera del Duomo Madonna: SS. Peter, Anthony Abbot, Paul, Augustine; in pinnacles, half-length Angels.

33. Polyptych: Madonna and Child; SS. Francis, John Evangelist, Lawrence, Clare; in pinnacles, blessing Redeemer, SS. Augustine, Peter, Baptist, Mary Magdalen. *Plate* 58.

DUOMO, MUSEO DELL'OPERA. 24. Centre-panel of polyptych from Pieve di S. Cecilia at Crevole, companion to Siena 29–32: Madonna and Child. (Fragment.) (Not to be confused with 37, by Duccio.) *Plate* 57.

Utrecht. 2, 3. Diptych: Crucifixion (r.); Madonna and Child with four Angels, SS. Francis and Agnes, and female donor (r.).

Vienna. LANCKORONSKI COLLECTION. Side-panel of polyptych: S. Francis (companion to New Haven).*

MASTER OF THE CODEX OF ST. GEORGE

School of Siena. Active apparently 1320–50. Close follower of Simone Martini; influenced by Baronzio.

Berlin. KUPFERSTICHKABINETT. 1984–2000. Various miniatures.
Boulogne. BIBLIOTHÈQUE. MSS. n. 86. S. Peter worshipped by a Pope (initial I).
    Bishop reading a book held by deacon (initial N).
    Bishop reading (initial P).
    Pope praying (initial O).
    Blessing Redeemer (initial O).
Bruges. RENDERS COLLECTION (EX?). Crucifixion.
Brussels. MME JACQUES STOCLET (EX). Angel and Virgin of Annunciation. *Plates* 114–115.
Cracow. 136. Front: Annunciation; back: SS. Stephen and Lawrence. *Plate* 112.
    JAGELLOŃSKA LIBRARY. Miniature: S. Michael.
Detroit (Mich.). 36.75. Right leaf of diptych: Crucifixion with Virgin of Annunciation above.
Florence. BARGELLO, CARRAND COLLECTION. 10, 11. Diptych: Coronation of Virgin; Noli me tangere. *Plates* 108–109.
    S. MARIA DEL CARMINE, SACRISTY. Reliquary: Madonna and Child enthroned with SS. John Baptist and Evangelist. *Plate* 113.
New York. MORGAN LIBRARY. MS. 713. Illuminated Missal. *Plate* 105.
    CLOISTERS. 61.200.1/2 (Rockefeller Bequest). 'Benson' diptych: Crucifixion; Entombment. *Plates* 110–111.
Paris. 1666. Madonna and Child enthroned with four Saints and Angels; Redeemer above. *Plate* 116.
    BIBLIOTHÈQUE NATIONALE. Pontifical n. 15619, f. 2: Pope cutting novice's hair.
Rome. VATICAN, PINACOTECA. 152. Crucifixion.
    — S. PIETRO, ARCHIVIO CAPITOLARE. 1290. Illuminated Codex of S. George. *Plates* 106–107.

MASTER OF THE CRIVELLESQUE POLYPTYCHS

Abruzzese follower of Crivelli, active last decades of the fifteenth century.

Aquila. MUSEO NAZIONALE ABRUZZESE. 29. Polyptych: Madonna adoring the Child in her lap; full-length SS. Bernardino of Siena, Francis, Anthony of Padua and John of Capistrano; in pinnacles, Dead Christ and half-length SS. Bonaventura, John Baptist, Jerome and Louis of Toulouse.
    32, 34, 35. Panels of dismembered polyptych from the Convento dei Minori at Tocco Casauria: S. Anthony of Padua and S. Bonaventura in pinnacle above;

Madonna adoring the Child in her lap; Dead Christ with Symbols of Passion (companions to Assisi and Chieti). 1489. *Plate 964.*

33. Polyptych: Madonna and Child worshipped by a nun; full-length SS. Francis, Michael, Jerome and Anthony of Padua; in pinnacles, Dead Christ and half-length SS. Bernardino of Siena, Louis of Toulouse, Ambrose and John of Capistrano; in predella, busts of Christ and Saints.

Assisi. BASILICA, MUSEO. Panel of dismembered polyptych from the Convento dei Minori at Tocco Casauria: S. Francis and S. Louis of Toulouse in pinnacle above (companion to Aquila and Chieti). d. 1489. *Plate 964.*

Chieti. MUSEO CIVICO. Two panels of dismembered polyptych from the Convento dei Minori at Tocco Casauria: S. John Baptist with S. Bernardino of Siena in pinnacle above; S. Jerome with S. John of Capistrano in pinnacle above (companions to Aquila and Assisi). 1489. *Plate 964.*

Harewood House (Yorks.). EARL OF HAREWOOD (EX). Polyptych: Madonna adoring the Child in her lap; full-length SS. Bonaventura, Michael, Francis and Bernardino of Siena; in pinnacles, Dead Christ with Symbols of Passion and half-length SS. Clare, Louis of France, Louis of Toulouse and John of Capistrano; in predella, twelve Apostles. *Plate 965.*

MASTER OF THE GARDNER ANNUNCIATION

Central Italian painter, active about 1480, running parallel with the young Perugino, influenced by Melozzo and Crivelli. May turn out to be Antoniazzo in Verrocchiesque moment. [Recently identified with Pier Matteo da Amelia, q.v.]

Altenburg. 110, 111. Side-panels of polyptych: full-length SS. Mary Magdalen and John Baptist (companions to Berlin, Cornbury Park and Philadelphia).

Baltimore (Md.). WALTERS ART GALLERY. 477. Madonna adoring the Child. *Plate 1065.*

Barcelona. IGLESIA DE LOS P.P. CAPUCHINOS DE SARRIA (CAMBÓ GIFT). Lunette: Blessing Redeemer and two Angels. *Plate 1071.*

Berlin-Ost. 129. Centre panel of polyptych: Madonna of the pomegranate (companion to Altenburg, Cornbury Park and Philadelphia). d. 1481. *Plate 1070.*

Boston (Mass.). GARDNER MUSEUM. Annunciation; in predella, Dead Christ and busts of SS. Peter and Paul (from Porziuncola, Assisi). *Plate 1072.*

Cornbury Park (Charlbury, Oxon.). WATNEY COLLECTION (EX). Side-panel of polyptych: full-length Bishop Saint trampling on the Powers of Arian Heresy (companion to Altenburg, Berlin and Philadelphia).*

Florence. UFFIZI. 1543 (2199?). Madonna and Child.

Perugia. 206. Triptych: Madonna and Child; S. Sebastian and donor; S. Bernardino.

Philadelphia (Pa.). J. G. JOHNSON COLLECTION. 140. Side-panel of polyptych: Full-length S. Nicholas of Tolentino (companion to Altenburg, Berlin and Cornbury Park).

Terni. S. FRANCESCO. Triptych: Madonna and Child enthroned; Bishop Saint and Baptist; SS. Francis and Louis of Toulouse; in lunette, God the Father and two Angels; in pilasters, SS. Anthony, Valentine, Anne, Bernardino, Sebastian, Monica; in predella, Nativity, Adoration of Magi, Crucifixion, Descent into Limbo (p.). d. 1485.*

MASTER OF THE GOODHART MADONNA
see DUCCIO'S IMITATORS

MASTER OF GRISELDA

Temporary designation for a pupil of Neroccio di Landi, strongly influenced by Signorelli, for whom he must have worked in Siena at the beginning of the sixteenth century.

Birmingham. BARBER INSTITUTE. Alexander the Great on a pedestal in landscape (with Signorelli; companion to Budapest, Florence, Milan, Washington, and to Pacchiarotto at Baltimore). *Plate* 904.

Budapest. 64 (67). Tiberius Gracchus on a pedestal in landscape (with Signorelli; see Birmingham). *Plate* 907.

Florence. BARGELLO, CARRAND. Scipio Africanus on a pedestal in landscape (background to Francesco di Giorgio's figure; see Birmingham). *Plate* 906.

London. 912, 913, 914. Three cassone fronts with Story of Griselda. *Plates* 910, 912.

Longleat (Wilts.). MARQUESS OF BATH. Two cassone fronts with Roman subjects (also listed Bartolomeo di Giovanni). *Plate* 911.

Milan. POLDI PEZZOLI. 473. Fides on a pedestal in landscape (with Signorelli; see Birmingham).

Washington (D.C.). 12 (MELLON COLLECTION). Vestal Claudia Quinta on a pedestal in landscape (background to Neroccio's figure; see Birmingham). *Plate* 905.

782 (KRESS COLLECTION. K 1400). Eunustus of Tanagra on a pedestal in landscape (cut at bottom; with Signorelli; see Birmingham). *Plate* 909.

MASTER OF OSSERVANZA TRIPTYCH

Possibly an early phase of Sano di Pietro.

Altenburg. 74. Madonna of Humility worshipped by two Angels.

Asciano. MUSEO D'ARTE SACRA. Polyptych: Birth of Virgin; above, Madonna of Humility with four Angels; Death of Virgin; Burial of Virgin; (predella at Dijon, Florence). *Plates* 574, 575.

Assisi. F. M. PERKINS. S. John Baptist. Lost 1944.

Berlin. 63D. Panel of polyptych: S. Anthony at Mass (see Washington).

Cambridge (Mass.). FOGG MUSEUM. 1922.172. Predella panel: Descent into Limbo (companion to Detroit, Kiev?, Philadelphia, Rome).

Detroit (Mich.). 60.61. Predella panel: Resurrection (companion to Cambridge, Kiev?, Philadelphia, Rome).

Dijon. MUSÉE, MACIET BEQUEST. Predella panel from Asciano polyptych: Man of Sorrows, with mourning Mary and John.

Florence. SERRISTORI COLLECTION. Pietà with S. Sebaldus and kneeling donor. (?)
BERENSON COLLECTION. Predella panel from Asciano polyptych: The dying Virgin taking leave of the Apostles.

Indianapolis (Ind.). 18. Roundel from an altarpiece: Bust of saintly monk.

Kiev. MUSEUM. Predella panel: Crucifixion (probably companion to Cambridge, Detroit, Philadelphia, Rome). *Plate 577.*

Lawrence (Kansas). UNIVERSITY OF KANSAS. 60.44 (KRESS COLLECTION. K 425). Roundel from altarpiece: Head of Angel.

London. 5114. 'Trivulzio' portable triptych: Birth of Virgin.

New Haven (Conn.). 1871.57. Panel of polyptych: S. Anthony beaten by Devils (p.) (see Washington).
1871.58. Panel of polyptych: S. Anthony tempted by the Devil in the shape of a girl (see Washington).

New York. R. LEHMAN COLLECTION. Panel of polyptych: S. Anthony Abbot tempted by the golden porringer (see Washington).
Centre panel of polyptych: Madonna and Child enthroned.

Paris. 1696. Panel of polyptych: S. Anthony Abbot reading (fr., see Washington).

Philadelphia (Pa.). J. G. JOHNSON COLLECTION. 1295. Predella panel: Christ on the way to Calvary (companion to Cambridge, Detroit, Kiev? and Rome). *Plate 578.*

Rome. VATICAN, PINACOTECA. 232. Predella panel: Flagellation (companion to Cambridge, Detroit, Kiev? and Philadelphia). *Plate 579.*

Siena. 177. Portable altarpiece from Convent of S. Maria Maddalena: Madonna of Humility with four Angels and blessing Redeemer; in wings, S. Catherine, S. John Baptist, Angel and Virgin of Annunciation.
216. Predella to Osservanza triptych: S. Ambrose chasing the Arians from the church, Crucifixion, S. Jerome in the Wilderness. 1436.
218. Predella: Martyrdom of S. Bartholomew, Man of Sorrows with mourning Virgin and Evangelist, Beheading of female Saint.
PALAZZO CHIGI SARACINI. Portable altarpiece: Madonna of Humility with four Angels and blessing Redeemer; in wings, S. Francis (formerly overpainted with S. Catherine of Siena), S. John Baptist, Angel and Virgin of Annunciation; in base, Man of Sorrows. *Plate 576.*
S. CRISTOFORO, R. WALL. Two panels of polyptych: S. George and the Dragon; S. Christopher.
(Environs) OSSERVANZA, THIRD ALTAR R. Triptych: Madonna and Child enthroned

with Angel and Virgin of Annunciation in roundels above; full-length SS. Ambrose and Jerome; in pinnacles, Redeemer, SS. Peter and Paul (predella, Siena n. 216). d. 1436. *Plate 573.*

Venice. CONTE VITTORIO CINI. Inv. 6663. Bust of Redeemer. (Formerly at Minneapolis.)

Washington(D .C.). 817/8 (KRESS COLLECTION. K 1367, K 1368). Two upright panels from polyptych: S. Anthony distributing his wealth to the poor; S. Anthony leaving his monastery (p.) (companions to following).

404 (KRESS COLLECTION. K 513). Panel from polyptych: Meeting of S. Anthony Abbot and Paul Hermit (companion to following).

1152 (KRESS COLLECTION. K 1568). Oblong panel from polyptych: Funeral of S. Anthony Abbot (companion to above, to Berlin, New Haven and New York, Lehman; central panel, Paris?).

MASTER OF PANZANO TRIPTYCH

Sienese painter active in the second half of the fourteenth century. Follower of Bartolo di Fredi and Andrea Vanni, close to Fei.

Baltimore (Md.). WALTERS ART GALLERY. 729. Portable altarpiece: Madonna and Child enthroned with SS. Catherine and Anthony Abbot; above, Crucifixion; in wings, SS. Nicholas and Bartholomew, SS. Francis and (Lucy?); above, Angel and Virgin of Annunciation.

Bolsena. S. CRISTINA. Frescoes: Madonna and Child, S. Christina, S. Nicholas, S. Catherine. (?)

Cambridge (Mass.). FOGG ART MUSEUM. Portable altarpiece: Madonna suckling the Child, with SS. John Baptist, Christopher, Augustine and Anthony Abbot; in wings, S. Andrew, S. Ansanus; in pinnacles, blessing Redeemer, Angel and Virgin of Annunciation.

Gotha. LANDESMUSEUM. Portable altarpiece: Christ on Cross with mourning Mary, S. John Evangelist, S. Francis and Magdalen; in wings, S. Anthony Abbot, S. Catherine, Angel and Virgin of Annunciation.

Montalcino. MUSEO CIVICO. Madonna and Child with S. Lawrence and S. Ansanus. d. 1372.

New York. MRS R. BONNER BOWLER. Three panels of polyptych in Renaissance frame: Angel and Virgin of Annunciation, S. Anthony of Padua.

Panzano. PIEVE DI S. LEOLINO, L. WALL. Triptych: Mystic Marriage of S. Catherine; S. Paul; S. Peter; in pinnacles, blessing Redeemer, S. Anthony Abbot, S. Blaise. *Plate 414.*

Polesden Lacey. NATIONAL TRUST. Adoration of Magi (version of Bartolo di Fredi's Adoration, now split between Dijon and New York, Lehman).

Ravenna. MUSEO CIVICO. Christ on Cross with Mary and S. John Evangelist.

Siena. S. BARTOLOMEO DELL'ISTRICE. Triptych: Madonna suckling the Child with SS. Peter and Paul and two female Saints; S. Christopher; S. Anthony Abbot; above, five roundels with Trinity, Angel and Virgin of Annunciation, two Prophets; below, five roundels with Christ and Evangelists.

Homeless. Madonna and Child with bird. (*Dedalo*, XI, p. 356.)

Madonna and Child enthroned with eight Saints. Angel and Virgin of Annunciation in roundels above (*Dedalo*, XI, p. 359.).

Portable altarpiece: Madonna with SS. Mary, Magdalen and Catherine; SS. Andrew and John Baptist, two hermit Saints; in pinnacles, blessing Redeemer, Angel and Virgin of Annunciation. (*Dedalo*, XI, p. 362.)

MASTER OF ST. FRANCIS

Artistic personality, possibly trained in Pisa and follower of Giunta, active in Umbria before Cimabue. So called after 'St. Francis's Bed' at Assisi, S. Maria degli Angeli.

Assisi. S. CHIARA. Crucifix (st.).

S. FRANCESCO, LOWER CHURCH, NAVE. Ruined frescoes, cut by later addition of chapels:

Right wall: Stories of Christ [Mounting on the Cross, Crucifixion, Descent from the Cross, Mourning of the dead Christ, Madonna and Child with Angel before the papal throne].

Left wall: Stories of S. Francis [S. Francis renounces his inheritance, Pope Innocent III has a vision of S. Francis supporting the Lateran Church, S. Francis preaches to the birds, receives Stigmata, Funerals of S. Francis]. *Plate 5.*

—— SOUTH TRANSEPT, CENTRAL WINDOW. Stained glass: The Baptist, Christ, Zacharias, Angel announcing John's birth.

— TESORO DELLA BASILICA. Fragment of low dossal: Isaiah (companion to Perugia 21, 22).

S. MARIA DEGLI ANGELI, MUSEO. S. Francis between two Angels, holding a scroll inscribed: 'Hic mihi viventi lectus fuit et morienti' (tunic repainted in sixteenth century). *Plate 3.*

Brussels. MME FERON-STOCLET. Fragment of dossal: S. Peter (companion to New York, Perugia and Washington).

Florence. ACTON COLLECTION. Crucifix with kneeling S. Francis.

London. 6361. 'Stoclet' Crucifix.

New York. ROBERT LEHMAN. Fragment of dossal: SS. Bartholomew and Simon (companion to Brussels, Perugia and Washington).

Perugia. 21, 22. Fragments of low dossal: S. Anthony of Padua, Deposition and Entombment (companions to Assisi, Tesoro). *Plate 4.*

23, 24. Fragments of dossal: S. Matthew, S. Francis (companions to Brussels, New York, Washington).

Perugia (contd.). 26. Crucifix (above, blessing Redeemer and Virgin of Assumption between two Angels; sides, mourning Mary and John; at feet, kneeling S. Francis). d. 1272.

Washington (D.C.). 810, 811 (KRESS COLLECTION 1359, 1360). Fragments of dossal: S. James, S. John Evangelist (companions to Brussels, New York, Perugia).

MASTER OF THE SFORZA ALTARPIECE

Milanese active end of fifteenth to beginning of sixteenth century. Close to Bernardino de' Conti and Butinone.

Berlin. 1433. Madonna and Child with rosary. *Plate* 1390.

Berlin-Ost. 284 A. Madonna and Child in niche. *Plate* 1389.

Florence. CORA COLLECTION. Madonna and Child presenting donor. *Plate* 1392.

London. 3899. S. Paul reading in niche.

    4444. Madonna and Child with Saints and worshippers. *Plate* 1391.

Milan. BRERA. 310. The Sforza Altarpiece: Madonna and Child enthroned with the Doctors of the Church, Lodovico il Moro, Beatrice d'Este and their children. 1494. *Plates* 1388, 1393.

    CASTELLO. 486. Five roundels with half-length Saints.

Paris. MUSÉE DES ARTS DÉCORATIFS. Inv. Pe 105. Right fragment of altarpiece: S. Anne and S. Joseph. *Plate* 1387.

MASTER OF STRATONICE

Follower of Francesco di Giorgio, influenced by early Filippino Lippi and later by Signorelli. Active ca 1475–90.

Altenburg. 87. Adoration of Magi. E.

Berne. SCHLOSS MERCHLINGEN, B. GUINNESS. Madonna and Child with two Angels; in background, Tobias and the Angel.

Birmingham (Ala.). MUSEUM OF ART. 61.124 (KRESS COLLECTION. K 2067). Madonna and Child with SS. Ursula and Agatha and four Angels (possibly for Nuns of via San Gallo; formerly Austen Collection). *Plate* 831.

Chapel Manor (Horsmonden, Kent). AUSTEN COLLECTION (EX). Madonna and Child with two Angels, SS. Roch and Sebastian.*

Florence. S. GIOVANNINO DE' CAVALIERI. Annunciation (also listed Master of Castello Nativity. See *Florentine School*, Pl. 878).

Geneva. LEDERER COLLECTION. Madonna and Child with Angel (version of Botticelli's Chigi Madonna in Boston). *Plate* 832.

London. COURTAULD INSTITUTE GALLERIES, LEE OF FAREHAM COLLECTION. Madonna and Child with S. Anne and two Angels.

   J. POPE-HENNESSY. Tondo: Madonna and Child with SS. Michael and Anthony Abbot.*

San Marino (Cal.). HUNTINGTON GALLERY. Cassone panels: Antiochus's illness and his doctor's talk with King Seleucus; Marriage of Antiochus and Stratonice. *Plates* 835, 837.

Venice. CONTE VITTORIO CINI. Inv. 6815. 'Moray' Nativity.

Homeless. Rape of Proserpina; Orpheus in Hades. *Plates* 834, 836.

   Three Saints.* *Plate* 833.

MATTEO DI GIOVANNI

Sienese School. First mentioned 1452–53. Citizen of San Sepolcro, active in Siena. Died there 1495. Pupil possibly of Domenico di Bartolo; strongly influenced by Vecchietta, and, later, by Pollajuolo and Girolamo da Cremona.

Altenburg. 81. Fragment (from portable altarpiece?): S. Nicholas (companion to Esztergom).

Anghiari. S. AGOSTINO, FIRST ALTAR L. Triptych: Madonna and Child enthroned with two Angels; SS. Augustine, Anthony Abbot, Francis and Blessed Gallerani. E.

Asciano (Siena). MUSEO D'ARTE SACRA. Polyptych: Madonna and Child (fr.); SS. James and Augustine; SS. Bernardino and Margaret; upper panels, blessing Eternal, Angel and Virgin of Annunciation; in predella, S. Catherine before the Judge, Martyrdom of the Wheels, Crucifixion, Beheading of S. Catherine, S. Catherine in the Temple.

— Side-panels to London Assumption: S. Michael, S. Augustine (deposited Pinacoteca, Siena?). 1474.

Assisi. F. M. PERKINS COLLECTION. Madonna and Child with two Angels and SS. Jerome and Galganus (st.).

Balcarres (Fife, Scotland). EARL OF CRAWFORD AND BALCARRES. Two panels of polyptych, joined together: SS. Lucy and Agatha.

Baltimore (Md.). WALTERS ART GALLERY. 698. Descent of Holy Ghost (fr.).

   1038. Madonna and Child with two Angels and SS. Bernardino and Jerome.

Bayonne. 967. Madonna and Child with two Angels, SS. Jerome and S. Louis of France (r.).

Bergamo. 556. Madonna and Child with two Angels and SS. Sebastian and Catherine.

Berlin. 1127. Madonna of the Rosary with SS. Jerome and Francis and two Angels.

   1441. (FROM KOENIGSBERG). Madonna and Child with SS. Jerome and Catherine of Siena and two Angels.

Birmingham. BARBER INSTITUTE. Madonna and Child with SS. Michael and John Baptist. L.

Bloomington (Ind.). INDIANA UNIVERSITY. L62.163 (KRESS COLLECTION. K 496). Judith.

Buonconvento (Sienese). PIEVE DEI SS. PIETRO E PAOLO, HIGH ALTAR. Madonna and Child enthroned with two Angels.

— PINACOTECA. Madonna and Child with two Angels (from Percena; st.).

Cambridge (Mass.). FOGG ART MUSEUM. 1905.13. S. Jerome in his Study. 1492.

Cassel. HENSCHEL COLLECTION (EX). Nativity (r.).

Castiglion Fiorentino. MUSEO. Madonna and Child with SS. Peter, Catherine of Siena, Bernardino and (James?). (?)

Chicago (Ill.). 33.1018/9. Two predella panels, possibly to Massacre in S. Agostino, Siena: Vision of S. Jerome, Vision of S. Augustine. 14(82?). *Plate* 813.

Cincinnati (Ohio). 1956.89. Madonna and Child with SS. Francis, Anthony of Padua and two Angels.

Cleveland (Ohio). 40.535. Predella panel: Crucifixion.

Cologne. WALLRAF–RICHARTZ MUSEUM. 515 (ex). Madonna and Child with S. Nicholas of Bari and Francis.

Columbia (S.C.). MUSEUM OF ART. 62.920 (KRESS COLLECTION. K 1746). Madonna and Child with SS. Catherine of Siena and Sebastian.

Corsano (Siena). PIEVE. Madonna and Child with two Angels (with Cozzarelli).

Detroit (Mich.). 25.24. Madonna and Child with SS. Catherine and Francis and two Angels.

Madonna and Child with two Angels.

Edinburgh. 1023. Madonna adoring the Child with SS. Francis and Sebastian, and two Cherubim.

Esztergom. 55.167. Predella panel: Crucifixion of S. Peter (st.).

55.175. Madonna and Child with two Angels (fr. of lunette, companion to London Allendale and Milan; formerly above Massacre in S. Agostino, Siena?). 14(82?). *Plate* 816.

55.176. Madonna and Child with two Angels (st.).

55.177. Fragment (from portable altarpiece?): S. Jerome (companion to Altenburg).

Florence. UFFIZI. 3578. Madonna and Child with four Angels.

3949. Oval fragment: Madonna and Child with SS. John Baptist and Jerome and two Angels.

MUSEO HORNE. 72. Madonna and Child with SS. Peter and Jerome. E.

BERENSON COLLECTION. Madonna and Child with SS. Jerome and Catherine and Cherubim.

Bust of Saint (possibly from polyptych of Assumption, see London).

Predella panel: S. Monica prays for S. Augustine who reads the epistles of S. Paul (st.; see Mells).

Gazzada (Varese). FONDAZIONE CAGNOLA. Madonna and Child with SS. Jerome Bernardino and two Angels (r.).

Genoa. GNECCO COLLECTION. Madonna and Child.

Grosseto. DUOMO, L. WALL. Madonna and Angels (fr. of Assumption). E.

London. 247. 'Ecce Homo.'

1155. Centre panel of polyptych: Assumption (companion to Asciano). Formerly Sd and d. 1474. [*Plate 276.*]

1461. S. Sebastian and Angels (Angels and Landscape by Cozzarelli).

LORD ALLENDALE (EX). S. Augustine (fr. of lunette, companion to Esztergom and Milan; formerly above Massacre at S. Agostino, Siena?). 14(82?). *Plate* 815.

MRS DEREK FITZGERALD (EX?). Madonna and Child with SS. Jerome and Sebastian (r.).

Mauchline (Ayr., Scotland). BALLOCHMYLE HOUSE, SIR CLAUD ALEXANDER (EX). Predella panel: Christ with Mary and Martha.

Meiningen. SCHLOSS (EX). Madonna and Child with SS. Francis and Anthony of Padua.

Mells (Frome, Somerset). EARL OF OXFORD AND ASQUITH. Predella panel companion to Chicago (and Florence, Berenson?): Crucifixion (possibly predella to Massacre in S. Agostino, Siena). 14(82?).

Milan. SAIBENE COLLECTION. S. Francis (fr. of lunette to Massacre of Innocents in S. Agostino, Siena; companion to Esztergom and London, ex Allendale). 1482. *Plate* 817.

Montepescali (Grosseto). UPPER CHURCH. Madonna and Child with SS. Sebastian. Mary Magdalen, Lucy, Roch and Angels (g.p.). L.

Naples. 38. Massacre of Innocents. 14(8)8. *Plate* 818.

New York. 41.100.17. Madonna and Child with SS. Jerome and Bernardino and two Angels (r.).

41.190.29. Madonna and Child with six Saints (st).

MISS HELEN FRICK. Madonna and Child with SS. Jerome and Sebastian and two Angels.

R. M. HURD (EX). 'Palmieri Nuti' Madonna and Child.

R. LEHMAN. Madonna and Child with SS. Jerome and Mary Magdalen. Madonna and Child with SS. Francis and Clare.

E. FOWLES. Madonna and Child.

Paris. 1660. Predella panel, companion to Philadelphia: Birth of Virgin. E.

Philadelphia (Pa.). J. G. JOHNSON COLLECTION. 107, 108. Predella panels: Marriage of Virgin (to left, portraits of Alberti and Donatello); Visitation (companions to Paris). E. *Plate* 809.

Pienza. PALAZZO PICCOLOMINI. Madonna and Child with S. Raphael and Tobias, S. Sebastian and three Innocents.

DUOMO, R. TRANSEPT. Madonna and Child with SS. Catherine, Matthew, Bartholomew and Lucy; in lunette, Flagellation; in predella, three roundels with Dead Christ, mourning Virgin and Evangelist. Sd and d. 1462.

— OVER ENTRANCE TO CAMPANILE. Madonna and Child enthroned with kneeling SS. Augustine and Nicholas, standing SS. Jerome and Martin (formerly Oratorio della Misericordia). *Plate* 812.

Providence (R.I.). 57.307. Virgin of Annunciation (possibly from Polyptych of the Assumption, see London). 1474?

Ravenna. 209. Madonna and Child with SS. Barbara and Jerome. E. *Plate* 808.

Rome. ACCADEMIA DI S. LUCA, GIFT LAZZARONI. Madonna and Child with S. Catherine.

San Diego (Cal.). FINE ARTS GALLERY. 'Platt' Madonna and Child with two Angels and SS. Jerome and John Baptist.

San Francisco (Cal.). DE YOUNG MEMORIAL MUSEUM. 61.44.8–9 (KRESS COLLECTION. K 1745 a, b). Predella panels to Massacre of Innocents in S. Maria dei Servi, Siena: The three Kings before Herod; Crucifixion. 1491.

San Marino (Cal.). HUNTINGTON GALLERY. Madonna and Child with two Angels and SS. Sebastian and Jerome.

San Sepolcro. DUOMO, L. WALL. Polyptych: full-length SS. Peter and Paul; Angel and Virgin of Annunciation in roundels above; six small Saints in pilasters of frame; in predella, Birth of Baptist, Baptist preaching in Wilderness, Crucifixion, Baptist preaching to Herod, Salome's Dance, and four small Saints in niches (central panel by Piero della Francesca, with Baptism of Christ, London 665). E.

   S. MARIA DEI SERVI, CHOIR. Triptych: Assumption of Virgin; SS. Philip Benizzi and John Baptist; SS. Paul and Lucy; in predella, Life of Virgin. 1487.

Siena. 280. Madonna and Child with SS. John Evangelist and James and two Angels.

   283. Madonna and Child against landscape. L.

   286. Madonna and Child enthroned with four Angels (from S. Maria dei Servi). Sd and d. 1470.

   399. Madonna and Child with SS. Jerome and Francis. L.

   400. Madonna and Child with two Angels, S. Mary Magdalen and S. Michael.

   414. Lunette to 'Placidi' Triptych in S. Domenico: Nativity. 1476. (Madonna and Saints below is by Girolamo di Benvenuto.)

   432. Madonna and Child with four Angels, SS. Cosmas, Damian, Galganus and Sebastian.

   446. Madonna and Child, Angel offering fruit, S. Sebastian and S. Catherine of Siena (g.p.).

   GIUSEPPINA LICCIOLI (EX). Madonna adoring Child with S. Raphael and Tobias, S. Sebastian and three Putti.

   CANONICO MANFREDO TARCHI (EX). Madonna and Child with SS. Jerome and Margaret and two Angels.

   CONTE TOLOMEI. Madonna and Child with SS. Jerome, John Baptist and two Angels.

   S. AGOSTINO, CAPPELLA PICCOLOMINI, L. WALL. Massacre of Innocents (for missing lunette, see Esztergom, London and Homeless; for missing predella, see Chicago and Mells). Sd and d. 1482. *Plate* 819.

   S. DOMENICO, L. TRANSEPT, SECOND CHAPEL. S. Barbara enthroned with SS. Mary Magdalen, Catherine and Angels; in lunette, Adoration of Magi. Sd and d. 1479. *Plate* 811.

— — THIRD CHAPEL. 'Placidi' Triptych: Madonna and Child enthroned and ten
Angels; kneeling SS. John Baptist and Jerome in landscape (lunette in Pinacoteca 414). 1476.

— RIGHT NAVE, LAST ALTAR BEFORE TRANSEPT. Lunette: Pietà with SS. Mary Magdalen and Michael (over Nativity by Francesco di Giorgio). [*Plate 275.*]

S. EUGENIO (PORTA PISPINI). Madonna and Child with SS. Jerome and Eugenia and
two Angels.

S. MARIA ASSUNTA (DUOMO). L. TRANSEPT, FLOOR. Marble intarsia: Judith liberates
Bethulia (with Urbano da Cortona and Federighi), 1473; Massacre of Innocents, 1481 (see also Beccafumi, Benvenuto di Giovanni, Domenico di Bartolo). *Plate 814.*

— L. NAVE, FLOOR. Marble intarsia: Samian Sibyl. 1483 (see also Cozzarelli, Benvenuto di Giovanni, Neroccio).

— MUSEO DELL'OPERA. 5. Madonna and Child enthroned with six Angels, SS.
Anthony of Padua and Bernardino. Sd and d. 1460. *Plate 810*

7, 8. Madonna and Child with two Angels, SS. John Evangelist, Nicholas,
Gregory and Jerome; in predella, S. John Evangelist in cauldron of boil-
ing oil, S. Nicholas and the three maidens without dowry, Resurrection,
S. Gregory heading procession of Cardinals stays the plague that was rava-
ging Rome, S. Jerome healing the lion (pilasters and top panel missing).
Formerly Sd and d. 1480.

S. MARIA DELLE NEVI, HIGH ALTAR. Madonna and Child with SS. Peter, John Evangelist, Lawrence and Catherine of Siena and Angels; in predella, Legend of
S. Maria delle Nevi. Sd and d. 1477.

S. MARIA DEI SERVI, FIFTH ALTAR R. Massacre of Innocents; in lunette, Madonna and
Child with SS. Andrew, Ansanus, two Angels and two donors (for missing
predella, see San Francisco). Sd and d. 1491. *Plate 820.*

S. PIETRO OVILE, FIRST ALTAR R. Annunciation (after Simone Martini's now at
Uffizi) with the addition of Crucifixion, S. Peter and S. Paul in pinnacles, and
of SS. John Baptist and Bernardino as side-panels. E.

Tarquinia (Viterbo). PALAZZO VITELLESCHI, MUSEO, ANTICAPPELLA. S. Paul (fr. from
polyptych, r.).

Turin. GALLERIA SABAUDA, GUALINO COLLECTION. 658. Madonna and Child with SS.
Bernardino and Jerome (formerly Goettingen 221).

Washington (D.C.). 9 (MELLON COLLECTION). Madonna and Child with four Angels
and Cherubim.

408 (KRESS COLLECTION 517). Madonna and Child with two Angels and SS.
Jerome and Catherine.

Williamstown (Mass.). STERLING AND FRANCINE CLARK ART INSTITUTE. 'Butler'
Madonna and Child with two Angels.

Homeless. Angel of Annunciation (companion to Providence, possibly from Assumption polyptych of 1474—see London; repr. *Proporzioni*, 1950, pp. 82–85).

MATTEO DA GUALDO

Gualdo Tadino. Born ca 1435, mentioned up to 1503. Pupil of Giovanni Boccatis; influenced by Girolamo di Giovanni da Camerino, by Benozzo Gozzoli, perhaps quite early by Crivelli and later by German woodcuts.

Aix-en-Provence. 393. Panels from pilasters of polyptych: S. Bernardino, Bishop Saint, S. Catherine, S. Paul Hermit.

Assisi. PINACOTECA. Two detached frescoes: Busts of Angels (frs.).

    ORATORIO DEI PELLEGRINI, ALTAR WALL. Frescoes: Annunciation around window; below, imaginary Renaissance portico with putti throwing flowers on cornice and Angels holding candelabra at sides; in this portico, Madonna and Child enthroned with ten Angels, S. James the More, S. Anthony Abbot. Sd and d. 1468. *Plate 643.*

— VAULT. Frescoes: Seraphim. 1468.

— FAÇADE. Christ in Glory of Angels between SS. James the More and Anthony Abbot (r.). 1468.

    S. PAOLO (CONFRATERNITA DI), ALTAR WALL. Fresco: Madonna and Child enthroned with SS. Lucy, Ansanus and kneeling donor; Angels musicians above. d. 10 November 1475.

    S. PIETRO, L. TRANSEPT. Triptych: Madonna and Child enthroned with Angel musicians, S. Peter and S. Victorinus. Sd.

    S. RUFINO (DUOMO), MUSEO CAPITOLARE. Triptych from Palazzo: Madonna and Child enthroned with Angels, S. Francis and S. Sebastian.

    (Environs). PALAZZO, CAPPELLA DELLA CONFRATERNITA DELLA BUONA MORTE, R. WALL. Frescoes: above, Annunciation (fr.); below, Madonna enthroned suckling the Child between S. Bernardino and another Saint (fr.).

Baltimore (Md.). 691. Madonna and Child in frame of carnations.* *Plate 641.*

Boston (Mass.). 47.233, 234. Detached frescoes from Acciano (Nocera Umbra): S. Sebastian and small donor; Madonna and Child enthroned (st.).

Casa Castalda (Valfabbrica, Umbria). PARISH CHURCH, L. WALL. Polyptych: Madonna and Child enthroned with five Angels, S. Peter, S. Paul; upper register, S. Michael, Pietà, S. John Baptist. Sd and d. 1478.

Coldellanoce (Sassoferrato). S. LORENZO MARTIRE. Triptych: Madonna and Child enthroned with five Angels and kneeling donor, S. Lawrence, S. Sebastian; in roundels above, God the Father, Angel and Virgin of Annunciation. Sd and d. 1471.

Gualdo Tadino. PINACOTECA (now transferred to S. FRANCESCO). Madonna and Child enthroned, with SS. Francis, Bernardino, Margaret and Catherine; two Bishop Saints in roundels above. Sd and d. 1462. *Plate 639.*

    Triptych: Madonna and Child enthroned with two Angels; Baptist and Evangelist; in predella, Baptism of Christ, half-length S. Francis, Last Supper, half-length S. Pasquale, Miracle of S. John Evangelist. Sd and d. 1471.

Triptych: Madonna and Child enthroned with two Angels and Christ on Cross
in roundel above; SS. Secundus and Anthony Abbot; SS. Sebastian and
Facondinus Bishop. Sd and d. 1477.

Annunciation.

Tree of Jesse (p.).

Processional standard from Nasciano: Madonna in Glory; Assumption (r.).
d. 1486.

S. FRANCESCO, SECOND ALTAR L. Fresco: Madonna and Child with S. Francis.

— THIRD ALTAR L. Fresco: S. Nicholas of Tolentino (fr.). Formerly d. 1466. (?)

— ENTRANCE. Frescoed lunette: Story of S. Giuliano between S. Bernardino and
S. John Baptist. d. 1469. (?)

— LEFT WALL, BETWEEN FIRST AND SECOND CHAPEL. Fresco: Madonna and Child in
the lap of S. Anne (found under whitewash 1955–60).*

— APSE. Fresco: Christ on Cross with kneeling knight.*

— ENTRANCE WALL. Frescoes: Madonna and Child with SS. Francis, Secundus and
kneeling youth; S. Anthony Abbot and the dragon; Trinity.*

S. ROCCO, L. WALL. Fresco: Madonna and Child enthroned with Angels.

Fresco: Madonna and Child with SS. Sebastian and (lost) Roch. d. 1511 (by his
son Girolamo?).

(Environs). NASCIANO, S. MARIA. Polyptych: Madonna and Child enthroned, S.
Roch, S. Sebastian; upper register, Circumcision, Angel and Virgin of
Annunciation. Sd and d. 1480.

Nocera Umbra. PINACOTECA (EX-CHURCH OF S. FRANCESCO). 7. Altarpiece from
Cappella della Concezione, Duomo: Meeting of Joachim and Anne, with
Virgin Immaculate, God the Father and Angels above; in pilasters, eight small
Saints in Gothic niches (SS. Agnes, Blaise, Magdalen, Blessed Angelo di
Nocera, SS. Bartholomew, Lucy, Rinaldo) (p.). L.

8. Votive fresco: Full-length Madonna and Child with S. John Baptist. d.
149(8?).

9. Votive fresco: Annunciation. L.*

10. Votive fresco: S. Francis receiving Stigmata. d. 1497.*

11. Votive fresco: S. Anthony reading a book. L.*

14. Votive fresco: S. Roch (fr.). d. 1508 (by his son Girolamo?).

Perugia. 878. Frescoed tabernacle from Colle Aprico: Madonna and Child enthroned with four Angels; in embrasure, blessing God the Father, S. Sebastian
and S. Anthony Abbot, Sd and d. 1488. *Plate 642.*

Sigillo (Gubbio). S. ANNA (CHIESA DEL CIMITERO), ALTAR WALL. Fresco: Madonna
and Child enthroned.

— L. WALL. Fresco: in lunette, Annunciation; below, SS. Nicholas of Tolentino,
Anthony Abbot and Sebastian. d. 1487.

— R. WALL. Fresco in lunette, S. Francis receiving Stigmata; below, Madonna del
Soccorso.

S. MARIA DELLA SCIRCA, R. WALL. Votive frescoes: Madonna and Child enthroned;

Madonna of Mercy; S. Anne with Madonna and Child in her lap. Sd and d. 1484. *Plate* 640.

Spoleto. PALAZZO ARCIVESCOVILE. Lateral Saints in triptych by Giovanni Francesco da Rimini. (?) *Plate* 638.

MATTEO GIOVANNETTI DA VITERBO

Mentioned in Viterbo 1322, 1326; active in Avignon from 1343 (or earlier) until he followed the Pope to Rome in 1367; died in Rome soon afterwards. School of Simone Martini.

Avignon (Gard). PALAIS DES PAPES, TOUR DE LA GARDEROBE, SALLE DE LA GARDE-ROBE OR DU CERF. Frescoed walls: scenes of hunting, fishing, fruit-gathering, against continuous background of trees, grass and bushes (p.). 1343–44. *Plate* 137.

— — CHAPELLE S. MICHEL (TOP FLOOR). Frescoes of Angels (only frs. of sinopie survive). 1344–45.

— — CHAPELLE S. MARTIAL (CAPELLA MAGNAE AULAE, CAPELLA TINELLI MAGNI), VAULT. Frescoes: Two stories of S. Martial in each quart of vault: (1) the boyish Saint listens to Christ preaching, is christened by S. Peter in the river; (2) Christ blesses the young Saint amidst the Apostles; (3) Christ orders S. Peter to send Martial to christianize Gaul and S. Peter sends S. Martial to preach with Alpinianus and Austriclianus; (4) S. Martial, now a Bishop, returns from Colle after the death of Austriclianus and S. Peter gives him the miraculous staff, which Martial uses to raise Austriclianus back to life; (5) S. Martial exorcizes the daughter of Arnulfus (Arnoux) in Tulle; (6) S. Martial raises to life the son of Nerva, Lord of Tulle, and christens his parents; (7) S. Martial admonishes the kneeling priests at Agen while two Angels force a demon to destroy a pagan idol; (8) S. Martial heals the paralytic at Agen and Christ orders him to go to Limoges. *Plate* 142.

— — — NORTH (L. OF ALTAR) WALL. Frescoes; in lunette, S. Martial raises Andreas and Aurelianus back to life; below, S. Martial ordains Aurelianus in the cathedral of Limoges, while the thirteen churches founded by S. Martial in France are shown to the right.

— — — WEST (ENTRANCE) WALL. Frescoes: in lunette, the wife of Sigebert Count of Bordeaux, using the staff of S. Martial, heals her paralytic husband and stops the fire of Bordeaux and obtains the destruction of pagan temples; below, Christ announces to S. Martial the martyrdom of SS. Peter and Paul, which is shown on the right.

— — — EAST (ALTAR) WALL. Frescoes: in lunette, Valeria having made the vow of chastity refuses to marry Duke Stephen, is beheaded, but her soul is taken to heaven by Angels while another Angel kills her executioner (fr.), Duke

Stephen repents, begs S. Martial to recall the executioner to life and is baptized; below, left, Christ announces to S. Martial his impending death, right, Christ, the Virgin and Saints, welcome the soul of S. Martial; over the altar, Crucifixion.

— — — SOUTH (R. OF ALTAR) WALL. Frescoes: in lunette, Duke Stephen implores S. Peter's absolution for Valeria's death and S. Martial raises to life the son of Accadius Count of Poitiers, strangled by a Demon near Vienne; below, left, miracles at the coffin of S. Martial, right, Alpinianus heals the sick by covering them with the shroud of S. Martial.

Frescoed decoration (r.). 1344–45.

— CHAPELLE S. JEAN (CAPELLA CONCISTORII) VAULT. Frescoes: SS. John Baptist, Elisabeth, Zacharias and Imerias; SS. John Evangelist, Mary Salome, Zebedaeus, Anne (two figures in each quart of vault).

— — NORTH WALL. Frescoes: in lunette (including window embrasure) Birth of Baptist, Zacharias and the Angel; below (including window embrasure) the Baptist hails Christ in the wilderness.

— — EAST WALL. Frescoes: in lunette (including window embrasure) Baptism of Christ, Baptist disputing with the Jews; below (including window embrasure) Beheading of the Baptist and his Head presented to Herodias and to Herod.

— — SOUTH WALL. Frescoes: in lunette (including window embrasure) Calling of the sons of Zebedee; below (including window embrasure) Christ appears to S. John Evangelist at Patmos, S. John Evangelist raises Drusiana.

— — WEST WALL. Frescoes: in lunette, Crucifixion; below, Miracle of S. John Evangelist (frs.). *Plate* 138.

Frescoed decoration (r.) 1347.

— SALLE DE L'AUDIENCE, VAULT. Frescoes above the destroyed Last Judgement on the North wall: in left pendentif, David, Solomon, Enoch, Job—Daniel, Oseas, Amos—Sophonias and Joel—Anne, mother of Samuel; in right pendentif, Ezechiel, Jeremiah, Isajah, Moses—Abdias, Michaes, Nahum—Habakkuk, Malachias—the Erythrean Sibyl. 1352. *Plate* 140.

— — EAST WALL, BETWEEN WINDOWS. Fresco: Christ on Cross with two Angels and two Prophets above, mourning Virgin and John Evangelist, four Church Fathers and worshipping (judges?) below (frs. of sinopia only). 1352.

Paris. FODOR COLLECTION. Centre panel of portable altarpiece: Madonna and Child ca 1345.

Udine. CONTE CERNAZAI (EX). Fragments of portable altarpiece: Angel and Virgin of Annunciation, S. Anthony Abbot, S. Catherine.*

Venice. MUSEO CORRER. 408, 409. Wings of portable altarpiece: S. Hermagoras with kneeling donor; S. Fortunatus (companions to Paris?). *Plate* 139.

Villeneuve-lès-Avignon (Gard). CHARTREUSE, CHAPELLE, POLYGONAL APSE. Frescoes: on the three central walls—full-length Saints holding scroll on either side of

windows and, below windows, Crucifixion and Madonna and Child enthroned worshipped by Pope Innocent VI.

— — WALL TO THE EXTREME RIGHT. Frescoes: in lunette, seated Evangelist (lost);
top register—Zacharias and the Angel, Visitation; middle register—Birth of
Baptist, Naming of Baptist; low register—full-length Blessed Pope Urban II,
SS. Vincent, Stephen and Lawrence. *Plate* 141.

— — WALL TO THE EXTREME LEFT. Frescoes: in lunette, seated Evangelist (lost); top
register—Baptist in prison and Miracles of Christ; middle register—Beheading
of Baptist, his head presented to Herodias, then to Herod, Burial of the
beheaded body; low register—lost frescoes.

Frescoed decoration (r.). 1355–56.

MAZZOLINO, Ludovico

*Ferrara. ca 1478–1528. Pupil of Ercole Roberti; influenced by Costa, Dosso and con-
temporary Flemings.*

Alnwick Castle (Northumberland). DUKE OF NORTHUMBERLAND. Christ driving the
Money-changers from the Temple. L. *Plate* 1738.

Amsterdam. 1534–E 2 (Formerly Mauritshuis, Hague). Massacre of Innocents; in
background, Adoration of Magi and Flight into Egypt.

     H. TIETJE (EX). 'Oldenburg' Holy Family with S. Elizabeth and Infant S. John.
Sd and d. 1511. *Plate* 1731.

Berlin. 270. Holy Family.

     273. Christ and the Doctors.

     S14. Small monstrance with S. Jerome on one side and S. Michael on the other
side. (Lost since 1945.)

Berlin-Ost. 266. Christ and the Doctors. Sd and d. 1524. *Plate* 1739.

     275. Triptych: Madonna and Child, SS. Anthony Abbot and Mary Magdalen.
d. 1509. *Plate* 1730.

Bologna. Inv. 563. Adoration of Shepherds. 1524.

     Inv. 118. The Eternal. 1524.

Brescia. 705. 'Noli me tangere.'

Budapest. 4247 (PÁLFFY 75). Christ before Pilate.

Cambridge. FITZWILLIAM MUSEUM. MARLAY BEQUEST. 55. Christ before Pilate (st.).

Chantilly. 36. 'Ecce Homo.'

     37. Madonna and Child with S. Anthony Abbot. d. 1526. *Plate* 1736.

Cremona. 128. Madonna and Child enthroned with SS. Peter and Andrew. L.

Dresden. 123. 'Ecce Homo'.

Dublin. 666. Pharaoh and his host overwhelmed in the Red Sea. *Plate* 1737.

Easton Neston (Towcester, Northants). LORD HESKETH (EX). Adoration of Magi.
d. 1522. *Plate* 1734.

Ferrara. 47. Nativity and Saints.

    S. FRANCESCO, PILLAR BETWEEN SIXTH AND SEVENTH CHAPEL R. Fresco: Two Executioners (at sides of marble Christ).

Florence. PITTI. 129. Christ and the Woman taken in Adultery.

    UFFIZI. 1347. Madonna and Child with S. Anne, S. Joachim and S. John Evangelist.

        1350. Massacre of Innocents (st.).

        1352. Nativity.

        1355. Circumcision.

Kiev. 78. Nativity.

Lisbon. ACADEMIA REAL. Holy Family with S. Francis.

London. 82. Holy Family with SS. Elizabeth, Infant John and Francis.

    169. Holy Family.

    641. Christ and the Woman taken in Adultery.

    1495. Christ disputing with the Doctors.

    3114. Nativity.

Milan. BRERA. 'Crespi.' Raising of Lazarus. d. 1527.

    G. BARGELLESI (EX MASSARI ZAVAGLIA). The Eternal.

    GUSTAVO FRIZZONI (EX). Madonna and Child with Saints and a pilgrim.

Munich. W.A.F. 575. Holy Family. 1516.

New York. HISTORICAL SOCIETY. Penitent S. Jerome.

Nice. MUSÉE CHÉRET. Adoration of Shepherds. (?)

Oxford. CHRIST CHURCH. 157. 'Nosworthy' Tribute Money.

Paris. 1387. Holy Family.

    BOURGEOIS COLLECTION (EX). Nativity. *Plate* 1732.

Philadelphia (Pa.). J. G. JOHNSON COLLECTION. 248. Washing of Feet.

Ponce (Puerto Rico). MUSEO DE ARTE. 62.0262. KRESS COLLECTION. K 1205. Eternal blessing.

Poznań. Inv. Mo 20. Christ drives the Money-changers from the Temple. d. 1524.

Rome. CAMPIDOGLIO, PINACOTECA. 13. Nativity.

    GALLERIA BORGHESE. 218. Adoration of Magi.

        223. Doubting Thomas. *Plate* 1735.

        247. Nativity.

        451. Christ and the Woman taken in Adultery.

    GALLERIA DORIA PAMPHILI. 120. Massacre of Innocents.

        137. Pietà.

    — PRIVATE APARTMENTS. Christ disputing with the Doctors.

    PRINCE LUDOVICO CHIGI DELLA ROVERE ALBANI (EX). Adoration of Magi. Sd and d.

        1512. *Plate* 1733.

Sarasota (Fla.). RINGLING MUSEUM. Nativity.

Turin. 154. Madonna and Child with three Saints (the frame painted by Garofalo).

Venice. CONTE VITTORIO CINI. Inv. 6700. Circumcision.

    Inv. 6488. 'Cook' Pietà.

Vienna. 88. Circumcision. d. 1526.

AKADEMIE. 495. Madonna and Child with S. Jerome in landscape.

MELONI see ALTOBELLO

MELOZZO DA FORLÌ

Melozzo (degli) Ambrogi, da Forlì. 1438–94. *Pupil of Piero della Francesca.*

Berlin. 54, 54A. Dialectic and Astronomy (from Library of Ducal Palace at Urbino, companions to London; execution by Berruguete). (Destroyed 1945.)

Bologna. PINACOTECA, DEPOT. Profile bust of elderly nobleman in prayer. (?)

Florence. UFFIZI. 3341, 3343. Cut down organ-shutters: outside—unfinished Angel of Annunciation, Virgin of Annunciation finished by other hand; inside—half-figure of S. Prosdocimus and S. John Evangelist.

MUSEO HORNE. 30. Bust of Christ. (?)

Forlì. PINACOTECA. Fresco: 'Pestapepe'. [*Plate* 284.]

SAN BIAGIO E GIROLAMO, CAPPELLA FEO. Frescoes (see under Palmezzano). Before 1495.

London. 755, 756. Rhetoric, Music (from Library of Ducal Palace at Urbino, companions to Berlin; execution by Berruguete).

Loreto. SANTUARIO, SAGRESTIA DI S. MARCO O DEL TESORO VECCHIO. Frescoes: Vault—eight Prophets (Zacharias, Abdias, Ezekiel, Baruch, Isaiah, Jeremiah, David, Amos) and eight Angels with Symbols (Olive-branch, Lamb, Chalice, Purse and Rope, Column, Cross, Nails, Tongs). Wall—Entry into Jerusalem (execution entirely by Palmezzano). Probably 1484–87. *Plates* 996, 997.

Madrid. 2843. Fragment of fresco: Music-making Angel.

Rome. GALLERIA COLONNA. 216. Profile of boy (Guidobaldo da Montefeltro?).

PALAZZO DEL QUIRINALE, SCALONE. Fragment of fresco once in cupola of SS. Apostoli: Christ of Ascension (companion to Vatican). Probably before 1480.

S. MARCO. S. Mark enthroned as Pope; S. Mark writing.

VATICAN, PINACOTECA. 269. Fragments of fresco once in cupola of SS. Apostoli: music-making Angels, Apostles and Cherubim (companions to Quirinale). Probably before 1480. [*Plate* 283.]

270. Inauguration of the Library of Sixtus IV, with the Pope surrounded by Girolamo Riario, Giovanni della Rovere, Platina, Giuliano della Rovere, Raffaele Riario. Not after 1477. *Plate* 995.

— BIBLIOTECA DI SISTO IV. Ornamental frescoes and lunette with SS. Gregory and Jerome (execution by Antoniazzo). 1480–81.

Turin. GALLERIA SABAUDA, GUALINO COLLECTION 660. Bust of Redeemer crowned by Angels (execution by other hand).

Urbino. GALLERIA NAZIONALE DELLE MARCHE. Bust of Redeemer. E.

LIPPO MEMMI

Sienese. Active 1317–57. Pupil, probably, of his father Memmo, assistant of Simone Martini, influenced by the Lorenzettis.

Altenburg. 43. Madonna and Child on draped throne. Sd. *Plate* 305.

44, 45. Pinnacles of polyptych: Two hermit Saints (st.) (see Berlin 1067).

Berlin. 1067. Centre panel of polyptych: Half-length Madonna and Child (companion to New Haven, New York, Paris, Siena and Washington side-panels, to Altenburg and Douai pinnacles; probably parts of dismembered polyptych from high altar of S. Paolo in Ripa d'Arno at Pisa, formerly signed and dated 1325). (g.p.)

1072. Left panel of diptych: Madonna of Humility suckling the Child (contemporary copy of lost original?).

1081A. Left panel of diptych: Madonna and Child; Angel of Annunciation in roundel above (from Camposanto, Pisa; companion to New York, Golovin). Sd. *Plate* 304.

1511. Madonna and Child (r.).

Boston (Mass.). 36.144. Madonna and Child (copy by Bartolo di Fredi?).

GARDNER MUSEUM. Madonna and Child; below, busts of SS. Catherine, Paul, Dominic, Stephen and kneeling Dominican.

Douai. 34. Pinnacle of polyptych: Blessing Christ (st.) (see Berlin 1067).

Florence. UFFIZI. 452, 453. Side-panels to Simone Martini's Annunciation (on his design): S. Ansanus, S. Margaret. 1333. *Plates* 301–302.

Kansas City (Mo.). 61–62 (KRESS COLLECTION. K 1343). Portable altarpiece: Madonna and Child; S. John Baptist and Bishop Saint in roundels above.

Munich. 986 (H.G. 671). Centre panel of triptych: Assumption and Coronation. (?)

New Haven (Conn.). 1943.239. Right panel of polyptych: S. John Evangelist (see Berlin 1067).

New York. 43.98.6. 'Griggs' portable altarpiece: Madonna and Child with S. John Baptist, S. Francis and Angels; below, seven busts of Saints.

88.3.99. Left panel of polyptych: S. Paul (see Berlin 1067).

W. B. GOLOVIN. Right leaf of diptych: S. John Baptist (r.; pinnacle missing; companion to Berlin 1081A).

R. LEHMAN COLLECTION (EX?). Madonna and Child (face repainted by Spinello?).

Orvieto. DUOMO, CAPPELLA DEL S. CORPORALE, R. WALL. 'Madonna dei Raccomandati' (r.). Sd. 1320.

Pisa. S. CATERINA, LEFT WALL. Triumph of S. Thomas Aquinas (Follower of Lippo Memmi and Barna, close to Traini; possibly author of Altenburg 44, 45, Douai 34). *Plate* 299.

Poznań. Inv. MO 46. Cut-down left panel of polyptych: S. John Evangelist writing on book supported by eagle.*

San Gimignano. PALAZZO DEL POPOLO, SALA DI DANTE, R. WALL. Fresco: 'Maestà' with Podestà Mino de' Tolomei (begun by Lippo's father Memmo, to whom the heads of the bearded old men to right may be ascribed; figures extreme right, repainted in 1467 by Benozzo Gozzoli). Sd and d. 1317. *Plate* 300.

S. AGOSTINO, FOURTH ALTAR L. Fresco: Madonna suckling the Child, with S. Michael and (lost) Knight of the Salvucci family (r.). 1330.

Siena. 48, 49. Left and right panel of polyptych: S. Louis of Toulouse, S. Francis (see Berlin 1067).

595. Centre panel of polyptych from S. Bernardo at Montepulciano: Madonna and Child; Christ as Judge in trefoil above (centre panel to Homeless Evangelist and Peter?). *Plate* 317.

S. DOMENICO, CLOISTER. Fresco: Maestà (fr.). Formerly Sd.

S. MARIA DEI SERVI, R. TRANSEPT, SECOND CHAPEL. 'Madonna del Popolo.' Sd. *Plate* 306.

S. PELLEGRINO ALLA SAPIENZA, R. WALL. Panel of polyptych: Full-length Blessed Andrea Gallerani.

Washington (D.C.). 11 (MELLON COLLECTION). 'Benson' Madonna and Child with donor. *Plate* 303.

402 (KRESS COLLECTION 511). Left panel of polyptych: S. John Baptist (see Berlin 1067).

Homeless. Left and right panels of polyptych: S. John Evangelist writing, and Angel blowing trumpet in trefoil above; S. Peter with keys and book, and Angel blowing trumpet in trefoil above (companions to Siena 595?) (r.). *Plates* 316, 318.

MEO DA SIENA

Sienese, active end of thirteenth and first decades of fourteenth century, chiefly at Perugia. Pupil of Duccio.

Frankfurt a/M. 1201, 1202. Dossal: Christ enthroned and six full-length Saints on either side, with Angels in spandrels; Madonna and Child enthroned, flanked by Angels, worshipped by kneeling Monk, and six full-length Saints on either side, with Prophets in spandrels. d. 1333. *Plates* 24–27.

Gubbio. PINACOTECA. Shrine for relics, from S. Francesco: Redeemer and six busts of Saints, above and below a Byzantine diptych; on inside wings, half-length SS. Francis and Clare and four other Saints; outside, Prophets, Madonna and Child.

Perugia. 1. Polyptych from Montelabbate: Madonna and Child, S. Gregory, missing Saint, S. John Evangelist, S. Milianus; upper row: two Prophets and six Saints (two missing); in pinnacles, blessing Redeemer and four Angels; in predella, SS. Peter and Paul and ten Apostles. Sd. *Plate* 28.

8. Madonna and Child (from Carità; r.).

13. Polyptych from S. Domenico: Madonna and Child, SS. John Baptist and Evangelist, Apostle and Bishop Saint.

30. Madonna and Child (from Abbazia di Montelabbate).

S. LORENZO (DUOMO), MUSEO DELL'OPERA. 7. Triptych: Madonna and Child, SS. John Baptist and John Evangelist; in pinnacles, blessing Redeemer, SS. Peter and Paul.

Worcester (Mass.). 1922.16. Madonna and Child and SS. Peter, Paul, John Baptist and John Evangelist, under a canopy held by Angels. L. (?)

MEZZASTRIS (Pier Antonio da Foligno)

1430–1506. Fellow-pupil of Niccolò da Foligno; developed under influence of Fra Angelico, Benozzo Gozzoli and, possibly, Sassetta.

Assisi. S. DAMIANO, CHOIR. Fresco: Christ on Cross with mourning Virgin and John. d. 1482.

S. MARIA DEGLI ANGELI, MUSEO. Detached fresco: Madonna and Child with four Angels.

ORATORIO DEI PELLEGRINI. Frescoed decoration ca 1468/70 (frescoes on altar-wall by Matteo da Gualdo. d. 1468). Sd.

— VAULT. Fresco: Four Church Fathers.

— L. WALL. Fresco: S. Anthony Abbot blessing camels and distributing alms. *Plate 646.*

— R. WALL. Fresco: S. James saves from death by hanging the young pilgrim falsely accused of theft. *Plate 644.*

— ENTRANCE WALL. Fresco: Christ in glory; below, S. James and S. Anthony Abbot.

Foligno. PALAZZO TRINCI, PINACOTECA. 4. Detached fresco: Crucifixion (fr.).

29. Detached fresco: Angel of Annunciation (fr.).

30. Detached frescoed lunette from S. Vincenzo, Bevagna: Christ on Cross with mourning Virgin, Magdalen, SS. Peter, Paul and John Baptist (fr.).

31. Detached fresco: S. Jerome as penitent and S. Jerome as Doctor.

32. Detached fresco: Madonna and Child with Angels, Baptist and S. Dominic.

33. Detached fresco: Madonna and Child with two Angels and Simeon.

34. Detached fresco: Madonna and Child with seven Saints (fr.).

35. Detached fresco: Madonna crowned by Angels. Sd and d. 1486.

36. Detached fresco: Madonna and Child with two Angels, S. Francis and S. John Baptist. Sd and d. 1499. *Plate 647.*

MONASTERO DI S. ANNA O DELLE CONTESSE, OVER ENTRANCE. Frescoed lunette: Madonna and Child with two female Saints and Angels.

— SECOND CLOISTER. Fresco: S. Francis receiving Stigmata. d. 1487.

MONASTERO DI S. LUCIA, OVER DOOR. Frescoed lunette: Madonna and Child with Angels, SS. Lucy and Clare. Sd and d. 1471. *Plate 645.*

Foligno (contd.). S. MARIA INFRAPORTAS, THIRD PILLAR L. Fresco: S. Roch and two Angels.

— R. PILLAR BY CHOIR. Fresco: S. Jerome crowned by Angels.

(Environs) MADONNA DELLA FIAMENGA, APSE. Fresco: Madonna and Child, Angels, Sibyls and Saints.

MAESTÀ BELLA. Frescoed tabernacle: Madonna and Child with SS. John Evangelist, John Baptist and two Angels; in embrasure, S. Peter and S. Paul; on face of arch, in roundels, blessing Christ, Angel and Virgin of Annunciation. Sd. *Plate* 648.

S. MARIA IN CAMPIS, CAPPELLA DI COLA DELLE CASSE, ALTAR WALL. Fresco: Crucifixion. ca 1456. *Plate* 649.

— L. WALL. Frescoes: Angel and Virgin of Annunciation and putti; below, S. Lucy.

— R. WALL. Fresco: 'Navicella' di S. Pietro (p.).

VESCIA, MAESTÀ DI S. ANNA. Frescoed tabernacle: Madonna and Child with S. Anne, S. Francis, S. Anthony Abbot and another Saint. L.

Montefalco. S. FRANCESCO (MUSEO), CAPPELLA DI S. ANTONIO (SECOND BAY L.). Frescoes: wall, Crucifixion, S. Anthony of Padua and two of his miracles; in soffit of arch fragments of (Annunciation?).

— CAPPELLA DI S. BERNARDINO (SECOND BAY R.). Frescoes: vault, S. Jerome (other Church Fathers lost); wall, Crucifixion, S. Bernardino and two Scenes from His Life; soffit of arch, Bust of Redeemer, S. Clare of Montefalco, S. Illuminata, Virgin adoring the Child, S. Bernardino. d. 1461.

— FOURTH BAY, R. WALL. Fresco: Madonna and Child with four Saints and four Angels.

— SIXTH BAY R. Fresco around a wooden crucifix: Mourning Virgin, Magdalen, S. Francis, S. John Evangelist (Mezzastris and Niccolò Alunno?).

S. FORTUNATO, L. ALTAR. Fresco: Pietà and two Angels.

Narni. PINACOTECA. Detached fresco from lunette: Madonna and Child with SS. Francis and Jerome.

S. FRANCESCO, CAPPELLA EROLI (FIRST R.). Frescoes: Scenes from Life of S. Francis (after Benozzo Gozzoli); two stories of S. Benedict.

Spello (Environs). S. GIROLAMO, PORTICO. Frescoes: S. Francis receiving Stigmata; Blessed Giacomo della Marca. d. 1498.

Trevi. PINACOTECA. Standard: Dead Christ with two Angels; back, Risen Christ with two Angels.

S. MARTINO, ALTAR R. OF CHOIR. Fresco: Madonna and Child with S. Francis, six Angels and another Franciscan Saint.

MICHELE PANNONIO or ONGARO or DI NICCOLÒ

Recorded at Ferrara 1415 to 1464. In his only known works, certainly late, close to Tura.

Budapest. 44 (101). 'Ceres' or 'Summer' for Studio of Borso d'Este at Belfiore (companion to London Tura and possibly to Florence, Strozzi 'Ferrarese before 1510'). Sd. *Plate 721.*

Ferrara. Inv. 72, 74. Side-panels of polyptych: S. Louis of France, S. Bernardino.

MICHELE DA VERONA

Verona. Died after 1536. Pupil of Domenico Morone, influenced by Montagna.

Berlin. LIPPMANN COLLECTION (EX). Two cassone panels: Story of Romans and Sabines.

London. 1214. Meeting of Coriolanus and Volumnia. *Plate 1291.*

Mells (Frome). EARL OF OXFORD AND ASQUITH. Allegorical scene (fr.). *Plate 1293.*

Milan. BRERA. 160. Crucifixion. Sd and d. 1501. *Plates 1292, 1294.*

Padua. 71 (Inv. 448). Madonna and Child with S. Rosa? and Catherine. (?)
   S. MARIA IN VANZO, OVER ENTRANCE. Crucifixion. Sd and d. 1505.

Piazzola sul Brenta (Padua). VILLA CAMERINI. S. Sebastian. *Plate 1296.*

Vaduz. LIECHTENSTEINSCHE SAMMLUNG (EX). 1120. Battle-scene. L. (?)

Venice. CONTE FOSCARI. Half-length S. Peter and two Saints (John Evangelist and Paul?) behind his shoulders.*

Verona. 187, 188, 190, 191. Legendary scenes.
   S. ANASTASIA, FIRST ALTAR L. Fresco: Crucifixion, Resurrection and Angels.
   S. CHIARA, FIRST CHAPEL L. Frescoes: (from top) Eternal and two Angels, Noah and Joshua in medallions, Blessing Christ in vault of niche, full-length Evangelists (with Francesco Morone, q.v.). Sd. 1508 (or 1509).
   S. MARIA DELLA VITTORIA NUOVA. Frescoed lunette: Eternal and Angels. (?)

Vienna. 212. Youth with helmet (after lost Giorgione). (?)

Villa Estense. S. ANDREA. Madonna and Child enthroned with SS. John Baptist, Andrew, Lawrence, Peter and music-making Angel. Sd and d. 1523. *Plate 1295.*

MICHELINO DA BESOZZO

Documented at Pavia 1388 (lost frescoes in S. Pietro in Ciel d'Oro) and 1394 (lost altar-piece of S. Mustiola), in Venice 1410; painter, designer and consultant of the Duomo di Milano 1404–1425; still living 1450.

Avignon. BIBLIOTHÈQUE. MS. III. Livre d'Heures.

Cologny. BIBLIOTECA BODMERIANA. Livre d'Heures.

Crevenna (Erba). S. SALVATORE. Fresco: Crucifixion.

New York. 43.98.7. Marriage of Virgin. L.

Paris. LOUVRE. 9833, 9833B. S. Peter, S. James (on parchment).

    BIBLIOTHÈQUE NATIONALE. MS. LAT. 5888 (from Castle of Pavia). Funeral oration for Gian Galeazzo Visconti, by Pietro del Castelletto: frontispiece, Madonna surrounded by Angels and Christ Child crowning Visconti, Monk in cathedra; following pages, genealogy of the Visconti. 1403.

Siena. 171. Marriage of S. Catherine. Sd. *Plate 535.*

MORANDO, Paolo, see CAVAZZOLA

MORETTO

Alessandro Bonvicino, called Moretto, Brescia 1498–1554. Pupil perhaps of Ferramola; strongly influenced by Savoldo and Titian, but also by Romanino and Lotto, and possibly by travelling Netherlanders.

Allington Castle. SIR MARTIN CONWAY (EX). S. Peter in meditation.

Asola (Brescia). S. ANDREA (DUOMO), IN VARIOUS CHAPELS. Eight temperas on canvas from Loggia of Palazzo Comunale, with figures in niches: Angel and Virgin of Annunciation, Prophet Isaiah, Erythrean Sibyl, S. Mark, S. Catherine with the wheel, S. Anthony of Padua, S. Norbert (r.).

Atlanta (Ga.). ART ASSOCIATION GALLERIES. 58.45 (KRESS COLLECTION. K 1630). Madonna and Child with SS. Roch and James (p. ?).

Basle. Inv. 1138. Madonna suckling the Child. L.

    Inv. 1351. Portrait of Pietro Aretino (fr.). 1544.

Belluno (Environs). S. GREGORIO NELLE ALPI. Madonna and Child with SS. Gregory and Valentin. E.

Bergamo. 192. Christ holding Cross worshipped by donor. Formerly d. 1518. *Plate 1699.*

    202. Madonna and Child with Infant S. John and donor as S. Joseph.

    602. Christ and Woman of Samaria. E.

    DR GIOVANNI FRIZZONI. Busts of SS. Stephen and Jerome.

    S. ALESSANDRO IN COLONNA, SACRISTY. Madonna adoring the Child (fr.). E.

    S. ANDREA, FIRST ALTAR R. Madonna and Child enthroned with SS. Andrew, Eusebia, Domnus and Domneus and bowl of fruit in foreground.

Berlin. 187. See Cassel.

    197. The Virgin and S. Elizabeth with the Holy Children appearing to two Camaldolese friars (Fra Bartolomeo Averoldi, Abbot of the Umiliati in Verona, and Aurelio his nephew). Sd and d. 1541. (Destroyed 1945.) *Plate 1706.*

    667. See Erfurt.

    OTTO HELD (EX). Holy Family with Infant S. John.

WESENDONCK COLLECTION (EX). Madonna and Child enthroned.

Bloomington (Ind.). INDIANA UNIVERSITY. 1.62.164 (KRESS STUDY COLLECTION. K 458). Adoring Angel in niche.

Bologna. MODIANO COLLECTION. 'Holford' Birth of Virgin. Sd. L.

Bordeaux. 113. Madonna and Child with S. Anthony Abbot (replica of Vaduz, Liechtenstein).

Brescia. 68. Detached fresco from ceiling: Moses and the burning Bush (companion to Brognoli Collection).

    71. Ecce Homo and Angel. L. *Plate* 1711.

    72. Nativity and Saints (from S. Maria delle Grazie). L. *Plate* 1710.

    73. Adoration of Shepherds. L.

    74. Banner of the Crosses (for Compagnia dell'Orifiamma). Formerly Sd. doc. 1520.

    76. Holy Family and donor (st. v.).

    79. Descent of the Holy Ghost (from S. Giuseppe).

    80. 'Terzi di Lana' altarpiece from S. Maria delle Grazie: SS. Anthony Abbot, Nicholas of Tolentino and Anthony of Padua.

    81. Half-length Salome.

    85. Risen Christ embracing His Mother (g.p.).

    87. Annunciation (after Titian's polyptych of 1522).

    88. Christ in Emmaus (fr.). *Plates* 1701–1702.

    89. Votive picture from S. Maria dei Miracoli: Two children recommended to the Madonna and Child by Galeazzo Rovelli as S. Nicholas. d. 1539.

    90. 'S. Euphemia altarpiece': Madonna appearing to SS. Euphemia, Justina, Benedict and Paterio.

    97. Madonna appearing to SS. Francis and S. Michael and Giulio Luzzago as donor (from S. Giuseppe). 1542.

    151. Bearded gentleman seated at table with letter in hand.

    517. Assumption (g.p.). L. (returned to Parish Church of Maguzzano).

BETTONI CAZZAGO COLLECTION. Moses striking water from the rock (companion to Chiari, Environs of Brescia, and to Milan, Conte Gussalli).

BROGNOLI COLLECTION. Detached frescoes from Chapel of Palazzo Martinengo Cesaresco: ten figures from Old Testament (companions to Pinacoteca 68, lent to Palazzo Martinengo). Commissioned 1529.

PALAZZO MARTINENGO DI PADERNELLO, NOW SALVADEGO. Frescoed hall: eight ladies seated on garden walls (the two ladies by the window, post 1543).

Bust of Mattia Ugoni Bishop of Famagosta looking up.

PALAZZO VESCOVILE. Madonna and Child in Glory, and S. John Evangelist, S. Lorenzo Giustiniani and Summa Sapientia.

ROTONDA (OR DUOMO VECCHIO), BEHIND HIGH ALTAR. Assumption. 1524/6.

— CAPPELLA DEL SACRAMENTO (R. OF CHOIR). Sacrifice of Abraham, Easter Meal, Vision of Elijah (1534), Abraham and Melchizedek, S. Mark, S. Luke (p.; possibly only Elijah). 1531-37.

Brescia (contd.). S. ANGELO. (See Seminario Vescovile.)

    S. CLEMENTE, HIGH ALTAR. Madonna appearing to SS. Clement, George, Dominic, Catherine and Magdalen. 1548.

    — SECOND ALTAR R. SS. Cecilia, Lucy, Agatha, Agnes and Barbara.

    — FIRST ALTAR L. S. Ursula and her maidens.

    — SECOND ALTAR L. Mystic Marriage of S. Catherine and Saints.

    — THIRD ALTAR L. Melchisedech and Abraham.

    S. CRISTO (CORPO DI CRISTO). Inside organ-shutters from S. Pietro in Oliveto: Flight and Fall of Simon Magus (companions to Seminario S. Angelo).

    S. FRANCESCO, FIRST ALTAR R. S. Margherita of Cortona between SS. Francis and Jerome. d. 1530.

    S. GIOVANNI EVANGELISTA, THIRD ALTAR R. Massacre of Innocents. 1530–32. *Plate* 1705.

    — HIGH ALTAR. Madonna and Child in Glory with SS. John Baptist, John Evangelist, Agnes, Augustine and two Augustinian Monks as donors; in lunette, blessing God the Father; in predella, monochrome David. Sd. 1521–24.

    — R. AND L. OF HIGH ALTAR. Organ-shutters: outside, Baptist, Evangelist; inside, S. John Baptist taking leave of his parents; S. John Baptist preaching.

    — CAPPELLA DEL SACRAMENTO (CORPUS DOMINI), ALTAR WALL. Lunette: Coronation of Virgin, SS. Gregory the Great, Sylvia, Monica and Augustine, and Francesco and Giovanni Casari as donors. Sd.

    — — R. WALL. In lunette, Last Supper; in embrasure of arch, six squares with Prophets (Jeremiah, Daniel, Hagias, Micheas, Hoseas, David King—p.); below, Fall of Manna, Vision of Elijah, Evangelist Luke, Evangelist Mark. Commissioned 1521 to be finished by 1524 (see also under Romanino). [*Plate* 382.] *Plate* 1700.

    S. MARIA IN CALCHERA, FIRST ALTAR L. Christ in House of Simon. L. *Plate* 1709.

    — SMALL CHAPEL R. Dead Christ worshipped by SS. Dorothy and Jerome. E.

    S. MARIA DELLE GRAZIE, SEVENTH ALTAR R. Madonna and Child in Glory with SS. Martin, Sebastian and Roch.

    SS. NAZZARO E CELSO, SECOND ALTAR L. 'Soncini altarpiece': Coronation of Virgin and SS. Michael, Joseph, Francis and Nicholas (panels from predella—Nativity in oval, Angel and Virgin of Annunciation in roundels—kept in Sacristy). 1534. *Plate* 1703.

    — THIRD ALTAR R. Blood of the Redeemer; below, Moses and David. 1541/2.

    — ATRIO. Outside organ-shutters: Angel and Virgin of Annunciation (inside by Paolo da Caylina the Younger). E.

    SEMINARIO VESCOVILE S. ANGELO (PALAZZO GAMBARA), AULA MAGNA. Outside organ-shutters from S. Pietro in Oliveto: SS. Peter and Paul support the Church (companions to S. Cristo).

    — CAPPELLA, HIGH ALTAR. Coronation of Virgin with SS. Peter and Paul, Justice and Peace (formerly High Altar of S. Pietro in Castello). L.

    (Environs). CHIARI, MAZZOTTI COLLECTION. Drunkenness of Noah (companion to Brescia, Bettoni Cazzago and to Milan, Gussalli).

Budapest. 1448 (131). Bust of S. Benedict.

90 (136). Bust of Man with zazzera looking up. E.

1253 (172). S. Roch and the Angel (from S. Alessandro at Brescia). L.

BARON ISTVÁN HERZOG. Lady with rosary.

Cambridge (Mass.). FOGG ART MUSEUM. 1930.187. Bust of man with letter looking upwards (r.).

Cassel. 511 (LOAN BERLIN 187). Adoration of Shepherds (from S. Maria della Ghiara, Verona). Sd. L.

Cleveland (Ohio). 51.329. Madonna and Child with Infant S. John.

Columbia (S.C.). MUSEUM OF ART. 54-402/14 (KRESS COLLECTION. K 24). Madonna and Child with SS. Stephen and Jerome (r.).

Comero (Brescia). SANTUARIO DI AURO. S. Anthony Abbot enthroned.

Erfurt. 15 (LOAN BERLIN 667). Madonna and Child with Infant S. John. Destroyed.

Escorial. CHAPTER HALL. Erythrean Sibyl and Prophet Isaiah (companions to Brescia, S. Francesco?).

Esine. ASSUNTA, CANONICA. Assumption (old c. of Brescia, Rotonda).

Frankfurt a/M. 869. Madonna and Child enthroned between SS. Anthony Abbot and Sebastian. E.

916. Madonna and Child enthroned and Fathers of Church. L.

Gardone (Lago di Garda). S. BERNARDINO. Panels of dismembered polyptych. Two Angels (companions to Milan, Brera and Paris, Louvre).

Genoa. PALAZZO BIANCO. n.i.258. Madonna and Child (after Titian).

PALAZZO ROSSO. n.l. 46. Male portrait. d. 1533. (?)

MARCHESE UGO PIETRO SPINOLA. Madonna adoring the sleeping Child (r.). E.

Isolabella (Lago Maggiore). PALAZZO BORROMEO. S. Jerome in Wilderness.

Leningrad. 113. Faith (from Casa Muselli, Verona).

London. 299. Conte Sciarra Martinengo Cesaresco.

625. Madonna, SS. Catherine and Clare appearing to S. Bernardino da Siena and four other Saints.

1025. Full-length portrait of gentleman. d. 1526.

1165. Madonna appearing to S. George? and S. Catherine.

2090–3. Panels of polyptych: Two Angels, S. Joseph and S. Jerome.

3094. Madonna and Child with SS. Nicholas of Tolentino and Anthony of Padua. E.

3095. Ettore Averoldi in prayer. L.

BROCKLEBANK COLLECTION (EX). A Bishop (formerly Cook).

3096. Christ in Wilderness blessing Baptist (companion to New York). E.

Lonigo (Vicenza). SS. FERMO E RUSTICO. Marriage at Cana. L.

S. Jerome and two other Saints.

Lovere. S. MARIA IN VALVENDRA. Inside organ-shutters from Duomo Vecchio, Brescia: S. Faustinus and S. Giovita on horseback (outside by Ferramola, d. 1518).

Maguzzano. PARISH CHURCH. (See Brescia 517.)

Manerbio (Brescia). PARISH CHURCH. Madonna and Child with Infant S. John appearing to SS. Peter, Paul, Lawrence, Catherine and donor.

Marmentino (Brescia). PARISH CHURCH. SS. Cosmas and Damian adoring Christ.

Mazzano (Brescia). S. GIOVANNI BATTISTA. Madonna and Child appearing to SS. Sebastian, Roch and Zeno.

Milan. AMBROSIANA. Death of S. Peter Martyr.

    BRERA. 91. Madonna and Child appearing to SS. Jerome, Francis and Anthony Abbot.

        92 A, B, C. Upper panels of dismembered polyptych from S. Bernardino at Gardone: SS. Jerome and Paul, Assumption, SS. Clare and Catherine (see Gardone and Paris). 1534.

        93. Centre panel of lower register in dismembered polyptych from S. Bernardino at Gardone: S. Francis (side-panels at Louvre, Paris; see Gardone and above). 1534.

        768. Madonna and Child with Angel.

    CASTELLO. 402. S. Anthony of Padua.

        403-5. Triptych: S. Ursula and her maidens between SS. Jerome and John Baptist. L.

    ALDO CRESPI. Bust of Saviour holding globe.

    BENIGNO CRESPI (EX). Visitation.

    AVV. GUSSALLI. The brazen Serpent (companion to Brescia, Bettoni Cazzago and Chiari).

    SOLA COLLECTION. Portrait of lady. *Plate* 1707.

    OTTAVIANO VENIER (EX). Male Saint (fr.).

Munich. W.A.F. 683. Seated ecclesiastic. [*Plate* 385.]

Naples. 97. Ecce Homo. L.

New York. 11.53. Christ in Wilderness (companion to London). E.

    12.61. Deposition. d. 1554.

    28.79. Man holding letter behind parapet with hour-glass.

Northwick Park (Blockley). CPT. SPENCER CHURCHILL (EX). 52. Visitation.

Orzinuovi (Brescia). CHIESA DELL'OSPEDALE, CHOIR. Madonna and Child with SS. Dominic, Joseph, Bonaventura, Catherine and donor. L.

Oxford. ASHMOLEAN. F. F. MADAN BEQUEST. Madonna and Child with S. Jerome.

Paitone (Brescia). CHIESA DEL PELLEGRINAIO. Madonna appearing to a boy. [*Plate* 383.]

Paris. 1175/6. Side-panels of Brera 93, from dismembered polyptych of S. Bernardino at Gardone: SS. Bernardino and Louis of Toulouse; SS. Bonaventura and Anthony of Padua. 1534.

    MUSÉE JACQUEMART-ANDRÉ. Male portrait.

Philadelphia (Pa.). J. G. JOHNSON COLLECTION. 236. Madonna and Child with male and female donors. E.

    1172. Lady with lapdog. E.

Polesden Lacey (Surrey). CHRISTOPHER NORRIS. Madonna and Child with S. Roch.

Porzano. PARISH CHURCH. Madonna and Child with SS. Martin and Catherine.

Possagno (Bassano). TEMPIO DI CANOVA. Banner: Madonna of Mercy and two Penitents; on back, Prophets Enoch and Elijah.

Pralboino (Brescia). PARISH CHURCH. Madonna and Child with SS. Sebastian and Roch.

Madonna and Child in Glory with SS. Joseph and Francis, and below, Jerome, Bishop Saint, S. Anthony, Clare and Cardinal Umberto Gambara.

Rome. ALBERTINI COLLECTION. Annunciation.

VISCONTI VENOSTA COLLECTION. Holy Family with Infant S. John. *Plate* 1708.

VATICAN, PINACOTECA. 359. Madonna and Child enthroned with SS. Bartholomew and Jerome.

Stockholm. UNIVERSITY GALLERY. 219. S. Jerome reading.

Turin. GALLERIA SABAUDA. Oval: Madonna in Glory (fr.). (?)

Vaduz. LIECHTENSTEINSCHE SAMMLUNG. G13. Madonna and Child with S. Anthony Abbot (replica at Bordeaux). L.

G 879. Madonna and Child with Infant S. John.

A 313. S. Jerome.

Varese. CARANTANI SCARINI COLLECTION. Madonna and Child with S. Elizabeth, Infant S. John and view of Brescia in background. L.

Venice. ACCADEMIA. 321. 'Madonna del Carmelo', worshipped by the Ottoboni family (contemporary with Brescia 74).

331, 332. Fragments of altarpiece from S. Agata, Brescia: S. Peter, S. John. Baptist. E.

10255. Nativity (after Lotto).

S. MARIA DELLA PIETÀ, CHOIR OF NUNS. Christ in the House of Simon. Sd and d. 1544.

Verona. 94. Bust of young man looking upwards. E. (?)

287. Bust of monk with palm of martyrdom. Sd and d. 1519.

S. EUFEMIA, FIRST ALTAR L. Madonna and Child in Glory, with S. Anthony Abbot and Hermit Saint.

S. GIORGIO IN BRAIDA, FIFTH ALTAR L. Madonna and Child appearing to SS. Catherine, Lucy, Cecilia, Barbara and Agnes. Sd and d. 1540.

Vienna. 218. S. Justina and donor. E.

BARON K. LAMPRECHT. Coronation of Virgin (from S. Giuseppe at Brescia). *Plate* 1704.

PRIESTER COLLECTION (EX O. BONDY). Federigo Martinengo. Sd and d. 1546.

Washington (D.C.). 341 (KRESS COLLECTION. K 421). Portrait of lady.

1093 (KRESS COLLECTION. K 1428). 'Cook' Entombment. [*Plate* 384.]

MORONE, Domenico

Verona. 1442–after 1517. Pupil of Benaglio; influenced by Mantegna and Gentile Bellini.

Altenburg. 156 (68). Holy Family with Putti and female donor. E.

Berlin. 1456. Madonna and blessing Child. Sd and d. 1484. *Plate* 1299.

Brno. MUSEUM. A 139. Oblong predella panel: Death of Dominican Saint.

Châalis (Ermenonville). MUSÉE JACQUEMART-ANDRÉ. 500. Presentation of Virgin. *Plate* 1303.

Columbia (Mo.). UNIVERSITY OF MISSOURI. 61.75 (KRESS STUDY COLLECTION. K 461). 'Ecce homo' and Madonna.

Florence. BERENSON COLLECTION. Roundel from cassone: Prisoner before king.

Fonthill (Wilts.). HUGH MORRISON (EX). Profile of elderly man.

London. 1211, 1212. Two roundels from cassone: Tournaments.

    3130. Bust of smooth-faced elderly Venetian. (?)

    COURTAULD INSTITUTE GALLERIES, LEE OF FAREHAM COLLECTION. Warrior before king.

Lovere. 28. Madonna and Child against landscape. E.

Mantua. PALAZZO DUCALE (REGGIA DEI GONZAGA). Battle of the Gonzaga and Buonacolsi. Sd and d. 1494. [*Plate* 349.]

  — CORTE REALE, SALA DEL GIURAMENTO. Fresco: Oath of Captain Luigi Gonzaga. (?)

Modena. SEMINARIO ARCIVESCOVILE. S. Vincent Ferrer.

New Haven (Conn.). 1871.41. Childhood of S. Thomas Aquinas (companion to New York, Paris, San Francisco, Washington).

New York. 23.140. S. Thomas Aquinas instructed by SS. Peter and Paul (see New Haven).

    22.60.59. Predella panel: S. Dominic raising Napoleone Orsini, nephew of Cardinal Fossanova.

    HEARST COLLECTION (EX). Madonna and Child enthroned with SS. Sebastian, Jerome, Francis, female Martyr, John Baptist and Roch (with his son Francesco). d. 1508.

Oxford. ASHMOLEAN. 289. Predella panel: S. Vincent Ferrer preaching in square. Pietà with Franciscan donor. (?)

Paladon (Valpolicella). S. NICOLA DA TOLENTINO. Frescoes (see Verona 2070, 2071).

Paris. MUSÉE JACQUEMART-ANDRÉ. 945. 'Madonna di Piazza.' E.

    MME ÉMILE PARAVICINI. S. Thomas Aquinas dining with King Louis (see New Haven).

    KLEINBERGER COLLECTION (EX). Two predella panels: Baptism of Christ, Baptist's Head brought to Herod.

Princeton (N.J.). 35.54. Cassone panel: Battle of Amazons. (?)

San Francisco (Cal.). M. H. DE YOUNG MUSEUM (KRESS COLLECTION. K 2055, 2056). Vision of Fra Paolino dell'Aquila of S. Thomas Aquinas preaching, approved

of by Pope; S. Thomas Aquinas disputing, approved of by Christ on Altar
(see New Haven).

Stuttgart. Inv. 219. Madonna crowned by Angels and crowning S. Brigid, while
Christ Child gives ring to S. Catherine. L. *Plate* 1305.

Szekesfervar (Hungary). BISHOP'S PALACE, CHAPEL. Christ on Cross.

Verona. 357. Roundel with battle scene.

816. Full-length Madonna and Child, with donor. L.

2070, 2071. Detached frescoes from Paladon: SS. Dominic, Catherine, Leonard and
Gottard; SS. Roch, Anthony of Padua, Onophrius and Lucy. Sd and d. 1502.

S. BERNARDINO. Organ-shutters: S. Francis, S. Bernardino. 1481. *Plates* 1301–1302.

— CAPPELLA DE' MEDICI OR DI S. ANTONIO (FOURTH R.), ANTECHAPEL. Frescoes: on face
of entrance arch, at top, Madonna and Child in oval; below, SS. Louis of
Toulouse and Catherine in niches (left), SS. Elizabeth and Clare in niches
(right) candelabra, monochrome Sacrifice of Isaac and Preparation of Sacrifice
(in spandrels), Saints in roundels. In vault, four medallions with Evangelists
(r.). On pillars, SS. Jerome, Louis of Toulouse, and Augustine; SS. Bonaventura, Gregory and Ambrose.

— — CHAPEL PROPER. Frescoes: vault, ornaments; altar wall—S. Anthony of Padua
appears to the daughter of the King of Portugal and she is healed; left wall—
above, Miracle of the mule and donor Niccolò de' Medici; below, lost scene;
right wall—Sermon at Limoges; below, Healing of the contracted son. (r.)

S. BERNARDINO, OLD LIBRARY. Frescoes: main wall—Madonna and Child in Glory
worshipped by Lionello and Anna Sagramoso, who are recommended to her
by SS. Francis and Clare; on left, five Franciscan Protomartyrs; on right, SS.
Anthony of Padua, Bonaventura, Bernardino, Louis of Toulouse. Other
walls—Saints and Blessed of the Order, full-length on pedestals, Busts above
doors, Heads in roundels. d. 1503. [*Plate* 348.] *Plates* 1307–1308.

TABERNACLE IN VIA MAZZA. Fresco: Madonna and Child with SS. Christopher and
Mary Magdalen (r.). 1471. (?)

Vicenza. 41. SS. Francis and Bonaventura. L.

163. Three scenes from life of S. Blaise. L. *Plates* 1304, 1306.

Vienna. Twelve panels with stories of S. Vincent Ferrer.

Washington (D.C.). 547 (WARBURG GIFT). S. Thomas Aquinas preaching in a square
(see New Haven).

MORONE, Francesco

*Verona. ca 1471–1529. Pupil of his father Domenico; influenced by Mantegna and Gentile
Bellini.*

Bergamo. 201. Madonna and Child with SS. Joseph, Anthony of Padua, Anne and
Francis. Sd and d. 1520.

554. Madonna and Child.

Berlin. 46. Madonna and Child. Sd.

1175. A Betrothal. E.

Berlin-Ost. 46B. Madonna and Child with SS. Anthony Abbot and Onuphrius. Sd. *Plate* 1332.

Budapest. 1359 (164). Predella panel: S. Francis reading his rule to the Tertiary Order (companion to Verona. 101).

Florence. MUSEO HORNE. 61. Communion of S. Onuphrius.

CONTINI BONACOSSI COLLECTION. Organ-shutters: Annunciation. (?)

London. 285. Madonna embracing Child.

Marcellise (Verona). PARISH CHURCH. Organ-shutters from S. Maria in Organo at Verona: outside—SS. John Evangelist and Benedict, SS. Mary Magdalen and Catherine; inside—Nativity and Prophets Daniel and Isaiah. Commissioned from Francesco Morone and Girolamo dai Libri November 1515, completed Easter 1516.

Milan. BRERA. 225. Madonna and Child with SS. Nicholas and Zeno. 150(2?).

POLDI PEZZOLI. 577. Samson and Delilah. False signature of Carpaccio. [*Plate* 350.]

New York. R. LEHMAN COLLECTION. Madonna and Child with SS. Rose and Catherine. Sd. *Plate* 1331.

Padua. 75 (Inv. 36). Madonna and Child. Sd. *Plate* 1330.

Princeton (N.J.). 35.24. Madonna and Child with SS. Mary Magdalen, Nicholas, John Baptist and Catherine. *Plate* 1325.

Quinto di Valpantena (Verona). PARISH CHURCH. Madonna and Child with SS. John Baptist and Evangelist. d. 1526.

Richmond (Surrey). COOK COLLECTION (EX). 120. Dead Christ and Angel.

Soave (Verona). PARISH CHURCH. Madonna and Child with SS. Roch and Joachim; in lunette, Eternal and Cherubim. L.

Trent. MUSEO DEL CASTELLO. Annunciation (not traced; probably identical with G. B. Moroni at S. Michele Arcangelo, Trent).

Tucson (Ariz.). UNIVERSITY OF ARIZONA ART GALLERY. 62.155 (KRESS STUDY COLLECTION. K 1164). Busts of two Olivetan Saints.

Venice. ACCADEMIA. 735. Ex-voto fresco: Madonna and Child with S. Roch (fr.). d. 1517.

916. Madonna and Child against curtain and landscape. Sd.

MUSEO CORRER. 71. Pietro Orseolo and Dogaressa Felicita Malipiero.

Verona. 101. Predella panel: S. Francis gives the rule to S. Clare and her nuns (companion to Budapest).

117. Lunette: Pietà.

135. Four canvases: S. Bernardino and worshipper, S. Clare and two female worshippers, SS. Sebastian and Paul, SS. Anthony Abbot and Roch.

182. Madonna and Child with Moscardo coat of arms (versions in Berlin and London).

259. S. Catherine and donor.

285, 291. Busts of SS. Francis and Bartholomew (from S. Bernardino). 1498.

305. Washing of Feet.

330. Deesis (from Chiesa della Vittoria Nuova, consecrated 1513). L.

348. S. Francis receiving Stigmata. E.

462–465. Detached frescoes from Capitolo di S. Nazzaro: Baptism of Christ and four medallions with Evangelists.

560. Detached fresco from house by Ponte delle Navi: Madonna of Loreto and SS. Joseph, Jerome, Anthony Abbot and Roch.

864. Detached fresco from façade of house by Ponte dell'Acqua Morta: Trinity with S. Albert Carmelite (or Anthony) and S. John Baptist (r.).

1636. Polyptych from Tregnago: Nativity with S. John Baptist, Pietà and Annunciation. E.

PALAZZO DELLA GRAN GUARDIA. Fresco (identical with 864 above; formerly deposited here).

PALAZZO N. 320, VIA XX SETTEMBRE. Fresco: Madonna and Child with SS. John Baptist and Roch.

S. ANASTASIA, SACRISTY. SS. Paul, Dionysius and Mary Magdalen with worshippers. L.

— FOURTH ALTAR L. Fresco in vault of niche: Descent of Holy Ghost.

S. BERNARDINO, CAPPELLA DELLA CROCE (R. OF CHOIR). Christ on Cross with mourning Virgin and Evangelist. Sd and d. 1498. *Plate* 1326. (Other pictures by Giolfino, G. F. Caroto and A. Badile.)

— REFECTORY. Frescoed lunette: Crucifixion with SS. Francis and Jerome.

— OLD LIBRARY. (See under his father Domenico Morone.)

— CAPPELLA DEI MEDICI O DI S. ANTONIO. (See under his father Domenico Morone.)

S. CHIARA, FIRST ALTAR L. Frescoes round altar: Blessing Christ, Mark, Matthew, Joshua (the rest by Michele da Verona). 1508/9.

S. FERMO MAGGIORE, OVER SIDE ENTRANCE. Fresco: Madonna and Child with SS. James and Elizabeth (r.). d. 1523.

S. MARIA MATRICOLARE (DUOMO), THIRD CHAPEL R. Side-panels of dismembered triptych: S. John Evangelist, S. James and donor.

— BIBLIOTECA CAPITOLARE. Madonna and Child. L. Sd. *Plate* 1329.

S. MARIA IN ORGANO, THIRD CHAPEL L. Madonna and Child with SS. Martin, Augustine and Angels. Sd and d. 1503. *Plate* 1328.

— CAPPELLA POMPEI. Frescoes in vault: Eternal and Evangelists.

— SACRISTY. Frescoes above stalls: Saviour and busts of Olivetan worthies. *Plate* 1327.

MORONI, Giovanni Battista

1520/25–1578. *Bergamask pupil of Moretto da Brescia, influenced by Lotto.*

Albino (Bergamo). S. BARBARA DI BONDO PONTELLO, BEHIND HIGH ALTAR. Madonna and Child in Glory and kneeling SS. Barbara and Catherine (sketch at Bergamo, 77). Sd.*

Albino (Bergamo) (contd.). S. GIULIANO, SIXTH CHAPEL L. SS. Anthony of Padua and Bernardino adoring Christ on Cross.

— SIXTH CHAPEL R. Trinity.

— SACRISTY. Banner: Madonna crowned by Angel; on reverse, Visitation.

Almenno San Bartolomeo (Bergamo). S. BARTOLOMEO, SECOND CHAPEL R. Madonna and Child enthroned. Sd.

Amsterdam. 1673 D–I. Lady in red with fan.

VOM RATH BEQUEST? Man with letter. Sd and d. 1565.

Baltimore (Md.). WALTERS ART GALLERY. 501. Knee-length portrait of gentleman with dog (from Conti Consolati, Trento).

Bergamo. 51. Bust of Isotta Brembati. ca 1550.*

65. Monk Saint.

68. Full-length portrait of Bernardo Spini.

69. Full-length portrait of Pace Rivola Spini.

71. Bust of girl of Redetti family.

75. S. Jerome reading in wilderness.

77. Madonna and Child in Glory and kneeling SS. Barbara and Catherine (sketch for Albino altarpiece).

78. Old man seated.

81. Half-length portrait of priest holding book.

82. Old man seated with book in left hand.

83. Bust of old man.

84. Bust of bearded man (st.).

86. Bust of youth.

87. Bust of Isotta Brembati Grumelli. ca 1560.

88. Bust of lady in ruff.

91. Seated lady. (?)

93. Seated old man in red, with white beard.

96. Bust of Paolo Vidoni Cedrelli. d. 1576.

596. Seated old man in fur-coat.

1042. Entombment. Sd and d. 1566.

ALMA AND MARIA FRIZZONI. Male portrait (destroyed).

CONTE AGLIARDI. Madonna and Child (after Giovanni Bellini).

CONTE MORONI. Isotta Brembati in Armchair. ca 1554.

Gian Girolamo Grumelli or 'il Cavaliere in rosa'. Sd and d. 1560. *Plate* 1959.

Lady in black.

Nativity.

Adoration of Magi.

— HEIRS. Full-length courtier in black. Sd.

CONTE RONCALLI. Old Albani in fur coat, seated.

Pietro Suardi, aged four, with little dog.

CONTE SUARDI. Male portrait.

S. ALESSANDRO DELLA CROCE, OVER ENTRANCE. Coronation of Virgin. Sd and d. 1576.

— SACRISITY. Bust of donor pointing at landscape with SS. Sebastian and John Baptist mourning Christ on Cross.

S. ALESSANDRO (DUOMO), FIRST ALTAR L. Madonna and Child appearing to SS. Jerome and Catherine. Sd and d. 1576.

S. PANCRAZIO, SECOND ALTAR R. Christ on Cross.*

Berlin-Ost. 193. Bust of bearded man.

193A. Young poet.

Boston (Mass.). 95.1371. Conte Alberghetti and his son.

GARDNER MUSEUM. Full-length nobleman. Sd and d. 1576.

Brescia. 144. The unknown poet. d. 1560.

147. Seated lawyer. Sd and d. 1560.

CONTE LECHI. Portrait of Carthusian monk.

Budapest. 1243 (179). Madonna and Child with Infant S. John.

1244, 1245 (113, 114). Two roundels: SS. Dorothy and Catherine.

53.501. Portrait of Jacopo Contarini. Sd and d. 1575.

SÁNDOR LEDERER (EX). Two panels: SS. Lucy and John Evangelist in niches.

F. GLUCK (EX). Bartolomeo Bongo seated by window with view of Bergamo's tower, as it was before 1553 (see New York).

Buffalo (N.Y.). A. C. GOODYEAR. Bust of ecclesiastic. Not traced.

Cambridge (Mass.). FOGG ART MUSEUM. 1942.200. 'Crespi' bust of man.

Castelli Calepio. S. PIETRO. Madonna and Child in niche, crowned by two Angels. Sd.*

Cenate d'Argon (Bergamo). S. LEONE. Assumption. E.

S. MARTINO. Madonna and Child in Glory, S. Martin and the Beggar, and donor Don Leone Cucchi. Sd.

Chantilly. 53. Knee-length gentleman.

54. Knee-length lady.

Charlottenburg. DR GERHART BOLLERT (EX). Old scholar.

Chicago (Ill.). 29.912. Lodovico Madruzzo.

Columbus (Ohio). GALLERY OF FINE ARTS, F. W. SCHUMACHER COLLECTION. S. Agnes in landscape.

Costa di Mezzate (Bergamo). CONTI CAMOZZI VERTOVA. Conte Girolamo Vertova (companion to Nantes).*

Desenzano al Serio. CHIESA DEL MIRACOLO. Madonna and Child. Paid 1567.*

Detroit (Mich.). 29.244. Bust of man with ruff.

Dublin. 78, 80. Young martyr; S. Bartholomew. E.

105. Portrait of widower with sons. *Plate 1966.*

Fino del Monte (Bergamo). PARISH CHURCH. Madonna and Child enthroned with SS. Andrea and Peter. Sd and d. 1577.

Firle Place (Sussex). LADY GAGE. Bust of bearded man.

Florence. PITTI. 120. Male portrait. (?)

121. Male portrait.

127. Bust of old man.

Florence (contd.). 128. Bust of woman.

    UFFIZI. 906. Full-length portrait of Pietro Secco Suardo pointing at brazier, with motto 'Et Quid Volo Nisi Ut Ardeat'. Sd and d. 1563.

      933. Bust of man with book on parapet.

      941. Portrait of Giovanni Antonio Pantera.

    CONTINI BONACOSSI COLLECTION. Head of old man with white beard.

Frankfurt a/M. 904. Head of monk.

Gaverina (Bergamo). S. VITTORE. Madonna and Child with SS. Victor and Fidentius. Sd and d. 1576.

Gazzaniga (Bergamo). S. GIORGIO A FIORANO. Polyptych: S. George and the dragon, between S. Alexander and S. Defendente; in upper register, Madonna and Child between S. Lucy and S. Apollonia. 1575. *Plate 196b.*

Genoa. BASEVI COLLECTION (formerly Conte Morlani, Bergamo). Donor contemplating Baptism of Christ. *Plate 196a.*

Gorlago (Bergamo). S. PANCRAZIO. Adoration of Magi. Sd.

    S. Gothard between SS. Lawrence and Catherine.

    Last Judgement (commissioned 1577, unfinished at death of artist in 1578, completed by other hand).*

Harewood House (Yorks.). EARL OF HAREWOOD. S. Jerome reading.

Havana (Cuba). OSCAR B. CINTAS (EX). Portrait of lady. [*Plate 387.*]

Honolulu (Hawaii). ACADEMY OF ARTS, KRESS COLLECTION. K 359 (formerly Berlin 167). Gentleman holding letter. d. 1553.

Leningrad. HERMITAGE (EX). Bust of seated old man with spectacles (according to copy in Accademia Carrara at Bergamo, he was the centenarian Cristoforo da Novate).

    154. Bust said to be Aretino, inscribed 'Nosce te auton'.

London. 697. Portrait of a tailor. [*Plate 388.*]

      742. Portrait of a lawyer.

      1022. Gentleman with the wounded foot.

      1023. Lady in red seated in armchair.

      1024. Ludovico di Terzi da Bergamo.

      1316. Gentleman with helmet on column.

      2094. Gentleman.

      3123. Allegory of Chastity.

      3124. Leonardo Salvani. L.

      3128. Bust of man with blond beard. L.

      3129. Bust of man (inscribed 'Dum Spiritus Hos Reget Artus').

    VISCOUNT POWERSCOURT (EX). Gentleman leaning on column, with letter in left hand. Sd and d. 1561.*

Madrid. 262. Knee-length portrait of Venetian Captain.

Memphis (Tenn.). BROOKS MEMORIAL ART GALLERY (KRESS COLLECTION. K 1768). Bearded man.

Mentmore (Leighton Buzzard). EARL OF ROSEBERY. Portrait of a rabbi. Sd and d. 1562.

Milan. BRERA. 89. Portrait of youth.

    100. Antonio Navagero. d. 1565.

    118. Madonna and Child with SS. Barbara and Lawrence.

    130. Assumption.

    131. Madonna with S. Catherine, S. Francis and donor. E.

   AMBROSIANA. Full-length portrait of gentleman. d. 1554.

   CASTELLO. 65. Conte Ercole Tassi. *Plate* 1964.

    365. Death of S. Peter Martyr.

   POLDI PEZZOLI. 558. S. Michael.

Minneapolis (Minn.). 16.22. Bust of ecclesiastic.

Nantes. 112. Lucia Vertova (fr., companion to Costa di Mezzate). *Plate* 1960.

New York. 13.177. Bartolomeo Bongo (the date 1584 is that of the death of the sitter). (See Budapest.)

    30.95.238. Portrait of a gentleman (inscribed 'Treu und Frumb').

    30.95.255. Lucrezia Cattanei Vertova, founder of Convent of S. Anna at Albino (the date 1557 is that of the death of the sitter).

Oneta (Bergamo). S. MARIA ASSUNTA. Assumption.

Orzivecchi (Brescia). PARISH CHURCH. Assumption and SS. John Evangelist, Peter, Paul and donor.

Ottawa (Canada). 3082. Gentleman behind parapet (inscribed 'Duritiem mollitie frangit'). (?)

Palazzago (Bergamo). S. GIOVANNI BATTISTA. Assumption.

Paris. 1395. Seated old man.

Parre (Bergamo). PARISH CHURCH. Madonna and Child enthroned with SS. Peter, Paul and John Evangelist. Sd. doc. 1564/5.

Philadelphia (Pa.). MUSEUM OF ART, WILSTACH COLLECTION. 216. Seated ecclesiastic.

  — J. G. JOHNSON COLLECTION. 237. Seated gentleman. Sd and d. 1547.

    238. Officer with gauntlet. (?)

  WIDENER COLLECTION (EX). Full-length gentleman with right hand on helmet.

Princeton (N.J.). UNIVERSITY GALLERY. 28.30. Profile of man in prayer (fr.).

Ranica. PARROCCHIALE DEI SETTE FRATELLI, L. ALTAR. Polyptych: Baptism, S. James and S. John Evangelist; above, Angel and Virgin of Annunciation.*

  — OVER ENTRANCE. Crucifixion with S. Defendente.*

Rheims. 661. Seated man with dog. L.

Richmond (Va.). VIRGINIA MUSEUM OF ART. 62.20. Husband and wife in adoration before Madonna and Child in Glory with S. Michael.

Romano Lombardo. S. MARIA ASSUNTA, FOURTH ALTAR R. Last Supper. 1568. *Plate* 1963.

Roncola. S. BERNARDO. Polyptych: lower register. S. Bernard between S. Defendente and S. Roch; upper register, Madonna in Glory, half-length SS. Andrew and John Evangelist. Sd.*

Rotterdam. BOYMANS–VAN BEUNINGEN MUSEUM. Inv. 2559. Bust of monk (ex Auspitz). *Plate* 1961.

Rovetta con Fino. See **Fino del Monte.**

San Francisco (Cal.). PALACE OF THE LEGION OF HONOR. 1941.22. Portrait of Giulio Gilardi (ex-Wimborne).

Sarasota (Fla.). RINGLING MUSEUM. 106. Portrait of Mario Benvenuti (ex Northbrook).

Seriate (Bergamo). S. CRISOGONO. Christ on Cross with SS. Chrysogonus, Christopher, Francis and donor. Sd.

Siena. 467, 484. Male busts.

Sovere (Bergamo). S. MARTINO. Resurrection. Sd.

Trent. S. MARIA MAGGIORE. Madonna and Child in Glory with S. John Evangelist and Doctors of the Church (after Moretto).

S. Clare. d. 1548.

S. MICHELE ARCANGELO. Annunciation (formerly at Museo del Castello, then at S. Chiara). Sd and d. 1548.*

Tucson (Arizona). UNIVERSITY (KRESS COLLECTION. K 1548). Bust of magistrate. L.

Vaduz. LIECHTENSTEINSCHE SAMMLUNG (EX). Bust of ecclesiastic.

Vienna. 216. Portrait of sculptor.

217. Portrait of lawyer.

Villa di Serio. S. STEFANO. Banner: Risen Christ; on back, S, Stephen. Sd (d. 1578?).

Warwick. EARL OF WARWICK. Portrait of Duke of Albuquerque. Sd and d. 1560.

Washington (D.C.). 225 (KRESS COLLECTION. K 240). Madonna and Child with donor.

641 (WIDENER COLLECTION). So-called Master of Titian. [*Plate* 386.]

1579 (TIMKEN COLLECTION). Gian Federico Madruzzo.

Woburn Abbey (Beds.). DUKE OF BEDFORD. 19. Male portrait.

Worcester (Mass.). 1912.60. 'The Bergamask Captain.'

NANNI DI JACOPO

Pisan follower of Turino Vanni and Martino di Bartolomeo.

Florence. MARCHESA PANCIATICHI (EX). Polyptych: Madonna and Child with four music-making Angels; SS. James and Augustine; SS. Donnino and Anthony Abbot; in pinnacles, Blessing Saviour, Angel and Virgin of Annunciation; in predella, Dead Christ with mourning Mary and John, SS. Clare and Lucy, SS. John Baptist and Francis. *Plate* 452.

Rome. MUSEO DI PALAZZO VENEZIA. Fragments of polyptych: Madonna and Child with six Angels; S. James and Evangelist; SS. Michael and Anthony Abbot. Signed. *Plates* 449–451.

Siena. 182. Madonna and Child enthroned, with SS. Catherine, Stephen, Anthony Abbot, Anthony of Padua; in pinnacle, Crucifixion (from Osservanza).

OTTAVIANO NELLI

Ottaviano de Martis or di Martino Nelli da Gubbio, ca 1375–1444. Active at Perugia 1400,
at Urbino 1416–22 and again 1428–32, at Assisi 1422, at Foligno 1424. Pupil of his
father's, strongly influenced in youth by contemporary French miniatures.

Assisi. SACRO CONVENTO. Detached frescoes: Madonna and Child with SS. James
and Anthony Abbot, God the Father blessing, Annunciation and other fragments. Formerly d. 1422.

S. FRANCESCO, LOWER CHURCH. Fresco: Madonna and Child with SS. Jerome,
Francis and Augustine.

Città di Castello. S. MARIA DELLE GRAZIE, R. CHAPEL. Detached fresco: Dormition.

Covignano (Rimini). S. MARIA DELLE GRAZIE. Banner: Annunciation (fr.); Crucifixion with S. Francis receiving Stigmata.

Fano. S. DOMENICO, L. WALL, NEAR ENTRANCE. Frescoes: in lunette, Trinity worshipped by Prophets, Patriarchs and Saints; below, six Stories on two tiers,
with Life of S. Dominic (Birth of S. Dominic, he receives the Dominican habit
from the Virgin, he is a pillar of the Church, the Pope confirms the Dominican
Rule, Funeral of S. Dominic, Dominican Supper).

— L. WALL, BETWEEN SECOND AND THIRD ALTAR. Frescoes: S. Mary Magdalen and
Arrival at Marseilles.

Florence. PROF. R. LONGHI: Herod on balcony with Baptist and Herodias.

Foligno. PALAZZO TRINCI, CHAPEL, VAULT. Frescoes: Joachim and Anne praying in
temple; Announcements to Joachim and Anne; Meeting of Joachim and Anne
at the Golden Gate; Birth of Virgin. *Plate 519.*

— LUNETTES. Frescoes: Presentation of Virgin, Zacharias announces competition
of suitors, Marriage of Virgin, Annunciation.

— WALL OPPOSITE ENTRANCE. Frescoes over altar: in lunette, Christ disputing with
Doctors; in middle register, Nativity, Adoration of Magi; in lower register,
SS. Anthony Abbot, John Baptist and Dominic, Crucifixion with S. Nicholas,
S. Messalina and Blessed Pietro Crisi, S. Francis receiving Stigmata. *Plate 520.*

— SIDE WALLS. Frescoes: Annunciation to the Virgin of her imminent Death,
Farewell from the Apostles, Dormitio, Funeral and Assumption of Virgin.

Sd and d. 1424 (25th February) in faded inscription between middle and lower
register on altar wall.

Gubbio. PALAZZO BENI, INNER COURTYARD. Fresco. S. Christopher. Not after 1431.

S. AGOSTINO, CHOIR. Frescoes: in vault, Symbols of Evangelists; Birth and youth
of S. Augustine; in soffit of arch, Christ and Apostles; on walls, Life of S.
Augustine. *Plate 521.*

— TRIUMPHAL ARCH. Fresco: Last Judgement.

— SECOND ALTAR R. Detached fresco: Madonna and Child, Saints and Angels.

S. DOMENICO, SECOND CHAPEL L. Frescoes: Scenes from life of S. Vincent Ferrer
and S. Peter Martyr.

Gubbio (contd.). S. FRANCESCO, L. APSE, VAULT. Frescoes: Coronation of Virgin (in five sections). *Plates* 513, 515.

—— WINDOW EMBRASURE. Frescoes: The naked Blessed Nicolas de Tavileis, the yoked Blessed Tomaso (or Benvenuto) da Gubbio, S. Eligius (Ubaldus?) with hammer, Blessed (Giordano?) da Gubbio.

—— WALLS. Frescoes in 17 sections: first register—Joachim and Anne pray in temple, Expulsion of Joachim, Annunciation to Joachim, Annunciation to Anne; second register—Meeting at Golden Gate, Birth of Virgin, Presentation of Virgin, Convocation of suitors; third register—Marriage of Virgin (lost), Annunciation, Nativity, Adoration of Magi (lost); fourth register—Annunciation to Virgin of her imminent death (lost), Farewell from Apostles, Dormitio, Funeral of Virgin, Assumption (fr.); in dado, frieze with bust of dead Christ and four busts indicating the Arts and Crafts of Painting, Building, Carpentry (partly lost); caryatids or mourners (spoilt by opening of windows). *Plates* 514–516.

— PILLAR BETWEEN L. AND CENTRAL APSE. Frescoes: from top, Marriage of S. Catherine, S. Christopher, S. Anthony Abbot enthroned, Dead Christ in Tomb with symbols of Passion (inscription on tomb, lost).

S. MARIA NUOVA, R. WALL. Fresco: Madonna of Humility with five Angels, two Saints, male and female donors. Dated MCCC.III (read 1413?). [*Plate* 290.]

S. MARIA DELLA PIAGGIOLA, APSE. Fresco: Madonna and Child with Angels (r.).

Montefalco. S. FRANCESCO (MUSEO), R. NAVE, FIFTH BAY, VAULT. Frescoes: Scenes from Life of S. Anthony Abbot; in soffit of arch, Christ and three Temptations of S. Anthony Abbot. (st.?) 1440.

Orléans. MUSÉE. Panel of polyptych: S. Jerome healing the lion (companion to Rome and Worcester?). (?)

Paris. MUSÉES NATIONAUX, CAMPANA COLLECTION. Madonna of Humility, and Crucifixion above (r.).*

Perugia. 1004. Polyptych from Pietralunga: Madonna and Child with lily, and Trinity in pinnacle above; SS. Anthony Abbot, Nicholas, Paul, Catherine; in pilasters, six small Saints. Sd and d. 1403. *Plate* 510.

Philadelphia (Pa.). J. G. JOHNSON COLLECTION. 123. Pinnacle: Coronation. E.

Rome. VATICAN, PINACOTECA. 213, 218. Two panels of polyptych: Marriage of S. Francis with Poverty, Circumcision (companions to Orléans and Worcester?). *Plate* 517.

PALAZZO VENEZIA. P.V. 7996. Madonna and Child.

São Paulo (Brazil). 3. Detached fresco from Assisi: Madonna and Child enthroned with S. Mary Magdalen and S. Stephen.

Urbino. ORATORIO DI S. CROCE, L. WALL. Fragment of frescoed decoration: Madonna and Child crowned by Angels. 1428–32.

ORATORIO DI S. GHERARDO (AGAINST APSE OF S. DOMENICO). Fresco: Madonna and Child crowned by Angels and two Saints. 1417.

(Environs). MADONNA DELL'HOMO OR S. MARIA DEL LOMO. Frescoes: Madonna of

Mercy, SS. James, Bartholomew, Peter and Paul; in soffit of arch, Mystic
Lamb and Symbols of Evangelists (p.). 1428.

Worcester (Mass.). 1920.2. Adoration of Magi (companion to Orléans and Rome?).
Plate 518.

Homeless. Madonna of Humility with music-making Angels: the Christ Child has
a goldfinch in His left hand and with His right hand tries to play a lute held
by an Angel. *Plate 512.*

Dossal: Nativity, Madonna and Child with SS. John Baptist, Jerome and
donors, Agony in the Garden. *Plate 511.*

NEROCCIO DI LANDI

Siena 1447–1500. Sculptor and painter. Pupil of Vecchietta, partner of Francesco di Giorgio.

Bergamo. 549. Madonna and Child.

Berlin. 63A. Madonna and Child with SS. Benedict and Catherine.

Boston (Mass.). 39.802. Panel of polyptych: Virgin Annunciate.

GARDNER MUSEUM. Roman hero in landscape (st.; companion to Tours).

Brussels. MME JACQUES STOCLET. Madonna and Child with SS. John Baptist and
Evangelist.

Cambridge. FITZWILLIAM MUSEUM. 554. Madonna and Child with SS. Bernardino
and Catherine of Siena (r.).

Castelnuovo dell'Abate (Montalcino). MISERICORDIA. Fresco: Madonna. L.

Champaign. See Urbana.

Cracow. CZARTORYSKI MUZEUM. 158. Madonna and Child with two Angels. (Lost.)

Esztergom. 55.200. Madonna and Child with SS. Sebastian and Catherine.

Florence. UFFIZI. 1602. Predella to Francesco di Giorgio's Coronation for Monte
Oliveto: S. Benedict at Subiaco, The Miracle of the broken Sieve, Totila's
Visit to S. Benedict. 1471–72? *Plate 896.*

MUSEO HORNE. 56. Madonna and Child with SS. Jerome and Mary Magdalen. L.

BERENSON COLLECTION. Madonna and Child with SS. Jerome, Anthony of Padua
and two Angels. *Plate 893.*

Predella panel: S. Catherine of Siena's Vision of SS. Dominic, Francis and
Bonaventura (companion to London, Christensen). *Plate 902.*

SERRISTORI COLLECTION. Madonna and Child with SS. Paul and Mary Magdalen.

Frankfurt a/M. 980. Madonna and Child with SS. Peter and Paul (st.).

1007. Madonna and Child with SS. Sebastian and Catherine (st.).

Gazzada (Varese). FONDAZIONE CAGNOLA. Madonna and Child with SS. Jerome
and John Baptist. *Plate 900.*

Indianapolis (Ind.). G. H. A. CLOWES. Madonna and Child with SS. John Baptist and
Mary Magdalen.

London. R. W. CHRISTENSEN (EX). Predella panel: Mystic Marriage of S. Catherine of Siena (companion to Florence, Berenson).* *Plate* 901.

Los Angeles (Cal.). COUNTY MUSEUM, GIFT OF NORTON SIMON FOUNDATION. Madonna and Child with SS. John Baptist and Catherine (formerly Somzée Brussels and Cremer Dortmund). *Plate* 899.

Madonna and Child (version of Rome, Visconti Venosta). E.

Magliano (Maremma Toscana). SS. ANNUNZIATA, HIGH ALTAR. Madonna suckling the Child and hand of S. Sigismund (fr.).

Montisi (Senese). PIEVE DELL'ANNUNCIATA. Madonna and Child with SS. Peter, Sigismund, Ansanus and Paul; in lunette, Eternal and Cherubim; in predella, S. Sebastian before Emperor Diocletian, Crucifixion, Martyrdom of S. Sebastian. Sd and d. 1496. *Plate* 903.

New Haven (Conn.). 1871.63. Lunette: Annunciation. ca 1470. *Plate* 895.

New York. 41.100.18. Madonna and Child with SS. Michael and Bernardino (g.p.).

61.43 (KRESS COLLECTION. K 411). Madonna and Child with SS. Jerome and Mary Magdalen (formerly in Meiningen).

Notre Dame (Ind.). UNIVERSITY. 62.17.2 (KRESS COLLECTION. K 1901). Madonna and Child with S. Mary Magdalen, S. John Baptist and kneeling monk.

Orvieto. DUOMO, MUSEO DELL'OPERA. Intarsia: Madonna and Child (from Neroccio's design).

Paris. 1398A. Madonna and Child with SS. Anthony Abbot and John Baptist (fr. cut on all sides).

PAUL BOURGET (EX). Madonna and Child with SS. James and Dominic.

CHALANDON (EX). Dead Christ upheld by Angels (fr. of lunette).

MARTIN LE ROY (EX). Tobias and the Angel. *Plate* 894.

Philadelphia (Pa.). J. G. JOHNSON COLLECTION. 109. Madonna and Child with SS. Jerome and Catherine.

1169. Panels of tabernacle, joined together: SS. Ursula, Catherine, Jerome and Galganus all kneeling.

Raleigh (N.C.). MUSEUM OF ART. GL.60.17.29-30 (KRESS COLLECTION. K 438-439). Two cassone panels: Battle of Actium; Cleopatra's arrival at court of Mark Antony.

Rome. VISCONTI VENOSTA COLLECTION. Madonna and Child holding bird. E.

Siena. 217. Cassone panel: Triumph of David.

278. Madonna and Child with SS. Peter, Sebastian, John Baptist, Sigismund, Bernardino and Paul. Sd and d. 1492.

281. Madonna and Child with SS. Bernardino and Jerome. [*Plate* 277.]

282. Triptych: standing Madonna and Child, S. Bernardino and S. Michael. Sd and d. 1476.

285. Madonna and Child with S. Catherine of Siena and S. Bernardino.

287. Madonna and SS. Jerome, Catherine of Alexandria, Catherine of Siena and Benedict (st.).

294. Madonna and Child with SS. John Baptist and Andrew.

295. Madonna and Child with SS. John Baptist and female Saint (with Francesco di Giorgio). E.

306. Wing of diptych: Virgin of Annunciation (from Osservanza).

ARCHIVIO DI STATO. Book-cover: Madonna protecting Siena. d. 1480. *Plate* 891.

CHIGI SARACINI COLLECTION. Madonna and Child with two female Saints.

SERGARDI BIRINGUCCI COLLECTION. Lunette with Christ on Cross and predella to Madonna by Sano di Pietro.

PALAZZO PUBBLICO, SALA DEI PILASTRI. S. Bernardino preaches in the Piazza del Campo, A Woman possessed by the Devil is healed at S. Bernardino's Funeral.

— STAIRCASE. Fresco: Madonna and Child (with Mariotto da Volterra). Paid 1485.

S. MARIA ASSUNTA (DUOMO), L. NAVE, FLOOR. Marble intarsia, on his design: Hellespontine Sibyl. 1483. *Plate* 897. (See also Benvenuto di Giovanni, Cozzarelli, Matteo di Giovanni.)

ORATORIO DELLA SS. TRINITÀ, SACRISTY. Portable Altarpiece: Madonna and Child with SS. Michael and John Baptist; in spandrel, two Victories; in predella, S. Mary Magdalen, S. Jerome and playing Putti.

(Environs). OSSERVANZA. Fresco: S. Agnes in roundel. Destroyed 1944.

Tours. 285 (CAMPANA n. 417). Horatius Cocles in landscape (st., companion to Boston).

Urbana (Illinois). UNIVERSITY, KRANNERT ART MUSEUM. Inv. 081140. Madonna and Child with S. Augustine, another Saint and a donor (formerly Thurn und Taxis).

Utrecht. 21. Madonna and Child with SS. Mary Magdalen and John Baptist (st.).

Washington (D.C.). 12 (MELLON COLLECTION). Vestal Claudia Quinta on a pedestal (background figures by Master of Griselda; companion to Pacchiarotto in Baltimore, Francesco di Giorgio in Florence and Master of Griselda). *Plate* 905.

643 (WIDENER COLLECTION.) Bust of Alessandra Piccolomini. [*Plate* 278.]

813 (KRESS COLLECTION. K. 1346). Rapolano altarpiece: Madonna and Child with SS. Anthony Abbot and Sigismund. 1492–96.

Homeless. Spalliera panels: Putti in landscape. *Plates* 886–887.

SCULPTURES

Borgo a Mozzano. S. JACOPO. Wooden pigmented statue of S. Bernardino. *Plate* 889.

Lucca. PINACOTECA. Inv. 166. Relief carved in wood, pigmented and gilded: Assumption of Virgin (by Vecchietta; finished by Neroccio). 1480–81.

S. MARIA CORTEORLANDINI. Wooden pigmented statue of S. Nicholas of Tolentino. 1481.

Siena. S. MARIA ASSUNTA, CAPPELLA DEL BATTISTA. Marble statue of S. Catherine of Siena. 1487–97. *Plate* 898.

— R. NAVE. Tomb of Bishop Piccolomini del Testa. 1484–85.

ORATORIO DI S. CATERINA IN FONTEBRANDA. Wooden pigmented statue of S. Catherine of Siena. 1474.

NICCOLÒ DI BUONACCORSO

Sienese. Died 1388. *Follower of Lippo Memmi and the Lorenzetti.*

Berlin. SCHLOSSMUSEUM. K 9223. Book-cover (biccherna): Trinity with S. Mary Magdalen, Bernard, Nicholas and John Evangelist. d. 1367. (?)

Boston (Mass.). 20.1860. Madonna and Child with SS. John Baptist and Augustine and four Angels. *Plate* 353.

Cologne. 619. Crucifixion.

Fiesole. MUSEO BANDINI. Angel and Virgin of Annunciation.

Florence. UFFIZI. 3257. Presentation of Virgin (companion to London and New York).

LOESER COLLECTION (EX). Madonna and Child enthroned with SS. Catherine, Anthony Abbot, two Angels and blessing Redeemer in pinnacle.

Konopist. CASTLE. 21200. Portable altarpiece: Madonna and Child enthroned with SS. John Baptist, Catherine and two Angels; Redeemer in pinnacle above; in wings, S. Anthony Abbot, S. Christopher, Angel and Virgin of Annunciation.

London. 1109. Marriage of Virgin (companion to Florence and New York). Sd. *Plate* 355.

Messina. 493. Small triptych: Trinity and two worshippers. (?)

Montecchio (Siena). S. ANDREA. S. Lawrence with a woman and three children at his feet (fr.).

New York. ROBERT LEHMAN COLLECTION. Coronation of Virgin (companion to Florence and London). *Plate* 356.

HERBERT LEHMAN (EX). Madonna and Child enthroned, crowned by two Angels, with SS. Ursula (?), Dominic and donor. (?)

Perugia. 70. Crucifixion with kneeling Cardinal.

Rome. VATICAN, PINACOTECA. 146, 151. Wings of portable altarpiece: SS. Paul and Nicholas; SS. Anthony Abbot and Francis. (?)

San Diego (Cal.). PUTNAM FOUNDATION. Portable altarpiece: Madonna of Humility, with Crucifixion and kneeling S. Francis above; in wings, S. Catherine, S. Christopher, Angel and Virgin of Annunciation (formerly T. S. Hyland Collection).

Siena. 121. Madonna and Child enthroned with SS. Catherine, Paul, James, Lucy, Peter and Nicholas; Crucifixion above.

Homeless. Madonna of Humility. *Plate* 354.

NICCOLÒ DA FOLIGNO

Niccolò di Liberatore, called l'Alunno. Foligno ca 1430–1502. Pupil of Benozzo Gozzoli; from 1466 active in the Marches, where he was influenced by Crivelli.

Alviano (Terni). S. MARIA ASSUNTA. (See Perugia.)

Angoulême. 2. (See Paris, Musées Nationaux.)

Assisi. PINACOTECA. Processional banner from S. Crispino: the Virgin protects the Brethren by intercession of SS. Francis and Clare; back, S. Blaise enthroned between S. Ruphinus and S. Victorinus; below, S. Blaise discovered by huntsmen and Martyrdom of S. Blaise (r.). 1475.

Crucifixion (fr.).

SACRO CONVENTO, F. M. PERKINS DONATION 22. S. Roch.

S. RUFFINO (DUOMO). Triptych: Madonna and Child enthroned with Angels; SS. Ruffinus and Cassidius, SS. John Evangelist and Pier Damiano; in pinnacles, Blessing God the Father with Angels and S. Michael above, Angel and Virgin of Annunciation in roundels; in predella, The Prefect Aspasio condemns S. Rufinus, first Bishop of Assisi, to the torture of fire; peasants find the Saint's body in the river Chiascio, Burial of S. Rufinus. Sd and d. 1460. *Plate 657.*

(Environs). LA BASTIA, PARISH CHURCH. Triptych: Madonna and Child enthroned with Angels; S. Sebastian and S. Michael; in pinnacles, God the Father, Angel and Virgin of Annunciation; in predella, Ezechias, David, Zacharias, Pietà, Isaiah, Daniel, Jeremiah. Sd and d. 1499 (but mostly by his son Lattanzio).

Baltimore (Md.). WALTERS ART GALLERY. 620. Upper panels from polyptych: Abraham, Jacob, Joseph, Daniel, Moses, Angel.

Bayeux. 39. (See Paris, Musées Nationaux.)

Bologna. 360. Processional standard: back, Annunciation with God the Father above; front, Madonna and Child with SS. Francis and Sebastian, two Angels and God the Father above. Sd and d. 1482.

Boston (Mass.). 20.1858/9. Six panels from pilasters of triptych formerly at S. Venanzio, Camerino: SS. Victorinus, Sebastian, Jerome, Lawrence, Gregory and Augustine (companions to Caen and Melun; see Rome, Vatican 299).

Budapest. 37 (82). Fresco transferred on canvas: S. Bernardino. Sd and d. 1497.

Caen. 21, 5. (See Paris, Musées Nationaux.)

Cambridge (Mass.). FOGG ART MUSEUM. 1927.207. Triptych: Madonna and Child enthroned with Angels and Donor; S. Francis, S. Sebastian.

Camerino. PALAZZO VESCOVILE. Predella panel from S. Venanzio triptych: Descent of the Holy Ghost. (See Rome, Vatican 299.)

Cannara (Perugia). S. GIOVANNI BATTISTA. Madonna and Child enthroned with SS. Sebastian and John Baptist (p.). d. 1482.

Claremont (Cal.). POMONA COLLEGE. 61.1.7 (KRESS STUDY COLLECTION. K 1284). Crucifixion (st.).

Compiègne. 28. (See Paris, Musées Nationaux.)

Deruta (Perugia). PALAZZO COMUNALE, PINACOTECA. Banner: Crucifixion and S. Anthony Abbot enthroned worshipped by Flagellants; back, Flagellation and SS. Egidius and Bernardinus.

Central panel of triptych, known as 'Madonna dei Consoli': Madonna and Child with SS. Francis and Bernardino, Angels and Donor (side panels with SS. Catherine and Louis of Toulouse, SS. Anthony of Padua and Sebastian, lost). Sd and d. 1457. *Plate 653.*

Esztergom. 55.204. Trinity.

Foligno. PALAZZO TRINCI, PINACOTECA. S. Francis receiving Stigmata.

Polyptych: Nativity and Resurrection above; side-panels—full-length SS. Sebastian, Nicholas, Michael, John Evangelist; upper row, half-length SS. Monica, John Baptist, Jerome, Blessed Pietro Grisci; pinnacles, half-length SS. Gregory, Paul, Peter (?) and Augustine (?): in pilasters, ten small Saints (predella, see Paris). 1492. *Plate 661.*

S. FELICIANO (DUOMO), SACRISTY. Fresco: Mourning Virgin and S. John Evangelist round a carved Crucifix (p.). *Plates 651–652.*

S. NICCOLÒ, ALTAR R. OF CHOIR. Coronation of Virgin, with S. Anthony Abbot and Bernardino; in predella, roundels with Dead Christ, mourning Virgin and mourning S. John Evangelist. L. [*Plate 298.*]

(Environs). S. BARTOLOMEO, L. CHAPEL. Martyrdom of S. Bartholomew (finished by his son Lattanzio in 1503).

— S. MARIA IN CAMPIS, CAPPELLA DI S. MARTA (UNDER BELL-TOWER). Frescoes: Crucifixion (fr.) and fragments of other scenes. 1456. *Plate 650.*

— VESCIA, COMPAGNIA ALLE VESCIE. Votive frescoes: Madonna di Loreto, Pietà (st.). d. 1494.

Gualdo Tadino. PINACOTECA. Polyptych: Madonna and Child enthroned with Angels; full-length SS. Paul, Peter, Francis and Bernardino; above, Pietà between eight half-length Saints; in pilasters, twelve small Saints; in predella, Blessed Bonaventura, Beltrando, King Robert, Alexander IV, Emperor Constantine, Nicholas IV, Cardinal Matteo d'Acquasparta, Franciscan monks and Cherubim. Sd and d. 1471.

Karlsruhe. 403. Standard from S. Gregorio at Assisi: Crucifixion; below, S. Gregory enthroned and Flagellants (p.). Sd and d. 1468.

Kevelaer. PRESBYTERY. Plague banner from altar of S. Ludovico (now S. Stefano) in Lower Church of Assisi: the Virgin and SS. Sebastian, Clare, Francis, Ruphinus Bishop, Victorinus Bishop, and Roch implore Christ to save Assisi from the plague. After 1460 and before 1472. *Plate 654.*

Laval. (See Paris, Musées Nationaux.)

London. 1107. Portable altarpiece: Crucifixion; in wings, Agony in the Garden, Way to Calvary, Resurrection, Pietà. Sd and d. 1487.

Lugnano in Teverina. PARISH CHURCH. Portable altarpiece: Assumption; in wings, S. Sebastian, S. Francis (g.p.).

Melun. (See Paris, Musées Nationaux.)

Milan. BRERA. 504. Polyptych: Madonna and Child, and Resurrection above; on either side, full-length SS. Louis of Toulouse, Francis, Bernardino, Sebastian; half-length SS. John Baptist, Peter (?), Jerome, Anthony; in pinnacles, female Saint, S. Peter Martyr, (two, lost). Sd and d. 1465.

Montefalco. S. AGOSTINO, CAPPELLA DEL SACRAMENTO, VAULT. Fragmentary frescoes: Church Fathers. (?)

S. FRANCESCO (MUSEO), SIXTH BAY R. Fresco around a wooden Crucifix: Mourning Virgin, Magdalen, S. Francis, S. John Evangelist (Mezzastris and Niccolò Alunno?).

Moulins. 79. (See Paris, Musées Nationaux.)

New York. R. LEHMAN COLLECTION. Front of processional standard: Madonna and S. Anne with Angels (companion of Princeton). E. *Plate 655.*

Nocera Umbra. PINACOTECA. Polyptych from cathedral: Nativity and Coronation of Virgin above; on either side, full-length Lawrence, Rinaldus Bishop, Felicissimus and Francis; half-length SS. Sebastian, John Baptist, Paul and Catherine; half-length Church Fathers; in pilasters, ten small Saints; first predella lost?; in second predella, twelve Apostles, two Seraphim, two Angels with emblem of Nocera and coat of arms of Bishop Francesco Scelloni. Sd and d. 1483. *Plate 658.*

Paris. 1120. Predella to Foligno polyptych: Agony in the Garden, Flagellation, Way to Calvary, Crucifixion, Joseph of Arimathea and Nicodemus, two Angels with inscription. Sd and d. 1492. *Plates 659, 660.*

MUSÉES NATIONAUX, CAMPANA 364, 367 (DEP. COMPIÈGNE, MOULINS). Two predella panels from triptych of S. Venanzio, Camerino (companions to Camerino): Ascension with SS. Michael and Raphael, Nativity. (See Rome, Vatican 299.)

— CAMPANA 365, 366 (DEP. TOURS). Two pinnacles from triptych of S. Venanzio, Camerino: Angel and Virgin of Annunciation. (See Rome, Vatican 299.)

— CAMPANA 368, 369, 370 (DEP. LAVAL, CAEN, MELUN). Panels from pilasters of triptych of S. Venanzio, Camerino (companions to Boston): David and S. Anthony; SS. Paul and Nicholas; S. Stephen and Bishop Saint (see Rome, Vatican 299).

— CAMPANA 371 (DEP. BAYEUX). Pietà.

— CAMPANA 372 (DEP. ANGOULÊME). Banner; front, Madonna of Mercy and Crucifixion above; back, Bishop enthroned and Annunciation above.

Perugia. 169. Banner of the Confraternita dell'Annunciata: Annunciation. d. 1466.

— DEP. FROM ALVIANO. Assumption.

VAN MARLE COLLECTION (EX). Two pages with coats of arms.

Princeton (N.J.). 65.266. Back of processional standard: S. Michael (companion to New York, Lehman). E. *Plate 656.*

Ravenna. 169. The Blood of the Redeemer (probably central panel of predella to Gualdo Tadino polyptych).

Rome. GALLERIA NAZIONALE, PALAZZO BARBERINI (FROM PALAZZO VENEZIA). Polyptych: Madonna and Child; SS. Francis, John Baptist, Jerome and Clare.

MUSEO DI CASTEL S. ANGELO, DONO CONTINI. Wings of portable altarpiece: S. Sebastian, S. John Baptist.

GALLERIA COLONNA. 91. 'Madonna del Soccorso'. L.

VILLA ALBANI. Polyptych: Madonna and Child with Angels; full-length SS. Benedict, Peter, Paul, Augustine; half-length SS. John Baptist, Catherine, Sebastian, Anthony Abbot. Sd and d. 1475.

VATICAN, PINACOTECA. 299. Fragmentary triptych from S. Venanzio, Camerino: Crucifixion and Resurrection above; on either side, full-length SS. Venantius and Peter, SS. John Baptist and Porphyrius; half-length Isaiah and David (lateral pinnacles, Saints in pilasters, predella panels, in Boston, Camerino, Paris Musées Nationaux).

307. Polyptych from Montelparo: Coronation and 'Cristo Pietoso' above; on either side, full-length SS. George, Basil, Benedict, John Baptist, Paul, Sebastian; half-length SS. Agatha, Catherine, Mary Magdalen, John Evangelist, Mary Cleophas, Ursula; in pinnacles, six Seraphim and six busts of Saints; in pilasters, 18 small Saints; in first predella, the twelve Apostles (Redeemer missing); in second predella, 15 female Saints. Sd and d. 1466.

San Marino. S. FRANCESCO, CHOIR. Two panels, each with two busts of Franciscan Saints.

San Severino Marche. PINACOTECA. Polyptych: Madonna and Child enthroned; full-length SS. James, Severinus, Victorinus, Sebastian; in pinnacles, God the Father, Angel and Virgin of Annunciation, David and Jeremiah; in predella, Apostles in gilded stucco. Sd and d. 1468.

Sarnano (Macerata). S. MARIA IN PIAZZA. Four side-panels of polyptych: full-length SS. Peter, John Baptist, Benedict and Blaise.

Spello. S. MARIA MAGGIORE, CAPPELLA DEL SEPOLCRO, MUSEO. Detached fresco from Cappella della Famiglia Tega (now shop): Crucifixion and Saints. Sd and d. 1461.

Spoleto. PINACOTECA. Monochrome Pietà. L.

Triptych: Coronation, Madonna and S. John Baptist.

Terni. PINACOTECA. Banner: Christ on Cross with S. Francis and S. Bernardino. Sd and d. 1497.

Tours. 247, 248. (See Paris, Musées Nationaux.)

Trieste (Environs). CASTELLO DI MIRAMARE. Four Franciscan Saints from pilasters of polyptych.

Vienna. EUGEN VON MILLER ZU AICHHOLZ (EX). Man of Sorrows and two Angels (from S. Agostino, Foligno).

NICCOLÒ DI NALDO

Painter from Norcia (Umbria), active in Siena. Partner of Gualtieri di Giovanni and Bene-
detto di Bindo in works for the Sienese Cathedral 1409–12.

Lugano. THYSSEN COLLECTION. Two panels from cupboard of Cappella dei Liri, sacristy of Siena cathedral (companions to Siena, Museo dell'Opera).

Siena. DUOMO, SACRISTY, CAPPELLA DEI LIRI (R. CHAPEL), L. WALL. Frescoes: Allegorical figure in pontifical dress seated on throne between an Angel holding a Bishop's staff and a (King?) holding a sceptre, surrounded by SS. Paolinus, Prosperus, Remigius, Bernard and other four Saints, while two warriors lie defeated before the throne (r.). 1410. *Plate 486.*

— — CENTRAL WALL. Frescoes: The Redeemer gives books to the Evangelists Mark and John; below them, seated at their desks, S. Ambrose and S. Gregory the Great (r.). 1410. *Plate 485.*

— — R. WALL. Frescoes: The Virgin offers a book to the Evangelist Matthew, while Jesus, in her lap, offers a book to the Evangelist Luke; below the Evangelists, seated at their desks, S. Augustine and S. Jerome (r.). 1410.

— MUSEO DELL'OPERA. 58. Panels from cupboard of the Cappella dei Liri: Four Apostles, four Prophets, four Angels and nine Articles of the Creed. Before 1412.

NICCOLÒ DI SEGNA

Sienese, documented 1331 to 1346. Pupil of his father Segna di Bonaventura and later close
imitator of Pietro Lorenzetti.

Amsterdam. OTTO LANZ (EX). Two panels from upper register of polyptch formerly Wallraf–Richartz Museum in Cologne: Half-length SS. James and Mary Magdalen (companions to New York). (See Siena 37.)

Assisi. PERKINS COLLECTION. Two panels from upper register of polyptych: S. John Evangelist, S. James (companions to Brussels, Cahen).

Atlanta (Georgia). ART ASSOCIATION GALLERIES. 58.51–52 (KRESS COLLECTION. K 40,41). Left and right panel of polyptych: S. Vitalis, S. Catherine. (See Siena 37.)

Baltimore (Md.). WALTERS ART GALLERY. 756. Panel of polyptych: Knee-length S. Lucy (companion to Atlanta; see Siena 37).

Brussels. PHILIPPE STOCLET (EX). Christ on Cross with Virgin and S. John. (?)
DR CAHEN. Panel of polyptych: S. Christopher (companion to Assisi).*

Buonconvento (Senese). PIEVE DEI SS. PIETRO E PAOLO, PINACOTECA. Painted Crucifix (fr.). (?)

Grosseto. See Segna.

Lucignano. MUSEO CIVICO. Annunciation. Madonna and Child with SS. Baptist and Peter; below, SS. Catherine, Michael, Magdalen and Francis.

Lugano. THYSSEN COLLECTION. Madonna and Child enthroned with Angels, S. John Baptist and Saint recommending kneeling monk.

Montalcino. MUSEO DIOCESANO. Centre panel of polyptych: Madonna and Child eating cherries (r.). d. 1346. *Plate 52.*

New York. ALBERT KELLER (EX). Two panels from upper register of polyptych formerly Wallraf Richartz Museum, Cologne: Half-length SS. John Baptist and Dominic (see Siena 37).

Paris. 1260. Madonna and Child enthroned with female Saint, SS. Peter Paul and Dominic worshipped by kneeling nun and monk.

Ponce (Puerto Rico). MUSEO DE ARTE. 255 KP.I. KRESS COLLECTION. K 577. Fragmentary polyptych: Madonna and Child, S. John Baptist, S. Peter; above, blessing Redeemer, two Angels.

Portland (Oregon). ART MUSEUM. 61.41. KRESS COLLECTION. K 1102. Panel of polyptych: S. Margaret (companion to Budapest Segna).

Rome. MUSEO DI PALAZZO VENEZIA. F.N. 18435. Madonna and Child (fr.).

San Galgano (Maremma Senese). ORATORIO DI MONTESIEPI, OVER ALTAR. Centre panel of polyptych commissioned by Ristoro da Selvatella: Madonna and Child. 1336.

San Gimignano. COLLEGIATA, R. AISLE, SEVENTH LUNETTE (OPPOSITE CHAPEL OF S. FINA). Fresco: S. Fina, lying on the wooden board where five mice had made their nest, has a vision of S. Gregory announcing to her her imminent death. *Plate 51.*

S. PIETRO, NICHE L. Fresco: Mourning Virgin and John Evangelist at foot of Cross.

Santa Colomba (Siena). PARISH CHURCH. Frescoes: Nativity; Crucifixion.

Siena. 21. Painted Crucifix. (?)

24. Panel from upper register of polyptych: half-length S. Catherine.

37. Right panel of polyptych: S. Bartholomew; above, SS. John Evangelist and Nicholas (companion to Amsterdam, Atlanta, Baltimore and New York).

38. Fragmentary polyptych: S. Benedict with SS. Lucy and Lawrence above; S. Michael with SS. Andrew and John Baptist above; S. Bartholomew with SS. John Evangelist and James above; S. Nicholas with SS. John Gualbert and Mary Magdalen above.

41. Madonna and Child (from Torri). (?)

44. Centre panel of polyptych: Madonna and Child.

46. Painted Crucifix. Sd and d. 1345. *Plate 54.*

S. MARTINO, CHAPEL OF CAMPANILE. Remains of frescoes: Legend of Blessed Pippo Ancarani. d. 1330. (?)

Venice. CONTE VITTORIO CINI. Inv. 6677. Madonna and Child. *Plate 53.*

Vertine (Senese). PARISH CHURCH. Madonna of Mercy. ca 1331. *Plate 50.*

Wiesbaden. VON HENCKELL COLLECTION. Nativity.

NICCOLÒ DI SER SOZZO see TEGLIACCI

NICCOLÒ DA VOLTRI

Ligurian, documented in Genoa from 1385 to 1417. Influenced by Barnaba da Modena (active in Liguria 1376/83) and later by Taddeo di Bartolo (in Liguria late 1390's).

Baltimore (Md.). WALTERS ART GALLERY. 443. Madonna suckling the Child, with two Angels and two small worshippers. *Plate 281.*

Genoa. PALAZZO BIANCO. 1739. Triptych from SS. Giacomo e Filippo: Madonna and Child; S. Catherine and female donor; S. Nicholas and male donor; in pinnacles, Crucifixion, S. Catherine of Siena, female Saint (with Barnaba da Modena, who signed it). *Plate 280.*

   s. DONATO. Madonna and Child, scratching His left foot and holding a scroll. Sd. *Plate 282.*

   s. ROCCO. Madonna and Child. E.

Rome. VATICAN, PAPAL APARTMENTS. Inv. 572. Panels of polyptych from Genoa, Chiesa delle Vigne: Annunciation; S. John Baptist, Angel Raphael with Tobias; in upper tier, half-length S. Dominic and S. Paul; in pinnacles, Trinity worshipped by Virgin and S. John Baptist; half-length Bishop Saint and Apostle. Sd and d. 1401. *Plate 283.*

Savona. PINACOTECA. Central panel of polyptych: Madonna and Child holding scroll inscribed 'Beati Pauperes in Spiritu' (st.).

NORTH-ITALIAN GOTHIC

CLOSE TO GENTILE DA FABRIANO, PISANELLO AND STEFANO DA ZEVIO

Denver (Col.). MUSEUM OF ART. E–GE–18–XV–950 (KRESS COLLECTION. K 1777). Nativity (fr.).

Florence. UFFIZI. Three panels of polyptych: S. Benedict exorcizing a monk, S. Benedict and the poisoned wine; S. Benedict and the broken sieve (companions to Milan, Poldi, Pezzoli). *Plate 541.*

Milan. POLDI PEZZOLI. 586. Madonna of Humility (Veronese follower of Gentile da Fabriano).

   591. S. Benedict in the wilderness (companion to Florence, Uffizi). *Plate 542.*

   PALAZZO BORROMEO. Frescoes: Card games and dances (Maestro dei Giuochi Borromeo).

Modena. 164. Cassone panel: Story of S. Giovanni Boccadoro. *Plate 548.*

Pavia. Inv. 176. Madonna and Child in Glory worshipped by SS. Francis and Clare. *Plate 534.*

Pordenone. DUOMO, CAPPELLA DEI SS. PIETRO E PAOLO, VAULT. Frescoes: Angel of S. Matthew, Young hermit Saint covered with cloak by Angel, Last Communion of Magdalen; Lion of S. Mark, S. Francis receiving Stigmata; Bull

of S. Luke, S. Benedict reading, monk reading; Eagle of S. John, two adoring
Angels. *Plates* 539–40.

— LUNETTES. Ruined frescoes: Townscape, Annunciation? (fr.).

Treviso. MUSEO CIVICO. Detached fresco: Madonna and Child blessing Saint with
cross (fr.).

Detached fresco from S. Caterina: Miracle of S. Eligius.

BAPTISTERY. Fresco: S. John Baptist and other figures.

Verona. 794. S. Dominic.

S. ANASTASIA, CAPPELLA SALERNI (SECOND L.). Fresco: Madonna and Child with S.
James and donor.

S. GIOVANNI IN VALLE, OVER ENTRANCE. Fresco: Madonna and Child enthroned with
SS. Anthony Abbot, Bartholomew, S. John Baptist and Isaiah (r.).

NUZI, Allegretto

*Fabriano (Marches) ca 1315–73. Registered among Florentine painters in 1346. Started
probably under Riminese painters, but developed under Florentine influence, especially
Daddi's and Maso's.*

Agen. MUSÉE. Madonna and Child enthroned with six Angels. *Plate* 207.

Ajaccio. 173. Triptych: Marriage of S. Catherine; S. John Baptist; S. Dominic. (?)

Altenburg. 52. Madonna and Child. (?)

Apiro (Macerata). PALAZZO MUNICIPALE. Polyptych: Madonna and Child enthroned;
SS. Catherine, Francis, Martin and Lucy; in pinnacles, Christ on Cross and
busts of S. Anthony of Padua, S. Louis of Toulouse and two Clarisse. Sd and
d. 1366. *Plate* 208.

Berlin. 1076, 1078. Diptych: Madonna and Child with SS. Catherine and Bartholomew; Crucifixion. Sd.

Berne. 198. Portable triptych: Crucifixion; four Saints; in pinnacles, blessing
Redeemer, Angel and Virgin of Annunciation.

Birmingham (Ala.). MUSEUM OF ART 61.113 (KRESS COLLECTION. K 1197). Crucifixion.

Brunswick (Maine). BOWDOIN COLLEGE, MUSEUM. 1961.100.4. (KRESS STUDY COLLEC-
TION. K 1226). Roundel from a pinnacle: Blessing Christ.

Chicago (Ill.). 33.1022. S. Augustine enthroned, worshipped by kneeling nun.
37.1006. Centre panel of dismembered dossal (companion to New York, Portland and Raleigh): Crucifixion; in spandrels, S. John Evangelist and S. Francis
(st.). L.

Crenna di Gallarate. CARMINATI COLLECTION. Right leaf of diptych: 'Fornari' Dead
Christ in Sepulchre (companion to Frankfurt).*

Detroit (Mich.). 89.19. Portable triptych: Madonna and Child with SS. John Baptist
and Catherine; Nativity and Crucifixion in wings; in pinnacles, Angel and
Virgin of Annunciation.

Fabriano. 2, 4. Two side-panels of triptych: SS. Venantius and John Baptist; SS. Anthony Abbot and John Evangelist.

3. S. Augustine between Nicholas of Tolentino and S. Stephen.

5. Madonna and Child; in pinnacle, blessing Redeemer (r.). L.

15. Polyptych: Madonna and Child, S. Venantius, S. John Baptist, S. John Evangelist, S. Nicholas; in pinnacles, Angel and Virgin of Annunciation, two busts of Saints.

17. Polyptych: Madonna and Child, S. Mary Magdalen, S. John Evangelist, S. Bartholomew, S. Venantius; in pinnacles, Christ on Cross, mourning Mary and John, S. Anthony Abbot and S. Catherine.

26 or 33. Fresco: Head of the Christ Child (fr.).

CORNER OF VIA S. FILIPPO AND VIA VALPOVERA, TABERNACLE. Fresco: Madonna and Child with two female Saints. L.

S. LUCIA (VULGO S. DOMENICO), EX CAPPELLA DI S. ORSOLA (L. OF CHOIR). Frescoes: in lunette, Death of Virgin; below, three roundels with S. Ursula, Dead Christ, S. Agnes; below, colossal S. Michael (p.).

— — L. WALL. Frescoes: in lunette, Massacre of Innocents (r.); below, S. Michael killing a tyrant; below, S. Nicholas and the three maidens; below, Announcing Angel (st.?).

— — R. WALL. Frescoes: in lunette, Stoning of S. Stephen; below, S. Michael fighting the Devils; below, S. Ursula's voyage; below, the Pope baptizes S. Ursula and her maidens; below, Meeting of S. Ursula and her bridegroom.

— SACRISTY (R. OF CHOIR). Frescoes: Death and Assumption of Virgin; Arsenius and his Hermits in the wilderness; Babylon riding the Hydra with the seven heads of the capital sins; the palm tree bending to the Madonna and Child (st.).

— — BETWEEN WINDOWS. Frescoes: below, Christ and the Apostles meet the Woman of Samaria at the well (st.).

S. VENANZIO (DUOMO), EX CAPPELLA DI S. LORENZO (R. OF CHOIR). Frescoes: vault— roundels with Evangelists (r.); left wall—in lunette, S. Lawrence distributing alms; below, Emperor Decius shown by S. Lawrence his poor; below, Madonna and Child between a Saint (destroyed) and S. Venantius; window wall—First Flagellation; Torture; Preaching to the Emperor; S. Lawrence baptizes (Hippolytus?); right wall—in lunette, S. Lawrence in prison; below, Second Flagellation (fr., due to opening of door); Martyrdom on the gridiron (fr.). *Plate* 209.

— CHAPEL L. OF CHOIR. Frescoes: Crucifixion; S. Catherine (st.); Nativity (r., st.); Beheading of Baptist (fr., r., st.).

Frankfurt a/M. GEORG HARTMANN (EX). Leaf of diptych: 'Fornari' Madonna and Child.

Houston (Texas). STRAUS GIFT. 8, 9. Side-panels of polyptych, each with ten Saints. L. (?).

London. GEORGE FARROW (EX). Fall of Simon Magus (fr.). *Plate* 210.

London (contd.). VISCOUNTESS D'ABERNON (EX). Madonna and Child enthroned. Sd and d. 1345. *Plate 206.*

Macerata. PINACOTECA. Triptych: Madonna and Child enthroned with Saints and Angels; S. Anthony Abbot; S. Julian; in pinnacles, Christ on Cross, Angel and Virgin of Annunciation. Sd and d. 1369.

Minneapolis (Minnesota). VANDERLIP COLLECTION. Crucifixion (inserted in fifteenth-century panel).

New York. MRS W. MURRAY CRANE. Three panels of dismembered dossal (companions to Chicago, Portland and Raleigh): S. John Evangelist raises to life the dead bridegroom, destroys the pagan idols with his prayers, helps the Man who had given up his riches (g.p.). L. *Plates 212–213.*

    ROBERT LEHMAN COLLECTION. Crucifixion with swooning Virgin and pelican.

Perugia. VAN MARLE COLLECTION (EX). Bust of Christ (r.).

Philadelphia (Pa.). JOHN G. JOHNSON COLLECTION. 2. Left wing of diptych: Madonna and Child with SS. John Baptist, Lucy, Ursula and Anthony Abbot; in pinnacle, Angel of Annunciation (r.).

    117. Panel of polyptych: S. John Evangelist. E.

    118. Diptych: Madonna and Child; Dead Christ in sepulchre (p.).

    119. Madonna and Child (p.).

Portland (Oregon). PORTLAND ART MUSEUM. 61.32 (KRESS COLLECTION. K 205A). Panel of dismembered dossal (companion to Chicago, New York, Raleigh): S. John Evangelist raising Drusiana (g.p.). L.

Raleigh (N.C.). NORTH CAROLINA MUSEUM OF ART, 60.17–20 (KRESS COLLECTION. K 205B, C, D). Three panels of dismembered dossal (companions to Chicago, New York and Portland): S. John Evangelist converts Atticus and Eugenius, confounds the philosopher Crato, drinks the poisoned cup (g.p.). L.

Rome. VATICAN, PINACOTECA. 204. Triptych: Madonna and Child enthroned; SS. Ursula, Michael and eight donors. Sd and d. 1365.

    208, 210. Diptych: Madonna and Child; Dead Christ in sepulchre (s.).

    209. Madonna and Child enthroned with SS. Catherine and John Baptist (p.?).

    244. Dead Christ in sepulchre worshipped by two Angels; below, Nativity (g.p.).

San Severino Marche. 22. Madonna suckling the Child. Sd and d. 1366.

Southampton. ART GALLERY. S–1403. Triptych: Coronation of Virgin; ten Saints in left panel; ten Saints in right panel; in pinnacles, Angel and Virgin of Annunciation. L. (?) *Plate 214.*

Strasbourg. 202. Predella panel: S. Bartholomew, S. Peter and three other Apostles (companion to Zurich).

Urbino. GALLERIA NAZIONALE DELLE MARCHE. Madonna and Child enthroned. Sd and d. 1372. *Plate 215.*

Washington (D.C.). 6 (MELLON COLLECTION). Triptych: Madonna and Child enthroned; S. Anthony Abbot; S. Venantius (only the S. Anthony Abbot, which is a version of left panel in Macerata triptych).

Zurich. KUNSTHAUS. Inv. 2598. Predella panel: SS. Paul, John Evangelist, Andrew, James and another Apostle (companion to Strasbourg).

Homeless. Scene of martyrdom (fr.). *Plate 211.*

ODERISI see ROBERTO DI ODERISIO

OGGIONO see MARCO D'OGGIONO

ORTOLANO

Giambattista Benvenuti, called l'Ortolano. Ferrara, born before 1488, died after 1526. Strongly influenced by Dosso, and in his last phase, scarcely to be distinguished from Garofalo.

Alton Towers (Staffs.). EARL OF SHREWSBURY (EX). Adoration of Magi (variant of Copenhagen).

Assisi. F. M. PERKINS COLLECTION. 'Noseda' S. Sebastian.

Baltimore (Md.). WALTERS ART GALLERY. 445. Predella panel: Nativity. *Plate 1763.*

Berlin. 1332. See Münster.

EUGEN SCHWEITZER (EX). Circumcision.

Bologna. Inv. 594. Madonna and Child in Glory with music-making Angels (fr.). L.

CASA MALVASIA (EX). Lunette: Pietà.

Bordeaux. 15. Madonna adoring the Child.

Cambridge. FITZWILLIAM MUSEUM. 160. S. John Baptist in the Wilderness.

Copenhagen. 520. S. Margaret and the dragon. d. 1524. *Plate 1771.*

521. Adoration of Magi.

Ferrara. 42. Lunette: Mourning over dead Christ.

VENDEGHINI BALDI COLLECTION. Madonna and Child.

Florence. BERENSON COLLECTION. Holy Family.

LOESER COLLECTION (EX). Nativity. *Plate 1761.*

Gazzada (Varese). FONDAZIONE CAGNOLA. Virgin and Child adoring each other. E.

London. 669. S. Sebastian between SS. Roch and Demetrius. *Plate 1764.*

COURTAULD INSTITUTE GALLERIES, LEE OF FAREHAM COLLECTION. Christ and the Woman taken in adultery. *Plate 1765.*

Magdeburg. MUSEUM (EX). Two panels: SS. Nicholas of Bari and Sebastian (old copies of Rome, Campidoglio?). Destroyed.

Milan. BRERA. 434. Crucifixion with S. John Baptist and Bishop Saint. *Plate 1768.*

G. BARGELLESI. Head of Baptist on a platter against landscape.

E. MALAGUTTI (EX). Madonna and Child adoring each other (variant of Gazzada).

A. ROBIATI. Madonna and Child with S. John Baptist (formerly Modena, Coccapani and Genoa, Nigro).

Münster. SEMINAR (BERLIN LOAN). Madonna and Child in landscape.

Nantes. 113. S. John at Patmos (old c. of Venice).

Naples. 73. Mourning over dead Christ. Sd and d. 1521. *Plate 1769.*

— DEPOT. S. Margaret.

New York. 30.95.296. 'Borghese' Adoration of Shepherds (small variant of Rome Doria Pamphili).

Paris. 1401. Nativity (r?).

Philadelphia (Pa.). J. G. JOHNSON COLLECTION. 246. Adoration of the Child with Angels carrying Symbols of Passion. *Plate 1762.*

Potsdam. SANS SOUCI (EX?). 48, Holy Family in landscape.

Rome. CAMPIDOGLIO, PINACOTECA. 16. Two panels: S. Nicholas of Bari, S. Sebastian.

GALLERIA BORGHESE. 390. Mourning over dead Christ.

GALLERIA DORIA PAMPHILI. 312. Adoration of the Child with Infant S. John, S. Francis and Magdalen. *Plate 1770.*

PALAZZO PATRIZI. Circumcision and Saints. *Plate 1766.*

PALAZZO ROSPIGLIOSI, COLLEZIONE PALLAVICINI. 31. Holy Family.

MARCHESA MARGHERITA VISCONTI VENOSTA. S. Anthony of Padua.

Venice. CONTE VITTORIO CINI. Inv. 2813. S. John at Patmos (replica at Nantes). *Plate 1767.*

PACCHIA, Girolamo del

Siena. 1477–1535. Pupil of Fungai; influenced by Signorelli, Pacchiarotto, Fra Bartolomeo, Sodoma, Andrea del Sarto, Raphael and Genga.

Allington Castle (Maidstone). LORD CONWAY (EX). Madonna and Child.

Asciano (Senese). SS. FABIANO E SEBASTIANO, R. OF ALTAR. Fresco to the right of Assumption by Benvenuto di Giovanni: full-length SS. Lucy and Roch; other wall, S. Jerome. d. 1496. (?)

Berlin. 105. Predella panel: Marriage of Virgin.

A. VON BECKERATH (EX). Madonna and Child with S. Bernardino, S. Catherine of Siena and four Angels.

Berlin-Ost. 227. Holy Family and S. Francis.

Bonn. PROVINZIALMUSEUM. 206A (EX). Madonna and Child.

Boston (Mass.). 94.180. Two Angels (fr.).

Budapest. 53 (68). Madonna and Child with S. Francis (st.).

1216 (116). Tondo: Holy Family and Saint. L.

Casole d'Elsa. COLLEGIATA. Visitation with SS. Lucy and Apollonia; in lunette, Madonna of Mercy (r.; st.?). (?)

Dubrovnik (Ragusa). BISKUPSKA PINAKOTEKA. Christ at Column.

Florence. UFFIZI. 3441. Tondo: Madonna and Child with Infant S. John. *Plate 1562.*

PEDULLI COLLECTION (EX). Madonna and Child with S. Jerome and S. Catherine of Siena.

London. COURTAULD INSTITUTE GALLERIES, GAMBIER PARRY COLLECTION. Tondo: Holy Family with S. Catherine of Siena.

LADY FREYBERG. Reclining Venus with three Cupids.

FAIRFAX MURRAY (EX). Madonna and Child with Infant S. John. *Plate 1563.*

J. POPE-HENNESSY. Marriage of the Virgin.

DUKE OF WESTMINSTER (EX). Holy Family with Infant S. John. *Plate 1559.*

Munich. W.A.F. 758. Bierhead: Madonna and Child with four Angels. *Plate 1556.*

W.A.F. 759. Bierhead: S. Bernardino of Siena with two Angels. *Plate 1555.*

Naples. 510. Holy Family with Infant S. John and S. Catherine of Siena.

New Haven (Conn.). 1871.75. Madonna and Child (r.).

Orléans. 1112. Holy Family with S. Catherine.

Paris. 1642. Crucifixion. L. (?)

Rome. VATICAN. 338. Holy Family with S. Catherine of Siena. L.

Sarteano (Val di Chiana). S. LORENZO. Angel and Virgin of Annunciation.

Siena. 350. Madonna and Child. L.

410. Annunciation and Visitation in background. 1518. *Plate 1558.*

448. Tondo: Holy Family with S. Catherine.

612. Bierhead: front, S. Augustine; back, S. Galganus (st.).

613. Bierhead: front, Pietà; back, S. Paul (st.). L.

PALAZZO CHIGI SARACINI. Banner: Madonna and Child enthroned with Putti drawing back Curtain, kneeling SS. Nicholas and Augustine (from Compagnia del Corpus Domini, S. Agostino). E.

Madonna and Child holding goldfinch (bierhead from Compagnia del Corpus Domini).

Tondo: Madonna embracing Child against landscape.

Madonna suckling Child with Infant S. John, S. Bernardino and S. Catherine of Siena.

E. MARTINI HEIRS. Annunciation. *Plate 1560.*

S. BERNARDINO, ORATORIO SUPERIORE. Frescoes: Birth of Virgin, S. Bernardino, Annunciation. (See also under Sodoma and Beccafumi.) 1518. *Plate 1557.*

S. CRISTOFORO, FIRST ALTAR L. Madonna and Child with SS. Luke and Romuald. 1508.

S. DONATO, R. TRANSEPT. Madonna and Child.

S. GIROLAMO, THIRD ALTAR L. Fresco: above, S. Jerome in his Study; below, on either side of altar, two Saints.

S. MARIA DEL CARMINE, THIRD ALTAR R. Ascension. E.

SANTUARIO CATERINIANO, S. CATERINA IN FONTEBRANDA (ORATORIO DELLA CONTRADA DELL'OCA), ALTAR. Frescoed lunette: S. Catherine of Siena receiving Stigmata (five Angels holding curtain below, by Sodoma; statue of altar, by Neroccio). (?)

— R. WALL. Frescoes: S. Agnes of Montepulciano raises a foot for S. Catherine to kiss, while lying in state on the bier; S. Catherine rescues Fra Tommaso della Forte and his companions attacked by robbers. *Plates 1554, 1561.*

— L. WALL. Fresco: S. Catherine heals Matteo Cenni from the plague (by Tamagni, on his design?) (S. Catherine blinding the Florentine soldiers is by Ventura Salimbeni, 1604). *Plate 1553.*

S. SPIRITO, THIRD ALTAR L. Coronation of Virgin and SS. John Baptist, Peter and Paul. *Plate 1565.*

Sinalunga (Val di Chiana). S. MARTINO, R. TRANSEPT. Deposition; in predella, two pairs of Flagellants adoring the Cross, Flagellation, Way to Calvary, Crucifixion, Deposition, Resurrection.

Stockholm. DR L. TEIANDER (EX). Assumption of Virgin.*

Sutton Place (Guildford). J. PAUL GETTY COLLECTION. Rape of the Sabine Women. *Plate 1564.*

Homeless. Tondo: Holy Family with S. Catherine of Siena (repr. *Dedalo* XI, p. 764).

PACCHIAROTTO, Giacomo

Sienese. 1474–1540. Pupil of Matteo di Giovanni; influenced by Fungai, Francesco di Giorgio, Pietro di Domenico and Perugino.

Baltimore (Md.). WALTERS ART GALLERY. 616. Sulpicia upon a pedestal. (See Master of Griselda.) *Plate 905.*

622. Predella panel: Crucifixion (companion to Cambridge and London, Butler).

MUSEUM OF ART (KRESS COLLECTION. K 62.16). Angel playing lute (fr. of Assumption; companion to El Paso, Dublin and London).

Buonconvento (Senese). SS. PIETRO E PAOLO, CHOIR. Madonna and Child with SS. John Baptist, Peter, Paul and Sebastian. E.

Cambridge. FITZWILLIAM MUSEUM. PD 980, 981/1963. Two predella panels: Baptism, Resurrection (companions to Baltimore and London, Butler). *Plates 924–925.*

Cambridge (Mass.). FOGG ART MUSEUM. 1921.9. Madonna and Child with SS. Mary Magdalen, Catherine and two Angels.

Dublin. JUDGE MURNAGHAN. Four Saints emerging from clouds (fr. of Assumption; companion to Baltimore, El Paso and London).

El Paso (Texas). MUSEUM OF ART (KRESS COLLECTION. K 1329, 1330). Angels (frs. of Assumption, companions to Baltimore, Dublin and London).

Englewood (N.J.). PLATT COLLECTION (EX). 'Palmieri Nuti' Madonna and Child with S. Jerome and female Saint holding Symbols of Passion. L.

Florence. SERRISTORI COLLECTION (EX). Madonna and Child with S. Bernardino and S. Jerome. E.

Hanover. LANDESMUSEUM. 262. Madonna and Child with SS. Catherine of Siena and S. Bernardino. (Between Benvenuto di Giovanni and Pacchiarotto.)

La Gaida (Parma). GINO MAGNANI. 'Palmieri Mocenni' Holy Family and four
Angels. *Plate* 923.

London. 1849. Nativity with SS. Stephen, John Baptist, Jerome and Nicholas; in
pilasters, Angel and Virgin of Annunciation, SS. Peter, Paul, Francis and
female Saint; in predella, Agony in the Garden, Betrayal of Christ, Crucifixion, Pietà, Resurrection.

COURTAULD INSTITUTE GALLERIES, GAMBIER PARRY COLLECTION. Three panels: Full-
length SS. Jerome, Francis and Anthony of Padua in niches.

CHARLES BUTLER (EX). Virgin of Assumption (fr.; companion to Baltimore, Dublin,
El Paso and below).

Predella panels: Nativity with S. Catherine; Descent of the Holy Ghost (companions to Baltimore and Cambridge).

SIR KENNETH MUIR MACKENZIE (EX). S. Onuphrius kneeling in landscape.

ANTHONY POST. Moses, David and two other figures emerging from Clouds (fr.
of Assumption, companion to Baltimore, Dublin, El Paso and above).

REPTON COLLECTION (EX). Madonna and Child with S. Catherine and S. Sigismund.

Massa Marittima. S. AGOSTINO. Small Nativity with SS. Bernardino and Anthony
of Padua. E. Not traced. *Plate* 918.

Nashville (Tennessee). GEORGE PEABODY COLLEGE (KRESS COLLECTION. K 1095).
Madonna and Child.

Ortignano di Raggiolo (Casentino). S. MATTEO. Madonna and Child with SS.
Jerome, Bernardino, Francis and S. Catherine (replica at Oxford ?).

Oxford. ASHMOLEAN MUSEUM. A 930. Madonna and Child with SS. Jerome, Bernardino, Francis and S. Catherine (replica of Ortignano ?).

Rome (Environs). MENTANA. F. ZERI. Ecce Homo (fr.).

Rossie Priory (Inchture, Scotland). LORD KINNAIRD. Nativity.

San Casciano dei Bagni (Chiusi). S. LEONARDO. Coronation of Virgin and SS.
John Baptist, Cassianus, Leonard, Bartholomew, four female Saints and
twelve Angels; in pilasters, six small Saints. *Plate* 917.

San Diego (Cal.). FINE ARTS GALLERY, LASAR O. KIPNIS GIFT. Madonna and Child
(formerly Platt).

Siena. 366. SS. Louis of Toulouse, Lucy, Jerome, Bartholomew and Galganus (frs.
of pilasters joined together).

388. Madonna and Child with SS. Jerome and Mary Magdalen (st.).

421, 422. Ascension; in predella: S. Michael defeats Satan, S. Catherine of Siena
gives clothing to Christ as Beggar, Marriage at Cana, Adoration of Magi,
Calling of SS. Peter and Andrew, Martyrdom of S. Catherine of Alexandria,
S. Raphael and Tobias. *Plate* 926.

424. Madonna and Child with SS. Onuphrius and Bartholomew and Angels;
in lunette, Christ with SS. Jerome and Francis. *Plate* 921.

426. Triptych from Campiglia d'Orcia: Visitation, S. Francis, S. Michael.

436. Visitation with SS. John Baptist, Anthony Abbot, Anthony of Padua,
Nicholas, Dominic and Leonard. ca 1530. *Plate* 922.

Siena (contd.). 576. Assumption (r.).

  ARCHIVIO DI STATO. Book-cover: Ambassador's arrival in Siena. d. 1498. (?)

  PALAZZO SALIMBENI (MONTE DEI PASCHI). Madonna and Child with SS. Jerome
    and John Baptist.

  S. MARIA ASSUNTA (DUOMO), SALA CAPITOLARE. Madonna and Child with SS. Roch
    and Sebastian (st.).

  (Environs). BELCARO, BARZELOTTI CAMAIORI COLLECTION (EX). Madonna and Child
    with SS. John Baptist and Jerome. *Plate* 919.

Stockholm. NATIONAL MUSEUM. Madonna and Child with SS. John Baptist and Paul

Zagreb. 60. Man of Sorrows.

Homeless. Madonna and Child with SS. Jerome and Anthony of Padua. L. *Plate* 920.

PAGANI, Giovanni, da Monterubbiano

Marchigian, follower of the Crivelli. Recorded 1506–1538. *Father of Vincenzo Pagani.*

Montpellier. 690. 'Madonna del Soccorso' from S. Agostino at Cingoli. Sd and d.
    1506. *Plate* 983.

Tolentino. BASILICA DI S. NICOLA. Lunette: Pietà; in roundels above, Angel and
    Virgin of Annunciation. (?)

Treia (Macerata). DUOMO, SACRISTY. Lunette: Entombment (with Vincenzo Pagani).

PAGANI, Vincenzo, da Monterubbiano

Marchigian. ca 1490–1568. *Pupil probably of his father Giovanni and teacher of his son
Lattanzio; strongly influenced by other followers of Crivelli; by Lotto, by the Umbrians,
and by Raphael.*

Altidona (Ascoli). PARISH CHURCH. Madonna and Child with S. Michael, another
    Saint and donor.

Appignano del Tronto. S. ANGELO, CRYPT. Assumption. Sd and d. 1539.

Ascoli Piceno. 59. Deposition. Sd and d. 1529.

    60. Madonna and Child with Angels.

    61. S. Mary Magdalen adoring the Crucifix (r.).

  S. AGOSTINO, FIRST ALTAR L. Madonna of Loreto and SS. Lucy, Cosmas, Damian
    and Homobonus. Sd and d. 1542.

Camerino. 30. Standard: front, Madonna and Child; back, S. Venantius. L.

Carassai (Ascoli). S. LORENZO. Madonna and Child with SS. Luke and Lawrence.

Corridonia (Macerata; former Mont'olmo; called Pàusola 1851 to 1931). S. FRAN-
    CESCO. Madonna and Child with SS. Peter, Francis and two music-making
    Angels. Sd and d. 1517. *Plate* 991.

Cossignano (Ascoli). SS. ANNUNZIATA. S. Anthony Abbot enthroned, with SS. Anthony of Padua and Job.

Esztergom. 56.766. Madonna and Child enthroned with SS. John Baptist, Dominic, Peter and Eternal with globe, above.

Fermo. 18. Madonna and Child with SS. John Evangelist and Mary Magdalen. L.

Florence. BERENSON COLLECTION. Bust of man.

Gàgliole. S. GIUSEPPE. Frescoed niche: Nativity; at sides, SS. Sebastian and Roch. d. 1530.

Gubbio. PINACOTECA. Lunette: Madonna and Cherubs. (?)

Macerata. 5. Madonna appearing to SS. Julian and Anthony of Padua and worshippers. E.

Milan. BRERA. 498. Coronation and SS. Genesio?, John Evangelist, Bonaventura and Ursula. 1517–18. *Plate 993.*

499–501. Predella panels: Adoration of Magi, Christ and the Doctors, Massacre of Innocents. *Plate 992.*

Montalto delle Marche. MUNICIPIO. Madonna and Child with SS. Sebastian and Sylvester. Sd and d. 1522.

Montelparo. S. MARIA NOVELLA. Madonna and Child, enthroned with SS. John Baptist, Prassede and female donor.

Monteprandone. CONVENTO DI S. GIACOMO. Coronation of Virgin and SS. Anthony of Padua, John Baptist, Francis and Catherine. 1525.

Monterubbiano. S. MARIA DEI LETTERATI, CHOIR. Assumption.

— SACRISTY. SS. George, Stephen, Vincent and Catherine.

— — Predella: Flagellation, Way to Calvary, Christ falling under Cross.

Moresco (Ascoli). MUNICIPIO. Madonna and Child in Glory and SS. Lawrence, Roch, Sophia and Nicholas. L.

Pàusola. See Corridonia.

Philadelphia (Pa.). J. G. JOHNSON COLLECTION. 198. Angel of Annunciation (companion to Rome, Spiridon).

199, 200. Predella panels: Flagellation, Circumcision.

Porchia (Ascoli). S. LUCIA. Madonna and Child enthroned with SS. Sebastian, John Baptist, Catherine and Lucy; Pietà in lunette.

Recanati. CHIESA DEL BEATO PLACIDO. 'Madonna del Soccorso' with SS. Bartholomew, Placido and kneeling Mother.

Ripatransone (Ascoli). 2. Madonna and Child in Glory, and SS. Michael, George and Martin. Sd and d. 1529.

Rome. NEVIN COLLECTION (EX). Madonna and Child in Glory and SS. Michael, Sebastian, Anthony of Padua, Roch and donor. L.

SPIRIDON (EX). Virgin of Annunciation (companion to Philadelphia).

VATICAN, PINACOTECA. 341, 345. Two pilasters from altarpiece with three small Saints each: SS Victor, Clare, Roch; SS. Augustine, Anthony and Sebastian.

Sarnano. 2. S. Lucy in Landscape, and music-making Putti. Sd and d. 1525.

3, 4. SS. John Baptist and Catherine; SS. Francis and Bonaventura.

Sarnano (contd.). 5. SS. Clare and Augustine.
     6. Deposition. Sd and d. 1529. *Plate* 994.
Treia (Macerata). DUOMO, LOWER CHURCH. Assumption.

PALMERUCCI, Guido

Painter from Gubbio, mentioned 1315 to 1349. Probably pupil of Meo da Siena. Close follower of Pietro and Ambrogio Lorenzetti.

Amsterdam. OTTO LANZ COLLECTION (EX). Madonna and Child.
Brussels. VAN GELDER COLLECTION (EX). Tondo: Madonna and Child. *Plate* 101.
Cambridge (Mass.). FOGG ART MUSEUM. 1962.158 (KRESS STUDY COLLECTION. M–5)
     Madonna and Child (r.) (from New York, M.M.A.).
Florence. CONTESSA SERRISTORI (EX). Three panels from polyptych: Madonna and
     Child. S. John Evangelist, S. Catherine. *Plate* 102.
Forlì. 126. Two panels from polyptych: S. (Gregory?) and S. Mary Magdalen.
Gubbio. PINACOTECA. Polyptych: Madonna and Child enthroned, SS. Marianus
     (Deacon), Ubaldus (Bishop), John Baptist and James; in pinnacles, Cruci-
     fixion, two Angels, SS. Agnes and Catherine.
     Tondo: Madonna and Child.
     Annunciation (fr.).
     Madonna embracing the Child (r.).
     Fragments of frescoes from S. Maria Nuova: Madonna and Child, Madonna
     and Child with Goldfinch and Angel, [S. John Baptist.]
     PALAZZO DEI CONSOLI, CAPPELLA. Madonna and Child enthroned with Saints and
     kneeling donor. *Plate* 103.
     S. MARIA DEI LAICI, TABERNACLE. Fresco: S. Anthony Abbot (r.). (?)
     S. MARIA NUOVA, ENTRANCE WALL. Fresco: Annunciation. (?)
     — (Environs). PIEVE DI AGNANO. Madonna and Child enthroned with Angels.
Nancy. 7, 8, 9. Predella panels: SS. James and Marianus led to their martyrdom;
     Crucifixion; Torture of S. Marianus. *Plate* 104.
New York. 27.250.2 (KRESS COLLECTION. M–5). Madonna and Child (now Cam-
     bridge).
Rome. NEVIN COLLECTION (EX). Triptych: Madonna and Child, SS. Francis and
     Louis of Toulouse.
Vienna. LANCKORONSKI COLLECTION (EX). Polyptych: Madonna and Child and four
     Saints; two more Saints from same polyptych; four Scenes from Life of S.
     Blaise. *Plate* 99.
Homeless. Right panel of polyptych: Deacon Martyr. *Plate* 100.

PALMEZZANO, Marco

Forlì (Romagna), 1459–after 1543. Pupil and assistant of Melozzo da Forlì; influenced slightly by Bellini and Rondinelli.

Athens. GALLERY. Frescoed lunette: Christ upheld by Angels.

Baltimore (Md.). WALTERS ART GALLERY. 437. Holy Family with Infant S. John and Magdalen. Sd.

    505. Holy Family (old copy?; see Rome, Vitetti).

    507, 547. Predella panels: Monk preaching; Novice taking the habit. (?)

Basle. 1129. Adoration of the Child. (?)

Bergamo. 268. Circumcision. Sd and d. 153(6?).

Berlin-Ost. 131. Nativity. Formerly Sd and d.

    137. Madonna and Child with parts of S. Petronius and another Saint showing (fr.).

    1087. Madonna and Child with S. Barbara and old Saint. Sd (date erased).

    1129A. Christus Triumphans. Sd and d. 1525. (Destroyed 1945.)

    GOBLET COLLECTION (EX). Mystic Marriage of S. Catherine with S. Joseph and Infant S. John. Sd and d. 1525.

Bologna. 502. Madonna and Child with ears of wheat (fr. of altarpiece from S. Varano near Forlì; companion to Forlì 121). E.

Bonn. 209. Christ carrying Cross. Sd and d. 1503.

Bordeaux. 90. Crucifixion.

Brescia. 110. Christ carrying Cross. Sd in Hebrew.

Brisighella (Faenza). S. MARIA DI RONTANA. Adoration of Magi; in lunette, Christ disputing in Temple. Sd and d. 1514.

    MINORI OSSERVANTI. Madonna and Child enthroned with SS. Anthony of Padua, Anthony Abbot, Jerome, Valerian and three Angels; in lunette, God the Father and Cherubim; in predella, Angel and Virgin of Annunciation. Sd and d. 1520.

Brooklyn (N.Y.). 34.499. Holy Family with S. Catherine and Infant S. John. 153(7?).

Budapest. 1032 (66). Holy Family with Infant S. John.

Cambridge (Mass.). FOGG ART MUSEUM. 1938.88. Panel of polyptych: S. Blaise.

Canford Manor (Ashby St. Ledgers). VISCOUNT WIMBORNE. Baptism of Christ (version of Forlì, Melbourne and Rome, Ferroni).

Castrocaro (Forlì). SS. NICCOLÒ E FRANCESCO. Madonna and Child enthroned with SS. Nicholas and Anthony of Padua; in lunette, Nativity. Sd and d. 1500.

Cesena. PINACOTECA. Bust of Filasio Roverella. (?)

Compton Wynyates (Oxon). MARQUESS OF NORTHAMPTON. 'Calzolai' altarpiece: Mystic marriage of S. Catherine and SS. Augustine, Dominic, Tobias and the Angel, three music-making Putti (from S. Agostino, Cesena). Sd and d. 1537.

Cracow. COUNT SIGISMUND PUSLOWSKI (EX). Christ carrying Cross. Sd and d. 1536.

Dijon. T 32. Sacra Conversazione with Simeon, Infant S. John, female martyr and S. Francis.

J 178. Christ on tomb, attended by Mary Magdalen, Nicodemus and Joseph of Arimathea (variant of Vicenza).

Dublin. 117. Madonna and Child enthroned with SS. Lucy and John Baptist and Angel. Sd and d. 1513.

Düsseldorf. WALTER GROSS (EX). Mourning over dead Christ.

Edinburgh. ERSKINE COLLECTION (EX). Holy Family with SS. Catherine, Dominic and Infant S. John. Sd and d. 1532.

Englewood (N.J.). D. F. PLATT COLLECTION (EX). Holy Family with S. Francis and Infant S. John.

Esztergom. 55.221. Martyrdom of S. Sebastian.

55.222. Holy Family with S. Catherine and Infant S. John. Sd and d. 1529.

55.223. Madonna and Child on parapet with SS. Anthony Abbot, Sebastian, female Martyr and Infant S. John.

Faenza. PINACOTECA. Madonna and Child enthroned with SS. Michael and James the Less; in lunette, God the Father. 1498.

Christ carrying Cross, and three other heads.

Panels from altarpiece: S. Augustine, Tobias and the Angel.

Panels from altarpiece; half-length S. Jerome and Bishop Saint.

GUIDI COLLECTION (EX). Blessing Redeemer.

Florence. UFFIZI. 1418. Crucifixion. Sd.

BIGALLO. Predella panel: Christ and the Apostles.

CORSINI COLLECTION. 417. S. Francis receiving stigmata. Sd and d. 1534.

GENTHNER COLLECTION (EX). Three predella panels: Nativity, Flight into Egypt, Flagellation.

Forlì. 110. So-called portrait of Cesare Borgia. (?)

111, 112. Predella panels: Circumcision, Flight into Egypt.

113. Annunciation. Sd. *Plate* 1001.

114. Selfportrait. d. 1536.

116. Christ carrying Cross, and other figures. Sd and d. 1535.

119. S. Anthony Abbot enthroned between SS. Sebastian and John Baptist. Sd. E. *Plate* 1000.

120. Annunciation (from Carmine).

121. Lunette: God the Father (companion to Bologna). E.

122. Communion of the Apostles (from High Altar of Duomo; companion to London 596). 1506.

123. Holy Family (st.).

124. Madonna and Child with SS. Severus and Valerian and three music-making Angels. L.

125. S. Helen. Sd and d. 1516.

143. 'Denti' altarpiece: Madonna and Child with SS. Bartholomew and Anthony of Padua. Sd and d. 1513 (?)

183. Madonna and Child.

— DEP. FROM S. MARIA DELLA RIPA. Detached fresco: Crucifixion with SS. Francis and Clare. Sd and d. 1492.

— FROM PALAZZO PIANCASTELLI, FUSIGNANO. Baptism of Christ. Sd and d. 1534.

— FROM PALAZZO PIANCASTELLI, FUSIGNANO. Nativity. Sd and d. 1532(33?).

SS. BIAGIO E GIROLAMO (rebuilt after the war). SECOND ALTAR L. Triptych: Madonna and Child enthroned with lute-playing Angel, donor and his family; SS. Catherine and Dominic, SS. Anthony of Padua and Sebastian; in predella, Christ and the Apostles, four Saints. Sd.

— CAPPELLA FEO. Frescoes: in vault, Prophets and Cherubim (on Melozzo's design?); on walls, Martyrdom of S. James, Miracle of S. James at San Domingo de la Calzada. Before 1495. Destroyed 1944. *Plate* 998.

— FOURTH CHAPEL R. Frescoed vault: Madonna and Cherubim. Destroyed 1944.

S. CROCE (DUOMO), SACRISTY. S. Roch.

S. MERCURIALE, CAPPELLA DEL SACRAMENTO. Votive picture: Warrior before Crucifix, recommended by SS. Mary Magdalen and John Gualbert.

— CAPPELLA DEI FERRI. Immaculate Conception with SS. Mercuriale, Rufillus and Stephen; in lunette, Resurrection; in predella, Meeting at Golden Gate, Stoning of Stephen, SS. John Gualbert and Peter, SS. Paul and Benedict; in spandrels, two Prophets. Sd and d. 1510. *Plate* 1003.

— THIRD CHAPEL R. Madonna and Child enthroned with SS. Catherine and John Evangelist. Sd.

CASA ALBICINI. Holy Family with Infant S. John; in background, S. Sebastian. Sd and d. 1515.

Forlimpopoli. S. MARIA DEI SERVI. Annunciation. Sd and d. 1533.

Gazzada (Varese). FONDAZIONE CAGNOLA. 49, 50. Angel and Virgin of Annunciation in roundels.

Geneva. MUSÉE D'ART ET D'HISTOIRE, LEGS REVILLIOD. C.R.120. Judith (variant of London). Sd and d. 1525.

— LEGS FOL. 3833. Christ on the Way to Calvary.

Greenville (S.C.). BOB JONES UNIVERSITY GALLERY. 31. Christ carrying Cross.

Grenoble. 507. Nativity. Sd and d. 1530.

Hanover. LANDESGALERIE. 265. Madonna and Child with Infant S. John. Sd and d. 1522.*

Karlsruhe. 405. Martyrdom of S. Sebastian. (Formerly Sd and d. 1521?)

Kilburn (London). S. AUGUSTINE. Holy Family with SS. Elizabeth and Infant S. John.

Kreuzlingen. H. KISTERS. Madonna and Child enthroned (variant of Munich).

Liverpool. 2793. Madonna and Child with SS. Francis, Matthew, Louis of Toulouse, John Evangelist, Anthony Abbot and Peter Martyr.

London. 596. Cut down lunette from high altar of Duomo in Forlì: Pietà with SS. Mercuriale and Valerian (companion to Forlì 122). 1506.

BUCKINGHAM PALACE, ROYAL COLLECTION. Judith (variant at Geneva). Sd and d. 1516. *Plate* 1007.

London (contd.). COURTAULD INSTITUTE GALLERIES, LEE OF FAREHAM COLLECTION.
Mourning over dead Christ.

W. B. PATERSON (EX). Crucifixion with SS. Jerome and Francis (variant of Uffizi).
Sd and d. 1531.

Loreto. SANTUARIO, SAGRESTIA DI S. MARCO O DEL TESORO VECCHIO. Frescoes (see under
Melozzo). Probably 1484-87. *Plates* 996, 997.

Lovere. 60. Christ carrying Cross. Sd and d. 1537.

Matelica. S. FRANCESCO. Madonna and Child enthroned; SS. Francis and Catherine;
in lunette, Pietà. Sd and d. 1501.

Melbourne. 982/3. Baptism of Christ (after lost Giovanni Bellini).

Milan. BRERA. 469. Nativity. Sd and d. 1542.

> 470. Coronation with SS. Benedict and Francis. Sd.

> 471. Madonna and Child with SS. John Baptist, Peter, Dominic and Mary
> Magdalen. Sd and d. 1493.

> 502. S. Sebastian.

POLDI PEZZOLI. 599, 697. Predella panels: Annunciation, Marriage of Virgin.

Munich. H.G.760. Madonna and Child enthroned with SS. Peter, Francis, Anthony
Abbot and Paul and Angel musician. Sd and d. 1513.

New York. ROERICH MUSEUM (EX). Wilderness with S. Jerome and S. Francis
receiving Stigmata. Sd.

Padua. 412. Holy Family with Infant S. John (later version of Hanover). Sd and d.
1536.

> 419. Madonna and Child with Infant S. John (p. or r.?). Sd.

> 444. S. Sebastian (fr.). (?)

Paris. 1400. Dead Christ on tomb and two Putti. Sd and d. 1510.

Philadelphia (Pa.). J. G. JOHNSON COLLECTION. 147. Predella panel: Nativity.

> 212. Christ carrying Cross, and three other figures. Sd and d. 1532.

Phoenix (Arizona). ART MUSEUM. Holy Family with Infant S. John (formerly
Heugel, Paris). Sd in Hebrew. *Plate* 1004.

Prague. 4440. Christ carrying Cross. Sd and d. 1534.

Ravenna. 31, 39. Predella panels: Circumcision, Nativity.

PALAZZO ARCIVESCOVILE. Madonna and Child with four Saints.

Rome. GALLERIA NAZIONALE, PALAZZO BARBERINI. S. Jerome. Sd and d. 150(3?).
Lunette: God the Father and Cherubim.

GALLERIA SPADA. 200, 201. Way to Calvary; in lunette, God the Father and
Cherubim. Sd.

VATICAN, PINACOTECA. 142. Madonna and Child with SS. John Baptist, Lawrence,
Francis, Peter, Anthony Abbot and Dominic and Angel musician. Sd and d.
1537.

> 271. Bust of Christ carrying Cross. Sd.

> 273. Madonna and Child enthroned with SS. Jerome and John Baptist and
> Angel musician. Sd and d. 1510.

> 274. Holy Family with S. Elizabeth and Infant S. John. Sd.

FERRONI COLLECTION (EX). Predella panel: Marriage of the Virgin.

MARCHESE CARLO VISCONTI VENOSTA (EX). S. Roch.

CONTE L. VITETTI. Holy Family. Sd.

Rouen. 485. Cassone panel: Trial of Vestal Tuccia. (?)

Sarasota (Fla.). RINGLING MUSEUM. 'Holford' altarpiece from S. Agostin di Cesena: Madonna and Child enthroned with Baptist and Evangelist. Sd.

Vaduz. LIECHTENSTEINSCHE SAMMLUNGEN. G 850, 855. Two panels of polyptych from S. Francesco at Castrocaro: S. Francis, S. Jerome. Sd and d. 1500.

G 878. Dead Christ seated on tomb.

Venice. CA' D'ORO. Dead Christ upheld by Angels. Sd and d. 1529.

MUSEO CORRER. 52. Christ on way to Calvary. Sd and d. 1525.

CONTE VITTORIO CINI. Inv. 3303. 'Stroganoff' S. Jerome in the Wilderness. Sd and d. 1537.

Vercelli. MUSEO BORGOGNA. Madonna and Child with S. Catherine and Infant S. John. Sd and d. 1533.

Vicenza. 179. Dead Christ with Magdalen, Nicodemus and Joseph of Arimathea.

Vienna. AKADEMIE. 1098. Bust of youth.

LANCKORONSKI COLLECTION (EX). Predella panel: Flight into Egypt (r.).

Warsaw. Inv. n. Wil. 1527. Madonna and Child with Infant S. John.

Weimar. GOETHEHAUS. Christ carrying Cross. Sd.

Zagreb. 83. Christ carrying Cross. Sd and d. 1525.

Homeless. Madonna and Child with Infant S. John. *Plate* 1002.

Madonna and Child with SS. Sebastian and Roch. *Plate* 999.

Madonna and Child with Infant S. John and SS. Sebastian and Magdalen. *Plate* 1006.

Christ carrying the Cross. *Plate* 1005.

PANNONIO see MICHELE PANNONIO

PARENTINO

Bernardo Parentino or Parenzano, born at Parenzo (Istria) 1437, died 1531 at Vicenza, where he spent his old age as a monk (and poet?). Pupil possibly of Giovanni Storlato; follower of Mantegna; influenced by Ercole da Ferrara, and by the Veronese painters Domenico Morone and Francesco Bonsignori.

Amsterdam. OTTO LANZ (EX). Apollo and Neptune leave Troy (companion to Cambridge).*

Baltimore (Md.). WALTERS ART GALLERY. 1162. Parchment: S. John Baptist in the wilderness and view of town (Vicenza?). L. (?)

Berlin. 1628, 1628A. Minstrels performing. *Plate* 713.

Boston (Mass.). GARDNER MUSEUM. Madonna and Child on clouds with two Cherubim (from Oratorio di S. Nicola, Vicenza; after Mantegna?). E.

Brooklyn (N.Y.). 26.517 and 26.518. Two stories of Jason: Battle scene and marriage with Medea. (?)

Cambridge. FITZWILLIAM MUSEUM, MARLAY BEQUEST. 69, 70. Two cassone-panels: Laomedon and the Building of Troy (companions to Amsterdam).

Cleveland (Ohio). 16.790. Darius riding out.

Denver (Col.). MUSEUM OF ART, KRESS COLLECTION. K 10–15. Six Triumphs: Chastity, Love, Time, Fame, Death, Divinity. (?)

Florence. BARGELLO. 2022. Flight from Troy.

Hampton Court. ROYAL COLLECTION. 1215. Martyrdom of S. Sebastian (after Mantegna in Louvre).

London. LOUIS MORANT (EX). Detached fresco from S. Giustina in Padua: S. Benedict at Agatone's School.

Lucca. 228, 229. Two panels from polyptych: S. Sebastian, S. Roch.*

Mantua. REGGIA. Two panels from polyptych: Half-length SS. Benedict and Clare.

Milan. PALAZZO BORROMEO (NOW ISOLABELLA?). 13. Betrayal of Christ.
56. Bis. Battle scene.

Modena. 12. Christ carrying the Cross, with SS. Jerome and Augustine (from Monte Ortone, then Castello del Catajo, Padua). Sd. 1502. *Plate* 715.

Monte Carlo. ONASSIS COLLECTION. Battle with Turks (formerly Verona, Da Lisca).

Padua. MUSEO ANTONIANO. S. Bernardino. (?)

S. GIUSTINA, CLOISTERS. Fragmentary frescoes: I Bay—Triumph of Church; II— S. Gregory writing the Life of S. Benedict; III—S. Benedict's departure from Nurcia and his arrival in Rome (fr. at Pavia); IV—S. Benedict at Agatone's school (fr. in London); V—Miracle of the broken Sieve; VI—S. Benedict retires into the Wilderness (detached); VII—S. Benedict does manual labour; VIII—S. Benedict in the Cave mistaken for a Wild Animal by the Shepherds; IX—S. Benedict fights Temptation in the Brambles; X—S. Benedict is elected Abbot; XI—Goes back to solitude after attempted poisoning; XII— Receives Maurus and Placidus; XIII—Funerals of S. Benedict (the remaining Stories of S. Benedict—50 altogether—are lost). In lunettes above, Busts of Benedictines and monochrome Scenes from the Old and New Testaments. Formerly Sd and dated 1489 and 1494.

S. MARIA DEL CARMINE, SCUOLA. Fresco: Presentation of Virgin. (?)

Paris. 1678. Adoration of Magi.

MUSÉE JACQUEMART-ANDRÉ. 1042. Pietà and donor as S. Francis.

Pavia. Inv. 86. Detached fresco from S. Giustina at Padua: Battle scene (monochrome). 1489–94. *Plate* 717.

Rome. GALLERIA DORIA PAMPHILI. 140. Temptations of S. Anthony Abbot. *Plate* 716.

— PRIVATE APARTMENTS. Two panels: S. Louis of France distributing alms; S. Anthony Abbot refusing alms. *Plate* 714.

Venice. MUSEO CORRER. 506. Centaurs and Lapiths.
> 624. Hercules in Hades.
> CONTE S. BAROZZI. S. Bernardino exorcizing (companion to following).
> CONTE VITTORIO CINI. Inv. 6738. S. Bernardino resuscitating the dead (companion to preceding). *Plate 718.*

Verona. 134. S. Lorenzo Giustiniani and worshipper.
> 331. Conversion of S. Paul.
> 358. Presentation in Temple.

Vienna. EMILE WEINBERGER (EX). Story of Jason? *Plate 720.*

Homeless. Trajan and the widow (*Bollettino d'Arte*, April 1931, fig. 3) (?)
> Six panels: I—Scipio at Cumae asks the Sibyl to call the soul of his Mother; II—Conquest of Carthagena; III—Continence of Scipio; IV—Scipio and Masinissa; V—Triumph of Scipio; VI—Scipio sheds his clothes before the Roman Senate (Pantheon, May 1931, p. 204). (?)
> Adoration of Magi. (?) *Plate 719.*

PARMIGIANINO (Francesco Mazzola)

Parma. 1504–40. Developed under influence of Correggio, Raphael and Michelangelo.

Bardi (Parma). S. MARIA, CANONICA. Mystic marriage of S. Catherine and SS. John Baptist and John Evangelist.

Bologna. 116 (Inv. 588). Madonna and Child with S. Petronius?, S. Margaret, S. Jerome and Angel. Before 1529.
> S. PETRONIO, FOURTH CHAPEL L. S. Roch and donor.

Columbia (S.C.). MUSEUM OF ART, GIFT OF BAY FOUNDATION. Lorenzo Cibo and page (replica of Copenhagen). d. 1523.

Copenhagen. 25. Lorenzo Cibo with a page. d. 1523.

Detroit (Mich.). 30.295. Circumcision. E.

Dresden. 160. Madonna and Child with SS. Stephen and John Baptist and donor.
> 161. Madonna of the rose. [*Plate 396.*]
> 162. Portrait of youth. (?)

Florence. PITTI. 230. Madonna of the long neck (u.). After 1534.
> UFFIZI. 1328. Madonna and Child with SS. Jerome, Mary Magdalen and Infant John. Not after 1527.
> 1377. Bust of youth (p.?).
> 1623. So-called self-portrait. 1527–8.

Fontanellato (Parma). CASTELLO SANVITALE, SMALL ROOM GROUND FLOOR. Frescoed ceiling and lunettes: Putti, Story of Diana and Actaeon. 1534–6 or earlier? *Plates 1804–1806.*

Hampton Court. Inv. 553. Lady with dog and orrery (c?).
> Inv. 1138. Bust of (?) Minerva.
> Inv. 1189. Portrait of youth.

Leningrad. HERMITAGE. Mystic Marriage of S. Catherine. E.

London. 33. Vision of S. Jerome and S. John Baptist pointing at Madonna.

    COUNT ANTOINE SEILERN. 'Cook' Holy Family. *Plate* 1800.

Lovere. 59. Knight of Calatrava (st.).

Madrid. 55. Youth with viola (c?).

    279, 280. Pier Maria Rossi Conte di San Secondo and his wife Camilla **Gonzaga** with three sons.

    282. Bust of S. Barbara.

    283. Holy Family.

Milan. AMBROSIANA. Portrait of sculptor. Not traced.

Naples. 108. Portrait of young woman. [*Plate* 395.]

    109. Portrait of scholar.

    110. Madonna and sleeping Child with Infant S. John.

    111. Galeazzo da Sanvitale. 1524. *Plate* 1801.

    119. Bust of Giovanni da Castelbolognese.

    124. Girolamo di Vincenti aged 25. 1535.

Paris. 1506. Sentimental youth. (?)

Parma. 114. 'Turkish Slave.'

    192. Mystic Marriage of S. Catherine (copy of early original).

    S. GIOVANNI EVANGELISTA, NAVE, ARCH OF FIRST CHAPEL. Frescoes: left—S. Agatha bound by executioner, right—SS. Lucy and Apollonia.

    — — ARCH OF SECOND CHAPEL. Frescoes: left—SS. John Evangelist and Stephen, right—S. Secundus.

    — — ARCH OF FOURTH CHAPEL. Frescoes: SS. Nicholas and Hilarius.

    — — ARCH OF SIXTH CHAPEL. Frescoes: Church Fathers; in soffit of Arch, monochromes (Cardinal Virtues, Fall of Man).

    S. MARIA DELLA STECCATA. Organ-shutters: David, S. Cecilia (r.).

    — BEFORE APSE. Frescoed decoration: six Canephorae; monochrome Adam, Eve, Moses, Aaron; fruit, flowers, putti, animals. After 1531. *Plates* 1802–1803.

Richmond (Surrey). COOK COLLECTION (EX). Charles V and Victory. *Plate* 1810.

Rome. GALLERIA BORGHESE. 85. Bust of young man.

    GALLERIA DORIA PAMPHILI. 279. Nativity.

    281. Madonna and Child. *Plate* 1807.

Somerley. EARL OF NORMANTON. Mystic Marriage of S. Catherine. *Plate* 1809.

Taggia. S. DOMENICO. Adoration of Magi.*

Vienna. 57. S. Catherine picking palm leaves, and two Putti.

    58. Self-portrait in round mirror. *Plate* 1799.

    62. Cupid bending his bow.

    65. Young woman in turban.

    66. Man reading. (?)

    67. Malatesta Baglione.

Wrotham Park. EARL OF STRAFFORD (EX). Portrait of a collector. *Plate* 1808.

York. 739. Portrait of a scholar.

PASTURA (Antonio da Viterbo called)

Viterbese follower of Pinturicchio, Perugino and Antoniazzo Romano. Documented Rome 1478, Orvieto 1489–92, Rome 1492–94, Orvieto 1497–99, Viterbo 1504, 1508–9.

Assisi. (Environs.) TORRE D'ANDREA, S. BERNARDINO, HIGH ALTAR. S. Bernardino worshipping the Christ Child held by Joseph after Circumcision (after Perugino).

Atlanta (Ga.). ART ASSOCIATION GALLERIES. 58.50 (KRESS COLLECTION. K 362). Predella panel (formerly Holford): Pietà.

Berlin. 143. Madonna and Child.

Cambridge (Mass.). FOGG ART MUSEUM. 45.4. Detached fresco: Annunciation.

Florence. BERENSON COLLECTION. Madonna and Child.*

Łódź. Inv. 649. Madonna and Child in mandorla (r.).*

Montefiascone (Viterbo). S. FLAVIANO, L. CHAPEL. Frescoes: in vault, Redeemer, Angels, frieze with head of youth in roundel; end wall, Massacre of Innocents, Beheading of S. Catherine; below altar, 'Ecce Homo' in medallion; (fr. r.).

New York. 32.100.74. Madonna and Child with SS. Jerome and Francis.

Orte. DUOMO. Madonna and Child.

Orvieto. S. MARIA ASSUNTA (DUOMO). CHOIR. Figures and scenes in frescoes by Ugolino di Prete Ilario (fourteenth century), repainted by Pastura: in vault, Eternal, some heads of Angels; right wall, around window, S. Gregory and fragments of Saints in medallions; right wall, below, Circumcision, Annunciation, Visitation. doc. 1498. *Plate* 1120.

— MUSEO DELL'OPERA. Madonna and Child enthroned.

Small Madonna and Child enthroned.

Detached fresco: S. Sebastian and donor.

S. ROCCO, APSE. Frescoes: Christ and Saints.

SS. TRINITÀ, L. WALL. S. Bernardino crowned by Angels and SS. Bartholomew, Louis of Toulouse, Francis and Peter.

— R. WALL. Fresco: Madonna crowned by Angels and four Saints.

Paris. M. F. GENTILI (EX). Madonna and Child with SS. Jerome and Francis. *Plate* 1116.

Philadelphia (Pa.). J. G. JOHNSON COLLECTION. 143. Madonna and Child with S. Jerome and Infant S. John. E. (?)

Rome. CAMPIDOGLIO, PALAZZO DEI CONSERVATORI, OLD CHAPEL ON FIRST FLOOR. Fresco: 'Madonna delle Scale' adoring sleeping Child with two Angels.

VATICAN, PINACOTECA. 323. Triptych: Madonna of the girdle, Communion of S. Gregory, Penitence of S. Jerome. (?)

— APPARTAMENTI BORGIA, SALA DEL TRIVIO E DEL QUADRIVIO (ROOM III). Frescoes: Arithmetic, Geometry, Music, Astronomy, Grammatica, Rhetorica (see also Pinturicchio). 1492–94. *Plate* 1118.

— — SALA DEI MISTERI (ROOM V). Frescoes: Angels in the Assumption, and one in spandrel (see also Pinturicchio). 1492–94.

S. COSIMATO. Fresco: Madonna and Child with SS. Francis and Clare. (?)

Sarasota (Fla.). RINGLING MUSEUM. Madonna and Child (r.)

Tarquinia (Viterbo). MUSEO. Madonna enthroned suckling Child (from S. Giovanni Gerosolimitano). d. 150(4?).

    DUOMO, CHOIR. Frescoes: in vault, Coronation of Virgin, King David and Sibyl.
Hoseah and Sibyl, Isaiah and Sibyl; in frieze, Putti, Nymphs and Coats of
Arms; on walls, Meeting of Joachim and Anne, Birth of Virgin, Marriage of
Virgin, Madonna in Glory, Pietà (r.). 1508–9. *Plate* 1121.

Tuscania (Viterbo). S. MARIA DEL RIPOSO. Madonna and Child crowned by Angels,
in Mandorla of Cherubim (variants at Ajaccio, Budapest, Darmstadt, London,
Milan Brera, Paris, New York Morgan Library, Richmond, Cook (ex),
Vercelli; possibly studio versions or by imitator). *Plate* 1115.

Vetralla (Viterbo). DUOMO. Fresco: S. Anthony Abbot enthroned; below, four
Scenes from his life.

Viterbo. 1. Detached fresco: Two Angels and two Cherubim round fourteenth
century Madonna by Andrea di Giovanni. *Plate* 1113.

    5. Nativity with SS. John Baptist and Bartholomew. 1488. *Plate* 1117.

    6. Madonna and Child with two Angels (from S. Clemente).

    7. Frescoed lunette from Chiesa del Paradiso: Madonna and Child with SS.
Jerome, Francis and Angels. ca 1490.

    s.n. Detached votive frescoes: S. Francis receiving Stigmata; Agony in the
Garden (fr.):

    PALAZZO CHIGI, COURT. Fresco: Madonna and blessing Child. L. *Plate* 1119.

    S. ANGELO IN SPATHA, L. CHAPEL. S. Roch and donor. (?)

Worcester (Mass.). 1914.44. Madonna and two Angels adoring the Child.

Homeless. Madonna and Child (replica of Berlin). *Plate* 1114.

GIACOMO DI MINO DEL PELLICCIAJO

*Sienese. Mentioned from 1344 (his marriage) to 1389. Follower of Lippo Memmi and the
Lorenzetti, taught Martino di Bartolomeo.*

Casole d'Elsa. COLLEGIATA (ASSUNTA). Fresco: Last Judgement (fr.). (?)

Perugia. 83. Portable altarpiece: Marriage of S. Catherine, with four Angels, and
S. Ansanus; S. Mary Magdalen, S. Eulalia; in pinnacles, Redeemer, Angel
and Virgin of Annunciation. *Plate* 399.

Sarteano. SS. MARTINO E VITTORIA. Centre panel of triptych from S. Francesco:
Madonna and Child. Sd and d. 13(42?). *Plate* 403.

    S. FRANCESCO. Fragment of polyptych: Madonna and Child, S. John Evangelist,
S. John Baptist; above, Annunciation, two pairs of Saints. *Plates* 400–
401.

Siena. 145. Triptych from S. Antonio Abate: Madonna and Child with SS. Mary Magdalen, Lucy, Agnes, Catherine and six Angels; S. Anthony Abbot; S. Michael; in pinnacles, Blessing Saviour, SS. Augustine, John Baptist, Onophrius, Jerome; in predella, five roundels with heads of Saints and Angels. Sd and d. 1362. *Plate 402.*

      S. MARIA DEI SERVI. Madonna del Belverde (later retouched by Taddeo di Bartolo). 1363.

PERINO DEL VAGA

Piero Buonaccorsi, called del Vaga after the painter Vaga who took him still young to Rome. Florence 1501–Rome 1547. Pupil perhaps of Ridolfo Ghirlandajo and Fra Bartolomeo. Assistant to Raphael in the decoration of the Vatican Loggie (completed 1519; see also under Raphael). Married 1525 sister of G. F. Penni (another assistant of Raphael). Influenced by Michelangelo. After Sack of Rome active in Genoa (1528–34), and Pisa (1534–38); and from 1439 to his end, again in Rome.

Chantilly. 44. Holy Family.

Florence. UFFIZI. Detached frescoes from Palazzo Baldassini in Rome: Justice of Seleucus; Tarquin founds the Temple of Jupiter on the Capitoline Hill. Before 1525.*

Genoa. ACCADEMIA LIGUSTICA, QUADRERIA. Inv. 53. Fragmentary polyptych from Oratorio di S. Erasmo at Quinto al Mare: S. Erasmus between SS. Peter and Paul; in lunette, Madonna and Child with SS. Nicholas and Clare; predella, Calling of S. Peter, S. Erasmus rescuing seafarers.

    The miraculous Draught of Fishes.

    Inv. 62. Two cartoons of Allegorical Figures.

    PALAZZO DORIA, VESTIBULE OR SALA DEI TRIONFI. Frescoes: in vault, Three Roman Triumphs (of Aemilius Paulus?); Triumph of Bacchus in pendentifs, pagan deities; in lunettes, Stories of Roman Kings. Sd and d. 1530.

    — LOGGIA OR GALLERIA DEGLI EROI. Frescoes: Mythological Figures, Putti, eagles, medallions with scenes from Roman history, seated heroes (r.). d. 1530.

    — SALA DEI GIGANTI. Frescoed ceiling: Jupiter destroys the Titans. *Plate 1820.*

    S. GIORGIO A BAVARI. Altarpiece from S. Francesco di Castelletto: Madonna and Child with SS. Francis and Dominic.

    DORIA BALBI DI PIOVERA (HEIRS). Holy Family and Infant John.

    (Environs). CELLE LIGURE, S. MICHELE. Polyptych: S. Michael defeating Satan, flanked by SS. Peter and Paul; upper register, Eternal, Angel and Virgin of Annunciation; predella, Calling of Peter, Beheading of Baptist.

Hampton Court. 690, 691. Two fragments of Deposition formerly in S. Maria sopra Minerva, Rome: Repentant and Unrepentant Crucified Thieves.

London. VICTORIA AND ALBERT MUSEUM. Detached fresco from Cappella Massimi in S. Trinità dei Monti, Rome: Raising of Lazarus (rest of decoration destroyed).

London (contd.). LORD NORTHBROOK (EX). Madonna and Child.

Melbourne. NATIONAL GALLERY. Holy Family.*

Milan. BRERA. Predella to Basadonne Altarpiece, once in S. Maria della Consolazione
   at Genoa (see Washington): Agony in Garden, Betrayal, Christ before
   Pilate, Flagellation, Ecce Homo. Sd. 1534. *Plates 1822–1823.*

Narbonne. 445. Frescoed lunette: Martyrdom of S. Cecilia (on Raphael's indications?).

Pesaro (Environs). VILLA IMPERIALE. Ornamental frescoes. *Plate 1818–a.*

Pisa. DUOMO, R. TRANSEPT, R. WALL. Fresco: Putti (fr.). 1534–38.

   MUSEO NAZIONALE DI S. MATTEO. Triptych: Holy Family, Bishop Saint, Warrior
   Saint.

Rimini. 51. Holy Family (c.?).

Rome. GALLERIA BORGHESE. 464. Holy Family with Infant S. John. E. (c.?).

   GALLERIA DORIA PAMPHILI. 168. Galatea. (?)

   MUSEO DI CASTEL S. ANGELO, APPARTAMENTO PAPALE, SALA DI AMORE E PSICHE.
   Frescoed frieze: Caryatids, Grotteschi and ten scenes from story of Cupid
   and Psyche (p.). 1545–47.

   — SALA DEL PERSEO. Frescoed frieze with Myth of Perseus (st.). L.

   — SALA PAOLINA O DEL CONSIGLIO. Frescoed decoration: ceiling, stuccoes and
   Stories of Alexander; short walls, Hadrian, S. Michael, 'sovrapporte'; long
   walls, Allegorical figures in niches, Stories of Alexander; dado, terms and
   simulated low-reliefs (with Marco Pino da Siena, Luzio, Siciolante, Pellegrino
   Tibaldi, Marcello Venusti, Domenico Zaga). 1545–47. *Plate 1829.*

   PALAZZO BALDASSINI. Frescoed decoration: Philosophers and Putti in niches; above
   (hidden by new ceiling): Roman stories (fr.; see Florence). Before 1526.

   PALAZZO DELLA CANCELLERIA, SALONE DELLO STUDIO, VAULT. Frescoed decoration
   Eternal in centre; Virtues in corners; four rectangular sections with Adam and
   Eve, Judgement of Solomon, Fall of Manna, Joseph's Brothers show Jacob
   the gold found in their Sacks; grotteschi; two hexagonal sections and three
   lunettes with Story of Adam and Eve; two hexagonal sections and three
   lunettes with Story of Joseph (with Peruzzi). Painted for Cardinal Raffaello
   Riario (died 1521). *Plate 1830.*

   PALAZZO MASSIMO ALLE COLONNE. Frescoed frieze: Episodes from Aeneid and other
   decorations. *Plates 1825–1827.*

   S. MARCELLO, CAPPELLA DEL CROCIFISSO (FOURTH R.), VAULT. Frescoes: Creation of
   Eve, Evangelists (commissioned 1525, finished 1544; partly executed by
   Daniele da Volterra).

   S. TRINITÀ DEI MONTI, CAPPELLA PUCCI (L. TRANSEPT). Frescoes: on vault, Meeting
   at the Golden Gate, Birth of Virgin, Presentation, Annunciation; entrance
   soffit, Creation of Adam, Fall of Man, Expulsion from Eden; lunette, Visitation. 1522/23.

   VATICAN, APPARTAMENTO BORGIA, SALA DEI PONTEFICI. Frescoed vault (with Giovanni da Udine). E.

— LOGGE DI RAFFAELLO. Frescoes in vault: IV Bay—Abraham and the Angels; VI Bay—Jacob and Rachel at the Well; VII Bay—Joseph and his Brothers, Joseph explains Pharaoh's Dreams; VIII Bay—Crossing of the Red Sea; IX Bay—Moses receives Tables of Law on Mount Sinai; and others (on Raphael's indications). Decoration completed 1519. *Plate 1819.*

— STANZA D'ELIODORO. Monochrome frescoes in dado, below Raphael's frescoes. E.

— STANZA DELLA SEGNATURA, DADO. Monochrome frescoes: Augustus and the Sibyl, S. Augustine and the boy on the beach, Pagan sacrifice; Siege of Syracuse and Death of Archimedes, Magi disputing, Philosophy; Augustus prevents Virgil's friends from burning the Aeneid, Alexander puts Homer's Poems on the Tomb of Achilles; Moses gives the Law to the Hebrews, Solon preaches to the Athenians. L. *Plates 1185, 1828.*

Vaduz. LIECHTENSTEINSCHE SAMMLUNG. G 24. Tondo: Holy Family. *Plate 1821.*

Washington (D.C.). 1392. KRESS COLLECTION. K 1621. 'Cook' Nativity with SS. John Baptist, Sebastian, Roch, James, Catherine of Alexandria and Eternal (from Cappella Basadonne in S. Maria della Consolazione at Genoa; predella at Milan). Sd and d. 1534. *Plate 1824.*

PERUGINO

Pietro Vannucci, Petrus de Castro Plebis. Città della Pieve 1445–1523 Fontignano. Registered as Florentine painter 1472. Citizen of Perugia. Developed under influence of Melozzo da Forlì and Verocchio.

Altenburg. 114, 115. Two panels from SS. Annunziata polyptych (see Florence): Blessed Filippo Benizzi (?), S. Helena (g.p.). 1506.

Assisi. SACRO CONVENTO, F. M. PERKINS DONATION. 10. Detached fresco: penitent S. Jerome. E.

(Environs). TORRE D'ANDREA, S. BERNARDINO, HIGH ALTAR. Presentation of Christ Child, with S. Bernardino (c. by Pastura).

Baltimore (Md.). MUSEUM OF ART, JACOBS COLLECTION. Detached fresco: Madonna and Child enthroned with SS. Sebastian, John Baptist, Peter and Roch (p.).

WALTERS ART GALLERY. 1089. S. Jerome in Wilderness, adoring Crucifix. E.

Bassano. 28. Small Deposition (sketch for Città della Pieve fresco). 1517.

Bellagio (Lake Como). S. GIACOMO. Deposition. Sd and d. 1495 (st. or c.?).

Berlin-Ost. 146A. Predella panel to 'Tezi' altarpiece (Perugia 279): Last Supper (st.). d. 1500.

Bettona (Perugia). PINACOTECA COMUNALE. S. Anthony of Padua worshipped by Bartolomeo di Pietro da Maraglia. Sd and d. 1512.

Madonna of Mercy with SS. Jerome, Marinus and Donors. L.

S. MARIA MAGGIORE, FIRST ALTAR R. Standard: S. Anne, Virgin and Child in Mandorla, SS. Crispolto and Anthony of Padua kneeling (p., r.).

Biella. C. ROBIOLO COLLECTION. 'Holford' Madonna and Child with two Cherubs (g.p.).

Birmingham (Ala.). MUSEUM OF ART, 61.103 (KRESS COLLECTION. K 544). S. Bartholomew (fragment of roundel from back of S. Agostino Polyptych; see Perugia 249).

Bologna. 197. Madonna and Child in mandorla appear to SS. Michael, Catherine, Apollonia and John Evangelist. Sd.

> S. PETRONIO, CAPPELLA DI S. ANTONIO. Stained Glass: S. Anthony of Padua and Annunciation (on design by the artist).

Bonn. 212. Tondo: Madonna adoring Child with two Angels (c.; other version Verona). Not traced.

Bordeaux. 145. Madonna and Child enthroned, between SS. Jerome and Augustine (Angels by other hand).

Brooklyn (N.Y.). 34.497. Bust of middle-aged Man (formerly Hanover Museum).

Brussels. 21. Tondo: Madonna and Child with Infant S. John (st.).

Caen. 35. S. Jerome in the Wilderness. Sd.

Cambridge. FITZWILLIAM MUSEUM. 120. Madonna and Child against landscape (p.). L.

Cerqueto (Perugia). PARISH CHURCH, ALTAR R. Fresco: S. Sebastian and other figures. Sd and d. 1478. *Plate* 1068.

> TABERNACLE. Fresco: Madonna and Child with S. Lucy and female Saint (p., r.). ca 1500.

Chantilly. 15. Madonna and Child enthroned between SS. Jerome and Peter (g.p.).

Chicago (Ill.). 33. 1023/6. Predella (to SS. Annunziata polyptych in Florence?): Baptism of Christ, Christ and Samaritan Woman at the Well, Nativity, 'Noli me tangere'.

Città della Pieve. DUOMO. Madonna and Child appearing to SS. Gervasius, Peter, Paul and Protasius (p.). Sd and d. 1514.

> Baptism of Christ (st.). 1495.

> S. MARIA DEI BIANCHI. Fresco: Adoration of Magi. d. 1504.

> S. MARIA DEI SERVI, CAPPELLA DELLA COMPAGNIA DELLA STELLA (FIRST R.). Frescoes: entrance wall—Annunciation; altar wall—Deposition; right wall—Pietà; left wall—Entombment (fragments, r.). d. 1517.

> S. PIETRO. Fresco transferred on canvas: S. Anthony Abbot enthroned between SS. Marcellus and Paul Hermit; above, Eternal blessing and Cherubs (p.).

Corciano. See Perugia, Environs.

Cremona. S. AGOSTINO, SIXTH ALTAR R. Madonna and Child enthroned between SS. James and Augustine. Sd and d. 1494.

Detroit (Mich.). EDSEL FORD COLLECTION. Madonna and Child.

Dublin. 942. Pietà (st. version of 'Ingesuati' Pietà in Florence, Uffizi).

Edinburgh. 1805. Apollo and three male nudes standing (fr.).

Fano. S. MARIA NUOVA, THIRD ALTAR R. Madonna and Child enthroned with SS. John Baptist, Louis of Toulouse, Francis, Peter, Paul and Mary Magdalen; in lunette, Dead Christ with mourning Virgin, Joseph of Arimathea, Nicodemus and John Evangelist; in predella, Birth of Virgin, Presentation, Marriage of Virgin, Annunciation, Assumption with S. Thomas receiving the Girdle. Sd and d. 1497.

— SECOND ALTAR L. Annunciation. Formerly Sd and d. 14(98?).

Fiesole. VIA VECCHIA FIESOLANA, TABERNACOLO DEL PREPOSTO (VILLA CAPPELLA). Frescoes: Blessing Eternal, Madonna and Child with SS. Peter, Lawrence and Infant John; in embrasure, male Saint and S. Sebastian.

Florence. ACCADEMIA. 8370. Centre panel from back of SS. Annunziata polyptych: Deposition (begun by Filippino; see SS. Annunziata). 1506.

PITTI. 42. Bust of S. Mary Magdalen.

164. Mourning over dead Christ. Sd and d. 1495.

219. 'Madonna del Sacco', adoring Child with Infant S. John and Angel (p.).

341. Adoration of Magi (c. of destroyed fresco at S. Giusto alle Mura).

8367. Agony in the Garden.

UFFIZI. 1453. Madonna and Child enthroned between SS. John Baptist and Sebastian. Sd and d. 1493.

1474. So-called Bust of Alessandro Braccesi.

1700. Portrait of Francesco delle Opere. Sd and d. 1494. [*Plate* 309.]

2185. Bust of young man.

3254. Christ on Cross with SS. Jerome, Francis, Blessed Giovanni Colombini, SS. John Baptist and Mary Magdalen. E. *Plate* 1096.

8365. 'Ingesuati' Pietà. E.

8366. Assumption of the Virgin with SS. Bernardo degli Uberti, John Gualbert, Benedict and Michael. Sd and d. 1500.

8375, 8376. Profile heads of Don Biagio Milanesi, General of the Vallombrosan Order, and of Don Baldassarre, Vallombrosan monk. 1500. *Plates* 1104–1105.

BERENSON COLLECTION. Pax: Christ in Tomb.

Two embroideries on design of the artist: S. John Evangelist and S. James in niches.

CENACOLO DI FOLIGNO. Fresco: Last Supper (g.p.).

PALAZZO ALBIZI (EX). Detached fresco from S. Pier Maggiore: Dead Christ on Tomb, upheld by Nicodemus, with mourning Virgin and Evangelist (see Moscow).* *Plate* 1103.

SS. ANNUNZIATA, CAPPELLA RABATTA (FOURTH L.). Centre panel from front of SS. Annunziata polyptych: Assumption (back panel at Accademia; side-panels at Altenburg, New York, Paris and Rome; predella at Chicago?) (g.p.). 1506.

S. CROCE, CAPPELLA MEDICI. S. Anthony of Padua (p.). L.

S. MARIA MADDALENA DEI PAZZI. Christ on Cross, Virgin and S. Jerome.

— FORMER CHAPTER HALL (VIA DELLA COLONNA). Fresco: Christ on Cross and kneeling Magdalen; Virgin and kneeling S. Bernard; Evangelist and kneeling S. Benedict. 1493/6.

Florence (contd.). s. spirito, west window. Stained glass on design of the artist: Descent of the Holy Ghost.

Foligno. chiesa della nunziatella, r. altar. Frescoed niche: Baptism of Christ. 1507.

Fontignano (Perugia). chiesa dell'annunziata, r. wall. Madonna and Child enthroned (st. replica of Spello). d. 1522.

Frankfurt a/M. 843. Madonna and Child with Infant S. John.

Gosford House (Scotland). earl of wemyss and march (ex). Madonna and Child with Infant S. John.

Granada. 537. capilla real, altar r. of high altar. Reliquary of Isabel: Christ in Tomb. (?)

Grenoble. 537. Full-length SS. Apollonia and Sebastian (from front of S. Agostino polyptych; see Perugia 258). L.

Hampton Court. royal collection. 1196. S. Jerome in Wilderness (g.p.).

Hanover. 274. S. Peter in garland of fruit and flowers (fr.). E.

Leningrad. 7. Bust of young man. *Plate* 1100.
    1938. Bust of S. Sebastian. Sd.

Liverpool. 2856. Predella panel to altarpiece painted in Verrochio's shop for Pistoia cathedral: Birth of S. John Baptist (see *Florentine School* under Lorenzo di Credi and Leonardo). 1478/85.

London. 181. Madonna and Child with Infant S. John. Sd.
    288. Lower register of polyptych from Certosa di Pavia: Madonna adoring Child, S. Michael, Tobias and the Angel (companion to Pavia). Sd. 1499.
    1075. Madonna and Child between SS. Jerome and Francis. Commissioned 1507 for S. Maria dei Servi at Perugia.
    1441. Detached fresco from Fontignano: Adoration of Shepherds (r.). L.
    walter sichel (ex). Madonna and Child standing on parapet (st.). L.

Lwów. count pininsky (ex). Crucifixion. (?)

Lyons. 18. Bust of young man.
    58. Lunette and centre panel from S. Pietro Polyptych in Perugia (see there): Ascension and Eternal above. 1496/8.
    59. Full-length SS. James and Hercolanus (from back of S. Agostino Polyptych; see Perugia 249). L.

Marseilles. 788. The Family of the Virgin (g.p.). Sd. L.

Montefalco. s. francesco (museo), niche l. of door. Fresco: Adoration of Shepherds; in lunette, Eternal with two Angels and Cherubs; in spandrels, Angel and Virgin of Annunciation.

Moscow. pushkin museum. 184. Dead Christ on Tomb, upheld by Nicodemus, between mourning Virgin and Evangelist (formerly Kotchoubey and Villa Quarto, Florence; version of 'Albizi' Pietà).
    2665. 'Stroganoff' Madonna and Child in landscape (other version in Borghese Gallery, Rome; old copy ex Leuchtenberg).

Munich. 526. Adoration of Child with SS. John Evangelist and Augustine.

764. Vision of S. Bernard. [*Plate* 308.]

Nancy. 94. Virgin adoring Child with Infant S. John and two Angels (inspired by Leonardo's Virgin of the Rocks). Sd.

Nantes. 62. R. fragment of altarpiece: Full-length SS. Sebastian and Anthony of Padua. E.

117, 118. Two roundels from S. Pietro Polyptych in Perugia: Isaiah, Jeremiah. 1495/8.

Naples. 47. Madonna and Child in landscape.

BIBLIOTECA NAZIONALE. Miniature in codex of Homer's poems: Full-page head of Piero de' Medici. 1488.

S. GENNARO (DUOMO). Assumption (r.).

New York. 11.65. Predella panel: Resurrection. L.

MORGAN LIBRARY. Virgin and two Saints adoring the Child.

JACK LINSKY. Side-panels from SS. Annunziata Polyptych: Full-length SS. Lucy and John Baptist (g.p., see Florence). 1506.

Panicale (Perugia). S. SEBASTIANO. Fresco: Martyrdom of S. Sebastian with Eternal above (g.p.). Sd and d. 1505.

Detached fresco from S. Agostino: Madonna in Glory, with SS. Augustine, Mary Magdalen and Angels.

Paris. 1415. Predella panels: Dead Christ with Symbols of Passion, S. Jerome saving two pilgrims, S. Jerome raises to life Cardinal Andrea in the presence of the Pope and the clergy. E.

1509. Apollo and Marsyas. [*Plate* 304.]

1564. Tondo: Madonna and Child with SS. Rosa and Catherine, and two Angels.

1565. Madonna and blessing Child with SS. John Baptist and Catherine. Sd.

1566. Roundel from front of S. Agostino Polyptych: S. Genesius? (See Perugia 249.)

1566A. S. Sebastian tied to column in portico. [*Plate* 305.]

1567. Combat of Love and Chastity (from Studiolo of Isabella at Mantua; see also Mantegna and Costa). 1505. *Plate* 1107.

1668A. Small S. Sebastian tied to tree in landscape.

MUSÉE JACQUEMART-ANDRÉ. 1019. Madonna and blessing Child. E. *Plate* 1062.

SAINT-GERMAIN-L'AUXERROIS, ST. GERVAIS. (See Lyons 58.)

E. BONAFÉ (EX). Side-panel from SS. Annunziata Polyptych: Full-length S. Catherine (g.p.; see Florence). 1506.

Pavia (Environs). CERTOSA, SECOND CHAPEL L. Centre panel of upper register from dismembered polyptych: Eternal with Cherubim (lost side-panels with Angel and Virgin of Annunciation, replaced with Doctors by Bergognone; companion to London). 1499.

Perugia. 180. Adoration of Magi (from S. Maria dei Servi). Before 1478. *Plate* 1095.

200, 263. Mourning Virgin, Evangelist, Magdalen and S. Francis round carved Crucifix; on back, Coronation of Virgin (from S. Francesco al Monte). Commissioned 1502, but later.

Perugia (contd.). 220. Pietà with SS. Jerome and Mary Magdalen. E.

223–226. Miracles of S. Bernardino: Healing of Polissena, wife of Onofrio da Spoleto (d. 1473); Antonio da Subiaco restored from drowning; Rescue of a prisoner; Healing of an epileptic.

222, 228, 229. Miracles of S. Bernardino (execution by Caporali, q.v., on Perugino's design; in 222, group to right and supposed portrait of Filippo il Buono may have been copied from a Burgundian miniature).

227. Miracle of S. Bernardino (execution by Bonfigli, q.v.).

238. Side-panel from back of S. Agostino Polyptych: Full-length SS. Jerome and Mary Magdalen (see 258). L.

239. Martyrdom of S. Sebastian. d. 1518.

241. Bust of Blessed Giacomo della Marca. L.

242. S. Jerome in Wilderness. L.

243. Top panel from front of S. Agostino polyptych: blessing Eternal with Cherubim (see 249). L.

245, 250, 246, 247, 251, 252. Predella panels to front of S. Agostino polyptych: Baptist preaching, Marriage at Cana; half-length SS. Monica, Nicholas of Tolentino, Lucy and Jerome (see 249).

248. Top panel from 'Decemviri' altarpiece: Dead Christ (see Rome, Vatican 317). 1495.

249. Centre panel (front) of polyptych from S. Agostino at Perugia: Baptism of Christ (top panel, 243; side-panels at Lyons and Toulouse; roundels at Birmingham and Perugia 253; predella panels at Perugia 245, 246, 247, 250, 251, 252; for side towards choir, see 258; for roundels with Evangelists, see Perugia, S. Agostino). Commissioned 1502, but left unfinished at painter's death.

253, 257. Two roundels from back of S. Agostino polyptych: Daniel, David. (See 258.) L.

254, 259; 255, 256, 260, 261. Predella panels from back of S. Agostino polyptych: Marriage at Cana, Circumcision; half-length SS. Lawrence, Louis of Toulouse, Constant, Catherine. (See 258.) L.

258. Centre panel (back) of polyptych from S. Agostino at Perugia: Nativity (top panel at Perugia, S. Pietro; side-panels at Grenoble and Perugia 238; roundels 264 and Strasbourg; predella panels at Perugia 254, 255, 256, 259, 260, 261; for side towards nave, see Perugia 249; for roundels with Evangelists, see Perugia, S. Agostino). Commissioned 1502, but left unfinished at painter's death.

262. Madonna and blessing Child with SS. Hercolanus and Constant (p.). L.

263. See 200.

264. Roundel from back of S. Agostino polyptych: Angel of Annunciation (see 258).

266. Transfiguration. 1517 (on earlier cartoon; companion to 267/9).

267/9. Predella to 266: Annunciation, Nativity, Baptism of Christ. 1517.

270. 'Madonna della Consolazione o dei Battuti' (g.p.). 1498.

278. Standard: Madonna and Child with Saints.

279. 'Tezi' Altarpiece: Madonna and Child in Glory, with SS. Thomas of Villa-nova, Bernardino, Jerome and Sebastian (on Perugino's design; execution by Eusebio; predella panel in Berlin). 1500.

280. S. John Baptist with SS. Francis, Jerome, Sebastian and Anthony of Padua. 1510.

281. 'Gonfalone della Giustizia': Madonna and Child appearing to SS. Francis and Bernardino and worshippers (g.p.). 1496/8.

358. Frescoed lunette from S. Francesco al Monte: Nativity.

COLLEGIO DEL CAMBIO. Frescoes: vault—six roundels with Planets and Grotteschi; walls, from left of entrance—Cato; Prudence and Justice with six Wise Men below; Fortitude and Temperance with six Heroes below (Lucius Sicinius, Leonidas, Horatius Cocles, Publius Scipio, Pericles and Cincinnatus); Self-portrait; Transfiguration; Nativity; Eternal and Angels with six Prophets (Isaiah, Moses, Daniel, David, Jeremiah, Solomon) and six Sibyls (Erythrea, Persica, Cumana, Libyca, Tiburtina, Delphica) below. [Plate 307.] Plate 1106.

CONTE RANIERI. Annunciation.

S. AGNESE, CAPPELLA DELLA CONCEZIONE. Frescoed triptych: Madonna of Mercy with SS. Elizabeth of Portugal and Elizabeth of Hungary; in lateral niches, S. Anthony Abbot and S. Anthony of Padua. 1522.

S. AGOSTINO. Four roundels from double polyptych once on High Altar: Evangelists (probably by Eusebio da S. Giorgio; see Perugia 249 and 258).

S. PIETRO, L. WALL. Top panel from back of S. Agostino Polyptych: Dead Christ upheld by Joseph of Arimathea between mourning Virgin and Evangelist. (See Perugia 258.)

— SACRISTY. Panels from Polyptych formerly on High Altar: Half-length SS. Hercolanus, Constant, Maurus, Scholastica (lost), Pietro in Vincoli (other Saints in Rome, Vatican; centre panel and lunette at Lyons; roundels with Prophets at Nantes; Predella panels at Rouen). 1495–98.

S. SEVERO, CLOISTER. Lower half of fresco begun by Raphael: SS. Scholastica, Jerome, John Evangelist, Gregory the Great, Bonifacius, Martha. Sd and d. 1521.

(Environs). CORCIANO, S. MARIA, HIGH ALTAR. Assumption. 1513.

Predella to Assumption: Annunciation, Nativity (fr.). 1513.

Philadelphia (Pa.). J. G. JOHNSON COLLECTION. 141. Madonna and Child in niche. L.

Pittsburgh (Pa.). CARNEGIE INSTITUTE. S. Augustine enthroned and kneeling Members of Confraternity (formerly Weimar, Schloss). Plate 1101.

Raleigh (N.C.). MUSEUM OF ART. GL.60.17.33-34 (KRESS COLLECTION K. 1153A, B). Two roundels from predella: Mourning Virgin and Evangelist (st.).

Rome. GALLERIA NAZIONALE (PALAZZO BARBERINI). Side-panel from SS. Annunziata polyptych: Francesco Patrizi or Gioacchino Piccolomini? (g.p.; see Florence, SS. Annunziata). 1506.

Rome. GALLERIA NAZIONALE (contd.). S. Jerome in Wilderness and Holy Children meeting in background (st.).

GALLERIA BORGHESE. 377. Christ on Cross, with penitent S. Jerome and S. Christopher. (Perugino's earliest surviving work?)

401. Madonna and Child in landscape (p.; see Moscow).

VATICAN, PINACOTECA. 317. 'Decemviri' altarpiece: Madonna and Child enthroned, with SS. Constant, Hercolanus, Lawrence and Louis of Toulouse (companion to Perugia 248). Sd. 1495.

318. Resurrection. 1499.

319–21. Panels from S. Pietro Polyptych in Perugia (see there): Half-length SS. Benedict, Placidus and Flavia. 1495/98.

— SISTINE CHAPEL, L. WALL. Fresco: Circumcision of the son of Moses (g.p., with Pinturicchio). 1482.

— — R. WALL. Baptism of Christ (g.p., with Pinturicchio). 1482.

Christ giving Keys to S. Peter. 1482. [*Plate* 306.]

— STANZA DELL'INCENDIO DI BORGO, VAULT. Frescoes: Four roundels—Eternal with Angels; Christ between Baptist and Satan; Trinity and Apostles; Christ as Judge. 1507–8. *Plate* 1108.

VILLA ALBANI, TORLONIA COLLECTION. Polyptych: Nativity and two Angels, SS. Michael and John Baptist, SS. Jerome and George; above, Crucifixion, Angel and Virgin of Annunciation. Sd and d. 14(91?). *Plate* 1098.

Rouen. 719–721. Predella to S. Pietro polyptych in Perugia (see there): Epiphany, Baptism of Christ, Resurrection (st.). 1495/8.

San Sepolcro. DUOMO, CHOIR, L. WALL. Ascension (g.p.).

São Paulo. 13. S. Sebastian (replica of Paris 1566A).

Resurrection (with young Raphael?)

Senigallia. PALAZZO COMUNALE. Madonna and Child enthroned with SS. John Baptist, Louis of Toulouse, Francis, Peter, Paul, James (g.p.; from S. Maria delle Grazie).

Shenfield (Berks.). J. HASSON COLLECTION (EX). Two panels: Full-length S. Jerome and S. Sebastian (st.).

Siena. S. AGOSTINO, SECOND ALTAR R. Christ on Cross with SS. Augustine, Monica, female Saint, Virgin, Magdalen, Evangelist, Baptist and S. Jerome. Probably 1506.

Spello. S. GIROLAMO. Frescoes: Nativity (p.); Marriage of Virgin (st.).

S. MARIA MAGGIORE (COLLEGIATA), CHOIR. Detached frescoes: Madonna and Child enthroned between SS. Blaise and Catherine; Pietà with mourning Evangelist and Magdalen. Sd and d. 1521.

Stockholm. 2703. Full-length S. Sebastian. Sd.

Strasbourg. MUSÉE. Virgin of Annunciation (fr. of roundel from back of S. Agostino Polyptych; see Perugia 258). Destroyed.

Toulouse. 393. Side-panel from front of S. Agostino Polyptych: SS. John Evangelist and Augustine (see Perugia 249). L.

Trevi (Perugia). S. MARIA DELLE LACRIME, SECOND ALTAR R. Fresco: Adoration of Magi; in embrasure, SS. Peter and Paul; in roundels above, Angel and Virgin of Annunciation. Sd. 1521.

Urbino. GALLERIA NAZIONALE DELLE MARCHE. Lady with long finger-index.

Venice. CONTE VITTORIO CINI. Inv. 4464. Fr. of reliquary?: Christ on Cross with Angels (st.).

Verona. 34. Tondo: Madonna adoring Child with two Angels (c.; other version at Bonn).

Vienna. 24. Baptism of Christ. *Plate* 1102.

25. S. Jerome in Wilderness.

27. Madonna and Child enthroned with SS. Peter, John Evangelist, John Baptist, Paul. d. 1493.

32. Madonna and blessing Child between SS. Rose and Catherine. Sd.

Washington (D.C.). 27 (MELLON COLLECTION). 'Galitzin' triptych: Crucifixion, S. Jerome, S. Mary Magdalen. *Plate* 1097.

266 (KRESS COLLECTION. K 302). Angel and Virgin of Annunciation in roundels among Grotteschi (st.).

326 (KRESS COLLECTION. K 403). Madonna and Child against landscape.

391 (KRESS COLLECTION. K 498). S. Jerome in Wilderness and Holy Children meeting in background (st.).

1151 (KRESS COLLECTION. K 1550). Tondo: Vintaging Putti.

Williamstown (Mass.). STERLING AND FRANCINE CLARK ART INSTITUTE. Dead Christ in Sepulchre with Evangelist and Nicodemus (formerly Stoke Park, Lord Taunton). Sd. *Plate* 1099.

PERUZZI, Baldassarre

Siena 1481–Rome 1536. Pupil probably of Pacchiarotto; assistant of Pinturicchio; influenced by Sodoma and Raphael, and towards the end by Rosso Fiorentino. Better known as architect.

Belcaro (Siena). CASTELLO, VESTIBULE. Fresco in ceiling: Judgement of Paris. *Plate* 1840.

— LOGGIA. Frescoed decoration (grotteschi etc.; completely modernized).

— CAPPELLA, APSE. Frescoes: Madonna and Child enthroned with SS. Catherine, Catherine of Siena, male martyr, Christopher and Infant John; on either side, four scenes of martyrdom, SS. Peter and Paul in niches; in vault of apse fifteen small frescoes (Allegorical figures, Way to Calvary, Deposition, Resurrection and two Stories of Saints). 1535.

Dresden. 99. Adoration of Magi. (?)

Florence. PITTI. 167. Dance of Apollo and Muses.

Gaeta. SS. ANNUNZIATA, SACRISTY. Annunciation. (?)

London. 167. Cartoon for Bentivoglio's Adoration of Magi. Sd. 1521. *Plate* 1838.
BRIDGEWATER HOUSE, EARL OF ELLESMERE (EX). 85. Adoration of Magi.
PHILIP POUNCEY. Holy Family (companion to below). *Plate* 1837.
SEBRIGHT COLLECTION (EX). Coronation (companion to above).

Rome. FARNESINA, SALA DI GALATEA. Frescoes: ceiling with allegorical figures of
Constellations; lunette with gigantic head in monochrome (other lunettes
by Sebastiano del Piombo). 1511. *Plates* 1184, 1831.

— SALA DEL FREGIO. Frescoed frieze: Labours of Hercules, Hermes steals the cattle
of Apollo, Rape of Europa, Danae, Semele, Diana and Actaeon, Midas, Apollo
and Pan, Amphitrite, Bacchus and Ariadne, Meleager, Orpheus. ca 1511.
Plate 1832.

— FIRST FLOOR, SALONE DELLE PROSPETTIVE. Frescoes: Frieze with Ovid's Fables
divided by Terms; below, on mantelpiece, Vulcan's Forge; in corners, Allegorical figures and Putti; in centre of walls, simulated loggias with views.
Plates 1833, 1834.

GALLERIA BORGHESE. Inv. 92. Venus.

PALAZZO DELLA CANCELLERIA, SALONE DELLO STUDIO. Frescoed lunettes: Stories of
Adam and Eve, Stories of Joseph (see under Perino del Vaga). *Plate* 1830.

VILLA ALBANI. Madonna and Child with SS. Sebastian, Lawrence, James and
donor. E.

VILLA MADAMA, LOGGIA, VAULT. Frescoes: Ovals with playing Putti. *Plate* 1839.

S. CROCE IN GERUSALEMME, CRYPT. Mosaics after P.'s design: Christ, Evangelists,
small Scenes. Not after 1508.

S. MARIA DELLA PACE, CAPPELLA PONZETTI (FIRST L.). Frescoes: Madonna and Child
with two SS. Catherine and Ponzetti as donor; in vault above, nine small
scenes (Sacrifice of Isaac, Creation of Eve, Moses and the Law; Nativity,
Adoration of Magi, Flight into Egypt; David and Goliath, Flood, Judith). d.
1516. *Plates* 1835–1836.

— R. WALL. Fresco: Presentation of Virgin.

S. ONOFRIO, CHOIR. Frescoes. In semidome, Coronation of Virgin; on walls below,
Adoration of Magi; Madonna and blessing Child with SS. Catherine,
Onuphrius, Jerome, John Baptist and donor; Flight into Egypt. E.

S. PAOLO FUORI LE MURA, PINACOTECA. Flagellation (Spanish follower?).

S. PIETRO IN MONTORIO, OVER SECOND AND THIRD CHAPEL R. Frescoes: Coronation
of Virgin and eight Virtues.

San Francisco (Cal.). ZELLERBACH COLLECTION. Detached fresco: Three Graces (fr.).

Sant'Ansano in Dofana (Siena). PARISH CHURCH. Madonna and Child. L.

Siena. PALAZZO POLLINI NERI. Three frescoed ceilings: Continence of Scipio, Nativity,
Punishment of the Elders. L.

ARCO DELLE DUE PORTE. Fresco in Tabernacle: Madonna and Child with S.
Catherine of Siena and Infant S. John. L.

CHIESA DI FONTEGIUSTA, FIRST ALTAR R. Augustus and the Sibyl. L.

(Environs). BELCARO, BARZELOTTI CAMAIORI COLL. See Belcaro.

PIAZZA, Albertino and Martino

Lodi. Martino, the younger brother but apparently senior partner, died 1529. Influenced by most of their Milanese contemporaries (chiefly by Boltraffio) and by Giovanni Agostino da Lodi, by Perugino and Raphael. Where the separate work of each can be distinguished, it is indicated with the initial A *or* M.

Baltimore (Md.). WALTERS ART GALLERY. 509. Magdalen. (?)

Bergamo. 309. Mystic Marriage of S. Catherine. (A)

    607. S. Dorothy. (A). (?)

    FRIZZONI SALIS COLLECTION (EX). Adoration of Magi. (A). *Plate 1461.*

    PICCINELLI COLLECTION (EX). Nativity. (A)

Brescia. S. AFRA, LOWER CHURCH. Polyptych: Pietà; Saints; in predella, Scenes of Passion and standing Saints.

Brno. A.138. Pietà.

Budapest. 6311. Madonna with Holy Children. (M.)

Castiglione d'Adda (Milan). INCORONATA. Polyptych commissioned by Cristoforo Pallavicino: Madonna and Child, SS. John Baptist and Roch; upper register, S. Anthony, Crucifixion, S. Bassianus; at top, God the Father blessing in lunette, Angel and Virgin of Annunciation; in predella, Christ and the Apostles.

Cavenago d'Adda (Milan). PARISH CHURCH. Madonna and Child with SS. Roch and Sebastian. Formerly d. 1512.

Denver (Col.). MUSEUM OF ART. E–IT–18–XVI–945 (KRESS COLLECTION. K 371). Tondo: Virgin in a glory of Angels.

Lockinge House (Wantage, Berks.). CHRISTOPHER LLOYD (EX). Madonna and Child with Angel and Infant S. John.

Lodi. MUSEO CIVICO. Two panels of polyptych: S. Bassianus blessing against landscape, Madonna and Child enthroned against landscape. (A). *Plate 1462.*

    Four frescoes from Cappella di S. Antonio Abate, Incoronata: S. Anthony Abbot beaten by the devils, disputing with the Elders, SS. Anthony Abbot and Paul Hermit fed by the raven, Death of S. Paul Hermit. (M) *Plate 1464.*

    PALAZZO DEL VESCOVO. Lower panels of polyptych (companions to Duomo): Dormition*, S. Sebastian in landscape, Bishop Saint (Bassianus?) (second Bishop not traced). 1508. *Plates 1457–1459.*

    DUOMO, CAPPELLA BATTESIMALE (FIRST R.), R. WALL. Upper panels of polyptych: Assumption, S. John Baptist, S. Catherine; above, Holy Ghost, Angel and Virgin of Annunciation (companions to Palazzo del Vescovo) 1508. *Plate 1454–6.*

    INCORONATA, ON BACK OF HIGH ALTAR. Coronation of Virgin. 1519. *Plate 1467.*

    — NICCHIONE DELLA CANTORIA, BELOW SINGING GALLERY, R. Madonna and Child with S. John Baptist and S. Roch (?) recommending Niccolò Trivulzio Count of Musocco freed by incurable disease (r.). d. 1509. (A)

Lodi (contd.). INCORONATA, CAPPELLA DI S. ANTONIO ABATE (FIRST L.). Polyptych: Madonna and Child, S. Anthony Abbot recommending Antonio Berinzaghi, S. Bassianus Bishop; upper register, SS. Roch and Sebastian, Crucifixion, SS. James and John Baptist; in predella, Christ and Apostles. 1513–14. *Plate* 1460.

S. AGNESE, FIRST ALTAR R. Polyptych: S. Augustine enthroned with two Angels, SS. Bassianus and Dominic, SS. Francis and Ambrose; upper register, SS. Catherine and Clare, Madonna and Child with Infant S. John and six Angels, worshipped by Fra Nicolao Galiani, SS. Theresa and Rosa; at top, blessing God the Father in lunette, Angel and Virgin of Annunciation; in predella, Christ and Apostles. 1520.

S. MARIA DELLA PACE. Fresco: Adoration of Magi. After 1523. (A)

London. 1152. S. John Baptist in the Wilderness. (M; inscribed MPP). *Plate* 1465.

Milan. AMBROSIANA. Adoration of the Child (M.; inscribed MPP).

BRERA. 337. Left panel of polyptych: S. John Baptist.

POLDI PEZZOLI. 645. Holy Family and Angels. (?)

ARCH. LUIGI BONOMI. Nativity.

PRINCIPI BORROMEO. 40 bis. Baptism.

   61. Madonna and Child. (A)

   145. Madonna and Child with Infant S. John.

   152. Christ and the Apostles. (M)

ALDO CRESPI. Angel and Virgin of Annunciation.

MARCHESE FOSSATI (EX). S. Jerome. (M)

SESSA FUMAGALLI COLLECTION. Adoration of Shepherds. d. 1520. *Plate* 1468.

S. AMBROGIO, FIRST CHAPEL R. Madonna and Child. Not traced.

Nantes. 121, 122. Fragments of altarpiece: S. John Evangelist, female Saint and donor; S. John Baptist and S. Anthony of Padua? (r.). L. (?)

New York. HEARST COLLECTION (EX). 'Chiesa' triptych: S. Nicholas enthroned, S. John Baptist and Bishop Saint; S. Clare and Tobias with the Angel. (A). *Plate* 1463.

Padua. 102 (Inv. 446). Predella panel: Blessing Redeemer with SS. John Evangelist and Peter.

Rome. MUSEO DI PALAZZO VENEZIA. F.N.19211. Madonna and Child with S. Elizabeth and Infant S. John. (M). *Plate* 1466.

MARCHESE GIOVANNI VISCONTI VENOSTA (EX). Predella panel: Dead Christ upheld by two Angels with SS. Catherine and Agatha. (A)

Savona. DUOMO, CAPPELLA SPINOLA (R. TRANSEPT). Madonna and Child with two male Saints.*

Turin. GALLERIA SABAUDA. 143. Blessing God the Father and Angels. (A)

Verona. 96. Madonna and Child with S. Elizabeth and Infant S. John. (A)

Vienna. AKADEMIE, GESCHENK KOENIGSCHMIED. S. John Baptist and Bishop Saint.

LEDERER COLLECTION (EX). Madonna and Child with Infant S. John. (A)

Wiesbaden. 9. Angel. (M)

PIAZZA, Calisto

Lodi. ca 1500–62. Son of Martino and nephew of Albertino Piazza. Was assisted by his brothers (Scipione, Cesare) and by his son Fulvio. Active in Brescia 1524–29, then mostly in Lodi and Milan. Follower of Romanino, influenced by the Venetians in general, and more particularly by Pordenone.

Abbadia Cerreto (Milano). SS. PIETRO E PAOLO. S. Peter recommending to the Virgin and Child the Bishop Federico Cesi, Infant S. John, S. Paul and two Bishop Saints behind (with his brother Scipione?).

Alessandria. DUOMO. S. Peter enthroned and Saints. Sd and d. 1546.

Azzate (Varese). PARISH CHURCH, HIGH ALTAR. Marriage of S. Catherine, S. Jerome and donor. Sd and d. 1542.

Berlin. 157A. Beheading of S. John Baptist. (Destroyed 1945.) (?)

Borno (Val Camonica). S. ANTONIO. Frescoed lunette: Madonna and Child with SS. Roch, Anthony of Padua, John Baptist and Martin. E.

Breno (Val Camonica). S. ANTONIO. Mourning over the Dead Christ.

— HIGH ALTAR. Madonna and Child enthroned, with SS. Anthony Abbot, Sebastian, Roch and Sirus; Angel and Virgin of Annunciation in roundels above; candelabra, grottesche and heads of Saints in frame and predella.

S. GREGORIO. Madonna and Child with Saints.

Brescia. 95. Virgin adoring the Child with SS. Stephen and Antoninus Bishop (from S. Clemente). Sd and d. 1524.

CONTI SALVADEGO (EX). Side-panels of polyptych: S. Joseph, S. John Evangelist.*

S. CLEMENTE. (Organ-shutters?): Angel and Virgin of Annunciation.

S. FRANCESCO, FIRST ALTAR R. Frescoed lunette (over Moretto's altarpiece): Visitation (companion to Milan, Brera 339).

S. MARIA IN CALCHERA, HIGH ALTAR. Visitation. Sd and d. 1525. *Plate 1678.*

SS. SIMONE E GIUDA (EX). Nativity, flanked by SS. Simon and Judas. Sd and d. 1524.

Budapest. 4241 (PÁLFFY 18). Nativity. E. (?)

Capriolo. PARISH CHURCH. Martyrdom of SS. Gervasio and Protasio.*

Cividate (Val Camonica). S. MARIA ASSUNTA, CHOIR, L. WALL. Madonna and Child with SS. Stephen, Lawrence, Jerome and John Baptist. Sd and d. 1529.

Codogno (Milano). COLLEGIATA. Assumption with Trivulzio and his Wife. Sd and d. 1553.

Copenhagen. 542. Head of man.

Crema. SS. TRINITÀ, THIRD ALTAR L. Nativity with SS. Peter, Paul, Sebastian and Roch. Commissioned from Calisto and Scipione 1537.

Dulwich. 84. Concert.

Erbanno (Val Camonica). S. MARIA DI RESTELLO, CHOIR. Frescoes: Beheading of S. John Baptist, Assumption, S. George killing the dragon. *Plates 1683–1684.*

Esine (Val Camonica). PARISH CHURCH, SECOND ALTAR R. Mourning over dead Christ and two Angels adoring Sacrament (from SS. Trinità). Sd and d. 1527.

— CHOIR. Organ-shutters: Angel and Virgin of Annunciation (outside, st.?, r.?); SS. Peter and Paul in niches (inside).

— SACRISTY. Madonna and Child under a tree, with SS. Peter and Paul and Lake of Iseo in background (from SS. Trinità).

Florence. PITTI, MAGAZZINO DEGLI OCCHI. 5065. Allegorical portrait of woman.

Lodi. PINACOTECA. Two panels: Angel and Virgin of Annunciation, in frame by Battista Coldiroli (from polyptych commissioned 1552).

'Saccani' altarpiece: Madonna and Child with S. Bassianus recommending donor and S. Catherine standing on wheel.

Small polyptych round a polychrome relief of Adoration of Magi: Marriage of Virgin, Joseph's Dream, Flight into Egypt (p.).

— DEP. FROM INCORONATA. Dead Christ upheld by Angels.

— DEP. MILAN (BRERA 338, 338A). Fragments of Crucifixion: Old woman; Youth picking up Nails.

— — (BRERA 342). Portrait of Ludovico Vistarini.

DUOMO, CAPPELLA BATTESIMALE (FIRST R.), BETWEEN WINDOWS. Polyptych of SS. Bovo and Lucia: top register—S. Michael and the Dragon, Madonna and Child with two female Saints, SS. Paul and Lawrence; bottom register—two Warrior Saints, Massacre of Innocents, Saintly Pope and Bishop (left unfinished by Albertino). 1529–32. *Plate 1682.*

INCORONATA, CAPPELLA DEL BATTISTA, OVER ALTAR. Beheading of S. John Baptist. Sd and d. 1530. *Plate 1681.*

— — Embrasures at sides of altar: top left, Birth of Baptist; bottom left, Baptism of Christ; top right, Baptist preaching to Multitudes; bottom right, Herod's Banquet. *Plate 1679.*

— — Frescoed lunette: Two Prophets with scrolls round circular window.

— CAPPELLA DELLA CROCIFISSIONE, OVER ALTAR. Deposition.

— — Embrasures at sides of altar: top left, Betrayal of Christ; bottom left, Flagellation; top right, Way to Calvary; bottom right, Nailing to Cross.

— — Frescoed lunette: Two Prophets round circular window, pointing at cartouche inscribed MDXXXVIII (1538).

— CAPPELLA MAGGIORE, EMBRASURES AT SIDES OF HIGH ALTAR. Top left, S. Joachim distributing Alms; bottom left, Expulsion from Temple; top right, Birth of Virgin; bottom right, Visitation (mostly executed by Calisto's son, Fulvio Piazza). 1558–62.

— CAPPELLA DI S. PAOLO, OVER ALTAR. Conversion of S. Paul (p.). 1552/3.

— — Embrasures at sides of altar (panels by Bergognone, formerly in the Cappella Maggiore).

— — Frescoed lunette: Sibilla Libica and Sibilla Samia round circular window, with cartouche inscribed MDLIX. 1559.

— NICCHIONE DELLA CANTORIA. Frescoed lunette round circular window: Two Prophets (st.)

— — Parapet of singing gallery: two roundels with busts of Sibyls (p.).

— NICCHIONE D'INGRESSO, OVER ENTRANCE. Adoration of Magi (st.).

Embrasure at sides of entrance (Four stories of Abraham by Calisto's son Fulvio).

— NICCHIONE DELL'ORGANO, BELOW ORGAN. Copy of Dead Christ upheld by Angels (original in Pinacoteca).

— — Parapet of Organ: Two roundels with busts of Sibyls.

— Pilasters and friezes. Frescoed Putti and ornaments (st.).

S. LORENZO, R. OF CHOIR. Fresco: Marriage of S. Catherine. (?)

Lovere. 73. Marriage of S. Catherine.

Milan. BRERA. 338, 338A, 342. See Lodi, Pinacoteca.

339. Madonna and Child with SS. John Baptist and Jerome (from S. Francesco at Brescia). Sd. *Plate* 1680.

341. Baptism of Christ.

CASTELLO, SALETTA NEGRA. Frescoes: Putti and garlands. L.

MUSEO DI SCIENZA E TECNICA (DEP. BRERA 340). S. Stephen between SS. Augustine and Nicholas of Bari. L.

UNIVERSITÀ CATTOLICA, AULA MAGNA. Detached fresco from refectory of S. Ambrogio: Marriage at Cana. 1545.

S. MARIA PRESSO S. CELSO, AMBULATORY, SIXTH BAY. S. Jerome.

— — FIFTH BAY. Frescoed ceiling around a relief of S. John: Putti and Prophets. After 1546.

S. MAURIZIO (MONASTERO MAGGIORE), CAPPELLA DEL VESCOVO SIMONETTI O DELLA PIETÀ (SECOND R.). Frescoed decoration on pilasters, friezes and spandrels. d. 1555.

(Environs). ABBAZIA DI CHIARAVALLE. CHIOSTRO GRANDE. Fresco: Madonna and Child with two female Saints and monks (r.). 1549.

Montichiari. S. PANCRAZIO. Votive fresco: Madonna and Child enthroned with S. Pancrazio recommending donor, SS. Anthony Abbot and Roch (r.).

Orzinuovi (Brescia). PALAZZO MUNICIPALE. Madonna and Child enthroned with SS. Bartholomew and Gregory and donor. L. (?)

Pandino. PARISH CHURCH. Mourning over dead Christ. Sd and d. 1556.*

Philadelphia (Pa.). J. G. JOHNSON COLLECTION. 233. Head of youth.

234. Concert. *Plate* 1675.

Postino Dovera (between Lodi and Crema). ORATORIO DI S. ROCCO. Frescoes: Prophets in lunettes; three stories of S. Roch and Ambrogio Beretta; S. Sebastian; (p.). d. 1545.*

Rome. MUSEO DI PALAZZO VENEZIA. F.N.720. Lady as S. Catherine (fr.). Sd.

Sarasota (Fla.). RINGLING MUSEUM. 67. Bust of young man in striped jerkin.

Venice. ACCADEMIA. Beheading of Baptist (for Benvenuto Brunetti). Sd and d. (on back) 1526. *Plate* 1677.

Verona. 83. Salome.

Vienna. LEDERER COLLECTION (EX). Madonna and Child in landscape.
  BERTHA MORELLI (FORMERLY EISSLER) (EX). Open-air concert. *Plate* 1676.

PIERMATTEO DA AMELIA

*Amelia, ca 1450, assistant to Fra Filippo Lippi at Spoleto, documented in Rome from 1469
to 1502, at Civita Castellana 1502/3. Follower of Pinturicchio. [Lately identified with the
Master of the Gardner Annunciation.]*

Amelia. MUSEO CIVICO. Madonna and Child with S. John Baptist and S. Francis; in
    lunette, God the Father blessing and two Putti; in predella, Man of Sorrows,
    mourning Virgin and Evangelist. *Plate* 1073.
Civita Castellana. PALAZZO PAPALE. Monochrome frescoes in vault and lunettes of
    portico with decorative motives (p. ?). 1502/3.
Narni. PINACOTECA. S. Anthony of Padua and kneeling child; Bernardino da Feltre
    and worshipper.
Rome. VATICAN, BELVEDERE. Frescoed lunettes: Putti with emblems and musical
    instruments. 1492.
  — BORGIA APARTMENTS, SALA DEL CREDO. Frescoed decoration (with Pinturicchio).
    d. 1494.
Terni. PINACOTECA. Frescoed lunette from S. Maria delle Grazie: Madonna and
    Child with SS. Francis and Bernardino.
Tuscania. S. MARIA DEL RIPOSO. Fragmentary polyptych.

PIERO DELLA FRANCESCA

San Sepolcro. 1416(?)–92. Pupil of Domenico Veneziano; influenced by Paolo Uccello.

Arezzo. DUOMO, L. TRANSEPT. Fresco: S. Mary Magdalen.
  S. FRANCESCO, APSE. Frescoes: Death of Adam and Growth of Tree from his
    Mouth; Building of Bridge (or Finding of Wood in Pool of Bethesda); Queen
    of Sheba adoring Bridge and meeting Solomon; Dream of Constantine;
    Victory of Constantine over Maxentius; Judas in the Well; Finding of the
    True Cross; Defeat of Chosroes; Heraclius carries the Cross into Jerusalem;
    Annunciation; Prophets. [*Plate* 281.] *Plate* 763.
  — ENTRANCE PIERS. Frescoes: Angel, Cupid, S. Louis of Toulouse, S. Peter Martyr
    (p.)
  S. MARIA DELLE GRAZIE (BUILDING NEAR BY). Fresco: Scene from Life of S. Donatus
    (fr.) (g.p.).

Berlin. 1904. S. Jerome in the Wilderness (Saint only, landscape finished later). Sd. and d. 145(?).

SCHLOSSMUSEUM. Ideal view of a Florentine square (p.). (?)

Berlin-Ost. 1615. Architectural view (p.)

Boston (Mass.). GARDNER MUSEUM. Fresco detached from Casa Graziani at S. Sepolcro: Hercules (fr.).

Florence. UFFIZI. 1615. Portraits of Federigo da Montefeltro and his wife, Battista Sforza; on back, Triumph of Federigo and Triumph of Battista. 1465–66. *Plate 765.*

CONTINI BONACOSSI COLLECTION. Profile Portrait of Sigismondo Pandolfo Malatesta.

Lisbon. MUSEU NACIONAL DE ARTE ANTIGA. Panel from S. Agostino Polyptych: S. Augustine (companion to London, Milan, New York, Washington).

London. 665. Baptism of Christ. [*Plate 279.*]

769. Panel from S. Agostino Polyptych: S. Michael (companion to Lisbon, Milan, New York, Washington). *Plate 768.*

908. Nativity (u.)

Milan. BRERA. 510. Madonna and Child enthroned with four Angels, SS. John Baptist, Bernardino, Jerome, Francis, Peter Martyr, John Evangelist and kneeling Federigo da Montefeltro (hand of Federigo by Berruguete). Probably ca 1469–73. *Plate 764.*

POLDI PEZZOLI. 598. Panel from S. Agostino Polyptych: S. Nicholas of Tolentino (companion to Lisbon, London, New York, Washington).

Monterchi (San Sepolcro). CAPPELLA DEL CIMITERO. Fresco: 'Madonna del Parto' with two Angels (p.).

New York. FRICK COLLECTION. Panels from S. Agostino Polyptych: S. Andrew (?); S. Monica, Augustinian monk (from pilasters of frame); Crucifixion (from predella) (companion to Lisbon, London, Milan, Washington).

Perugia. 111. Annunciation (Madonna and four Saints of this altarpiece are largely the works of pupils). L.

112-114. Predella to altarpiece 111: S. Francis receiving Stigmata, S. Elizabeth saving a child fallen into a well; S. Anthony resuscitating a boy. L.

Richmond. COOK COLLECTION (EX). 48. Presentation in the Temple (executed by Marco Marziale, inspired by Piero della Francesca).

Rimini. S. FRANCESCO, CHAPEL R. (CAPPELLA DELLE RELIQUIE). Fresco: Sigismondo Malatesta kneeling before his Patron Saint. Sd and d. 1451. *Plates 759a, 760.*

San Sepolcro. PINACOTECA COMUNALE. Polyptych: lower register—Madonna of Mercy; SS. Sebastian, John Baptist, Andrew, Bernardino; upper register— Christ on Cross with Virgin and S. John; Angel and Virgin of Annunciation; SS. Francis and Benedict; predella—Agony in the Garden, Flagellation, Entombment, Noli me tangere, the Three Maries at the Tomb (st.); six Saints from Pilasters (st.). Commissioned 1445. *Plate 761.*

San Sepolcro. PINACOTECA COMUNALE (contd.). Fresco detached from Palazzo Pretorio: S. Louis of Toulouse. Formerly dated 1460.

Detached fresco: Resurrection. [*Plate 282.*]

EX CONVENTO DI S. CHIARA. Fragment of fresco: Bust of Saint.

Turin. GALLERIA SABAUDA, GUALINO COLLECTION. Bust of young woman (r.).

Urbino. GALLERIA NAZIONALE DELLE MARCHE. Madonna and blessing Child with two Angels (from Sinigallia).

Flagellation with Duke Oddantonio and his ministers Manfredi Pio da Carpi and Tommaso di Guido dell'Agnello da Rimini. Sd. [*Plate 280.*]

Architectural view. *Plate 762.*

Venice. ACCADEMIA. 47. S. Jerome with kneeling Girolamo Amadi. Sd. *Plate 766.*

Washington (D.C.). 815 (KRESS COLLECTION. K 1365). Panel from S. Agostino polyptych: S. Apollonia (companion to Lisbon, London, Milan, New York).

Williamstown (Mass.). STERLING AND FRANCINE CLARK ART INSTITUTE. Madonna and Child enthroned with four Angels (st.). *Plate 767.*

PIETRO DI DOMENICO DA MONTEPULCIANO

Documented works from 1418 till after 1422. Remote follower of Simone Martini; influenced by Gentile da Fabriano.

Altidona. PARISH CHURCH. Madonna and Child enthroned with Angels; SS. Lawrence, Stephen, Michael, Cosmas (formerly at Potenza Picena, and Ancona, Duca Ferretti). *Plates 525–527.*

Cherbourg. 82 (CAMPANA 144). Madonna of Mercy. E. (?)

New York. 07.201. Madonna of Humility with four Angels (from Camaldolese convent, Naples). Sd 'Petrus Dominici de Monte Politiano' and d. 1420. *Plate 523.*

Osimo. BAPTISTERY (MUSEO). Polyptych: Madonna of Humility with five Angels; SS. Anthony Abbot, Catherine, Nicholas and Leopard; upper register, Crucifixion and four Saints. d. 1418. *Plate 524.*

Perugia. 84. Triptych: Madonna and Child, S. Francis, S. Anthony Abbot.

Potenza Picena. ISTITUTO DELL'ADDOLORATA. See Altidona.

Recanati. PINACOTECA COMUNALE. Polyptych from S. Vito: Madonna of Humility, SS. John Baptist, John Evangelist, Lawrence and Vitus; in predella, SS. Bartholomew, James, Peter, mourning Virgin, Dead Christ, mourning S. John, SS. Paul, Andrew, Thomas. Sd 'Petrus' and d. 1422.

S. MARIA DI CASTELNUOVO, CASA PARROCCHIALE. Fresco: Madonna and Child enthroned with two Angels.

Riofreddo (Tivoli). ORATORIO DELL'ANNUNZIATA, VAULT. Fresco: Christ in Glory and Angels. d. 1422.

Washington (D.C.). HOWARD UNIVERSITY. 61.148.P (KRESS STUDY COLLECTION. K 59). Coronation of the Virgin.

PIETRO DI DOMENICO DA SIENA

1457–1506? *Developed under influence of Matteo di Giovanni, Francesco di Giorgio and Benvenuto di Giovanni.*

Balcarres (Fife, Scotland). EARL OF CRAWFORD AND BALCARRES. Madonna and Child with SS. Sebastian and Jerome.

Buonconvento (Senese). PIEVE DEI SS. PIETRO E PAOLO, PINACOTECA. Assumption of Virgin.

Englewood (N.J.). PLATT COLLECTION (EX). Madonna and Child with two Angels.

Grosseto. MUSEO DI ARTE SACRA. Lunette: Dead Christ in sepulchre worshipped by S. Crescentius and S. Roch.*

Le Mans. 26. Madonna and Child with SS. Sebastian and Augustine.

London. LORD BROWNLOW (EX). Madonna and Child.

New York. 88.3.100. Madonna suckling the Child with SS. Peter and Paul.

41.190.22. Madonna suckling the Child and two Angels.

OSCAR B. CINTAS (EX). Madonna and Child with two Angels (formerly Brooklyn, F. L. Babbott; possibly identical with Englewood).

Radicondoli (Senese). COLLEGIATA (SS. SIMONE E GIUDA). Assumption; below, Nativity and six Saints. *Plate* 914.

Rome. STERBINI COLLECTION (EX). Coronation of Virgin, with SS. John Baptist, Jerome, Benedict, Bernard and Catherine and Angels. Sd. L.

Siena. 279. Nativity with SS. Galganus and Martin. Sd. *Plate* 915.

390. Adoration of Shepherds, with Procession of Magi in background. *Plate* 916.

397. Madonna and Child with SS. Jerome and Anthony of Padua.

428. Disrobing of Christ (on Francesco di Giorgio's cartoon). *Plate* 913.

CASA DI RIPOSO IN CAMPANSI (EX MONASTERO DI S. GIROLAMO), CLOISTER. Fresco: Assumption (Eternal, Prophets and Angels only; Virgin by Fungai; fourteen Saints below by Balducci).

MUSEO DELL'OPERA DEL DUOMO. Madonna and Child with SS. John Baptist and Jerome. E. (?)

PIETRO DI GIOVANNI see AMBROSI

PIETRO DA RIMINI see RIMINI

PINTURICCHIO (Bernardino Betti)

Perugia. 1454–1513. Pupil perhaps of Fiorenzo di Lorenzo; close follower of Perugino.

Assisi. S. MARIA DEGLI ANGELI. CAPPELLA DI S. BONAVENTURA, CEILING. Fresco: The Eternal.

Assisi (contd.). ORATORIO DEI PELLEGRINI. Fresco: S. Ansanus (next to S. Anthony Abbot by Mezzastris).

Balcarres (Fife, Scotland). EARL OF CRAWFORD AND BALCARRES. Madonna suckling the Child and two Angels (st.)

Baltimore (Md.). WALTERS ART GALLERY. 430. Tondo: Christ carrying the Cross (st.) 514. Nativity (p., r.)

Berlin. 136. Bust of young man (temporarily deposited at Goettingen 143). 1481. Madonna and Child writing in book, with S. Jerome (st.)

Berlin-Ost. 132A. Reliquary from S. Donato in Polverosa at Florence: S. Augustine in Glory with two Angels and SS. Benedict and Bernard (st.)

Boston (Mass.). GARDNER MUSEUM. Small Madonna and Child reading.

Brooklyn (N.Y.). 34.486. Bust of young man.

Cambridge. FITZWILLIAM MUSEUM. 119. Madonna and Child reading with Infant S. John.

Cambridge (Mass.). FOGG ART MUSEUM. 33. Holy Family with Infant S. John (g.p.).

Chicago (Ill.). LAKE FOREST, JOHN R. THOMPSON COLLECTION (EX). Madonna and Child (r.)

Città di Castello. DUOMO. Madonna and Child blessing Infant S. John (st.).
PALAZZO BUFALINI (EX). Madonna and Child blessing against landscape.

Cleveland (Ohio). 44.89 (SEVERANCE PRENTISS BEQUEST). Madonna and Child against landscape. L.

Denver (Col.). MUSEUM OF ART. E–IT–18–XV–936 (KRESS COLLECTION. K 1375). Madonna and Child blessing. E.

Dresden. 41. Portrait of a boy. *Plate* 1128.

Glasgow. BEATTIE COLLECTION (EX). Portrait of lady supposed to be Agnese Piccolomini (replica of portrait in fresco of Eleonora meeting Frederick III, in the Piccolomini Library at Siena).

Göttingen. 143. Portrait of young man (dépôt from Berlin 136).

Honolulu (Hawaii). HONOLULU ACADEMY OF ARTS. 2988.1 (KRESS COLLECTION. K 542). Madonna and Child with goldfinch.

Imbersago (Monza). MOMBELLO, PRINCIPE PIO DI SAVOIA (EX). Small Madonna and Child. d. 1492.

Isolabella (Lago Maggiore). PALAZZO BORROMEO. Way to Calvary. Sd and d. 1513. *Plate* 1144.

Leningrad. BOTKINE COLLECTION (EX) (HERMITAGE?). Madonna and Child.

London. 693. Full-length S. Catherine with kneeling donor (st.).
703. Madonna and Child standing on parapet. E. *Plate* 1063.
911. Fresco detached from Palazzo Petrucci at Siena (see there): The Return of Odysseus. ca 1509.
2483. Madonna and Child under rose-garland. E.
R. KINGETT. Miniature: Porta Sancti Petri Auguste Perusie: Madonna and Child in Mandorla between SS. Peter and Paul; below, Infants with Monks and Amico Graziani (companion to Perugia and Vienna). 1486.

Lyons. M. E. AYNARD (EX). Knee-length S. Bartholomew. *Plate* 1130.

Massa Carrara. DUOMO. CAPPELLA DEL SACRAMENTO. In Baroque altar, fragment of fresco detached from Cappella Cybo in S. Maria del Popolo, Rome: Madonna and Child with Angels.

Milan. AMBROSIANA. Madonna and Child blessing donor (p.). L.

Naples. 49. Assumption of the Virgin and Saints (execution chiefly by Eusebio da San Giorgio).

New York. 14.114.1–22. Frescoed ceiling from Palazzo del Magnifico at Siena (see there): Four putti with garlands, Rape of Proserpine; Chariot of Apollo; Triumph of Mars; Chariot of Ceres; Triumph of Cybele; Triumph of Alexander; Triumph of Amphitrite; Triumph of a warrior; Galatea; Hunt of the Calydonian Boar; Judgement of Paris; Helle on a ram; Hercules and Omphale; Rape of Europa; Bacchus, Pan and Silenus; Jupiter and Antiope; The three Graces; Venus and Cupid. *Plate* 1145.

Oberlin (Ohio). ALLEN MEMORIAL MUSEUM. Tondo: Marriage of S. Catherine (p.).

Orvieto. DUOMO, CHOIR, R. WALL. Ruined frescoes round circular window: SS. Luke, Matthew, Ambrose (frs., st.; see Pastura). 1492/96.

Oxford. ASHMOLEAN MUSEUM. 330. Bust of young man.

331. Madonna with blessing Child in landscape.

Paris. 1417. Madonna and Child writing, between SS. John Baptist and Gregory (st.).

JOLY DE BAMMEVILLE (EX) (?). Detached fresco from Palazzo Petrucci, Siena (see there): Continence of Scipio.

POURTALÈS COLLECTION (EX). Madonna and Child in landscape (r.).

Perugia. 274. Polyptych from S. Maria dei Fossi (or S. Maria degli Angeli a Porta S. Pietro): Madonna and Child enthroned with Infant S. John; full-length SS. Augustine and Jerome; above, Angel and Virgin of Annunciation; on top, Dead Christ and two Angels; predella, four tondi with Busts of the four Evangelists, S. Augustine and the Child who wanted to empty the sea, central panel missing; S. Jerome in the Wilderness. 1495. *Plates* 1131–1133.

276. S. Augustine with two kneeling Flagellants. 1500.

293. Madonna and Child with two trees (r.).

MUNICIPIO, SALA DEL CONSIGLIO. Fresco in lunette: Madonna and Child with two Angels and six Cherubim. 14(86?). *Plate* 1122.

PALAZZO GRAZIANI (EX). Three miniatures with Graziani coat of arms and Perugia's Griffon: 'Porta Solis Auguste Perusie' (Coronation of Virgin with Amico Graziani Capitano delle Porte, monks and children below; d. 1486), 'Porta Heburnea Auguste Perusie' (Holy Family and Infants, with Capitano delle Porte, monks and children below, d. 1486), 'Porta S. Susanne Auguste Perusie' (Madonna and Child between S. Francis and S. Susanna holding lily and book, with A. Graziani, monk, assistant and foundlings below) (companions to London and Vienna). *Plate* 1124.

OPERA DEL DUOMO. Full-length S. Jerome; Full-length S. Lawrence (on sides of a stucco relief of a Madonna and Child with Infant S. John).

Philadelphia (Pa.). JOHN G. JOHNSON COLLECTION. 142. S. John Evangelist between two male Saints.

    Inv. 1336. Madonna teaching the Holy Child to read with Flight into Egypt in background (g.p.).

Raleigh (N.C.). NORTH CAROLINA MUSEUM OF ART. GL.60.17.35 (KRESS COLLECTION. K 47). 'Stroganoff' Madonna and Child reading, against landscape.

Rome. VATICAN, PINACOTECA. 312. Coronation of Virgin with Saints and Angels (g.p.). 1503.

    314. Marriage of S. Catherine.

    324. Detached fresco: Madonna and blessing Child.

— BELVEDERE, GALLERIA DELLE STATUE. Fragments of decorative frescoes not touched under Pius VI by Unterberger (p.; execution of lunettes with pairs of Putti probably by Piermatteo d'Amelia, who received payments). Between 1487 and 1492.

— BIBLIOTECA. *Ms. Vat. Barber. Lat.* Miniature: Christ on Cross with Virgin and Evangelist. *Plate* 1143.

— BORGIA APARTMENTS. Frescoes. 1492–95.

— — SALA DELLE SIBILLE (I). Small scenes in vault, Sibyls and Prophets in lunettes (execution by assistants under his guidance).

— — SALA DEL CREDO (II). Twelve lunettes with Prophets and Apostles holding scrolls with Articles of the Creed (by Piermatteo d'Amelia under his guidance).

— — SALA DEL TRIVIO E DEL QUADRIVIO (III). Lunettes with Liberal Arts (by Pastura under his guidance).

— — SALA DEI SANTI (IV). Vault—in two bays, eight Episodes from Myth of Isis and Osiris, and five octagonal sections with Myth of Io and Apis (p.); Walls— opposite window, S. Catherine disputing with the Emperor; Left, Flight of S. Barbara, Chastity of Susanna; Right, Visitation (all entirely his), Meeting of SS. Anthony Abbot and Paul Hermit (g.p.); above window, Martyrdom of S. Sebastian (p.); over door, Madonna and Child with Cherubim (p.). *Plates* 1126, 1129.

— — SALA DEI MISTERI DELLA FEDE (V). Vault, David, Solomon, Isaiah, Jeremiah, Malachias, Sophonias, Micheas, Joel (st.); Walls, Resurrection (only portrait of Alexander VI by his hand); Adoration of Magi (st.); Annunciation (st.); Descent of the Holy Ghost (st.); Assumption (only donor by his hand; Angels by Pastura; rest by other assistants). *Plate* 1127.

— SISTINE CHAPEL. Fresco: Baptism of Christ (assisting Perugino).

    Fresco: Circumcision of the son of Moses (assisting Perugino).

CASTEL S. ANGELO. Slight fragments of frescoes. 1495.

CONTESSA RASPONI SPALLETTI (EX). Madonna and Child reading.

MARCHESE VISCONTI VENOSTA. Tondo: Madonna and Child blessing Infant S. John. L.

PRINCIPE CHIGI. The Holy Child blessing (fr.).

PALAZZO COLONNA, GROUND FLOOR ROOM. Monochrome frescoes in vault: Episodes from the Old Testament, Greek and Roman history, ornaments.

PALAZZO DEI PENITENZIERI, SALA DEGLI APOSTOLI. Frescoed lunettes: Apostles and Prophets (with Pastura).

— SALA DEGLI DEI MARINI. Panelled ceiling with marine deities (st.).

— SALA DEI MESI. Frescoed vault: fragments of decoration. d. 1490.

S. CECILIA IN TRASTEVERE, CAPPELLA PONZIANI (SACRISTY). Vault: Eternal and Evangelists (p., r.).

S. MARIA IN ARACOELI, CAPPELLA BUFALINI (FIRST R.). Frescoes: vault—Evangelists; Altar wall—S. Bernardino flanked by SS. Louis of Toulouse and Anthony of Padua and blessed by Redeemer in Glory; right wall—right of window, S. Francis receiving Stigmata; left of window, S. Bernardino taking the Franciscan habit; below window, five figures round monk telling story of S. Bernardino; lunette above window, Eternal blessing; left wall—lunette, S. Bernardino in penitence at Porta Tufi near Siena; below, Funeral of Bernardino (in background, the Saint raises to life the youth of Prato killed by a Bull and liberates Genuzia from the Devil); in dado, two Putti with monogram of S. Bernardino. E. [*Plate* 301.] *Plate* 1125.

S. MARIA DEL POPOLO, FIRST CHAPEL R. Frescoes: in five lunettes, Scenes from life of S. Jerome (p.); on altar wall, Nativity.

— THIRD CHAPEL R. Frescoes: in five lunettes, Scenes from Life of Virgin (st.).

— CHOIR. Frescoes in vault: Coronation of Virgin, Evangelists, Church-Fathers, four reclining Sibyls. 1508–9.

San Gimignano. 33. Madonna in Glory with SS. Gregory and Bernard. 1512.

San Marino (Cal.). HUNTINGTON GALLERY. Madonna and Child in landscape. L.

San Severino Marche. DUOMO, SACRISTY. Madonna and Child blessing kneeling donor with two Angels; in lunette, blessing Eternal and six Cherubim. ca 1488–90.

Siena. 387. Madonna and Child with Infant S. John (p.).

422. Tondo from Monastery of Campansi: Holy Family with Infant S. John. L.

PALAZZO PETRUCCI ('Palazzo del Magnifico'), CEILING. Fragments of ornamental frescoes (companions to New York; frescoes detached from wall, see London and Paris; for other frescoes of same series see Genga, Siena and Signorelli, London; maiolica floor tiles on P.'s design in Berlin, Schlossmuseum and Paris, Louvre). ca 1509.

S. MARIA ASSUNTA (DUOMO), CAPPELLA DI S. GIOVANNI BATTISTA. Frescoes: Birth of Baptist (r.); Alberto Aringhieri kneeling against view of Rhodes; kneeling knight; Baptist in Wilderness; Baptist preaching (execution of last two scenes possibly by Peruzzi). 1504–6.

— — FLOOR. Marble intarsia on his design: Allegory of Fortune. 1505.

— LIBRERIA PICCOLOMINI, OVER ENTRANCE. Fresco: Coronation of Pius III. 1504.

— — CEILING. Frescoes of allegories, mythologies, decorative motives (execution by Balducci and other assistants). *Plate* 1146.

Siena, s. maria assunta (duomo), libreria piccolomini (contd.). walls. Frescoes: Ten scenes from life of Pius II. [Enea Silvio Piccolomini on his way to Basle with Cardinal Capranica; acting as Ambassador before King James of Scotland; crowned Poet Laureate by Emperor Frederic III; submitting to Pope Eugenius IV; Eleonora d'Aragona and Frederick III meet outside Porta Camollia; Enea Silvio created Cardinal by Callistus III; visiting S. John Lateran after being elected Pope Pius II in 1458; calling for Crusade at Mantua; canonizing S. Catherine of Siena; arriving at Ancona just before his death.] 1503–08. [*Plate* 302.] *Plates* 1141, 1142.

Spello. s. andrea, r. transept. Madonna and Child enthroned with Infant S. John and SS. Andrew, Louis of Toulouse, Francis, Lawrence, two Angels and four Cherubs (execution largely by Eusebio da S. Giorgio). 1507–08.

> oratorio di s. bernardino. Fresco: Madonna and Child between SS. Jerome and Bernardino (st.). 1503.

> collegiata di s. maria, cappella baglioni. Frescoes: in quarts of vault, four Sibyls; on walls, Annunciation with self-portrait; Adoration of Shepherds; Christ among Doctors, with Troilo Baglioni as donor. Sd and d. 1501. *Plates* 1134–1140.

> — cappella del sacramento. Fresco: Angel.

> — sacrestia vecchia. Fresco: Madonna and Child blessing.

Spoleto. duomo, cappella eroli (first r.). Ruined frescoes: Madonna and Child enthroned between SS. John Baptist and Lawrence; above, the Eternal blessing with two Angels and Cherubs; below, Dead Christ. d. 1497.

Valencia. 11. Madonna and Child with kneeling Cardinal Giovanni Borgia (st.).

Vienna. akademie. 1095. Miniature: 'Porta S. Angeli Auguste Perusie': Madonna and Child in Glory between SS. Michael and Herculanus with worshippers below (companion to London and Perugia). 1485. *Plate* 1123.

Warsaw. muzeum narodowe. Inv. 5. Madonna and Child with Infant S. John.

Washington (D.C.). 405 (kress collection. k 514). Bust of young man. [*Plate* 303.]

PISANELLO

Antonio Pisano, called Pisanello, born probably in Pisa before November 22, 1395, died 1455. Assistant to Gentile da Fabriano 1415/20 in lost frescoes of Sala del Gran Consiglio, Venice. Finished 1431/2 lost frescoes begun by Gentile in S. Giovanni Laterano, Rome. Other lost frescoes documented in castles of Pavia (1424) and Mantua (ca 1425). Influenced by his elder Franco-Flemish contemporaries. Famous as medallist.

Bergamo. 519. Profile of Lionello d'Este. After 1440.

London. 776. Madonna and Child appearing to SS. George and Anthony Abbot. Sd. [*Plate* 324.]

> 1436. Vision of S. Eustace. Sd. [*Plate* 325.]

Paris. 1422a. Profile of ? Ginevra d'Este. Before 1438. *Plate 545.*

Verona. 90. Madonna della Quaglia. (?)

   S. ANASTASIA, R. TRANSEPT, CAPPELLA PELLEGRINI. Fresco: S. George and the Princess.
      Sd. 1433–38. [*Plate 323*].

   S. FERMO MAGGIORE, L. OF ENTRANCE. Fresco around tomb of Niccolò Brenzoni:
      Annunciation, S. George and S. Michael (r.). Sd. 1426. *Plate 544.*

Washington (D.C.). 23 (MELLON COLLECTION). Profile of Lady.

Homeless. Madonna and Child with two small Saints in a pergola. Sd. *Plate 543.*

SIGNED MEDALS IN CHRONOLOGICAL ORDER

*Specimens exist in Brescia (Museo), Florence (Bargello), Milan (Medagliere Municipale),
Washington (National Gallery of Art).*

   Gianfrancesco Gonzaga, Marquess of Mantua.
   John VIII Paleologus. 1438.
   Filippo Maria Visconti Duke of Milan. ca 1441.
   Niccolò Piccinino. 1441.
   Medal for the marriage of Lionello d'Este and Maria d'Aragona. 1444. *Plate 546.*
   Sigismondo Pandolfo Malatesta. 1445.
   Novello Malatesta. ca 1445.
   Vittorino da Feltre. ca 1445/6.
   Ludovico Gonzaga. 1447/8.
   Cecilia Gonzaga. 1447.
   Decembrino Umanista. 1447/8.
   Don Inigo Davalos. 1448/9.

PREDIS see DE PREDIS

PUCCINELLI, Angelo

*Lucchese follower of Andrea Vanni, recorded in Siena 1379 and in Lucca from 1382 to 1407.
First documented work 135(?0).*

Altenburg. 49. Madonna and Child enthroned with six Angels, eight Saints and
     Eve reclining in foreground; in pinnacle, Christ on Cross with mourning
     Mary and John.

Antràccoli (Lucca). PARISH CHURCH. Madonna and Child with two Angels.

Bonn. 121. Madonna and Child enthroned with SS. Peter, Paul, John Baptist,
     Anthony Abbot, two female Martyrs and two Angels.

Greenwich (Conn.). T. S. HYLAND COLLECTION (EX). Left panel of polyptych: S.
     Catherine and S. Moses.*

Lucca. MUSEO DI VILLA GUINIGI. Triptych: Marriage of S. Catherine; SS. Peter and John Baptist; SS. Gervasius and Protasius. Sd and d. 135(0?). *Plate 375.*

    S. FREDIANO, SAGRESTIA. S. Caterina. (?)

    S. MARIA FUORISPORTAM, L. TRANSEPT. Centre panel of triptych from the Monastery del Salvatore: Death and Assumption of the Virgin. Sd and d. 1386.

    SS. PAOLINO E DONATO, CHAPEL R. OF CHOIR. Burial of SS. Paolino, Severus and Theobald. (?)

Siena. 67. Triptych from S. Pellegrino alla Sapienza: S. Michael enthroned; S. Anthony Abbot; S. John Baptist; in pinnacles, blessing Redeemer, Angel and Virgin of Annunciation. (1379?). *Plate 374.*

Tulsa (Oklahoma). PHILBROOK ART CENTER, 3347 (KRESS COLLECTION. K 153). Predella panel: Tobit blesses his son. (?)

Varano (Lunigiana). PARISH CHURCH. Polyptych: Madonna and Child; SS. Lucy and Nicholas; SS. Michael and Augustine. Sd and d. 1394. *Plates 376–377.*

RANUCCIO D'ARVARO or ARVARI

Veronese painter active late fourteenth to early fifteenth century.

Legnano. CHIESA DELLA DISCIPLINA. Madonna suckling the Child, with kneeling Dominican, and two Prophets above. Sd. *Plate 522.*

    Madonna of Humility with many Angels and Eternal above. (?)

RAPHAEL (RAFFAELLO SANZIO)

Urbino. 1483–1520. Pupil possibly of Timoteo Viti of Urbino; formed by Perugino; influenced by Leonardo, Fra Bartolommeo, and Michelangelo.

Avignon. 444. Madonna and Angels (c.)

Baltimore (Md.). MUSEUM OF ART, J. EPSTEIN COLLECTION. 51.114. Portrait of Emilia Pia of Montefeltro. E.

    WALTERS ART GALLERY. 484. Tondo: 'Madonna dei Candelabri' (p.).

Bergamo. 314. Bust of S. Sebastian. E.

Berlin. 141. 'Solly' Madonna and Child. E.

    145. Madonna and Child with SS. Jerome and Francis. E.

    147. 'Diotallevi' Madonna and Child with Infant S. John. E.

    247A. Tondo: 'Terranuova' Madonna and Child with Infant S. John. E.

    248. 'Colonna' Madonna and Child. E.

Bignor Park. VISCOUNTESS MERSEY. Predella panel to London 1171: S. John Baptist preaching (p.). 1506.

Bologna. 152. S. Cecilia with SS. Paul, John Evangelist, Augustine and Mary Magdalen.

Boston (Mass.). GARDNER MUSEUM. Portrait of Tommaso (or 'Fedra') Inghirami (died
    1516).
    Predella panel to Colonna altarpiece: Mourning over Dead Christ (companion to
    Dulwich, London 2919 and New York 16.30). 1505.

Brescia. 149. Bust of an Angel (fr. of the S. Nicola da Tolentino altarpiece). 1501.
    150. The Redeemer blessing. E.

Budapest. 71 (53). 'Esterhazy' Madonna and Child with Infant S. John (u.). E.
    72 (86). Portrait of young man (g.p.).

Chantilly. 38. The three Hesperides (companion to London 213?). E.
    39. 'Vierge de la Maison d'Orléans.' E. *Plate* 1180.
    40. Madonna of Loreto (c.).

Città di Castello. 79, 80. Standard: Trinity with SS. Sebastian and Roch; Creation
    of Eve (r.). E.

Cracow. NATIONAL MUSEUM, CZARTORYSKI GALLERY (EX). Portrait of (?) Federigo
    Gonzaga. 1513. Lost in Second World War.

Dresden. 93. The 'Sistine' Madonna.

Dulwich (London). 241, 243. Predella panels to Colonna altarpiece: Full-length S.
    Francis and S. Anthony of Padua (p.; companions to Boston, London 2919 and
    New York). 1505.

Edinburgh. DUKE OF SUTHERLAND LOAN. 35. Tondo: Holy Family under palm tree. E.
    37. 'Madonna del Passeggio.'
    38. 'Bridgewater' Madonna and Child. *Plate* 1182.

Florence. PITTI. 40 (exh. in Uffizi). Leo X with Cardinals Giulio de' Medici and
    Luigi de' Rossi. 1518.
    59. Portrait of Maddalena Doni. E.
    61. Portrait of Angelo Doni. E.
    94. 'Madonna dell' Impannata' (st.).
    151. 'Madonna della Seggiola.'
    158. Bust of Cardinal Bibbiena (c.).
    165. 'Madonna del Baldacchino' (p.). E.
    171. Portrait of Tommaso (or 'Fedra') Inghirami (c. after the Boston picture).
    174. Vision of Ezechiel (execution perhaps by Giulio Romano).
    178. 'Madonna del Granduca.' E. [*Plate* 316.]
    229. 'La Donna Gravida.' E.
    245. 'La Donna Velata.'
    1127. S. John Baptist (st.).
   UFFIZI. 1441. Portrait of Elisabetta Gonzaga, Duchess of Urbino. E.
    1447. 'Madonna del Cardellino.' E.
    1450. Portrait of Julius II (other replicas known; original in S. Maria del Popolo
    at Rome, lost). Not later than 1513.
    1706. Self-Portrait. E.
    8538. Bust of young man holding an apple. E.
    8760. Portrait of Guidobaldo da Montefeltro, Duke of Urbino. E.

Florence (contd.). CONTINI BONACOSSI COLLECTION (EX). Full-length S. Mary
 Magdalen; Full-length S. Catherine.
Leningrad. 1667. Tondo: The 'Conestabile' Madonna and Child. E.
Lisbon. Inv. 568. Predella panel to London 3943: S. Cyril, assisted by S. Jerome,
 raises three youths from the Dead (companion to Raleigh) (g.p.). 1503.
London. 168. Knee-length S. Catherine. E.
 213. Dream of young warrior (companion to Chantilly?). E. *Plate* 1178.
 744. 'Aldobrandini' or 'Garvagh' Madonna and Child with Infant S. John.
 1171. The 'Ansidei' Madonna and Child enthroned with SS. John Baptist and
  Nicholas (predella panel at Bignor Park). d. 1506.
 2069. 'Madonna della Torre.'
 2919. Predella panel to the Colonna altarpiece: Christ carrying the Cross (g.p.;
  companion to Boston, Dulwich and New York). 1505.
 3943. 'Mond' Christ on Cross with the Virgin, SS. Jerome, Mary Magdalen
  and John Evangelist (from S. Domenico at Città di Castello) (predella panels
  at Lisbon and Raleigh). Sd. 1503.
 VICTORIA AND ALBERT MUSEUM. Cartoons for Tapestries: The miraculous Draught
  of Fishes; Christ giving the Keys to S. Peter; The healing of the Lame; Elymas
  struck with Blindness; Death of Ananias; The Sacrifice at Lystra; S. Paul
  preaching; Stoning of S. Stephen; The Fall of S. Paul (p.). L. (On permanent
  loan from the Royal Collection.) *Plates* 1189–1190.
 Cartoon for the Massacre of Innocents (p.fr.). L. (On loan from the Spedale
  degli Innocenti.)
Madrid. 296. Holy Family of the Lamb. Sd and d. 1506.
 297. 'Madonna del Pesce' (g.p.). Before 1517.
 298. Way to Calvary (from S. Maria dello Spasimo in Palermo) (execution
  chiefly by Giulio Romano). Sd. 1517.
 299. Portrait of a young Cardinal. [*Plate* 310.]
 300. Visitation (execution probably by Pierin del Vaga). Sd.
 301. 'La Perla' (execution by Giulio Romano).
 302. 'Madonna della Rosa' (st.).
 303. Holy Family with Infant S. John under oak-tree (execution chiefly by
  Giulio Romano). Sd.
 315. Transfiguration (c.).
Milan. BRERA. 472. Marriage of the Virgin (from Città di Castello). Sd and d. 1504.
 [*Plate* 317.]
 AMBROSIANA, Cartoon for the School of Athens in the Vatican.
Munich. 476. 'Canigiani' Holy Family. Sd. E.
 H.G. 796. 'Tempi' Madonna and Child. E. *Plate* 1181.
 H.G. 797. 'Madonna della Tenda.'
Naples. 50. The Eternal with the Virgin and four Cherubim (fr. from S. Nicola da
 Tolentino altarpiece). 1501.
 145. Portrait of Cardinal Farnese, later Paul III (g.p., r.).

146. 'Madonna del Divino Amore' (p.).

New York. 16.30. 'Colonna' altarpiece from S. Antonio, Perugia: Madonna and Child enthroned with Infant S. John; SS. Peter, Catherine, Cecilia and Paul; in lunette above, the Eternal blessing and two Angels (predella panel at Boston, Dulwich, London 2919 and below) (g.p.). 1505.

31.130.1. Predella panel to above: Agony in Garden. 1505.

49.7.12. Portrait of Giuliano de' Medici (c.). Not later than 1516.

Paris. 1496. 'La Belle Jardinière.' Sd and d. 1507. [*Plate* 318.]

1497. 'La Vierge au Diadème' (execution largely by Giulio Romano).

1498. 'Sainte Famille de François' Ier (execution by Giulio Romano). Sd and d. 1518.

1500. S. John Baptist in the Wilderness.

1501. S. Margaret (st.).

1502. S. Michael. E. *Plate* 1753.

1503. S. George and the Dragon. E.

1504. S. Michael crushing Satan (execution by Giulio Romano). Sd and d. 1518.

1505. Portrait of Baldassarre Castiglione. 1515.

1506. Portrait of young man (?)

1507. Portrait of Giovanna d'Aragona (execution chiefly by Giulio Romano). 1518.

1508. Portraits of Raphael and another man (execution probably by Giulio Romano).

1511. Full-length S. Catherine (st.).

Perugia. 284. Madonna and Child reading (g.p.). E.

288. The Eternal blessing and Cherubs (p.?, top to Deposition in Galleria Borghese, Rome). 1507.

S. SEVERO, CLOISTER. Fresco: Trinity with SS. Maurus, Placidus, Benedict, Romualdus, Benedict Martyr, John (r.; left unfinished; lower half painted by Perugino in 1521). Sd and d. 1505.

Princeton (N.J.). 783. Madonna with right hand lifting veil from sleeping Child and left hand on Infant S. John (c.).

Raleigh (N.C.). MUSEUM OF ART. Predella panel to London 3943: S. Jerome saves Bishop Silvanus from being beheaded and inflicts that death on Sabinianus (companion to Lisbon). 1503. *Plate* 1175.

Rome. ACCADEMIA DI S. LUCA. Fresco detached from mantelpiece in Vatican: Putto with garland (fr.).

FARNESINA, LOGGIA DI PSICHE. Frescoed vault: in centre, Council of the Gods and Marriage of Cupid and Psyche; in pendentifs, Episodes from Myth of Cupid and Psyche; in triangular sections over lunettes, Genietti with attributes of various Gods (p.; figures chiefly by Giulio Romano). 1515–17.

— SALA DI GALATEA. Fresco: Triumph of Galatea (see also Peruzzi and Sebastiano del Piombo). Well before 1514. [*Plate* 319.] *Plate* 1184.

Rome (contd.). GALLERIA NAZIONALE (PALAZZO BARBERINI). 'La Fornarina' (g.p.). Sd.

GALLERIA BORGHESE. 369. Deposition (upper part at Perugia 288, predella in Vatican Pinacoteca 330–32). Sd and d. 1507.

371. Lady with unicorn (u.).

397. Portrait of man (possibly Perugino). E.

GALLERIA DORIA PAMPHILI. 403. Portrait of Navagero and Beazzano. 1516.

S. AGOSTINO, CENTRAL NAVE, THIRD PILLAR L. Fresco: Isaiah.

S. MARIA DELLA PACE, FIRST CHAPEL R., OVER ARCH. Frescoes: in lunette, Habakkuk, Jonah, David and Daniel with Angels (st., r.); below, four Sibyls and Angels (g.p.; r.). ca 1514. *Plate* 1188.

S. MARIA DEL POPOLO, CAPPELLA CHIGI (SECOND LEFT), CEILING. Mosaic on design of the artist: The Eternal and the Planets guided by Angels. Finished 1516. *Plate* 1187.

VATICAN, PINACOTECA. 329. 'Madonna di Foligno' with SS. John Baptist, Francis and Jerome recommending Sigismondo de' Conti. 1511–12. *Plate* 1186.

330–32. Three monochrome panels: Faith, Hope, Charity (from predella to Borghese Deposition). 1507. *Plate* 1179.

333. Transfiguration (execution of lower part by Giulio Romano). 1519/20.

334. Coronation of Virgin (from S. Francesco at Perugia). 1503. *Plate* 1176.

335. Predella to 334: Annunciation, Adoration of Magi, Circumcision. 1503.

356. Full-length S. Peter (begun by Fra Bartolomeo). 1514.

— STANZA DELLA SEGNATURA. Frescoes: Vault—four roundels (Theology, Philosophy, Justice, Poetry) and four rectangles (Fall of Man, Judgement of Solomon, Apollo and Marsyas, Astronomy); Walls—Dispute over the Holy Sacrament; School of Athens; Parnassus (d. 1511); Cardinal and Theological Virtues in lunette and below Justinian publishing the Pandects, Gregory IX approving the Decretals. 1509–11. [*Plates* 311–314.] *Plate* 1185.

— STANZA D'ELIODORO. Frescoes: Vault—Four stories on R.'s design: The burning Bush, Jacob's ladder, Sacrifice of Isaac, God speaks to Noah; Walls—Heliodorus driven out of the Temple (Pope Julius and his bearers by Raphael himself, the rest largely by assistants); Miracle of Bolsena; Attila turned away from Rome (the heads of Leo X and his Cardinals in part by Raphael's own hand, the rest by pupils); S. Peter delivered from prison (execution largely by pupils). 1511–14.

— STANZA DELL'INCENDIO DI BORGO. Frescoes: Vault—(1507–08, see Perugino); Walls—Fire in the Environs of S. Peter's (execution largely by Giulio Romano); Coronation of Charlemagne (st.), Self-defence of Leo III (st.); Battle of Ostia (execution chiefly by Giulio Romano). 1514–17.

— LOGGIE. Fresco and Stucco Decoration: Twelve vaults, each with four scenes from the Old Testament, and one vault with four scenes from the New Testament; pilasters with Grotteschi. (Their present condition is such that little can be said of the execution, save that it could not have been Raphael's. Some of the best seem to have been painted by Perino del Vaga. After 1519.)

Urbino. CASA DI RAFFAELLO. See Giovanni Santi.

Vaduz. LIECHTENSTEINSCHE SAMMLUNGEN. G 36. Bust of man against landscape. E.

Vienna. 29. 'Madonna im Gruenen' or 'Madonna del Prato'. d. 1505. *Plate* 1177.

Washington (D.C.). 24 (MELLON COLLECTION). Tondo: 'Alba' Madonna and Child
with Infant S. John.

    25 (MELLON COLLECTION). 'Niccolini Cowper' Madonna and Child. d. 1508.
Plate 1183.

    26 (MELLON COLLECTION). S. George and the Dragon. E. [*Plate* 320.]

    534 (KRESS COLLECTION. K 1239). Bust of Bindo Altoviti. [*Plate* 315.]

    653 (WIDENER COLLECTION). Small 'Cowper' Madonna and Child. E.

Worcester (Mass.). 1946.39. 'Northbrook' Madonna and Child.

Homeless. Madonna and Child. E. *Plate* 1174.

RIMINESE TRECENTO

[*See Introduction*, p. x.]

Ajaccio. 67. Last Judgement.

    176. Dossal: Adoration of Magi, Crucifixion, Vision of Blessed Chiara of
Rimini.

Albury (Herts.). MRS CRITCHLEY. Panel of dossal from S. Francesco, Rimini: 'Ashburnham' Vision of Blessed Chiara of Rimini (companion to Miami).

Allentown (Pa.). MUSEUM OF ART. 60.02.KBS (KRESS COLLECTION. K 29.). Crucifixion.

Bagnacavallo (Ravenna). S. FRANCESCO. Painted Crucifix.

    S. PIETRO IN SILVIS, CHOIR. Frescoes: Christ in Glory and the Evangelists; below, the
twelve Apostles and Crucifixion; in soffit of arch, busts of Angels and Saints;
Madonna and Child crowned by Angels (fr.); S. John Evangelist (fr.) (r.).
Plate 175.

Baltimore (Md.). WALTERS ART GALLERY. 634. Finials of painted Crucifix: Busts of
Redeemer, Virgin and S. John Evangelist.

Barcelona. MUSEO DE ARTE, CAMBÒ BEQUEST. Three side-panels to Venice, Cini,
Madonna: Annunciation, Circumcision, Dormition (companions to Lausanne)
Plate 197.

Bath. STREET COLLECTION. Annunciation to Zacharias; Baptist visited in prison.
(Master of Life of Baptist; see Washington 1147.)

Berlin. 1110. Panels of dossal: Christ before Pilate, Resurrection, Descent into
Limbo, Ascension, Descent of the Holy Ghost. (Master of the Life of Christ,
see Venice 26.)

    1116. Panels of dossal: Circumcision; Mourning over dead Christ (companions
to Rome, Vatican 167 and to Wiesbaden).

Birmingham. BARBER INSTITUTE. Left leaf of diptych: Angel of Annunciation,
Nativity, Adoration of Magi (companion to Urbino) (r.).

Bologna. 231. Crucifixion flanked by SS. Francis, John Evangelist, Catherine and Clare; below, Mourning over dead Christ and Descent into Limbo.

Boston (Mass.). 28.887. Bust of dead Christ.

40.91. Detached fresco from S. Lucia at Fabriano: Crucifixion (companion to Rochester and Rome, Palazzo Barberini). (Master of Urbino Coronation.)

Budapest. 26 (19). Painted Crucifix, with Bishop Saint above and S. Francis below.

Cambridge. FITZWILLIAM MUSEUM. PD.8–1955. Crucifixion with S. Francis at foot of Cross (Master of Verucchio Crucifix).

Castagneto Carducci (Grosseto). GHERARDESCA COLLECTION (EX). Crucifix (rustic follower of Giuliano da Rimini).

Cleveland (Ohio). 43.280. 'Loeser' Painted Crucifix, with Angel above and S. Francis below.

Collalto (Treviso). CAPPELLA DI S. SALVATORE. Frescoes in vault and entrance wall: Christ and Fathers of the Church; Presentation, Jesus disputing in Temple, Baptism of Christ, Marriage at Cana, Maries at the Tomb, Resurrection of Christ, Dormition; Madonna suckling the Child with SS. Nicholas and Prosdocimus; scenes from Life of S. Prosdocimus; S. George killing the dragon; Triumph of S. Ursula. d. 1530. Mostly destroyed 1915–18.

Coral Gables (Fla.). UNIVERSITY, LOWE ART GALLERY. 61.10 (KRESS COLLECTION. K 201). Right leaf of diptych: Crucifixion.

— K 1084. Panel of dossal from S. Francesco, Rimini: Adoration of Magi (companion to Albury).

Denver (Col.). ART MUSEUM. Fragment of dossal: Christ receiving a procession of Virgin Martyrs led by His Mother; below, S. George and the princess, S. Peter enthroned as pope, S. Augustine (?), S. Dominic and Evangelist.

Dublin. 1022. Right leaf of diptych: Crucifixion, 'Noli me tangere' below. (Master of Verucchio Crucifix; companion to Florence, Stibbert). *Plate* 200.

Fabriano. PINACOTECA. Detached fresco from S. Emiliano: Madonna and Child enthroned with two Angels, two female Saints and Bishop Saint. (Master of Urbino Coronation.)

S. AGOSTINO. Frescoes: Life of S. Augustine. (Master of Urbino Coronation?)

Fano. S. DOMENICO. Fresco above sepulchre of Pietro e Ugolino de' Pili: Madonna and Child with SS. Dominic, James, Peter Martyr and Leonard and female donor. (Master of Urbino Coronation.) *Plate* 202.

Ferrara. PINACOTECA. Detached fresco from refectory of S. Francesco: Descent of the Holy Ghost and other scenes (fr.).

Florence. MUSEO STIBBERT. Left leaf of diptych: Above, Standing Madonna and Child with two Virgin Martyrs; below, SS. Catherine, Francis and Clare. (Master of Verucchio Crucifix; companion to Dublin.)

CHARLES LOESER (EX). Devils watching the Baptist preaching (fr., companion to Seattle (?)). (Master of Life of Baptist, see Washington.)

R. LONGHI. Left leaf of diptych: Madonna suckling the Child with four Angels, SS. John Baptist, Peter as Pope, Agnes, Catherine and two Virgin Martyrs. (Master of S. Maria in Porto Fuori.)

Forlì. MUSEO CIVICO. Detached fresco from S. Pellegrino: Crucifixion (r.).

Griessmannsdorf (Friedenthal). GRAF INGENHEIM. Centre panel of dossal (from destroyed S. Colomba Cathedral at Rimini): Crucifixion (companion to Paris, André; Turin and Homeless).

Hamburg. 756, 757. Diptych: Dormition; Crucifixion.

Indianapolis (Ind.). CLOWES FUND (formerly Minneapolis Institute of Arts). Panel from dossal: St. Francis receiving Stigmata. (Master of S. Maria in Porto Fuori?)

Jesi. S. MARCO, APSE. Fresco: Crucifixion.

— R. NAVE. Frescoes: Annunciation, Dormition, Madonna di Loreto. (Master of Urbino Coronation?)

Kiev. 5. Triptych: Coronation of Virgin and scenes from her life.

Lausanne. MUSÉE, CAMBÒ BEQUEST. Side-panel to Venice, Cini, Madonna: Birth of the Virgin (companion to Barcelona). *Plate* 197.

London. COURTAULD INSTITUTE GALLERIES, GAMBIER PARRY COLLECTION. Nativity and Adoration of Magi. (Master of the Life of Christ, see Venice 26.)

Lyons. AYNARD COLLECTION (EX). Leaf of diptych: above, Madonna and Child enthroned with Saint and donor; below, S. Louis of Toulouse, S. Marino holding castle, with bear killing donkey at his feet, and S. Clare. *Plate* 201.

Milan. BRERA (formerly Sessa Collection). Three side-panels to dossal from destroyed Rimini Cathedral: S. Colomba, daughter of the Spanish King, is arrested and brought before Emperor Aurelian; S. Colomba in prison resists the advances of Baruga and stops the bear come to her rescue from killing him; Beheading of S. Colomba (central panel with figure of S. Colomba and other scenes from her life, lost).

Montpellier. 744. Panel of dossal: Dormition (r.).

Moulins. 78. See Paris, Musées Nationaux.

Munich. WAF 837, 838. Diptych: Left leaf—top, Madonna and Child enthroned with two female Saints; bottom, Washing of Feet; bottom, Last Judgement; Right leaf—top, Crucifixion; middle, Flagellation and Way to Calvary; bottom, S. Francis receiving Stigmata and four other Saints. (Master of Verucchio Crucifix.)

New York. 09.103. Dossal: Coronation of Virgin; Four Saints; Deposition; Mourning over Dead Christ; Descent into Limbo; Ascension; Descent of the Holy Ghost; Last Judgement.

39.42. Painted Crucifix (fr.).

EMMET JOHN HUGHES. S. Catherine (fr.).

ROBERT LEHMAN. Small Crucifixion.

Panel of dossal: Herod's Feast (Master of Life of Baptist, see Washington). *Plate* 205.

Paris. 2287. Deposition (formerly Viterbo, Gentili). *Plate* 186.

Paris (contd.). MUSÉE JACQUEMART-ANDRÉ. 757. Panel of dossal (from destroyed
Cathedral of S. Colomba, Rimini): Angels at Christ's Tomb (fr., companion
to Griessmannsdorf, Turin and Homeless).

MUSÉES NATIONAUX, CAMPANA COLLECTION 70 (DEP. MOULINS). Dead Christ in
sepulchre, and two Bishop Saints in spandrels.

Perugia. 68. Left leaf of Mezzaratta diptych from Convento dell'Osservanza at
Bologna: Ascension of Mary of Egypt, surrounded by SS. James, John Bap-
tist, Elizabeth, Francis, Dominic, Herculanus and Christopher (companion to
Zurich).

Pomposa (Codigoro). S. MARIA, L. WALL. Fresco: Madonna and Child enthroned
with four Saints and kneeling donor (r.).

— REFETTORIO, END WALL. Frescoes: Last Supper; Redeemer with Virgin, S. John
Baptist, S. Benedict and S. Guido degli Strambiati; S. Guido pours out water
to himself and transforms water into wine for his guest Gebeardo, archbishop
of Ravenna. 1316–20. *Plate* 174.

— — SIDE WALLS. Frescoes: Agony in the Garden (fr.); Monks at their desks. (d.
1317?).

— AULA CAPITOLARE. Frescoes: Crucifixion; S. Benedict standing in niche; The
Abbot S. Guido standing in niche; SS. Peter and Paul, ten Prophets, two by
two, in painted windows.

Ravenna. DUOMO. 'Madonna del Sudore.'

S. CHIARA, VAULT. Frescoes: One Evangelist and one Father of the Church in each
quarter of vault (detached and transferred to Museo Nazionale di S. Vitale).

— EAST WALL. Frescoes: in lunette, Annunciation; below, SS. Francis and Clare,
SS. Anthony of Padua and Louis of Toulouse. *Plates* 181–182.

— SOUTH WALL. Frescoes: in lunette, Nativity (fr.); below, Adoration of Magi
(fr.). *Plate* 184.

— NORTH WALL. Frescoes: in lunette, Crucifixion; below, Baptism of Christ,
Agony in the Garden.

— TRIUMPHAL ARCH, SOFFIT. Frescoes: Twelve busts of Saints, Virgin and Redeemer.

— ON PILLARS. Frescoes: S. James, a Saint.

— FORMER CONVENT. Detached frescoes: S. Sigismund; Stoning of S. Stephen (fr.).

S. FRANCESCO, CAPPELLA POLENTANI. Ruined frescoes: in lunette, Abraham and the
Angels; below, Crucifixion; Swooning Virgin from another Crucifixion; Dead
Christ in Tomb; Seated man in meditation (so-called Dante); Female Saint;
Bishop Saint (fragments saved after 1944 bombardment, now shown in left
Nave). *Plate* 183.

— FIRST CHAPEL R. Fresco: S. Mary Magdalen (fr., r.).

S. MARIA IN PORTO FUORI, CHOIR, TRIUMPHAL ARCH. Fresco: Christ as Judge in
mandorla; on His right, two Saints beheaded by Antichrist, and the Elect;
on His left, S. Michael beheads the Antichrist, and the Damned. *Plate* 179.

— — SOFFIT. Fresco: Busts of Saints.

— APSE, VAULT; Frescoes: One Evangelist and one Father of the Church in each quarter of vault. *Plate* 178.

—— SOFFIT OF INNER ARCH. Fresco: Busts of Saints.

—— WALLS. Frescoes: Annunciation (fr.); The Maries at the Tomb (fr.); S. Paul; Doubting Thomas. Left—Expulsion of Joachim, Birth of Virgin, Presentation of Virgin. Right—Dormitio and Coronation of Virgin, Massacre of Innocents watched by so-called Francesca and Suor Chiara da Polenta, Christ giving Communion to Apostles. *Plate* 180.

— L. CHAPEL. Frescoes: in lunette, Martyrdom of Saint,; below, Pope John I in prison.

— R. CHAPEL. Frescoes: Vault—Four Angels. Walls—Piero degli Onesti healing the sick and maimed, S. John Evangelist preaching, S. John Evangelist baptizing a King, Ascension of S. John Evangelist, Calling of S. Matthew (only few fragments of all these frescoes survived the 1944 bombardment and are shown in the rebuilt church).

Rimini. PALAZZO DELL'ARENGO, SALONE, R. WALL. Detached triangular fresco from S. Agostino: Last Judgement. *Plates* 170–171.

PINACOTECA. 83. Dossal: Crucifixion, SS. Cosmos, Catherine, Barbara, Damian; in spandrels, Symbols of the Evangelists, busts of SS. Sigismund (?) and Augustine (rustic follower of Giuliano da Rimini).

SPINA COLLECTION. Painted Crucifix (rustic follower of Giuliano da Rimini).

S. AGOSTINO, APSE, CENTRAL WALL. Frescoes: in lunette, Redeemer enthroned with SS. John Evangelist and John Baptist; middle register, full-length Saint, Madonna and Child enthroned with Angels, full-length Saint; lower register, full-length Saint, Noli me tangere, full-length Saint.

—— L. WALL. Frescoes: S. John Evangelist stops the earthquake at Ephesus and is put in the cauldron of boiling oil; below, S. John Evangelist disputing with Aristodemus. *Plate* 172.

—— R. WALL. S. John the Evangelist raises Drusiana, the Saint in a boat between Ephesus and Patmos, the Saint writing the Apocalypse at Patmos; below, S. John the Evangelist takes leave of his faithful, dies, and ascends to heaven.

— ABSIDIOLA A CORNU EPISTOLAE, CENTRAL WALL. Frescoes: Marriage of Virgin and Circumcision (fr.); below, left of window, S. Ambrose, Hermit Saint, kneeling woman; below, right of Window, S. Augustine giving his rule to monks, S. Monica and donor.

—— L. WALL. Frescoes: in lunette, Joachim and the Angel, Joachim and Anne bring offerings at the Temple; below, Nativity and Adoration of Magi.

—— R. WALL. Frescoes: in lunette, Annunciation; below, Presentation of Virgin, Dormition.

— BAPTISTERY. Painted Crucifix (fr.).

Rochester (N.Y.). MEMORIAL ART GALLERY. Detached fresco from S. Lucia at Fabriano: Zacharias and the Angel (companion to Boston and Rome) (Master of Urbino Coronation).

Rome. GALLERIA NAZIONALE, PALAZZO BARBERINI. Detached fresco from S. Lucia at Fabriano: Birth of Baptist (companion to Boston and Rochester) (Master of Urbino Coronation).

'Corvisieri Dossal': Deposition, Mourning over Dead Christ, Resurrection, Descent into Limbo, Ascension, Descent of the Holy Ghost (companion to Valdagno). *Plate 195.*

STERBINI COLLECTION (EX). Panel of dossal: Baptist in Limbo (Master of Life of Baptist; see Washington).

VATICAN, PINACOTECA. Inv. 44. Panel of dossal: SS. Francis, John Baptist, Louis of Toulouse with donor and Saint with flag (fr.).

167. Panel of dossal: Deposition (companion to Berlin 1116 and to Wiesbaden).

172. Crucifixion (r.).

175. Right leaf of diptych: Above, Crucifixion with S. Francis; below, S. Peter as Pope with SS. Paul and Louis of Toulouse.

178. Right leaf of diptych: Christ on Cross with mourning Virgin and S. John Evangelist (r.).

181. Crucifixion with SS. Peter and Paul; below, Noli me tangere and the Maries at the Tomb.

185. Panel of dossal: Infant S. John going into Wilderness (Master of Life of Baptist, see Washington).

San Severino Marche. ROCCA. Painted Crucifix (fr., r.).

Sant'Arcangelo di Romagna. COLLEGIATA. Painted Crucifix.

Sassocorvaro. ROCCA. Painted Crucifix (fr., r.).

Sassoferrato. S. FRANCESCO. Painted Crucifix.

Seattle (Wash.). ART MUSEUM. IT.37/M394.LI.1 (KRESS COLLECTION. K 460). Panel of dossal: S. John Baptist talking to two Pharisees (fr., companion of Florence, Loeser). (Master of Life of Baptist, see Washington.)

Strasbourg. 204. Pinnacle: Crucifixion with S. Francis. (Master of Verucchio Crucifix.) *Plate 199.*

Talamello (Urbino). S. LORENZO. Painted Crucifix, with Redeemer, Virgin and S. John in finials.

Tolentino. BASILICA DI S. NICOLA DA TOLENTINO, CAPPELLONE, VAULT. Frescoes: One Evangelist and one Father of the Church in each quarter. Along vaulting ribs, busts of Saints. At bottom of ribs, Virtues (Hope, Prudence, Faith, Temperance, Charity, Fortitude, Justice and Injustice).

— — WALLS. Frescoes. Life of Virgin and Christ.

Lunettes; Annunciation; Visitation, Nativity, Annunciation to the Shepherds, Arrival of Magi; Circumcision; Dormition.

Middle register: Christ entering Jerusalem, preaching on Gethsemane and Agony in the Garden; Descent into Limbo; the Maries at the Tomb; Descent of the Holy Ghost and Massacre of the Innocents; Christ among Doctors and led home by his parents; Marriage of Cana with donors. *Plates 191–193.*

Lower register: Crucifixion. *Plate 187.*

— — WALLS. Frescoes. Life of S. Nicholas of Tolentino.

Lower register: S. Nicholas of Bari announces to a kneeling couple that they will be blessed with the birth of the future S. Nicholas of Tolentino; the Saint as a boy learns to read and write; listens to an Augustinian Monk preaching, is received in the Augustinian Order; is crowned by an Angel, helps with his prayers the Souls in Purgatory (?; fr.); the Saint laid out on a bier and his Soul received in Heaven by Christ, the Virgin and S. Nicholas of Bari; the Saint returns a young woman to life, heals a blind woman, frees a prisoner, saves a ship at sea, rescues a man from hanging, Miracles performed at the Saint's Tomb. *Plates* 188–190.

Turin. GALLERIA SABAUDA, GUALINO COLLECTION. Panel of dossal from destroyed cathedral of S. Colomba at Rimini: Ascension (companion to Griessmannsdorf; Paris, André; and Homeless).

Urbania. CHIESA DEL CARMINE. Fresco: Maestà (r.).

Urbino. GALLERIA NAZIONALE DELLE MARCHE. Fragmentary polyptych: Coronation of Virgin; SS. Catherine of Alexandria and Agnes; two Heads of Angels in roundels; in pinnacles, SS. Clare and Francis. (Master of Urbino Coronation; see Boston, Fabriano, Fano, Rochester and Rome.) *Plate* 204.

Painted Crucifix from Old Hospital.

Painted Crucifix.

Painted Crucifix with pelican, four Evangelists in roundels and skull below.

Top panel of polyptych: Crucifixion.

Right leaf of diptych: Virgin of Annunciation and Crucifixion below (companion to Birmingham).

Vaduz. LIECHTENSTEINSCHE SAMMLUNG. Crucifixion with Adoration of Magi above and seven Saints below; in tympanum, 'Woman this is thy Son'.

Valdagno. CONTE G. MARZOTTO. Left part of 'Corvisieri' dossal, Rome: Last Supper, Agony in the Garden, Christ before Herod, Crowning with Thorns, Way to Calvary.

Venice. 26. Six panels of dossal: Betrayal of Christ, Pilate washing his hands, Christ ascending Cross, Crucifixion, Deposition and Last Judgement (companions to Berlin 1110 and Homeless).

CONTE VITTORIO CINI. Inv. 6309. Madonna and Child enthroned with five Angels (fr. of Maestà).

Inv. 6436. Central panel of dossal, formerly Galitzine, then Popoff collections: Madonna and Child enthroned with four Angels above and small SS. Francis and Clare below (companion to Barcelona and Lausanne). *Plate* 197.

Inv. 6497. Left leaf of diptych: Angel of Annunciation, Mocking of Christ, Way to Calvary.

Verucchio (Rimini). SS. MARTINO E FRANCESCO. Painted Crucifix. *Plate* 198.

Villa Verucchio. CONVENTO DI S. FRANCESCO, CHIESA DI S. CROCE, L. WALL. Fresco: Crucifixion.

Washington (D.C.). 242 (KRESS COLLECTION. K 264). Panel of dossal: Baptism of Christ (see 1147).

 711 (KRESS COLLECTION. K 1312). Madonna and Child enthroned with six Angels (central panel, companion to Scenes from Life of Baptist?).

 1147 (KRESS COLLECTION. K 1435). Panel of dossal: Birth, Naming and Circumcision of Baptist (companion to Bath; Florence, Loeser; New York, Lehman; Rome, Sterbini and Vatican; Seattle; Washington 242 and ? 711). (Master of the Life of Baptist.)

Wiesbaden. HENCKELL COLLECTION. Panel of Dossal: Birth of Virgin (companion to Berlin 1116 and to Rome, Vatican).

 Panel of dossal: Agony in the Garden.

Winter Park (Fla.). ROLLINS COLLEGE. 38.2.P (KRESS COLLECTION. K 1074). Panels of Polyptych: Four Apostles.

Zurich. KUNSTHAUS. Right leaf of Mezzaratta diptych: Crucifixion (companion to Perugia, 68).

Homeless. Side panel of dossal from destroyed Cathedral of S. Colomba at Rimini: Deposition (companion to Griessmannsdorf, Paris and Turin). (*Paragone*, 1958, 99, fig. 34.)

 Panel of dossal: Entombment (companion to Berlin 1110 and Venice 26). (*Beiträge für G. Swarzenski*, Berlin, 1951, p. 66, fig. 1.)

RIMINI, FRANCESCO DA

Riminese, active second quarter of fourteenth century, died before 1348. Influenced by Giotto's frescoes at Assisi.

Bologna. PINACOTECA. Twelve fragments of frescoes detached from refectory of ex-convent of S. Francesco (signed cycle):

 746. Christ (from Resurrection). *Plate 203.*

 747, 748, 749, 750. Four mourning Angels (from Crucifixion).

 751. Worshipping Franciscan (from Apparition of S. Francis on chariot of fire).

 752. S. Francis, a gentleman and a monk (from Death of Knight of Celano).

 753. Four onlookers (from extreme left of Healing of youth at Lerida).

 754. Three onlookers (from left side of Crucifixion).

 755. Half-length warrior (from lower right corner of Crucifixion).

 756. Two heads of warriors (from lower right corner of Crucifixion).

 757. Onlookers (from Healing of Youth at Lérida).

 S. FRANCESCO, EX-CONVENT, REFECTORY, END-WALL. Fragmentary frescoes: upper tier—S. Francis appears to his Brethren in a chariot of fire, ? Visitation, Pope Honorius confirms the Franciscan rule (?); middle tier—S. Francis receives Stigmata and appears to Pope Honorius in a dream, Crucifixion, Death of the

Knight of Celano; lower tier—S. Francis crosses the fire before the Sultan, Resurrection, S. Francis appears to the youth of Lérida and heals him. Formerly Sd.

RIMINI, GIOVANNI DA

Riminese, documented 1295, 1300, 13(14?).

Alnwick Castle. DUKE OF NORTHUMBERLAND. Leaf of diptych: Presentation; Coronation of the Virgin; Scene from Life of S. Catherine; St. Francis receiving Stigmata and Baptist in the Wilderness (companion to Rome). *Plate* 177.

Faenza. PINACOTECA. Madonna and Child between two Angels; below, SS. Francis, Michael, Augustine, Catherine and Clare (repr. *Critica d'Arte*, 1937, plate 140).

Mercatello sul Metauro. S. FRANCESCO. Painted Crucifix. Signed JOHANNES, Sd. d. 13(09) (14?). *Plate* 176.

Rimini. MUSEO. 'Diotallevi' Crucifix; in finials, Redeemer, Virgin, S. John Evangelist and Mary Magdalen.

Rome. GALLERIA NAZIONALE, PALAZZO BARBERINI. Leaf of diptych: Nativity; Crucifixion; Entombment; Christ in Limbo; Resurrection; Last Judgement (companion to Alnwick Castle).

Utrecht. ARCHIEPISCOPAL MUSEUM. Painted Crucifix (fr.).

RIMINI, GIOVANNI BARONZIO DA

Riminese, active middle of the fourteenth century. (*See Introduction*, p. x.)

Mercatello sul Metauro. S. FRANCESCO. Polyptych: Madonna and Child enthroned with Angels; SS. Catherine, Paul, Louis of Toulouse, Peter, John Evangelist, Francis, Michael, Clare.

New Haven (Conn.). 1959.15.14. 'Hurd' Coronation of Virgin. *Plate* 194.

Urbino. GALLERIA NAZIONALE DELLE MARCHE. Polyptych: Madonna enthroned and Child standing beside her, SS. Francis and Louis of Toulouse and two Angels; Nativity, Circumcision, Last Supper, Betrayal of Christ; in pinnacles, Crucifixion, Angel and Virgin of Annunciation; four busts of Saints. Sd and d. 1345. *Plate* 196.

RIMINI, GIULIANO DA

Riminese, active end of thirteenth and early fourteenth century.

Boston (Mass.). GARDNER MUSEUM. Dossal: Centre. Madonna and Child with Angels and donors; at left, S. Francis receiving stigmata, S. John Baptist, S. Clare, S. Catherine; at right, S. John Evangelist, S. Mary Magdelen visited by the Angel, S. Agnes, S. Lucy. Sd and d. 1307. *Plate 173.*

RIMINI, PIETRO DA

Riminese, active second quarter of the fourteenth century.

Montottone. CONVENTO DI S. FRANCESCO. Fresco detached from column in church of S. Niccolò, Jesi: S. Francis. Formerly Sd and d. 1333. (?)
Padua. MUSEO CIVICO. Eighteen fragments of frescoes from chapel in cloisters of Eremitani: Coronation of Virgin (lunette); Ascension; Descent into Limbo; Resurrection; Nativity; Crucifixion (in seven frs.); decorative motives.
Urbania. CHIESA DEI MORTI. Painted Crucifix. Sd. *Plate 185.*

ROBERTI see ERCOLE DA FERRARA

ROBERTO DI ODERISIO DA NAPOLI

Active in and around Naples, middle decades of fourteenth century. Pupil probably of some follower of Cavallini; formed under the influence of Giotto and Simone Martini.

Aix-en-Provence. MUSÉE GRANET. S. Louis of Toulouse with his brother Robert of Anjou and Queen Sanche (from Chapelle de S. Claire). Before 1343. (?)
Cambridge (Mass.). FOGG ART MUSEUM. 1937.49. Pietà with symbols of the Passion. *Plate 147.*
Eboli (Salerno). S. FRANCESCO, SACRISTY. Crucifixion with Franciscan donor. Sd. *Plate 146.*
Naples. CAPPELLA DELLA DISCIPLINA DELLA CROCE. Painted Crucifix.
    S. DOMENICO MAGGIORE. Lunette: Madonna of Humility and twelve Angels.
    S. LORENZO MAGGIORE, FIFTH CHAPEL IN AMBULATORY OF CHOIR. Frescoes: Left wall —from top, Journey to Bethlehem, Annunciation, Adoration of Magi; right wall—from top, Birth of Virgin, Marriage of Virgin, Nativity. E. (?)
    S. MARIA INCORONATA, R. NAVE, NEAR ENTRANCE. Frescoes: vault—Triumph of religion and seven Sacraments (Baptism, Confirmation, Eucharist, Matrimony, Penance, Ordination, Extreme Unction); walls—Joseph in jail inter-

prets dreams, The infant Moses rescued from the Nile, Moses and the Burning Bush, Samson destroys the Temple, and fragments of other subjects. ca 1360. *Plates* 143, 144, 145.

Venosa (Melfi). ss. TRINITÀ. Fresco: Standing S. Catherine and Pietà below.

ROMANINO

Girolamo di Romano, called Romanino. Brescia 1484/7–1559. Pupil perhaps of Civerchio. Influenced by Giorgione, Titian, Savoldo and Lotto.

Allentown (Pa.). MUSEUM OF ART. 60.23.KB (KRESS COLLECTION. K 524). Half-length portrait of bearded gentleman with large hat.

Arcore (Monza). VITTADINI COLLECTION (EX). Madonna and Child embracing little dog.

Asola (between Mantua and Brescia). DUOMO, ORGAN. Outside shutters: S. Andrew and S. Erasmus; inside shutters: Augustus and the Sibyl, Sacrifice of Isaac; parapet; twenty-one panels with ten Sibyls and eleven Prophets, twelve panels with Saints and one with standing Madonna and Child—altogether thirty-two figures in niches; two half-length portraits at base of organ. *Plate* 1691.

— ORGAN LOFT. Frescoes: on spandrels, SS. Peter and Paul, Moses and Isaiah; on pedestals, monochrome roundels. Organ decorations 1526.

— PULPIT. On parapet, Redeemer, Apostles, S. Marc; on column behind pulpit, Man of Sorrow (fresco). 1536–37.

Atlanta (Ga.). ART ASSOCIATION GALLERIES. 58.45 (KRESS COLLECTION. K 1630). Madonna and Child with SS. Jerome and James. E.

Bergamo. 599. Gentleman with plumed hat (st. variant of Budapest).

ACHILLE LOCATELLI MILESI (EX). Bust of youth with jaunty cap.

S. ALESSANDRO IN COLONNA, L. TRANSEPT. Assumption of Virgin.

Berlin-Ost. 151. Pietà (from SS. Faustino e Giovita, Brescia). 1534. (Destroyed 1945.) 155. Salome. (?)

157. Madonna and Child with SS. Louis of Toulouse, Roch and three Angels. E. (Destroyed 1945.) *Plate* 1686.

KUNSTGEWERBEMUSEUM (EX). Two roundels from frame of altarpiece: Heads (see Padua 165).

Bienno (Val Camonica). S. MARIA ANNUNZIATA, CHOIR. Frescoes: left wall—Presentation of Virgin; right wall—Marriage of Virgin; end wall—figures in courtyard. ca 1540. *Plate* 1697.

Breno (Val Camonica). S. ANTONIO, CHOIR. Frescoes: left wall—Trial and martyrdom of the three youths in the fiery furnace; right wall—Entry into Jerusalem; end wall—above, God the Father and Angels; below, Flagellation and Last Supper. ca 1530–35.

S. VALENTINO. Madonna and Child with Infant S. John and two Saints. E.

Brescia. 32, 33. Fragments of fresco from Loggia of Orsini Palace at Ghedi (companions to Budapest 1234/5/6, listed late Bartolomeo Montagna): busts of Erasmo da Narni called Gattamelata and of Niccolò Orsini da Pitigliano (r.). 1506–09. (?)

78, 92. Two frescoes from refectory of Abbazia di Rodengo (see there): Christ in Emmaus; Christ in the house of Simon. ca 1533.

82. Bust of man in striped jerkin.

83. Roundel from Cancelleria della Chiesa di S. Luca, companion to Ospedale Nuovo: Christ carrying the Cross.

84. Nativity (from S. Giuseppe).

94. Pietà with SS. Paul and Joseph (p.).

96. Coronation of Virgin with SS. Dominic, Faustino, Giovita and six more Saints.

514. 'Avogadro' altarpiece from S. Giuseppe: S. Paul, surrounded by SS. Jerome, John Baptist, Catherine and Mary Magdalen. ca 1548–50.

1214. 'Crespi Morbio' penitent S. Jerome.

BETTONI COLLECTION (EX). Male portrait (identical with Budapest 1254?).

CONGREGAZIONE DI CARITÀ APOSTOLICA. Madonna and Child enthroned with Angels.

OSPEDALE NUOVO. Roundel from Cancelleria della Chiesa di S. Luca, companion to Pinacoteca 83: Madonna adoring the Christ Child.

ROTONDA (DUOMO VECCHIO). Two temperas on canvases: Gathering of Manna (r.). L.

S. PIETRO DE DOM (DUOMO NUOVO). Organ shutters from Duomo Vecchio: Marriage of Virgin (outside); Birth of Virgin and Visitation (inside). 1539–41.

SS. FAUSTINO E GIOVITA, CHOIR, R. WALL. Banner: Resurrection; on back, S. Apollonius and kneeling SS. Faustinus and Giovita.

S. FRANCESCO, HIGH ALTAR. Madonna and Child enthroned with SS. Francis of Assisi, Anthony of Padua, Bonaventura, Louis of Toulouse and two Frati Minori. d. 1502.

— CHOIR, PENTAGONAL APSE. Frescoes: in vault, Redeemer and Evangelists; in lunettes, Doctors of the Church (r.).

— FOURTH ALTAR R. Fresco (transferred on canvas): Descent of the Holy Ghost.

S. GIOVANNI EVANGELISTA. S. Jerome (fr.).*

— CAPPELLA DEL SACRAMENTO O CORPUS DOMINI, L. WALL. Soffit of arch above lunette, six squares with Prophets (p.?); in lunette, Miracle of the Holy Sacrament at Bolsena; below lunette, Raising of Lazarus and Supper in the House of Simon; on pilasters, the Evangelists John and Matthew. 1521–24. *Plate* 1687.

— BATTISTERO (L. WALL). Marriage of Virgin.

— FOURTH ALTAR L. Madonna and Child with SS. Margaret of Cortona, Onophrius, Anthony of Padua and Roch (from suppressed church of S. Rocco). E.

S. MARIA IN CALCHERA, SECOND ALTAR L. Apollonius at Mass with four donors.

SS. NAZARO E CELSO. Overpainted, cut-down, shutters: Adoration of Magi. (?)

S. SALVATORE, FIRST CHAPEL R. Frescoes: outside, S. Obizio as a knight on a white horse and below it, gentleman with three Putti; Christ at the Column; inside, S. Obizio worshipped by the faithful and Christ above; S. Obizio recommending a female donor and her daughters to the Virgin in Glory (r.).

Brooklyn (New York). 11.517. Detached fresco from Bedizzole near Brescia: Madonna and Child with SS. Roch and Anthony Abbot (r.).

Budapest. 1254 (126). Male portrait (see Bergamo 599 and Brescia, Bettoni).

1313 (174). Bust of man writing letter.

1451. Fragment of fresco: four portraits.

SÁNDOR LEDERER (EX). Madonna and Child.

Calvisano (Brescia). PARISH CHURCH. Marriage of S. Catherine, and Bishop Saint (p.).

Cambridge. FITZWILLIAM MUSEUM, MARLAY BEQUEST. 11. Gentleman in fur coat (same sitter as Cassel 512).

Capriolo (Brescia). PARISH CHURCH. Resurrection.

Cassel. 502A, 503. Side-panels of triptych: SS. Peter and Paul. E.

Cizzago (Brescia). PARISH CHURCH. Pietà. L.

Cornbury Park (Oxon.). WATNEY COLLECTION (EX). Contest of Apollo and Marsyas.

Crema. PALAZZO VESCOVILE. Marriage of Virgin.

Cremona. 179–183. Five fragments of frescoes: Heads of Saints.

DUOMO, CENTRAL NAVE, R. WALL. Frescoes: Crowning with Thorns and 'Ecce Homo' (over fourth arch); Christ before Caiaphas and Flagellation (over fifth arch). Sd and d. 1519. *Plate* 1690.

Florence. UFFIZI. 896. Bust of boy.

3384. Self-portrait. L. (?)

Frankfurt a/M. 925. Old man seated at table. L. (?)

Genoa. PALAZZO ROSSO. Inv. 86. Prisoner adoring Crucifix.

Glasgow. 579. Musicians in landscape. E. (?)

Gosford House. EARL OF WEMYSS AND MARCH. 117. Adoration of Shepherds (inscribed 'Georgius Barbarelli').

Hanover. LANDESGALERIE. 324. 'Ecce Homo.' Sd.

Isolabella (Lago Maggiore). PALAZZO BORROMEO. Portrait of gentleman. d. 1532. Madonna and Child with Angel.

Karlsruhe. Bishops receiving Blood of Redeemer. Not traced.

Leningrad. 1916. Madonna and Child.

London. 297. Polyptych from S. Alessandro at Brescia: Nativity, SS. Jerome, Alexander, Blessed Felice Servita, S. Gaudentius Bishop of Brescia. Formerly d. 1525. *Plate* 1689.

BUCKINGHAM PALACE, ROYAL COLLECTIONS. Bust of officer.

Madonna della Stella (Cellàtica, Brescia). SANTUARIO. Madonna and Child with Angels. Post 1536.*

Malpaga (Bergamo). CASTLE, INNER COURT. Fresco: Pope Paul II investing Colleoni as General.

Memphis (Tenn.). BROOKS MEMORIAL ART GALLERY. 61.202 (KRESS COLLECTION. K
1551). 'Cook' Marriage of S. Catherine with S. Lawrence, S. Ursula and
female donor (r.).

Milan. BRERA. 98. Madonna and Child on cushion. E.

775. Portrait of a Martinengo Cesaresco. L.

801. Circumcision. Sd and d. 1529.

CASTELLO SFORZESCO. Madonna and Child with SS. Francis, Anthony of Padua
and donor (r.).

BENIGNO CRESPI (EX). Christ carrying the Cross.

PROF. MARIANO CUNIETTI. Two upper side-panels of polyptych: Knee-length SS.
John Baptist and Augustine, Bartholomew and Jerome (companions to
Cassel?). E.*

FAUSTO GRASSETTI. Madonna and Child (after Titian).

Montauban. MUSÉE INGRES. 127. Front of cassone: Two couples dancing.

Montichiari (Brescia). PARISH CHURCH. Last Supper.

New Orleans (La.). DELGADO MUSEUM OF ART. 61.75 (KRESS COLLECTION. K 1769).
Warrior.

Ospitaletto Bresciano. PARISH CHURCH. Entombment (fr.). L. (?)

Padua. 166 (Inv. 663). Last Supper (from refectory of Convento di S. Giustina).
Commissioned 1513.

165 (Inv. 669). Altarpiece from S. Giustina: Madonna and Child enthroned with
SS. Benedict, Justina, Prosdocimus and Scholastica; in pediment, roundel with
dead Christ upheld by Angel; in spandrels, two roundels with heads of youth
and bearded man; in predella, five roundels with massacred Innocents, heads
of Saints (two missing; see Berlin). Sd. Commissioned 1513. [*Plate* 381.]

Palermo. CHIARAMONTE BORDONARO COLLECTION. Sketch for a Nativity.

Pisogne (Lago d'Iseo). S. MARIA DELLA NEVE. Frescoes. Before 1534.

— VAULT. Twelve Prophets and twelve Sibyls; monochrome putti on mosaic
ground.

— ENTRANCE WALL. Above, Crucifixion; left and right of entrance, Flagellation,
Crowning with Thorns.

— RIGHT WALL. Upper register: Resurrection, Descent to Limbo, Ascension; lower
register: Last Supper, Washing of Feet, Christ enters Jerusalem. *Plate* 1698.

— LEFT WALL. Upper register: Way to Calvary, 'Ecce Homo', destroyed scene;
lower register: Jesus before Pilate, Supper in the House of Simon.

— END WALL. Upper register: Eternal, Angel and Virgin of Annunciation; lower
register: Entombment, Descent of the Holy Ghost.

— Detached frescoes from outside walls: Adoration of Magi and other fragments.

Prague. TYNKIRCHE, CHOIR. Organ shutters: Circumcision, Visitation. L.

Richmond (Surrey). COOK COLLECTION. Madonna and Child (after Giorgione).
E. (?)

Rodengo. ABBAZIA, ROOM BY THE CHIOSTRO GRANDE. Frescoed lunette: Madonna
and Child with Infant S. John (see Brescia 78, 92). ca 1533.*

Rome. ACCADEMIA DI S. LUCA. Madonna and Child. Not traced.

CAMPIDOGLIO, PINACOTECA. 228. Head of boy. Not traced.

GALLERIA DORIA PAMPHILI. 162. Madonna and Child.

298. Angel musician (fr.). E. (?)

MUSEO DI CASTEL SANT'ANGELO, MENOTTI BEQUEST. Predella panel: Circumcision. (?)

Roncadelle. PARISH CHURCH. Nativity.*

Rovato. S. MARIA DELL'ANNUNCIATA, CHOIR. Frescoes: in lunettes, Prophets; end wall, Annunciation (r.).*

Salò (Lago di Garda). DUOMO, L. WALL. S. Anthony of Padua worshipped by Conte Cicala. Sd and d. 1529. *Plate 1692.*

Madonna and Child with SS. Bonaventura and Sebastian. E.

San Felice del Benaco. PARISH CHURCH. Madonna and Child in Glory and below SS. Felix, Adautus, Anthony Abbot, John Evangelist and another young Saint (st.). 1531–34.*

Savannah (Georgia). TELFAIR ACADEMY. P.102 (KRESS COLLECTION. K 1067). Madonna suckling the Child (st.).

Seattle (Washington). ART MUSEUM. IT.37/R.6616.I (KRESS COLLECTION. K 1436). 'Wemyss' Nobleman.

Stenico (Val Giudicaria, Trento). CASTELLO. Fresco: decorative frieze. (?)

Tavernola (Bergamo). S. PIETRO, ENTRANCE WALL. Fresco: Madonna and Child enthroned with SS. George and Mauritius; below, SS. Peter and Paul recommending six donors. E.

Trento. CASTELLO DEL BUONCONSIGLIO, LOGGIA, VAULT. Frescoes: Apollo in his chariot and the four Seasons at short ends; in ten spandrels, naked Gods and Goddesses, alternating with monochrome figures in roundels. [*Plate* 379.] *Plate* 1693.

—— LUNETTES. Judith and Holofernes, Concert, Virginio kills his daughter, Tarquinius pursues Lucretia, The three Graces, Death of Cleopatra, Samson and Delilah, Concert, Venus and Cupid.

— INNER COURT. Fresco: Charlemagne enthroned.

— CORRIDOIO DELLA CUCINA. Frescoed vault: putti, emblems, Flying figure in oval. Frescoed lunettes: Prometheus, monochrome busts of Emperors.

— CORRODIO DEL BAGNO. Frescoed lunettes: Bathing Women.

— CORRIDOR AT TOP OF STAIRS. Frescoes: upper register, men and women behind parapets; lower register, simulated niches with Chastity embracing the Unicorn, Prodigality, Avarice with a snake, Two women fighting for Cupid (Lust), Woman killing herself, The Vestal Tuccia with the sieve.

— STAIRS. Frescoes: Diana hunting and two monochrome Scenes; Satyr and Nymph; Buffoon with a monkey; Martino Malpaga and two workmen; Fête champêtre. *Plates* 1695, 1696.

—— WINDOW EMBRASURE. Frescoes: Lot and his daughters; Venus and Cupid, Mercury and other Gods; castration of a cat.

Trento. CASTELLO DEL BUONCONSIGLIO (contd.). SALA DELL'UDIENZA. Frescoed ceiling: Allegory of Fame and commemorative portraits (with Fogolino). *Plate 1694.* Frescoed decorations. 1531–32.

— CAPPELLA. Madonna and Child with SS. Emerenziana and Nicholas worshipped by Canon Tavernelli.

Venice. 708. Madonna and Child.

737. Mourning over dead Christ, with donor. Sd and d. 1510. *Plate 1685.*

Verona. S. GIORGIO IN BRAIDA. Organ-shutters: outside: S. George before the judge; inside, two episodes of the martyrdom of S. George. d. 1540.

Vienna. 213A. Youth leaning on parapet. (?)

HARRACH COLLECTION. 305. Two putti.

Villongo San Filastrio (Bergamo). CAPPELLA DI S. ROCCO. Frescoes: left wall— Scene from Life of a Saint, and Bishop Saint; end wall—Madonna and Child enthroned with SS. Roch and Sebastian; right wall—penitent S. Jerome (r.).

Homeless. Madonna and Child. E. *Plate 1688.*

SALIMBENI, Lorenzo and Jacopo

Lorenzo di Salimbene, also called Lorenzo da Sanseverino the Elder, born at San Severino Marche 1374, died before 1420. Follower of Nuzi, influenced perhaps by work of German painters like Meister Bertram, belongs to same Gothic trend as Gentile da Fabriano. His brother and partner Jacopo died after 1427.

Baltimore (Md.). WALTERS ART GALLERY. 694, 701. Panels of polyptych: S. James the More enthroned, S. James the Less enthroned.

Cingoli. S. DOMENICO. Fresco: Crucifixion (fr.).

Foligno. PALAZZO TRINCI, LOGGIA. Frescoes: Stories of Romulus and Remus. (?)

Perugia. GALLERIA NAZIONALE. Detached monochrome fresco from Monastery of S. Benedetto: Crucifixion.

Pesaro. MUSEO. Detached fresco from S. Domenico: Mystic Marriage of S. Catherine.

San Ginesio (Marche). COLLEGIATA, CRIPTA, FORMER ORATORIO DI S. BIAGIO. Frescoes: Altar wall, Madonna and Child enthroned with S. Stephen being stoned and S. Ginesius playing the violin; Left wall (cut by window), S. Blaise in episcopal dress, S. Blaise tortured with iron combs; in embrasures, Eternal, S. Stephen, S. Anthony Abbot; Right wall, S. Blaise heals a child choked by a fishbone, S. Blaise is captured and promises a woman that her pig, taken by a wolf, will return to her vault, the woman, having got back her pig, visits S. Blaise in prison; Martyrdom of the seven women who threw idols in a pool, S. Blaise miraculously dries up the pool (r.), S. Blaise before the governor; Soffit of triumphal arch, Racemes, Man of Sorrows, Busts of mourning Virgin and Evangelist. Sd and d. 1406.*

San Severino Marche. 4. Portable triptych from S. Lorenzo: Mystic Marriage of
S. Catherine; in wings, inside—S. Simeon and S. Taddeus, outside—S. Luke
and Pietà (r.). Sd ('nelli mei anni 26 io Lorenzo feci') and d. 1400. *Plate* 496.
13, 14. Fragments of frescoes from Colleluce: head of child, head of youth.

S. LORENZO IN DOLÍOLO, SACRISTY, ENTRANCE WALL. Frescoed lunette: Crucifixion
with SS. Lawrence, Eustace (Benedict?), Bernard, two Saints, Anthony Abbot,
Andrew (fr., r.).

— — R. WALL. Monochrome fresco: Story of S. Lawrence (fr.).

— — L. WALL. Monochrome fresco: Story of S. Eustace? (fr.). Frescoed decoration
formerly Sd and d. 1407.

— CRYPT, L. WALL. Frescoed lunette: S. Margaret, S. Lucy, Crucifixion (detached
and shown in sacristy).

— —L. PILLAR. Votive frescoes: S. Nicholas, S. James, S. Severinus, Trinity. *Plate* 497.

— — ENTRANCE TO SECOND CRYPT, R. AND L. PILLAR. Frescoes: Madonna and Child
enthroned, crowned by Angels, with female Worshipper and Man in chains
(r.); Standing Madonna crowned by Angels and Child blessing S. Lucy (both
frescoes now detached and—temporarily?—stored in Pinacoteca).

— — CONVEX ENTRANCE WALL TO CHAPEL OF S. ANDREA. Votive frescoes: S. Anthony
Abbot, S. Lucy (fr.), Standing Madonna (fr.), S. Dominic (fr.), S. Thomas
Aquinas (other frescoes by another hand).

— CRYPT, L. AISLE, FIRST BAY (CAPPELLA DI S. ANDREA), VAULT: Monochrome
frescoes: S. Andrew performs miracles while in prison, Preparations for his
martyrdom, Death of S. Andrew with Maximilla at feet of cross, S. Andrew
lowered from the cross.

— — — FACE OF ARCH. Monochrome fresco: Punishment of Egeus (detached and
transferred to sacristy).

— — — SOFFIT OF ARCH. Monochrome frescoes: S. Andrew discovers the Devil
in the shape of a woman, S. Andrew confounds the Devil.

— — — WALL. Frescoed lunette: S. Andrew holding cross and fish, surrounded
by Saints, flagellant and worshippers (fr., detached and transferred to sacristy).

S. MARIA DEL MERCATO (S. DOMENICO), CHAPEL L. OF CHOIR (SACRISTY). Fragmentary
frescoes: left wall, above—Madonna and Child with kneeling donor, below
—SS. Eustace and Tatiana with their children in a portico; right wall, above
—kneeling Warrior recommended by female Saint to (Virgin?).

— CHAPEL R. OF CHOIR. Fragmentary frescoes. (?)

S. MARIA DELLA MISERICORDIA (FORMER LOGGIA PUBBLICA), SOFFIT OF ARCH. Frescoes:
Blessing Redeemer and busts of Prophets among intertwining racemes (remaining frescoes, lost). Sd by Lorenzo and d. 1404.

S. MARIA DELLA PIEVE, OR PIEVE VECCHIA. Votive frescoes:
Madonna and Child enthroned and two Angels (fr.). *Plate* 499.
Madonna of Humility and two Angels (fr.).
Madonna enthroned and Child standing on her knee (r.).
Madonna suckling the Child and two Angels (fr.).

San Severino Marche. S. MARIA DELLA PIEVE (contd.). Full-length S. Bartholomew.
Full-length beardless Apostle. *Plate* 498.
Full-length Bishop Saint with kneeling Woman and Child.
Two Saints in prison.
　　　Mostly detached and transferred to Pinacoteca.

S. SEVERINO OR DUOMO VECCHIO, FIRST CHAPEL L, VAULT: Frescoes: S. John Evan-
　　gelist writes in Patmos, distributes coins to the poor, changes stones into gold,
　　raises to life the dead bridegroom. *Plate* 509.

— WALLS. Frescoes: S. John Evangelist blames the philosopher Crato for advising
　　the two youths to break up their diamonds and returns the diamonds to their
　　integrity (remaining frescoes, lost). Sd 'Lorenzo e Jacomo so fratello'. *Plate*
　　508.

Urbino. GALLERIA NAZIONALE DELLE MARCHE. Standard from S. Chiara: Full-length
　　S. Clare holding lily and book.

　　Banner from S. Chiara: Full-length S. Anthony of Padua; below, the Saint heals
　　a nun, the nun joins her astonished companions (st.).

ORATORIO DI S. GIOVANNI BATTISTA. Frescoes Sd by Lorenzo and Jacopo and d.
　　1416.

— END WALL. Fresco: Crucifixion. *Plate* 503.

— R. WALL. Frescoes: Upper register—I, Annunciation to Zacharias, and Zach-
　　arias writing the news to Elizabeth; II, Visitation, and Virgin greeting
　　Zacharias; III, Birth, Naming and Circumcision of Baptist; IV, Virgin taking
　　leave of Elizabeth and Zacharias; V, Virgin and Jesus meeting the infant
　　S. John in the wilderness. Lower register—VI, S. John Baptist preaching in
　　the wilderness; VII, Baptism of the multitudes; VIII, Baptism of Christ; IX,
　　Baptist preaching to Herod. *Plates* 500–502, 504–507.

— ENTRANCE WALL. Fragmentary fresco: X, Banquet of Herod, Salome's Dance
　　and Beheading of Baptist.

— L. WALL, UPPER REGISTER. Frescoes: XI, the Body of the Baptist carried away;
　　XII, Burial of S. John Baptist.

— L. WALL, LOWER REGISTER. Votive frescoes (p., s.):
　　S. John Baptist (r.).
　　Blessed Pietro Spagnuolo.
　　Madonna of Humility with S. John Baptist and S. James.
　　Madonna and Child with SS. Sebastian and John Baptist.

SANO DI PIETRO

Siena, 1406–81. Pupil of Sassetta (see also Master of Osservanza).

Acquapendente (Viterbo). S. FRANCESCO, SACRISTY. S. Bernardino.

Alesani (Corsica). CONVENT. Madonna of the cherries (fr.).

Altenburg. 70, 71. Two predella panels from lost polyptych in Chapel of Palazzo Pubblico, Siena: Mary's homecoming from the Temple; Assumption of Virgin (companions to Northwick Park and Rome, Vatican 136, 138). (1448–51?).

    72. Madonna and Child with two Saints and four Angels.

    73. Madonna and Child with SS. Jerome, Bernardino and four Angels.

    74. Madonna and Child with two Angels. E.

Amherst (Mass.). AMHERST COLLEGE. 1961–83 (KRESS COLLECTION. K 311). Adoration of the Christ Child.

Amsterdam. UNIVERSITY, LOANED BY NEDERLANDS KUNST-BEZIT. 'Lanz' Madonna and Child with SS. Francis and Bernardino.

    OTTO LANZ (EX). Tondo: S. Catherine of Siena.

    Crucifixion with mourning Virgin, SS. John Evangelist and Peter, in roundel.

Arundel Castle (Sussex). DUKE OF NORFOLK (EX). Virgin of Annunciation (fr.).

Ashburnham Place (Sussex). LADY ASHBURNHAM (EX). Predella panel: S. Bernardino rescuing a drowned boy.

Assisi. S. FRANCESCO, SACRO CONVENTO, PERKINS DONATION 24. S. Bernardino standing on the World and two Angels.

    S. MARIA DEGLI ANGELI, MUSEO. Madonna and Child.

    F. M. PERKINS COLLECTION (EX). Oval: Bust of S. Bernardino (fr., r.).

Badia a Isola (Colle Val d'Elsa). SS. SALVATORE E CIRINO. Polyptych: Madonna and Child enthroned with two kneeling Benedictines; SS. Benedict and Cyrinus Bishop, SS. Donatus Bishop and Justina; above, Blessing Christ, Angel and Virgin of Annunciation; in pilasters, SS. Jerome, Eugene, Maurus, SS. Gregory, Anthony Abbot and Placidus; in predella, Dead Christ with mourning Virgin and S. John Evangelist, S. Benedict rescuing a Monk from the Devil, S. Cyrinus thrown into the River, S. Donatus and the Dragon, Stabbing of S. Justina. Sd and d. 1471. *Plate 588.*

Barcelona. CATHEDRAL. Madonna and Child with SS. Jerome, Bernardino and six Angels.

Bayeux. MUSÉE. Madonna and Child with Redeemer and Angels.

Berlin. BOTTENWIESER (EX). Madonna and Child.

Birmingham (Ala.). MUSEUM OF ART. 61.91–92 (KRESS COLLECTION. K 100, 101). Side-panels of triptych: SS. Benedict and Augustine with Angel and Virgin of Annunciation above (st.).

Bologna. BIBLIOTECA COMUNALE. Antiphonary 52: miniatures—Nativity, Baptism of Christ, S. John Evangelist in Patmos.

Bologna (contd.). SS. VITALE E AGRICOLA, L. CHAPEL. Madonna and Child in oval (surrounding Angels are by Francia). *Plate* 1614.

Bolsena. S. CRISTINA, CAPPELLA DEL ROSARIO. Polyptych: Madonna and Child (S. Dominic is a sixteenth-century addition); SS. George, Peter, Paul and Christine; above, Redeemer, Virgin and Angel of Annunciation (predella is by Benvenuto di Giovanni).

Bordeaux. 76. Angel Gabriel (fr.).

    CATHÉDRALE ST-ANDRÉ, TRÉSOR. Madonna and Child with SS. Jerome, Bernardino and four Angels (r.). (?)

Boston (Mass.). 07.515. Triptych: Madonna and Child with Redeemer, two Angels and female donor; SS. Jerome and Catherine of Siena.

    97.229. Madonna and Child with four Angels (r.). (?).

    39.801. S. Bernardino standing on the World.

Brooklyn (N.Y.). 06.80. Fragmentary polyptych: Madonna and Child enthroned; SS. James and John Evangelist.

Brussels. 793. Madonna and Child with SS. Jerome and Bernardino, and four Angels.

Budapest. 23. Predella panel: Dance of Salome.

    1210 (24). Madonna.

Buonconvento. SS. PIETRO E PAOLO, CHOIR. Fragmentary polyptych: Madonna and Child enthroned; SS. Bernardino and Catherine of Siena.

Cambridge. FITZWILLIAM MUSEUM. MS. 196. Illuminated page: Christ in Judgement.

    MS. 198. Illuminated page: King David in the initial D.

    MS. 6–1954 (Lee of Fareham Bequest). Missal of Friars Hermits of Siena: f. 160 v. —large miniature of Christ on Cross with mourning Virgin and S. John Evangelist; nineteen illuminated initials.

Cambridge (Mass.). 1962.284. Madonna and Child with SS. Jerome and Bernardino and six Angels.

Capistrano (Abruzzi). S. FRANCESCO, SACRISTY. S. Bernardino.

Cetona (Siena). S. FRANCESCO, HIGH ALTAR. Madonna and Child (fr., r.).

Chicago (Ill.). 33.1027. Madonna and Child with SS. Jerome and Bernardino and four Angels.

Chiusi. S. SECONDIANO (DUOMO), SALA CAPITOLARE. Antiphonaries U and V: miniatures. 1459–63.

Città Castellana. S. PIETRO. S. Bernardino held by two Angels over the world.

Cleveland (Ohio). 24.199. Madonna and Child with kneeling SS. Nicholas and Mary Magdalen; Crucifixion above.

    44.56. Madonna and Child (r.).

Cologne. 726. Risen Christ (fr.).

    DIÖZESANMUSEUM. Predella panel: Vision of S. Jerome.

Coral Gables (Fla.). LOWE ART UNIVERSITY. 61.12 (KRESS COLLECTION. K 286). Madonna and Child with SS. John Baptist, Peter Martyr, Catherine, Anthony of Padua, Francis and Jerome.

Detroit (Mich.). 24.107. Madonna and Child with SS. Jerome and Bernardino and two Angels.

LILIAN HENKEL HAASS. (EX). Madonna and Child.

T. S. HYLAND COLLECTION. Predella panel: S. Donatus chastising the dragon.

Dorking (Surrey). WATERHOUSE COLLECTION (EX). Right panel of polyptych: Full-length S. Jerome.

Dresden. 24. Reliquary panel: Assumption of Virgin with S. Margaret and Bishop Saint below; in frame, Redeemer, SS. Peter, Paul and ten other Saints.

25. Painted Crucifix.

26. Painted Crucifix.

31. Roundel from predella: Dead Christ in Tomb.

Edinburgh. 1565. Pinnacle: Coronation of the Virgin. L.

El Paso (Texas). MUSEUM OF ART. 1961-6/7 (KRESS COLLECTION. K 522). Madonna and Child with SS. John Baptist, Bartholomew and four Angels.

Englewood (N.J.). D. F. PLATT COLLECTION (EX). Portable altar: Madonna and Child with two Angels and Christ on Cross above; in wings, S. John Baptist and S. Peter. (r.).

Madonna and Child with two Angels (r.).

Esztergom. 55.180. Madonna and Child with SS. Jerome and Bernardino.

Florence. ACTON COLLECTION. Madonna and Child with SS. Peter and Paul and four Angels. E. *Plate 580.*

Madonna and Child with two Angels.

Madonna and Child (fr.).

Madonna and Child with SS. Jerome, Bernardino, Dorothy and Ansanus. L.

BERENSON COLLECTION. Madonna suckling the Child.

Madonna and Child with SS. Jerome, Bernardino and two Angels.

LOESER COLLECTION (EX). Assumption of Virgin.

CONTESSA RUCELLAI (EX). Predella panels: S. Bernardino rescuing a drowned boy, Death of S. Bernardino, Miracles at the bier of S. Bernardino (companions to London, Hutton).

Frontignano (Senese). PARISH CHURCH. Madonna and Child with SS. Apollonia, Bernardino and four Angels.

Gazzada (Varese). FONDAZIONE CAGNOLA. Madonna and Child (fr., r.).

Grosseto. S. LORENZO, CHOIR. Side-panels of triptych: S. Jerome, S. Anthony Abbot.

Gualdo Tadino. 9. Coronation of Virgin with two Saints.

Hamburg. 764. Madonna and Child (r.).

Hampton Court. ROYAL COLLECTION. 1216. Madonna and Child with SS. Jerome and Bernardino and six Angels.

Houston (Texas). MUSEUM OF ART, STRAUS BEQUEST. Madonna and Child with SS. Jerome and Bernardino and six Angels.

Isola Maggiore (Lago Trasimeno). S. FRANCESCO. Central panel of polyptych: Madonna and Child enthroned and four Angels.

Kreuzlingen. H. KISTERS. Madonna embracing the Child (fr.).*

Kreuzlingen. H. KISTERS. (contd.). Madonna and Child with two Angels (variant of Florence, Acton and Hamburg).*

London. COURTAULD INSTITUTE GALLERIES, LEE OF FAREHAM BEQUEST. Christ on the way to Calvary.

    HENRY HARRIS COLLECTION (EX). Madonna and Child with two Angels.

    E. HUTTON COLLECTION. Predella panel: S. Bernardino preaching in the Piazza del Campo (companion to Florence, Rucellai).

    H. TOPIC MIMARA (EX). Madonna and Child with S. Jerome, S. Bernardino and two Angels (r.).

    MRS DONNELL POST (EX). 'Graham' Madonna and Child in octagonal frame.

    DORA WILSON COLLECTION (EX). Nativity.

Louisville (Ky.). ARTHUR D. ALLEN COLLECTION. Madonna and Child with two Angels (r.).

Massa Marittima. DUOMO (EX). Circumcision.

Milan. ALDO CRESPI COLLECTION. Madonna and Child with SS. Jerome, Bernardino, Catherine, female Saint, and two Angels.

Minneapolis(Minn.)(ex).23.87. S. Bernardino standing on the World and two Angels.

Montalcino (Senese). MUSEO CIVICO. Madonna of Humility and Angels, in rose garden (r.). E.

    OSSERVANZA. S. Bernardino standing on the World and two Angels.

Montemerano (Maremma). S. GIORGIO, FIRST ALTAR R. Polyptych: Madonna and Child with SS. Peter, George, Lawrence and Anthony of Padua; above, S. Francis, Virgin and Angel of Annunciation, S. Anthony Abbot, S. Bernardino; in predella, Dead Christ, mourning Virgin, S. John Evangelist and six more Saints. Sd and d. 1458. *Plate 584.*

    Polyptych: Half-length Christ blessing, SS. Blaise, Michael, Paul and Peter.

Montorsaio (Senese). SS. MICHELE E CERBONE, HIGH ALTAR. Madonna and Child.

Mount Trust (Churchill, Oxon.). CAPT. AND MRS BULKELEY-JOHNSON. Madonna and Child.

Nantes. 151. S. Francis receiving Stigmata.

New Haven (Conn.). 1871.60. Coronation of the Virgin.

    1871.61. Predella: Adoration of the Magi.

New York. 14.44. Cassone panel: Story of the Queen of Sheba (st.).

    41.100.19. Madonna and Child with S. Catherine, female Saint and four Angels.

    64.189.4. 'Straus' portable altar: Madonna and Child, S. John Baptist, S. Jerome in the wilderness.

    65.181.7. (A. AND A. LEHMAN BEQUEST). Predella panel: Burial of S. Martha.

    KRESS FOUNDATION. K 1036. Madonna and Child.

    ROBERT LEHMAN COLLECTION. Madonna and blessing Child.

    Tondo: Madonna and Child.

    Madonna and Child holding Bird (fr.).

    Madonna and Child with SS. Jerome, Bernardino, John Baptist, Francis (?) and two Angels.

Madonna and Child holding bird with SS. John Baptist, Jerome, Peter Martyr, Bernardino and four Angels.

Knee-length S. Francis.

Knee-length S. Bernardino.

Bust of S. Bernardino.

Roundel from predella: Mourning S. John Evangelist.

Three predella panels: SS. Cosmas and Damian before Lycias; SS. Cosmas and Damian thrown into the sea; Stoning of SS. Cosmas and Damian.

Madonna of Humility (?). E.

Predella Panel: Naming of S. John Baptist.

UZIELLI COLLECTION. Two predella panels: S. Bernardino saves a boy fallen into the well; during funeral of S. Bernardino a possessed woman is exorcized on approaching the corpse of the Saint.

MORGAN COLLECTION (EX). Madonna and Child enthroned.

FELIX WARBURG COLLECTION. Madonna and Child with two Angels.

Northampton (Mass.). SMITH COLLEGE. Madonna and Child with SS. Jerome, Bernardino and two Angels.

Northwick Park (Blockley). CAPT. SPENCER CHURCHILL (EX). Predella panel (to lost polyptych in Chapel of Palazzo Pubblico, Siena?): Birth of Virgin (companion to Altenburg and Rome, Vatican 136, 138). (1448-51?).

Oxford. ASHMOLEAN MUSEUM. 395. Madonna and Child with SS. Catherine, Jerome and two Angels.

CHRIST CHURCH. 31. Madonna and Child with SS. Clare, Francis, Ambrose, Jerome, John Baptist and Bernardino.

32. Madonna and Child with SS. Jerome, and Bernardino and two Angels.

Palermo. CHIARAMONTE-BORDONARO COLLECTION. Madonna and Child with two Angels.

Paris. 1128–1132. Predella to Siena Polyptych 246: Dream of S. Jerome, S. Jerome in the wilderness, S. Jerome and the lion, Death of S. Jerome, Jerome as Cardinal and S. John Baptist wearing triple tiara appear to S. Augustine while he is writing to S. Jerome unaware of his death. 1444. *Plate 582.*

M. PAUL BOURGET COLLECTION (EX). Madonna and Child.

Perugia. VAN MARLE COLLECTION (EX). Madonna and Child with two Angels.

Philadelphia (Pa.). JOHN G. JOHNSON COLLECTION. 106. Madonna and Child with four Angels.

Pienza. MUSEO DIOCESANO. Miniature: Baptism of Christ.

Miniature: Prophet receiving Vision of Christ Child.

DUOMO, L. TRANSEPT. Madonna and Child with SS. Mary Magdalen, Philip, James, Anne and two Angels; in tympanum: Dead Christ and two Angels; in predella, Blessing Christ, Angel and Virgin of Annunciation. Sd. 1462-63.

Rome. GALLERIA NAZIONALE (PALAZZO BARBERINI). Crucifixion.

VATICAN, PINACOTECA. 133, 135. Two predella panels: S. George converting the father of the Princess and his court; Baptism of the King. E.

Rome. VATICAN, PINACOTECA (contd.). 134. Roundel from predella: Half-length S. Benedict.

136, 138. Predella panels: Presentation and Marriage of the Virgin (companions to Altenburg and Northwick Park). 1448–51.

139–142. Predella panels: The Sick and the Cripples at the tomb of S. Peter Martyr; Virgin, SS. Agnes, Catherine and Cicily appear to S. Peter Martyr; three women at Utrecht mocking the Saint's memory pray later for forgiveness; S. Peter Martyr saves a woman whom the husband wanted to kill.

144, 145. Predella panels: Nativity, Flight into Egypt.

237–240. Predella: Birth of the Virgin, Presentation of the Virgin, Marriage of the Virgin, Visitation (st.). E.

— BIBLIOTECA. Cod. Vat. Lat. 1742 (cat. 2). Miniature: a Reader.

PRINCESS DORIA PAMPHILI. Portable altar: Blessing Redeemer; S. John Baptist, S. Bernardino.

MARCHESE PIETRO MISCIATTELLI. Head of S. Bernardino.

Madonna and Child with SS. Jerome, Bernardino and four Angels.

NEVIN COLLECTION (EX). Central panel of predella: Dead Christ in Tomb, mourning Virgin, S. John.

CONTE L. VITETTI. S. Bernardino standing on the world and two Angels.*

San Diego (Cal.). FINE ARTS GALLERY. Knee-length S. Catherine of Siena; knee-length S. Augustine.

San Quirico di Val d'Orcia. COLLEGIATA. Altarpiece: Madonna and Child enthroned with four Angels; SS. John Baptist and Quiricus; SS. Crescentius and John Evangelist, with two kneeling Saints; in lunette above, Resurrection and Christ in Limbo; in predella, Birth, Presentation, Marriage, Assumption and Coronation of the Virgin. L.

San Severino (Marche). 15. Madonna and Child with four Angels. E.

Siena. 202. S. Francis receiving the Stigmata (?). E.

223. Coronation of the Virgin.

224. Madonna and Child enthroned with eight Angels.

225, 229. Side-panels of polyptych from S. Pietro alle Scale: Full-length female Saint and S. John Baptist, full-length SS. John Evangelist and Peter.

226. Polyptych: Madonna and Child enthroned with six Angels and the Blessed Giovanni Colombini and Francesco Vincenti; full-length SS. Stephen, Benedict with two female donors, John Baptist with two male donors, and Lawrence; in pinnacles, Blessing Redeemer, half-length Angel and Virgin of Annunciation, SS. Peter and Paul; in pilasters, SS. Augustine and Andrew, Stephen and Agnes, Catherine, SS. Jerome and Bernardino, Lawrence and Lucy, Mary Magdalen; in predella, Adoring Angels and six Scenes from Passion.

228. Madonna and Child with four Angels, SS. Anthony Abbot and Bernardino; in lunette, Pietà.

230. Predella: Busts of SS. Louis of Toulouse, Bartholomew, Virgin, Christ, John Evangelist, Bernardino and Francis.

231. Polyptych: Madonna and Child enthroned with six Angels; full-length SS. Gregory, Augustine, Jerome and John Evangelist; in pinnacles, Redeemer, Angel and Virgin of Annunciation, SS. Francis and Dominic; in pilasters, SS. Agnes, Michael, Anthony Abbot and Ansanus.

232. Triptych: Madonna and Child; SS. Lucy and Bartholomew; in pilasters, SS. John Baptist, George, Anthony Abbot and Catherine. Sd and d. 1447.

233. Polyptych from Convent of S. Girolamo: Madonna and Child with many Angels worshipped by penitent S. Jerome and Blessed Giovanni Colombini; full-length SS. Cosmas and Damian; in pinnacles, Redeemer (lost), Angel and Virgin of Annunciation; in pilasters, SS. Stephen, Augustine, Agatha, Lawrence, Nicholas and Lucy; in predella, busts of SS. Bernardino and Catherine of Siena and six scenes from life of SS. Cosmas and Damian.

234. Right panel of polyptych: S. Lawrence.

235. Full-length S. Ansanus.

236. Central panel of polyptych: Madonna and Child enthroned (st.). L.

237. Triptych: Madonna and Child enthroned and six Angels, SS. Margaret and Catherine; full-length SS. Francis and Bernardino; in arched top, two roundels with Angel and Virgin of Annunciation. L.

238. S. Bernardino.

239. Right panel of triptych: SS. Francis, Louis of Toulouse and kneeling Jerome.

240. Panel of polyptych from S. Pietro in Castelvecchio: Full-length SS. Francis and Bartholomew.

241. Virgin commanding Pope Callistus III to protect Siena (from the Palazzo Pubblico). Sd and d. 1456. *Plate 585.*

242. SS. Jerome and Ansanus.

243. Roundel: Bust of S. Catherine.

244. Bust of S. Lawrence.

245. Side-panel of polyptych: Full-length S. Bartholomew.

246. Polyptych from Convent of S. Girolamo: Madonna and Child enthroned with Angels and kneeling Giovanni Colombini; full-length SS. Francis, Augustine, Dominic and Jerome; in pinnacles, Redeemer, Angel and Virgin of Annunciation, SS. Cosmas and Damian; in pilasters, SS. Catherine, Anthony of Padua, Paul, Mary Magdalen, Anthony Abbott and Peter. (Predella in Paris.) Sd and d. 1444.

247, 266. Pilaster-panels from polyptych: SS. Juliana and Agatha; SS. Francis and Louis of Toulouse.

248. Roundel: Bust of S. Augustine.

249. Panel from polyptych: Half-length S. Peter.

250. Side-panel of polyptych: Full-length S. Paul.

251. See 323.

252. Madonna of Humility crowned by two Angels.

253. S. Bernardino standing on the world (from Cappella delle Carceri, Mon-

talcino; see also Acquapendente, Città Castellana, Rome, Vitetti and Siena S. Maria Assunta). d. 1450.

254. Madonna and Child with SS. Ansanus, Lawrence, Jerome, Bernardino and two Angels.

255. Polyptych from S. Biagio a Scrofiano: Madonna and Child enthroned; full-length SS. John Baptist and Blaise with S. Jerome in roundel above; full-length SS. Martha and Lawrence with Bishop Saint in roundel above; in pinnacles, Redeemer, Angel and Virgin of Annunciation; in pilasters, SS. Bartholomew, Dionysius, Cyprianus, Peter, Paul and Sebastian; in predella, Dead Christ with mourning Virgin and the Evangelist, four scenes from Life of S. Blaise, half-length SS. Francis and Bernardino. Sd and d. 1449.

256, 257. Two panels of polyptych from Osservanza: Half-length SS. Louis of Toulouse and Francis.

258. Panel from polyptych: SS. John Baptist and Lawrence.

259, 260. Polyptych from S. Petronilla: Assumption of Virgin with SS. John Baptist and John Evangelist recommending Suor Battista di Benedetto Incontri; full-length SS. Catherine, Michael, Jerome and Petronilla; in predella, Adoration of Magi, Christ and the Woman of Samaria, Crucifixion and four scenes from Life of Saints. d. 1479. *Plate 587.*

261. Madonna and Child with two Angels and eight small Saints (Catherine, Lucy, Dorothy, Augustine, Jerome, Benedict, Ursula, Apollonia); below, half-length SS. Catherine of Siena, Bernardino, Francis, Dead Christ, SS. Dominic, Mary Magdalen, Petronilla and Peter.

262. Fragment of Nativity: Annunciation to the Shepherds.

263. Madonna and Child with four Angels, S. Jerome and two other Saints.

264. S. Catherine.

265. Predella panel: S. Jerome in Wilderness.

266. See 247.

267. SS. Luke, Michael, Jerome and Anthony Abbot (companion to 270).

268. Six pilaster-panels from polyptych: Full-length SS. Sebastian, Louis of Toulouse, Lucy, Clare, Francis and Bernardino.

269. Triptych: Coronation of Virgin; S. Francis and kneeling S. Jerome; S. Bernardino and kneeling S. Augustine; in arched top, two Prophets, Angel and Virgin of Annunciation.

270. SS. Augustine, Benedict, Bernardino and Louis of Toulouse (companion to 267).

271. Madonna and Child surrounded by SS. Agnes, Andrew (?), Peter, Catherine, Lawrence, Augustine and kneeling SS. Jerome, John Baptist, Bernardino and Bishop Saint; above, Crucifixion, Angel and Virgin of Annunciation.

272. Two side-panels of triptych: SS. Anthony of Padua and Michael; SS. Nicholas and Jerome; in pinnacles, Angel and Virgin of Annunciation; in pilaster, SS. Christopher, Clare, Catherine, Louis of Toulouse, Crescentius and Ursula.

273. Madonna and Child enthroned with twenty-four Saints; above, Crucifixion with Saints, Agony in the Garden and Noli me tangere (predella by
later hand).

323 and 251. Fragmentary polyptych: Madonna and Child enthroned with
Angels (r.); SS. Clare, Bartholomew, Nicholas and Francis; Angel and Virgin
of Annunciation.

ARCHIVIO DI STATO. Book-cover: Two Ambassadors on horseback. d. 1429. (?)

Book-cover: S. Michael and the Dragon. d. 1444. (?)

Book-cover: Camarlingo Bellanti washing his hands. d. 1451.

Book-cover: Blessed Francesco Patrizi and Blessed Giovacchino Piccolomini
with the Holy Ghost. d. 1457.

Book-cover: God sending forth Angel of Wisdom. d. 1471.

Book-cover: Marriage of Count Roberto da Sanseverino and Lucrezia Mala-
volti. d. 1473.

Miniature: *Statuto dell'Arte di Mercanzia*. d. 1474.

BIBLIOTECA COMUNALE. Franciscan Breviary with miniatures of Months.

PALAZZO PUBBLICO, GROUND FLOOR, SALA DI BICCHERNA. Fresco: Coronation of
Virgin (g.p., begun by Domenico di Bartolo); on either side, S. Bernardino
and S. Catherine of Siena (the latter repainted by Ventura Salimbeni). Sd
and d. 1445.

— GROUND FLOOR, VESTIBULE, THIRD BAY, R. WALL. S. Peter Alexandrinus enthroned, holding town of Siena, with the Blessed Ambrogio Sansedoni and
Andrea Gallerani.

— FIRST FLOOR, SALA DEL MAPPAMONDO. Fresco: S. Bernardino standing on the
world. *Plate* 352.

PALAZZO CHIGI SARACINI. Madonna and Child with SS. Jerome, Bernardino and
four Angels.

Four busts of Saints (frs. of altarpiece).

Ecce Homo (st.).

PORTA OVILE. Fresco: Madonna and Child with SS. Bernardino and Ansanus (begun
by Taddeo di Bartolo).

PORTA ROMANA. Fresco: Coronation of Virgin (begun by Sassetta). 1459.

RICOVERO (MADONNA DI CAMPANSI), FIRST FLOOR. Fresco: Annunciation.

S. BERNARDINO, ORATORIO INFERIORE, VESTIBULE. Madonna and Child.

S. CRISTOFORO. Triptych: S. George killing the Dragon; S. Christopher (companion
panel lost).

S. DOMENICO, CRYPT. Painted Crucifix.

— SECOND ALTAR R. Madonna and Child.

S. GIROLAMO, SACRISTY. Coronation of the Virgin with the Blessed Giovanni
Colombini and S. Jerome.

S. MARIA ASSUNTA (DUOMO), CHAPTER HALL. Two panels: S. Bernardino preaching in
Piazza del Campo; S. Bernardino preaching in Piazza S. Francesco. *Plate* 583.

S. Bernardino standing on the world with two Angels.

Siena. S. MARIA ASSUNTA (DUOMO) (contd.). PICCOLOMINI LIBRARY. Miniatures:
> Graduale n. 1—ff. 67, 72.
> Graduale n. 2—ff. 58, 93, 109.
> Graduale n. 3—f. 117.
> Graduale n. 6—ff. 151, 184.
> Graduale n. 10—f. 14.
> Graduale n. 11—ff. 1, 10, 18, 34, 87, 98, 103. *Plate* 586.

> S. PIETRO ALLE SCALE, CANONICA. Angel of Annunciation in roundel. E.
> > Madonna and Child.
> > S. Lucy.

> S. RAIMONDO AL RIFUGIO. (CONSERVATORIO FEMMINILE.) Crucifixion.
> > Madonna and Child with SS. Jerome, Dominic, Francis, Bernardino and two Angels.

> ORATORIO DELLA SS. TRINITÀ, R. CHAPEL. Madonna and Child with two Saints and Angels.

> SPEDALE DI S. MARIA DELLA SCALA, MADONNA SOTTO LE VOLTE, SACRISTY. Lunette: Dead Christ against landscape.

> SOCIETÀ ESECUTORI PIE DISPOSIZIONI. Madonna and Child with Saints and Angels.
> > Madonna and Child with SS. Jerome and Bernardino and Angels; below, Crucifixion.

> CARLO CINUGHI (EX). Madonna and Child with two Angels; lunette above by later hand.

> BICHI RUSPOLI COLLECTION. Madonna and Child with SS. Peter, Jerome, Anthony Abbot, Bernardino, Augustine, Paul and two Angels.

> SERGARDI COLLECTION. Madonna and Child with SS. John Baptist, Anthony Abbot, Bernardino, Augustine, two Angels and God the Father (lunette and predella by Neroccio).

> (Environs) OSSERVANZA, FIRST CHAPEL L. Madonna and Child enthroned with four Angels (r.).

> — THIRD ALTAR R. Triptych: Madonna and Child enthroned; Full-length SS. Jerome and Bernardino; Angel and Virgin of Annunciation in roundels above.

Sinalunga (Val di Chiana). S. BERNARDINO, L. CHAPEL. Salvator Mundi.
> Triptych: Madonna and Child with SS. Francis and Bonaventura.

Tivoli. MUSEO CIVICO. S. Bernardino.

Tucson (Ariz.). UNIVERSITY OF ARIZONA 62.153–4 (KRESS STUDY COLLECTION. K 1155, K 1156). S. Dominic, S. Thomas Aquinas.

Uopini (Monteriggioni). S. MARCELLINO. Left panel of polyptych: SS. Jerome and John Baptist.

Utrecht. 22. S. John Baptist (fr.).

Varallo (Biella). 203. Annunciation. [Not in 1960 catalogue.]

Vienna. LANCKORONSKI COLLECTION (EX). Man of Sorrows (fr.).
> Small Madonna and Child.
> Bust of S. Francis.

— (Environs), FANITEUM (Ober St. Veit). Madonna and Child.

Viterbo. 62. S. Bernardino and two Angels.

Washington (D.C.). 156 (KRESS COLLECTION. K 88). Predella panel: Crucifixion.

    385 (KRESS COLLECTION. K 492). Madonna and Child with SS. Jerome and Bernardino, and four Angels.

Homeless. Madonna and Child with SS. Jerome and Bernardino and four Angels. *Plate 581.*

SANTI, Giovanni

Urbino, ca 1430–94. Pupil of Melozzo da Forlì, influenced by Perugino, Justus van Ghent and slightly by Giovanni Bellini. Father of Raphael.

Berlin-Ost. 139. Madonna and Child with SS. Thomas Aquinas, Catherine, Anthony Abbot, Thomas Apostle, and donor. *Plate 1008.*

    140A. Madonna and Child. (Destroyed 1945.) *Plate 1009.*

Budapest. 51.799. Man of Sorrows. *Plate 1010.*

Cagli (Urbino). MUSEO CIVICO. Fresco: Head of S. Sebastian (fr.).

    S. DOMENICO, SECOND ALTAR L. Frescoes: Madonna and Child with SS. Peter, Francis, Dominic, John Baptist and two Angels; Resurrection above; in embrasure of arch, blessing Redeemer and Putti. *Plate 1013.*

    — L. WALL, OVER TOMB OF CLARA TIRANNI (1481). Fresco: Dead Christ with S. Jerome and Franciscan Saint.

    PALAZZO COMUNALE, ATRIO. Fresco: Madonna and Child with two Saints.

Fano. MUSEO CIVICO. Madonna and Child with SS. Helena, Andrew, Sebastian and Roch. Sd.

    S. MARIA NUOVA, FIRST ALTAR L. Visitation. Sd. *Plate 1016.*

Florence. GALLERIA CORSINI. Decorative panels from Tempietto delle Muse, Palazzo Ducale di Urbino (execution by Evangelista da Pian di Meleto and Timoteo Viti). *Plate 1017, 1019.*

    MARCHESE GINORI. Two decorative panels with a Shepherd and a Nymph (between Santi and Timoteo Viti). *Plates 1018, 1020.*

Gradara (Pesaro). MUNICIPIO. Madonna and Child enthroned with SS. Stephen, Sophia, Michael and John Baptist. Sd and d. 1484.

London. 751. Madonna and sleeping Child.

Lugano. THYSSEN COLLECTION. 279. Profile of boy.

Milan. BRERA. 503. Annunciation from S. Maria Maddalena at Sinigaglia.

Pian di Meleto (Marches). CONVENTO DI MONTEFIORENTINO, CAPPELLA DEI CONTI OLIVA. Madonna and Child with SS. Jerome, Anthony Abbot, Francis, George, music-making Angels and donor; in predella, roundels with Franciscan and Dominican Saints. Sd and d. 1489. *Plate 1011.*

Rome. VATICAN, PINACOTECA. 326. S. Jerome enthroned (from S. Bartolo at Pesaro).

Urbino. GALLERIA NAZIONALE DELLE MARCHE. Madonna and Child with SS. John Baptist, Francis, Jerome, Sebastian and the Buffi family (from S. Francesco). 1489. *Plate* 1012.

Dead Christ upheld by Angels (from S. Bernardino).

Bust of dead Christ and Virgin (from S. Chiara).

Martyrdom of S. Sebastian, and donors (execution by Bartolomeo di Gentile; from S. Bartolomeo).

CASA DI RAFFAELLO. Fresco: Madonna and sleeping Child (with young Raphael?).

SASSETTA

Sienese, 1395–1450. Pupil of Paolo di Giovanni Fei; probably influenced by Masolino, Paul de Limbourg and similar Franco–Flemish artists, as well as by elder contemporary Franco–Lombard miniaturists.

Assisi. S. FRANCESCO, SACRO CONVENTO, PERKINS DONATION 7. S. Christopher (st.).

Barnard Castle (Durham). BOWES MUSEUM. 52. Predella panel from Arte della Lana polyptych: Miracle of the Holy Sacrament (companion to Budapest, Rome Vatican and Siena). 1423–26.

Basciano (Siena). CHIESA DEL CASTELLO. Madonna of Humility.

Berlin. 63B. Madonna of Humility.

63C. Madonna and Child with S. John Baptist and female Saint (close follower; companion to New York, Lehman?).

1122. Assumption (design and upper part only; rest by later hand). (Destroyed 1945.)

1945. Predella panel from San Sepolcro polyptych: Blessed Ranieri appears to sleeping Cardinal (see Paris). 1437–44. *Plate* 559.

Bordeaux. 53. S. Francis.

Budapest. 32 (25). Predella panel from Arte della Lana Polyptych: S. Thomas Aquinas praying in church (companion to Barnard Castle, Rome Vatican, Siena). 1423–26. *Plate* 550.

Chantilly. 10. Side-panel from back of San Sepolcro polyptych: Marriage of S. Francis with Poverty (see Paris). 1437–44. [*Plate* 271.] *Plate* 557.

Cleveland (Ohio). 62.36. S. Francis worshipping Christ on the Cross.

Corridonia (Marche; former Mont'olmo, called Pàusola 1851 to 1931). S. FRANCESCO, SACRISTY. S. Francis. (?)

Cortona. GESÙ (MUSEO). Triptych: SS. Francis, Bernardino and Anthony of Padua (st.).

S. DOMENICO. Polyptych: Madonna and Child with two music-making Angels; SS. Nicholas and Michael; SS. John Baptist and Margaret; in pinnacles, the Lamb, Angel and Virgin of Annunciation. ca 1433–37.

Detroit (Mich.). 24.94, 46.56, 53.270. Three predella panels: Way to Calvary, Betrayal of Christ, Agony in the Garden. ca 1435–36.

El Paso (Texas). MUSEUM OF ART. 1961–6/5 (KRESS COLLECTION. K 1434). 'Pratt' portable altarpiece: Nativity and Last Judgement above; in wings, S. John Baptist, S. Bartholomew, Angel and Virgin of Annunciation (anonymous follower, same hand as Pienza and Siena n. 185).

Florence. BERENSON COLLECTION. Three panels from San Sepolcro polyptych: Blessed Ranieri, S. John Baptist (from front); Ecstasy of S. Francis, with Poverty, Humility and Chastity above, Lust, Pride and Avarice below (from back) (see Paris). 1437–44. *Plates 556, 557, 618–a.*

CONTINI BONACOSSI COLLECTION. Polyptych from cathedral of Siena: 'Madonna of the Snow', enthroned, with two Angels crowning her, two Angels offering platters with snow, SS. Peter and Paul standing, SS. John Baptist and Francis kneeling beside her; in predella, Legend of the founding of S. Maria Maggiore in Rome (the Virgin appearing to the patrician Giovanni in his sleep, Snow-fall on the Esquiline hill (r.), Dream of Pope Liberius (r.), the Pope receives the patrician Giovanni (r.), the Pope lays the foundation of the church, the building of the church, Consecration of the church); in spandrels, SS. Catherine, Augustine, Matthew, Bartholomew, Dominic and Lucy. Pinnacle: missing (see Massa Carrara and New Haven). Sd. 1430/32. *Plates 554, 555.*

CONTE FILICAIA (EX). Madonna of Humility (r.).

Frankfurt a/M. 1003, 1004. Cassone panels: Rape of Helen, Arrival of Helen in Troy (st.).

Genoa. COSTA COLLECTION. Side-panel of polyptych (of Holy Sacrament?): S. Anthony Abbot (see Siena).

Grosseto. MUSEO DI ARTE SACRA. Central panel of polyptych (signed, lost, formerly in S. Francesco, Siena?): 'Madonna delle Ciliegie' (fr.). ca 1430–40.

The Hague. MEERMAN VAN WESTREENEN MUSEUM. Portable altarpiece: Madonna and Child with two female Saints and two Angels; S. Liberale; S. Lawrence; Angel and Virgin of Annunciation (follower).

Lille. 993. Fresco: Female head (fr.). (?)

London. 4757–4763. Seven panels from back of San Sepolcro polyptych: S. Francis gives his cloak to a poor nobleman and has a vision of the Celestial City; S. Francis renounces his inheritance; receives Stigmata; the Pope recognizes the Franciscan Rule; S. Francis pacifies the wolf of Gubbio; crosses the fire before the Sultan; S. Francis laid on the bier, with Monna Jacopa da Settesoli kissing his hand and the knight Jerome probing his Stigmata (see Paris). 1437/44. *Plate 557.*

1842. Fragment of fresco: Three heads of Angels. L.

Massa Marittima. PINACOTECA COMUNALE. Pinnacle: Angel of Annunciation (companion to New Haven).

Milan. LIVRAGHI COLLECTION. Two roundels: Angel and Virgin of Annunciation. (?)

Montpellier. 120. (See Paris, Musées Nationaux.)

Moscow. PUSHKIN MUSEUM. 1494, 1496. S. Stephen, S. Lawrence.*

New Haven (Conn.). YALE UNIVERSITY GALLERY, RABINOWITZ GIFT. Pinnacle: Virgin of Annunciation (companion to Massa Marittima).

New York. 43.98.1. The Journey of the Magi (fr., companion to Siena, Chigi). *Plate 551.*

    41.100.20. Madonna and Child with two Angels.

    MISS HELEN FRICK. Madonna of Humility crowned by two Angels. *Plate 553.* Fragment of portable altarpiece: Annunciation.

    R. LEHMAN COLLECTION. Annunciation.

    Fragment of wing of portable altarpiece: Virgin of Annunciation.

    Side-panels of portable altarpiece (companions to Berlin 63C?): S. Michael, S. Nicholas of Bari (close to Sassetta).

    MR AND MRS JACK LINSKY. (Formerly KRESS COLLECTION. K 330.) Predella panel: Joachim and the Angel.

Paris. LOUVRE. Three panels from front of San Sepolcro polyptych (companions to Berlin, Chantilly, Florence): Madonna and Child enthroned with Angels; S. John Evangelist; S. Anthony of Padua. 1437–44. *Plate 556.*

    R.F.1965.2. Predella panel from San Sepolcro polyptych: Blessed Ranieri delivers the poor from a Florentine prison.

    MUSÉES NATIONAUX, CAMPANA 37 (DEP. MONTPELLIER). Pinnacle: Crucifixion. E.

Pàusola (Marche). See Corridonia.

Perugia. DUOMO, FIRST PILLAR L. Fresco: S. Bernardino. (?)

Pienza. MUSEO DIOCESANO. Portable altarpiece: Madonna and Child with Redeemer, Angels and Prophets above; in wings, S. John Baptist, S. Catherine, Angel and Virgin of Annunciation (anonymous follower; same hand as El Paso and Siena 185).

Rome. VATICAN, PINACOTECA. 234. Predella panel from Arte della Lana polyptych of Holy Sacrament (companion to Barnard Castle, Budapest, Genoa and Siena): 'Bene scripsisti de me Thomas'. 1423–26.

    CONTE ALFONSO CASTELLI MIGNANELLI (EX). Madonna and Child. (?)

Siena. 87, 95. Pinnacle from Arte della Lana polyptych of Holy Sacrament: Elijah and Elisha. 1423–26.

    166, 167. Two predella panels from Arte della Lana polyptych: S. Anthony Abbot beaten by the Devils; Last Supper. 1423–26.

    168, 169. Pilasters from Arte della Lana polyptych: SS. Ansanus, Crescentius, Victor and Savinus; SS. Ambrose, Augustine, Jerome and Gregory. 1423–26.

    185. Madonna and Child crowned by Angels and Redeemer above (anonymous follower; same hand as El Paso and Pienza).

    325. Madonna of Humility crowned by Angels. Sd. L.

    PALAZZO CHIGI SARACINI. Adoration of Magi (fr.; companion to New York). *Plate 552.*

    Three fragments of painted Crucifix: Bust of mourning Virgin, Bust of mourning S. John Evangelist, S. Martin and the Beggar. doc. 1433.

PORTA ROMANA. Fresco: Coronation (finished by Sano di Pietro; Angels and Saints on canopy by Sassetta). Begun 1447. *Plate 558*.

Venice. CONTE VITTORIO CINI. Inv. 6325. 'Perriolat' Madonna and Child.

Washington (D.C.). 357 (KRESS COLLECTION. K 443). Madonna of Humility.

505, 506 (KRESS COLLECTION. K 1285A, B). Side-panels of portable altarpiece: S. Margaret, S. Apollonia (between Sassetta and Ambrosi).

Washington Crossing (Pa.). MRS F. JEWETT MATHER. Predella panel: Penitent S. Jerome (g.p.).

Zagreb. 22. Madonna of Humility crowned by two Angels.

Homeless. Centre panel of portable altarpiece: Madonna and Child with SS. Catherine, Margaret and two Angels; Crucifixion above (st., r.). *Plate 564*.

SCACCO

Cristoforo Scacco da Verona. Active in and around Naples at turn of the sixteenth century. Follower of Paduans, influenced by Antoniazzo Romano.

Capua. MUSEO CAMPANO. Altarpiece pieced together from fragments of polyptychs: upper register—SS. Helena and Constantine worship the Cross, between SS. Francis and Anthony of Padua; lower register—Madonna and Child enthroned with Joachim and Anne holding scrolls; on either side, S. Clare, S. Elizabeth. Sd and d. (below Madonna's throne) 1500.

Fondi. S. PIETRO (DUOMO), L. WALL. Triptych: Annunciation; SS. Honoratus and Maurus; in predella, Christ and Apostles. Sd and d. 1499. *Plate 1078*.

Triptych: Madonna and Child enthroned with Angels; reading S. Jerome, penitent S. Jerome (r.).

(Environs). MONTE SAN BIAGIO, S. GIOVANNI BATTISTA, APSE. Triptych: Mystic Marriage of S. Catherine; SS. John Evangelist and Baptist; in lunette, Dormition; in predella, Last Supper. Sd and d. 1500.

Greenville (S.C.). BOB JONES UNIVERSITY. Fragment of altarpiece: God the Father blessing.

Harewood House (Yorks.). EARL OF HAREWOOD (EX). 59. Full-length S. John Baptist in landscape.

London. MRS LLOYD GRISCOM. Madonna and Child enthroned (fr.; possibly from lost triptych, Sd and d. 1483, formerly at S. Francesco, Fondi). *Plate 1077*.

Naples. 62, 810. Triptych from Penta: Madonna and Child with Angels and Souls in Purgatory; SS. Benedict and John Baptist; SS. John Evangelist and (Romuald?); in predella, Christ and Apostles. Sd and d. 1493. *Plate 1079*.

63, 69. Fragmentary triptych from Itri: Madonna and Child; S. Francis, S. John Baptist; blessing God the Father.

64. Triptych: Coronation of Virgin; S. Mark, S. Julian. *Plate 1080*.

Nola. CHIESA DELL'ANNUNZIATA. Annunciation.

Salerno. s. PIETRO IN VINCOLI. S. Michael. *Plate* 1082.

Venice. CONTE VITTORIO CINI. Inv. 6305. 'Filangieri' triptych from Piedimonte d'Alife: Madonna and Child enthroned; SS. James and John Evangelist; SS. Mark and Thomas. Sd.

Vienna. LANCKORONSKI COLLECTION. Madonna and Child enthroned. L.

Homeless. Dead Christ with mourning Virgin and S. John Evangelist. *Plate* 1081.

SCARSELLINO

Ippolito Scarsella, Ferrara ca 1551–1620. Follower of Girolamo da Carpi, was strongly influenced in Venice by the late Titian, Paolo Veronese and the Bassano, at home by contemporary Bolognese.

Arezzo. PINACOTECA. Circumcision.

Avignon. 472 (Dep. from Louvre). S. Barbara.*

Baltimore (Md.). WALTERS ART GALLERY. 442. Adoration of Magi. Sd and d. on back 1618.

Barcelona. D. B. HERNÁNDEZ (EX). Assumption of the Virgin.

Bologna. F. MOLINARI PRADELLI. Holy Family with Infant S. John. E.* *Plate* 1979.
   NOVELLI COLLECTION. Story of S. John Evangelist.*

Brussels. 902 (DEPOT). 'Madonna di Reggio' (variants at Gualdo and Karlsruhe). E.

Budapest. 169. Mystic Marriage of S. Catherine with S. Joseph, S. Francis and kneeling Bishop.

Burghley House (Stamford). MARQUESS OF EXETER. 28. Madonna and Child with Infant S. John (variant of Leningrad). E. *Plate* 1983.
   429. Nativity. (?)

Dijon. MUSÉE MAGNIN. Madonna and Child with S. Anne.*

Dresden. 146, 147. Companion pictures: Flight into Egypt; the Carpenter's shop.
   148. Holy Family with S. Barbara and S. Carlo Borromeo 1615. *Plate* 1988.
   149. Madonna and Child with SS. Francis, Clare, Catherine of Siena and Anthony of Padua. (?)
   311. The three Maries at Sepulchre. (?)

Ferrara. Inv. 142. Marriage at Cana (from refectory of S. Benedetto). 1605.
   Inv. 197, 199. Antonio Ariosti, Virginia Ariosti (from predella of Madonna di Reggio) (r.).
   Inv. 198. Self-portrait. d. 1618.
   Inv. 200. Annunciation (from S. Andrea).
   Inv. 203. Immaculate Conception; all around, the fifteen Mysteries of the Rosary (joys and sorrows of the Virgin) and portrait busts of donors. L. (Framing pictures, destroyed 1944.)
   PALAZZO ARCIVESCOVILE, CAPPELLA. Agony in the Garden.*
   Adoration of Magi.*

Birth of Virgin, Annunciation, Assumption (from S. Crispino).*

S. BENEDETTO, L. TRANSEPT. Assumption of the Virgin. Destroyed 1944.

S. CHIARA DELLE CAPPUCCINE, HIGH ALTAR. The Capuchin nuns, worshipping the Host on the altar, have a vision of the Madonna and Child in Glory with S. Francis and S. Clare. ca 1609.

— R. ALTAR. Madonna with the Holy Children and SS. Elizabeth, Lucy and Anthony Abbot; in predella, Baptism of Christ, Beheading of Baptist.

CORPUS DOMINI, ORATORIO DEL MONASTERO. Crucifixion. d. 1600.*

S. DOMENICO, FOURTH CHAPEL L. Madonna and Child in Glory and SS. Paul, Francis and Lucy.

Vision of the dying Magdalen in wilderness. *Plate* 1978.

— FIFTH CHAPEL L. S. Carlo Borromeo in prayer. 1616.

— FIFTH CHAPEL R. Madonna in Glory and SS. Paul, Lucy and Francis. L.

Madonna in Glory and SS. Roch, Louis and Bertrand. L.

S. FRANCESCO, SIXTH ALTAR L. Assumption and female donor (after Girolamo da Carpi).

— SEVENTH ALTAR LEFT. Rest on Flight (r.).

S. GIOVANNI BATTISTA, ALTARE NEGRELLI (L. OF CHOIR). Beheading of S. John Baptist. (Lent to Istituto della Provvidenza.)

— ALTARE NIGRISOLI (R. OF CHOIR). Deposition. (Lent to Istituto della Provvidenza.)

S. MAURELIO, SECOND CHAPEL R. Rest of the Flight. L.

S. PAOLO, VAULT OF APSE. Fresco: Assumption of Elijah. Sd. 1592.

— ARCH OF CHOIR. Fresco: Madonna and six Carmelite Saints. Destroyed.

— THIRD CHAPEL L. Descent of the Holy Ghost.

— THIRD CHAPEL R. Birth of Baptist.

DUOMO, SAGRESTIA DEI CANONICI (dep. from Pinacoteca 109). SS. Lawrence and Francis with donor.

MASOTTI COLLECTION. 'Noli me Tangere' (from Cappella Riminaldi in S. Niccolò).

Florence. UFFIZI. 1374. Holy Family. E.

1382. Judgement of Paris.

PROF. R. LONGHI. Calling of Matthew.

SOLDI COLLECTION. Christ crowning S. Helena.

Glasgow. UNIVERSITY. 31. Birth of Virgin.

Gualdo (Ferrara). MAZZA COLLECTION. 'Madonna di Reggio' worshipped by SS. Catherine of Siena and Clare of Assisi (from right altar in suppressed church of S. Guglielmo, Ferrara).

Last Supper (from S. Guglielmo). 1605.

Hanover. 348–355. Eight Stories of Job, from frame of altarpiece in S. Giobbe, Ferrara: Job's prosperity; Banquet of his sons; God speaks to Satan; Loss of cattle; Destruction by fire; Attack by the Chaldaeans; Destruction of Job's house and his children; Job, poor and despised, still worships God. 1600.

Karlsruhe. 423. 'Madonna di Reggio' (variants at Brussels and Gualdo).

Leipzig. HARCK COLLECTION (EX). Holy Family and Saints.

Leipzig (contd.). PLATKY COLLECTION (EX). Venus mourning Adonis.

Le Mans. 1039. Madonna and Child in Glory, with SS. Jerome and Anthony of Padua.

Leningrad. 273. Madonna and Child with Infant S. John, and S. Joseph in back-
　　ground. E.

Le Puy. Inv. 826–17. Annunciation.

Linlathen (Dundee). COL. ERSKINE (EX). Adoration of Magi. *Plate 1985.*

Lisbon. 191. Two boys.

London. MOND COLLECTION (EX). Mystic Marriage of S. Catherine.

　　B. NICOLSON. Holy Family with Infant S. John. E.

　　JULIUS WEITZNER. Christ entering Jerusalem.

　　Virgin in Glory and the Founders of the Holy Orders.

Lucca. PINACOTECA. Nativity.

Madrid. BRERA. 344. Madonna seated in landscape and cuddling the Child. E.

Milan. 435. Virgin in Glory and Fathers of Church (from S. Bernardino, Ferrara).
　　808. Holy Family.

　　OSPEDALE MAGGIORE (formerly Castello 406). SS. Lucy, Margaret and Apollonia.
　　　E. (?)

　　BARGELLESI COLLECTION. Flagellation, Crowning with Thorns (from frame of
　　　Deposition in S. Giovanni Battista, Ferrara).

Modena. 157. Birth of Virgin. L.

　　203, 206, 208. Ceiling panels from the Palazzo dei Diamanti: Fame, Roman
　　　Emperor, Apollo. 1592–93.

　　209. Adoration of the Child (from S. Bartolomeo). L.

Nîmes. 483. Massacre of Innocents (version of Rome, Galleria Nazionale 948).

Paray-le-Monial. 221. Miracle of S. Anthony of Padua.

Paris. 1580. Mystic marriage of S. Catherine. E.

Parma. 37. Madonna and Child with S. Catherine. E.*

　　399. Madonna and the Holy Children in a landscape.

　　405. Holy Family.

　　998. Venus (r.).

Philadelphia (Pa.). J. G. JOHNSON COLLECTION. 255. Susanna and the Elders. E.
　　Plate 1977.

　　WILSTACH COLLECTION (EX). 278, 279, 280, 281. The four Evangelists.

Pieve di Cento. S. MARIA VERGINE. Birth of the Virgin.*

Prague. S. HERMANN (EX). Adoration of sleeping Christ Child with SS. Zacharias,
　　Elizabeth and Infant S. John.

Ravenna. S. MARIA IN PORTO, FOURTH ALTAR R. S. James chased from Temple.*

Rome. GALLERIA NAZIONALE (PALAZZO BARBERINI). 647. Pietà. E.

　　948. 'Barberini' Massacre of Innocents (dep. at Villa d'Este Tivoli; version at
　　　Nîmes).

　　1227. 'Noli me Tangere.' L.

　　10067. Augustus and the Sibyl. E.

　　42256. Raising of Lazarus (companion to Barberini 'Massacre'). L.

— (DONO SESTIERI). Agony in the Garden.

GALLERIA BARBERINI (EX). Vision of S. Francis. *Plate* 1986.

S. Simon Stock received in the Franciscan Order (companion to Rome, Colonna?).

GALLERIA BORGHESE. 169. Christ in the House of Simon.

212. Venus mourning Adonis.

209. Massacre of Innocents. ca 1600–10.

214. Venus and Endymion (Salmacis and Hermaphroditus). *Plate* 1981.

219. The toilet of Venus.

222. Holy Family with Infant S. John.

226. Christ on the way to Emmaus.

GALLERIA COLONNA. Inv. 2077. The Virgin gives the scapulary to S. Simon Stock (companion to Rome, Barberini?).

GALLERIA DORIA PAMPHILI, GROUND FLOOR STUDY. 72. The Flood.

GALLERIA PALLAVICINI, PALAZZO ROSPIGLIOSI. Joseph sold by his brothers.
Assumption of Enoch. *Plate* 1982.

MUSEO DI PALAZZO VENEZIA (DEPOT FROM BRERA, MILAN). Version of Barocci's 'Perdono di S. Francesco' at Urbino.

PINACOTECA CAPITOLINA. 8. Conversion of S. Paul.

9. 'Sacchetti' Adoration of Magi.

24. Flight into Egypt. *Plate* 1984.

25. 'Pio' Adoration of Magi.

185 (dep. Palazzo dei Conservatori). Birth of Virgin (s.).

PRINCIPE LADISLAO ODESCALCHI. Four Scenes from Life of Virgin: Annunciation to Joachim; Marriage of Virgin; Adoration of Magi; Christ taking leave of His Mother. ca 1595/1600.

E. PEDICONI. Adoration of the Christ Child.

VATICAN, PINACOTECA. 366. Visitation.

(Environs). MENTANA. F. ZERI. Disrobing of Christ.

Schleissheim. 1204 (from Mannheim). S. Joseph and Mary reading, while Jesus plays with Infant S. John.

Schloss Sebenstein. PRINCE LIECHTENSTEIN. 384. Nativity. E. Not traced, possibly identical with Holy Family in private collection, Swinemünde.

Siena. 551. Last Supper. (?)

Vienna. 453. Christ on the way to Calvary.

GALERIE S. LUKAS (EX). Ariadne.

Wiesbaden. 98. Rest on Flight into Egypt. (Not traced.)

York. 818. Augustus and the Sibyl. (?)

Homeless. Christ and the plague-stricken. *Plate* 1987.

Madonna and Child with Infant S. John. *Plate* 1980.

SCHIAVONE (Giorgio Chiulinovich)

Skradin (Dalmatia) ca 1433/36. Became disciple to Squarcione in Venice 1456 and was his assistant in Padua until 146(0?); then returned to Sebenic, went into business and died there 1504.

Amsterdam. 2158–DI. 'Regina Celi.' (?)
Baltimore (Md.). WALTERS ART GALLERY. 519. Madonna and Child seated on parapet.
    1026. Madonna and Child with two music-making Angels. Sd. *Plate 692.*
Bergamo. 177, 178. Side-panels of polyptych: SS. Jerome and Alexis.
Berlin. 1162. Centre-panel of Triptych from S. Francesco, Padua (side-panels at Padua): Madonna and Child enthroned with two Angels. Sd. *Plate 690.*
    KAUFMANN COLLECTION (EX). Madonna and Child seated on parapet (variant of Baltimore, r.).
Florence. MUSEO STIBBERT. 12717. So-called portrait of Cosmé Tura.
London. 630. Polyptych (from S. Nicola, Padua?): Madonna and Child enthroned, full-length SS. Anthony of Padua, Bernardino, John Baptist and Peter Martyr; upper register, half-length SS. Jerome, Catherine, Sebastian, Cecilia and Dead Christ upheld by Angels. Sd.
    904. Madonna and Child holding a pear (r.).
    GRAHAM COLLECTION (EX). Madonna and Child (st.).
Padua. DUOMO, SACRISTY. Side-panels to Berlin: SS. Francis and Anthony Abbot; SS. Louis and Prosdocimus. *Plate 690.*
Paris. MUSÉE JACQUEMART-ANDRÉ. 1030. Madonna and Child enthroned with SS. Peter Martyr and Anthony of Padua and two Angels. E.
    1040. Profile of man. Sd.
Turin. GALLERIA SABAUDA. 162. Madonna and Child with Putti. Sd. *Plate 691.*
Venice. MUSEO CORRER. 545. Madonna and Child before parapet (r.).

SEGNA DI BONAVENTURA

Sienese active 1298–1327. Pupil of Duccio, later influenced by Simone Martini. Father of Niccolò di Segna.

Angers. MUSÉE DES BEAUX-ARTS. Centre panel of polyptych: Last Judgement.
Arezzo. BADIA. Painted Crucifix. 13(19?).
Asciano. MUSEO D'ARTE SACRA. Madonna and Child.
Assisi. SACRO CONVENTO, PERKINS DONATION. 55. Left panel of polyptych: S. John Baptist (companion to New York).
Bibbiena. S. LORENZO, SACRISTY. Painted Crucifix.
Boston (Mass.). 15.952. Panel of polyptych: Head of S. Mary Magdalen (fr.).

Budapest. 14 (31). Left panel of polyptych: S. Lucy (companion to Portland S. Margaret by Niccolò di Segna).

16 (46). Fragment of a Coronation of the Virgin.

Castiglione Fiorentino. COLLEGIATA DI S. GIULIANO, L. TRANSEPT. Madonna and Child enthroned with six Angels, SS. John Baptist and Gregory (?) and four tiny donors ('Maestà'). Sd. *Plate* 47.

Florence. BONDI COLLECTION (EX). Madonna and Child enthroned, with SS. Bartholomew and Ansanus, and small Donor.

Grosseto. MUSEO DI ARTE SACRA. Madonna and Child from S. Maria della Misericordia (fr., st.).

Helsinki. ATENEUM. 1764. Left panel of polyptych: Half-length S. John Baptist.*

Honolulu. ACADEMY OF ARTS. 2977.1 (KRESS COLLECTION. K 3). Madonna and Child.

London. 567. Painted Crucifix. (?)

VISCOUNTESS LEE OF FAREHAM (EX). Madonna and Child with SS. Catherine and Dorothy; Annunciation; Christ on the way to Calvary and mounting the Cross.

Lucignano (Val di Chiana). MUSEO CIVICO. Madonna and Child enthroned worshipped by Monna Muccia (g.p.).

Lugano. THYSSEN COLLECTION (EX). Madonna and Child with bird.

Massa Marittima. DUOMO. Painted Crucifix.

Montalcino (Senese). MUSEO DIOCESANO. Polyptych from Compagnia di S. Antonio Abate: Madonna and Child, SS. Regina, Augustine, John Evangelist, Dominic.

Montecchio Senese. S. MARIA DELLA GROTTA. Madonna and Child (temporarily at Opera del Duomo, Siena) (r.). E.

Moscow. PUSHKIN MUSEUM. Painted Crucifix. Sd.

Munich. 9038. Panel of polyptych: S. Mary Magdalen.

New Haven (Conn.). 1871.10. Diptych: Madonna and Child enthroned with six Angels; Crucifixion (st.).

1959.15.17. Madonna enthroned, suckling the Child, and four small Saints (ex Platt and Rabinowitz). (?)

New York. 18.117.1. Portable altarpiece: Madonna and Child enthroned with six Angels and four Saints; below, four other Saints; in wings, five scenes of Passion (st.).

24.78. Fragmentary polyptych: Madonna and Child, S. Sylvester Gozzolini, S. Benedict; over centre panel, Christ with SS. Peter and Paul; over side-panels, two Apostles and two Angels (companion to Blumenthal and Assisi). Sd. *Plate* 48.

41.100.22. Panel of polyptych (companion to Assisi and to above): S. John Evangelist.

65.181.2 (A. AND A. LEHMAN BEQUEST). Pinnacle: Blessing Redeemer.

Palermo. CHIARAMONTE BORDONARO COLLECTION. 68. Madonna and Child. (?)

Pienza. S. FRANCESCO. Painted Crucifix.

Raleigh (N.C.). MUSEUM OF ART. GL.60.17.1. KRESS COLLECTION. K 1349. Centre panel
of polyptych: Madonna and Child.

Rome. HELBIG COLLECTION. Pinnacle: Virgin of Annunciation.

San Gimignano. CONSERVATORIO DI S. CHIARA. Madonna and Child with eight
Saints and Franciscan nun. (Still there?)

Siena. 40. Four panels of dismembered polyptych from Badia S. Salvatore at
Berardenga: Mourning Virgin (r.), S. John Evangelist (r.), S. Paul and S.
Bernard. Sd.

45. Central panel of polyptych: Madonna and Child; in spandrels, Prophets.
MUSEO DELL'OPERA DEL DUOMO. Centre panel of polyptych: Madonna and Child.
S. MARIA DEI SERVI, R. TRANSEPT, OVER SACRISTY DOOR. Madonna and Child.

Tyninghame (East Lothian). EARL OF HADDINGTON (EX). Madonna and Child.

Vienna. LANCKORONSKI COLLECTION. Madonna and Child.

Volterra. PALAZZO DEI PRIORI, PINACOTECA. Two panels of polyptych: S. Hugo, S.
Justus; in pinnacles, Prophets.

Homeless. Busts of three Saints.* *Plate 49.*

SIGNORELLI, Luca

*Cortona. 1450 (scarcely earlier) to 1523. Pupil of Piero della Francesca; influenced by
Antonio Pollajuolo, Perugino and Francesco di Giorgio.*

Altenburg. 138–142. Five predella panels: Agony in Garden, Flagellation, Crucifixion, Entombment, Resurrection (p.). L.

143–46. Four panels from pilasters of altarpiece: SS. Bernardino, Casilda, Clare,
Louis of Toulouse (companion to Carshalton?).

Amsterdam. 2199–DI. S. George and the Dragon (g.p.).

Arcevia (Ancona). S. MEDARDO, CHOIR. Polyptych: Madonna and Child enthroned;
SS. Sebastian, Medardus, Andrew, Roch; above, the Eternal blessing; SS.
Paul, John Baptist, Peter, James of Compostella; fourteen knee-length Saints
in pilasters; predella: Annunciation, Adoration of Magi, Flight into Egypt,
Massacre of Innocents. Sd. and d. 1507

Altarpiece: Baptism of Christ; for pilasters, see Antonio da Fabriano (?) and
Francesco di Gentile da Fabriano; predella: Birth of S. John Baptist, S. John
Baptist preaching, Reproach of Herod and Herodias, Dance of Salome,
Beheading of S. John Baptist (p.). 1508. *Plate 956.*

Arezzo. PINACOTECA. Madonna and Child in Glory with, below, David between
two Prophets, SS. Jerome, Donatus, Stephen and Nicholas presenting kneeling
Donor, above, the Eternal and two Angels (g.p.; predella at London n. 3946).
Commissioned 1519.

Altarpiece from Monastery of S. Margherita: Madonna and Child in Glory with SS. Mary Magdalen, Francis, Clare, Francis and four Angels (p.; predella in Duomo). 1518–19.

DUOMO, SACRISTY. Predella panels to altarpiece from Monastery of S. Margherita: Birth, Presentation and Marriage of the Virgin, S. Francis, S. Bernardino (p.). 1518–19.

S. FRANCESCO, CHAPEL R. OF CHOIR. Detached fresco from Casa da Monte near Gragnone: Annunciation. E.

Assisi. SACRO CONVENTO, F. M. PERKINS DONATION. 3. Bust of S. Jerome (fr.).

LADY BERKELY. Predella: Marriage of Virgin, Visitation, Adoration of Magi (st.). L.

Atlanta (Ga.). ART ASSOCIATION GALLERIES. 58.53–4 (KRESS COLLECTION. K 494, 499). Predella panels (from S. Niccolò at Cortona?): Birth of S. Nicholas; S. Nicholas returning young Adeodatus to his father's house. L.

Balcarres (Fife, Scotland). EARL OF CRAWFORD AND BALCARRES. Two predella panels: Angel appearing to Zacharias, Zacharias expelled from Temple, Meeting at the Golden Gate; Birth of S. John Baptist.

Baltimore (Md.). WALTERS ART GALLERY. 520. Announcing Angel (companion to Uccle?).

DR REULING (EX). Flagellation (st. version of Venice).

Bergamo. 521, 523. Roch, S. Sebastian (p.).

522. Madonna and Child (g.p.).

Berlin. 79. Side-Panels from Bichi Polyptych in S. Agostino, Siena: SS. Catherine, Mary Magdalen and kneeling Jerome; SS. Augustine, Catherine of Alexandria and kneeling Francis (central relief of S. Christopher now Louvre; see Dublin, Pollockshaws, Toledo, Williamstown). 1498.

79A. Pan and the Gods. Sd. (Destroyed 1945.) [*Plate 288.*]

79B. Tondo: Visitation with SS. Joachim, Joseph and Infant S. John. Sd.

79C. Male portrait. E. *Plate 949.*

Birmingham. BARBER INSTITUTE. Profile portrait of Niccolò Vitelli (companion to Florence, Berenson).

Alexander the Great on pedestal (with Griselda Master, q.v.). *Plate 904.*

Bologna. COLLEZIONI COMUNALI. Head of mourning Magdalen (fr.). (?)

Boston (Mass.). 22.697. Madonna and Child on parapet, with Angel. E.

Budapest. 64 (67). Tiberius Gracchus on pedestal (with Griselda Master). *Plate 907.*

Capesthorne Hall (Chelford, Cheshire). SIR WALTER BROMLEY DAVENPORT. Bearded old man with two women and another man (fr. of Deposition, possibly from S. Agostino at Matelica, 1504–05; companion to Connell and Padua?; version at Castiglione Fiorentino). *Plate 950.*

Carshalton (Surrey). REV. COURBOULD. Panel from pilaster of altarpiece (companion to Altenburg?): S. Anthony of Padua.

Castiglione Fiorentino (Val di Chiana). PIEVE (back of Collegiata), CAPPELLA BATTESIMALE (R.), L. WALL. Detached fresco: Mourning over Dead Christ (r.; version of Capesthorne Hall).

Città di Castello. 77. Martyrdom of S. Sebastian (from S. Domenico). Formerly dated on stone frame 1498.

81. Banner: S. John Baptist; on back: Baptism of Christ (p.).

85–90. Full-length SS. Michael, Lucy, John Baptist, Bernardino, Margaret, James (p.).

115. Madonna and Child crowning S. Cecilia, and seven other Saints (p.; pilasters, nn. 85–90; predella, New York, Chrysler).

Fragments of frescoes detached from Torre del Vescovo: S. Paul, Head of the Holy Child, Fragments of Candelabra. 1474.

Connell (Argyllshire). MRS JEAN NELSON. Man on ladder (fr. of Deposition; companion to Capesthorne Hall and Padua?)

Cortona. GESÙ (MUSEO). Assumption (g.p.). L.

Mourning over Dead Christ, Crucifixion and Resurrection in background; in predella: Agony in Garden, Last Supper, Betrayal of Judas and Flagellation. Formerly Sd and d. 1502.

Communion of the Apostles (p.; lost lunette; for predella, see Detroit and Rome). Sd and d. 1512.

Predella: Life of S. Benedict (r.).

Madonna and Child with SS. Michael, Anthony of Padua, Bernardino and Nicholas (p.).

Madonna and Child enthroned with SS. Francis, Anthony of Padua and two Saints; in tympanum, Eternal blessing (g.p.). L.

Adoration of Shepherds with three singing Angels above (from Chiesa del Gesù; p.). L.

Adoration of Shepherds (from S. Francesco; st.). L.

Immaculate Conception (st.). Commissioned 1521.

PALAZZONE, CONTE PASSERINI, CAPPELLA. Baptism of Christ and other frescoes (unfinished at artist's death) (p., r.).

S. DOMENICO. Madonna and Child in Glory, with two Angels and S. Dominic, a Bishop Saint with kneeling Giovanni Sernini as donor. d. 1515.

S. NICCOLÒ. SS. Anthony of Padua, Dominic, Francis, Nicholas, Michael, Jerome and three Angels adoring Dead Christ in Tomb; on back: Madonna and Child enthroned between SS. Peter and Paul (companion to Atlanta?; p.). L.

— L. WALL. Fresco: Madonna and Child with Saints (r.; st.). L.

Detroit (Mich.). 29.41–42. Two predella panels to Cortona Communion of Apostles: 'Noli me tangere'; Christ appearing to the Disciples (companions to Rome). 1512.

Dresden. 36, 37. Pilaster panels: Archangel with Tobias, S. Jerome, S. Bernardino; S. Bernardus, S. Onuphrius, S. Dorothy (st.).

Dublin. 266. Predella panel from Bichi Polyptych in S. Agostino at Siena (see Berlin): Feast in the House of Levi. 1498.

Florence. PITTI. 355. Tondo: Holy Family with S. Catherine.

UFFIZI. 502. Madonna and Child with nudes in background, in tondo; above, two

Prophets in roundels and bust of S. John Baptist in Shell (from Villa Medicea di Castello).

1605. Tondo di Parte Guelfa: Holy Family.

1613. Predella from S. Lucia at Montepulciano: Annunciation, Nativity, Adoration of Magi. [*Plate* 289.]

3107. Monochrome: Allegory of Fertility and Abundance.

8368. Christ on Cross with kneeling Magdalen (from Convent of Annalena; sketch of S. Jerome on back). *Plates* 951, 952.

8369. Madonna and Child enthroned with SS. Augustine, Michael, Archangel Gabriel, Athanasius, Trinity above (from Church of Trinità at Cortona; predella 8371). L.

8371. Predella to 8369: Last Supper, Agony in Garden, Flagellation. L.

MUSEO HORNE. 51. Predella panel: S. Catherine seated on wheel. L.

GALLERIA CORSINI. Tondo: Madonna and Child with SS. Jerome and Bernard (later version at Castel di Poggio).

BERENSON COLLECTION. Profile portraits of Camillo and Vitellozzo Vitelli (companions to Birmingham).

CASTEL DI POGGIO, BADUEL COLLECTION (EX). Tondo: Madonna and Child with SS. Jerome and Bernard (later version of Corsini Tondo).

Foiano (Val di Chiana). COLLEGIATA, L. ALTAR. Coronation of the Virgin with four Angels and SS. Joseph, Mary Magdalen, Michael, John Evangelist, Martin, Leonard, Nicholas of Tolentino, Jerome and kneeling rettore Angelo Mazzarelli; predella: S. Martin and the Beggar, Baptism of S. Martin, Miracle of S. Martin, Funeral of S. Martin (st.). 1523.

Greenville (S.C.). BOB JONES UNIVERSITY. Predella panel: Flagellation.

Kansas City (Mo.). 52.1952. Predella panel: Flight into Egypt and Christ among Doctors (companion to Richmond and Washington 1401).

Liverpool. 2810. Madonna and Child against landscape (p.; variant of New York).

London. 910, 3929. Frescoes detached from Palazzo Petrucci at Siena: Triumph of Chastity; Coriolanus and his family (g.p.; two more frescoes 'Calumny of Apelles' and 'Festival of Pan', also signed by Signorelli, supposedly whitewashed *in situ*; see Pinturicchio and Genga at London, New York, Siena). Sd. 1509.

1128. Circumcision from S. Francesco at Volterra (Child entirely repainted by Sodoma). Sd. E.

1133. Adoration of the Shepherds (from S. Francesco at Città di Castello; g.p.). Sd. Commissioned 1496.

1776. Predella panel: Adoration of Shepherds.

1847. 'Montone' altarpiece: Madonna and Child in Glory with SS. Jerome, Sebastian, Catherine, Nicholas and two Angels (g.p.; predella at Brera, Milan 506). Sd and d. 1515.

2488. Holy Family (r.).

London (contd.). 3946. Predella to Arezzo altarpiece of 1519: Esther before Ahasuerus; SS. John Baptist and Jerome appearing to S. Augustine, Christ and S. Jerome appearing to Severus at Tours; Christ and S. Jerome appearing to Cyril, Bishop of Jerusalem. *Plate 955.*

VINCENT KORDA. Tondo: Madonna and Child with SS. Jerome, Anthony of Padua and Bernard (st.).

Loreto. BASILICA DELLA SANTA CASA, SAGRESTIA DELLA CURA (L.). Frescoes: vault, eight Angels, Evangelists and Church Fathers; walls, Doubting Thomas, Apostles; over door, Conversion of S. Paul; in window embrasure, male nude. E. [*Plate 285.*]

— OVER ARCHES OF NAVE. Frescoes: monochrome Prophets in roundels (r.).

Lucignano (Val di Chiana). MUSEO CIVICO. Lunette: S. Francis receiving Stigmata. Madonna and Child (from S. Francesco) (fr. of altarpiece which was probably crowned by the lunette with S. Francis receiving Stigmata; r.; p.).

Milan. BRERA. 476, 477. Flagellation; Madonna suckling the Child with Cherubs (from S. Maria del Mercato at Fabriano). Sd. E. *Plate 947.*

505. Madonna and Child enthroned with SS. Simon, Judas, Francis and Bonaventura (from S. Francesco, Arcevia). Sd and d. 1508.

506. Predella to 'Montone' altarpiece, London 1847: S. Christine and the idols, Prefect Urbanus has her whipped, S. Christine tied to a wheel and roasted, S. Christine thrown into the lake with a millstone tied to her neck, An Angel brings her a wreath and makes her float on the millstone, Collapse of Apollo's statue, S. Christine thrown into an oven, Two archers shoot S. Christine (g.p.). 1515.

POLDI-PEZZOLI. 473. 'Fides' (with Griselda Master).

Montecassino. BADIA. Adoration of the Shepherds (st.). L.

Monteoliveto Maggiore (Siena). ABBAZIA, CHIOSTRO GRANDE, WEST SIDE. Frescoes: God punishing Fiorenzo; S. Benedict converting the inhabitants of Montecassino; S. Benedict exorcising the devil upon the Stone; S. Benedict resuscitating a monk killed by the falling of a wall; S. Benedict reproaching two monks who had banqueted; S. Benedict reproving the brother of the monk Valerian for his violated fast; S. Benedict discovering the deceit of Totila; S. Benedict welcomes Totila; Fresco damaged by opening of door: S. Benedict blessing (and healing?) (fr.); in lunette, Consecration of a Monk (fr.). 1497–99.

Montepulciano. S. LUCIA, R. CHAPEL. Centre panel of polyptych: Madonna and Child (r.; predella in Florence, Uffizi?).

Morra (Città di Castello). S. CRESCENTINO. Frescoes: in niche over altar, Eternal blessing and two Angels; below, Hermit Saint and Magdalen (r.); walls— Flagellation, Crucifixion (p.), Madonna di Loreto (p.), Madonna of Mercy (p.), Agony in the Garden (r.). After 1507.

Munich. 7931. Tondo: Madonna and Child in landscape with naked youth.

Naples. GALLERIA NAZIONALE (CAPODIMONTE). Nativity (from Palazzo Reale).

New Haven (Conn.). 1871.69. Adoration of Magi. L.

New York. 29.164. Assumption of Virgin with SS. Michael and Benedict, six Angels and four Cherubim.

49.7.13. Madonna and Child (variant at Liverpool).

CHRYSLER COLLECTION. Predella panels to Città di Castello 115: Story of SS. Cecilia, Valerian and Tiburtius (formerly Mancini and Lanz; p.). L.

North Mimms (Herts.). MRS WALTER BURNS. Lunette: Coronation of Virgin (r.). 1508.

Orvieto. DUOMO, CAPPELLA DI S. BRIZIO. Frescoes: in six sections of vault—Angels, Apostles, Patriarchs, Church Fathers, Martyrs, Virgins (two quarts of vault with Judging Christ and Prophets by Angelico and Benozzo, 1447); Entrance wall—The End of the World; left wall—the Antichrist, the Blessed; Altar wall—Paradise, Hell; in embrasure of large window, two music-making Angels, SS. Brizio and Constant; in embrasure of small windows, roundels with Raphael and Tobias, Gabriel, Michael weighing Souls, Michael defeating Satan; right wall—the Damned, Resurrection of the Bodies; in niche, Mourning over dead Christ with SS. Piero Parenzo and Faustinus; Dado—Grotteschi and grisailles with poets, philosophers and scenes from their poems (Homer, Empedocles, Orpheus?, Horace, Lucan, Ovid, Virgil, Dante). 1499–1503. [*Plate 286.*] *Plate 953.*

— OPERA. Frescoed tile: Busts of Signorelli and Niccolò Franchi. d. 1503.

S. ROCCO, R. WALL. Fresco: S. Mary of Egypt.

Oxford. CHRIST CHURCH. 33. Madonna and Child with three Angels. E.

Padua. PROF. G. FIOCCO. Hanging head of dead Christ (fr., possibly companion to Capesthorne Hall and Connell).

Paris. 1525. Predella panel (to Perugia, Opera del Duomo?): Birth of Baptist.

1526. Adoration of Magi (from S. Agostino at Città di Castello).

1527. Ten male Figures (fr.).

1527A. Bust of S. Jerome.

MUSÉE JACQUEMART-ANDRÉ. 1043. Oval: Holy Family with Infant S. John.

Perugia. 203. Madonna and Child in Glory with SS. Francis, Lawrence, Michael, Sebastian, Anthony Abbot, Anthony of Padua; predella: S. Bernardino; Dream of Innocent III; Martyrdom of S. Lawrence; View of Pacciano; SS. Anthony and Paul Hermits; Miracle of the stingy man; Blessed Giacomo della Marca (st.). Sd and d. 1517.

OPERA DEL DUOMO. Madonna and Child enthroned with SS. Onuphrius, John Baptist, Lawrence, Herculanus (or Bishop Jacopo Vannucci) and three Angels. Formerly dated 1484. *Plate 948.*

Philadelphia (Pa.). JOHN G. JOHNSON COLLECTION. 135. The Magdalen reading.

136. Predella panel: Annunciation (from Città di Castello).

137. Adoration of Shepherds.

138. Head of young Man.

Pollockshaws (Scotland). POLLOCK HOUSE, MRS JOHN MAXWELL-MACDONALD. Predella panel from Bichi Polyptych in S. Agostino, Siena: Mourning over Dead Christ (see Berlin). 1498.

Richmond (Va.). 54.193. Predella panel (to Volterra Annunciation?): Presentation of Virgin (companion to Kansas City and Washington 1401; formerly at Kassel).

Rome. MUSEO DI CASTEL S. ANGELO, CONTINI COLLECTION. Madonna and Child in Glory with SS. Peter, Benedict, Lawrence, Paul and two Angels; predella: Christ giving Keys to S. Peter; Birth of S. John Baptist; Baptism of Christ; Feast of Herod; Doubting S. Thomas (g.p.). L.

PALAZZO ROSPIGLIOSI, PALLAVICINI COLLECTION. Madonna and Child with S. Jerome and Infant S. John.

VATICAN, SISTINE CHAPEL. Fresco: Last Days of Moses (with Bartolomeo della Gatta). 1482. *Plate 941.*

CONTE L. VITETTI. Two predella panels to Cortona Communion of Apostles: Christ on the way to Emmaus; Supper at Emmaus (companions to Detroit). 1512.

San Sepolcro. MUSEO CIVICO. Standard (from Confraternity of S. Antonio Abate): Crucifixion; on back: SS. Anthony Abbot and Eloy with four kneeling members of Confraternity.

Sinaia (Rumania). CASTLE OF PELES. Predella panels: Dominican monk; Abraham and the Angels; Stoning of S. Stephen.

Sinalunga (Val di Chiana). S. CROCE. Marriage of the Virgin (st.). L.

Stockholm. UNIVERSITY GALLERY. 107. Madonna and Child with Infant S. John (st.). L.

Toledo (Ohio). MUSEUM OF ART. Two naked men; woman with child and naked man (frs. of Baptism, from Bichi Polyptych in S. Agostino at Siena; see Berlin). 1498. [*Plate 287.*]

Turin. GALLERIA SABAUDA. GUALINO COLLECTION. Nativity.

Uccle (Belgium). VAN GELDER. Virgin of Annunciation (g.p.; companion to Baltimore?).

Umbertide (Perugia). S. CROCE. Deposition; in predella, Story of the True Cross. Sd and d. 1516.

Urbino. GALLERIA NAZIONALE DELLE MARCHE. Banner from S. Spirito: Crucifixion; Pentecost. Commissioned in 1494; painted probably several years later.

Venice. CA' D'ORO, ROOM X. Flagellation (p.).

CONTE VITTORIO CINI. Inv. 6499. 'Villamarina' Madonna and Child. E.

Vienna. LANCKORONSKI (EX). Tondo: Madonna and Child with six Saints (st.).

Volterra. GALLERIA COMUNALE. Madonna and Child enthroned with SS. Augustine, John Baptist, Anthony of Padua, Francis, Peter, Jerome and two Angels (from Oratorio di S. Antonio alla Ripa). Sd. and d. 1491.

Annunciation (from Oratorio di S. Carlo near Duomo; predella at Kansas City, Richmond, Washington?). Sd and d. 1491.

PALAZZO DEL COMUNE, SALA DELLA GIUNTA. Fresco detached from stairway: S. Jerome. d. 1491.

Washington (D.C.). 782 (KRESS COLLECTION. K 1400). Eunustus of Tanagra (with Griselda Master, see there). *Plate* 909.

1154 (KRESS COLLECTION. K 1566). Crucifixion (fr.).

1401 (KRESS COLLECTION. K 2123). Predella panel (to Volterra Annunciation?): Marriage of Virgin (formerly Kassel; companion to Kansas City and Richmond).

1639 (KRESS COLLECTION. K 1657). Madonna and Child enthroned with two Evangelists, SS. Michael, S. Augustine and four Angels.

Williamstown (Mass.). STERLING AND FRANCINE CLARK ART INSTITUTE. Predella panel from Bichi Polyptych in S. Agostino, Siena: Martyrdom of S. Catherine (see Berlin). 1498.

Homeless. Resurrection. *Plate* 954.

SIMONE MARTINI

Sienese. Probably born 1284, died at Avignon 1344. Pupil of Duccio, slightly influenced by Giovanni Pisano and Giotto.

Altomonte (Cosenza). S. MARIA DELLA CONSOLAZIONE. Wing of diptych or portable altarpiece: S. Ladislas King of Hungary. Probably 1326. *Plate* 130.

Antwerp. 257–260. Four panels from a portable altarpiece: Angel and Virgin of Annunciation, Crucifixion, Deposition with kneeling Bishop Orsini (companions at Berlin and Paris, Louvre).

Assisi. S. FRANCESCO, LOWER CHURCH, CAPPELLA DI S. MARTINO. Frescoes. ENTRANCE ARCH: four pairs of full-length Saints: SS. Francis and Anthony of Padua, SS. Catherine and Mary Magdalen, SS. Louis of France and Louis of Toulouse, SS. Clare and Elizabeth of Hungary. CEILING: S. Martin raises a child to life, the Emperor Valentinian thrown down from his throne by a fire, Death of S. Martin, Funeral of S. Martin. WALLS: S. Martin shares his cloak with a beggar, sees Christ in a dream, is knighted, refuses to take up arms, meditates before saying Mass, the Mass of S. Martin, Cardinal da Montefiore offers the chapel to S. Martin. WINDOWS: eighteen busts of Saints; stained glass on Simone's design, with Christ, Virgin and Saints. [*Plate* 255.] *Plates* 122, 123.

— — R. TRANSEPT. Fresco: Five half-length Saints separated by twisted columns: SS. Francis, Louis of Toulouse, Clare, Elizabeth of Hungary (Louis of France; r.).

Avignon. NOTRE-DAME-DES-DOMS. Frescoes in portico: in tympanum above, Redeemer surrounded by six flying Angels; in lunette below, Madonna of Humility with two Angels and kneeling Cardinal Stefaneschi; heads of Angels in soffit of arch (r.). Probably 1341. *Plates* 132, 133.

Berlin. 1070A. Panel from portable altarpiece: Entombment (see Antwerp). *Plate* 134.

Birmingham. CITY ART GALLERY. P37′59. Bust of Apostle on octagonal panel (companion to Boston).

BARBER INSTITUTE. The mourning S. John Evangelist. d. 1320. *Plate* 120.

Boston (Mass.). 51.2397. Bust of Apostle on octagonal panel (companion to Birmingham).

GARDNER MUSEUM. Polyptych (from S. Francesco, Orvieto): Madonna and Child, SS. Paul, Lucy, Catherine, John Baptist; in pinnacles, Christ the Judge, two Angels blowing trumpets, two Angels carrying the instruments of the Passion. *Plate* 124.

Brussels. MLLE MICHÈLE STOCLET (EX). Panel of polyptych: Bust of S. James the Less (st.; companion to New York and Washington).

Right panel of diptych: Virgin of Annunciation.

Cambridge. FITZWILLIAM MUSEUM. 552. Three panels of polyptych (from S. Agostino at San Gimignano?): SS. Michael, Augustine and Ambrose; in pinnacles, Angels (g.p.; companions to Cologne and Homeless). ca 1325/30. *Plate* 125.

Cambridge (Mass.). FOGG ART MUSEUM. 1919.51. Pinnacle: Christ on the Cross.

Cologne. WALLRAF RICHARTZ MUSEUM. 880. Central panel of polyptych (from S. Agostino at San Gimignano?): Madonna of the goldfinch (g.p.; companion to Cambridge and Homeless). ca 1320–25. *Plate* 126.

Florence. UFFIZI. 451. Annunciation (central panel of triptych; wings by Lippo Memmi). d. 1333. [*Plate* 257.]

BERENSON COLLECTION. Two panels: S. Lucy, S. Catherine.

Leningrad. 1964. Right wing of diptych: 'Stroganoff' Virgin of Annunciation (companion to Washington).

Liverpool. 2787. Christ returning from the Temple. Sd and d. 1342. *Plate* 131.

London. COURTAULD INSTITUTE GALLERIES, LEE OF FAREHAM COLLECTION. Predella panel: Christ on the Cross worshipped by a monk, a woman and a child. E.

Lucignano d'Arbia. PIEVE. (Deposited at Siena Pinacoteca.)

Massa Marittima. DUOMO, CHAPEL L. OF CHOIR. Fragment of a 'Maestà': front, Madonna enthroned; on back, Scenes from the Passion. (Assisting Duccio?) Not finished in 1316.

Milan. BIBLIOTECA AMBROSIANA. Illuminated frontispiece of Codex Virgilianus which belonged to Petrarch. 1340–44. *Plate* 135.

Moscow. PUSHKIN MUSEUM. 220, 222. Side-panels of polyptych: S. Mary Magdalen, S. Augustine. *Plates* 117–118.

Naples. 32. Bust of the Redeemer.

34. S. Louis of Toulouse enthroned crowned by Angels and crowning his brother Robert King of Naples; in predella, Louis, followed by Franciscan Monks, refuses the bishop's mitre; Louis leaves the convent of Aracoeli and is made bishop of Toulouse by Pope Boniface VIII; Louis feeds the poor; Funeral of Louis; Louis appears to a man who holds up his image and raises a child to life (from the Franciscan Convent of S. Lorenzo Maggiore). Sd; 1317. [*Plate* 256.]

New York. 43.98. 9–12. Four panels of polyptych: Busts of SS. Bartholomew, Thomas, Matthias and Andrew (st.; companions to Brussels, Lehman and Washington).

ROBERT LEHMAN. Panel of polyptych: Bust of S. Philip (st.; companion to panels above).

Orvieto. OPERA DEL DUOMO. Five fragments of dismembered polyptych from the Dominican Convent: Madonna and Child, S. Paul (right panel), SS. Peter, Dominic and Mary Magdalen with the donor, Bishop Monaldeschi (left panels). Sd and d. 1320.

Central panel of polyptych from the Jesuit Church: Madonna and Child holding scroll; two roundels with Angels; in pinnacle, blessing Saviour and two Angels (companion to Ottawa).

Ottawa. 6430. Left panel of polyptych (from Jesuit church, Orvieto): S. Catherine with a sword (formerly Liechtenstein). *Plate* 128.

Paris. 1383. Panel from a portable altarpiece: Christ on the way to Golgotha (companion to Antwerp and Berlin).

VICOMTESSE DE NOAILLES. S. Bartholomew.

Pisa. MUSEO NAZIONALE DI S. MATTEO. Polyptych from S. Caterina. Centre panel: Madonna and Child with Gabriel, Michael and Redeemer; side-panels: SS. Dominic (Philip and James), Mary Magdalen (Taddeus and Simon), John Evangelist (Andrew and Peter), John Baptist (Paul and James the Less), Catherine (Thomas and Matthias), Peter Martyr (Matthew and Bartholomew). Pinnacles: Redeemer and six Prophets. Predella: SS. Gregory, Lucas, Stephen, Apollonia, Nicholas, Mary Magdalen, Agnes, Ambrose, Thomas Aquinas, Augustine, Ursula, Lawrence; in centre, Dead Christ between mourning Virgin and S. John. Sd; 1319.

S. CATERINA, CHOIR. Stained glass windows on Simone's design: God the Father, Annunciation, enthroned Saints, Virgin and Baptist.

Rome. VATICAN, ARCHIVIO CAPITOLARE DI S. PIETRO. Full-length SS. Peter and Paul (transferred on copper, r.).

— PINACOTECA. 165. Blessing Saviour.

San Casciano Val di Pesa. S. MARIA DELLA MISERICORDIA. Painted Crucifix.

Siena. 583. Madonna and Child. E. (?)

— DEP. FROM LUCIGNANO. Centre panel of polyptych: Madonna and Child. *Plate* 119.

PALAZZO PUBBLICO, SALA DEL MAPPAMONDO. Fresco: 'Maestà' [Madonna and Child enthroned surrounded by the four patron Saints of Siena (Savinus, Ansanus, Victor, Crescentius), eight other Saints (Peter, Paul; Evangelist, Baptist, Catherine, Magdalen, Agnes, Elizabeth of Hungary), the twelve Apostles, Michael and Gabriel and four other Angels; in frame, twenty roundels with busts of Redeemer, Evangelists, Saints and Prophets]. Sd and d. 1315. Restored by Simone himself in 1321. [*Plate* 253.] *Plate* 121.

Fresco: Guidoriccio da Fogliano on horseback. d. 1328. [*Plate* 254.]

Siena (contd.). S. AGOSTINO, CAPPELLA PICCOLOMINI, R. WALL. Triptych: Blessed Agostino Novello, four of his miracles and two Augustinian Saints in roundels. [*Plates 251–252.*] *Plate 129.*

Washington (D.C.). 327 (KRESS COLLECTION 405). Left wing of diptych: Angel of Annunciation (companion to Leningrad).

　　820–823 (KRESS COLLECTION 1350–1353). Four panels of polyptych: Busts of S. Matthew (p.), S. Simon (st.), S. James the Great (st.), Thaddeus (st.) (companions to Brussels and New York).

Homeless. Panel of polyptych: S. Catherine; in pinnacle, Angel (g.p.; companion to Cambridge and Cologne). *Plate 127.*

SIMONE MARTINI'S Close Imitators and Immediate Followers

Aix-en-Provence. 467, 468. Annunciation; Nativity (companion to New York, Lehman). (Avignonese follower.)

Arezzo. S. DOMENICO, CAPPELLA DRAGONCELLI, SOFFIT OF ARCHES. Frescoes: Busts of Evangelists in roundels (close to Barna and Andrea Vanni).

Assisi. PIAZZA DEL COMUNE, CORNER VIA PORTICA, TABERNACLE. Fresco: 'Madonna del Popolo' (fragment of a Maestà).

Boston (Mass.). 16.117. Christ on Cross with mourning Virgin and S. John Evangelist, both seated on ground.

　　51.738. Pinnacle: Bishop Saint holding three books.

Cleveland (Ohio). 52.110. 'Lederer' Madonna and Child (between Lippo Memmi and Ceccarelli).

Copenhagen. 1, 2. Side-panels to Florence, Berenson: S. Catherine, S. Vittore. *Plates 307, 309.*

Dublin (New Hampshire). MRS SAMUEL HALE. Centre panel of portable altarpiece: Madonna and Child with SS. Peter and Paul and Angels (fr., companion to Le Mans).*

Florence. BERENSON COLLECTION. Centre panel of polyptych: Madonna and Child enthroned with Michael, Gabriel, two Angels, two Cherubim; two Prophets in roundels above (companion to Copenhagen; same hand as Rome, Palazzo Venezia). *Plate 308.*

　　MUSEO HORNE. 58. Christ on Cross.

Hartford (Mass.). TRINITY COLLEGE (KRESS COLLECTION. K 1237). Right panel of polyptych: S. John Baptist; Winged Evangelist in pinnacle (companion to London, Courtauld).

Houston (Texas). MUSEUM OF ART. 44.566 (STRAUSS COLLECTION 2). Centre panel of polyptych: Madonna and Child holding bird. (Not to be confused with Florentine Master of Strauss Madonna.) *Plate 314.*

Le Mans. 286, 287. Side-panels of portable altarpiece: S. Catherine and Bishop Saint with Angel and Virgin of Annunciation above (companion to Dublin).

London. 4491, 4492. Side-panels to Rome, Palazzo Venezia: S. Mary Magdalen, S. Peter. *Plates* 311–312.

    COURTAULD INSTITUTE GALLERIES, GAMBIER PARRY COLLECTION. Left panel of polyptych: S. Peter as a Pope; Winged Evangelist in pinnacle (companion to Hartford).

    J. TAYLEUR (EX). Pinnacle: Dead Christ in Sepulchre.

New Haven (Conn.). 1946.12. Right panel of polyptych (possibly companion to Houston, 'Straus' Madonna): S. John Evangelist. *Plate* 315.

New York. ROBERT LEHMAN COLLECTION. Adoration of Magi (same hand as Aix). *Plate* 136.

    PERCY S. STRAUS (EX). Madonna and Child enthroned with two Angels, SS. Francis and Clare.

Paris. BIBLIOTHÈQUE NATIONALE. Fr. 9561. Illustrated Bible (same hand as Aix).

Rome. PALAZZO VENEZIA. Centre panel of polyptych: Madonna and Child holding scroll (companion to London 4491, 4492). *Plate* 310.

Siena. 108. Centre panel of polyptych from Spedale di S. Maria della Scala: Marriage of S. Catherine.

South Hadley (Mass.). MOUNT HOLYOKE COLLEGE. Madonna and Child (r.).

Tours. MUSÉE, LINET BQ. Diptych: Adoration of Magi, with Angel and Virgin of Annunciation above (close to Aix Master).

Worcester (Mass.). 1923.35. Side-panel of polyptych: S. Agnes. *Plate* 313.

SODOMA

Giovanni Antonio Bazzi da Vercelli, called il Sodoma. Vercelli 1477–Siena 1549. Pupil of Spanzotti but formed by Leonardo; influenced somewhat by Bergognone and Fra Bartolomeo, slightly by Signorelli, and more by Raphael. Spent most of his life at Siena.

Arcore (Monza). VITTADINI COLLECTION (EX). Holy Family with S. Mary Magdalen and Infant S. John.

Baltimore (Md.). WALTERS ART GALLERY. 522. Tondo: Holy Family with S. Elizabeth and Infant S. John.

Bergamo. 568. Fantastic portrait of the artist.

Berlin. 109. Charity. E. (Destroyed 1945.)

Budapest. 1161 (90). Predella panel: Flagellation. *Plate* 1537.

Buscot Park (Glos.). LORD FARINGDON. Madonna and Child blessing Infant S. John, with Raphael, Tobias and S. Francis.

    Madonna and Holy Children (formerly at Lockinge House).

Detroit (Mich.). 59.444. Holy Family with Infant S. John.

Florence. PITTI. 374. 'Ecce Homo.'

    1279. Banner for Confraternita di S. Sebastiano at Siena: front—Madonna

appearing to SS. Sigismund and Roch and to Brethren of S. Sebastiano; back
—Martyrdom of S. Sebastian. 1525–31.

UFFIZI. 738. Betrayal of Christ.

MONTEOLIVETO, FORMER REFECTORY. Fresco: Last Supper (fr., r.). *Plate* 1539.

Frankfurt a/M. 946. Portrait of lady.

Gosford House (Haddington, Scotland). EARL OF WEMYSS AND MARCH. Tondo:
Holy Family and Infant S. John.

Grosseto. MUSEO D'ARTE SACRA. Bierheads: Dead Christ; Madonna in Glory.

Hamburg. 742. Holy Family with Infant S. John.

Hanover. LANDESGALERIE. 368. Lucretia. E.

Harewood House (Yorks.). EARL OF HAREWOOD. S. Jerome in Wilderness.

London. 1128. Child in Circumcision by Signorelli.

 1144. S. Peter presenting Carthusian to Virgin and S. Catherine of Siena.

 1337. Head of Christ crowned with Thorns.

 3947. S. Jerome in Wilderness.

 4647. Adoration of Shepherds.

CAPT. HOLFORD (EX). Tondo: Holy Family with Infant S. John and two Angels.
E. *Plate* 1530.

Lucca. PINACOTECA. Christ carrying Cross (r.).

Milan. BRERA. 286. Madonna and Child with lamb. E. (?)

AMBROSIANA, BRIVIO BEQUEST. Tondo: Holy Family with S. Elizabeth and Infant
S. John (st.; another version at Baltimore).

CASTELLO. 283. S. Michael and Devil.

POLDI PEZZOLI. 576. Tondo; Madonna and Child with SS. John Baptist and
Catherine of Siena (r.).

TRECCANI COLLECTION. Holy Family with S. John Baptist.

Montalcino (Senese). MUSEO DIOCESANO. Banner of the Republic. ca 1501.

Monteoliveto (Senese). ABBAZIA, CHIOSTRO GRANDE. Frescoes 1505–8. EAST PORCH.
 1.—S Benedict leaves home and goes to study in Rome; 2—leaves the school;
 3—Miracle of the broken sieve; 4—S. Benedict takes the habit from S.
 Romano; 5—The broken bell; 6—The priest at the Easter Meal; 7—S. Benedict instructs the peasants; 8—overcomes temptation by throwing himself in
 the stinging nettles; 9—is elected abbot; 10—breaks the poisoned cup; 11—
 builds twelve monasteries.

— — SOUTH PORCH. Frescoes: 12—SS. Maurus and Placidus entrusted to S. Benedict; 13—S. Benedict frees a monk possessed by devils; 14—strikes water
 from top of mountain; 15—recovers scythe fallen in lake; 16—Maurus walks
 on waters to rescue Placidus from drowning; 17—S. Benedict changes a
 flask of wine into a snake; 18—Fiorenzo tries to poison S. Benedict; 19—
 Fiorenzo sends whores to monastery. *Plate* 1533.

— — WEST PORCH. Frescoes: 20–29 (by Riccio, Signorelli, destroyed through
 opening door); 30—S. Benedict predicts destruction of Montecassino.

— — NORTH PORCH. Frescoes: 31—S. Benedict obtains flour for his monks; 32

—appears in a dream, with the model of a monastery, to sleeping monks; 33
—excommunicates two nuns and absolves them after death; 34—puts Host
on the body of a monk which the earth refuses to take; 35—forgives a monk
who wanted to leave the monastery; 36—frees a peasant from his bonds.
Plates 1531–1532.

— Frescoes: Christ at Column; PASSAGE FROM CHIOSTRO GRANDE TO CHAPTER HOUSE.
Christ carrying Cross; S. Benedict gives the rule.

— STAIRCASE. Fresco: Coronation of Virgin (r.).

Montepulciano. 7. Holy Family and Infant S. John.

Munich. W.A.F. 1025. Holy Family. *Plate* 1535.
1073. Holy Family (variant of Turin 56).

Naples. 90. Resurrection. d. 1534. *Plate* 1545.

New York. 11.119 (EX). Venus and Mars caught by Vulcan (companion to Worcester).

Paris. 1681. Tondo Chigi Zondadari: Love and Chastity. (?)
MUSÉE JACQUEMART-ANDRÉ. 1021. S. Sebastian. E. (?)
DUC DE TRÉVISE. Lucretia. *Plate* 1538.

Philadelphia (Pa.). J. G. JOHNSON COLLECTION. 277. Predella: Adoration of Magi. E.
278. Madonna and Child in landscape. E.

Pienza (Environs). S. ANNA IN CAMPRENA, REFECTORY. Frescoes: end wall—Three
episodes of Multiplication of Loaves and Fishes; entrance wall—Madonna and
Child in lap of S. Anne, and two Olivetan monks, S. Benedict and six
monks, Pietà; long walls—frieze with busts of Saints and monochrome
scenes with Life of Virgin and S. Anne. 1503–4.

Pisa. B.P. VII, 19. Madonna and Child enthroned with SS. Mary Magdalen, John
Baptist, Peter, Sebastian, Joseph? and Catherine. 1542.
DUOMO, CHOIR. Entombment. 1540.
Sacrifice of Isaac. 1542.

Portland (Ore.). PORTLAND ART MUSEUM. 61.39 (KRESS COLLECTION. K 1059). Fr. of
altarpiece: S. Sebastian, S. Margaret and head of another Saint.

Princeton (N.J.). 35.55. Dead Christ upheld by Angels.

Rome. GALLERIA NAZIONALE (PALAZZO BARBERINI). 11478. Mystic Marriage of S.
Catherine.

— FROM PALAZZO VENEZIA. Front of cassone: Rape of Sabine women. ca 1508.
Plate 1534.

GALLERIA BORGHESE. 434. Leda (after Leonardo).
459. Holy Family.
462. Pietà.

FARNESINA, FIRST FLOOR, SALA DI ALESSANDRO. Frescoes: Marriage of Alexander and
Roxane; Family of Darius before Alexander (r.); Forge of Vulcan; Alexander
and Bucephalus (r.). [*Plate* 372.]

MARCHESE MISCIATTELLI. Madonna and Child with SS. Jerome and John Baptist
(st.).

Rome (contd.). CONTE L. VITETTI. Holy Family with S. Catherine of Siena (or Clare).*

S. MARIA MAGGIORE, CAPPELLA PAOLINA, SACRISTY. Way to Calvary. L.

S. MARIA DELL'ORTO. Pietà (r.). E.

VATICAN, STANZA DELLA SEGNATURA, CEILING. Frescoes: Putti holding Papal Arms; monochrome Subjects; arabesques framing in Raphael's Tondi. 1508.

San Gimignano. PALAZZO DEL PODESTÀ, LOGGIA. Fresco: Madonna and Child with Saints and Angels; Eternal in lunette (r.). 1513.

PALAZZO DEL POPOLO (PINACOTECA), TORRE. Fresco: S. Yves. 1507.

Sarasota (Fla.). RINGLING MUSEUM. Risen Christ.

Siena. 326. Bier-head: Madonna and Child with two Angels.

   327. Bier-head: Two Brethren adoring Cross.

   352. Detached fresco from S. Francesco: Christ at Column. 1514.

   354. Judith.

   357. S. Catherine of Siena reading with a skull.

   358. Sketch: Adoration of Magi.

   360. Bier-head: Madonna and Child with two Angels.

   361. Bier-head: Pietà.

   401, 443. Detached frescoes from Compagnia della Croce: Agony in the Garden; Christ in Limbo. ca 1525.

   413. Deposition. E.

   512. Tondo: Nativity with Infant S. John and Angel. E.

   610. Banner: Crucifixion.

CASA BAMBAGINI GALLETTI (VIA DI STALLOREGGI). Fresco on façade: Pietà.

PALAZZO PUBBLICO, GROUND FLOOR, UFFICIO DEL SEGRETARIO GENERALE. Fresco: Resurrection. 1535.

— — COURTYARD. Fresco: Two Putti and Angel holding shields.

— — SALA DI BICCHERNA. Fresco: Madonna and Child with SS. Michael, Galganus and Infant John. 1537.

— FIRST FLOOR, SALA DEL MAPPAMONDO. Frescoes: S. Victor, S. Ansanus, 1529; Blessed Bernardo Tolomei, 1534. *Plates* 1542–1543.

— — CAPPELLA. Holy Family with S. Leonard. L.

PIAZZA DEL CAMPO, CAPPELLA, ALTAR. Fresco: Madonna and Child with SS. Sebastian and Bernardino (r.). 1539.

PIAZZA TOLOMEI. Fresco: Holy Family with SS. John, Francis, Roch and Crispinus. 1530. Not traced.

PORTA PISPINI. Fresco: Adoration of Shepherds. d. 1531.

S. AGOSTINO, CAPPELLA PICCOLOMINI. Adoration of Magi. Before 1533. *Plate* 1544.

S. BERNARDINO, ORATORIO SUPERIORE. Frescoes: Presentation, Visitation, S. Louis of Toulouse, S. Francis of Assisi, Assumption (see also Pacchia and Beccafumi) 1518–32.

— CONTRADA DELLA TORRE, ORATORIO. Way to Calvary (r.).

S. DOMENICO, CAPPELLA DEL ROSARIO. Eternal, SS. Dominic, Sigismund, Catherine and Sebastian, round a Madonna by Francesco di Vannuccio.

— CAPPELLA DI S. CATERINA. Frescoes: Scenes from Life of S. Catherine of Siena; in soffits and pilasters, Putti, Prophets, Evangelists. 1526. *Plates 1540–1541.*

S. DONATO (FORMER S. MICHELE). Two Bierheads: Trinity, Madonna of Mercy; Trinity, Dead Christ upheld by Angels.

S. FRANCESCO, SACRISTY. Putto and Angels.

CONFRATERNITA DEI SS. GIOVANNINO E GENNARO. Bierheads: S. John Baptist, S. Bernardino, Pietà, Madonna and Child.

S. NICCOLÒ AL CARMINE, CAPPELLA DEL SACRAMENTO. Birth of Virgin.

S. SPIRITO, CAPPELLA DEGLI SPAGNUOLI. Altarpiece: in lunette, Madonna gives habit to S. Ildefonso, with SS. Lucy, Cecilia and two Angels; at sides, SS. Michael and Nicholas of Tolentino (centre panel now lost and replaced by an eighteenth-century S. Rosalia).

— WALL SURROUNDING ALTARPIECE. Frescoes: in lunette, S. James riding against Saracens; at sides, SS. Sebastian and Anthony Abbot (p.). 1530.

SANTUARIO CATERINIANO, ABOVE ALTAR. Fresco: Five Angels holding curtain (above, S. Catherine receiving Stigmata is by Pacchia).

SOCIETÀ ESECUTORI PIE DISPOSIZIONI. Holy Family with Infant S. John. *Plate 1536.*

(Environs). MONISTERO DI S. EUGENIO, L. WALL. Fresco: Way to Calvary.

Sinalunga (Val di Chiana). COLLEGIATA DI S. MARTINO. Madonna and Child with SS. Roch, Sigismund, Anthony Abbot, Sebastian and Infant John (predella, st.). L.

(Environs). ORATORIO DELLA FRATTA. Frescoes: Madonna and Child enthroned with SS. Michael, Raphael with Tobias, John Baptist, Catherine of Siena, two more Saints, and Angels; at sides, S. Jerome in the Wilderness, S. Francis receiving Stigmata.

Strasbourg. 244. Holy Family with Infant S. John and Angel.

Trequanda (Val di Chiana). COLLEGIATA DI S. PIETRO. Fresco: Ascension.

Turin. GALLERIA SABAUDA. 56. Holy Family. E.

59. Lucretia.

63. Madonna and Child with SS. Lucy, Catherine and John Evangelist. Probably 1511–12.

MUSEO CIVICO. Inv. 566. S. Catherine of Siena.

Ubeda (Andalusia). SAN SALVADOR, FOURTH CHAPEL R. Penitent Magdalen.

Vercelli. MUSEO BORGOGNA. Tondo: Holy Family with Angel and Infant S. John. E.

Vienna. 51. Holy Family with Infant S. John.

Washington (D.C.). 416 (KRESS COLLECTION. K 531). Madonna and Holy Children. E.

1155 (KRESS COLLECTION. K 1426). S. George and the Dragon. E. [*Plate 373.*]

Worcester (Mass.). 1925.120/122. Apollo and Daphne, Fall of Phaethon, Pan and Nymph. E. (Companion to New York.)

SOFONISBA see ANGUISSOLA

SOLARI or SOLARIO, Andrea, da Milano

Milan, ca 1465–1524. 'Andreas Mediolanensis' or 'de Solario'. Pupil perhaps of his brother, the sculptor Cristoforo, but formed under Alvise Vivarini; strongly influenced by Bellini, Antonello and Leonardo. Went to Normandy to paint in the Château de Gallion 1508/10.

Arcore (Monza). VITTADINI COLLECTION (EX). Head of Baptist on a platter (versions at Greenville, Locko Park, Milan, Paris).

Barnard Castle (Yorks.). BOWES MUSEUM. 42. S. Jerome in the Wilderness.

Bergamo. 300. 'Ecce Homo' behind parapet.

FRIZZONI COLLECTION (EX). Madonna and Child. E.

Berlin. EUGEN SCHWEITZER (EX). Madonna del Sonno. ca 1505. *Plate* 1440.

Boston (Mass.). 11.450. Venetian Senator. E.

LONGYEAR FOUNDATION. Holy Family.

Brescia. 148. Way to Calvary and worshipping Carthusian monk.

Budapest. BARON F. HATVANY. Lady with prayer-book. L. *Plate* 1434.

Columbia (S.C.). MUSEUM OF ART. 62.925 (KRESS COLLECTION. K 1374). Madonna suckling the Child (formerly Crespi and Pratt).

Dijon. T.9. 'Ecce Homo' (replica of Leipzig).

Dublin. 351. Bust of man with instruments.

Florence. GUALINO COLLECTION. Penitent S. Jerome (after Leonardo's in Vatican).

Greenville (S.C.). BOB JONES UNIVERSITY (EX MINNEAPOLIS ART INSTITUTE). Head of S. John Baptist on a platter. L.

Grenoble. Inv. 45 (cat. of 1911 n. 533). Way to Calvary. L.

Leipzig. Inv. 1660 (formerly Speck von Sternburg). 'Ecce Homo' (replicas at Dijon and Philadelphia). *Plate* 1435.

Locko Park (Derby). J. PACKE DRURY-LOWE (EX). Head of S. John Baptist on a platter.

London. 734. Portrait of Cristoforo Longoni. Sd and d. 1505. *Plate* 1438.

923. Portrait of Venetian Senator holding a pink. E. [*Plate* 376.]

2504. Madonna and Child.

Lugano. THYSSEN COLLECTION. 391. Bust of youth. E.

Milan. AMBROSIANA. Head of S. John Baptist on a platter.

Bust of penitent S. Jerome.

BRERA. 282. Portrait of youth.

283. Madonna of the pinks. E.

285. Holy Family with S. Jerome (from S. Pietro Martire in Murano). Sd and d. 1495. *Plate* 1432.

954. Wilderness with S. Jerome, S. Francis receiving Stigmata and other Saints. (?)

POLDI PEZZOLI. 602. Madonna suckling the Child.

636, 638. S. John Baptist and S. Anthony Abbot (for Cardinal Federico Sanseverino of Naples). ca 1512.

637. 'Ecce Homo.'

653, 657. S. John Baptist, S. Catherine. Sd. 1499.

658. Madonna of the Book (after Giovanni Bellini). E.

655. Rest on Flight. Sd and d. 1515. *Plate 1442.*

DUCA GALLARATI SCOTTI. Portrait of Chancellor Domenico Morone.
Head of S. John Baptist on a platter (version of Locko Park).

BENIGNO CRESPI (EX). 'Ecce Homo.'
Pietà.

S. MARIA DELLE GRAZIE, FORMER REFECTORY. Detached fresco from Convent of
Castellazzo near Milan: Copy of Leonardo's Last Supper.

Nantes. 160. Christ carrying the Cross.

Newbattle Abbey (Dalkeith, Scotland). MARQUESS OF LOTHIAN. 562. Bust of Christ.

New York. 22.16.12. 'Crespi' full-length blessing Redeemer.

32.100.81. Salome with the head of the Baptist (versions at Syon House and
Turin). Sd. *Plate 1433.*

Oxford. ASHMOLEAN MUSEUM. 410.* Mocking of Christ (formerly Allington Castle).

Paris. 1530. 'La Vierge au coussin vert.' Sd. [*Plate 377.*]

1531. Portrait of Charles d'Amboise (1460–1510).

1532. Crucifixion. Sd and d. 1503. *Plate 1437.*

1533. Head of S. John Baptist on a platter. Sd and d. 1507.

MUSÉES NATIONAUX. Annunciation. Sd and d. 1506. *Plate 1439.*

DUC D'ORLÉANS (EX). Salome receiving the head of S. John Baptist. *Plate 1436.*

Pavia (Environs). CERTOSA, R. TRANSEPT, SAGRESTIA NUOVA. Assumption (interrupted
by his death in 1524 and finished by Bernardino Campi in 1576).

Philadelphia (Pa.). MUSEUM OF ART, J. G. JOHNSON COLLECTION. 272. Madonna and
Child with donor and his family (r.). E.

274. 'Ecce Homo' (replica of Leipzig). Sd.

— WILSTACH COLLECTION (EX). 295. Christ at Column.

Rome. GALLERIA NAZIONALE (PALAZZO BARBERINI). Woman playing the lute.

GALLERIA BORGHESE. 461. Christ carrying the Cross. Sd and d. 1511.

Syon House (Middlesex). DUKE OF NORTHUMBERLAND. Salome receiving the head of
the Baptist. Sd.

Tongerloo. ABBAYE. Copy of Leonardo da Vinci's Last Supper, painted for Cardinal
Georges d'Amboise. 1506–7.

Turin. GALLERIA SABAUDA, GUALINO COLLECTION. 672. Salome receiving the head
of the Baptist. L.

Verona. DEPOT. Bust of man with large hat. (?)

Vienna. 82A. Salome receiving the head of S. John Baptist. L.

BARON OFENHEIM. Madonna suckling the Child (variant of Paris, Louvre, 1530).

Washington (D.C.). 1402 (KRESS COLLECTION. K 2061). Mourning over the dead
Christ (formerly Rossie Priory, Lord Kinnaird).

Worcester (Mass.). 1940.36. Madonna and Child (c.).

Zagreb. 124. Madonna and Child holding a rose. L.

Homeless. Bust of donor (fr. of altarpiece). *Plate* 1441.
Madonna and Child. *Plate* 1431.

LO SPAGNA

Giovanni di Pietro, called Lo Spagna. Died 1532–33. *Pupil and follower of Perugino, influenced by Raphael.*

Assisi. S. FRANCESCO, MUSEO. Madonna and Child enthroned with two Angels, SS. Catherine, Francis, Clare, Louis and two other Saints. d. 1516. *Plate* 1110.
> S. MARIA DEGLI ANGELI, CAPPELLA DEL TRANSITO. Frescoes: Saints and Blessed of the Franciscan Order.
> (Environs). See Rocchicciola.

Baltimore (Md.). WALTERS ART GALLERY. 526. Holy Family and Infant S. John.

Berkeley (Cal.). MISS LUCY SPRAGUE (EX). Fragments from pilasters of Todi Coronation (companions to Melchett Court, Todi and Paris): SS. Catherine, Bernardino of Feltre and John Capistrano. 1511.

Berlin-Ost. 150. 'Ancaiani' Adoration of Magi. Before 1503.

Bettona. COLLEGIATA (EX). S. Anne protecting Bettona, Madonna, Blessed Peter Hegles and S. Anthony of Padua.

Caen. 34. Marriage of Virgin from Cappella di S. Giuseppe in Perugia Cathedral (with Perugino).

Chicago (Ill.). 37.1008. S. Catherine of Siena.

Detroit (Mich.). RALPH H. BOOTH (EX). Madonna and Child.

Eggi (Spoleto). S. GIOVANNI BATTISTA. Frescoes: over apse, Annunciation; inside apse, Madonna and Child in Glory and Baptism of Christ with SS. Sebastian and Roch (at sides, SS. Jerome and James, st.). d. 1532.

Florence. PITTI. 499. Mystic Marriage of S. Catherine and SS. Francis and Anthony of Padua.

Gavelli (Spoleto). S. MICHELE ARCANGELO, APSE. Frescoes: triumphal arch—Eternal and Annunciation; soffit of arch, Holy Ghost and six Saints; inside apse, Coronation of Virgin, SS. Peter and Paul, S. Michael appears on Gargano (g.p.). Sd and d. 1518. *Plate* 1112.
> — CAPPELLA DI S. GIROLAMO (FIRST L.). Fresco: Madonna and Child in Glory and SS. Francis, Jerome and Anthony. d. 1523.
> — CAPPELLA DI S. SEBASTIANO (FOURTH L.). Fresco: Madonna and Child in Glory and SS. Sebastian, Catherine, Apollonia and John Baptist.

Indianapolis (Ind.). J. HERRON ART MUSEUM. 24.9. S. Jerome in landscape.

Locko Park (Derbys.). DRURY LOWE COLLECTION (EX). Madonna and Blessing Child with SS. Jerome, Nicholas of Tolentino, Catherine and Brizio (version of Spoleto fresco).

London. 1032. Agony in the Garden.

1812. Agony in the Garden (fr.; companion to Stafford House). (?)

WALLACE COLLECTION. 545. S. Mary of Egypt.

LORD ABERCONWAY. Eternal and S. Sebastian, Tobias and the Angel, and S. Roch receive the prayers of a Bishop Saint who wants them to protect his city from the plague.

Melchett Court (Romsey, Hants.). LORD MELCHETT (EX). Fragments of pilasters from Todi Coronation: SS. James of the Marches, Louis of France and Mary Magdalen (companions to Berkeley and Paris). 1511.

Mells (Frome, Somerset). EARL OF OXFORD AND ASQUITH. Knee-length monk in prayer.

Milan. POLDI PEZZOLI. 603. Madonna and Child with two Angels.

Montefalco. CÉLINE CAPPELLI COLLECTION (EX). Madonna and Child.

Narni. MUNICIPIO. Detached fresco: S. Francis receiving Stigmata. d. 1528.

Paris. 1539. Nativity (finished by Mariano di Ser Austerio). 1510.

1540. Madonna and Child.

1568–70. Predella to Todi Coronation: S. Francis receiving Stigmata, Dead Christ, S. Jerome in the Wilderness. 1511.

N. D'ESTAILLEUR (EX). Madonna and Child.

Perugia. 271. Madonna and Child with SS. John Baptist, Francis, Anthony and Jerome. (?)

273. Blessed Colomba of Rieti.

353. Detached fresco: S. Francis receiving Stigmata.

MONASTERO DELLA BEATA COLOMBA. Christ carrying Cross (unfinished). E.

Philadelphia (Pa.). J. G. JOHNSON COLLECTION. 146. S. Mary Magdalen (r.).

Rocchicciola (Rocca S. Angelo). S. FRANCESCO. Frescoed triptych: Madonna and Child, with Eternal above, and SS. Francis and Anthony of Padua at sides.

Rome. CAMPIDOGLIO, PINACOTECA. 111–120. Frescoes: Apollo and the nine Muses. (?)

VATICAN, PINACOTECA. 311. Madonna suckling the Child and SS. Mary Magdalen and Anthony of Padua.

316. Nativity called 'Madonna della Spineta'. E.

BARONE ALBERTO FASSINI (EX). Madonna and blessing Child in landscape. (?)

MARCHESE VISCONTI VENOSTA (EX). Panel from pilaster of altarpiece: S. Catherine.

Rovigo. 42. Madonna and Child.

San Diego (Cal.). FINE ARTS GALLERY. S. Jerome in the Wilderness.

San Giacomo di Spoleto. S. GIACOMO, APSE. Frescoes: Coronation of Virgin; below, S. James and two scenes of his Life (Rescue of the hanged pilgrim, Birds raised to life before the judge). d. 1526.

— TRIUMPHAL ARCH. Frescoes: Annunciation; below, SS. Mary Magdalen and Apollonia. 1526–7.

— NICHES OF CHOIR: L. (CAPPELLA DI S. ANTONIO). Madonna and Child in Glory and below SS. Peter, Anthony Abbot and Bartholomew (finished by Dono Doni and Bernardino d'Assisi). 1527–30.

San Giacomo di Spoleto. S. GIACOMO, NICHES OF CHOIR (contd.): R. (CAPPELLA DI S. SEBASTIANO). Frescoes: Madonna and Child in Glory and below SS. Gregory, Sebastian and Roch. d. 1527.

Spoleto. PALAZZO COMUNALE, PINACOTECA. 36. Detached fresco: Madonna and Child.

> 40. Fresco detached from Rocca: Charity, Justice and Pietà round arms of Pope Julius II.

> 43. Fresco detached from Rocca: Madonna and Child with SS. Jerome, Nicholas of Tolentino, Catherine and Brizio (version at Locko Park). 1514–16. *Plate* IIII.

> S. ANSANO, R. WALL, NEAR ENTRANCE. Fresco: Madonna and Child with two Angels (g.p.). Sd and d. 1518.

> (Environs). CLITUNNO, ORATORIO. Fresco: Madonna and Child in Glory and SS. Sebastian and Roch (g.p.). L.

Stafford House. DUKE OF SUTHERLAND (EX). Christ carrying the Cross (fr.; companion to London 1812). (?)

Terni. PINACOTECA. Fresco round wooden Crucifix: Mourning Virgin, Evangelist, Magdalen, S. Francis and two Angels (r.).

Todi. PINACOTECA. Coronation of Virgin with Angels, Prophets, Sibyls and twenty-five Saints below; in pilasters of frame, six small Saints (see also Berkeley and Melchett Court; predella panels in Paris). d. 1511. *Plate* 1109.

> Blessed Bernardino da Feltre.

Trevi. PALAZZO COMUNALE, PINACOTECA. Coronation of Virgin and Saints below, with view of Assisi; in predella, S. Martin and the Beggar, S. Francis receiving Stigmata (from Convent of Minori Osservanti) (g.p.). 1522.

> 63, 66. S. Catherine, S. Cecilia (from Madonna delle Lacrime). L.

> MADONNA DELLE LACRIME, L. TRANSEPT, CHAPEL. Frescoes: end wall—in lunette, S. Augustine and saintly Monk; below, Entombment with S. Francis (and view of Foligno); side walls—S. Ubaldus, S. Joseph; above entrance, Name of Jesus and Prophets (g.p.). d. 1520.

> S. MARTINO, CHAPEL OUTSIDE. Fresco: Madonna and Child appearing to SS. Jerome, John Baptist, Francis and Anthony of Padua (with view of Foligno). d. 1512.

Tucson (Ariz.). ST. PHILIP'S IN THE HILLS (KRESS COLLECTION. K 1186). Dead Christ with mourning Virgin and Evangelist. L.

Vienna. TUCHER COLLECTION (EX). Madonna and Child.

Visso (Macerata). COLLEGIATA DI S. MARIA, FIRST ALTAR L. Detached fresco from S. Agostino: in top lunette, God the Father and Cherubim; two roundels with Angel and Virgin of Annunciation; lower lunette, Madonna and Child with Angels, and below SS. John Evangelist, Francis, Tobias and the Angel, Anthony of Padua and Bishop Saint.

SPANZOTTI, Gian Martino

School of Vercelli. Documented 1480 to 1526. Mainly active at Casale Monferrato, developed under direct or indirect influence of Macrino d'Alba, Foppa, Leonardo and the Franco-Flemings. Taught Sodoma 1490–97.

Bianzè. CHIESA DELLA MISERICORDIA. Triptych: Pietà, S. Anthony Abbot, S. Lucy (st.).

Budapest. 1324. Assumption. d. 1500. *Plate 1240.*
   4266 (P.85). Pietà. *Plate 1228.*

Conzano Monferrato. PARISH CHURCH. Side-panels of polyptych: Half-length S. Stephen, S. Mauritius, full-length S. Lucy, S. Catherine (st.).

Denver (Col.). MUSEUM OF ART. E-IT-18-XVI-946 (KRESS COLLECTION. K 70). Christ in the house of Simon (with Defendente; companion to Turin 213, 217, 218?).

Florence. CONTINI BONACOSSI COLLECTION. Adoration of Magi from Sommariva Perno (with Defendente?).

Genoa. MARCHESE MEDICI DEL VASCELLO. Baptism (st.v. of Turin, Duomo).

Ivrea. S. BERNARDINO. Frescoes: upper row—Annunciation, Nativity, Adoration of Magi, Flight into Egypt, Christ among Doctors, Baptism, Raising of Lazarus, Entry into Jerusalem; centre of middle and lower row—large Crucifixion; on either side, twelve Scenes of the Passion—Last Supper, Washing of Feet, Agony in the Garden, Betrayal of Christ, Christ before Caiaphas, Christ before Pilate, Flagellation, 'Ecce Homo', Way to Calvary, Deposition, Resurrection, Ascension; in spandrels of arches—Expulsion from Eden, Last Judgement, Hell, Redemption; on piers, S. Bernardino, Dead Christ in Sepulchre. ca 1485–95. *Plates 1217–1220.*

London. 1200, 1201. Panels of polyptych, companions to Milan 718, 719 and to Turin, Accademia: Half-length SS Nicholas of Tolentino and John Baptist; half-length SS Peter Martyr and Bishop (with Defendente?).
   COURTAULD INSTITUTE GALLERIES, LEE OF FAREHAM COLLECTION. 88. Madonna and Child enthroned.

Milan. See under Defendente.

Rivarolo Canavese. S. FRANCESCO. Fresco: Adoration of the Child with the four Church Fathers and two Bishops. *Plate 1237.*

Rome. CASTEL S. ANGELO, MUSEO. Pietà. L.

Sommariva Perno. SANTUARIO DELLA MADONNA DEL TAVOLETO. Pietà and blessing Saviour above.

Strasbourg. 258. Version of Leonardo's Last Supper. (?)

Stresa. ISTITUTO ROSMINI. Side-panels of triptych: SS. Francis, Sebastian, John Baptist and Anthony Abbot with male donor; SS. Barbara, Catherine, Mary Magdalen and Apollonia. (?)

Trino Vercellese. S. DOMENICO. Copy of Turin, Inv. 373.

Turin. ACCADEMIA ALBERTINA. Centre panel of triptych: Madonna enthroned (companion to Museo Civico, Inv. 487). L.

Turin (contd.). GALLERIA SABAUDA. Inv. 28 bis. Predella panel: Epiphany.
29 bis: Triptych: Madonna and Child; S. Ubaldus; S. Sebastian. Sd. *Plate* 1216.
MUSEO CIVICO. Inv. 213. Fragment of octagonal panel, companion to 217, 218:
Christ and the Doctors. Sd. Before 1513 (see Giovenone, Avignon). *Plate* 1221.
Inv. 217, 218. Octagonal panels, companions to 213: Marriage of the Virgin;
Landing of Mary Magdalen at Marseilles. Before 1513. *Plate* 1223.
Inv. 239. Predella panel: Martyrdom of S. Sebastian.
Inv. 276. Madonna and Child with S. Anne (fr.).
Inv. 357. Female Saint. (?)
Inv. 373. Nativity from Trino Vercellese.
Inv. 404. Dead Christ in sepulchre with four Angels.
Inv. 487. Side-panel to Madonna in the Accademia Albertina: S. Catherine. L.
S. DOMENICO, FIRST ALTAR L. (BEHIND MODERN ALTARPIECE). Fresco: S. Nicholas
distributing alms to two children.
S. GIOVANNI BATTISTA (DUOMO), SECOND CHAPEL R. Madonna enthroned suckling
the Child and two music-making Putti; full-length SS. Ursus and Crispinus;
half-length SS. Crispinianus and Tebaldus; in soffit above, Annunciation,
Visitation, Nativity; in predella, Agony in the Garden, Betrayal of Christ,
Flagellation, Mocking of Christ, Way to Calvary (with Defendente?).
— Eighteen panels (from a cupboard?) in framework of altarpiece mentioned
above: Birth of SS. Crispinus and Crispinianus; They receive their mother's
blessing; They worship at an altar; They make and sell shoes; They are baptized; They cast down an idol They are led to a judge; They are beaten with
sticks; They pray in prison; They are tied round a tree and tortured on hands
and feet with burning irons; They are scourged and skinned; They are thrown
into a river; They are thrown into a furnace; they are thrown into a cauldron
of boiling tar; Beheading of S. Crispin; Beheading of S. Crispinianus; Burial
of S. Crispin; Burial of S. Crispinianus. (?) *Plates* 1225–1227.
— SACRISTY. Baptism. 1508–10. *Plate* 1224.
Vercelli. MUSEO BORGOGNA. Triptych from Conzano: Nativity, SS. Francis and
George; SS. Clare and Augustine (st.).
Washington Crossing (Pa.). MRS F. J. MATHER. Predella panel: Nativity.

SQUARCIONE, Francesco

*Founder of the Paduan School. 1394–1474. Developed under influence of the Antique and
of the earliest Quattrocento Florentines. Probably more organizer than painter.*

Berlin. 27A. Madonna and Child. Sd. *Plate* 688.
Padua. Inv. 399. Polyptych from Cappella Lion de Lazzara ai Carmini; SS. Jerome,
Lucy, John Baptist, Anthony Abbot and Justina (s.). Between 1449 and 1452.
Plate 689.

Inv. 402. Fresco: Madonna and Child (fr.).

s. FRANCESCO GRANDE, CONVENT. Monochrome frescoes in twenty-four lunettes of Portico, with Scenes from Life of S. Francis (other Franciscan Stories in rooms of Convent, lost): (1), (2), (3)—lost; (4) Dialogue between S. Francis and Crucifix in S. Damiano (almost entirely lost); (5) Imprisonment of S. Francis; (6) S. Francis renounces his inheritance; (7) S. Francis and the Lepers; (8) Clothing of S. Francis' first Disciples; (9) Vision of Pope Innocent III; (10) Recognition of the Franciscan Rule; (11) S. Francis appears to his Disciples; (12) Vision of Brother Pacifico; (13) S. Francis appears to S. Anthony of Padua; (14) S. Francis praying in his cell and tempted by the Devil; (15) S. Francis receiving S. Clare and her Nuns; (16) Institution of the Third Franciscan Order; (17) Vision of the Virgin?; (18) Unidentified Subject; (19) The Trial of the Fire; (20) S. Francis refuses the riches offered by the Sultan; (21) Mystic Marriage of S. Francis and Poverty; (22) S. Francis receiving Stigmata; (23) S. Francis blesses the Monks; (24) Funeral of S. Francis. (r.). ca 1460/5.

Rome. CONTE LEONARDO VITETTI. Madonna and Child with SS. Roch and Anthony Abbot.

STEFANO DI GIOVANNI see SASSETTA

STEFANO DA ZEVIO

Verona. 1374–1451. Influenced by Gentile da Fabriano, Pisanello and by his elder Franco-Flemish contemporaries [see also under North Italian Gothic].

Illasi (Verona). PARISH CHURCH, SACRISTY. Detached fresco: Madonna and Child with six singing Angels and peacock (r.).

Mantua. s. FRANCESCO, CAPPELLA RAMA. Detached fresco: S. Francis receiving Stigmata (fr.). ca 1420–30.

Milan. BRERA. 223. Adoration of Magi. Sd and d. 1435. *Plate 538.*

Rome. MUSEO DI PALAZZO VENEZIA. Madonna and Child.

PALAZZO COLONNA. 221. Madonna and Child with ten Angels. *Plate 536.*

Verona. 359. Madonna and Child with S. Catherine in rose garden.

1087. Detached fresco from SS. Cosma e Damiano: Madonna and Child with Angels and donor (fr.).

1203. Detached fresco: Angel (fr.; r.).

s. ANASTASIA, FIFTH ALTAR L. Fresco in right niche: S. Dominic and Angels (fr.).

s. EUFEMIA. Detached fresco: S. Augustine enthroned with SS. Euphemia and Nicholas presenting kneeling worshippers; Annunciation above; below, Prophets; at sides, S. Tomaso di Villanuova and S. Monica (r.). Sd. ca 1426.

Verona (contd.). s. FERMO MAGGIORE. Detached fresco: Angels with scrolls, twelve half-length Prophets, reclining Adam and Eve, and peacock (r.). ca 1410–20.

CHIESA DEI FILIPPINI. Fragment of fresco from S. Fermo minore in Braida: Madonna and Child crowned by two Angels. Formerly Sd.

Worcester (Mass.). 1912.63. Madonna and Child with God the Father and Angels in rose garden. *Plate* 537.

TADDEO DI BARTOLO

Sienese. About 1362–1422. Pupil probably of Giacomo di Mino del Pellicciajo; follower of Andrea Vanni and Bartolo di Fredi. Often active outside Siena: at San Gimignano (1393), Genoa (where he was influenced by Barnaba da Modena), Pisa (1395–97), Perugia (1403) and Volterra (1411).

Altenburg. 62. Madonna of Humility and two Seraphim.

63. Pinnacle: Blessing Redeemer.

Asciano. MUSEO D'ARTE SACRA. Central panel of S. Agata polyptych: Madonna and Child enthroned with two Angels (fr.) (see Fei).

Assisi. F. M. PERKINS COLLECTION. Panel of polyptych: Full-length S. Elizabeth of Hungary.

Panel of polyptych: Half-length S. Bernard.

Aurillac. 28. (See Paris, Musées Nationaux.)

Badia a Isola (Colle Val d'Elsa). ss. SALVATORE E CIRINO. Fresco: Madonna and Child with Cherubim, S. Catherine, S. Anthony Abbot, S. Augustine and traces of other Saint (r.).

Bergen (Norway). BILLEDGALLERI. Diptych: Annunciation. E. (?) *Plate* 474.

Berlin. 1083 (FORMERLY LENT TO BONN 275). Virgin of Annunciation.

Bracciano. CASTELLO. Panel of polyptych: S. Clare.

Budapest. 18(30). Crucifixion.

27(32). Tondo from frame of altarpiece: S. John Evangelist.

1090(29). Madonna and Child sucking His forefinger.

53.500 (FORMERLY ZICHY MUSEUM). Polyptych: Madonna del Latte crowned by two Angels; SS. John Baptist and Andrew; below, six standing Saints (g.p.). *Plate* 471.

Cambridge (Mass.). FOGG ART MUSEUM. 1965.2. Madonna and Child in Glory. Sd and d. 1418.

Castelfiorentino (Empoli). PINACOTECA. S. Verdiana with two snakes. (?)

Chicago (Ill.). 33.1033. Predella panel: Crucifixion.

Colle Val d'Elsa. S. AGOSTINO, FIRST ALTAR R. Madonna and Child with goldfinch. *Plate* 470.

Collegalli (San Miniato al Tedesco). ss. VITO E MODESTO, CAPPELLA DI S. PAOLO (EX). Polyptych: Madonna and Child, SS. Sebastian, Paul, John Baptist and Nicholas. Sd and d. 1389. *Plate* 469.

Cologne. 504. Predella panel: Crucifixion.

    613. Predella panel: Resurrection.

Copenhagen. THORWALDSEN MUSEUM. 2. Predella: S. Catherine, Resurrection, Crucifixion, Betrayal, S. Mary Magdalen.

Englewood (N.J.). PLATT COLLECTION (EX). Two panels of polyptych: Full-length SS. Nicholas and Galganus.

Florence. MUSEO BARDINI. Shield with coat of arms and Beato Ranieri.

    BERENSON COLLECTION. Predella: Christ and the Apostles.

    Predella panel: Mourning over the dead Christ (r.).

    GENTNER COLLECTION (EX). Two panels: S. Nicholas of Tolentino, S. James.

    SERRISTORI COLLECTION. Panels of polyptych: SS. Luke, Matthew, Lawrence, two Bishop Saints, three Dominican Saints.

    (Environs) VINCIGLIATA. Side-panel of polyptych: S. Nicholas with two Cherubim and S. Fina above (companion to Rome, Fassini).

Frankfurt a/M. DR OSKAR LOEWE BEER (EX). Four panels of polyptych: Half-length SS. Helena, Catherine, Lawrence and Agatha.

Ginestreto (Siena). S. GIOVANNI (FORMERLY DON PIETRO TANGANELLI, SIENA). Left panel of polyptych: Full-length S. John Baptist (version of Triptych in S. Caterina della Notte, Siena). Sd.

Göttingen. 173. Trinity.

Grenoble. 454. Triptych from S. Paolo all'Orto, Pisa: Madonna and Child enthroned with Cherubim; SS. Gherardus and Paul, with bust of Bishop Saint above; SS. Andrew and Nicholas with bust of S. Louis of Toulouse above. Sd and d. 1395.

Hanover. LANDESGALERIE. 375. Predella panel: Funeral of Virgin.

    376–381. Six scenes from Life of S. Francis (predella to polyptych from S. Francesco al Prato, now Perugia Gallery): S. Francis before the Sultan, Pope Honorius III confirms the Franciscan rule, Christmas Mass at Greccio, Miracle of the water, Preaching to the birds, Assumption in a golden chariot. 1403. *Plate 476.*

Hartford (Conn.). WADSWORTH ATHENEUM. 1962–444 (GIFT OF R. LEHMAN). Madonna and Child with goldfinch.

s'Heerenberg. VAN HEEK. S. Francis appearing at Arles (companion to Hanover and Perugia).

Karlsruhe. 402. Predella panel: Martyrdom of S. James.

Kreuzlingen. H. KISTERS. Predella panel: Resurrection (companion to London, L. Douglas?).

Le Mans. 9. S. James.

Le Puy. 194. Madonna and Child.

London. BROCKLEBANK COLLECTION (EX). Half-length S. Ursula (companion to Homeless).

    HENRY HARRIS (EX). SS. Augustine and Clemens.

Marseilles. COMTE DE DEMANDOLX (EX). Blessing Redeemer. L.

Memphis (Tenn.). BROOKS MEMORIAL ART GALLERY. 61.195–6 (KRESS COLLECTION. K 551, K 552). Panels of polyptych: Full-length SS. John Baptist and James (ex Platt, companions to New Orleans).

Minneapolis (Ohio). ART INSTITUTE, VANDERLIP BEQUEST (EX). Panel of polyptych: Half-length S. Peter. E.

Montepulciano. DUOMO, CHOIR. Polyptych: Assumption of Virgin with Apostles below; S. John Baptist with SS. Donatus Bishop, Michael, Francis, Stephen, Dominic, Lawrence, Martin Bishop, Anthony Abbot; S. John Evangelist with SS. Catherine, Lucy, Mary Magdalen, Agatha, Ursula, Mustiola and Antilla holding town model; in pinnacles, Coronation of Virgin, Angel and Virgin of Annunciation; in first predella, ten Scenes from the Old Testament and four Angels at base of pilasters; in second predella, Entry into Jerusalem, Last Supper, Betrayal, Way to Calvary, Crucifixion, Mourning over dead Christ, Resurrection, Descent into Limbo, Christ on the way to Emmaus; in four pilasters, twelve small Saints. 1401. *Plates* 473, 475.

Nancy. 10. Madonna and Child enthroned (wrongly inscribed 'Duccio').

Nantes. 306. (See Paris, Musées Nationaux.)

Naples. Inv. 84267. Panel from pilaster of altarpiece: S. Sebastian.

New Haven (Conn.). 1943.249. Pinnacle: Blessing Redeemer.

1943.250/1. Two panels of polyptych: S. John Baptist; S. Jerome as Cardinal. E.

New Orleans (La.). I. DELGADO MUSEUM OF ART. 61.63–4 (KRESS COLLECTION. K 553, 554). Two panels of polyptych: Full-length S. Catherine and S. Augustine (companions to Memphis).

New York. MRS SIMON GUGGENHEIM. Predella panels: Half-length SS. Dominic, Galganus, Catherine, Lawrence (from Grenoble polyptych of 1395?).

ROBERT LEHMAN COLLECTION. Fragments of fresco: Three female heads.

H. L. MOSES COLLECTION. Predella: Christ and the Apostles. *Plate* 477.

Northampton (Mass.). SMITH COLLEGE MUSEUM. Predella panel: Assassination of S. Peter Martyr.

Notre Dame (Ind.). UNIVERSITY ART GALLERY. 61.47.2 (KRESS COLLECTION. K 104.) Panel of polyptych: Half-length S. Giminianus.

S. MARY'S COLLEGE. S. Francis. (?)

Oldenburg (ex). Four pinnacles: The Evangelists.

Orte. DUOMO. Virgin in prayer. Sd and d. 1420.

Palermo. CHIARAMONTE BORDONARO COLLECTION. 77. Madonna and Child.

Paris. 1622. Predella panel: Crucifixion.

MUSÉES NATIONAUX, CAMPANA COLLECTION 44 (DEP. AURILLAC). Crucifixion.

— CAMPANA COLLECTION 137 (DEP. NANTES). Virgin of Annunciation.

Perugia. 62, 63, 64, 66. Fragments of polyptych from S. Francesco al Prato: front panels—Madonna and Child enthroned with four Angels; SS. Mary Magdalen, John Baptist, John Evangelist and Catherine; back panels—S. Francis in Glory defeating Vices; SS. Hercolanus, Anthony of Padua, Louis of

Toulouse and Costantius; SS. Peter and Paul. (See also Amsterdam and Hanover.) Sd and d. 1403.

67. Pinnacle from S. Agostino: Descent of Holy Ghost. Sd and d. 1403.

72. Annunciation.

Petroio (Senese). SS. PIETRO E PAOLO, OVER DOOR. Madonna and Child.

Philadelphia (Pa.). J. G. JOHNSON COLLECTION. 99. Madonna and Child with SS. James and John Baptist.

100. Madonna and Child with four Angels; Crucifixion above (st.).

101. Predella panel: S. Dominic before the Pope.

Pisa. B.P., V, 18, 19. Side-panels of polyptych: SS. Francis and Peter, SS. Paul and Anthony of Padua (frs.).

B.P., V. 20, 21. Two panels of polyptych: S. Peter, S. Paul (st.).

B.P., V, 22. Processional standard of the Compagnia di S. Donnino: front, S. Donnino enthroned; back, Crucifixion. *Plate 472.*

B.P., VI, 6. Panel of polyptych: S. John Baptist (from Convent of S. Domenico).

S. FRANCESCO, CAPPELLA SARDI CAMPIGLI (OLD SACRISTY), VAULT. Frescoes: Evangelists and Church Fathers in pairs and busts of Saints and Prophets.

—— CENTRAL WALL. Frescoes: above, the Virgin is warned of her imminent death; below, SS. John Baptist and Andrew.

—— SIDE WALLS. Frescoes on two registers: the Apostles taking leave of the dying Virgin, Dormition, Mourning over the dead Virgin, Burial of Virgin (r.). Sd and d. 1397.

S. MARTINO, CAPPELLA DEL SACRAMENTO. Side-panels to Madonna at S. Michele in Borgo: SS. Bartholomew, Andrew, Christopher and Augustine.

S. MICHELE IN BORGO, SECOND ALTAR R. Central panel to Saints above: Madonna and Child enthroned with two music-making Angels, SS. Catherine, Michael, Warrior Saint and S. Peter.

Poppi (Casentino). CASTELLO. Madonna and Child with SS. Anthony Abbot, John Evangelist, John Baptist and Francis.

Ravenna. 203, 207. Pinnacles: Angel and Virgin of Annunciation (p.).

Rome. VATICAN, PINACOTECA. 155. Predella panel: Assumption of Virgin.

169. Predella panel: Dormition.

BARONE ALBERTO FASSINI (EX). Side-panel of polyptych: S. John Baptist with two Cherubim and S. Agatha above (companion to Florence, Vincigliata).

San Antonio (Texas). MARION KOOGLER MCNAY INSTITUTE. Predella panel: S. Dominic raising to life the son of Cardinal Orsini.

San Francisco (Cal.). M. H. DE YOUNG MEMORIAL MUSEUM. 61.44.6 (KRESS COLLECTION. K 310.). Madonna suckling the Child and two Seraphim.

San Gimignano. PINACOTECA CIVICA. SALA V. Polyptych: Madonna and Child enthroned; SS. Nicholas, Christopher, John Evangelist and a Bishop Saint; in pinnacles, blessing Redeemer, Angel and Virgin of Annunciation, SS. Peter and Paul. E.

S. Giminianus and eight scenes from his life.

San Gimignano (contd.). s. maria assunta (collegiata o duomo), entrance
wall. Fresco: Last Judgement.

— wall towards r. nave, near entrance. Frescoes: Paradise; in soffit of arch,
Cardinal Virtues.

— wall towards l. nave, near entrance. Frescoes: Hell; in soffit of arch,
four Prophets.

Frescoed decoration: 1393.

Savona. pinacoteca. Madonna and Child with four Angels, male and female
donors (from Finalborgo). ca 1397.

Siena. 55. Painted Crucifix (cut at bottom) (from Spedale di S. Maria della Scala).
Formerly Sd and d. 1420.

129, 132. Predella panels: Adoration of Magi, Adoration of Shepherds.

128. Portable altarpiece; Madonna and Child with SS. Francis and Catherine
and Crucifixion above; in wings, S. Anthony Abbot, S. Christopher, Angel
and Virgin of Annunciation.

129. S. Peter Martyr.

130. Right pinnacle of polyptych (companion to 135): S. Agnes. (r.; st.)

131. Polyptych: Annunciation; SS. Cosmas and Damian; in pinnacles, Trinity,
Angel Gabriel, S. James. Sd and d. 1409.

134. Predella panel to n. 134: Martyrdom of SS. Cosmas and Damian. 1409.

135. Left pinnacle of polyptych (companion to 130): S. Matthew (r.; st.).

143, 144. Pinnacles: Angel and Virgin of Annunciation (st.).

162. S. Francis receiving Stigmata (from Osservanza). E.

archivio di stato. Book-cover ('Provisioni contra le donne del portare vestimenti
di seta'): Lady in golden mantle. 1421.

palazzo pubblico, cappella, vault. Frescoes: Music-making Angels.

— — altar wall. Frescoes: in lunettes, Angel and Virgin of Annunciation; in
roundels, Isaiah and Jeremiah; full-length SS. Peter and Paul.

— — side walls. Frescoes: in eight lunettes, Faith, Hope, Charity, S. Peter
Alexandrinus symbolizing the Church, Evangelists and Church Fathers in
pairs (John Evangelist and Augustine, Matthew and Gregory, Luke and
Jerome, Mark and Ambrose): in six roundels, Fortitude, Prudence, Justice,
Temperance, Elisah and Zarobabel; Four scenes from Life of Virgin (Taking
leave of the Apostles, Dormition, Funeral, Christ raises her from tomb).

— — pillars and arches. Frescoes: in roundels, half-length SS. Agatha, Lucy
and female Saints; full-length SS. Bernard, Francis, Blessed Ambrogio Sansedoni and Judas Maccabeus.

Frescoed decoration: 1407–08.

— anticappella, entrance wall. Frescoes: in lunettes. Justice and Magnanimity;
below, Cicero, Cato, Scipio Nasica, Curius Dentatus, Marcus Furius Camillus,
Scipio Africanus, Boy indicating mottoes of good government.

— — l. wall. Fresco: Large S. Christopher.

— — l. pillar. Fresco: Caesar, Pompey and bust of Roman soldier.

— — R. WALL. Frescoed lunette: Religion.

— — R. PILLAR. Fresco: Aristotle and bust of Roman soldier.

— — WALL OPPOSITE CAPPELLA: Frescoes: in lunette, Wisdom and Strength; below, Lelius Brutus.

— — SOFFIT OF ARCH. Frescoes: Jupiter with lightning bolts, Mars on a chariot, Apollo, Pallas, round a map of Rome. *Plate 479.*
   Frescoed decoration. 1414.

— SALA DEI MATRIMONI. Frescoes: S. Francis in Glory, S. Albert the Great.

COMPAGNIA DI S. CATERINA DELLA NOTTE. Triptych: Madonna and Child with two music-making Angels and two Cherubim; S. John Baptist, S. Andrew; in pinnacles, Holy Ghost and Seraphim; in pillars, SS. Stephen, Agnes, Mary Magdalen, Margaret. Sd and d. 1400.

SS. GHERARDO E LUDOVICO (NEAR S. FRANCESCO). Panel of polyptych: S. Louis of Toulouse (fr.).

S. MARIA DEI SERVI, FIFTH CHAPEL R. Nativity. Sd and d. 1404.

— SECOND CHAPEL L. 'Madonna di Belverde' by Giacomo di Mino del Pellicciajo (retouched by early Taddeo di Bartolo?).

SPEDALE DELLA SCALA, INFERMERIA DI S. GALGANO. Fresco: Crucifixion.

Triora (Liguria). BATTISTERO. Baptism of Christ. Sd and d. 1397.

Tucson (Ariz.). UNIVERSITY OF ARIZONA. 61.96 (KRESS COLLECTION. K 1292). Coronation of Virgin. L. [*Plate 269.*]

Tulsa (Okla.). PHILBROOK ART CENTER. 3364 (KRESS COLLECTION. K 1179). Madonna and Child with goldfinch and Cherubim.

Turin. GALLERIA SABAUDA. 95. 'Gualino' triptych: Madonna and Child, S. James, S. Dominic. E.

Vaduz. LIECHTENSTEINSCHE SAMMLUNGEN. G869. S. Agnes.

Vienna. LANCKORONSKI COLLECTION (EX). Bust of S. Francis (p.).

Viterbo. PALAZZO GENTILI. Predella panel: Christ on Cross with mourning Virgin and Evangelist and female donor.

Volterra. PALAZZO DEI PRIORI. 20. Madonna and Child with two Cherubim (fr. oval).
   21. Polyptych: Madonna and Child; SS. Anthony Abbot, John Baptist, Michael and Francis; in pinnacles, Redeemer, Angel and Virgin of Annunciation; in roundels, busts of Saints; in pillars, four small Saints; in predella, five Scenes. Sd and d. 1411. *Plate 478.*
   24. Left panel of polyptych: SS. Nicholas of Tolentino and Peter, with bust of Isaiah in roundel above. Sd.

MUSEO DIOCESANO D'ARTE SACRA. Madonna and Child upheld by Cherubim.

S. AGOSTINO. Centre panel of polyptych: Madonna and Child with two Cherubim.

Homeless. Top panel of polyptych: Half-length S. Agnes (companion to London, Brocklebank) (repr. by Symeonides, *Taddeo di Bartolo*, pl. XLVI-B).

TAMAGNI, Vincenzo, da San Gimignano

1492–*after* 1537. *Pupil of Mainardi, close imitator of Sodoma whom he assisted at Monte-oliveto* 1505–08; *influenced by Antoniazzo, Pinturicchio and Ridolfo del Ghirlandajo.*

Arrone (Terni). S. MARIA DELLA QUERCIA, CHOIR. Frescoes: in vault, Coronation of Virgin; on walls, Nativity and Dormition (with Giovanni da Spoleto). Sd and d. 1516.

Badia a Isola (between Siena and Colle Val d'Elsa). ABBAZIA DEI SS. SALVATORE E CIRINO, L. WALL. Fresco: Madonna della Cintola with kneeling SS. Catherine of Siena, Salvatore?, Cirino? and Stephen; on either side, in superimposed niches, SS. Bernardo Tolomei, Bernardino of Siena, Ambrose Sansedoni and Sebastian.

Istia d'Ombrone (Grosseto). S. SALVATORE, R. ALTAR. Meeting of Joachim and Anne at the Golden Gate. 1523.

Montalcino (Senese). CORPUS DOMINI. Madonna of Mercy.

    MADONNA DEL SOCCORSO, R. OF HIGH ALTAR. 'Madonna della Cintola' and SS. Sebastian and Roch. Sd and d. 1527. *Plate* 1552.

    S. FRANCESCO, TWO EX-CHAPELS (SACRISTY). Frescoes: I—Birth of Virgin, Marriage of Virgin, S. Nicholas of Bari. Sd and d. 1511. *Plate* 1548.

    II—Frescoes: 'Quo Vadis Domine' with Septizonium in background; Fall of Simon Magus (r.). 1510.

    VECCHIO SPEDALE, EX FARMACIA (MUSEO CIVICO ETRUSCO). Frescoes: end wall, Madonna and Child enthroned, crowned by two Angels, flanked by SS. Jerome and Gregory; side walls, monochrome Prophets, Philosophers, Heroes and Heroines in niches and friezes with Grottesche; wall opposite Madonna, fragments of unspecified story. 1510–12. *Plates* 1546–1547.

Monteoliveto Maggiore (Siena). GENERAL'S APARTMENT. Frescoed tondo: Madonna and head of Olivetan monk. (?)

Narbonne. 453. Predella: Last Supper, Way to Calvary, Christ in Sepulchre upheld by Angels, with Maries, S. John Evangelist and Joseph of Arimathea.

Philadelphia (Pa.). MUSEUM OF ART, WILSTACH COLLECTION (EX). 308. Portrait of young woman.

Pomarance (Volterra). S. GIOVANNI BATTISTA, CHAPEL R. OF HIGH ALTAR. Madonna and Child with SS. John Baptist, Sebastian, Lucy and Martin. Sd and d. 1525.*

Rome. GALLERIA NAZIONALE (PALAZZO BARBERINI). Marriage of Virgin. Sd and d. 1526.

San Gimignano. PINACOTECA. Madonna and Child with SS. Michael, Augustine, Nicholas of Tolentino, Monica and Lucy (from Collegiata).*

    Frescoed Tondo: Madonna and Child.

    MUSEO D'ARTE SACRA. Madonna and Child with SS. Nicholas and Sebastian.

    PALAZZO PRATELLESI. Fresco: Mystic Marriage of S. Catherine and SS. Nicholas, Jerome and Bernard. d. 1528.

S. AGOSTINO, FIRST ALTAR R. Frescoed lunette: Pietà, with S. Monica.

— FIRST ALTAR L. Fresco: The Cross adored by the Virgin, SS. Mary Magdalen, Monica and John Evangelist; in embrasure, S. Margaret and S. Hippolytus.

— R. APSE, ALTAR. Birth of Virgin and female donor. Sd and d. 1523. *Plate 1550.*

— SECOND ALTAR R. (CAPPELLA DI S. NICOLA DA TOLENTINO). Fresco round statue of S. Nicholas of Tolentino: Madonna and Child with Angels in Glory; below, SS. Onuphrius, Nicholas of Tolentino, Roch and Paul Hermit (p. ?). d. 1529.

S. MARIA ASSUNTA (COLLEGIATA), L. TRANSEPT. S. Martin and Madonna appearing to Saints. Not traced.

S. GIROLAMO, L. WALL. Madonna and Child enthroned, with SS. John Baptist, John Gualbert, Benedict, Jerome and two Putti (Angels and God the Father above, added later). Sd and d. 1522. *Plate 1551.*

PIEVE DI S. LORENZO MONTAUTO. Madonna del Rosario. L. Not traced.

Siena. SANTUARIO CATERINIANO, S. CATERINA IN FONTEBRANDA (ORATORIO DELLA CONTRADA DELL'OCA). L. WALL. Fresco: S. Catherine of Siena heals Matteo Cenni from the plague (on Pacchia's design?). *Plate 1553.*

Subiaco. S. FRANCESCO, THIRD CHAPEL L. Frescoes: in vault, Redeemer, Evangelists and Putti; right wall, Crucifixion; left wall, Birth of Virgin and Marriage of Virgin; in dado, monochrome scenes, sacred and mythological.

— ALTAR. Nativity. E. (?)

Volterra. DUOMO, CAPPELLA DI S. CARLO (BOMBED 1943). Small Crucifixion. Not traced.

Homeless. Portrait of a lady. *Plate 1549.*

TEGLIACCI, NICCOLÒ DI SER SOZZO

Sienese, of noble family. Died 1363. Pupil of the Lorenzetti.

Balcarres (Fife, Scotland). EARL OF CRAWFORD AND BALCARRES. Four predella panels to Siena 51: Stories of S. Thomas (with Luca di Tommè). 1362. *Plates 366–367.*

Boston (Mass.). 83.175. Polyptych: Death and Assumption of Virgin; SS. Augustine (?) and Peter; Evangelist and Deacon Saint (upper panels by another hand).

Brooklyn (N.Y.). 34.841. Madonna of the cherries and two Angels (fr.). (?)

Cleveland (Ohio). 24.430. Miniature: two Angels.

Florence. UFFIZI, DEPOT. Madonna and Child holding pomegranate (from S. Antonio del Bosco). *Plate 358.*

Greenwich (Conn.). T. S. HYLAND COLLECTION. Madonna and Child with two Angels (fr.; formerly Prince Léon Ourusoff). *Plate 359.*

Kansas City (Mo.). 61.149 (KRESS COLLECTION. K 1085). Centre panel of polyptych: Madonna and Child with four Angels (fr.).

Newark (N.J.). 12811 w. Illuminated initial: Virgin of Assumption in the letter O.
    Plate 363.

Rome. VATICAN, PINACOTECA. 195. Predella panel to Siena 51: Crucifixion (with
    Luca di Tommè). 1362.

San Gimignano. MUSEO DI ARTE SACRA. Corale 68–I. Miniatures:
    f. 1. Nativity.
    f. 6. Martyr Saint.
    f. 12. Evangelist.
    f. 17. Adoration of Magi.
    f. 18. S. Paul.
    f. 22. S. Gimignanus enthroned with four Angels and six worshipping monks.
        Plate 361.
    f. 28. Presentation.
    f. 40. Resurrection. *Plate* 362.
    f. 54. Ascension.
    f. 57. Descent of the Holy Ghost.
    f. 66. The dead Saviour.
    f. 68. SS. Philip and James.
    f. 70. The Cross.
    f. 74. S. John Baptist.
    f. 78. SS. Peter and Paul.
    f. 82. S. Lawrence.
    f. 84. Assumption.
    f. 88. Madonna and Child.
    f. 91. S. Michael.
    f. 95. S. Francis receiving Stigmata.
    f. 97. All Souls.
    120. S. Peter.
    f. 176. Saint kneeling by open door.
    f. 179. A dead female Saint.
   PINACOTECA CIVICA. Dismembered polyptych from S. Maria Assunta di Monte-
    oliveto a Barbiano: Virgin of Assumption (fr.); S. Thomas, S. Benedict,
    S. Catherine, S. Bartholomew (p.). *Plate* 357.

Siena. ARCHIVIO DI STATO. Caleffo dell'Assunta: Full-page miniature with Assump-
    tion. Sd. *Plate* 360.
   51. Polyptych: Madonna and Child enthroned with six Angels; S. John Baptist,
    S. Thomas, S. Benedict, S. Stephen (see Luca di Tommè). Sd by both artists
    and d. 1362. *Plate* 365.
   SOCIETÀ ESECUTORI PIE DISPOSIZIONI. 29. Madonna and Child enthroned with two
    Angels and kneeling S. Anthony Abbot and Catherine; blessing Redeemer
    above.

TIBERIO D'ASSISI

Umbrian, ca 1470–1524. Pupil perhaps of Mezzastris; strongly influenced by Pinturicchio and Perugino.

Assisi. PINACOTECA CIVICA. Madonna and Child enthroned and two Saints.
   Half-length Madonna (r.).
   Detached frescoes: S. Roch with hat; S. Roch with cap; S. Sebastian; SS.
   Roch and Anthony Abbot; Madonna of Mercy; Madonna and Child with
   two Saints; Annunciation; S. Roch and Female Saint; Madonna and Child
   with two Cherubim; A Bishop.
   S. DAMIANO, CAPPELLA DI S. GIROLAMO, END WALL. Fresco: Madonna and Child
   with SS. Francis, Clare, Bernardino and Jerome. d. 1517.
   — L. WALL. Fresco: SS. Sebastian and Roch (st.). d. 1522.
   S. FRANCESCO, MUSEO. Christ on Cross, SS. Leonard, Anthony Abbot, Francis,
   Clare and Flagellants.
   S. MARIA DEGLI ANGELI, CAPPELLA DEL ROSETO, ATRIO. Frescoes: S. Francis throws
   himself in the rosebushes, is guided by two Angels to the Porziuncola, prays
   to obtain Indulgence of Sins, Pope Honorius III grants his requests, The
   Pardon is announced to the Faithful by S. Francis and the seven Bishops of
   Umbria (version of Montefalco). d. 1516. *Plates 1026, 1028.*
   — CAPPELLA DEL ROSETO, ORATORIO DI S. BONAVENTURA. Frescoes: over altar, S.
   Francis and his first companions; in vault, Eternal; right wall, SS. Clare and
   Elizabeth; left wall, SS. Bonaventura, Bernardino of Siena, Louis of Toulouse,
   Anthony of Padua. Sd and d. 1506. *Plate 1021.*
Bettona. PINACOTECA. Frescoes: S. Roch; Trinity (r., d. 1513, ?).
   S. MARIA MAGGIORE, FIRST ALTAR R. Banner: Madonna and Child with S. Anne in
   Glory, and SS. Anthony and Crispoldus.
Birmingham. BARBER INSTITUTE. Detached frescoes: S. Clare, S. Francis, S. Ansanus.
   Plate 1023.
Castel Ritaldi (Perugia). S. MARINA. Frescoed niche: in lunette, Eternal; below,
   Tobias and the Angel, S. Catherine and saintly Pope. Sd. *Plate 1024.*
Farfa (Sabina). ABBAZIA, OVER DOOR. Frescoed lunette: Madonna and Child, two
   Saints and Donor, with two Putti above.
Montefalco. S. FRANCESCO (MUSEO), L. WALL. Fresco: Madonna and Child with SS.
   Bonaventura and Andrea. Sd and d. 1510.
   — R. WALL. Detached frescoes: Assumption and Annunciation; Coronation (r.);
   S. Jerome (r.); S. John (r.). Not traced.
   SANTUARIO DI S. FORTUNATO, CAPPELLA DELLE ROSE. Frescoes: in vault, Eternal; at
   spring of arches, Franciscan Martyrs in medallions; on walls, from left, SS.
   Bonaventura, Bernardino, Louis of Toulouse, Anthony of Padua; S. Francis
   invited by the Angels and accompanied by the them to the Porziuncola; S.
   Francis prays to obtain the Indulgence of Sins; Pope Honorius III grants his

request; The Pardon is announced to the Faithful by S. Francis and the seven
Bishops of Umbria; SS. Elizabeth and Clare. Sd and d. 1512. *Plate* 1025, 1027.
— R. OF ENTRANCE OF CHURCH. Fresco: S. Sebastian.

Perugia. MARCHESE MONALDI. 'Maestà.' Sd and d. 1513.*

Princeton (N.J.). 14.40. Detached fresco: Madonna and blessing Child.

Rome. VATICAN, PINACOTECA. 315. Madonna and Child enthroned with SS. Francis
and Jerome. d. 1502.

    SCHIFF COLLECTION (EX). S. Roch.

Sigmaringen. MUSEUM. Coronation of Virgin. Sd and d. 1512.*

Stroncone (Terni). S. FRANCESCO, CHAPEL NEAR ENTRANCE. Fresco: Madonna and
Child with SS. Michael, Bonaventura, Jerome and Anthony of Padua. Sd
and d. 1509. *Plate* 1022.

Todi. S. FORTUNATO, L. WALL. Fresco: Holy Trinity.

Trevi. S. MARTINO, OVER DOOR. Frescoed lunette: Madonna and Child with two
Angels.
— ALTAR L. OF HIGH ALTAR. S. Martin and the Beggar.
— OUTSIDE CHAPEL. Fresco: S. Emilian and a Nun.

TISI see GAROFALO

TOMASO DA MODENA

*Modena 1325/6–1379. Mentioned in Treviso 1349 to 1354. Mentioned again in Modena
1358 to 1360 and 1366–68. Pupil of some Emilian follower of Giotto. Influenced by trans-
alpine art.*

Baltimore (Md.). WALTERS ART GALLERY. 1686. Eight panels in a reliquary: in
corners, Symbols of Evangelists; above, S. Francis and S. Michael; at sides,
four half-length male and female Saints. *Plate* 257.

Bologna. 228. Portable altarpiece: in tympanum, Last Supper; middle register,
Madonna reading, Madonna and Child enthroned, Madonna dressing the
Child; lower register, SS. Anastasia, Lucy, Agnes and Catherine; in pinnacles,
Blessing Redeemer, Angel and Virgin of Annunciation. Before 1349. *Plate*
258.

Burg Karlstein (Prague). Wings of triptych: Madonna and Child; Man of Sorrows
(r.); in pinnacles, two busts of Angels; in pillars of frame, eight full-length
Saints and music-making Angels. Sd.

    Panels of a triptych inserted in golden background and painted over: Madonna
and Child, S. Wenceslas, S. Palmatius. Sd. (formerly dated 1357?).

Florence. PROF. R. LONGHI. Miniature: Madonna and Child in a letter D.

Mantua. S. FRANCESCO, CAPPELLA DI S. BERNARDINO. Frescoes: Five Franciscan
stories (r.). (?)

Milan. SAIBENE COLLECTION. Madonna and Child.

Modena. 42. Portable triptych: Madonna and Child, with Christ in Limbo below; in wings, S. Romuald, the young Baptist in wilderness, S. Jerome healing the lion, S. Catherine. Sd and d. 13(?)5. *Plate 259*.

Treviso. MUSEO CIVICO. Detached frescoes from the demolished church of S. Margherita, Treviso:

P. 31. Virgin of Annunciation (from lunettes of side-walls, Cappella di S. Orsola —Angel of Annunciation is lost). L.

P. 32–37, P. 39–44. Legend of S. Ursula (from side walls of Cappella di S. Orsola): the English King gives instructions to the departing Ambassadors; the King of Brittany reads the message and Ursula argues with her mother the Queen; Ursula takes leave of her friends; the English bridegroom is baptized; An Angel appears to Ursula during her sea voyage; S. Ursula is met by the Pope outside Rome; the Pope's dream; the Pope's abdication; Departure from Rome; Homeward journey; Martyrdom of S. Ursula and her Maidens outside Cologne (r.); fragment of decorative frieze with S. Michael in roundel. L. *Plate 261*.

P. 46. Madonna and Child enthroned (from altar wall of Cappella di S. Orsola) (fr.—only Child survives). L.

P. 38. S. Ursula surrounded by her Maidens (from altar wall of Cappella di S. Orsola). L.

P. 48. Full-length Christ in garden (fr. of a 'Noli me tangere'). L.

P. 49. Christ talking to a pilgrim (fr. of a 'Way to Emmaus'). L.

S. FRANCESCO, CAPPELLA DI S. GIOVANNI EVANGELISTA. Fresco: Madonna and Child enthroned with SS. Anthony Abbot, Francis, Bonaventura (?) and Christopher. d. 1351.

— CAPPELLA DI S. GIOVANNI BATTISTA. Fresco: Madonna and Child enthroned, and SS. Anthony Abbot, Catherine, SS. Stephen and John Baptist, SS. Louis of Toulouse and James, S. Christopher.

S. LUCIA (FORMERLY S. MARIA AD CARCERES), CAPPELLA DELLA CROCIFISSIONE. Fresco: Madonna and Child enthroned (both repainted in fifteenth century) and two Angels.

S. NICCOLÒ, THIRD PIER L. Votive frescoes: S. Jerome in his study; S. Romuald worshipped by two Men, one saved from prison; S. Agnes; S. John Baptist. *Plate 262*.

Fresco: Madonna and Child and S. Augustine. (?)

— SACRISTY. Fresco: God the Father sends the Angel Gabriel to the Virgin; below, Christ explains the mystery of the Incarnation to S. Nicholas (g.p.).

SEMINARIO (EX-CONVENT OF S. NICCOLÒ), CAPITOLO DEI DOMENICANI. Frescoed frieze: East wall—SS. Dominic, Peter Martyr, Thomas Aquinas (r.); Popes Innocent V and Benedict XI; Cardinal Hugo of Provence. South wall— Cardinal Annibaldo degli Annibaldi, Pietro di Tarantasia, Robert of England, Latino Malabranca, Ugo di Billom, Nicolò Bocassino, Nicolò da Prato,

Walter of England, Nicholas of Rouen, Thomas of England. West wall—
Cardinals William of England, Matteo Orsini, Guillaume de Bayonne, Boni-
fazio da Pisa, Tomaso de Molendini and monks Guido da Napoli, Maurice of
Hungary, Pietro de la Palude, Agostino da Tragurio, Giacomo da Venezia,
Ambrogio da Siena, Vincent of Beauvais. North wall—monks Bernardo da
Traverso, Pelagiano di Spagna, Francesco Sedre di Spagna, Walter of Ger-
many, Isnardo da Vicenza, Giovanni da Schio, Alberto Magno, John of
Saxony, Raymondo da Penafort, Jordan of Saxony. Sd and d. 1352. *Plate* 260.
VESCOVADO. Frescoed lunette: Christ in Sepulchre.*

TORBIDO, Francesco, called IL MORO

*Venice 1482/3–Verona 1561/2. Son of Marco India da Venezia, pupil of Giorgione, came
young to Verona. Assistant, then heir (1526) to Liberale. Influenced by Lorenzo Lotto, Titian
and Giulio Romano.*

Amsterdam. 1896 AG 1. Sacra Conversazione with SS. Joseph, Catherine, Infant
   John and Angel.
Berlin. 1.233. Tondo: Madonna and Child with Infant S. John.
Brussels. 92. Male bust.
Cambridge. FITZWILLIAM MUSEUM. 1111. Portrait of bearded man.
Florence. MUSEO FERRONI. 123. S. Anthony Abbot. L.
London. 3949. Half-length portrait of Girolamo Fracastoro. E.
Mantua. S. ANDREA, SECOND ALTAR R. Baptist, Evangelist; Eternal in lunette (round
   a wooden statue of the Virgin).
Messina. 134. Circumcision. *Plate* 1871.
Milan. BRERA. 90. Head of old man.
   99. Bust of man with black hat. Sd. *Plate* 1870.
Munich. 1013. Portrait of youth. Sd and d. 1516. *Plate* 1869.
   5164. Lunette from Cappella Fontanelli in S. Maria in Organo at Verona:
   Transfiguration (companion to Potsdam).
Naples. 159. Half-length portrait of old man. Sd.
Padua. Inv. 694. Bust of old man. (?)
Potsdam. NEUES PALAIS. Mystic Marriage of S. Catherine, with Giacomo Fontanelli
   and his wife Giulia Pellegrini as S. James and S. Mary Magdalen (from family
   chapel in S. Maria in Organo at Verona; lunette at Munich). Sd. *Plate* 1873.
Princeton (N.J.). 35.35. Madonna and Child with S. Anthony Abbot presenting
   donor.
   35.36. Bust of Dorotea Quistelle. d. 1536.
Rome. GALLERIA DORIA PAMPHILI. 401. Bust of young man. E.
Rosazzo (Udine). BADIA, CHOIR. Frescoes: in vault, Symbols of Evangelists; on
   triumphal arch, SS. Peter and Paul; on walls, Madonna in roundel, Trans-

figuration, Calling of the Children of Zebedee, Miraculous draught of fishes. Sd and d. 1535.

Verona. 3. Madonna and Child. *Plate* 1867.

49. Tobias and the Angel.

210. S. Francis recommends the Conte Sanbonifacio to the Holy Family. *Plate* 1868.

CASA DI TORELLO SARAINA (VIA DELLA STELLA). Frescoes between Windows: pagan Sacrifices (p.)

S. EUFEMIA, SECOND ALTAR R. S. Euphemia with SS. Roch and Anthony Abbot.

S. FERMO MAGGIORE, SECOND ALTAR R. Madonna and Child in Glory with Trinity above, Tobias and the Angel and S. Apollonia below. d. 1523. *Plate* 1872.

S. MARIA MATRICOLARE (DUOMO), CHOIR. Frescoes: on triumphal arch, Annunciation, Isaiah and Ezekiel in niches; on barrel vault, Birth of Virgin, three Angels holding the Virgin's crown of seven stars; in semidome, Assumption; on end wall, S. Zeno (on cartoons by Giulio Romano). Sd and d. 1534.

S. MARIA IN ORGANO, R. TRANSEPT, CAPPELLA FONTANELLI. Frescoes: outside—SS. Jerome and S. John Evangelist (p.); inside—S. Peter Martyr and S. Francis in niches (see also Munich and Potsdam).

S. ZENO, FIRST ALTAR R. Holy Family and SS. Anne, Zeno, Roch, Christopher, Sebastian; in lunette above, fresco—Resurrection (p.).

TRAINI, Francesco

Pisan, active middle fourteenth century. Follower of Simone Martini and the Lorenzetti; influenced perhaps by Maso di Banco.

Chapel Hill (N.C.). WILLIAM HAYES ACKLAND MEMORIAL ART CENTER. 61.12.1. Pinnacle: Blessing Redeemer.* *Plate* 288.

Florence. UFFIZI, DEPOT. Full-length Bishop Saint.* *Plate* 287a.

Madrid. PRADO. Madonna and Child holding scroll (fr.; possibly central panel of Nancy and Homeless).*

Nancy. MUSÉE. Right panel of polyptych from Carmine, Pisa: Half-length S. Paul (companion to Homeless and possibly to Madrid). *Plate* 290.

Pisa. CAMPOSANTO, MUSEO. Detached frescoes: Crucifixion; Resurrection; Doubting Thomas; Ascension; Last Judgement (p., r.). *Plates* 294–295.

Assumption (r.) (?) (finished by Antonio Veneziano?).

Triumph of Death; Thebaid (p., r.). [*Plate* 266.] *Plates* 296–298.

MUSEO NAZIONALE DI S. MATTEO. Polyptych: S. Dominic, eight Scenes from his Life; in pinnacles, Redeemer and four Prophets. Sd. 1345. *Plates* 292–293.

— DEPOT. S. Michael (r.).*

S. CATERINA. Triumph of S. Thomas Aquinas (see under Lippo Memmi). *Plate* 299.

S. GIUSTO A SCANNICCI. Madonna and Child.*

Princeton (N.J.). 63.2. Madonna and Child with S. Anne (also listed Giovanni del Biondo (?)). *Plate 291.*

Homeless. Panel of polyptych: Half-length S. Gregory (companion to Nancy, and possibly to Madrid).* *Plate 289.*

TURA, Cosmè

Ferrara, ca 1430–95. Absent from Ferrara 1452–56; then Court painter of the Este's till 1486. Studied in the school of Squarcione at Padua; strongly influenced by Donatello, Castagno and other Florentines; possibly also by Tavernier and other miniaturists of the Burgundian Court.

Ajaccio. MUSÉE FESCH. Inv. Mfa. 852.1.560. 'Cicognara' altarpiece from S. Maria della Consolazione at Ferrara: standing Madonna and Child with Virgin Martyr and S. Jerome (st.). L.

Bergamo. 263. Madonna and blessing Child on gold ground (fr. of centre panel of polyptych, companion to Florence, Nantes, New York, Paris).

Berlin. 111. 'S. Lazzaro' Altarpiece: Madonna and Child with Saints (begun by Tura?; completed by Ercole Roberti). (Destroyed 1945.)

    1170B, C. Panels from polyptych (companions to Caen?): S. Sebastian, S. Christopher.

Boston (Mass.). GARDNER MUSEUM. Circumcision in roundel (companion to Cambridge, Fogg and New York n. 49.7.17).

Caen. 1. Central panel of polyptych (from S. Giacomo d'Argenta?): S. James enthroned (companion to Berlin?).

Cambridge. FITZWILLIAM MUSEUM. PD30–1947. 'Cook' Crucifixion (r.).

Cambridge (Mass.). FOGG ART MUSEUM. 1905.14. Adoration of Magi in roundel (companion to Boston and New York 49.7.17).

Dresden. 42A. S. Sebastian (finished and signed by Costa). L.

Dublin. 470. Viol player tuning his instrument. L. (?)

Ferrara. Inv. 69, 71. Two roundels from predella to lost altarpiece in Chapel rededicated to SS. Maurelio e Lorenzo in 1479; S. Maurelius before the Judge, Martyrdom of S. Maurelius. *Plate 728.*

    BIBLIOTECA DELL'UNIVERSITÀ. Cl. II, n.167. 'De Civitate Dei': miniature: S. Augustine (st.).

    DUOMO, MUSEO DELL'OPERA. Organ-shutters: inside, Annunciation; outside, S. George killing the Dragon and the Princess. doc. 1468–69. [*Plate 336.*] *Plate 723.*

Florence. UFFIZI. 3273. Right panel of polyptych, cut at bottom: S. Dominic on gold ground (companion to Bergamo?, Nantes, New York and Paris).

London. 772. Centre panel of 'Roverella' altarpiece: Madonna and Child enthroned with six Angels (companion to Paris, Rome, San Diego).

    773. S. Jerome (fr., companion to Milan).

905. Virgin of Annunciation.

3070. 'Primavera', for Studio of Borso d'Este at Belfiore. 1459/60. *Plate 722.*

Milan. BRERA. 447. Christ on Cross (fr., companion to London).

POLDI PEZZOLI. 597. Charity and Putti (p.).

600. S. Maurelius (companion to Rome, Colonna and to Venice, Cini). *Plate 727.*

DE ANGELI FRUA COLLECTION. S. John at Patmos.

Modena. 9. S. Anthony of Padua and Chapel by the sea in background (from S. Niccolò at Ferrara, in Chapel later dedicated to Blessed Jacopo della Marca). Before 1490.

Nantes. 177. Right panel of polyptych: S. Nicholas of Bari on gold ground (companion to Bergamo?, Florence, New York and Paris).

New York. 14.40.649. Profile of youth.

30.95.259. Left panel of polyptych: S. Louis of Toulouse on gold ground (companion to Bergamo?, to Florence, Nantes and Paris) (st.).

49.7.17. Flight into Egypt in roundel (companion to Boston, and to Cambridge, Fogg). *Plate 724.*

Paris. 1556. Lunette to 'Roverella' Altarpiece: Pietà (see London). *Plate 725.*

1557. Left panel of polyptych: S. Anthony of Padua on gold ground (companion to Bergamo?, Florence, Nantes and New York).

Philadelphia (Pa.). J. G. JOHNSON COLLECTION. 241. Two panels from pilaster of frame: S. John Baptist, S. Peter.

242. Madonna and Child with goldfinch (st.).

Rome. PRINCIPE COLONNA. Madonna and Child in Mandorla with Signs of Zodiac. Right panel of 'Roverella' altarpiece: SS. Maurelius and Paul recommending Abbot Niccolò Roverella (see London).

Virgin of Annunciation (companion to Milan, Poldi Pezzoli and to Venice, Cini). L.

San Diego (Cal.). 44.3. Left panel of 'Roverella' altarpiece: SS. Peter and George recommending Bishop Lorenzo Roverella (Head of S. George only, fr.; see London).

Venice. ACCADEMIA. 628. Madonna and sleeping Child; in lunette, two Angels and Monogram of S. Bernardino. [*Plate 337.*]

MUSEO CORRER. Inv. 9. Dead Christ upheld by Angels.

CONTE VITTORIO CINI. Inv. 6269. S. George and the Dragon (companion to Milan, Poldi Pezzoli and to Rome, Colonna). *Plate 726.*

Vienna. 90 (Inv. 1867). Lunette: dead Christ upheld by Angels.

Washington (D.C.). 450. (KRESS COLLECTION. K 1082.) Bust of man.

827. (KRESS COLLECTION. K 1373.) 'Pratt' Madonna and sleeping Child; Annunciation in roundels above.

1089. (KRESS COLLECTION. K 1429.) Four panels from portable altarpiece: Angel and Virgin of Annunciation, S. Francis, S. Maurelius (formerly Cook). (1475?).

B.13.524. (ROSENWALD COLLECTION.) Miniature: S. Francis receiving Stigmata.

TURINO VANNI DA RIGOLI (or DA PISA)

Pisan follower of Taddeo di Bartolo, documented 1390–1438, active in Genoa 1405–19.

Altenburg. 24 (94). Madonna and Child enthroned with S. James and S. Ranieri.*

Bayonne. 201. Assumption (fr.).

Birmingham (Ala.). MUSEUM OF ART (KRESS COLLECTION. K 176, 177). Side-panels of polyptych: Full-length SS. Lucy and Agnes; full-length Bishop Saint and S. Francis. *Plates 464–465.*

Genoa. S. BARTOLOMEO DEGLI ARMENI. Triptych: Madonna and Child with Angels; ten male Saints; ten female Saints; in predella, S. Bartholomew heals the woman possessed by the Devil, baptizes the King and Queen of the Armenians, sits surrounded by Basilian monks and worshippers, preaches, is beheaded. Sd and formerly d. 1415.

Palermo. Inv. 12 (old inv. 202). Altarpiece from S. Martino alla Scala, Pisa: Madonna and Child enthroned, with three Archangels, three Angels, SS. John Baptist, John Evangelist, Peter, Anthony Abbot, Mary Magdalen, Catherine, Ursula and Lucy. Sd and formerly dated. L. *Plate 468.*

Paris. 1563. Altarpiece from S. Silvestro, Pisa: Madonna and Child enthroned with six Angels. Sd. E. *Plate 466.*

MUSÉE DE CLUNY. 1669/1674. Five panels of dismembered polyptych: Madonna and Child with two Angels, S. Philip, S. Nicholas, two Archangels (frs., also listed Rossello di Jacopo Franchi).

Pisa. 69, 70 (BP IV, 30, 27). Angel and Virgin of Annunciation.

73 (BP IV, 29). Polyptych from Convent of S. Miniato: Madonna and Child enthroned with SS. Lucy and Elizabeth; SS. Euphrasia, Bartholomew, John Baptist and Ursula; in pinnacles, Redeemer, Angel and Virgin of Annunciation; in predella, three roundels with Dead Christ, mourning Virgin and John Evangelist, S. Bartholomew casting down idols, Flaying of S. Bartholomew; (two further scenes are later addition); in pilasters, eight Saints.

85 (BP III, 14). Baptism of Christ. ca 1395.

S. DONNINO IN S. GIUSTO. Madonna and Child enthroned. d. 1402.

S. PAOLO A RIPA D'ARNO. Altarpiece from the destroyed church of S. Cassiano: Madonna and Child enthroned with SS. Ranieri and Torpè and two female Blessed. Sd and d. 1397. *Plate 467.*

(Environs). RIGOLI, PIEVE DI S. MARCO. Madonna and Child enthroned with eight Angels. Sd. ca 1410.

Randazzo (Sicily). S. GREGORIO. Triptych from Casa Fisauli: Madonna suckling the Child, crowned by two Angels; a Saint on either side; above, Deposition, Angel and Virgin of Annunciation.

Rome. VATICAN, PINACOTECA. S. Margaret and scenes from her life. (?)

'UGOLINO LORENZETTI'

Sienese, active 1320–60. Temporary name for an artistic personality emerging from Ugolino di Nerio and passing over to the Lorenzetti. [Lately identified with Bartolomeo Bulgarini.]

Amsterdam. OTTO LANZ COLLECTION (EX). S. Helena.

Athens (Ga.). UNIVERSITY OF GEORGIA. R.I (KRESS STUDY COLLECTION. K 447). Panel of polyptych: S. Clare.

Basle. ROBERT VON HIRSCH COLLECTION. Predella panel: Blinding of S. Leodegarius (companion to Paris).

Boston (Mass.). GARDNER MUSEUM. Tabernacle: Madonna and Child enthroned with Angels, SS. Peter, Paul, Mary Magdalen and Catherine; in embrasure, SS. John Evangelist and John Baptist, Anthony Abbot and Bishop Saint; in trefoil above, blessing Redeemer.

Cambridge (Mass.). FOGG ART MUSEUM. 1917. 89. Nativity. *Plate 70.*

E. WALDO FORBES (EX). Wing of diptych: Christ on Cross, with Virgin, S. Mary Magdalen and S. John Evangelist (lent to Fogg 472.1931).

Cologne. 494. Centre panel of Ramboux polyptych (companion to Siena, S. Pellegrino?): Madonna and Child enthroned, with bird tied to a string (fr.).

610, 611. Top panels of Ramboux polyptych: S. Peter, S. Matthew.

SCHNÜTGEN MUSEUM. Pinnacle: S. Francis.

Columbia (S.C.). MUSEUM OF ART. 54–402/3. KRESS COLLECTION. K 106. Left panel of polyptych: S. Mary Magdalen.

Esztergom. 55.142, 55.143. Pinnacles: Moses, Daniel.

Florence. UFFIZI. 6136, 6137. Side-panels to Siena 76: S. Peter and half-length Saint in predella; S. John Baptist and half-length Saint in predella.

BERENSON COLLECTION. Crucifixion with S. Francis.

MUSEO HORNE. 54. Christ on Cross with mourning Virgin, S. John Evangelist and Mary Magdalen (r.).

S. CROCE, MUSEO DELL'OPERA. 8. Polyptych: Madonna and Child; SS. Matthew, John Baptist, John Evangelist, Francis; in pinnacles, Hermit Saint, S. Paul, blessing Redeemer, S. Peter, S. Michael; in predella, Christ in Sepulchre and four small Saints. E.

Fogliano (Siena). PIEVE. Centre panel of polyptych: Madonna and Child (companion to Siena, 42, 43). E. *Plate 65.*

Grosseto. MUSEO D'ARTE SACRA. Madonna and Child enthroned.

Le Mans. 4. Crucifixion.

London. HENRY HARRIS (EX). Panel of polyptych: Half-length S. John Baptist.

Lucca. PINACOTECA. Two panels from S. Cerbone polyptych: Madonna and Child; Evangelist (companions to Rome and Washington). *Plates 68, 69.*

New Haven (Conn.). 1943.244. Centre panel of polyptych: Madonna and Child (fr.; companion to Pisa?). L. *Plate 72.*

New York. HISTORICAL SOCIETY. B–14. Crucifixion. E. (?)

B–16. Portable altarpiece: Madonna and Child with four Angels, SS. John Baptist and Catherine; in wings, Conversion of S. Paul, S. Michael; in pinnacles, Crucifixion, Angel and Virgin of Annunciation (r.).

S. H. KRESS FOUNDATION. K 1045. Right wing of diptych: Crucifixion and Virgin of Annunciation above.

ROBERT LEHMAN COLLECTION. Top panel of polyptych: SS. Matthew and Thomas. L.

Oxford. CHRIST CHURCH. 3. Portable altarpiece: Madonna and Child with six Angels and donor; in wings, S. Francis receiving Stigmata, Crucifixion. E.

Palermo. CHIARAMONTE BORDONARO COLLECTION. 100. Polyptych from S. Agostino at San Gimignano: Madonna and Child holding crown; four Saints; in pinnacles, Blessing Redeemer and small Saints (r.). *Plate 71.*

Paris. 1665. Predella panel: Crucifixion (companion to Basle).

Perugia. VAN MARLE COLLECTION (EX). Pinnacle: S. Luke.

Panels of polyptych: Two Prophets.

Philadelphia (Pa.). J. G. JOHNSON COLLECTION. 92. Wings of portable altarpiece: SS. Andrew, Augustine (?), Bartholomew, Stephen and Angel of Annunciation above; SS. Dominic, Francis, Lucy, Agatha and Virgin of Annunciation above.

Pienza. SEMINARIO, CAPPELLA. Madonna and Child (r.).

Pisa. (B.P., V, 32, 33, 35, 36.) Side-panels of polyptych (companions to New Haven?): SS. Michael, Agatha, Catherine, Bartholomew. L. *Plates 73–74.*

Rome. PINACOTECA CAPITOLINA. 345, 346. Side-panels from S. Cerbone polyptych: S. Bartholomew, S. Clare (companions to Lucca and Washington).

Sestano (Siena). S. BARTOLOMEO. Three panels of polyptych: S. Peter enthroned, S. Paul, S. John Evangelist.

Siena. 42, 43. Side-panels to Fogliano: S. Ansanus, S. Galganus. E. *Plates 64, 66.*

54. Parts of dismembered polyptych from S. Caterina at Radicondoli: Crucifixion with Madonna and Child in pinnacle; S. Mary Magdalen with S. Bartholomew above; S. Catherine with S. Anthony Abbot above (r.).

59. Side panel of polyptych: S. Gregory (companion to 75, 76 and to Florence, Uffizi).

61. Centre panel of polyptych from S. Maria della Scala: Assumption. L.

72, 74. Panels of polyptych: S. Peter enthroned, S. Paul enthroned.

75. Predella panel to 59: Half-length Saint.

76. Centre panel of polyptych: Madonna and Child enthroned with eight Angels; six Angels in spandrels (companion to 59, 75 and to Florence, Uffizi).

80. Centre panel of polyptych, from S. Maria della Scala: Madonna and Child with eleven Angels; six Angels in spandrels. L.

ARCHIVIO DI STATO. Biccherna: Tax collector and taxpayer. 1340. (?)

Biccherna: Chancellor and scribe. 1353.

S. MARIA DEI SERVI. Painted Crucifix. (?)

S. PELLEGRINO ALLA SAPIENZA. Side panels of polyptych: S. Peter, S. Paul (companions to Cologne?).

s. PIETRO OVILE. Madonna and Child enthroned, with four Angels. L. *Plate 75*.

Tucson (Arizona). UNIVERSITY, 61.111 (KRESS COLLECTION. K 1364). Madonna of Humility.

Washington (D.C.). 521 (KRESS COLLECTION. K 1302). Side-panel from S. Cerbone polyptych: S. Catherine (companion to Lucca and Rome). *Plate 67*.

Zurich. STEHLI COLLECTION. Crucifixion. L.

UGOLINO DI NERIO

Sienese. Mentioned 1317–27. Son of a painter, his brothers Guido di Nerio and Minuccio di Nerio were painters as well. Close follower of Duccio.

Bagnano (Val d'Elsa). s. MARIA. Triptych: Madonna and Child, SS. Peter and Romulus; in pinnacles, Redeemer, SS. Francis and Mary Magdalen (st., r.).

Balcarres (Fife, Scotland). EARL OF CRAWFORD AND BALCARRES. Christ on Cross between mourning Virgin and S. John Evangelist (variant formerly at Ponte-dera).

Berlin. 1635, 1635C, D, E. Three parts of polyptych from High Altar of S. Croce, Florence: SS. John Baptist, Paul, Peter, with Angels in spandrels and couples of half-length Saints in register above (SS Elizabeth of Hungary and Matthias, SS. Matthew and James the Less, SS. James the More and Philip) (see London).
1635A, B. Two predella panels from S. Croce polyptych: Flagellation, Entomb-ment (see London). *Plate 40*.

Birmingham. BARBER INSTITUTE. Left panel of polyptych: S. Francis; half-length Angel above.

Boston (Mass.). 16.65. Madonna and Child (st.).

Brolio (Chianti). CASTELLO, BARONE RICASOLI. Polyptych: Madonna and Child, SS. Peter, Paul, John Baptist, John Evangelist; in pinnacles, Redeemer and four Angels (r.).

Cambridge (Mass.). 1921.8. S. John Baptist worshipped by S. Clare and S. Francis (r.). (?)

Champaign. See Urbana.

Chianciano. MUSEO DI ARTE SACRA. Roundel from pinnacle: Bust of blessing Redeemer (st.).

Chicago (Ill.). 37.1007. Madonna and Child enthroned with SS. John Baptist, Peter, Paul, Dominic and kneeling Dominican (st.).

Cleveland (Ohio). 61.40. Polyptych: Madonna and Child; SS. Francis, John Baptist, James, Mary Magdalen; in pinnacles, Christ on Cross, SS. Matthew, Paul, Peter, Andrew.

Cracow. Inv. XII.183. Left panel of polyptych: S. Michael (companion to Princeton, San Francisco and Urbana).

Dublin. 1112. Pinnacle: Isaiah.

Florence. CONTINI BONACOSSI COLLECTION. Fragmentary 'Gori Pannilini' polyptych from San Giovanni d'Asso: Madonna and Child, SS. Peter and Paul; in pinnacles, Redeemer and two small Saints (st.). *Plate* 44.

'Tadini Buoninsegni' Madonna and Child (with Duccio?).

BERENSON COLLECTION. Left panel of polyptych: S. Thomas (st.).

Greenwich (Conn.). MR AND MRS T. S. HYLAND (EX). Panel of polyptych: Saint with book (companion to Poznań).*

Grosseto. MUSEO D'ARTE SACRA. S. Michael slaying the dragon. (?) *Plate* 42.

London. 1188, 1189, 3375, 4191. Four predella panels of dismembered polyptych from High Altar of S. Croce, Florence: Betrayal of Christ, Way to Golgotha, Deposition, Resurrection.

3376. Pinnacle of S. Croce polyptych: Isaiah.

3377, 3473. Top panels of S. Croce polyptych: SS. Simon and Thaddeus; SS. Bartholomew and Andrew.

3378. Spandrels with Angels, from S. Croce polyptych. For other surviving panels of S. Croce polyptych, see Berlin, Los Angeles, New York, Philadelphia, Richmond. ca 1325.

Los Angeles (California). A.5141.49–660. Spandrels of lost centre panel of S. Croce polyptych: Adoring Angels (see London).

Lucca. PINACOTECA. Predella: SS. Agnes, Mary Magdalen, Nicholas, Stephen, Louis of Toulouse, Michael and Crucifixion (st.).

Maidenhead. SIR THOMAS MERTON. Roundel with Prophet inserted in male portrait by Botticelli. (?)

Montepulciano. S. MARIA DEI SERVI. Centre panel of polyptych: Madonna and Child (formerly deposited Florence, Uffizi).

Monterongríffoli (Senese). S. LORENZO. Polyptych: Madonna and Child, SS. Ansanus, Lawrence, Leonard and Augustine; in pinnacles, Blessing Redeemer, SS. Peter and Paul and two Angels (st.).

Montisi (Senese). CHIESA DELL'ANNUNZIATA. Painted Crucifix. (?)

New York. 41.190.31. Portable altarpiece: Crucifixion with S. Francis; in wings, Annunciation, Nativity, Adoration of Magi, Coronation and six Saints (st.).

R. LEHMAN. Predella panel of S. Croce polyptych: Last Supper (see London). *Plate* 41.

Madonna and Child.

Right panel of polyptych: S. Matthew (fr.).

Olena (Chianti). S. PIETRO. Triptych: Madonna and Child, SS. Peter and John Evangelist; in pinnacles, blessing Redeemer and two Angels (st.).

Philadelphia (Pa.). J. G. JOHNSON COLLECTION. 89. Pinnacle of S. Croce polyptych: Daniel (see London).

90. Pinnacle: Christ on Cross with mourning Virgin, Magdalen and S. John Evangelist.

Poggibonsi. S. LUCCHESE, SACRISTY. Busts of Saints and Prophets decorating cupboard doors (st.).

Pontedera. TOSCANELLI COLLECTION (EX). Christ on Cross with mourning Virgin, S. John Evangelist and Angels (variant of Balcarres).

Poznań. 546. Panel of polyptych: S. John Baptist (companion to Greenwich).*

Princeton (N.J.). ART MUSEUM. Centre panel of polyptych, companion to Cracow, Urbana and San Francisco: 'Platt' Madonna and Child (r.).

Richmond (Surrey). COOK COLLECTION. 1, 2. Two pinnacles of S. Croce polyptych: Moses, Aaron (see London).

   3. Symbols of Passion and two Angels (fr.).

Saint Louis (Mo.). 46.41. S. John Baptist preaching (fr.). E.

San Casciano Val di Pesa. S. MARIA DELLA MISERICORDIA. Two panels of polyptych: SS. Francis and Peter, knee-length.

— HIGH ALTAR. Madonna and Child enthroned and tiny donor. *Plate 43.*

San Francisco (Cal.). CALIFORNIA PALACE OF THE LEGION OF HONOR. 1952.36–37. Left and right panel of polyptych: S. Mary Magdalen, S. Louis of Toulouse (companions to Cracow, Princeton and Urbana). After 1317 (when Louis of Toulouse was canonized).

San Giovanni d'Asso (Senese). PIEVE DI S. GIOVANNI BATTISTA. Triptych: Madonna and Child, SS. John Baptist and Evangelist; in pinnacles, blessing Redeemer and two Angels (st.).

S. PIETRO IN VILLORE. Fragmentary polyptych, now Florence.

Siena. 34. Christ on Cross with mourning Virgin, S. John Evangelist and S. Francis (the latter formerly covered by sixteenth century Magdalen). L.

   36. Painted Cross.

   39. Polyptych: Madonna and Child, SS. Clare, Stephen, John Evangelist and Francis.

   596. Fragment of painted Cross from Conservatorio di S. Girolamo at Montepulciano: Mourning Virgin.

PALAZZO PUBBLICO, SALA DEL MAPPAMONDO. Retouching of flesh parts in Guido da Siena's Maestà.

Urbana. UNIVERSITY OF ILLINOIS, KRANNERT ART MUSEUM. Right panel of polyptych: S. Catherine (companion to Cracow, Princeton and San Francisco).

Williamstown (Mass.). STERLING AND FRANCINE CLARK ART INSTITUTE. Polyptych: Madonna and Child, SS. Francis, Andrew, Paul, Peter, Stephen and Louis of Toulouse; in spandrels, fourteen Angels; in pinnacles, Blessing Redeemer, Isaiah, Ezechiel, Moses, David, Daniel, Jeremiah. After 1317.* *Plates 45–46.*

URBANI, Ludovico da San Severino

Marchigian documented 1460 to 1493 at Sanseverino, Recanati, Macerata and Potenza Picena. Follower of Matteo da Gualdo and of his own townsman, Lorenzo da Sanseverino the Younger (Lorenzo d'Alessandro).

Colmar. 263. Pinnacle: Crucifixion (companion to Matelica). *Plate 967.*
Matelica. S. TERESA, SACRISTY. Two side-panels of polyptych: SS. Sebastian and Catherine, with bust of Daniel above; SS. John Baptist and Romuald with bust of Elisha above (companions to Colmar). *Plates 966, 968.*
Nevers. 22 (CAMPANA N. 435). Centre panel of polyptych: Madonna and Child with five Angels (companion to Recanati, Museo Diocesano).
Recanati. MUSEO DIOCESANO. Triptych: Madonna and Child with ten Angels, S. Benedict, S. Sebastian; six small Saints in pilasters; Dead Christ, Angel and Virgin of Annunciation in pinnacles; four Saints and three Stories of S. Sebastian in predella. Sd. 1474.
Side-panels of polyptych: Bishop Saint kneeling, S. Francis receiving stigmata (companions to Nevers).
S. MARIA DI CASTELNUOVO (EX). Madonna and Child enthroned with SS. Anthony Abbot and Nicholas. Sd and d. 1480. *Plate 970.*
Rome. VATICAN, PINACOTECA. 261 (173). Predella panel: Adoration of Magi.
Homeless. Assumption of Magdalen. (?) *Plate 969.*
Madonna suckling the Child. (*Proporzioni*, 1948, fig. 196, Zeri).

VANNI, Andrea

Siena, ca 1332–1414. Perhaps pupil of Lippo Memmi, strongly influenced by Barna and by works of Simone Martini and the Lorenzetti. Partner of Bartolo di Fredi in 1353, worked with Antonio Veneziano in the Duomo of Siena 1370. First journey to Naples 1375. Documented again in Naples 1383.

Altenburg. 46. Left panel of Casaluce polyptych: S. Francis (companion to Naples) *Plate 397.*
Aversa (Naples). (Environs.) CAPPELLA DI CASALUCE. Frescoes: Dormitio, Assumption of Virgin and other scenes; S. Anthony Abbot, S. Catherine of Siena (r.). 1375.
Berlin. 1054A. Madonna and Child with pear. E.
Boston (Mass.). 22.3/4. Two panels of polyptych from Monistero di S. Eugenio, Siena: SS. Peter and Paul (companions to New York).
GARDNER MUSEUM. Portable altarpiece: Crucifixion; in central pinnacle, Redeemer; in wings, SS. Stephen and Anthony Abbot with Angel of Annunciation above; SS. Catherine and John Baptist with Virgin of Annunciation above. *Plate 392.*

Right pinnacle of polyptych: S. Elizabeth of Hungary. (?)

Cambridge. FITZWILLIAM MUSEUM. 560. Madonna suckling the Child. E.

Cambridge (Mass.). FOGG ART MUSEUM. 1914.9. Two pinnacles; Angel and Virgin of Annunciation. *Plate 388.*

Florence. BERENSON COLLECTION. Madonna and Child.

Frankfurt a/M. 1467/8/9. Three panels of polyptych: Full-length S. Anne holding Virgin Mary, S. Ursula and S. Agnes.

Ingenheim. GRAF INGENHEIM (EX). Resurrection (companion to Leningrad and Washington). ca 1383. *Plate 389.*

Leningrad. HERMITAGE. Ascension (companion to Ingenheim and Washington). ca 1383. *Plate 390.*

Minturno (Gaeta). SS. ANNUNZIATA. Fragmentary frescoes: Annunciation, S. Christopher. (?)

Naples. 40. Left panel of Casaluce polyptych: S. James (companion to Altenburg). *Plate 396.*

New Orleans (Louisiana). I. DELGADO MUSEUM OF ART. 61.61 (KRESS COLLECTION. K 233). Predella panel: Adoration of Magi.

New York. DR LILLIAN MALCOVE. Panel of polyptych from Monistero di S. Eugenio, Siena: Evangelist (companion to Boston). *Plate 394.*

Oxford. ASHMOLEAN MUSEUM. 447. Leaf of diptych: Madonna suckling the Child and Angel of Annunciation above.

Paris. CHALANDON COLLECTION (EX). Madonna and Child enthroned crowned by two Angels, with SS. Catherine, Dominic and kneeling donor.

Perugia. MUSEO DELL'OPERA DEL DUOMO. 9. Madonna and Child with two small Prophets; Angel and Virgin of Annunciation in roundels above (r.; face of Virgin probably repainted by Fiorenzo di Lorenzo).

VAN MARLE COLLECTION (EX). Left panel of polyptych: Blessed Andrea Gallerani.

Pontedera. TOSCANELLI COLLECTION (EX). Pinnacle: Blessing Redeemer. *Plate 395.*

Siena. 114. Triptych from S. Francesco all'Alberino: Crucifixion and four Prophets. 1396. *Plate 393.*

PALAZZO PUBBLICO, SALA DEI CARDINALI. Fresco painted over previous figure: full-length S. Paul (the date 136.. seems to belong to previous fresco). (?)

S. DOMENICO, CAPPELLA DELLE VOLTE. Fresco: S. Catherine of Siena holding out her hand to female Donor.

S. DONATO. Madonna and Child (st.).

— ORATORIO DI S. MICHELE O DEI SS. CHIODI. Madonna enthroned suckling the Child (fr. cut into an oval).

S. FRANCESCO, FIRST CHAPEL R. OF CHOIR. Madonna and Child enthroned. 1398.

— LAST CHAPEL L. OF CHOIR. Fresco: Madonna and Child enthroned (r.).

S. SPIRITO, THIRD CHAPEL L. Madonna enthroned and Child holding bird, worshipped by donor.

S. STEFANO, HIGH ALTAR. Polyptych: Madonna and Child, fourteen Saints, Annunciation, four Evangelists (predella by Giovanni di Paolo). 1400. *Plate 398.*

Washington (D.C.). CORCORAN GALLERY. 26.181. Three panels of polyptych: Crucifixion, Agony in the Garden, Descent into Limbo (companions to Ingenheim and Leningrad). Sd. ca 1383. [*Plate 268.*] *Plate 391.*

Zara (Dalmatia). MONASTERY OF S. MARIA. Painted Crucifix. (?)

Homeless. Madonna and Child. *Plate 387.*

VANNI, Lippo

Sienese. Documented as a miniaturist 1341 and 1345, as a painter up to 1373. Follower of Simone Martini, Lippo Memmi, and the Lorenzetti. Influenced slightly by Taddeo Gaddi and Bernardo Daddi.

Altenburg. 59. Predella panel: Dormition (companion to Göttingen). *Plate 341.*

Amsterdam. VAN REGTEREN ALTENA COLLECTION. Two miniatures: Madonna; SS. Peter and Paul.

— N. BEETS COLLECTION (EX). Two miniatures: S. Francis (or Anthony of Padua), in initial I; Monk saying Mass, in initial O. *Plate 345.*

Angers. MUSÉE. Madonna and Child. (?)

Baltimore (Md.). WALTERS ART GALLERY. 750. Portable altarpiece from Dominican convent of S. Aurea, Rome: Madonna and Child enthroned with SS. John Baptist and Aurea; in wings, SS. Dominic and Ansanus, S. Jerome and Apostle, Angel and Virgin of Annunciation.

Bayonne. MUSÉE BONNAT. Miniature: Christ appears to His Disciples, in initial O.

Berlin-Ost. 1094A. Portable altarpiece: Nativity and Annunciation.

Cambridge (Mass.). FOGG ART MUSEUM. Madonna and Child with Angels and SS. Peter and Paul.

— WALTER BERRY BEQUEST. Antiphonary with many miniatures.

Cleveland (Ohio). 24.1011. Illuminated initial: Nativity. E. (?)

Coral Gables (Florida). LOWE ART GALLERY, UNIVERSITY OF MIAMI, 61.24 (KRESS COLLECTION. K 1355). Triptych: Madonna and Child with donors, S. Elizabeth of Hungary and S. Dominic. E. *Plate 342.*

Cracow. JAGELLOŃSKA LIBRARY. Miniatures 19–27: Entry into Jerusalem, Agony in the Garden, Mocking of Christ, Way to Calvary, Ascension, Descent of the Holy Ghost, Pope Gregory, S. Clare, S. Agnes. (?)

Detroit (Ohio). INSTITUTE OF ART. Illuminated initial: Annunciation.

Florence. CHARLES LOESER (EX). Panel of polyptych: S. Dorothy (companion to New Haven, New York and Providence). (?)

Frankfurt a/M. 1470. Madonna and Child enthroned with SS. Paul, Catherine, Bishop, Peter and two Angels.

Geneva. LEDERER COLLECTION. Panel of polyptych: Half-length S. Luke (companion to New York). E. *Plate 339.*

Göttingen. 165. Predella panel: Crucifixion (companion to Altenburg).

Konopist. CASTLE. 21201, 21210. Diptych: Crucifixion, with Virgin of Annunciation above; Madonna and Child enthroned with four Saints, four Angels, and Angel of Annunciation above. (?)

Le Mans. 13. Madonna and Child with goldfinch and two Angels. *Plate* 348.

Milan. AMBROSIANA. Ivory diptych: Virgin and S. John Evangelist, with female Saint below; Ecce Homo with Magdalen below.

Naples. 275. Noli me tangere.

New Haven (Conn.). 1943.240/11 (EX). (Formerly M. F. Griggs, New York.) S. Agnes, S. Anthony of Padua. (?) (Companion to Florence, New York and Providence.)

New York. 32.100.100. Madonna and Child with two Angels and SS. Peter and Paul.

    41.100.23. Panel of polyptych: Half-length Apostle (companion to Geneva and R. Lehman). E.

    64.189.2. Panel of polyptych: S. Clare (companion to Florence, New Haven, Providence). (?)

    ROBERT LEHMAN COLLECTION. Three panels of polyptych: Half-length Madonna and Child, S. Peter, S. Ansanus (companions to Geneva and Metropolitan Museum). E. *Plate* 338.

Paris. CABINET DES DESSINS. 1313. Miniature: Annunciation, in the initial M.

    CONTE MARIO PINCI. Madonna and Child enthroned with Magdalen, S. Augustine and two Angels.

    M. MERCIER (EX). Madonna and Child, with blessing Redeemer in roundel above.

Perugia. 59. Madonna and Child (fr.). ca 1355. *Plate* 347.

Providence (R.I.). 21.250. Panel of polyptych: S. Mary Magdalen (companion to Florence, New Haven, New York). (?)

Rome. VATICAN, PINACOTECA. 224. Reliquary triptych: S. Peter Martyr, S. Dominic and S. Thomas Aquinas.

    SS. DOMENICO E SISTO, EX-CONVENT, ANGELICA LIBRARY. Reliquary triptych from church of S. Aurea: Madonna and Child enthroned with two Angels, SS. Dominic and Aurea and reclining Eve with Serpent; in wings, four scenes from life of S. Aurea (Flagellation, Bishop Cyriacus, Aurea and Maxima raise to life the tailor's son, they undergo the trial of the fire, S. Aurea is thrown into the sea with a stone attached to her neck); in predella, Dead Christ, busts of S. Thomas Aquinas and S. Bartholomew. Sd and d. 1358. *Plate* 351.

Saltwood Castle (Kent). SIR KENNETH CLARK. Illuminated initials: Christ opens the eyes of the Apostles, Christ talks to the Apostles, S. Agatha. Plate 344.

San Gimignano. PALAZZO COMUNALE O DEL POPOLO, CAPPELLA DELLE CARCERI. Fresco: Madonna and Child enthroned with SS. Giminianus and Augustine.

Siena. ARCHIVIO DI STATO. Book cover (gabella): Circumcision. d. 1357. (?)

    'Statuto del Campaio': miniature: Madonna in Glory. 1361. (?)

    PALAZZO PUBBLICO, SALA DEL MAPPAMONDO. Monochrome fresco: S. Paul, sur-

Montefeltro in 1363 in the Val di Chiana (the next fresco, of the victory at rounded by seven Virtues, directs the victory of the Sienese over Nicola da Poggio Imperiale, was painted in 1480 by Giovanni di Cristofano and Francesco di Andrea). Sd and d. 1373. *Plate* 352.

MUSEO DELL'OPERA DEL DUOMO, CODEX 180. Miniatures: f.1—Last Judgement; Baptism, in initial H; f.154—Annunciation; f.171—Christ sends Apostles to preach.

— CODEX 181. Miniatures: f.1—The three Maries at the Tomb; Christ appears to Apostles, in initial P; Descent of Holy Ghost, in initial A; half-length Baptist, in initial P.

— GRADUAL 4 (FROM SPEDALE DELLA SCALA). Miniatures: f.3—Descent of the Holy Ghost; f.8—Annunciation; f.14—Birth of Virgin; f.22—Assumption; f.27—Presentation (possibly also f.82—Resurrection). 1345. *Plates* 343.

PONTIFICIO SEMINARIO REGIONALE PIO XII, CAPPELLA, L. WALL. Frescoed polyptych: Madonna and Child enthroned; SS. Francis, John Baptist, Catherine, Anthony (?); in pinnacles, blessing Christ and busts of four Saints; in predella, Pietà and four Evangelists.

— Illuminated antiphonary. *Plate* 340.

S. DOMENICO, CLOISTERS. Fragmentary frescoes: Annunciation (only heads of Angels and Virgin left); S. Paul and two heads of Saints. Formerly Sd and d. 1372.

(Environs). LECCETO, ENTRANCE DOOR. Frescoed lunette: Christ and two Angels. (?)

— — CLOISTERS, SOUTH WALL. Frescoed lunette: Risen Christ. (?)

— S. LEONARDO AL LAGO, APSE, VAULT. Frescoes: Hierarchies of Angels. *Plate* 346.

— — — L. WALL. Frescoes: Presentation of Virgin; in frieze, half-length SS. Colomba, Mary Magdalen, Cecilia. *Plate* 346.

— — — CENTRE WALL. Frescoes: Angel and Virgin of Annunciation; in frieze, half-length SS. Agnes, Agatha, Ursula.

— — — R. WALL. Frescoes: Marriage of Virgin; in frieze, half-length SS. Lucy, Martha, Margaret.

— — SOFFIT OF ENTRANCE ARCH. Frescoes: six monochrome Virtues with wings (Constantia, Temperantia, Patientia, Justitia, Fortitudo, Humilitas).

— — ENTRANCE PILLARS. Frescoes: left, S. Catherine and kneeling donor; right, S. Monica and kneeling donor.

— — TRIUMPHAL ARCH. Frescoes: above, Assumption; left, S. Leonard and four stories of his life (st.); right, S. Augustine and Prayers of S. Monica for her son (st.).

Tours. MUSÉE, LINET BEQUEST. Coronation, with Christ blessing above.

Vienna-Lainz. ROSSIANA LIBRARY. Sammelband II, f.66: miniature—Blessing Bishop, in initial E.

Homeless. Predella panel: S. Monica and S. Augustine. *Plate* 349.

VECCHIETTA

Lorenzo di Pietro, called Vecchietta. Castiglione d'Orcia ca 1412–1480 Siena. Registered as Sienese painter in 1428; also sculptor and architect. Pupil of Sassetta.

Beaulieu (Alpes-Maritimes). VILLA SYLVIA, RALPH CURTIS (EX). Lunette; Crucifixion flanked by Busts of SS. John Baptist and Bishop Saint.

Castiglione d'Olona (Varese). COLLEGIATA, CHOIR. Frescoes: Burial of S. Stephen, Martyrdom and Burial of S. Lawrence, Self-portrait(?; see also Masolino, Neri di Bicci and Paolo Schiavo).

Castiglione d'Orcia (Senese). S. MARIA MADDALENA. Centre panel of triptych: Madonna and Child with four Angels.

Florence. UFFIZI. 474. Triptych of Giacomo d'Andreuccio Setaiuolo: Madonna and Child; SS. Bartholomew, James and kneeling Eligius; SS. Andrew, Lawrence and kneeling Dominic; four small Saints in pilasters. Sd and d. 1457. *Plate 803.*

    BERENSON COLLECTION. Processional Cross (in finials, on front—Eternal, Virgin, S. John, S. Mary Magdalen; on back—four Evangelists) (st.).

Liverpool. 2758. Predella panel, companion to Munich and Rome: S. Bernardino da Siena preaching. [*Plate 272.*]

Memphis (Tennessee). BROOKS MEMORIAL ART GALLERY. 61.192 (KRESS COLLECTION. K 290). Bierhead: Deposition (st.).

Munich. 1020. Predella panel, companion to Liverpool and Rome: Miracle of S. Anthony of Padua (g.p.).

New York. R. LEHMAN. S. Bernardino preaching (on parchment).

Paris. MUSÉE DE CLUNY. 1699. Triptych: Madonna and Child with Angels, SS. John Baptist and Jerome; Angel and Virgin of Annunciation in roundels.

Pienza. MUSEO DIOCESANO D'ARTE SACRA. Madonna and Child enthroned with SS. Blaise, John Baptist, Nicholas and Florian; in lunette, Annunciation; in predella, Martyrdom of S. Blaise, Crucifixion, S. Nicholas and the three Maidens without dowry. *Plate 804.*

    DUOMO (ASSUNTA), CHAPEL L. OF CHOIR. Triptych: Assumption; SS. Agatha and Pius, SS. Callistus and Catherine. Sd. 1461/2. *Plate 805.*

    (Environs). S. ANNA IN CAMPRENA. Predella panel: Monks building a monastery.*

Princeton (N.J.). 62.85 (formerly Platt). S. Bernardino (st.).

Rome. VATICAN, PINACOTECA. 233. Predella panel, companion to Liverpool and Munich: Miracle of S. Louis of France.

Siena. 204. 'Arliquiera' (doors of cupboard for relics) from sacristy of S. Maria della Scala: outside (divided into eighteen sections) from left to right and from top to bottom—Angel of Annunciation, Crucifixion, Resurrection, Virgin of Annunciation; S. Ansanus, S. Ambrose Sansedoni, S. Bernardino da Siena, Blessed Agostino Novello, Blessed Andrea Gallerani, S. Savinus, S. Julian, S. Catherine of Siena, S. Pier Pettignano, Blessed Sorore, S. Galganus, S.

Crescentius; inside, right door—Last Supper, Washing of Feet, Betrayal of Christ, Christ before Caiaphas; inside, left door—Christ before Pilate, Flagellation, Crowning with Thorns, Way to Calvary. 1445. *Plate* 799.

205. S. Bernardino; below, S. Bernardino preaching. (?)

210. Madonna and Child enthroned with SS. Peter, Paul, Lawrence and Francis (r.) (from S. Maria della Scala). Sd. After 1476.

404. Design for the ciborium of the cathedral. 1472.

577. Left panel of polyptych: S. Lawrence.

ARCHIVIO DI STATO. Book-covers:

Spedale di S. Maria della Scala: The Rector of the Spedale gives candles to a monk. Libro della Cera n. 464. Begun May 1441.

Spedale di S. Maria della Scala: A lay-brother taking the habit. (Libro delle Oblazioni n. 176, 1347–1437.) (?)

Spedale di S. Maria della Scala: A lay-brother offers money to the Rector of the hospital. (Libro de' Danari n. 466.)

Compagnia della Morte: Beheading of S. John Baptist (Libro delle Entrate e Uscite, 1463–1527.)

Spedale di S. Maria della Scala: Wheat is given to the hospital. Libro del Grano, n. 465. (Book begun May 1441.)

Opera metropolitana: Angels holding a shield. d. 1458.

Biccherna: Coronation of Pope Pius II. d. 1460. *Plate* 806.

Gabella: Pope Pius II dons his nephew Francesco Todeschini Piccolomini, Bishop of Siena, with the Cardinal's Hat. d. 1460.

PALAZZO PUBBLICO, SALA DEI MATRIMONI (GROUND FLOOR). Frescoes: in lunette; Madonna of Mercy with SS. Savinus, Jerome, Peter Martyr, Catherine, Lawrence and Ansanus; in embrasure, 15 busts of Saints; in spandrels above, Adoring Angels, S. Bernardino and S. Martin with the beggar. 1453–57.

— SALA DEL MAPPAMONDO (FIRST FLOOR). Fresco: S. Catherine of Siena. Sd. Paid 1460. Inscribed 1461 after sanctification of Catherine. *Plate* 352.

BATTISTERO, VAULTS OF THREE BAYS ALONGSIDE FAÇADE. Frescoes: in each quart of vault, one full-length Apostle.

— VAULTS OF THREE BAYS ALONGSIDE APSE. Frescoes: Articles of the Creed (L. BAY— I believe in God the Father Almighty Maker of Heaven and Earth; in Jesus Christ his only Son; Who was conceived by the Holy Ghost, born of the Virgin Mary, i.e. Annunciation; Suffered under Pontius Pilate, was crucified, dead and buried. CENTRAL BAY—Rose again from the dead and descended into Hell; Ascended into heaven; Shall come to judge the quick and the dead; I believe in the Holy Ghost. R. BAY—I believe in the Holy Catholic Church; in the forgiveness of sins; in the resurrection of the body; in the communion of Saints and the Life everlasting). In corners, Prophets holding scrolls; ornamental friezes with Putti and Heads. *Plate* 801.

— APSE, FACE OF TRIUMPHAL ARCH. Fresco: Assumption of Virgin.

— —, WALLS. Frescoes (left to right): Flagellation, Angel and Virgin of Annunciation, Way to Calvary. Frieze with medallions: the seven Acts of Mercy and four Saints. In soffit of High Altar, busts of SS. Savinus, Crescentius, Blessed Ambrogio Sansedoni, S. Catherine of Siena, Blessed Pier Pettinaio, S. Francis of Assisi, S. Bernardino of Siena, Blessed Andrea Gallerani, S. Galganus, S. Victor. *Plate 802.*

— PILLARS OF APSE. Frescoes: Blessed Bernardo Tolomei, Franco da Grotti, Pietro Petroni and Giovacchino Piccolomini in niches (p.).

— LEFT OF APSE. Frescoed lunette: Miracles of S. Anthony of Padua (st.; with Benvenuto di Giovanni?).

S. ANSANO IN CASTEL VECCHIO, L. WALL. Frescoes: Adoration of Magi; S. Ansanus and worshpper. E.

S. MARIA ASSUNTA (DUOMO), ARCHIVIO DEL CAPITOLO. Codex with Constitution granted by Pius II in 1464. Illuminated frontispiece: Pope Pius II enthroned and kneeling Agapito Cenci di Ruspoli and Antonio Piccolomini.

— MUSEO DELL'OPERA. Detached frescoed lunette from Chapel in S. Francesco: Mourning over dead Christ. Probably 1448.

SPEDALE DI S. MARIA DELLA SCALA, PELLEGRINAIO. First fresco on left wall: The Virgin receives the souls of the foundlings ('La scala del Paradiso'). 1441. *Plate 797.*

— SALA DI S. PIETRO (FORMER CAPPELLA DEL SACRO CHIODO, NOW BIBLIOTECA). Frescoed decoration Sd and d. 1449.

— — VAULT. Frescoes in central lozenge, Christ in mandorla with Angels; in four nearest lozenges, the Evangelists (Luke and Mark obliterated by dampness); in farthest lozenges, the Church Fathers, two by two; in the ten pendentifs, roundels with Prophets holding scrolls (four destroyed).

— — WALL OPPOSITE ENTRANCE. Frescoes. I—Lunette: God the Father in Glory, the Redeemer in Glory and busts of Prophets in corners. Below: Adam and Eve worship their Maker in the Garden of Eden, surrounded by the Animals; the Youths in the fiery furnace (fr.). Monochrome female allegorical figure, below capital. II—Lunette: in foreground Angel and Virgin of Annunciation with God the Father blessing in sky; in middle distance, Nativity; in corners, busts of Isaiah and Jacob. Below, ruined fresco. Monochrome female allegorical figure below capital. III—Lunette: Crucifixion (r.). Below, Moses and the brazen Serpent.

— — WALL R. OF ENTRANCE. Frescoes. I—Lunette: Descent into Limbo, with busts of Prophets in corners; below, Scene outside walled city. II—Lunette: lost fresco; below, Jonah and the whale (repainted). (See Domenico di Bartolo for fresco under ciborium.)

— — ENTRANCE WALL. Frescoes. I—lost frescoes. Monochrome female allegorical figure below capital. II—Lunette: Last Judgement, with busts of Prophets in corners. Below: half Mankind destroyed by the fiery river issued from the Throne of God. Monochrome female allegorical figure below capital. III— Lunette: Descent of the Holy Ghost and busts of Prophets in corners. Below:

King Solomon praying by the altar of his Temple, and God's Fire descending on it (II Chronicles 6, 12–7, 3). *Plate 800.*

— — WALL L. OF ENTRANCE. Frescoes much ruined.

Venice. CONTE VITTORIO CINI. Inv. 2067. S. Peter Martyr (from pilaster of altarpiece).

SCULPTURES

Florence. BARGELLO. Wooden statue of S. Bernardino (from Narni). Sd. ca 1475.
   Bronze effigy of Mariano Socino or Sozzini (for a tomb in S. Domenico). 1467.
   MUSEO HORNE. Wooden statue of S. Paul from Castelfiorentino.

Istia d'Ombrone. PARISH CHURCH. Wooden, pigmented statue of Madonna and Child.

Lucca. PINACOTECA. Inv. 166. Relief in wood, pigmented and gilded: Assumption of the Virgin (left unfinished at his death; finished by Neroccio).

Montemerano. S. GIORGIO, APSE. Wooden pigmented statue of S. Peter.

— FIRST ALTAR R. Wooden pigmented relief of Assumption.

Narni. DUOMO. Wooden pigmented statue of S. Anthony Abbot. Sd and d. 1475.

New York. FRICK COLLECTION. Bronze relief: Resurrection. Sd and d. 1472.

Rome. S. MARIA DEL POPOLO, THIRD CHAPEL R. Bronze effigy of Bishop Girolamo Foscari. 1463–64.

Siena. LOGGIA DELLA MERCANZIA. Two marble statues: S. Peter, S. Paul. Sd. 1460–62.
   S. MARIA ASSUNTA (DUOMO), HIGH ALTAR. Bronze Ciborium. Sd and d. 1472.
   SPEDALE DI S. MARIA DELLA SCALA, CHURCH, HIGH ALTAR. Bronze Statue: Risen Christ. Sd and d. 1476. *Plate 807.*

Vico Alto. PARISH CHURCH. Wooden pigmented statue of Risen Christ (from Duomo of Siena). 1442. *Plate 798.*

VIGOROSO DA SIENA

Mentioned from 1276 (when he became citizen of Siena) to 1293. Painter and miniaturist.

Perugia. GALLERIA NAZIONALE DELL'UMBRIA. 32. Dossal from the Collegio della Sapienza: Madonna and Child with SS. Mary Magdalen, John Baptist, John Evangelist and Juliana; in pinnacles, blessing Redeemer and four Angels. Sd and d. 128(0?). *Plate 23.*

VINCENZO DA BRESCIA see FOPPA

VINCENZO DA CREMA see CIVERCHIO

VITALE DA BOLOGNA

Born ca 1305, last mentioned 1359, died before July 1361.

Bologna. COLLEZIONI COMUNALI. Two left panels of S. Maria dei Denti polyptych: S. Peter blessing a pilgrim and Angel above; SS. Anthony Abbot and James the More and Angel above (both panels cut at bottom; companions to Bologna, Davia Bargellini and to Vienna). 1345. *Plate 263.*

MUSEO DAVIA BARGELLINI. 129. Central panel of S. Maria dei Denti polyptych: Madonna and Child enthroned with male and female donors (companion to above and to Vienna). Sd and d. 1345.

PINACOTECA. Frescoes from S. Apollonia (or S. Maria) a Mezzaratta: Annunciation with Nativity below; Dream of Virgin; The Virgin appearing to a sick Man; Madonna and Child; Baptism of Christ. *Plate 265.*

Fresco from S. Francesco, Chiostro dei Morti: Resurrection (fr.).

Fresco from S. Francesco, Foresteria: Last Supper (fr.); on either side, SS. Catherine and Anthony of Padua, SS. Francis and Angel Raphael.

Coronation of the Virgin (from Budrio).

Four Scenes from Life of S. Anthony Abbot, possibly side panels of dispersed, signed altarpiece in S. Antonio (from the Museo di S. Stefano). *Plates 266–268.*

S. George killing the Dragon. Sd. *Plate 270.*

S. MARIA DEI SERVI, CHAPEL R. OF CHOIR. Frescoes: in vault, Fathers of the Church; under arches, Heads of Saints; on walls, Assumption (fr.), Scenes from Life of Magdalen (fr.).

— ARCH BETWEEN CHOIR AND L. CHAPEL. Fresco: Trinity.

S. MARTINO, R. WALL. Fresco: Head of Christ (fr. of Crucifixion). L.

S. MICHELE DEI LEPROSETTI. Fresco: Madonna and Child.

S. SALVATORE. Polyptych: Coronation of Virgin, S. Thomas of Canterbury with kneeling monk, S. John Baptist with worshipper, Nativity and two Saints in conversation below, Martyrdom of S. Catherine and two Saints in conversation below. Commissioned 1353.

Dublin. 1113. Four heads of Saints in roundels. (?)

Edinburgh. 952. Left wing of diptych: Adoration of Magi; in spandrels, Angels and Virgin of Annunciation.

Florence. R. LONGHI. Right wing of diptych: Pietà and worshipping Saints; in spandrels, the Eagle and the Lion.

Forlì. CHIESA DELL'ADDOLORATA. 'Madonna della Pace.'

Lugano. THYSSEN COLLECTION. Crucifixion.

Milan. MUSEO POLDI PEZZOLI. 594. Madonna of Humility with S. Catherine and female Martyr.

Pesaro. MUSEO CIVICO. S. Ambrose.

Petts Wood. MAX GOLD (EX). Madonna and Child.

Pomposa. ABBAZIA, APSE. Frescoes: Christ in Glory with Saints, Angels and Donor; middle register: half-length Madonna embracing the Child, the four Evangelists seated writing, S. Martin; lower register: S. Eustace has a vision of Christ in the antlers of the stag, is baptized with his family, is separated from his wife and children when crossing the water, mourns the death of his children by a wolf and a lion, is accused of being a Christian, S. Eustace and his family are thrown into prison and roasted alive in a brazen bull. d. 1351. *Plate 269.*

Rome. VATICAN, PINACOTECA. 96. 'Madonna dei Battuti'. Sd.

Udine. CATTEDRALE, CAPPELLA DI S. NICCOLÒ. Frescoes: Descent of the Holy Ghost, Scenes from life of S. Nicholas, heads of Saints (frs.). Documented 1348–1349.

Vienna. LANCKORONSKI COLLECTION. Two panels of S. Maria dei Denti polyptych: S. Mary Magdalen, S. Apollonia (companions to Bologna, Collezioni Comunali and Museo Davia Bargellini). 1345.

Viterbo. MUSEO CIVICO. 28. Madonna and Child worshipped by a Pope and a Cardinal (from S. Maria della Pace). *Plate 264.*

Timoteo VITI da Urbino

1467–1523. Pupil possibly of Giovanni Santi; formed by Costa and Francia at Bologna; influenced by Perugino.

Bergamo. 532. S. Margaret.

Bologna. 204 (inv. 590). S. Mary of Egypt. [*Plate 347.*]

Bristol. CITY ART GALLERY, SCHILLER BEQUEST. Agony in Garden (version of Cleveland).

Cagli (Urbino). S. ANGELO, HIGH ALTAR. 'Noli me tangere', SS. Michael and Anthony Abbot. Sd. 1518–19. *Plate 1057.*

   S. DOMENICO, R. WALL. Fresco: Annunciation with Eternal.

Cleveland (Ohio). 27.161. Miniature: Agony in the Garden (version of Bristol).

Florence. GALLERIA CORSINI. 407, 409. Apollo, Thalia (other Muses listed under Evangelista da Pian di Meleto). *Plate 1058.*

Fossombrone (Pesaro). VESCOVADO, CAPPELLA. Fresco: Crucifixion with Saints and Donor. d. 1493. (?)

Gubbio. DUOMO, SEVENTH BAY, L. WALL. S. Mary Magdalen. Sd and d. 1521. *Plate 1061.*

Milan. BRERA. 507. Annunciation, with SS. John Baptist and Sebastian.

   508. Madonna and Child with SS. Crescentius and Vitalis.

   509. Trinity with S. Jerome and donor. E.

Munich. WAF.315. Head of S. Michael (fr.).

Urbino. 732. SS. Roch and Joseph.

738. S. Sebastian (st.).

744. SS. Thomas and Martin with Archbishop Arrivabene and Duke Guidobaldo. 1504.

766. Stained glass window: Annunciation, Putti. *Plate* 1060.

— DEP. CONVENTO DELLA TRINITÀ: S. Apollonia. *Plate* 1059.

S. AGOSTINO, FIRST ALTAR L. Fresco. Madonna rescuing Child from Devil. d. 1564.

ZAGANELLI

Francesco (ca 1470–1532) and his brother Bernardino (died probably before 1514) Zaganelli, da Cotignola (near Faenza). Romagnol painters. Several pictures (up to 1509) are signed with both names. Francesco appears to be a pupil of Palmezzano, influenced by Ercole Roberti, Rondinelli and Fra Bartolomeo. Works by Bernardino or Francesco alone are here denoted with B or F.

Aix-en-Provence. 470. Deposition (after Mantegna).

Allington Castle (Maidstone). LORD CONWAY (EX). Bust of S. Catherine in prayer.

Amsterdam. 2741. Mourning over dead Christ. (B.?)

2741–A 1. Bust of S. Catherine holding palm. (B.)

Assisi. F. M. PERKINS COLLECTION. Mourning over dead Christ in Sepulchre. (?)

Baltimore (Md.). WALTERS ART GALLERY. 581. Madonna and Child with Mary
Magdalen, S. Sebastian and two other Saints (r.).

739. Predella panel: SS. Catherine, Anne with Virgin and Child, and Lucy. (B.)
Plate 1039.

Barnard Castle. BOWES ART MUSEUM. 44. Knee-length S. Catherine in landscape.

Bergamo. 255. Holy Family with Child asleep on parapet. Sd by both and d. 1509.

517. Predella panel: S. Anthony of Padua preaching to the fish (companion to
Berlin).

Berlin. I, 110. Two roundels: busts of SS. Stephen and Maurice.

236, 241. Two predella panels: S. Anthony gives speech to the newborn baby;
Miracle of the mule (companions to Bergamo).

1164. Annunciation with SS. John Baptist, Anthony of Padua and donor. Sd
by Francesco and d. 1509. (Destroyed 1945.) *Plate* 1043.

A. VON BECKERATH (EX). S. Catherine of Siena accepts the crown of thorns (fr.).

SCHWEITZER COLLECTION (EX). Knee-length S. Catherine behind parapet.

Beziers. 224. S. Francis.

Bologna. 236. Madonna and Child with SS. Dorothy and Catherine.

1023. Entombment (from Madonna del Monte, Cesena). L.

Bonn. 47 (sold in 1936). Madonna and Child.

Boston (Mass.). 25.214. Holy Family (after Pinturicchio). (?)

Brussels. 796. Madonna and Child with Bishop Saint and nun (r.). (B.).

Budapest. 5418. Madonna enthroned with Child standing on her knee.

Cambridge (Mass.). FOGG ART MUSEUM. 36. Holy Family.

Castel di Mezzo (Pesaro). PARISH CHURCH. Madonna and Child enthroned with SS. Christopher and Apollinaris and music-making Angel. *Plate* 1048.

Cesena. PINACOTECA. Bust of Riverelli, Archbishop of Ravenna.

Chambéry. 191. Predella panel: Penitent Magdalen in the Wilderness. (B.). *Plate* 1042.

Chantilly. 22. Madonna and Child with SS. Sebastian and John Baptist (version of Milan, Brera 455).

Cotignola. S. FRANCESCO. Lunette: Pietà.

Dublin. 106. Madonna and Child with SS. Francis, Anthony of Padua and another Saint (from Church of Riformati, Imola; companion to Rome, Albani). Sd by both and d. 1509. *Plate* 1033.

Ferrara. 182. S. Sebastian. Sd by Francesco and d. 1513. *Plate* 1049.

    MASSARI ZAVAGLIA COLLECTION (EX). Madonna and Child with two female Saints and Infant S. John.

Forlì. 135. Immaculate Conception (from S. Biagio). Sd by Francesco and d. 1513. *Plate* 1047.

Genoa. ACCADEMIA LIGUSTICA. Tondo: Pietà (after Giovanni Bellini).

Laon. 32. Madonna and Child. (B.).*

Lille. MUSÉE. Lunette: Pietà.

London. 1092. S. Sebastian. Sd by Bernardino and d. 1506. *Plate* 1034.

    3892, 3892 A. Altarpiece from S. Domenico at Faenza: Baptism of Christ; in lunette, Dead Christ upheld by Angels. Sd by Francesco and d. 1514. *Plate* 1051.

Mantua. REGGIA. Madonna and Child with six Saints. L.

Milan. BRERA. 455. Madonna and Child with SS. Nicholas and Francis and donor (from Riformati di Civitanova). Sd by Francesco and d. 1505.

    457. Madonna and Child with SS. John Baptist and Florian and three Angels (from Osservanza at Cotignola). Sd by both and d. 1499.

    456. Dead Christ (from S. Domenico di Lugo).

    458. Madonna and Child with SS. John Baptist and Francis. Sd by both and d. 1504 (from S. Apollinare Nuovo, Ravenna).

    BASSI DI SAN GENNARO COLLECTION. Veronica.

    BORROMEO COLLECTION. S. Jerome.

    Circumcision. (?)

Modena. 47. Christ carrying the Cross.

Montechiarúgolo (Parma). COURT OF CASTLE. Fresco: Madonna and Child with S. Francis.

Naples. 82. Marriage of Virgin.

    88. Man of Sorrows and kneeling Cardinal (F. and B.).

    1096. Christ carrying the Cross. Sd by Francesco and d. 1514. *Plate* 1052.

New York. COLLIS P. HUNTINGTON (EX). Madonna and Child against parapet and curtain.

ROBERT MINTURN (EX). Madonna and Child with SS. Sebastian and Roch (B.). *Plate* 1038.

Oxford. CHRIST CHURCH. 55. Madonna and Child with two female Saints and two Angels. *Plate* 1036.

Paris. 1164. Christ carrying the Cross. (B.)

Parma. SS. ANNUNZIATA. Fragmentary polyptych: Madonna and Child with SS. Bernard, John Evangelist and Francis; Rolando Pallavicini and his daughter; Domicilla Gambara Pallavicini. Commissioned 1518. (F.) *Plates* 1054–1055.

Pesaro. 24. Madonna and Child in Glory and Saints.

Ravenna. 4. Large Nativity (from S. Niccolò).

5, 6. S. Sebastian, S. Catherine (once at S. Apollinare).

7. Crucifixion and Saints (from S. Agata).

41. Madonna adoring the Child and S. Francis.

59. Agony in the Garden (r.).

54. Head of Angel.

Former n. 208. Christ Child and small Saints. (not there?)

Former n. 305. Circumcision. (not there?)

Former n. 306. Profile of youth. (not there?)

Former n. 315. Baptism (not there?)

SEMINARIO ARCIVESCOVILE. Mystic Marriage of S. Catherine. (F.) *Plate* 1056.

S. ROMUALDO. Raising of Lazarus. (F.)

Rimini. PINACOTECA. SS. Sebastian, Lawrence and Jerome.

Rome. GALLERIA COLONNA. Madonna and Child with SS. Agatha and Agnes. *Plate* 1040.

NEVIN COLLECTION (EX). Madonna suckling the Child and Infant S. John.

MARCHESE PATRIZI (EX). Dead Christ upheld by Angels. *Plate* 1050.

SCHIFF-GIORGIONI COLLECTION (EX). Head of Christ crowned with Thorns.

VILLA ALBANI. Mourning over dead Christ. (B)

Dead Christ and two Angels (lunette to Dublin). 1509. *Plate* 1033.

Sarasota (Fla.). RINGLING MUSEUM. 48. S. Sebastian in niche. (?)

49. Madonna and Child enthroned with SS. Helena and Constantine.

Strasbourg. 259. Madonna and Child.

265. Mystic Marriage of S. Catherine.

Tucson (Arizona). UNIVERSITY OF ARIZONA ART GALLERY. 62.156 (KRESS STUDY COLLECTION. K 1263). Pietà (r.).

Vaduz. LIECHTENSTEINSCHE SAMMLUNGEN. S. Clare.

Venice. CA' D'ORO. Madonna and Child with two music-making Angels. (B?)

Verona. 118. Dead Christ with Magdalen and Joseph of Arimathea. (B?)

Viadana (Cremona). SS. MARTINO E NICOLA, FIRST ALTAR R. Madonna and Child with SS. Sebastian, Roch, Francis and John Baptist. Sd by Francesco and d. 1518.

Vicenza. 195. Assumption of Virgin (by both).

Vienna. AKADEMIE, GIFT KOENIGSCHMIED. Circumcision.

Vienna (contd.). LEDERER COLLECTION (EX). Madonna and Child with SS. Catherine and Mary Magdalen. (B.). *Plate* 1037.

TRAU COLLECTION (EX). Madonna in Glory with SS. Jerome and Francis. Sd by Francesco and d. 1512.

TUCHER COLLECTION (EX). Side-panels of polyptych: S. Catherine, S. Ursula.

Homeless. Christ carrying the Cross. (F.). *Plate* 1044.

Madonna and Child enthroned with S. Mary Magdalen and Bishop Saint. (B.). *Plate* 1035.

Right panel of polyptych: Female martyr. (F.). *Plate* 1045.

Lucretia. (B.). *Plate* 1041.

Holy Family with female martyr. (F.). *Plate* 1053.

Madonna and Child enthroned with SS. Peter and Paul. (F.). *Plate* 1046.

ZAVATTARI

Family of painters and decorators active in Lombardy for two generations or more, 1404 (document concerning Cristoforo) to 1479 (document quoting Gregorio and Francesco).

Monza. DUOMO, CAPPELLA DELLA REGINA TEODOLINDA, WALLS. Frescoes: Ambassadors of Autari, King of the Longobards, meet with the refusal of Childebert, King of the Franks, who does not want his sister to marry Autari; Garibald, King of Bavaria, promises his daughter Theodolinda to Autari; Garibald sends Ambassadors to Verona to confirm his promise; Autari, disguised as his own ambassador, brings gifts to his future Bride in order to see her; Festivities in Bavaria before the departure of the Bride; Childebert King of the Franks attacks and defeats the Bavarian army; Theodolinda is accompanied by her Brother and Ladies-in-waiting to Italy and is met half-way by Longobard Knights; Marriage between Autari and Theodolinda outside Verona (A.D. 590), Dances in the palace, Autari touches a column with his sceptre to mark the sacred boundaries of the Longobard Kingdom; sudden death of Autari; the council of dignitaries chooses Agilulf, cousin of Autari and Duke of Turin, as new husband for Theodolinda; Theodolinda rides out to meet Agilulf and drinks with him out of the same goblet; Conversion of Agilulf, nuptial banquet and hunt; Queen Theodolinda is told in a dream that she must build a church in honour of S. John Baptist where she will see a dove standing in a meadow; Queen Theodolinda surveys the builders; surveys the various artists; the church is inaugurated and endowed by the Queen; after the death of her second husband and of her son, Theodolinda gives the church the famous Royal Treasures of Monza; funeral of Queen Theodolinda (A.D. 628); the Byzantine emperor Constant II, landed in Apulia to fight the Longobards, consults a hermit; the hermit has a vision that S. John Baptist, so richly honoured in Monza by Theodolinda, will never suffer the Longobards to be defeated; he transmits this information to the Emperor who gives up the expedition and returns to the Orient. Sd 'de Zavatariis' and d. 1444. (probably commissioned by Filippo Maria Visconti, whose emblems appear above windows; and finished under Francesco Sforza, whose emblems appear below windows, after 1447—episode of Constant II appears below date). [*Plate* 355.] *Plates* 547, 549.

ZENALE, Bernardino, da Treviglio

Milanese school. First mentioned in Treviglio 1485, died in Milan 1526. Perhaps chiefly architect. Pupil of Foppa; influenced by Bramante and Leonardo; worked in partnership with Butinone.

Florence. CONTINI BONACOSSI COLLECTION. Side-panels to Lawrence: S. Michael, S. William of Aniane and Carthusian donor (formerly Frizzoni). *Plates* 1359, 1361.

Isolabella. BORROMEO COLLECTION. 30. Mocking of Christ. Sd and d. 1503. *Plate* 1362.

Lawrence (Kansas). UNIVERSITY. 60.49 (KRESS COLLECTION. K 315). Centre panel to Contini Bonacossi, Florence: Madonna and All Saints. *Plate* 1360.

Milan. AMBROSIANA. Triptych: Madonna and Child blessing male and female donors, SS. Catherine and John Baptist, SS. Peter and Anthony of Padua (with Civerchio). *Plate* 1366.

Two panels of polyptych (companions to Rome, Lazzaroni): Bishop Saints.

BRERA. 734. Nativity (p.).

CASTELLO. 56. Panel from polyptych: S. Anthony of Padua.

366. Upper and lower side-panel of polyptych: S. Clare; SS. Francis and Bruno. (?)

POLDI PEZZOLI. 662, 666. Roundels: S. Jerome, S. Ambrose (st.).

661, 665. Side-panels (from Cantù polyptych, signed by Zenale and dated 1507?; companions to Bagatti Valsecchi): SS. Stephen and Anthony of Padua (with Civerchio?).

BAGATTI VALSECCHI COLLECTION. Side-panels (from Cantù polyptych, signed by Zenale and dated 1507?; companions to Poldi Pezzoli): SS. John Baptist and Francis (with Civerchio?).

S. AMBROGIO, MUSEO. Triptych for Oratorio della Passione: Madonna and Child (Zenale and Civerchio?), S. Jerome (Zenale), S. Ambrose (Butinone). Paid to Zenale 1494.

S. MARIA DELLE GRAZIE, NAVE. Lunettes over arches. Some frescoed roundels (see Butinone).

S. PIETRO IN GESSATE, L. TRANSEPT, CAPPELLA GRIFI. Frescoes commissioned to Butinone and Zenale by Senator Ambrogio Grifi in 1489 and finished before death of donor in 1493. Signed by Butinone and Zenale (but the latter's hand is hard to distinguish in fragments now visible).

— — VAULT. In centre of umbrella-shaped ceiling, bust of Christ; in each of the five segments, one adoring and two music-making Angels.

— — WALLS. Simulated loggia opening on a landscape with episodes from Life of S. Ambrose. [Right Wall, from top of mountain downwards: Investiture of S. Ambrose as Bishop, S. Ambrose baptizing, healing, praying for Victory of Theodosius, blessing acolytes, acting as judge—the tortured man pulled by a chord, and a monkey, are shown in lunette above. Left Wall, from top of mountain: S. Ambrose prevents Theodosius from entering the church, performs a miracle?, baptizes (S. Augustine?), preaches, condemns the heretic (Manes?); two peacocks in lunette above. Altar Wall: in lunette, S. Ambrose on horseback; on either side of altar, continuation of the landscape, with figures.]

Paris. 1545 (CAMPANA N. 309). Altarpiece from S. Maria della Canonica in Porta Nuova, Milano: Circumcision with four Saints and Fra Jacopo Lampugnani (with Civerchio). Dated 1491. *Plate* 1364.

MUSÉE JACQUEMART-ANDRÉ. Four Church Fathers seated. E.

Prague. Inv. 01167. Cut head of S. Paul.

Rome. LAZZARONI (EX). Two panels of polyptych: SS. Francis and Anthony of Padua (companions to Milan, Ambrosiana).

Treviglio. COLLEGIATA DI S. MARTINO, END OF R. NAVE. Polyptych commissioned from Butinone and Zenale 1485, not yet completely paid 1507. Lower register: Madonna and Child enthroned with six Angels (probably heads of Madonna and Child by Zenale), flanked by SS. Lucy, Catherine, Magdalen (left panel, by Zenale) and by SS. John Baptist, Stephen and John Evangelist (Butinone). Upper register: S. Martin and the Beggar (Zenale) flanked by SS. Zeno, Gustav (or Mauritius?) and Peter (left panel, Zenale) and by SS. Sebastian, Anthony of Padua and Paul (right panel, Butinone). Predella: Nativity (mostly Butinone), Crucifixion (Butinone), Resurrection (mostly Zenale), separated by half-length Fathers of the Church (Zenale). [*Plate* 364.] *Plates* 1357, 1358.

Venice. CONTE VITTORIO CINI. Inv. 3346. Two ovals: Heads of S. Jerome and of another Saint (st.).

Homeless. Madonna and Child with S. Francis. (with Civerchio) *Plate* 1363.

ZOPPO, Marco d'Antonio di Ruggero, called

Cento 1433–78 Bologna. Assistant to Squarcione in Padua 1452–55. Active in Venice 1455, 1468/73; influenced by Jacopo and Giovanni Bellini.

Altenburg. 189 (51). Madonna and Child standing on parapet. Sd 'Marco Zoppo da Bolognia'.

Baltimore (Md.). WALTERS ART GALLERY. 542. Right panel of polyptych, companion to London, Oxford and Washington: S. Jerome (possibly from S. Cristina polyptych of 1468). *Plate 696.*

543. S. Jerome in the Wilderness. (?)

544. Predella panel: S. Francis receiving Stigmata. *Plate 697.*

Berlin-Ost. 1170. Madonna and Child enthroned with SS. John Baptist, Francis, Paul and Jerome (from Padri Zoccolanti, Pesaro). Sd 'Marco Zoppo da Bolognia Pinxit . . . Venezia' and d. 1471. *Plate 700.*

Bologna. Inv. 778. Penitent S. Jerome.

COLLEGIO DI SPAGNA, CAPPELLA. Polyptych: Madonna and Child enthroned; SS. Andrew and Clemens; SS. John Baptist and Jerome; in roundels above, blessing Redeemer, Angel and Virgin of Annunciation; in pilasters of frame, eight small Saints; in predella, S. Christopher, Miraculous draught of Fishes, S. Dominic, Nativity, S. Peter Martyr, S. Jerome in the Wilderness, S. Sebastian. Sd (deposited at Pinacoteca?). *Plate 698.*

S. GIUSEPPE DI SARAGOZZA. Painted Crucifix.

Brunswick. VIEWEG COLLECTION (EX). Man of Sorrows.

Bucarest. Inv. 657. Madonna and Child with six Saints and two donors. Inscribed: 'Madonna del Zopo di Squarcione'. (?)

Cambridge. FITZWILLIAM MUSEUM, SIDNEY BEQUEST R-D. 4.1955. Salvator Mundi.

Canford Manor (Ashby St. Ledgers). VISCOUNT WIMBORNE. Madonna suckling the Child and Angels. Sd 'Del Zoppo di Squarcione'. 1453/5. *Plate 693.*

Edinburgh. 1719. Predella panel: 'Noli me tangere'.

London. 590. Dead Christ with SS. John Baptist and Jerome.

3541. Left panel of polyptych, companion to Baltimore, Oxford and Washington (possibly S. Cristina polyptych of 1468): S. Augustine. *Plate 695.*

COUNT ANTOINE SEILERN. S. Sebastian in landscape.

Lugano. THYSSEN COLLECTION. 462. S. Jerome in the Wilderness. Sd 'Marco Zoppo da Bononia'. *Plate 699.*

Oxford. ASHMOLEAN MUSEUM. 98. Right panel of polyptych, companion to Baltimore, London and Washington: S. Paul (possibly from S. Cristina polyptych of 1468).

Pesaro. 10. Head of Baptist in roundel.

18. Dead Christ upheld by Angels.

Rome. SCHIFF COLLECTION (EX). Man of Sorrows.

Vienna. 84. Madonna and blessing Child with two Angels. L. (?)

Washington (D.C.). 382 (KRESS COLLECTION 489). Left panel of polyptych, companion to Baltimore, London and Oxford: S. Peter (possibly from S. Cristina polyptych of 1468).

1414 (KRESS COLLECTION. K 2033). 'Cook' Madonna and Child. Sd 'Marco Zoppo da Bologna'. *Plate 694.*

TOPOGRAPHICAL INDEX

Alviano (Terni). S. MARIA ASSUNTA: Niccolò da Foligno.

Amelia. PALAZZO COMUNALE: Caporali, Piermatteo da Amelia.

Amherst (Massachusetts). COLLEGE, KRESS COLLECTION: Cozzarelli, Dosso, Sano di Pietro.

Amiens. MUSÉE DE PICARDIE: Andrea di Bartolo, Francesco di Giorgio.

Amsterdam. RIJKSMUSEUM: Bergognone, Giovan Francesco Caroto, Costa, De Predis, Farinati, Fei, Garofalo, Gaudenzio Ferrari, Giampietrino, Mazzolino, Moroni, Schiavone, Signorelli, Torbido, Zaganelli.

— VOM RATH BEQUEST: Defendente Ferrari, Francesco Napolitano, Moroni.

UNIVERSITY, LOANED BY NEDERLANDS KUNST-BEZIT: Sano di Pietro.

N. BEETS (EX): Lippo Vanni.

OTTO LANZ (EX): Barna da Siena, Fungai, Garofalo, Liberale da Verona, Niccolò di Segna, Palmerucci, Parentino, Sano di Pietro, 'Ugolino Lorenzetti'.

ERNST PROEHL: Ambrosi.

H. TIETJE (EX): Mazzolino.

VAN REGTEREN ALTENA: Lippo Vanni.

Ancaiano (Siena). S. BARTOLOMEO: Cozzarelli.

Ancona. S. DOMENICO: Beccafumi.

Angers. MUSÉE DES BEAUX-ARTS: Andrea di Bartolo, Segna di Bonaventura, Lippo Vanni.

Anghiari (San Sepolcro). S. AGOSTINO: Matteo di Giovanni.

Angoulême. MUSÉE DE LA VILLE: Niccolò da Foligno.

Antibes. NOTRE-DAME DE LA GARDE: Brea.

Antràccoli (Lucca). PARISH CHURCH: Puccinelli.

Antwerp. MUSÉE MAYER VAN DEN BERGH: Macrino d'Alba.

MUSÉE ROYAL DES BEAUX-ARTS: Simone Martini.

Apiro (Macerata). PALAZZO MUNICIPALE: Nuzi.

Appignano del Tronto. S. ANGELO: Vincenzo Pagani.

Aquila. MUSEO NAZIONALE ABRUZZESE: Delitio, Master of the Crivellesque Polyptychs.

S. AMICO: Delitio.

MARCHESE DRAGONETTI DE TORRES (EX): Antoniazzo Romano.

Arcevia (Ancona). S. MEDARDO: Antonio da Fabriano, Francesco di Gentile da Fabriano, Signorelli.

Arcore (Monza). VITTADINI COLLECTION (EX): Bergognone, Cesare Magni, Romanino, Sodoma, Solario.

Arcs, see Les Arcs.

Arezzo. PINACOTECA: Bartolomeo della Gatta, Guariento, Guido da Siena, Margarito, Scarsellino, Signorelli.

BADIA: Bartolomeo della Gatta, Segna di Bonaventura.

DUOMO: Bartolomeo della Gatta, Piero della Francesca, Signorelli.

PIEVE: Pietro Lorenzetti.

S. DOMENICO: Simone Martini Follower.

S. FRANCESCO: Piero della Francesca, Signorelli.

S. MARIA DELLE GRAZIE (BUILDING NEARBY): Piero della Francesca.

S. PIERO PICCOLO: Bartolomeo della Gatta.

Argenta. PALAZZO MUNICIPALE: Garofalo.

Argiano (Montalcino Senese). S. PANCRAZIO: Beccafumi.

Ariccia. PALAZZO CHIGI (EX): Garofalo.

Arona. SS. GRATINIANO E FELINO: Bergognone, Farinati.

S. MARIA, CAPPELLA BORROMEO: Gaudenzio Ferrari.

Arrone (Terni). S. MARIA DELLA QUERCIA: Tamagni.

Arundel Castle (Sussex). DUKE OF NORFOLK: Sano di Pietro.

Asciano (Senese). MUSEO DI ARTE SACRA: Ambrosi, Barna da Siena, Fei, Giacomo del Pisano, Giovanni di Paolo, Ambrogio Lorenzetti, Martino di Bartolomeo da Siena, Master of Osservanza Triptych, Matteo di Giovanni, Segna di Bonaventura, Taddeo di Bartolo.

SS. FABIANO E SEBASTIANO: Benvenuto di Giovanni, Pacchia.

CASA BARGAGLI, GRANARY: Ambrogio Lorenzetti.

Ascoli Piceno. PINACOTECA CIVICA: Cola d'Amatrice, Vincenzo Pagani.

MUSEO VESCOVILE: Cola d'Amatrice.

S. AGOSTINO: Cola d'Amatrice, Ghissi, Vincenzo Pagani.

SS. ANNUNZIATA: Cola d'Amatrice.

S. FRANCESCO: Cola d'Amatrice.

S. PIETRO MARTIRE: Cola d'Amatrice.

S. VITTORE: Cola d'Amatrice.

Ashburnham Place (Sussex). LADY ASHBURNHAM (EX): Sano di Pietro.

Asola (Brescia). S. ANDREA (DUOMO): Moretto, Romanino.

Assisi. PINACOTECA: Matteo da Gualdo, Niccolò da Foligno, Tiberio d'Assisi.

PIAZZA DEL COMUNE, CORNER VIA PORTICA, TABERNACLE: Simone Martini Follower.

ORATORIO DEI PELLEGRINI: Matteo da Gualdo, Mezzastris, Pinturicchio.

S. CHIARA: Master of St. Francis.

S. DAMIANO: Eusebio da San Giorgio, Mezzastris, Tiberio d'Assisi.

S. FRANCESCO: LOWER CHURCH: Andrea da Bologna, Pietro Lorenzetti, Master of St. Francis, Nelli, Simone Martini.

— SACRO CONVENTO DI S. FRANCESCO: Nelli.

— — MUSEO DEL SACRO CONVENTO: Caporali, Cozzarelli, Master of the Crivellesque Polyptychs, Lo Spagna, Tiberio d'Assisi.

— — F. M. PERKINS DONATION: Cozzarelli, Giovanni di Nicola da Pisa, Giovanni di Paolo, Pietro Lorenzetti, Niccolò da Foligno, Perugino, Sano di Pietro, Sassetta, Segna di Bonaventura, Signorelli.

— — TREASURY: Master of St. Francis.

S. MARIA DEGLI ANGELI: Ambrosi, Giunta Pisano, Mezzastris, Pinturicchio, Lo Spagna, Tiberio d'Assisi.

— MUSEO: Master of St. Francis, Sano di Pietro.

S. PAOLO (CONFRATERNITA DI): Matteo da Gualdo.

S. PIETRO: Matteo da Gualdo.

S. RUFINO (DUOMO): Matteo da Gualdo, Niccolò da Foligno.

LADY BERKELY: Signorelli.

F. M. PERKINS COLLECTION: Costa, Fei, Ferrarese-Bolognese, Francesco di Gentile da Fabriano, Fungai, Girolamo di Benvenuto, Master of Osservanza Triptych, Matteo di Giovanni, Niccolò di Segna, Ortolano, Taddeo di Bartolo, Zaganelli.

— (EX): Sano di Pietro.

— (EX?): Cozzarelli.

Assisi (Environs). LA BASTIA, PARISH CHURCH: Bernardino di Mariotto, Niccolò da Foligno.

PALAZZO, CAPPELLA DELLA CONFRATERNITA DELLA BUONA MORTE: Matteo da Gualdo.

ROCCHICCIOLA: Lo Spagna.

TORRE D'ANDREA, S. BERNARDINO: Pastura, Perugino.

Athens. GALLERY: Palmezzano.

Athens (Georgia). UNIVERSITY OF GEORGIA, KRESS COLLECTION: Bergognone, Ferrarese, Giusto de' Menabuoi, 'Ugolino Lorenzetti'.

Atlanta (Georgia). ART ASSOCIATION GALLERIES, KRESS COLLECTION: Costa, Cozzarelli, Fei, Francesco di Giorgio, Garofalo, Giovanni Francesco da Rimini, Moretto, Niccolò di Segna, Pastura, Romanino, Signorelli.

Atri. S. AGOSTINO: Delitio.

S. MARIA ASSUNTA (CATHEDRAL): Delitio.

Attingham Park (Shrewsbury). NATIONAL TRUST: Brescianino, Cesare Magni.

Auckland (New Zealand). ART GALLERY: Lanino, Marco d'Oggiono.

Augusta (Georgia). G. HERBERT ART INSTITUTE, KRESS COLLECTION: Giovan Francesco Caroto.

Autun. MUSÉE ROLIN: Giovanni Francesco da Rimini.

Aversa (Naples). CAPPELLA DI CASALUCE: Andrea Vanni.

Avigliana (Turin). S. GIOVANNI: Defendente Ferrari.

MADONNA DEI LAGHI: Defendente Ferriari.

Avignon. MUSÉE CALVET: Raphael, Scarsellino.

— (EX): Giovenone.

PALAIS DES PAPES: Matteo Giovannetti da Viterbo.

BIBLIOTHÈQUE: Michelino da Besozzo.

NOTRE-DAME DES DOMS: Simone Martini.

Azzate (Varese). PARISH CHURCH: Calisto Piazza.

Badia a Isola (Colle Val d'Elsa). SS. SALVATORE E CIRINO: Duccio Follower, Sano di Pietro, Taddeo di Bartolo, Tamagni.

Bagnacavallo (Ravenna). S. FRANCESCO: Riminese Trecento.

S. PIETRO IN SILVIS: Riminese Trecento.

Bagnano (Val d'Elsa). S. MARIA: Ugolino di Nerio.

Bagnoregio. S. AGOSTINO: Giovanni di Paolo, Martino di Bartolomeo da Siena.

Balcarres (Fife, Scotland). EARL OF CRAWFORD AND BALCARRES: Balducci, Cesare da Sesto, Cozzarelli, Duccio, Girolamo di Giovanni da Camerino, Luca di Tommè, Matteo di Giovanni, Pietro di Domenico da Siena, Pinturicchio, Signorelli, Tegliacci, Ugolino di Nerio.

Baltimore (Maryland). WALTERS ART GALLERY: Andrea di Bartolo, Anguissola, Antoniazzo Romano, Antonio da Fabriano, Aspertini, Barna da Siena, Bartolomeo di Tommaso da Foligno, Benvenuto di Giovanni, Bernardino di Mariotto, Bertucci, Bonsignori, Brescianino, Brusasorci, Butinone, Giovan Francesco Caroto, Ceccarelli, Cozzarelli, Defendente Ferrari, Delitio, Ercole da Ferrara, Fiorenzo di Lorenzo, Foppa, Francesco di Gentile da Fabriano, Francesco di Giorgio, Francesco dai Libri (Il Vecchio), Fungai, Garofalo, Giacomo del Pisano, Giovanni Agostino da Lodi, Giovanni di Paolo, Giovanni Francesco da Rimini, Giovenone, Girolamo di Benvenuto, Pietro Lorenzetti,

Lorenzo d'Alessandro, Macrino d'Alba, Master of Panzano Triptych, Matteo di Giovanni, Matteo da Gualdo, Moroni, Niccolò da Foligno, Niccolò di Segna, Niccolò da Voltri, Ortolano, Pacchiarotto, Palmezzano, Parentino, Perugino, Albertino and Martino Piazza, Pinturicchio, Raphael, Riminese Trecento, Salimbeni, Scarsellino, Schiavone, Signorelli, Sodoma, Lo Spagna, Tomaso da Modena, Lippo Vanni, Zaganelli, Zoppo.

MUSEUM OF ART: Antoniazzo Romano, Luini, Master of the Gardner Annunciation, Pacchiarotto, Perugino, Raphael.

DR REULING (EX): Giovanni Caroto, Signorelli.

Banzi (Lucania). CHIESA ABBAZIALE: Andrea da Salerno.

Bar, see Le Bar.

Barcelona. MUSEO DE ARTE, CAMBÒ BEQUEST: Riminese Trecento.

CATHEDRAL: Sano di Pietro.

IGLESIA DE LOS P.P. CAPUCHINOS DE SARRIA: Master of the Gardner Annunciation.

DON B. GRASES HERNÁNDEZ: Costa, Giampietrino.

— (EX): Scarsellino.

Bardi (Parma). S. MARIA, CANONICA: Parmigianino.

Bari. MUSEO: Garofalo.

— DEP. FROM GALLERIA NAZIONALE, ROME: Garofalo.

Barnard Castle (Durham). BOWES MUSEUM: Sassetta, Solario, Zaganelli.

Baschi (Orvieto): PARISH CHURCH: Giovanni di Paolo.

Basciano (Siena). CHIESA DEL CASTELLO: Sassetta.

Basle. KUNSTMUSEUM: Ambrosi, Bergognone, Moretto, Palmezzano.

DR TOBIAS CHRIST (EX): Garofalo.

ROBERT VON HIRSCH: Giovanni di Paolo, Luca di Tommè, 'Ugolino Lorenzetti'.

SARASIN VARNERY COLLECTION (EX): Foppa.

Bassano del Grappa. MUSEO CIVICO: Guariento, Perugino.

S. FRANCESCO: Guariento.

Bath. STREET COLLECTION: Riminese Trecento.

Bayeux. MUSÉE: Fei, Lorenzo da Viterbo, Niccolò da Foligno, Sano di Pietro.

Bayonne. MUSÉE BONNAT: Antoniazzo Romano, Beccafumi, Bonfigli, Giulio Campi, Costa, Martino di Bartolomeo, Matteo di Giovanni, Turino Vanni, Lippo Vanni.

Beaulieu (Alpes-Maritimes). VILLA SYLVIA, RALPH CURTIS (EX): Vecchietta.

Beffi (Aquila). MADONNA DEL PONTE: Francesco di Gentile da Fabriano.

Belcaro, see Siena (Environs).

Belfiore d'Adige (Verona). S. VITO: Farinati.

Belforte sul Chienti. S. EUSTACHIO: Boccati.

Belgrade. ROYAL PALACE (EX): Eusebio da San Giorgio.

WHITE PALACE: Beccafumi.

Bellagio (Lago di Como). S. GIACOMO: Perugino.

— Environs. See San Giovanni

Belluno (Environs). S. GREGORIO NELLE ALPI: Moretto.

Bennebroek (Haarlem). DE HARTEKAMP, FRAU VON PANNWITZ: Girolamo dai Libri.

Berea (Kentucky). BEREA COLLEGE, KRESS COLLECTION: Francia.

Bergamo. ACCADEMIA CARRARA: Altobello Melone, Anguissola, Aspertini, Balducci, Benaglio, Bergognone, Bernardino de' Conti, Bernardino di Mariotto, Boltraffio,

Brusasorci, Butinone, Galeazzo Campi, Giovan Francesco Caroto, Cavazzola, Cesare Magni, Cicognara, Civerchio, Costa, Defendente Ferrari, De Predis, Battista Dossi, Ercole da Ferrara, Fei, Ferrarese-Bolognese, Fiorenzo di Lorenzo, Foppa, Francia, Fungai, Garofalo, Gaudenzio Ferrari, Genga, Giampietrino, Giolfino, Giovenone, Girolamo dai Libri, Luini, Mantegna, Marco d'Oggiono, Matteo di Giovanni, Moretto, Francesco Morone, Moroni, Neroccio, Palmezzano, Albertino and Martino Piazza, Pisanello, Raphael, Romanino, Schiavone, Signorelli, Sodoma, Solario, Tura, Viti, Zaganelli.

PALAZZO DEL PRETORE (MUSEO DI STORIA NATURALE): Bramante.

S. ALESSANDRO DELLA CROCE (DUOMO): Costa, Gaudenzio Ferrari, Marco d'Oggiono, Moroni.

S. ALESSANDRO IN COLONNA: Moretto, Romanino.

S. ANDREA: Moretto.

S. PANCRAZIO: Moroni.

S. SPIRITO: Bergognone.

CONTE AGLIARDI: Moroni.

FRIZZONI COLLECTION: Solario.

FRIZZONI–SALIS COLLECTION: Albertino and Martino Piazza.

ALMA AND MARIA FRIZZONI (EX): Brusasorci.

ALMA AND MARIA FRIZZONI: Moroni.

DR GIOVANNI FRIZZONI: Moretto.

SIGRA BICE EYNARD FRIZZONI (EX): Dosso, Battista Dossi.

ACHILLE LOCATELLI MILESI (EX): Romanino.

LORENZELLI COLLECTION: Dosso.

CONTE MORONI: Moroni.

ING. PESENTI: Francesco di Gentile da Fabriano.

PICCINELLI COLLECTION (EX): Albertino and Martino Piazza.

CONTE RONCALLI: Moroni.

CONTE SUARDI: Moroni.

Bergen. BILLEDGALLERI: Arcangelo di Cola da Camerino, Taddeo di Bartolo.

Berkeley (California). MISS LUCY SPRAGUE (EX): Lo Spagna.

Berlin. STAATLICHE MUSEEN (DAHLEM): Ambrosi, Andrea di Bartolo, Anguissola, Antoniazzo Romano, Barna da Siena, Barnaba da Modena, Beccafumi, Bergognone, Bernardino de' Conti, Bernardino di Mariotto, Brescianino, Butinone, Caporali, Civerchio, Correggio, Cossa, Costa, Deodato Orlandi, Dosso, Duccio, Ercole da Ferrara, Foppa, Francesco di Giorgio (sculpture), Francesco di Vannuccio, Francia, Garofalo, Gaudenzio Ferrari, Gentile da Fabriano, Giampietrino, Giolfino, Giovanni Agostino da Lodi, Giovanni di Paolo, Girolamo di Benvenuto, Girolamo da Cremona, Gualtieri di Giovanni da Pisa, Liberale da Verona, Pietro Lorenzetti, Luini, Maineri, Mantegna, Martino di Bartolomeo da Siena, Master of Osservanza Triptych, Master of the Sforza Altarpiece, Matteo di Giovanni, Mazzolino, Melozzo da Forlì, Lippo Memmi, Moretto, Domenico Morone, Francesco Morone, Neroccio, Nuzi, Ortolano, Pacchia, Parentino, Pastura, Calisto Piazza, Piero della Francesca, Pinturicchio, Raphael, Riminese Trecento, Sassetta, Schiavone, Signorelli, Simone Martini, Sodoma, Squarcione, Taddeo di Bartolo, Torbido, Tura, Ugolino di Nerio, Andrea Vanni, Zaganelli.

Berlin-Ost. STAATLICHE MUSEEN: Aspertini, Bernardino de' Conti, Bernardino di Mariotto, Bertucci, Bianchi Ferrari, Boccaccino, Boltraffio, Giovan Francesco Caroto, Cesare Magni, Costa, Defendente Ferrari, Dosso, Ercole da Ferrara, Francia, Garofalo, Genga, Giolfino, Giovanni Agostino da Lodi, Girolamo dai Libri, Guariento, Lanino, Liberale da Verona, Luini, Marco d'Oggiono, Master of the Gardner Annunciation, Master of the Sforza Altarpiece, Mazzolino, Francesco Morone, Moroni, Pacchia, Palmezzano, Perugino, Piero della Francesca, Pinturicchio, Romanino, Santi, Lo Spagna, Lippo Vanni, Zoppo.

Berlin. KUPFERSTICHKABINETT: Master of the Codex of St. George.

KÖPENICK SCHLOSS, KUNSTGEWERBEMUSEUM: Cossa.

— (EX): Romanino.

KULTURMINISTERIUM (EX): Bernardino de' Conti.

REICHSKANZLER PALAIS (KAISER-FRIEDRICH MUSEUM) (EX): Farinati.

SCHLOSSMUSEUM: Giovanni di Paolo, Niccolò di Buonaccorso, Piero della Francesca.

— (EX): Bernardino de' Conti.

A. VON BECKERATH (EX): Girolamo di Benvenuto, Pacchia, Zaganelli.

BOTTENWIESER (EX): Sano di Pietro.

DE BURLET COLLECTION (EX): Andrea di Bartolo.

GLOGOWSKY COLLECTION (EX): Bramantino.

GOBLET COLLECTION (EX): Palmezzano.

PRINZ HEINRICH VON PREUSSEN (EX): Girolamo da Carpi.

OTTO HELD (EX): Moretto.

R. VON KAUFMANN (EX): Barna da Siena, Francesco di Vannuccio, Garofalo, Girolamo di Benvenuto, Schiavone.

LIPPMANN COLLECTION (EX): Luini, Michele da Verona.

EUGEN SCHWEITZER (EX): Brescianino, Garofalo, Gaudenzio Ferrari, Giampietrino, Girolamo da Cremona, Girolamo dai Libri, Liberale da Verona, Marco d'Oggiono, Ortolano, Solario, Zaganelli.

E. SIMON (EX): Bramantino.

ALFRED SOMMERGUTH (EX): Benvenuto di Giovanni.

H. WENSTENBERG COLLECTION (EX): Boccaccino.

WESENDONCK COLLECTION (EX): Beccafumi, Moretto.

Bernay (Eure). MUSÉE (CAMPANA COLLECTION): Foppa.

Berne. KUNSTMUSEUM: Boltraffio, Duccio, Nuzi.

SCHLOSS MERCHLINGEN, B. GUINNESS: Master of Stratonice.

Besançon. MUSÉE DES BEAUX-ARTS: Duccio Follower, Francia, Gaudenzio Ferrari, Giovanni di Paolo.

Besate (Milan). PARISH CHURCH: Marco d'Oggiono.

Bettona (Perugia). PALAZZO DEL PODESTÀ, PINACOTECA: Fiorenzo di Lorenzo, Perugino, Tiberio d'Assisi.

COLLEGIATA (EX): Lo Spagna.

S. MARIA MAGGIORE: Gregorio di Cecco di Luca, Perugino, Tiberio d'Assisi.

Béziers. MUSÉE DES BEAUX-ARTS: Bartolo di Fredi, Zaganelli.

Bianzè. CHIESA DELLA MISERICORDIA: Spanzotti.

Bibbiano (Siena). S. LORENZO: Brescianino.

Bibbiena. SS. IPPOLITO E DONATO: Arcangelo di Cola da Camerino.

S. MARIA DELLA MISERICORDIA: Costa, Francia, Lippo Dalmasio.

S. MARIA DEI SERVI: Vitale da Bologna.

S. MARTINO MAGGIORE: Aspertini, Costa, Francia, Girolamo da Carpi, Vitale da Bologna.

S. MICHELE DEI LEPROSETTI: Vitale da Bologna.

S. PETRONIO: Aspertini, Costa, Ferrarese, Lippo Dalmasio, Parmigianino, Perugino.

S. PIETRO: Ercole da Ferrara.

S. PROCOLO: Lippo Dalmasio.

S. SALVATORE: Garofalo, Girolamo da Carpi, Vitale da Bologna.

SS. VITALE E AGRICOLA: Francia, Sano di Pietro

Bologna. Private Collections.

PALAZZO HERCOLANI (EX): Francia.

CASA MALVASIA (EX): Ortolano.

MODIANO COLLECTION: Moretto.

MOLINARI PRADELLI COLLECTION: Garofalo, Scarsellino.

NOVELLI COLLECTION: Scarsellino.

CONTE GIUSEPPE SCARSELLI: Costa.

Bolsena. S. CRISTINA: Bartolo di Fredi, Benvenuto di Giovanni, Master of Panzano Triptych, Sano di Pietro.

Bolzano. S. DOMENICO: Guariento.

Bonn. PROVINZIALMUSEUM: Cesare Magni, Farinati, Garofalo, Pacchia, Palmezzano, Perugino, Puccinelli, Zaganelli.

LANDESMUSEUM: Andrea da Salerno.

DR P. CLEMEN (EX): Duccio Follower.

Bonson (Alpes-Maritimes). PARISH CHURCH: Brea.

Bordeaux. MUSÉE DES BEAUX-ARTS: Aspertini, Moretto, Ortolano, Palmezzano, Perugino, Sano di Pietro, Sassetta.

CATHÉDRALE ST-ANDRÉ: Sano di Pietro.

Borgo a Mozzano. S. JACOPO: Neroccio (sculpture).

Borgosesia (Vercelli). SS. PIETRO E PAOLO: Lanino.

Borno (Val Camonica). S. ANTONIO: Calisto Piazza.

Boston (Massachusetts). MUSEUM OF FINE ARTS: Barna da Siena, Barnaba da Modena, Beccafumi, Benvenuto di Giovanni, Bernardino di Mariotto, Boccaccino, Bramantino, Costa, Cozzarelli, Duccio, Eusebio da San Giorgio, Ferrarese, Fiorenzo di Lorenzo, Francesco di Giorgio, Giovanni di Paolo, Giovenone, Gregorio di Cecco di Luca, Ambrogio Lorenzetti, Luini, Mantegna, Matteo da Gualdo, Lippo Memmi, Moroni, Neroccio, Niccolò di Buonaccorso, Niccolò da Foligno, Pacchia, Riminese Trecento, Sano di Pietro, Segna di Bonaventura, Signorelli, Simone Martini, Simone Martini Follower, Solario, Tegliacci, Ugolino di Nerio, Andrea Vanni, Zaganelli.

ISABELLA STEWART GARDNER MUSEUM: Fei, Francia, Giovanni di Paolo, Liberale da Verona, Mantegna, Master of the Gardner Annunciation, Lippo Memmi, Moroni, Neroccio, Parentino, Piero della Francesca, Pinturicchio, Raphael, Giuliano da Rimini, Simone Martini, Tura, 'Ugolino Lorenzetti', Andrea Vanni.

CABOT LODGE COLLECTION: Macrino d'Alba.

LONGYEAR FOUNDATION: Solario.

EDWARD WHEELWRIGHT: Francesco di Giorgio.

Boughton House (Northamptonshire). DUKE OF BUCCLEUCH: Garofalo.

Briançonnet (Alpes-Maritimes): PARISH CHURCH: Brea.

Bribano (Belluno). ORATORIO DI S. NICCOLÒ: Giovanni Agostino da Lodi.

Bridgeport (Connecticut). MUSEUM OF ART, SCIENCE AND INDUSTRY, KRESS COLLECTION: Bergognone, Domenico di Bartolo, Pietro Lorenzetti.

Brigue (Ventimiglia). S. MARTINO: Brea.

Brisighella (Faenza). S. MARIA DI RONTANA: Palmezzano.
MINORI OSSERVANTI: Palmezzano.

Bristol. CITY ART GALLERY: De Predis, Viti.

Brno. MUSEUM: Girolamo di Giovanni da Camerino, Liberale da Verona, Domenico Morone, Albertino and Martino Piazza.

Brolio (Chianti). CASTELLO, BARONE RICASOLI: Ugolino di Nerio.

Brooklyn (New York). BROOKLYN MUSEUM: Ambrosi, Andrea di Bartolo, Bernardino de' Conti, Galeazzo Campi, Cozzarelli, Domenico di Bartolo, Giovanni Francesco da Rimini, Luini, Martino di Bartolomeo da Siena, Palmezzano, Parentino, Perugino, Pinturicchio, Romanino, Sano di Pietro, Tegliacci.

Broomhall (Dunfermline, Fife). LORD ELGIN (EX): Boltraffio.

Bruges. RENDERS COLLECTION: Master of the Codex of St. George.

Brunswick. VIEWEG COLLECTION (EX): Zoppo.

Brunswick (Maine). BOWDOIN COLLEGE, MUSEUM OF FINE ARTS, KRESS STUDY COLLECTION: Ambrosi, Garofalo, Nuzi.

Brussels. MUSÉES ROYAUX DES BEAUX-ARTS: Giovan Francesco Caroto, Fei, Perugino, Sano di Pietro, Scarsellino, Torbido, Zaganelli.
MUSÉE SOMZÉE: Luini.
DR CAHEN: Niccolò di Segna.
M. A. DE DONCKER (EX): Brescianino.
FIEVEZ COLLECTION (EX): Garofalo.
STOCLET COLLECTION: Andrea di Bartolo, Giunta Pisano.
— (EX): Andrea di Bartolo.
M. ADOLPHE STOCLET: Giovanni di Paolo.
JACQUES STOCLET: Andrea di Bartolo, Duccio, Ambrogio Lorenzetti.
MADAME JACQUES STOCLET (EX): Master of the Codex of St. George, Neroccio.
MLLE MICHÈLE STOCLET: Giovanni di Paolo, Simone Martini.
PHILIPPE STOCLET (EX): Duccio Follower, Niccolò di Segna.
MADAME FERON-STOCLET: Master of St. Francis.
VAN GELDER COLLECTION, see Ucclé.
HENRI WAUTERS: Francesco di Giorgio, Girolamo da Cremona, Liberale da Verona.

Bucarest. MUSEUM: Boccaccino, Bramantino, Dosso, Maineri, Zoppo.

Budapest. MUSEUM OF FINE ARTS: Andrea di Bartolo, Andrea da Salerno, Bartolomeo di Gentile da Urbino, Bergognone, Bernardino di Mariotto, Bertucci, Boccaccino, Boccati, Boltraffio, Giulio Campi, Caporali, Giovanni Caroto, Giovan Francesco Caroto, Ceccarelli, Civerchio, Correggio, Costa, Cozzarelli, Dosso, Duccio, Eusebio da San Giorgio, Farinati, Ferrarese, Ferrarese–Bolognese, Foppa, Francia, Fungai, Garofalo, Gaudenzio Ferrari, Giampietrino, Giovanni di Paolo, Girolamo dai Libri, Giulio Romano, Liberale da Verona, Ambrogio Lorenzetti, Lorenzo da Viterbo, Luca di Tommè, Luini, Martino di Bartolomeo da Siena, Master of Griselda, Mazzolino, Michele Pannonio, Moretto, Francesco Morone, Moroni, Niccolò da Foligno,

Pacchia, Palmezzano, Albertino and Martino Piazza, Calisto Piazza, Raphael, Riminese Trecento, Romanino, Sano di Pietro, Santi, Sassetta, Scarsellino, Segna di Bonaventura, Signorelli, Sodoma, Spanzotti, Taddeo di Bartolo, Zaganelli.

COUNT JULIUS ANDRASSY (EX): Antonio da Fabriano.

F. GLUCK (EX): Moroni.

BARON HATVANY: Solario.

BARON ISTVÁN HERZOG: Moretto.

SÁNDOR LEDERER (EX): Giovanni Francesco Caroto, Defendente Ferrari, Moroni, Romanino.

PÉTERI COLLECTION (EX): Liberale da Verona.

Budrio (Bologna). PINACOTECA CIVICA INZAGHI: Dosso.

Buffalo (New York). A. C. GOODYEAR: Moroni.

Buonconvento (Senese). PINACOTECA: Andrea di Bartolo, Cozzarelli, Duccio Follower, Girolamo di Benvenuto, Niccolò di Segna, Pietro di Domenico da Siena.

PIEVE A PIANA: Luca di Tommè.

PIEVE DEI SS. PIETRO E PAOLO: Matteo di Giovanni, Pacchiarotto, Sano di Pietro.

Burg Karlstein (Prague). Tomaso da Modena.

Burg Liechtenstein, see Mödling, Austria.

Burghley House (Stamford, Northamptonshire). MARQUESS OF EXETER: Anguissola, Brescianino, Marco d'Oggiono, Scarsellino.

Burgos. CATHEDRAL: Giampietrino.

Buscot Park (Gloucestershire). LORD FARINGDON: Sodoma.

Busto Arsizio (Milan). S. MARIA IN PIAZZA: Gaudenzio Ferrari, Lanino, Luini.

ARCH. PAOLO CANDIANI: Bergognone, Garofalo.

Buttigliera Alta (Turin). S. ANTONIO DI RANVERSO: Defendente Ferrari.

Caen. MUSÉE DES BEAUX-ARTS: Niccolò da Foligno, Perugino, Lo Spagna, Tura.

Cagli (Urbino). MUSEO CIVICO: Santi.

PALAZZO COMUNALE, ATRIO: Santi.

S. ANGELO: Viti.

S. DOMENICO: Santi, Viti.

Caiolo. PARISH CHURCH: Civerchio.

Calci (Pisa). PIEVE: Gera.

Caldarola (Tolentino). S. MARIA DEL MONTE: Lorenzo d'Alessandro.

Calvisano (Brescia). PARISH CHURCH: Romanino.

Cambridge. FITZWILLIAM MUSEUM: Andrea di Niccolò, Balducci, Bartolomeo della Gatta, Beccafumi, Boccaccino, Galeazzo Campi, Ceccarelli, Ferrarese, Francesco Napolitano, Giolfino, Giovanni di Paolo, Girolamo da Cremona, Liberale da Verona, Luca di Tommè, Martino di Bartolomeo da Siena, Mazzolino, Neroccio, Ortolano, Pacchiarotto, Parentino, Perugino, Pinturicchio, Riminese Trecento, Romanino, Sano di Pietro, Simone Martini, Torbido, Tura, Andrea Vanni, Zoppo.

— (EX): Bernardino de' Conti, Garofalo.

SIR SIDNEY COCKERELL (EX): Cozzarelli.

GIRTON COLLEGE: Francesco di Vannuccio.

Cambridge (Massachusetts). HARVARD UNIVERSITY, FOGG ART MUSEUM: Andrea di Bartolo, Antoniazzo Romano, Bartolomeo di Gentile da Urbino, Benvenuto di Giovanni,

Bernardino di Mariotto, Boltraffio, Brescianino, Ceccarelli, Defendente Ferrari, De Predis, Dosso, Foppa, Francesco Napolitano, Fungai, Giampietrino, Giolfino, Giovanni di Paolo, Girolamo di Benvenuto, Guariento, Guido da Siena, Ambrogio Lorenzetti, Pietro Lorenzetti, Luini, Martino di Bartolomeo da Siena, Master of the Osservanza Triptych, Master of Panzano Triptych, Matteo di Giovanni, Moretto, Moroni, Niccolò da Foligno, Pacchiarotto, Palmerucci, Palmezzano, Pastura, Pinturicchio, Roberto di Oderisio da Napoli, Sano di Pietro, Simone Martini, Taddeo di Bartolo, Tura, 'Ugolino Lorenzetti', Ugolino di Nerio, Andrea Vanni, Lippo Vanni, Zaganelli.

E. WALDO FORBES (EX): 'Ugolino Lorenzetti'.

Camerino. PINACOTECA: Arcangelo di Cola da Camerino, Girolamo di Giovanni da Camerino, Vincenzo Pagani.

PALAZZO VESCOVILE: Niccolò da Foligno.

DUOMO: Girolamo di Giovanni da Camerino.

SS. ANNUNZIATA: Bernardino di Mariotto, Girolamo di Giovanni da Camerino.

S. MARIA IN VIA: Boccati.

(Environs). ACQUACANINA, S. MARGHERITA: Girolamo di Giovanni da Camerino.

— BOLOGNOLA, VILLA MALVEZZI, Girolamo di Giovanni da Camerino.

— S. MARIA DI RAGGIANO: Girolamo di Giovanni da Camerino.

Campagnano (Rome), see Viterbo.

Campagnatico (between Siena and Grosseto). S. MARIA: Martino di Bartolomeo.

Campiglia Cervo (Biella). SS. GIUSEPPE E BERNARDINO: Lanino.

Campli (Teramo, Abruzzi). PARISH CHURCH: Cola d'Amatrice.

Camporosso (Bordighera). PARISH CHURCH: Brea.

Campriano (Murlo). PARISH CHURCH: Pietro Lorenzetti.

Canford Manor (Ashby St. Ledgers). VISCOUNT WIMBORNE: Dosso, Garofalo, Maineri, Palmezzano, Zoppo.

Cannara (Perugia). S. GIOVANNI BATTISTA: Niccolò da Foligno.

Cannes. MUSÉE DE LA CASTRE: Liberale da Verona.

Canobbio (Lago Maggiore). S. MARIA DELLA PIETÀ: Gaudenzio Ferrari.

Canterbury. CATHEDRAL: Garofalo.

Capena. S. MICHELE: Antonio da Viterbo.

Capesthorne Hall (Chelford, Cheshire). SIR WALTER BROMLEY DAVENPORT: Benvenuto di Giovanni, Marco d'Oggiono, Signorelli.

Cape Town. JOSEPH ROBINSON (EX): Civerchio.

Capistrano (Abruzzi). S. FRANCESCO: Sano di Pietro.

Capriolo (Brescia). PARISH CHURCH: Calisto Piazza, Romanino.

Capua. MUSEO CAMPANO: Scacco.

DUOMO: Antoniazzo Romano.

S. SALVATORE MINORE (CARMINELLO): Cavallini Follower.

Carassai (Ascoli). S. LORENZO: Vincenzo Pagani.

Cardiff. NATIONAL MUSEUM OF WALES: Dosso.

Carmagnola (Turin). COLLEGIATA: Defendente Ferrari.

Carpi. FORESTI COLLECTION: Aspertini.

— (EX): Boccaccino, Mantegna.

Carshalton (Surrey). REV. COURBOULD: Francia, Signorelli.

Casa Castalda (Valfabbrica, Umbria). PARISH CHURCH: Matteo da Gualdo.

Casale Monferrato. S. DOMENICO: Giovan Francesco Caroto.

    S. EVASIO (DUOMO): Gaudenzio Ferrari.

    CONFRATERNITA DI GESÙ: Lanino.

Casalmaggiore. BIGNAMI COLLECTION: Galeazzo Campi.

Casciano in Vescovado (Murlo). S. MARIA ASSUNTA IN PIANTASALA: Andrea di Niccolò.

Càscina (Pontedera). S. GIOVANNI DEI CAVALIERI GEROSOLIMITANI: Luca di Tommè, Martino di Bartolomeo da Siena.

Caselle Torinese. MUNICIPIO: Defendente Ferrari.

Casole (Colle Val d'Elsa). COLLEGIATA ASSUNTA: Andrea di Niccolò, Pacchia, Pellicciajo.

Cassel. GEMÄLDEGALERIE: Antoniazzo Romano, Moretto, Romanino.

    HABICH COLLECTION (EX): Beccafumi.

    HENSCHEL COLLECTION (EX): Matteo di Giovanni.

Castagneto Carducci (Grosseto). GHERARDESCA COLLECTION (EX): Riminese Trecento.

Castel del Piano (Siena). MADONNA DELLE GRAZIE: Andrea di Niccolò.

Castel di Mezzo (Pesaro). PARISH CHURCH: Zaganelli.

Castelfiorentino (Empoli). PINACOTECA: Taddeo di Bartolo.

    COLLEGIATA DEI SS. IPPOLITO E BIAGIO: Duccio Follower.

Castellarano (Reggio Emilia). S. VALENTINO: Garofalo.

Castelli Calepio. S. PIETRO: Moroni.

Castelnuovo dell'Abate (Montalcino). MISERICORDIA: Neroccio.

Castelnuovo Berardenga. PREPOSITURA: Giovanni di Paolo.

Castelnuovo di Porto (Lazio). S. MARIA ASSUNTA: Antoniazzo Romano.

Castel Ritaldi (Perugia). S. MARINA: Tiberio d'Assisi.

Castel Santa Maria (by Castelraimondo near Camerino). CHIESA DELL'ASSUNTA: Boccati.

Castiglion del Bosco (Buonconvento). S. MICHELE ARCANGELO: Pietro Lorenzetti.

Castiglione d'Adda (Milan). INCORONATA: Albertino and Martino Piazza.

Castiglione d'Olona (Varese). COLLEGIATA: Vecchietta.

Castiglione d'Orcia. PIEVE: Pietro Lorenzetti.

    S. MARIA MADDALENA: Pietro Lorenzetti, Vecchietta.

    S. SIMEONE: Bartolo di Fredi, Giovanni di Paolo.

Castiglione Fiorentino. PINACOTECA: Bartolomeo della Gatta, Giovanni di Paolo, Matteo di Giovanni.

    S. FRANCESCO: Margarito.

    COLLEGIATA DI S. GIULIANO: Bartolomeo della Gatta, Segna di Bonaventura.

    — PIEVE (back of COLLEGIATA): Signorelli.

Castiglione Garfagnana. S. MICHELE: Giuliano di Simone da Lucca.

Castle Ashby (Northamptonshire). MARQUESS OF NORTHAMPTON: Dosso and Battista Dossi, Gaudenzio Ferrari, Mantegna.

Castle Howard (Yorkshire). MAJOR HOWARD: Battista Dossi.

Castrocaro (Forlì). SS. NICCOLÒ E FRANCESCO: Palmezzano.

Catajo (Padua). CASTELLO: Guariento.

Cava dei Tirreni (Salerno). ABBAZIA DELLA TRINITÀ, MUSEO: Andrea da Salerno.

Cavenago d'Adda (Milan). PARISH CHURCH: Albertino and Martino Piazza.

Cavour (Saluzzo). S. LORENZO: Defendente Ferrari.

Cedar Rapids (Ohio). COES COLLEGE, MUSEUM: Bernardino de' Conti.

Cellàtica (Brescia), see Madonna della Stella.

Cenate d'Argon (Bergamo). s. LEONE: Moroni.

s. MARTINO: Moroni.

Cernusco Montevecchia. CONTE LURANI: Luini.

Cerqueto (Perugia). PARISH CHURCH: Perugino.

TABERNACLE: Perugino.

Cerreto d'Esi (Fabriano). PARISH CHURCH: Antonio da Fabriano.

Cesena. PINACOTECA: Palmezzano, Zaganelli.

MADONNA DEL MONTE: Francia.

Cetona (Val di Chiana). s. FRANCESCO: Balducci, Sano di Pietro.

s. FRANCESCO (CLAUSURA): Girolamo di Benvenuto.

Châalis (Ermenonville). MUSÉE JACQUEMART-ANDRÉ: Balducci, Bernardino de' Conti, Foppa, Francia, Domenico Morone.

Chalon-sur-Saône. MUSÉE DENON: Giovanni di Paolo.

Châlons-sur-Marne. MUSÉE MUNICIPAL: Bernardino di Mariotto.

Chambéry. MUSÉE DES BEAUX-ARTS: Fungai, Zaganelli.

Chantilly. MUSÉE CONDÉ: Bonfigli, Butinone, Dosso, Francia, Giampietrino, Giovanni di Paolo, Luini, Marco d'Oggiono, Mazzolino, Moroni, Perino del Vaga, Perugino, Raphael, Sassetta, Zaganelli.

Chapel Hill (North Carolina). WILLIAM HAYES ACKLAND MEMORIAL ART CENTER: Traini.

Chapel Manor (Horsmonden, Kent). AUSTEN COLLECTION (EX): Master of Stratonice.

Charlottenburg. DR GERHART BOLLERT (EX): Moroni.

Charlton Park (Malmesbury). EARL OF SUFFOLK (EX): Giampietrino.

Chartres. MUSÉE DES BEAUX-ARTS: Cavazzola.

Chatsworth (Bakewell). DEVONSHIRE COLLECTION: Beccafumi, Boltraffio, Giulio Campi.

Cherbourg. MUSÉE THOMAS HENRY: Giovanni di Paolo, Pietro di Domenico da Montepulciano.

Chesterfield. G. LOCKER-LAMPSON: Giampietrino.

Chianciano (Chiusi). MUSEO DI ARTE SACRA: Duccio Follower, Ugolino di Nerio.

Chiaravalle (Milan). ABBAZIA: Luini.

Chicago (Illinois). ART INSTITUTE: Butinone, Cavazzola, Correggio, Ercole da Ferrara, Giovanni di Paolo, Matteo di Giovanni, Moroni, Nuzi, Perugino, Sano di Pietro, Lo Spagna, Taddeo di Bartolo, Ugolino di Nerio.

MARTIN RYERSON COLLECTION (EX): Ferrarese–Bolognese, Garofalo.

LAKE FOREST, J. R. THOMPSON (EX): Luini, Pinturicchio.

Chieti. MUSEO CIVICO: Master of the Crivellesque Polyptychs.

Chiusi. s. SECONDIANO (DUOMO): Benvenuto di Giovanni, Francesco di Giorgio, Fungai, Girolamo da Cremona, Liberale da Verona, Sano di Pietro.

Chiusure (near Monteoliveto di Siena). CANONICA DI GROSSENANO: Giovanni di Paolo.

Chivasso (Turin). ASSUNTA: Defendente Ferrari.

Cimiez, see Nice.

Cincinnati (Ohio). ART MUSEUM: Andrea di Niccolò, Duccio Follower, Luini, Mantegna, Matteo di Giovanni.

Cingoli. s. DOMENICO: Salimbeni.

Ciriè (Turin). s. GIOVANNI BATTISTA (DUOMO): Defendente Ferrari.

CONFRATERNITA DEL S. SUDARIO: Defendente Ferrari.

Città della Pieve. DUOMO: Perugino.

S. MARIA DEI BIANCHI: Perugino.

S. MARIA DEI SERVI: Perugino.

S. PIETRO: Perugino.

Città di Castello. PALAZZO BUFALINI (EX): Pinturicchio.

PALAZZO VITELLI DELLA CANNONIERA (PINACOTECA): Cola d'Amatrice, Master of Città di Castello, Raphael, Signorelli.

DUOMO: Pinturicchio.

S. MARIA DELLE GRAZIE: Nelli.

Cividate (Val Camonica). S. MARIA ASSUNTA: Calisto Piazza.

Civita Castellana. PALAZZO PAPALE: Piermatteo da Amelia.

S. PIETRO: Antoniazzo Romano, Sano di Pietro.

Civitella Benazzone (Perugia). PARISH CHURCH: Bonfigli.

Cizzago (Brescia). PARISH CHURCH: Romanino.

Claremont (California). POMONA COLLEGE, KRESS COLLECTION: Barnaba da Modena, Ferrarese, Niccolò da Foligno.

Cleveland (Ohio). MUSEUM OF ART: Berlinghiero, Brescianino, Giulio Campi, Dosso, Duccio Follower, Francesco Napolitano, Giovanni Agostino da Lodi, Giovanni di Paolo, Girolamo dai Libri, Lorenzo d'Alessandro, Luini, Mantegna, Matteo di Giovanni, Moretto, Parentino, Pinturicchio, Riminese Trecento, Sano di Pietro, Sassetta, Simone Martini Follower, Tegliacci, Ugolino di Nerio, Lippo Vanni, Viti.

WILLIAM G. MATHER COLLECTION: Boltraffio.

Codogno (Milan). COLLEGIATA: Calisto Piazza.

Coldellanoce (Sassoferrato). S. LORENZO MARTIRE: Matteo da Gualdo.

Collalto (Treviso). CAPPELLA DI S. SALVATORE: Riminese Trecento.

Collegalli (San Miniato al Tedesco). SS. VITO E MODESTO: Taddeo di Bartolo.

Colle Val d'Elsa. S. AGOSTINO: Taddeo di Bartolo.

S. PIETRO: Giovanni di Paolo.

Colmar. MUSÉE D'UNTERLINDEN: Urbani.

Cologne. WALLRAF RICHARTZ MUSEUM: Bergognone, Bramantino, Duccio Follower, Fei, Fungai, Matteo di Giovanni, Niccolò di Buonaccorso, Sano di Pietro, Simone Martini, Taddeo de Bartolo, 'Ugolino Lorenzetti'.

— (EX): Giovanni di Paolo.

ERZBISCHÖFLICHES DIÖZESANMUSEUM: Giovanni Francesco da Rimini, Sano di Pietro.

SCHNÜTGEN MUSEUM: Fei, 'Ugolino Lorenzetti'.

Cologny (Geneva). BIBLIOTECA BODMERIANA: Michelino da Besozzo.

Columbia (Missouri). UNIVERSITY OF MISSOURI, KRESS COLLECTION: Altobello Melone, Bramantino, Fungai, Domenico Morone.

Columbia (South Carolina). MUSEUM OF ART, KRESS COLLECTION: Cozzarelli, Francia, Genga, Matteo di Giovanni, Moretto, Parmigianino, Solario, 'Ugolino Lorenzetti'.

Columbus (Ohio). GALLERY OF FINE ARTS, HOWALD COLLECTION: Fungai, Martino di Bartolomeo da Siena.

— SCHUMACHER COLLECTION: Garofalo, Liberale da Verona, Moroni.

Combe House (Presteigne). URSULA HARRISON (EX): Boccaccino.

Comero (Brescia). SANTUARIO DI AURO: Moretto.

Como. DUOMO: Gaudenzio Ferrari, Luini.

Compiègne. MUSÉE VIVENEL: Boccati, Giovanni di Paolo, Niccolò da Foligno.

Compton Wynyates (Warwickshire). MARQUESS OF NORTHAMPTON: Andrea da Salerno, Balducci, Palmezzano.

Connell (Argyllshire). MRS JEAN NELSON: Signorelli.

Conzano Monferrato. PARISH CHURCH: Spanzotti.

Copenhagen. STATENSMUSEUM: Boccaccino, Cecco di Pietro, Luini, Maineri, Mantegna, Master of Città di Castello, Ortolano, Parmigianino, Calisto Piazza, Simone Martini Follower.

THORWALDSEN MUSEUM: Fiorenzo di Lorenzo, Taddeo di Bartolo.

Coral Gables (Florida). UNIVERSITY OF MIAMI, LOWE ART GALLERY, KRESS COLLECTION: Cozzarelli, Dosso, Francesco di Giorgio, Fungai, Garofalo, Riminese Trecento, Sano di Pietro, Lippo Vanni.

Corciano (Perugia). S. MARIA: Bonfigli, Perugino.

Cori (Latina). S. OLIVA: Francesco da Tolentino.

Cornbury Park (Charlbury, Oxfordshire). WATNEY COLLECTION (EX): Master of the Gardner Annunciation, Romanino.

Correggio (Reggio Emilia). CONGREGAZIONE DI CARITÀ: Mantegna.

Corridonia (Macerata), (former Mont'olmo, called Pàusola 1851–1931). S. AGOSTINO: Andrea da Bologna.

S. FRANCESCO: Vincenzo Pagani, Sassetta.

SS. PIETRO, PAOLO E DONATO, CANONICA (now Pinacoteca): Lorenzo d'Alessandro.

Corsano (Siena). PIEVE: Matteo di Giovanni.

Corsham Court (Wiltshire). METHUEN COLLECTION: Anguissola, Luini.

Cortona. GESÙ (MUSEO DIOCESANO): Pietro Lorenzetti, Sassetta, Signorelli.

S. DOMENICO: Bartolomeo della Gatta, Sassetta, Signorelli.

S. FRANCESCO: Margarito.

S. NICCOLÒ: Signorelli.

PALAZZONE, CONTE PASSERINI, CAPPELLA: Signorelli.

Cossato (Novara). ASSUNTA: Lanino.

Cossignano (Ascoli). SS. ANNUNZIATA: Vincenzo Pagani.

Costa di Mezzate (Bergamo). CONTI CAMOZZI VERTOVA: Moroni.

Cotignola. S. FRANCESCO: Zaganelli.

Coursegoules. S. JEAN-BAPTISTE: Brea.

Covignano (Rimini). S. MARIA DELLE GRAZIE: Nelli.

Cracow. NATIONAL MUSEUM: De Predis, Garofalo, Liberale da Verona, Neroccio, Raphael, Ugolino di Nerio.

JAGELLOŃSKA LIBRARY: Master of the Codex of St. George, Lippo Vanni.

COUNT SIGISMUND PUSLOWSKI (EX): Palmezzano.

Crea (Casale Monferrato). SANTUARIO DI S. MARIA ASSUNTA: Macrino d'Alba.

Crema. PALAZZO ZURLA DE POLI: Civerchio.

PALAZZO VESCOVILE: Romanino.

DUOMO: Civerchio.

SS. TRINITÀ: Calisto Piazza.

STRAMEZZI COLLECTION: Foppa.

Cremia (Lago di Como). S. MICHELE: Farinati.

Cremona. MUSEO CIVICO: Aleni, Altobello Melone, Anguissola, Bianchi Ferrari, Boccaccino, Galeazzo Campi, Giulio Campi, Cicognara, Giovanni Agostino di Lodi, Mazzolino.

PINACOTECA: Romanino.

S. ABBONDIO: Aleni, Galeazzo Campi, Giulio Campi.

S. AGATA: Boccaccino, Galeazzo Campi, Giulio Campi.

S. AGOSTINO: Galeazzo Campi, Perugino.

DUOMO: Aleni, Altobello Melone, Boccaccino, Giulio Campi, Romanino.

S. MARGHERITA: Giulio Campi.

S. MARIA MADDALENA: Aleni, Galeazzo Campi.

S. MICHELE: Boccaccino, Giulio Campi.

S. PIETRO AL PO: Giulio Campi.

S. SEBASTIANO: Galeazzo Campi.

S. SIGISMONDO: Aleni, Giulio Campi.

G. CAROTTI: Boccaccino.

CRIGNANI COLLECTION: Civerchio.

Crenna di Gallarate. CARMINATI COLLECTION: Gentile da Fabriano, Nuzi.

Crespino (Rovigo). SS. MARTINO AND SEVERO: Garofalo.

Crevacuore (Biella). S. SEBASTIANO: Lanino.

Crevenna (Erba). S. SALVATORE: Michelino di Besozzo.

Cuneo. MUSEO CIVICO: Defendente Ferrari.

S. MARIA DEGLI ANGELI: Defendente Ferrari.

CASSA DI RISPARMIO: Macrino d'Alba.

Cusona (Siena). S. BIAGIO: Bartolo di Fredi.

Dallas (Texas). MUSEUM OF FINE ARTS, KRESS COLLECTION: Garofalo.

Darmstadt. HESSISCHES LANDESMUSEUM: Dosso.

Denver (Colorado). MUSEUM OF ART: Defendente Ferrari, Foppa, Girolamo di Benvenuto, North-Italian Gothic, Parentino, Albertino and Martino Piazza, Pinturicchio, Riminese Trecento, Spanzotti.

Derby. A. W. PUGIN (EX): Francesco di Gentile da Fabriano.

Deruta (Perugia). PALAZZO COMUNALE, PINACOTECA: Niccolò da Foligno.

S. ANTONIO: Caporali.

S. FRANCESCO: Fiorenzo di Lorenzo.

— (Environs). LA FANCIULLATA, CHAPEL: Caporali.

Desenzano al Serio. CHIESA DEL MIRACOLO: Moroni.

Detroit (Michigan). INSTITUTE OF ARTS: Andrea di Bartolo, Antoniazzo Romano, Benvenuto di Giovanni, Bernardino de' Conti, Correggio, Costa, Dosso, Eusebio da San Giorgio, Francesco dai Libri (Il Vecchio), Garofalo, Gaudenzio Ferrari, Giovanni di Paolo, Giulio Romano, Luca di Tommè, Luini, Master of Città di Castello, Master of the Codex of St. George, Master of Osservanza Triptych, Matteo di Giovanni, Moroni, Nuzi, Parmigianino, Sano di Pietro, Sassetta, Signorelli, Sodoma, Lippo Vanni.

RALPH H. BOOTH (EX): Lo Spagna.

L. P. FISCHER COLLECTION: Foppa.

EDSEL FORD COLLECTION: Perugino.

ROBERT GRAHAM: Girolamo di Benvenuto.

LILIAN HENCKEL HAASS COLLECTION: Giovanni di Paolo, Sano di Pietro.

HIGBIE COLLECTION: Luini.

Diano Borello. PARISH CHURCH: Brea.

Diano Borganzo. PARISH CHURCH: Brea.

Dijon. MUSÉE DES BEAUX-ARTS: Bartolo di Fredi, Farinati, Pietro Lorenzetti, Lorenzo d'Alessandro, Luini, Master of Osservanza Triptych, Palmezzano, Solario.

MUSÉE MAGNIN: Scarsellino.

Dorking (Surrey). WATERHOUSE COLLECTION (EX): Sano di Pietro.

Douai. MUSÉE: Lippo Memmi.

Downton Castle (Ludlow). MAJOR KINCAID LENNOX (EX): Costa.

Dresden. GEMÄLDEGALERIE: Balducci, Giovan Francesco Caroto, Cavazzola, Ceccarelli, Correggio, Cossa, Costa, Battista Dossi, Dosso, Ercole da Ferrara, Francia, Garofalo, Girolamo di Benvenuto, Girolamo da Carpi, Giulio Romano, Mantegna, Mazzolino, Parmigianino, Peruzzi, Pinturicchio, Raphael, Sano di Pietro, Scarsellino, Signorelli, Tura.

ALBERTINUM: Francesco di Giorgio (sculpture).

Dublin. NATIONAL GALLERY OF IRELAND: Andrea di Bartolo, Antoniazzo, Beccafumi, Costa, Eusebio da San Giorgio, Francia, Giacomo del Pisano, Giovanni di Paolo, Girolamo di Benvenuto, Mantegna, Mazzolino, Moroni, Palmezzano, Perugino, Riminese Trecento, Signorelli, Solario, Tura, Ugolino di Nerio, Vitale da Bologna, Zaganelli.

JUDGE JAMES A. MURNAGHAN: Aspertini, Brescianino, Pacchiarotto.

Dublin (New Hampshire). MRS SAMUEL HALE: Simone Martini Follower.

Dubrovnik (Ragusa). BISHUPSKA PINACOTECA: Pacchia.

Dudley Castle (Stafford). EARL OF DUDLEY: Luini.

Duino. PRINZ VON THURN UND TAXIS: Francesco di Giorgio.

Dulwich. COLLEGE ART GALLERY: Calisto Piazza, Raphael.

Dunfermline (Fife). EARL OF ELGIN (EX): Farinati.

Düsseldorf. WALTER GROSS (EX): Palmezzano.

Easton Neston (Towcester, Northants). LORD HESKETH (EX): Mazzolino.

Eboli (Salerno). S. FRANCESCO: Roberto di Oderisio da Napoli.

Edinburgh. NATIONAL GALLERY OF SCOTLAND: Butinone, Ferrarese, Fiorenzo di Lorenzo, Matteo di Giovanni, Perugino, Raphael, Sano di Pietro, Vitale da Bologna, Zoppo.

ERSKINE COLLECTION: Palmezzano.

Eger (Hungary). GALERIE: Dosso.

Eggi (Spoleto). S. GIOVANNI BATTISTA: Lo Spagna.

El Paso (Texas). MUSEUM OF ART, KRESS COLLECTION: Boltraffio, Bonfigli, Battista Dossi, Garofalo, Giovanni Agostino da Lodi, Giovanni di Paolo, Ambrogio Lorenzetti, Macrino d'Alba, Martino di Bartolomeo da Siena, Pacchiarotto, Sano di Pietro, Sassetta.

Elton Hall (Peterborough). SIR RICHARD PROBY, BT.: Cesare da Sesto, Luini.

Eltville. GRÄFIN VON FRANCKEN SIERSTORPFF: Gaudenzio Ferrari.

Englewood (New Jersey). DAN FELLOWS PLATT COLLECTION (EX): Andrea di Bartolo, Andrea di Niccolò, Antoniazzo, Bartolo di Fredi, Beccafumi, Benvenuto di Giovanni, Brescianino, Cozzarelli, Fei, Garofalo, Giovanni di Paolo, Girolamo di Benvenuto, Girolamo di Giovanni da Camerino, Luini, Pacchiarotto, Palmezzano, Pietro di

Domenico da Siena, Sano di Pietro, Taddeo di Bartolo.

Erbanno (Val Camonica). S. MARIA DI RESTELLO: Calisto Piazza.

Erbizzo (Verona). PARISH CHURCH: Giovan Francesco Caroto.

Erfurt. MUSEUM: Moretto.

Erlenbach. HANS CORAY (EX): Defendente Ferrari.

Escorial. Garofalo, Moretto.

Esine (Val Camonica). ASSUNTA, CANONICA: Moretto.

PARISH CHURCH: Calisto Piazza.

Esztergom. KERESTENY MUSEUM: Ambrosi, Andrea di Bartolo, Andrea di Niccolò, Boccati, Duccio Follower, Giampietrino, Giovanni di Paolo, Girolamo dai Libri, Matteo di Giovanni, Neroccio, Niccolò da Foligno, Vincenzo Pagani, Palmezzano, Sano di Pietro, 'Ugolino Lorenzetti'.

Fabriano. PINACOTECA: Antonio da Fabriano, Nuzi, Riminese Trecento.

S. AGOSTINO: Riminese Trecento.

S. DOMENICO: Ghissi.

S. LUCIA (VULGO S. DOMENICO): Antonio da Fabriano, Nuzi.

S. VENANZIO (DUOMO): Nuzi.

CORNER OF VIA S. FILIPPO AND VIA VALPOVERA, TABERNACLE: Nuzi.

(Environs). BASTIA, PARISH CHURCH: Bernardino di Mariotto.

Faenza. PINACOTECA: Bertucci, Dosso, Palmezzano, Giovanni da Rimini.

GUIDI COLLECTION: Palmezzano.

Fano. MUSEO CIVICO: Santi.

S. DOMENICO: Nelli, Riminese Trecento.

S. MARIA NUOVA: Perugino, Santi.

Farfa (Sabina). ABBAZIA: Tiberio d'Assisi.

Feletto Canavese (Turin). PARISH CHURCH: Defendente Ferrari.

Fermo. MUSEO E PINACOTECA COMUNALE: Andrea da Bologna, Antoniazzo Romano, Ghissi, Vincenzo Pagani.

Ferrara. PINACOTECA CIVICA: Baldassarre d'Este, Boccaccino, Cicognara, Cossa, Dosso, Battista Dossi, Ercole da Ferrara, Ferrarese, Ferrarese-Bolognese, Garofalo, Girolamo da Carpi, Guariento, Mazzolino, Michele Pannonio, Ortolano, Riminese Trecento, Scarsellino, Tura, Zaganelli.

BIBLIOTECA DELL'UNIVERSITÀ: Tura.

CASTELLO: Girolamo da Carpi.

PALAZZO ARCIVESCOVILE: Giralomo da Carpi.

— CAPPELLA: Scarsellino.

PALAZZO (TROTTI) DEL SEMINARIO: Garofalo.

PALAZZO DI LUDOVICO IL MORO, AULA COSTABILIANA: Garofalo.

PALAZZO SCHIFANOIA: Baldassarre d'Este, Cicognara, Cossa, Ercole da Ferrara, Ferrarese.

ESTE PALACE (EX): Battista Dossi.

CORPUS DOMINI, ORATORIO DEL MONASTERO: Scarsellino.

DUOMO: Francia, Garofalo, Scarsellino.

— MUSEO DELL'OPERA: Tura.

ORATORIO DELLA CONCEZIONE: Boccaccino.

S. BENEDETTO: Scarsellino.

s. CHIARA DELLE CAPPUCCINE: Scarsellino.

s. DOMENICO: Scarsellino.

s. FRANCESCO: Garofalo, Girolamo da Carpi, Mazzolino, Scarsellino.

s. GIOVANNI BATTISTA: Scarsellino.

s. MAURELIO: Scarsellino.

s. MONICA: Garofalo.

s. PAOLO: Girolamo da Carpi, Scarsellino.

AVV. MARIO BALDI: Mantegna.

BARBI CINTI COLLECTION (EX): Bertucci.

MASOTTI COLLECTION: Scarsellino.

MASSARI-ZAVAGLIA COLLECTION: Ferrarese-Bolognese.

— (EX): Zaganelli.

TADDEI COLLECTION: Maineri.

VENDEGHINI BALDI COLLECTION: Ercole da Ferrara, Ortolano.

Fiesole. MUSEO BANDINI: Cavallini Follower, Niccolò di Buonaccorso.

VIA VECCHIA FIESOLANA, TABERNACOLO DEL PREPOSTO (VILLA CAPPELLA): Perugino.

Finale Pia (Savona). SANTUARIO: Barnaba da Modena.

Fino del Monte (Bergamo). PARISH CHURCH: Moroni.

Fiordimonte (Macerata). CASTELLO: Girolamo di Giovanni da Camerino.

Firle Place (Sussex). LADY GAGE: Moroni.

Florence. Galleries, Museums, Palazzi.

GALLERIA DELL'ACCADEMIA: Giovanni Francesco da Rimini, Guido da Siena, Perugino.

GALLERIA DEGLI UFFIZI: Anguissola, Antoniazzo Romano, Aspertini, Beccafumi, Bernardino de' Conti, Boccaccino, Boltraffio, Brescianino, Brusasorci, Giulio Campi, Caporali, Giovan Francesco Caroto, Cavazzola, Correggio, Costa, De Predis, Dosso, Duccio, Ercole da Ferrara, Farinati, Francia, Fungai, Garofalo, Genga, Gentile da Fabriano, Giampietrino, Giovanni di Paolo, Giulio Romano, Ambrogio Lorenzetti, Pietro Lorenzetti, Lorenzo d'Alessandro, Luini, Maineri, Mantegna, Master of the Gardner Annunciation, Matteo di Giovanni, Mazzolino, Melozzo da Forlì, Lippo Memmi, Moroni, Neroccio, Niccolò di Buonaccorso, North-Italian Gothic, Pacchia, Palmezzano, Parmigianino, Perino del Vaga, Perugino, Piero della Francesca, Raphael, Romanino, Scarsellino, Signorelli, Simone Martini, Sodoma, Tegliacci, Traini, Tura, 'Ugolino Lorenzetti', Vecchietta.

— GABINETTO DEI DISEGNI: Beccafumi.

GALLERIA PALATINA DI PALAZZO PITTI: Beccafumi, Giulio Campi, Dosso, Garofalo, Genga, Girolamo da Carpi, Mazzolino, Moroni, Parmigianino, Perugino, Peruzzi, Calisto Piazza, Raphael, Signorelli, Sodoma, Lo Spagna.

MUSEO ARCIVESCOVILE (SEMINARIO MAGGIORE, CESTELLO): Ambrogio Lorenzetti.

MUSEO BARDINI: Beccafumi, Benvenuto di Giovanni, Girolamo di Benvenuto, Girolamo di Giovanni da Camerino, Luca di Tommè, Taddeo di Bartolo.

BARGELLO, MUSEO NAZIONALE: Girolamo da Cremona, Parentino, Pisanello (signed medals), Vecchietta (sculpture).

— CARRAND COLLECTION: Bonsignori, Francesco di Giorgio, Genga, Giovanni di Paolo, Lanino, Martino di Bartolomeo da Siena, Master of the Codex of St. George, Master of Griselda.

BIBLIOTECA NAZIONALE: Girolamo da Cremona.

Florence. Galleries, Museums, Palazzi (contd.).

BIGALLO: Palmezzano.

CENACOLO DI FOLIGNO: Perugino.

GALLERIA CORSI: Bartolo di Fredi.

MUSEO FERRONI: Torbido.

MUSEO HORNE: Ambrosi, Barna da Siena, Bartolomeo della Gatta, Beccafumi, Boccac-
cino, Ceccarelli, Dosso, Giampietrino, Giolfino, Girolamo di Benvenuto, Pietro
Lorenzetti, Lorenzetti Follower, Matteo di Giovanni, Melozzo da Forlì, Francesco
Morone, Neroccio, Signorelli, Simone Martini Follower, 'Ugolino Lorenzetti',
Vecchietta (sculpture).

MUSEO STIBBERT: Beccafumi, Francesco di Giorgio, Luini, Riminese Trecento, Schiavone.

PALAZZO VECCHIO (LOESER BEQUEST): Pietro Lorenzetti.

Florence. Churches.

SS. ANNUNZIATA: Perugino.

S. CROCE: Cavallini Follower, Perugino.

— MUSEO DELL'OPERA: Brescianino, 'Ugolino Lorenzetti'.

S. GIOVANNINO DE' CAVALIERI: Master of Stratonice.

S. LUCIA DEI MAGNOLI: Pietro Lorenzetti.

S. MARIA DEL CARMINE: Master of the Codex of St. George.

S. MARIA MADDALENA DEI PAZZI: Perugino.

S. SPIRITO: Perugino.

EX-CONVENT OF S. GIORGIO ALLA COSTA (CASERMA VITTORIO VENETO): Caporali.

EX-CONVENT OF MONTEOLIVETO: Sodoma.

Florence. Private Collections.

ACTON COLLECTION: Ambrosi, Andrea di Bartolo, Bartolomeo della Gatta, Master of
St. Francis, Sano di Pietro.

PALAZZO ALBIZI (EX): Perugino.

BERENSON COLLECTION: Balducci, Barna da Siena, Benvenuto di Giovanni, Bergognone,
Boccati, Bonfigli, Bonsignori, Brescianino, Ercole da Ferrara, Fei, Foppa, Francesco
di Gentile da Fabriano, Francesco di Giorgio, Fungai, Gentile da Fabriano, Giolfino,
Giovanni di Paolo, Girolamo di Benvenuto, Girolamo da Cremona, Liberale da
Verona, Pietro Lorenzetti, Lorenzetti Follower, Master of Osservanza Triptych,
Matteo di Giovanni, Domenico Morone, Neroccio, Ortolano, Vincenzo Pagani,
Pastura, Perugino, Sano di Pietro, Sassetta, Signorelli, Simone Martini, Simone
Martini Follower, Taddeo di Bartolo, 'Ugolino Lorenzetti', Ugolino di Nerio,
Andrea Vanni, Vecchietta.

BONDI COLLECTION (EX): Segna di Bonaventura.

CONTINI BONACOSSI COLLECTION: Antoniazzo, Boccaccino, Boltraffio, Bramantino, De-
fendente Ferrari, Duccio, Foppa, Francia, Gaudenzio Ferrari, Luini, Francesco
Morone, Moroni, Piero della Francesca, Raphael, Sassetta, Spanzotti, Ugolino di
Nerio, Zenale.

CORA COLLECTION: Master of Sforza Altarpiece.

GALLERIA CORSINI: Evangelista da Pian di Meleto, Palmezzano, Santi, Signorelli, Viti.

ENRICO COSTA (EX): Liberale da Verona.

FERRONI COLLECTION (EX): Domenico di Bartolo.

CONTE FILICAIA (EX): Sassetta.

Foligno (Environs) (contd.). VESCIA, MAESTÀ DI S. ANNA: Mezzastris.

— COMPAGNIA ALLE VESCIE: Niccolò da Foligno.

Fondi. S. PIETRO: Antoniazzo Romano, Scacco.

— Environs. MONTE SAN BIAGIO, S. GIOVANNI BATTISTA: Scacco.

Fondra (Bergamo). PARISH CHURCH: Garofalo.

Fontanellato (Parma). CASTELLO SANVITALE: Parmigianino.

Fonthill (Wiltshire). HUGH MORRISON (EX?): Bernardino de' Conti, Domenico Morone.

Fontignano (Perugia). CHIESA DELL'ANNUNZIATA: Perugino.

Forlì. PINACOTECA COMUNALE: Francia, Melozzo da Forlì, Palmerucci, Palmezzano, Riminese Trecento, Zaganelli.

CASA ALBICINI: Palmezzano.

CHIESA DELL'ADDOLORATA: Vitale da Bologna.

SS. BIAGIO E GIROLAMO: Palmezzano.

S. CROCE (Duomo): Palmezzano.

S. MERCURIALE: Palmezzano.

Forlimpopoli. S. MARIA DEI SERVI: Palmezzano.

Fossombrone (Pesaro). VESCOVADO: Viti.

Frankfurt am Main. STÄDELSCHES KUNSTINSTITUT: Aspertini, Barnaba da Modena, Bartolo di Fredi, Giovan Francesco Caroto, Cavazzola, Correggio, Deodato Orlandi, Dosso, Fei, Fiorenzo di Lorenzo, Garofalo, Gaudenzio Ferrari, Girolamo di Benvenuto, Ambrogio Lorenzetti, Pietro Lorenzetti, Macrino d'Alba, Mantegna, Martino di Bartolomeo da Siena, Meo da Siena, Moretto, Moroni, Neroccio, Perugino, Romanino, Sassetta, Sodoma, Andrea Vanni, Lippo Vanni.

CONSUL HARRY FULD (EX): Barna da Siena.

GEORG HARTMANN (EX): Nuzi.

DR OSKAR LOEWE BEER (EX): Taddeo di Bartolo.

CARL VON WEINBERG: Fei.

Frassino (Peschiera del Garda). SANTUARIO DELLA MADONNA: Farinati.

Fratticciola Selvatica (between Perugia and Gubbio). ORATORIO DI S. MARIA DELLE GRAZIE: Fiorenzo di Lorenzo.

Frontignano (Senese). PARISH CHURCH: Sano di Pietro.

Fürstenau (Michelstadt). ERBACH VON FÜRSTENAU COLLECTION: Cavallini Follower.

Gaeta. SS. ANNUNZIATA: Peruzzi.

Gàgliole (San Severino Marche). CERQUETA: Lorenzo d'Alessandro.

S. GIUSEPPE: Vincenzo Pagani.

Gallarate. CARMINATI COLLECTION: Girolamo di Benvenuto.

Ganghereto (Valdarno). PARISH CHURCH: Margarito.

Garda. S. STEFANO: Farinati.

Gardone (Lago di Garda). S. BERNARDINO: Moretto.

Garegnano (Milan). OLD PARISH CHURCH (EX): Bergognone.

Gargagnano (Valpolicella). VILLA SEREGO ALIGHIERI: Liberale da Verona.

Garscube (Dunbarton). SIR GEORGE CAMPBELL: Luini.

Gattinara (Biella). MADONNA DEL ROSARIO: Giovenone.

S. PIETRO: Lanino.

Gavelli (Spoleto). S. MICHELE ARCANGELO: Lo Spagna.

Gaverina (Bergamo). S. VITTORE: Moroni.

Gazzada (Varese). FONDAZIONE CAGNOLA: Aspertini, Bergognone, Brescianino, Butinone, Cavazzola, Cossa, Cozzarelli, Fungai, Giampietrino, Giovanni Agostino da Lodi, Matteo di Giovanni, Neroccio, Palmezzano, Sano di Pietro.

DON GUIDO CAGNOLA (EX): Bramantino, Ortolano.

Gazzaniga (Bergamo). S. GIORGIO A FIORANO: Moroni.

Genazzano (Roma). CONVENTO DI S. PIO: Antoniazzo Romano.

Geneva. MUSÉE D'ART ET D'HISTOIRE: Palmezzano.

MUSÉE ARIANA: Giovenone.

DURAND MATTHIESEN COLLECTION: Foppa.

LEDERER COLLECTION: Giulio Campi, Giulio Romano, Master of Stratonice, Lippo Vanni.

Genga (Fabriano). S. CLEMENTE: Antonio da Fabriano.

Genoa. PALAZZO BIANCO: Barnaba da Modena, Brea, Massone, Moretto, Niccolò da Voltri.

PALAZZO ROSSO: Giolfino, Moretto, Romanino.

ACCADEMIA LIGUSTICA, QUADRERIA: Perino del Vaga, Zaganelli.

PALAZZO DORIA: Perino del Vaga.

CHIESA DELLA MADONNETTA: Brea.

S. BARTOLOMEO DEGLI ARMENI: Turino Vanni.

SS. COSMA E DAMIANO: Barnaba da Modena.

S. DONATO: Niccolò da Voltri.

S. GIORGIO A BAVARI: Perino del Vaga.

S. MARIA DI CASTELLO: Brea, Lorenzetti Follower, Massone.

NOSTRA SIGNORA DELLA CONSOLAZIONE: Lorenzetti Follower.

S. ROCCO: Niccolò da Voltri.

S. STEFANO: Giulio Romano.

BASEVI COLLECTION: Moroni.

COSTA COLLECTION: Sassetta.

DORIA BALBI DI PIOVERA (HEIRS): Perino del Vaga.

GNECCO COLLECTION: Dosso, Matteo di Giovanni.

MARCHESE MEDICI DEL VASCELLO: Spanzotti.

MARCHESA NEGROTTO CAMBIASO: Brea.

NIGRO COLLECTION: Anguissola.

MARCHESE UGO PIETRO SPINOLA: Moretto.

VIEZZOLI COLLECTION: Giovanni Agostino da Lodi.

Genoa (Environs). (SAMPIERDARENA): S. BARTOLOMEO DEL FOSSATO: Barnaba da Modena.

CELLE LIGURE, S. MICHELE: Perino del Vaga.

Gerenzano (Saronno). BEATA VERGINE DEL SOCCORSO: Luini.

Ginestreto (Pesaro). PIEVE VECCHIA: Bartolomeo di Gentile da Urbino.

Ginestreto (Siena). S. DONATO: Girolamo di Benvenuto.

S. GIOVANNI: Taddeo di Bartolo.

Glasgow. ART GALLERY: Brescianino, Cesare da Sesto, Correggio, Francia, Garofalo, Girolamo da Carpi, Romanino.

BEATTIE COLLECTION (EX): Pinturicchio.

UNIVERSITY: Scarsellino.

Goodwood (Chichester). DUKE OF RICHMOND: Anguissola.

Gorlago (Bergamo). S. PANCRAZIO: Moroni.

Gosford House (Longniddry, East Lothian). EARL OF WEMYSS AND MARCH: Butinone, Giampietrino, Mantegna, Perugino, Romanino, Sodoma.

Gotha. LANDESMUSEUM: Farinati, Francesco di Gentile da Fabriano, Fungai, Maineri, Master of Panzano Triptych.

— (EX): Fei.

Göttingen. UNIVERSITY: Benvenuto di Giovanni, Pinturicchio, Taddeo di Bartolo, Lippo Vanni.

Gradara (Pesaro). MUNICIPIO: Santi.

CASTELLO: Genga.

Granada. CAPILLA REAL: Perugino.

Grasse (Alpes-Maritimes). CATHEDRAL: Brea.

Graz. LANDESBILDGALERIE, PALAIS ATTEMS: Anguissola, Brescianino, Costa, Dosso.

SALZER COLLECTION: Bertucci.

Greenville (South Carolina). BOB JONES UNIVERSITY MUSEUM AND GALLERY: Andrea di Bartolo, Beccafumi, Cavazzola, Fiorenzo di Lorenzo, Francesco di Vannuccio, Gaudenzio Ferrari, Marco d'Oggiono, Palmezzano, Scacco, Signorelli, Solario.

Greenwich (Connecticut). T. S. HYLAND COLLECTION: Tegliacci.

— (EX): Puccinelli, Ugolino di Nerio.

Grenoble. MUSÉE DE PEINTURE: Giulio Campi, Cola d'Amatrice, Farinati, Liberale da Verona, Palmezzano, Perugino, Solario, Taddeo di Bartolo.

Griessmanndorf (Friedenthal). GRAF INGENHEIM: Riminese Trecento.

Grignasco (Valsesia). ASSUNTA: Giovenone.

Grosseto. MUSEO DIOCESANO DI ARTE SACRA: Bartolo di Fredi, Girolamo di Benvenuto, Guido da Siena, Niccolò di Segna, Pietro di Domenico da Siena, Sassetta, Segna di Bonaventura, Sodoma, 'Ugolino Lorenzetti', Ugolino di Nerio.

S. LORENZO (DUOMO): Benvenuto di Giovanni, Matteo di Giovanni, Sano di Pietro.

Gualdo (Ferrara). MAZZA COLLECTION: Scarsellino.

Gualdo Tadino. PINACOTECA: Antonio da Fabriano, Bernardino di Mariotto, Matteo da Gualdo (now transferred to S. FRANCESCO), Niccolò da Foligno, Sano di Pietro.

S. FRANCESCO: Matteo da Gualdo.

S. ROCCO: Matteo da Gualdo.

— Environs. NASCIANO, S. MARIA: Matteo da Gualdo.

Guardiagrele. COLLEGIATA DI S. MARIA MAGGIORE: Delitio.

Gubbio. PINACOTECA: Meo da Siena, Vincenzo Pagani, Palmerucci.

PALAZZO BENI: Nelli.

PALAZZO DEI CONSOLI, PINACOTECA: Balducci, Palmerucci.

DUOMO: Viti.

S. AGOSTINO: Nelli.

S. DOMENICO: Nelli.

S. FRANCESCO: Nelli.

S. MARIA DEI LAICI: Palmerucci.

S. MARIA DELLA PIAGGIOLA: Nelli.

S. MARIA NUOVA: Nelli, Palmerucci.

(Environs). PIEVE DI AGNANO, see Agnano.

The Hague. MAURITSHUIS: Ferrarese.

MUSEUM MEERMAN VAN WESTREENEN: Francesco di Vannuccio, Sassetta.

KRÖLLER COLLECTION: Giovanni di Paolo.

Hamburg. KUNSTHALLE: Boccaccino, Riminese Trecento, Sano di Pietro, Sodoma.

RUTH NOTTEBOHM: Battista Dossi.

CONSUL WEBER (EX): Beccafumi, De Predis.

Hampton Court. ROYAL COLLECTION: Giulio Campi, Correggio, Costa, Dosso, Duccio, Francia, Garofalo, Gentile da Fabriano, Giampietrino, Giulio Romano, Luini, Marco d'Oggiono, Parentino, Parmigianino, Perino del Vaga, Perugino, Sano di Pietro.

— ORANGERY: Mantegna.

Hanover. NIEDERSÄCHSISCHES LANDESMUSEUM: Aspertini, Benvenuto di Giovanni, Ercole da Ferrara, Fiorenzo di Lorenzo, Giovanni Francesco da Rimini, Giulio Romano, Pacchiarotto, Palmezzano, Perugino, Romanino, Scarsellino, Sodoma, Taddeo di Bartolo.

PROVINZIALMUSEUM (EX): De Predis.

KESTNER MUSEUM: Giovanni di Paolo.

Harewood House (Yorks). EARL OF HAREWOOD: Moroni, Sodoma.

— (EX): Cavazzola, Master of the Crivellesque Polyptychs, Scacco.

Harrow. STOGDON COLLECTION (EX): Aspertini.

Hartford (Connecticut). WADSWORTH ATHENEUM: Dosso, Fungai, Girolamo di Benvenuto, Taddeo di Bartolo.

TRINITY COLLEGE, KRESS COLLECTION: Simone Martini Follower.

CHARLES C. CUNNINGHAM: Girolamo di Benvenuto.

Haughton Hall (Cheshire). BROCKLEBANK COLLECTION (EX): Bernardino de' Conti.

Hautecombe (Savoie). ABBAYE: Luca di Tommè.

s'Heerenberg. VAN HEEK: Taddeo di Bartolo.

Havana (Cuba). OSCAR B. CINTAS (EX): Moroni.

Helena (Arkansas). PHILLIPS COUNTY MUSEUM, KRESS COLLECTION: Boccaccino.

Helsinki. ATENEUM: Boccati, Segna di Bonaventura.

Henfield (Sussex). LADY SALMOND: Beccafumi.

Hildesheim. RÖMER UND PELIZÄUS MUSEUM: Battista Dossi.

Holkham (Norfolk). EARL OF LEICESTER: Aspertini.

Honolulu (Hawai). ACADEMY OF ARTS, KRESS COLLECTION: Moroni, Pinturicchio, Segna di Bonaventura.

Houston (Texas). MUSEUM OF FINE ARTS: Simone Martini Follower.

— EDITH AND PERCY STRAUSS COLLECTION: Antoniazzo Romano, Fungai, Giovanni di Paolo, Luini, Nuzi, Sano di Pietro.

— ROBERT LEE BLAFFER MEMORIAL COLLECTION: Giovanni di Paolo.

Illasi (Verona). PARISH CHURCH: Stefano da Zevio.

Imbersago (Monza). MOMBELLO, PRINCIPE PIO DI SAVOIA (EX): Pinturicchio.

Indianapolis (Indiana). JOHN HERRON ART MUSEUM: Barnaba da Modena, Duccio Follower, Master of Osservanza Triptych, Lo Spagna.

THE CLOWES FUND: Duccio Follower, Riminese Trecento.

G. H. A. CLOWES: Neroccio.

Ingenheim. GRAF INGENHEIM (EX): Andrea Vanni.

Innsbruck. TIROLER LANDESMUSEUM FERDINANDEUM: Garofalo, Guariento.

Isolabella (Lago Maggiore): PALAZZO BORROMEO: Bergognone, Bernardino de' Conti, Boltraffio, Bramantino, Butinone, Cesare Magni, Foppa, Gaudenzio Ferrari, Giampietrino, Lanino, Luini, Macrino d'Alba, Marco d'Oggiono, Moretto, Pinturicchio, Romanino, Zenale. (See also Milan, Borromeo.)

Isola del Gran Sasso. CONA (CHAPEL) DI S. SEBASTIANO: Delitio.

Isola Maggiore (Lake Trasimeno). S. ANGELO: Caporali.

S. FRANCESCO: Sano di Pietro.

Istia d'Ombrone (Grosseto). S. SALVATORE: Giovanni di Paolo, Tamagni.

PARISH CHURCH: Vecchietta (sculpture).

Ivrea. ASSUNTA (DUOMO): Defendente Ferrari.

S. BERNARDINO: Spanzotti.

Jesi. S. MARCO: Riminese Trecento.

Kansas City (Missouri). WILLIAM ROCKHILL NELSON GALLERY OF ART. Bartolo di Fredi, Benvenuto di Giovanni, Francesco di Giorgio, Signorelli.

— KRESS COLLECTION: De Predis, Giovanni di Paolo, Lippo Memmi, Tegliacci.

Karlsruhe. KUNSTHALLE: Antoniazzo Romano, Benvenuto di Giovanni, Bernardino de' Conti, Farinati, Niccolò da Foligno, Palmezzano, Romanino, Scarsellino, Taddeo di Bartolo.

Kassel, see Cassel.

Keir (Dunblane, Scotland). STIRLING COLLECTION: Anguissola, Butinone.

— (EX): Giampietrino.

Kevelaer. PRESBYTERY. Niccolò da Foligno.

Kew Gardens (Surrey). A. WELKER: Luca di Tommè.

Kiev. MUSEUM: Master of Osservanza Triptych, Mazzolino, Riminese Trecento.

Kilburn (London). S. AUGUSTINE: Francesco di Gentile da Fabriano, Palmezzano.

Klagenfurt. HISTORISCHES MUSEUM: Mantegna.

Knole (Kent). LORD SACKVILLE: Garofalo.

Konopist. CASTLE: Andrea di Bartolo, Giovanni Francesco da Rimini, Luca di Tommè, Niccolò di Buonaccorso, Lippo Vanni.

Kreuzlingen. H. KISTERS: Palmezzano, Sano di Pietro, Taddeo di Bartolo.

La Gaida (Parma). GINO MAGNANI: Pacchiarotto.

Langeais (Touraine). CHÂTEAU: Duccio.

Laon. MUSÉE MUNICIPAL: Zaganelli.

La Rochelle. MUSÉE DES BEAUX-ARTS. Andrea di Bartolo.

Lausanne. MUSÉE, CAMBÒ BEQUEST: Riminese Trecento.

Lavagno. S. BRIZIO: Giolfino.

Lavagnola (Savona). S. DALMAZZO: Barnaba da Modena.

Laval. MUSÉE DES BEAUX-ARTS: Niccolò da Foligno.

Lawrence (Kansas). UNIVERSITY GALLERY: Lippo Dalmasio, Master of the Osservanza Triptych, Zenale.

Le Bar (Alpes-Maritimes). PARISH CHURCH: Brea.

Le Havre. MUSÉE. Andrea di Bartolo, Costa, Giampietrino, Girolamo da Cremona, Liberale da Verona, Lorenzo d'Alessandro.

Le Mans. MUSÉE DE TESSÉ: De Predis, Giovanni Francesco da Rimini, Pietro Lorenzetti, Pietro di Domenico da Siena, Scarsellino, Simone Martini Follower, Taddeo di Bartolo, 'Ugolino Lorenzetti', Lippo Vanni.

MAISON DE LA REINE BÉRENGÈRE: Boccaccino.

M. HERVÉ-MATHÉ (EX): Marco d'Oggiono.

Le Puy. MUSÉE CROZATIER: Scarsellino, Taddeo di Bartolo.

Lecco. S. GIOVANNI SOPRA LECCO: Civerchio.

Leghorn. GIULIO TORTOLINI (EX): Beccafumi.

LARDEREL COLLECTION (EX): Giuliano di Simone da Lucca.

Legnano (Milan). CHIESA DELLA DISCIPLINA: Ranuccio d'Arvaro.

S. MAGNO: Lanino, Luini.

Leicester. CITY ART GALLERY: Beccafumi.

Leinì. SS. PIETRO E PAOLO: Defendente Ferrari.

Leipzig. MUSEUM DER BILDENDEN KUNST: Giovan Francesco Caroto, Costa, Francia, Gaudenzio Ferrari, Liberale da Verona, Solario.

FRITZ HARCK (EX): Battista Dossi.

HARCK COLLECTION (EX): Scarsellino.

PLATKY COLLECTION (EX): Scarsellino.

Leningrad. HERMITAGE: Beccafumi, Boccaccino, Caporali, Cesare da Sesto, Correggio, Dosso, Francia, Fungai, Garofalo, Luini, Maineri, Moretto, Moroni, Parmigianino, Perugino, Raphael, Romanino, Scarsellino, Simone Martini, Andrea Vanni.

BOTKINE COLLECTION (EX) (HERMITAGE?): Pinturicchio.

PRINCE A. GAGARIN (EX): Duccio Follower.

Lérins (Alpes-Maritimes). ABBAYE DE S. HONORÉ: Brea.

Les Arcs (Var). PARISH CHURCH: Brea.

Lessona (Biella). S. LORENZO: Lanino.

Lewes (Sussex). E. P. WARREN (EX): Antoniazzo Romano.

Lewisburg (Pennsylvania). BUCKNELL UNIVERSITY, KRESS STUDY COLLECTION: Antoniazzo Romano, Ercole da Ferrara, Giampietrino, Girolamo di Benvenuto.

Liège. MUSÉE. Girolamo di Benvenuto.

Lieuche (Alpes-Maritimes). PARISH CHURCH: Brea.

Lille. PALAIS DES BEAUX-ARTS: Aleni, Antoniazzo Romano, Bartolomeo di Gentile da Urbino, Bernardino di Mariotto, Boltraffio, Brea, Cozzarelli, Francesco di Gentile da Fabriano, Sassetta, Zaganelli.

Lincoln (Nebraska). UNIVERSITY OF NEBRASKA, KRESS STUDY COLLECTION: Andrea di Bartolo.

Linlathen (Dundee, Scotland). ERSKINE COLLECTION (EX): Bertucci, Scarsellino.

Lisbon. MUSEU DE ARTE ANTIGA: Cesare da Sesto, Genga, Piero della Francesca, Raphael, Scarsellino.

ACADEMIA REAL: Mazzolino.

GULBENKIAN FOUNDATION: Francia.

Lisciano Niccone (Cortona). VAL DI ROSE, PARISH CHURCH: Eusebio da San Giorgio.

Lisieux. MUSÉE: Antoniazzo Romano.

Liveri di Nola. SANTUARIO DI S. MARIA A PARETE: Francesco da Tolentino.

Liverpool. WALKER ART GALLERY: Beccafumi, Giovan Francesco Caroto, Ercole da Ferrara, Eusebio da San Giorgio, Ferrarese–Bolognese, Garofalo, Giovanni Francesco da Rimini, Massone, Palmezzano, Perugino, Signorelli, Simone Martini, Vecchietta.

del Vaga, Raphael.

WALLACE COLLECTION: Beccafumi, Benvenuto di Giovanni, Bertucci, Foppa, Francesco di Vannuccio, Luini, Lo Spagna.

London. Private Collections.

LORD ABERCONWAY: Lo Spagna.

LORD ALDENHAM (EX): Bertucci.

LORD ALLENDALE (EX): Matteo di Giovanni.

SIR THOMAS BARLOW: Ercole da Ferrara.

— (EX): Boccati, Butinone, Cozzarelli.

BENSON COLLECTION (EX): Aleni, Costa, Francia, Giampietrino, Giolfino, Marco d'Oggiono.

BLAKESLEE COLLECTION (EX): Cola d'Amatrice.

BRIDGEWATER HOUSE, EARL OF ELLESMERE (EX): Andrea da Salerno, Peruzzi (see also Edinburgh, former Earl of Ellesmere, now Duke of Sutherland, loan).

LT.-COL. HUGH BROCKLEBANK, HEIRS [destined for Magdalen College, Oxford]: Lorenzetti Follower, Moretto, Taddeo di Bartolo.

EARL BROWNLOW (EX): Pietro di Domenico da Siena, Lo Spagna.

W. S. M. BURNS (EX): Andrea di Bartolo.

CHARLES BUTLER (EX): Ercole da Ferrara, Pacchiarotto.

I. O. CHANCE: Battista Dossi.

R. W. CHRISTENSEN (EX): Neroccio.

PETER CORBETT: Dosso.

DAVID M. CURRIE: Girolamo da Cremona.

VISCONTESS D'ABERNON (EX): Nuzi.

DONALDSON COLLECTION (EX): Dosso.

SIR GEORGE DONALDSON (EX): Bernardino de' Conti.

DORCHESTER HOUSE, CAPT. HOLFORD (EX): Giampietrino, Sodoma.

L. DOUGLAS (EX): Taddeo di Bartolo.

W. J. M. ENRIGHT (EX): Brescianino.

C. FAIRFAX-MURRAY (EX): Garofalo, Pacchia.

FARRER COLLECTION (EX): Andrea da Salerno, Farinati.

GEORGE FARROW (EX): Foppa, Nuzi.

MRS DEREK FITZGERALD (EX?): Matteo di Giovanni.

FORBES COLLECTION (EX): Ferrarese.

LADY FREYBERG: Pacchia.

MR AND MRS J. GERE: Girolamo da Carpi.

GRAHAM COLLECTION (EX): Garofalo, Giovanni Agostino da Lodi, Schiavone.

MRS LLOYD GRISCOM: Scacco.

MRS HANS GRONAU: Girolamo da Carpi.

MRS MARK HAMBURG (EX): Girolamo dai Libri.

HENRY HARRIS (EX): Ambrosi, Brea, Brescianino, Fungai, Giovanni di Nicola da Pisa, Giovanni di Paolo, Martino di Bartolomeo da Siena, Sano di Pietro, Taddeo di Bartolo, 'Ugolino Lorenzetti'.

SIR HENRY HAWORTH (EX): Genga.

LADY HOUSTON BOSWALL: Ercole da Ferrara.

E. HUTTON: Sano di Pietro.

SEBASTIAN ISEPP (EX): Altobello Melone.

London. Private Collections (contd.).

DUKE OF WESTMINSTER (EX): Pacchia.

C. P. WILSON: Ercole da Ferrara.

DORA WILSON (EX): Sano di Pietro.

W. H. WOODWARD (EX): Cozzarelli, Fungai.

EARL OF YARBOROUGH (EX): Brescianino, Giulio Campi.

Longare (Vicenza). VILLA COSTOZZA, CONTE DA SCHIO: Cossa.

Long Island (New York). ROSLYN, CLARENCE MACKAY (EX): Francia.

Longleat (Wilts). MARQUESS OF BATH: Master of Griselda.

Lonigo (Vicenza). SS. FERMO E RUSTICO: Moretto.

Loreto. SANTUARIO, SAGRESTIA DI S. MARCO O DEL TESORO: Melozzo da Forlì, Palmezzano.

BASILICA DELLA SANTA CASA, SAGRESTIA DELLA CURA: Signorelli.

Los Angeles (California). COUNTY MUSEUM OF ART: Bartolo di Fredi, Benvenuto di Giovanni, Correggio, Francia, Garofalo, Luca di Tommè, Martino di Bartolomeo da Siena, Ugolino di Nerio.

— N. SIMON FOUNDATION: Antoniazzo Romano, Francesco di Giorgio, Luini, Neroccio.

Louisville (Kentucky). J. B. SPEED ART MUSEUM: Foppa.

ARTHUR D. ALLEN COLLECTION: Sano di Pietro.

Lovere. ACCADEMIA TADINI: Badile, Brusasorci, Civerchio, Farinati, Francesco dai Libri (Il Vecchio), Giolfino, Liberale da Verona, Domenico Morone, Palmezzano, Parmigianino, Calisto Piazza.

S. MARIA IN VALVENDRA: Moretto.

Lucardo (Certaldo). SS. MARTINO E GIUSTO: Balducci.

Lucca. PINACOTECA: Aspertini, Beccafumi, Berlinghiero, Deodato Orlandi, Neroccio (sculpture), Parentino, Scarsellino, Sodoma, 'Ugolino Lorenzetti', Ugolino di Nerio, Vecchietta (sculpture).

S. FREDIANO: Aspertini, Francia, Puccinelli.

COLLEGIO DI S. FREDIANO: Aspertini.

S. MARIA CORTEORLANDINI: Neroccio (sculpture).

S. MARIA FUORISPORTAM: Puccinelli.

SS. PAOLINO E DONATO: Puccinelli.

MUSEO DI VILLA GUINIGI: Puccinelli.

Luceram (Alpes-Maritimes). PARISH CHURCH: Brea.

Lucerne. SCHLOSS MEGGENHORN, MATHILDE FREY-BAUMANN: Giampietrino.

ABEGG STOCKAR: Ambrogio Lorenzetti, Pietro Lorenzetti.

Lucignano (Val di Chiana): MUSEO CIVICO: Ambrosi, Bartolo di Fredi, Luca di Tommè, Niccolò di Segna, Segna di Bonaventura, Signorelli.

S. FRANCESCO: Bartolo di Fredi.

Lucignano d'Arbia. PIEVE: Simone Martini.

Lugano. MUSEO DI BELLE ARTI: Giampietrino.

THYSSEN COLLECTION: Andrea di Bartolo, Antoniazzo Romano, Boltraffio, Bramantino, Giulio Campi, Cossa, Costa, De Predis, Ercole da Ferrara, Giovanni Agostino da Lodi, Giovanni di Paolo, Niccolò di Naldo, Niccolò di Segna, Santi, Segna di Bonaventura, Solario, Vitale da Bologna, Zoppo.

S. MARIA DEGLI ANGELI: Luini.

— (Environs). DINO DI SONVICO, S. NAZZARO: Luini.

Lugnano in Teverina. PARISH CHURCH: Niccolò da Foligno.

Marseilles. MUSÉE DES BEAUX-ARTS: Perugino.

COMTE DE DEMANDOLX (EX): Taddeo di Bartolo.

PARANQUE COLLECTION: Brea.

Massa Carrara. DUOMO: Pinturicchio.

Massa Marittima. PINACOTECA COMUNALE: Ambrogio Lorenzetti, Sassetta.

DUOMO: Duccio, Segna di Bonaventura, Simone Martini.

— (EX): Sano di Pietro.

S. AGOSTINO: Pacchiarotto.

Matelica. MUSEO PIERSANTI: Antonio da Fabriano, Bernardino di Mariotto, Francesco di Gentile da Fabriano, Lorenzo d'Alessandro.

S. FRANCESCO: Eusebio da San Giorgio, Francesco di Gentile da Fabriano, Palmezzano.

S. GIOVANNI: Eusebio da San Giorgio.

S. TERESA: Urbani.

OSPEDALE CIVILE, CAPPELLA: Lorenzo d'Alessandro.

Mauchline (Ayr, Scotland). BALLOCHMYLE HOUSE, SIR CLAUDE ALEXANDER (EX): Matteo di Giovanni.

Mazzano (Brescia): S. GIOVANNI BATTISTA: Moretto.

Mazzurega (Verona). S. BARTOLOMEO: Badile.

Meggenhorn (Switzerland). FRAU BAUMANN: Giolfino.

Meiningen. SCHLOSS (EX): Matteo di Giovanni.

Melbourne (Victoria). NATIONAL GALLERY OF VICTORIA: Cola d'Amatrice, Domenico di Bartolo, Francesco di Giorgio, Palmezzano, Perino del Vaga.

Melchett Court (Romsey, Hants). LORD MELCHETT (EX): Giovan Francesco Caroto, Francesco di Gentile da Fabriano, Girolamo dai Libri, Lo Spagna.

Melegnano (Milan). PARISH CHURCH: Bergognone.

Mellerstain (Berwickshire). EARL OF HADDINGTON: Aspertini. (See also Tyninghame.)

Mells (Frome, Somerset). EARL OF OXFORD AND ASQUITH: Beccafumi, Matteo di Giovanni, Michele da Verona, Lo Spagna.

Melun. MUSÉE MUNICIPAL: Niccolò da Foligno.

Memphis (Tennessee). BROOKS MEMORIAL ART GALLERY: Costa, Fei, Ferrarese, Moroni, Romanino, Taddeo di Bartolo, Vecchietta.

Mendrisio. S. SISINIO: Luini.

Mentana, see **Rome** (Environs).

Mentmore (Leighton Buzzard). EARL OF ROSEBERY: Moroni.

Merate. MARCHESE PRINETTI: Gaudenzio Ferrari.

Mercatello sul Metauro. S. FRANCESCO: Luca di Tommè, Giovanni da Rimini, Giovanni Baronzio da Rimini.

Mertoun (Scotland). DUKE OF SUTHERLAND: Andrea da Salerno.

Messina. MUSEO NAZIONALE: Niccolò di Buonaccorso, Torbido.

EUGENIA SCAGLIONE FRIZZONI (EX): Boltraffio, Luini.

Mezzana di Sotto (Verona). PARISH CHURCH: Giovan Francesco Caroto.

Mezzana Superiore (Somma Lombardo). S. STEFANO: Bramantino, Marco d'Oggiono.

Milan. Galleries, Museums, Palazzi, Institutes.

PINACOTECA AMBROSIANA: Bergognone, Bernardino de' Conti, Bramantino, Butinone, Giulio Campi, Cesare Magni, Cesare da Sesto, Civerchio, De Predis, Giampietrino, Giovanni Agostino da Lodi, Luini, Marco d'Oggiono, Moretto, Moroni, Parmigianino, Albertino and Martino Piazza, Pinturicchio, Raphael, Simone Martini, Solario, Lippo Vanni, Zenale.

— BRIVIO COLLECTION: Cesare Magni, Sodoma.

PINACOTECA DI BRERA: Aleni, Altobello, Andrea di Bartolo, Anguissola, Bartolomeo di Tommaso da Foligno, Bergognone, Bernardino de' Conti, Boccaccino, Boltraffio, Bramante, Bramantino, Brusasorci, Butinone, Galeazzo Campi, Giulio Campi, Cesare Magni, Cesare da Sesto, Civerchio, Correggio, Cossa, Costa, Cozzarelli, Defendente Ferrari, De Predis, Dosso, Battista Dossi, Ercole da Ferrara, Farinati, Foppa, Francesco di Gentile da Fabriano, Francesco Napolitano, Francia, Garofalo, Gaudenzio Ferrari, Genga, Gentile da Fabriano, Giampietrino, Giovanni Agostino da Lodi, Girolamo di Giovanni da Camerino, Lanino, Liberale da Verona, Ambrogio Lorenzetti, Luini, Maineri, Mantegna, Marco d'Oggiono, Master of Sforza Altarpiece, Mazzolino, Michele da Verona, Moretto, Francesco Morone, Moroni, Niccolò da Foligno, Ortolano, Vincenzo Pagani, Palmezzano, Perino del Vaga, Albertino and Martino Piazza, Calisto Piazza, Piero della Francesca, Raphael, Riminese Trecento, Romanino, Santi, Scarsellino, Signorelli, Sodoma, Solario, Stefano da Zevio, Torbido, Tura, Viti, Zaganelli, Zenale.

MUSEI CIVICI DEL CASTELLO SFORZESCO: Bergognone, Bernardino de' Conti, Boltraffio, Bramante, Bramantino, Brusasorci, Butinone, Cesare Magni, Cesare da Sesto, Civerchio, Correggio, De Predis, Foppa, Gaudenzio Ferrari, Giampietrino, Giovanni Agostino da Lodi, Giovenone, Luini, Marco d'Oggiono, Master of the Sforza Altarpiece, Moretto, Moroni, Calisto Piazza, Romanino, Sodoma, Zenale.

— TRIVULZIO COLLECTION: Baldassarre d'Este, Cavazzola, Foppa, Mantegna.

— TRIVULZIO DELLA SOMAGLIA COLLECTION: Bernardino de' Conti, Bramantino.

— BIBLIOTECA TRIVULZIANA: De Predis.

MUSEO POLDI PEZZOLI: Anguissola, Bergognone, Bernardino de' Conti, Boltraffio, Giulio Campi, Cesare da Sesto, Civerchio, Farinati, Foppa, Francia, Gaudenzio Ferrari, Giampietrino, Lanino, Pietro Lorenzetti, Luini, Mantegna, Marco d'Oggiono, Master of Griselda, Francesco Morone, Moroni, North-Italian Gothic, Palmezzano, Albertino and Martino Piazza, Piero della Francesca, Signorelli, Sodoma, Solario, Lo Spagna, Tura, Vitale da Bologna, Zenale.

MUSEO DELLA SCIENZA E DELLA TECNICA LEONARDO DA VINCI (MONASTERO DI S. VITTORE): Luini, Calisto Piazza.

MEDAGLIERE MUNICIPALE: Pisanello (signed medal).

OSPEDALE MAGGIORE: Scarsellino.

PALAZZO FONTANA SILVESTRI (CORSO VENEZIA 16): Bramante, Butinone.

PALAZZO ARCIVESCOVILE: Altobello Melone, Civerchio, Marco d'Oggiono.

UNIVERSITÀ CATTOLICA: Calisto Piazza.

Milan. Churches.

S. AGOSTINO DELLE MONACHE: Civerchio.

S. AMBROGIO: Gaudenzio Ferrari, Lanino, Luini, Albertino and Martino Piazza.

— MUSEO: Bergognone, Butinone, Civerchio, Zenale.

S. CELSO: Bergognone.

S. EUFEMIA: Civerchio, Marco d'Oggiono.

S. EUSTORGIO: Bergognone, Foppa.

S. GIORGIO AL PALAZZO: Gaudenzio Ferrari, Luini.

S. MARIA PRESSO S. CELSO: Bergognone, Gaudenzio Ferrari, Calisto Piazza.

S. MARIA DEL CARMINE: Civerchio, Luini.

S. MARIA DELLE GRAZIE: Bramantino, Butinone, Cesare Magni, Gaudenzio Ferrari, Marco d'Oggiono, Solario, Zenale.

S. MARIA DELLA PASSIONE: Bergognone, Bramantino, Giulio Campi, Gaudenzio Ferrari.

S. MARIA DELLA VISITAZIONE IN S. SOFIA: Butinone.

S. MAURIZIO: Boltraffio, Luini, Calisto Piazza.

S. NAZZARO MAGGIORE: Lanino.

S. PIETRO IN GESSATE: Bergognone, Butinone, Civerchio, Zenale.

S. SIMPLICIANO: Bergognone.

Milan. Private Collections.

BARONE BAGATTI VALSECCHI: Galeazzo Campi, Civerchio, Farinati, Giampietrino, Zenale.

G. BARGELLESI: Dosso, Ercole da Ferrara, Garofalo, Mazzolino, Ortolano, Scarsellino.

AVV. BARNABÒ: Liberale da Verona.

BASSI DI SAN GENNARO COLLECTION: Zaganelli.

BERNASCONI COLLECTION (EX): Foppa.

ARCH. LUIGI BONOMI: Albertino and Martino Piazza.

SENATORE BORLETTI: Macrino d'Alba.

PALAZZO BORROMEO (some of the following may be at Isolabella, q.v.): Bernardino de' Conti, Giulio Campi, Farinati, Macrino d'Alba, North-Italian Gothic, Parentino, Albertino and Martino Piazza, Zaganelli.

MARCHESE BRIVIO: Costa.

CANTO COLLECTION (EX): Ercole da Ferrara.

CAVALIERI COLLECTION: Anguissola.

ACHILLE CHIESA (EX): Girolamo di Giovanni da Camerino.

CONTE CICOGNA: Luini.

COLOGNA COLLECTION (EX): Cicognara.

ALDO CRESPI: Butinone, Foppa, Giampietrino, Luini, Moretto, Albertino and Martino Piazza, Sano di Pietro.

MARIO CRESPI: Boltraffio.

CRESPI MORBIO COLLECTION: Barnaba da Modena, Giovan Francesco Caroto.

CRESPI COLLECTION (EX): Bergognone, Boltraffio, Giovan Francesco Caroto, Francia, Liberale da Verona, Luini, Moretto, Romanino, Solario.

PROF. MARIANO CUNIETTI: Romanino.

DE ANGELI FRUA COLLECTION: Tura.

DEL MAJNO COLLECTION: Giovanni Agostino da Lodi.

TULLIO FOSSATI BELLANI: Matteo di Bartolomeo da Siena.

MARCHESE FOSSATI (EX): Giulio Campi, Albertino and Martino Piazza.

GUSTAVO FRIZZONI (EX): Bergognone, Boltraffio, Liberale da Verona, Mazzolino.

DUCA GALLARATI SCOTTI: Bergognone, Butinone, Cesare da Sesto, Solario.

GERLI COLLECTION (EX): Foppa.

CONTE PAOLO GERLI: Luini.

MADAME GINOULHIAC (EX): Brusasorci.

FAUSTO GRASSETTI: Romanino.

Milan. Private Collections (contd.).

DR GRIECO: Maineri.

AVV. GUSSALLI: Moretto.

G. LANGHI (EX): Foppa.

LITTA MODIGNANI COLLECTION: Luini.

LIVRAGHI COLLECTION: Sassetta.

LURATI COLLECTION: Maineri, Marco d'Oggiono.

E. MALAGUTTI (EX): Ortolano.

MELZI D'ERIL COLLECTION: Cesare da Sesto, Marco d'Oggiono.

PRINCIPE DI MOLFETTA: Giovanni Agostino da Lodi.

ALDO NOSEDA (EX): Bergognone, Liberale da Verona, Luini.

CONTI PORRO (EX): De Predis.

RASINI COLLECTION: Bergognone, Bramantino, Foppa.

A. ROBIATI: Ortolano.

SAIBENE COLLECTION: Bernardino di Mariotto, Cozzarelli, Dosso, Battista Dossi, Ercole da Ferrara, Matteo di Giovanni, Tomaso da Modena.

DONNA SESSA FUMAGALLI: Cesare Magni, Albertino and Martino Piazza.

SOLA COLLECTION: Bramantino, Moretto.

CONTESSA TERESA SORANZO MOCENIGO (EX): Boltraffio.

TRECCANI COLLECTION: Maineri, Sodoma.

OTTAVIANO VENIER: Butinone, Moretto.

DUCA VISCONTI DI MODRONE: Lippo Dalmasio.

VONWILLER COLLECTION: Giampietrino, Marco d'Oggiono.

WERNER COLLECTION: Bramantino.

YUCKER COLLECTION: Luini.

Milan (Environs). ABBAZIA DI CHIARAVALLE: Calisto Piazza.

Milwaukee (Wisconsin). ALFRED BADER: Dosso.

Minneapolis (Minnesota). INSTITUTE OF ARTS: Foppa, Ambrogio Lorenzetti, Moroni.

— VANDERLIP BEQUEST: Benvenuto di Giovanni, Giovanni di Paolo, Nuzi, Taddeo di Bartolo.

— (EX ?): Eusebio da San Giorgio.

— (EX): Giampietrino, Sano di Pietro.

Minturno (Gaeta). SS. ANNUNZIATA: Andrea Vanni.

Mizzole (Verona), S. FENZO (EX): Francesco dai Libri (Il Vecchio).

Modena. GALLERIA ESTENSE: Arcangelo di Cola da Camerino, Barnaba da Modena, Bianchi Ferrari, Boccaccino, Giovan Francesco Caroto, Correggio, De Predis, Dosso, Battista Dossi, Ercole da Ferrara, Fei, Ferrarese, Garofalo, Giovanni Agostino da Lodi, Giovanni di Paolo, Girolamo da Carpi, Maineri, North-Italian Gothic, Parentino, Scarsellino, Tomaso da Modena, Tura, Zaganelli.

DUOMO: Bianchi Ferrari, Dosso.

S. BIAGIO (CARMINE): Dosso.

S. PIETRO: Bianchi Ferrari.

SEMINARIO ARCIVESCOVILE: Domenico Morone.

Mödling (Austria). BURG LIECHTENSTEIN (EX): Bartolo di Fredi.

Monaco-Ville (Alpes-Maritimes). CATHEDRAL: Brea.

PRINCE DE MONACO: De Predis.

Monastero dell'Isola (Cessapalombo, Macerata). PARISH CHURCH: Arcangelo di Cola da Camerino.

Mondello Valdese (Palermo). TORRE DELL'ADDAURA, PRINCIPE DI BELMONTE: Cesare da Sesto.

Montalcino (Senese). MUSEO CIVICO: Andrea di Bartolo, Bartolo di Fredi, Benvenuto di Giovanni, Duccio Follower, Giovanni di Paolo, Girolamo di Benvenuto, Luca di Tommè, Master of Panzano Triptych, Sano di Pietro.

MUSEO DIOCESANO D'ARTE SACRA (SEMINARIO): Bartolo di Fredi, Girolamo di Benvenuto, Niccolò di Segna, Segna di Bonaventura, Sodoma.

VECCHIO SPEDALE EX FARMACIA (MUSEO CIVICO ETRUSCO): Tamagni.

CORPUS DOMINI: Tamagni.

MADONNA DEL SOCCORSO: Tamagni.

OSSERVANZA: Sano di Pietro.

S. AGOSTINO: Bartolo di Fredi.

S. FRANCESCO: Tamagni.

S. PIETRO: Beccafumi.

Montalto delle Marche. MUNICIPIO: Vincenzo Pagani.

Montalto Ligure (Porto Maurizio). S. GIORGIO: Brea.

Montauban. MUSÉE INGRES: Butinone, Romanino.

Monte Carlo (Alpes-Maritimes). ONASSIS COLLECTION: Parentino.

Montecassino. ABBAZIA (BADIA): Andrea da Salerno, Garofalo, Giusto de' Menabuoi, Signorelli.

CAPPELLA DI S. BERTARIO (EX): Andrea da Salerno.

BIBLIOTECA: Girolamo dai Libri.

Montecchio (Senese). S. ANDREA: Andrea di Niccolò, Niccolò di Buonaccorso.

S. MARIA DELLA GROTTA: Segna di Bonaventura.

Montechiarúgolo (Parma). COURT OF CASTLE: Zaganelli.

Monteciccardo (Pesaro). S. SEBASTIANO: Bartolomeo di Gentile da Urbino.

Montefalco. S. AGOSTINO: Lorenzetti Follower, Niccolò da Foligno.

S. FRANCESCO, MUSEO: Antoniazzo Romano, Mezzastris, Nelli, Niccolò da Foligno, Perugino, Tiberio d'Assisi.

SANTUARIO DI S. FORTUNATO: Mezzastris, Tiberio d'Assisi.

CÉLINE CAPPELLI COLLECTION (EX): Lo Spagna.

Montefiascone (Viterbo). S. FLAVIANO: Cavallini Follower, Pastura.

Montefiore Conca (Forlì). S. PAOLO: Bartolomeo di Gentile da Urbino.

Montefollonico. S. SIGISMONDO: Andrea di Bartolo.

CHIESA DELL'OPERA DEL TRIANO: Cozzarelli.

Monteforte d'Alpone (Verona). MENSA VESCOVILE: Girolamo dai Libri.

Montefortino (Marches). MUSEO CIVICO: Antoniazzo Romano.

Montegiorgio (Ascoli Piceno). S. SALVATORE: Ghissi.

Montelabbate (Perugia). S. MARIA: Caporali, Fiorenzo di Lorenzo.

Montelparo. S. MARIA NOVELLA: Vincenzo Pagani.

Montelungo (Arezzo). S. MARIA: Margarito.

Montemerano (Maremma). S. GIORGIO: Sano di Pietro, Vecchietta (sculpture).

Montenero (Livorno). SANTUARIO: Gera.

Montenero sull'Amiata. S. LUCIA: Giovanni di Paolo, Ambrogio Lorenzetti.

CHIESA DELLA MADONNA: Fungai.

Monteoliveto Maggiore (Siena). ABBAZIA: Signorelli, Sodoma, Tamagni.

Montepertuso (Senese). S. MICHELE ARCANGELO: Andrea di Niccolò, Benvenuto di Giovanni.

Montepescali (Grosseto). UPPER CHURCH: Matteo di Giovanni.

Monteprandone. CONVENTO DI S. GIACOMO: Vincenzo Pagani.

Montepulciano. MUSEO CIVICO: Ceccarelli, Duccio Follower, Francesco di Vannuccio, Girolamo di Benvenuto, Luca di Tommè, Margarito, Sodoma.

 DUOMO: Taddeo di Bartolo.

 S. AGOSTINO: Giovanni di Paolo.

 S. LUCIA: Signorelli.

 S. MARIA DEI SERVI: Ugolino di Nerio.

Monterchi (San Sepolcro). CAPPELLA DEL CIMITERO: Piero della Francesca.

Monterongriffoli (Senese). S. LORENZO: Ugolino di Nerio.

Monterubbiano. S. MARIA DEI LETTERATI: Vincenzo Pagani.

Montesanmartino (Macerata). S. MARIA DEL POZZO: Girolamo di Giovanni da Camerino.

Monte San Savino (Arezzo). S. CHIARA: Cozzarelli.

 S. MARIA DELLE VERTIGHE: Margarito.

Monteveglio (Bologna). ABBAZIA: Costa.

Montichiari (Brescia). S. PANCRAZIO: Calisto Piazza.

 PARISH CHURCH: Romanino.

Montichiello (Pienza). PIEVE DEI SS. LEONARDO E CRISTOFORO: Pietro Lorenzetti.

Montingegnoli (Senese). S. SISTO: Cozzarelli.

Montisi (Senese). CHIESA DELL'ANNUNCIATA: Neroccio, Ugolino di Nerio.

Montone (Perugia). S. FRANCESCO: Caporali.

Montorsaio (Senese). SS. MICHELE E CERBONE: Sano di Pietro.

Montottone. CONVENTO DI S. FRANCESCO: Pietro da Rimini.

Montpellier. MUSÉE FABRE: Brescianino, Garofalo, Giovanni Pagani, Riminese Trecento, Sassetta.

Montreal. MUSEUM OF FINE ARTS: Andrea di Bartolo, Boltraffio, Mantegna.

 DR S. P. RETY (EX): Brescianino.

Montserrat (Barcelona). ABBEY: Andrea da Salerno.

Monza. DUOMO: Foppa, Luini, Zavattari.

Morbegno (Sondrio). S. ANTONIO: Gaudenzio Ferrari.

 ASSUNTA E S. LORENZO: Gaudenzio Ferrari.

Moresco (Ascoli). MUNICIPIO: Vincenzo Pagani.

Mori (Trento). PARISH CHURCH: Farinati.

Morimondo. S. MARIA: Luini.

Morra (Città di Castello). S. CRESCENTINO: Signorelli.

Mortara. S. CROCE: Lanino.

 S. LORENZO: Giovenone.

Moscow. PUSHKIN MUSEUM: Boltraffio, Dosso, Duccio Follower, Gaudenzio Ferrari, Giulio Romano, Perugino, Sassetta, Segna di Bonaventura, Simone Martini.

Moulins. MUSÉE: Bartolomeo di Tommaso da Foligno, Benvenuto di Giovanni, Brea, Niccolò da Foligno, Riminese Trecento.

Mount Trust (Churchill, Oxon.). CAPT. AND MRS BULKELEY-JOHNSON: Sano di Pietro.

Muncie (Indiana). BALL STATE TEACHERS COLLEGE: Luini.

Munich. BAYERISCHE STAATSGEMÄLDESAMMLUNGEN (ALTE PINAKOTHEK): Aspertini, Beccafumi, Bernardino de' Conti, Boccaccino, Bonfigli, Brescianino, Correggio, Ferrarese, Francia, Garofalo, Giulio Romano, Liberale da Verona, Mazzolino, Lippo Memmi, Moretto, Pacchia, Palmezzano, Perugino, Raphael, Riminese Trecento, Segna di Bonaventura, Signorelli, Sodoma, Torbido, Vecchietta, Viti.

— PRINT ROOM: Mantegna.

KAULBACH COLLECTION (EX): Andrea di Bartolo, Francesco di Vannuccio.

WALTER SCHNACKENBERG (EX): Arcangelo di Cola da Camerino.

BARON VON LIPHARDT (EX): Boccaccino.

VON NEMES COLLECTION (EX): Giampietrino.

Münster i/W. DIÖZESANMUSEUM: Cavazzola, Defendente Ferrari, Fei.

LANDESMUSEUM: Giovanni di Paolo.

SEMINAR: Pietro Lorenzetti, Ortolano.

Murcia. CATHEDRAL: Barnaba da Modena.

Murlo (Senese). PIEVE DI SAN FORTUNATO: Andrea di Niccolò.

Mutignano (Atri). PARISH CHURCH: Delitio.

Nancy. MUSÉE DES BEAUX-ARTS: Giampietrino, Palmerucci, Perugino, Taddeo di Bartolo, Traini.

Nantes. MUSÉE DES BEAUX-ARTS: Bergognone, Brescianino, Garofalo, Genga, Moroni, Ortolano, Perugino, Albertino and Martino Piazza, Sano di Pietro, Solario, Taddeo di Bartolo, Tura.

Naples. GALLERIA NAZIONALE (CAPODIMONTE): Andrea da Salerno, Anguissola, Boccaccino, Brescianino, Caporali, Cesare Magni, Cesare da Sesto, Correggio, Dosso, Battista Dossi, Fei, Garofalo, Giampietrino, Giovanni Agostino da Lodi, Giulio Romano, Luini, Mantegna, Matteo di Giovanni, Moretto, Ortolano, Pacchia, Parmigianino, Perugino, Pinturicchio, Raphael, Scacco, Signorelli, Simone Martini, Sodoma, Taddeo di Bartolo, Torbido, Andrea Vanni, Lippo Vanni, Zaganelli.

ARCHIVIO: Garofalo.

BIBLIOTECA NAZIONALE: Perugino.

MUSEO FILANGIERI: Lanino.

— (EX): Luini.

PALAZZO ARCIVESCOVILE: Cavallini.

CAPPELLA DELLA DISCIPLINA DELLA CROCE: Roberto Oderisio.

CAPPELLA PONTANIANA: Antoniazzo Romano.

CERTOSA DI S. MARTINO: Francesco Napolitano.

S. CHIARA: Cavallini Follower.

S. DOMENICO MAGGIORE: Andrea da Salerno, Cavallini Follower, Roberto di Oderisio.

S. FRANCESCO DELLE MONACHE: Antoniazzo Romano.

S. GENNARO (DUOMO): Cavallini, Fei, Perugino.

S. GENNARO DEI POVERI: Andrea da Salerno.

GIROLAMINI, QUADERIA: Andrea da Salerno.

S. LORENZO MAGGIORE: Cavallini Follower, Roberto Oderisio.

S. MARIA DI DONNA REGINA: Cavallini, Francesco da Tolentino.

S. MARIA INCORONATA: Roberto Oderisio.

S. MARIA NUOVA: Francesco da Tolentino.

S. RESTITUTA: Andrea da Salerno.

Naples (contd.). SS. SEVERINO E SOSIO: Andrea da Salerno.

SS. TRINITÀ DEI PELLEGRINI: Eusebio da San Giorgio.

GORO COLLECTION: Andrea da Salerno.

Narbonne. MUSÉE D'ART ET D'HISTOIRE: Brea, Perino del Vaga, Tamagni.

Narni. PINACOTECA: Mezzastris, Piermatteo da Amelia.

MUNICIPIO: Lo Spagna.

DUOMO: Vecchietta (sculpture).

S. FRANCESCO: Mezzastris.

Nashville (Tennessee). GEORGE PEABODY COLLEGE FOR TEACHERS, KRESS COLLECTION: Giovanni Agostino da Lodi, Giovenone, Luca di Tommè, Pacchiarotto.

Negrano di Villazzano (Trento): CAPPELLA DEL PALAZZO CAZUFFI: Farinati.

Nemi (Fiordimonte, Macerata). PARISH CHURCH: Boccati.

Nervi. HEIRS OF MARCHESE FRANCESCO SPINOLA: Giampietrino.

Neuwied. SCHLOSS SEGENHAUS, PRINZ WIED: Giampietrino.

Nevers. MUSÉE: Francesco di Gentile da Fabriano, Urbani.

Neviglie (Alba). PARISH CHURCH: Macrino d'Alba.

Newark (N.J.). MUSEUM: Tegliacci.

Newbattle Abbey (Dalkeith, Scotland). MARQUESS OF LOTHIAN: Macrino d'Alba, Solario.

New Haven (Connecticut). YALE UNIVERSITY ART GALLERY: Andrea di Bartolo, Arcangelo di Cola da Camerino, Bartolo di Fredi, Benvenuto di Giovanni, Bertucci, Brea, Cavallini Follower, Farinati, Ferrarese–Bolognese, Fiorenzo di Lorenzo, Francia, Fungai, Gentile da Fabriano, Giovanni di Paolo, Giovanni di Pietro da Napoli, Girolamo di Benvenuto, Girolamo da Cremona, Guido da Siena, Pietro Lorenzetti, Lorenzetti Imitator, Luca di Tommè, Martino di Bartolomeo da Siena, Master of Città di Castello, Master of Osservanza Triptych, Lippo Memmi, Domenico Morone, Neroccio, Pacchia, Giovanni Baronzio da Rimini, Sano di Pietro, Sassetta, Segna di Bonaventura, Signorelli, Simone Martini Follower, Taddeo di Bartolo, 'Ugolino Lorenzetti', Lippo Vanni.

New Orleans (Louisiana). ISAAC DELGADO MUSEUM OF ART, KRESS COLLECTION: Foppa, Fungai, Garofalo, Girolamo di Benvenuto, Luini, Romanino, Taddeo di Bartolo, Andrea Vanni.

New York. METROPOLITAN MUSEUM OF ART: Andrea di Bartolo, Antoniazzo Romano, Bartolo di Fredi, Bartolomeo di Tommaso da Foligno, Benvenuto di Giovanni, Bergognone, Berlinghiero, Boccaccino, Boltraffio, Bramantino, Correggio, Costa, Cozzarelli, Defendente Ferrari, De Predis, Dosso, Duccio Follower, Ercole da Ferrara, Fei, Foppa, Francesco di Giorgio, Francia, Fungai, Garofalo, Gentile da Fabriano, Giovanni Agostino da Lodi, Giovanni di Paolo, Girolamo da Cremona, Girolamo dai Libri, Guariento, Liberale da Verona, Ambrogio Lorenzetti, Pietro Lorenzetti, Luca di Tommè, Mantegna, Martino di Bartolomeo da Siena, Matteo di Giovanni, Lippo Memmi, Michelino da Besozzo, Moretto, Domenico Morone, Moroni, Neroccio, Ortolano, Palmerucci, Pastura, Perugino, Pietro di Domenico da Montepulciano, Pietro di Domenico da Siena, Pinturicchio, Raphael, Riminese Trecento, Sano di Pietro, Sassetta, Segna di Bonaventura, Signorelli, Simone Martini, Sodoma, Solario, Tura, Ugolino di Nerio, Lippo Vanni.

— CLOISTERS: Master of the Codex of St. George.

FRICK COLLECTION: Barna da Siena, Duccio, Gentile da Fabriano, Matteo di Giovanni,

Piero della Francesca, Vecchietta (sculpture).

HISTORICAL SOCIETY: Bernardino di Mariotto, Farinati, Fei, Francesco Napolitano, Macrino d'Alba, Mazzolino, 'Ugolino Lorenzetti'.

SAMUEL H. KRESS FOUNDATION: Bramantino, Marco d'Oggiono, Sano di Pietro, 'Ugolino Lorenzetti'.

LEHMAN COLLECTION: Andrea di Bartolo, Barna da Siena, Bartolo di Fredi, Benvenuto di Giovanni, Cozzarelli, Delitio, Duccio Follower, Fei, Ferrarese, Francia, Giovanni di Paolo, Girolamo di Benvenuto, Master of Osservanza Triptych, Master of St. Francis, Francesco Morone, Niccolò di Buonaccorso, Niccolò da Foligno, Nuzi, Riminese Trecento, Sano di Pietro, Sassetta, Simone Martini, Simone Martini Follower, Taddeo di Bartolo, 'Ugolino Lorenzetti', Ugolino di Nerio, Lippo Vanni, Vecchietta.

MORGAN LIBRARY: Cicognara, Francia, Girolamo da Cremona, Macrino d'Alba, Master of the Codex of St. George, Perugino.

ROERICH MUSEUM (EX): Giovanni di Nicola da Pisa, Palmezzano.

O. BERBERYAN: Anguissola.

BLUMENTHAL COLLECTION (EX): Barna da Siena, Fei.

MRS R. BONNER-BOWLER: Master of Panzano Triptych.

MRS BORCHARD (EX): Francia, Macrino d'Alba.

ANDREW CARNEGIE (EX): Costa.

CHRYSLER COLLECTION: Dosso, Signorelli.

OSCAR B. CINTAS (EX): Pietro di Domenico da Siena.

E. FOWLES: Matteo di Giovanni.

MISS HELEN FRICK: Arcangelo di Cola da Camerino, Francesco di Vannuccio, Giovanni di Paolo, Matteo di Giovanni, Sassetta.

FRIEDSAM COLLECTION (EX): Aspertini.

W. B. GOLOVIN: Lippo Memmi.

MRS E. A. GOODHARDT (HEIRS): Girolamo di Benvenuto.

MRS SIMON GUGGENHEIM: Taddeo di Bartolo.

GEORGE A. HEARN (EX): Cozzarelli.

HEARST COLLECTION (EX): Domenico Morone, Albertino and Martino Piazza.

EMMET JOHN HUGHES: Fei, Riminese Trecento.

COLLIS P. HUNTINGTON (EX): Zaganelli.

RICHARD M. HURD (EX): Barnaba da Modena, Boltraffio, Deodati Orlandi, Giampietrino, Girolamo di Benvenuto, Matteo di Giovanni.

OTTO H. KAHN COLLECTION (EX): Bonfigli, Ceccarelli.

ALBERT KELLER (EX): Niccolò di Segna.

MRS RUSH H. KRESS: Luini.

J. P. LABEY (EX): Luini.

MRS LANGBOURNE WILLIAMS: Francia, Giampietrino.

HERBERT LEHMAN (EX): Niccolò di Buonaccorso.

ROBERT LEHMAN (EX ?): Lippo Memmi.

JACK LINSKY: Giovanni di Paolo, Perugino, Sassetta.

DR LILLIAN MALCOVE: Andrea Vanni.

ROBERT MINTURN (EX): Giovan Francesco Caroto, Zaganelli.

FRED MOND (EX): Altobello Melone.

MORGAN COLLECTION (EX): Sano di Pietro.

New York (contd.). STANLEY MORTIMER (EX): Francia.

H. L. MOSES COLLECTION: Taddeo di Bartolo.

MRS W. MURRAY CRANE: Nuzi.

MR AND MRS J. D. ROCKEFELLER JR.: Duccio.

A. SACHS (EX ?): Giovanni di Paolo.

PAUL SACHS (EX): Francesco di Giorgio.

H. G. SPERLING (EX): Anguissola.

JESSE I. STRAUS (EX): Luca di Tommè.

PERCY S. STRAUS (EX): Fungai, Simone Martini Follower.

SUIDA-MANNING COLLECTION: Bergognone, Butinone.

BISHOP JOHN TARAK: Giampietrino.

TOLENTINO COLLECTION (EX): Giusto de' Menabuoi, Guariento.

UZIELLI COLLECTION: Sano di Pietro.

FELIX WARBURG COLLECTION: Sano di Pietro.

Nice. MUSÉE MASSÉNA: Brea.

MUSÉE CHÉRET: Mazzolino.

ARCICONFRATERNITA DELLA MISERICORDIA: Brea.

S. AGOSTINO: Brea.

— (Environs). CIMIEZ, CHURCH OF FRANCISCAN MONASTERY: Brea.

— SOSPEL, PÉNITENTS NOIRS: Brea.

Nîmes. MUSÉE DES BEAUX-ARTS: Ferrarese–Bolognese, Marco d'Oggiono, Scarsellino.

Nivaagaard (Copenhagen). HAGE COLLECTION: Anguissola, Luini.

Nocera Inferiore (Salerno). S. ANTONIO: Andrea da Salerno.

Nocera Umbra. PINACOTECA: Duccio Follower, Matteo da Gualdo, Niccolò da Foligno.

Nogarole Rocca (Verona). PARISH CHURCH: Brusasorci.

Nola. CHIESA DELL'ANNUNZIATA: Scacco.

Nonantola (Modena). ABBAZIA: Ferrarese.

Northampton (Massachusetts). SMITH COLLEGE MUSEUM OF ART: Giunta Pisano, Sano di Pietro, Taddeo di Bartolo.

North Mimms (Hertfordshire). MRS WALTER BURNS: Signorelli.

Northwick Park (Blockley). CAPT. SPENCER CHURCHILL (EX): Moretto, Sano di Pietro.

Norton Hall (Gloucestershire). SIR WALTER POLLEN: Lippo Dalmasio.

Notre Dame (Indiana): UNIVERSITY GALLERY, KRESS COLLECTION: Gaudenzio Ferrari, Gualtieri di Giovanni da Pisa, Neroccio, Taddeo di Bartolo.

ST. MARY'S COLLEGE: Taddeo di Bartolo.

Novara. MUSEO DEL BROLETTO: Gaudenzio Ferrari.

S. GAUDENZIO: Gaudenzio Ferrari.

S. MARIA ASSUNTA (DUOMO): Gaudenzio Ferrari, Lanino.

Oakly Park (Shropshire). EARL OF PLYMOUTH: Luini.

Oberlin (Ohio). ALLEN MEMORIAL ART MUSEUM, KRESS COLLECTION: Anguissola, Boccati, Giampietrino, Giolfino, Pinturicchio.

Occimiano (Monferrato). SS. LORENZO E GIORGIO: Lanino.

Offida (Ascoli Piceno). S. MARIA DELLA ROCCA: Andrea da Bologna.

Oggiono. S. EUFEMIA: Marco d'Oggiono.

Oldenburg. LANDESMUSEUM FÜR KUNST UND KULTURGESCHICHTE: Francia.
— (EX): Taddeo di Bartolo.

Olena (Chianti). S. PIETRO: Ugolino di Nerio.

Oneonta (New York). HARTWICK COLLEGE: Boccaccino.

Oneta (Bergamo). S. MARIA ASSUNTA: Moroni.

Orford (Suffolk). S. BARTHOLOMEW: Luini.

Orléans. MUSÉE DES BEAUX-ARTS: Correggio, Costa, Nelli, Pacchia.
ORANGERIE: Cozzarelli.

Orte. DUOMO: Pastura, Taddeo di Bartolo.

Ortignano di Raggiolo (Casentino). S. MATTEO: Pacchiarotto.

Orvieto. S. MARIA ASSUNTA (DUOMO): Gentile da Fabriano, Lippo Memmi, Pastura, Pinturicchio, Signorelli.
— MUSEO DELL'OPERA DEL DUOMO: Neroccio, Pastura, Signorelli, Simone Martini.
S. ROCCO: Pastura, Signorelli.
SS. TRINITÀ: Pastura.

Orzinuovi (Brescia). PALAZZO MUNICIPALE: Calisto Piazza.
CHIESA DELL'OSPEDALE: Moretto.

Orzivecchi (Brescia). PARISH CHURCH: Moroni.

Osimo. S. MARCO: Arcangelo di Cola da Camerino.
BAPTISTERY (MUSEO): Pietro di Domenico da Montepulciano.

Oslo. MUSEUM: Andrea di Bartolo.
HARRY FETT: Marco d'Oggiono.

Ospitaletto Bresciano. PARISH CHURCH: Romanino.

Ottawa. NATIONAL GALLERY OF CANADA: Dosso, Luini, Moroni, Simone Martini.

Oxford. ASHMOLEAN MUSEUM: Altobello Melone, Ambrosi, Andrea di Bartolo, Barna da Siena, Giovan Francesco Caroto, Giovanni di Paolo, Moretto, Domenico Morone, Pacchiarotto, Pinturicchio, Sano di Pietro, Solario, Andrea Vanni, Zoppo.
CHRIST CHURCH: Balducci, Giovan Francesco Caroto, Cozzarelli, De Predis, Giovanni di Paolo, Mazzolino, Sano di Pietro, Signorelli, 'Ugolino Lorenzetti', Zaganelli.
EXETER COLLEGE: Lorenzetti Follower.
MAGDALEN COLLEGE: see London, Brocklebank Collection.

Pacina. S. MARIA MADDALENA: Andrea di Niccolò.

Padenghe (Brescia). SS. MARIA E EMILIANO: Farinati.

Paderno Dugnano. S. MARIA NASCENTE: Luini.

Padua. MUSEO CIVICO: Badile, Boccaccino, Caporali, Ercole da Ferrara, Garofalo, Guariento, Mantegna, Michele da Verona, Francesco Morone, Palmezzano, Albertino and Martino Piazza, Pietro da Rimini, Romanino, Squarcione, Torbido.
MUSEO BOTTACCIN: Guariento.
ACCADEMIA DI SCIENZE, LETTERE ED ARTE, SALA (FORMER CAPPELLA DEL CAPITANIO IN THE CARRARESE PALACE): Guariento.
LIVIANO: Altichiero.
SALA DELLA RAGIONE: Altichiero.
BAPTISTERY: Giusto de' Menabuoi.
BASILICA DEL SANTO (S. ANTONIO): Altichiero, Giusto de' Menabuoi, Mantegna, Parentino.

Padua (contd.). CAPPELLA DEGLI SCROVEGNI: Giusto de' Menabuoi.

DUOMO: Schiavone.

EREMITANI: Altichiero, Giusto de' Menabuoi, Guariento, Mantegna.

ORATORIO DI S. GIORGIO: Altichiero.

S. BENEDETTO VECCHIO: Giusto de' Menabuoi.

S. FRANCESCO GRANDE: Squarcione.

S. GIUSTINA: Parentino.

S. MARIA DEL CARMINE: Parentino.

S. MARIA IN VANZO: Michele da Verona.

PROF. G. FIOCCO: Signorelli.

Paganico (Grosseto). S. MICHELE: Ambrosi, Andrea di Niccolò, Bartolo di Fredi, Cozzarelli.

Paitone (Brescia). CHIESA DEL PELLEGRINAIO: Moretto.

Paladon (Valpolicella). S. NICOLA DA TOLENTINO: Domenico Morone.

Palazzago (Bergamo). S. GIOVANNI BATTISTA: Moroni.

Palazzolo d'Oglio. S. FEDELE: Civerchio.

Palermo. GALLERIA NAZIONALE: Anguissola, Garofalo, Gera, Giovanni di Nicola da Pisa, Turino Vanni.

MUSEO DIOCESANO: Brescianino, Gera.

CHIARAMONTE BORDONARO COLLECTION: Barna da Siena, Bartolo di Fredi, Boccati, Brescianino, Cesare Magni, Civerchio, Fei, Giovanni di Paolo, Girolamo di Benvenuto, Marco d'Oggiono, Romanino, Sano di Pietro, Segna di Bonaventura, Taddeo di Bartolo, 'Ugolino Lorenzetti'.

Pallanza (Lago Maggiore). Environs. MADONNA DI CAMPAGNA: Gaudenzio Ferrari.

Pandino. PARISH CHURCH: Calisto Piazza.

Panicale (Perugia). S. SEBASTIANO: Perugino.

Panzano. PIEVE DI S. LEOLINO: Master of Panzano Triptych.

Paray-le-Monial. MUSÉE MUNICIPAL: Giovan Francesco Caroto, Girolamo di Benvenuto, Scarsellino.

Parcieux. LA GRANGE BLANCHE, HENRI CHALANDON (EX): Antoniazzo Romano, Bartolo di Fredi.

Paris. LOUVRE: Antoniazzo Romano, Balducci, Bartolo di Fredi, Beccafumi, Bergognone, Bernardino de' Conti, Boccaccino, Boltraffio, Butinone, Giulio Campi, Cesare da Sesto, Civerchio (see Zenale), Correggio, Costa, Defendente Ferrari, Domenico di Bartolo, Dosso, Battista Dossi, Ercole da Ferrara, Farinati, Francesco di Giorgio, Francesco di Giorgio (sculpture), Francia, Garofalo, Gaudenzio Ferrari, Gentile da Fabriano, Giampietrino, Giovanni di Paolo, Giovanni Francesco da Rimini, Girolamo di Benvenuto, Giuliano di Simone da Lucca, Giulio Romano, Lorenzetti Imitators, Luini, Mantegna, Marco d'Oggiono, Massone, Master of the Codex of St. George, Master of the Osservanza Triptych, Matteo di Giovanni, Mazzolino, Michelino da Besozzo, Moretto, Moroni, Neroccio, Niccolò da Foligno, Niccolò di Segna, Ortolano, Pacchia, Palmezzano, Parentino, Parmigianino, Perugino, Pinturicchio, Pisanello, Raphael, Riminese Trecento, Sano di Pietro, Sassetta, Scarsellino, Signorelli, Simone Martini, Sodoma, Solario, Lo Spagna, Taddeo di Bartolo, Tura, Turino Vanni, 'Ugolino Lorenzetti', Zaganelli, Zenale.

— ARCONATI VISCONTI BEQUEST: Luini.

— CABINET DES DESSINS: Mantegna, Lippo Vanni.

Paris. Private Collections (contd.).

MARTIN LE ROY COLLECTION (EX): Ambrosi, Boccati, Brescianino, Giovanni di Paolo, Neroccio.

FRITS LUGT: Anguissola.

M. MERCIER (EX): Lippo Vanni.

VICOMTESSE DE NOAILLES: Simone Martini.

DUC D'ORLÉANS (EX): Solario.

MME ÉMILE PARAVICINI: Domenico Morone.

CONTE MARIO PINCI: Lippo Vanni.

POURTALÈS COLLECTION (EX): Pinturicchio.

REINACH COLLECTION: Duccio Follower.

SALOMON REINACH (EX): Giampietrino.

RICHTEMBERGER (EX): Maineri.

BARONNE ÉDOUARD DE ROTHSCHILD: Luini.

LIONEL DE ROTHSCHILD: Mantegna.

BARON EDMOND ROTHSCHILD: Luini.

BARON SCHICKLER: De Predis.

STRÖLIN COLLECTION: Guido da Siena.

LEON SUZOR: Lorenzetti Follower.

DUC DE TRÉVISE: Sodoma.

TROTTI COLLECTION (EX): Cozzarelli.

VAN MOPPES COLLECTION (EX): Ferrarese.

Parma. GALLERIA NAZIONALE: Araldi, Butinone, Correggio, Dosso, Battista Dossi, Francia, Garofalo, Giovanni di Paolo, Giuliano di Simone da Lucca, Giulio Romano, Parmigianino, Scarsellino.

BIBLIOTECA: Correggio.

PALAZZO DELLA CONGREGAZIONE DI CARITÀ S. FILIPPO NERI, PINACOTECA STUARD: Ambrosi, Fei.

DUOMO: Correggio.

SS. ANNUNZIATA: Zaganelli.

S. GIOVANNI EVANGELISTA: Correggio, Parmigianino.

S. MARIA DELLA STECCATA: Parmigianino.

CONVENTO DI S. PAOLO: Correggio.

Parre (Bergamo). PARISH CHURCH: Moroni.

Passignano (Lago Trasimeno): MADONNA DELL'OLIVO: Caporali.

Pàusola (Macerata), see Corridonia.

Pavia. MUSEO MALASPINA: Bergognone, Boltraffio, Butinone, Giovanni Caroto, Correggio, Defendente Ferrari, Farinati, Foppa, Giovenone, Guariento, Luini, North-Italian Gothic, Parentino.

DUOMO: Giovanni Agostino da Lodi.

S. MARINO: Giampietrino.

Pavia (Environs). CERTOSA, CHURCH: Bergognone, Luini, Macrino d'Alba, Perugino, Solario.

— MUSEO: Bergognone, Luini.

Pergola (Pesaro). CAPPELLA DEL PALAZZOLO: Lorenzo d'Alessandro.

Périgueux. MUSÉE: Caporali.

Perugia. GALLERIA NAZIONALE DELL'UMBRIA: Antoniazzo Romano, Bartolo di Fredi, Benvenuto di Giovanni, Bernardino di Mariotto, Boccati, Bonfigli, Caporali, Domenico di Bartolo, Duccio, Eusebio da San Giorgio, Fiorenzo di Lorenzo, Francesco di Giorgio (sculpture), Gentile da Fabriano, Giovanni Francesco da Rimini, Luca di Tommè, Master of the Gardner Annunciation, Master of St. Francis, Matteo da Gualdo, Meo da Siena, Nelli, Niccolò di Buonaccorso, Niccolò da Foligno, Pellicciajo, Perugino, Piero della Francesca, Pietro di Domenico da Montepulciano, Pinturicchio, Raphael, Riminese Trecento, Salimbeni, Signorelli, Lo Spagna, Taddeo di Bartolo, Lippo Vanni, Vigoroso da Siena.

— BERENSON GIFT: Francesco di Gentile da Fabriano.

COLLEGIO DEL CAMBIO: Perugino.

PALAZZO DEI PRIORI: Cavallini Follower, Pinturicchio.

DUOMO: Sassetta.

MUSEO DELL'OPERA DEL DUOMO: Caporali, Meo da Siena, Pinturicchio, Signorelli, Andrea Vanni.

S. AGNESE: Eusebio da San Giorgio, Perugino.

S. AGOSTINO: Perugino.

CARMINE: Bonfigli.

MONASTERO DELLA BEATA COLOMBA: Lo Spagna.

S. DOMENICO: Benedetto di Bindo.

S. FIORENZO: Bonfigli.

S. FRANCESCO AL PRATO: Bonfigli.

S. MARIA DI MONTELUCE: Fiorenzo di Lorenzo.

S. MARIA NUOVA: Bonfigli.

S. PIETRO: Bonfigli, Eusebio da San Giorgio, Perugino.

S. SEVERO: Perugino, Raphael.

PALAZZO GRAZIANI (EX): Pinturicchio.

MARCHESE MONALDI: Tiberio d'Assisi.

CONTE RANIERI: Perugino.

CONTE SALVADORI (EX): Fiorenzo di Lorenzo.

VAN MARLE COLLECTION (EX): Andrea di Bartolo, Ferrarese, Francesco di Vannuccio, Giampietrino, Martino di Bartolomeo da Siena, Niccolò da Foligno, Nuzi, Sano di Pietro, 'Ugolino Lorenzetti', Andrea Vanni.

Perugia (Environs). CIVITELLA D'ARNA, PARISH CHURCH: Caporali.

CORCIANO, see under **Corciano.**

Pesaro. MUSEO CIVICO: Beccafumi, Ferrarese, Giovanni Francesco da Rimini, Salimbeni, Vitale da Bologna, Zaganelli, Zoppo.

— (Environs) VILLA IMPERIALE: Dosso, Genga, Girolamo da Carpi, Perino del Vaga.

Peschiera (Lago di Garda). MADONNA DEL FRASSINO: Farinati.

Pescia. S. FRANCESCO: Bonaventura Berlinghieri.

Petroio (Senese). S. ANDREA: Andrea di Niccolò.

SS. PIETRO E PAOLO: Taddeo di Bartolo.

Petts Wood (Kent). MAX GOLD (EX): Vitale da Bologna.

Philadelphia (Pennsylvania). MUSEUM OF ART: Giovanni di Paolo, Martino di Bartolomeo.

— WILSTACH COLLECTION: Giulio Campi, Moroni, Scarsellino, Solario.

ACADEMY OF FINE ARTS: Francia, Luini.

Philadelphia (Pennsylvania) (contd.). FLEISCHER MEMORIAL: Gualtieri di Giovanni da Pisa.
JOHN G. JOHNSON COLLECTION: Altobello Melone, Andrea di Bartolo, Arcangelo di Cola da Camerino, Aspertini, Barna da Siena, Benaglio, Bergognone, Bernardino de' Conti, Bernardino di Mariotto, Boltraffio, Bonsignori, Bramantino, Brescianino, Brusasorci, Giovan Francesco Caroto, Cavallini Follower, Cavazzola, Civerchio, Correggio, Costa, Cozzarelli, Defendente Ferrari, De Predis, Domenico di Bartolo, Dosso, Duccio, Ercole da Ferrara, Eusebio da San Giorgio, Foppa, Francesco di Gentile da Fabriano, Francesco di Vannuccio, Francia, Giampietrino, Giolfino, Giovanni di Paolo, Liberale da Verona, Pietro Lorenzetti, Luini, Master of the Gardner Annunciation, Master of Osservanza Triptych, Matteo di Giovanni, Mazzolino, Moretto, Moroni, Nelli, Neroccio, Nuzi, Ortolano, Vincenzo Pagani, Palmezzano, Pastura, Perugino, Calisto Piazza, Pinturicchio, Sano di Pietro, Scarsellino, Signorelli, Sodoma, Solario, Lo Spagna, Taddeo di Bartolo, Tamagni, Tura, 'Ugolino Lorenzetti', Ugolino di Nerio.
WIDENER COLLECTION (EX): Moroni.

Phoenix (Arizona). ART MUSEUM: Palmezzano.

Piacenza. S. SISTO: Farinati.

Pian di Meleto (Marches). CONVENTO DI MONTEFIORENTINO: Santi.

Piazzola sul Brenta (Padua). VILLA CAMERINI: Cavazzola, Michele da Verona.

Piediluco (between Terni and Rieti). S. FRANCESCO: Aspertini.

Pienza. MUSEO DIOCESANO DI ARTE SACRA: Bartolo di Fredi, Giovanni di Paolo, Sano di Pietro, Sassetta, Vecchietta.
PALAZZO PICCOLOMINI: Matteo di Giovanni.
SEMINARIO: 'Ugolino Lorenzetti'.
S. MARIA ASSUNTA (DUOMO): Giovanni di Paolo, Matteo di Giovanni, Sano di Pietro, Vecchietta.
S. FRANCESCO: Segna di Bonaventura.
— (Environs). S. ANNA IN CAMPRENA: Sodoma, Vecchietta.

Pieve a Piana, see Buonconvento.

Pieve di Cento. S. MARIA VERGINE: Scarsellino.

Piòraco (Camerino). CHIESA DEL CROCIFISSO: Girolamo di Giovanni da Camerino.
— (Environs). See Seppio.

Pisa. MUSEO NAZIONALE DI S. MATTEO: Andrea di Bartolo, Barna da Siena, Barnaba da Modena, Cecco di Pietro, Deodato Orlandi, Domenico di Bartolo, Gentile da Fabriano, Gera, Getto di Jacopo da Pisa, Giovanni di Nicola da Pisa, Giovanni di Pietro da Napoli, Giunta Pisano, Luca di Tommè, Martino di Bartolomeo da Siena, Perino del Vaga, Simone Martini, Sodoma, Taddeo di Bartolo, Traini, Turino Vanni, 'Ugolino Lorenzetti'.
CAMPOSANTO, MUSEO: Traini.
SEMINARIO VESCOVILE: Giovanni di Nicola da Pisa.
DUOMO: Beccafumi, Domenico di Bartolo, Perino del Vaga, Sodoma.
S. CATERINA: Lippo Memmi, Simone Martini, Traini.
S. DONNINO IN S. GIUSTO: Turino Vanni.
S. FRANCESCO: Taddeo di Bartolo.
S. GIUSTO A SCANNICCI: Traini.
S. MARTINO: Cecco di Pietro, Giovanni di Nicola da Pisa, Taddeo di Bartolo.

S. MICHELE IN BORGO: Taddeo di Bartolo.

S. PAOLO A RIPA D'ARNO: Turino Vanni.

— (Environs). RIGOLI, PIEVE DI S. MARCO: Turino Vanni.

RIPOLI, PIEVE DI S. MARIA: Barnaba da Modena.

S. PIETRO IN GRADO: Deodato Orlandi.

Pisogne (Lago d'Iseo). S. MARIA DELLA NEVE: Romanino.

Pistoia. MUSEO: Lippo Dalmasio.

S. DOMENICO, CONVENT: Lippo Dalmasio.

Pitigliano (Grosseto). SS. PIETRO E PAOLO: Cozzarelli.

Pittsburgh (Pennsylvania). CARNEGIE INSTITUTE: Giulio Campi, Perugino.

Poggibonsi. S. LUCCHESE: Bartolo di Fredi, Fei, Ugolino di Nerio.

Poggioferro (Grosseto). PARISH CHURCH: Giacomo del Pisano.

Poggio Nativo (Sabina). SS. ANNUNZIATA: Antoniazzo Romano.

Poitiers. MUSÉE DES AUGUSTINS: Bernardino de' Conti.

MUSÉE DES BEAUX-ARTS: Giulio Campi.

Polesden Lacey (Surrey). NATIONAL TRUST: Lucca di Tommè, Master of Panzano Triptych.

CHRISTOPHER NORRIS: Moretto.

Pollenza (Macerata). SS. FRANCESCO E ANTONIO DA PADOVA: Lorenzo d'Alessandro.

Pollockshaws (Scotland). POLLOCK HOUSE, MRS JOHN MAXWELL-MACDONALD: Signorelli.

Pomarance (Volterra). S. GIOVANNI BATTISTA: Duccio Follower, Tamagni.

Pommersfelden. SCHLOSSMUSEUM: Giovan Francesco Caroto.

Pomposa (Codigoro). ABBAZIA, BASILICA DI S. MARIA: Riminese Trecento, Vitale da Bologna.

— MONASTERY (REFETTORIO, SALA CAPITOLARE): Riminese Trecento.

Ponce (Puerto Rico). MUSEO D'ARTE, KRESS COLLECTION: Boccati, Giampietrino, Luca di Tommè, Mazzolino, Niccolò di Segna.

Pontedera. TOSCANELLI COLLECTION (EX): Ugolino di Nerio, Andrea Vanni.

Ponte Valtellina. S. MAURIZIO: Luini.

Pontremoli (Massa Carrara). SS. ANNUNZIATA: Massone.

Poppi (Casentino). CASTELLO: Taddeo di Bartolo.

Porchia (Ascoli). S. LUCIA: Vincenzo Pagani.

Pordenone. DUOMO, CAPPELLA DEI SS. PIETRO E PAOLO: North-Italian Gothic.

Port Washington (New York). SOLOMON R. GUGGENHEIM (EX): Francesco di Giorgio, Luini.

Portland (Oregon). ART MUSEUM, KRESS COLLECTION: Giovan Francesco Caroto, Cecco di Pietro, Francesco di Giorgio, Giampietrino, Niccolò di Segna, Nuzi, Sodoma.

Portomaggiore. MUNICIPIO: Dosso.

Porzano. PARISH CHURCH: Moretto.

Possagno (Bassano). TEMPIO DEL CANOVA: Moretto.

Postino Dovera (between Lodi and Crema). ORATORIO DI S. ROCCO: Calisto Piazza.

Potenza Picena. ISTITUTO DELL'ADDOLORATA: Pietro di Domenico da Montepulciano.

MINORI OSSERVANTI: Bernardino di Mariotto.

Potsdam. NEUES PALAIS: Torbido.

SANS SOUCI: Bernardino de' Conti.

— (EX?): Ortolano.

Poughkeepsie (New York). VASSAR COLLEGE: Martino di Bartolomeo da Siena.

Powis Castle (Shropshire). EARL OF POWIS (EX): Boltraffio.

Poznań. NATIONAL MUSEUM: Anguissola, Bergognone, Boccati, Garofalo, Giovanni Agostino da Lodi, Mazzolino, Lippo Memmi, Ugolino di Nerio.

Pozzuolo (Mantua). PARISH CHURCH: Farinati.

Prague. NATIONAL GALLERY: Giovan Francesco Caroto, Cavazzola, Costa, Farinati, Palmezzano, Zenale.

TYNKIRCHE: Romanino.

S. HERMAN (EX): Scarsellino.

Pralboino (Brescia). PARISH CHURCH: Moretto.

Princeton (New Jersey). UNIVERSITY ART MUSEUM: Ambrosi, Andrea di Bartolo, Boccati, Brusasorci, Giovanni Caroto, Giovan Francesco Caroto, Ceccarelli, Civerchio, Cozzarelli, Domenico di Bartolo, Farinati, Foppa, Giolfino, Guido da Siena, Liberale da Verona, Luca di Tommè, Mantegna, Marco d'Oggiono, Domenico Morone, Francesco Morone, Moroni, Niccolò da Foligno, Raphael, Sodoma, Tiberio d'Assisi, Torbido, Traini, Ugolino di Nerio, Vecchietta.

F. JEWETT MATHER COLLECTION: Balducci.

Providence (Rhode Island). SCHOOL OF DESIGN: Brusasorci, Delitio, Dosso, Matteo di Giovanni, Lippo Vanni.

— (EX): Antoniazzo Romano.

Prun de Negrar (Verona). PARISH CHURCH: Farinati.

Pszczyna. CASTLE: Fungai.

Quarona (Vercelli). S. GIOVANNI: Massone.

Quimper (Finistère). MUSÉE: Bartolo di Fredi.

Quinto di Valpantena (Verona). PARISH CHURCH: Francesco Morone.

Quinzano (Verona). S. ROCCO: Francesco dai Libri (Il Vecchio).

Radicondoli (Senese). CHIESA DEL CIMITERO: Ceccarelli.

COLLEGIATA (SS. SIMONE E GIUDA): Pietro di Domenico da Siena.

Raleigh (North Carolina). MUSEUM OF ART, KRESS COLLECTION: Benvenuto di Giovanni, Boltraffio, Costa, Duccio Follower, Foppa, Francia, Guariento, Lanino, Lorenzetti Follower, Luca di Tommè, Neroccio, Nuzi, Perugino, Pinturicchio, Raphael, Segna di Bonaventura.

Randazzo (Sicily). S. GREGORIO: Turino Vanni.

Ranica. PARROCCHIALE DEI SETTE FRATELLI: Moroni.

Ranverso, see Buttigliera Alta.

Rapolano (Senese). CHIESA DELLA FRATERNITA: Luca di Tommè.

ORATORIO DI S. BARTOLOMEO: Cozzarelli.

Ravello. DUOMO: Andrea da Salerno.

Ravenna. ACCADEMIA: Brea, Matteo di Giovanni, Niccolò da Foligno, Palmezzano, Taddeo di Bartolo, Zaganelli.

MUSEO CIVICO: Master of Panzano Triptych.

PALAZZO ARCIVESCOVILE: Palmezzano.

SEMINARIO ARCIVESCOVILE: Zaganelli.

DUOMO: Riminese Trecento.

S. CHIARA: Riminese Trecento.

S. FRANCESCO: Riminese Trecento.

S. MARIA IN PORTO: Scarsellino.

S. MARIA IN PORTO FUORI: Riminese Trecento.

S. ROMUALDO: Zaganelli.

Recanati. PINACOTECA COMUNALE: Pietro di Domenico da Montepulciano.

MUSEO DIOCESANO: Urbani.

CHIESA DEL BEATO PLACIDO: Vincenzo Pagani.

S. MARIA DI CASTELNUOVO, CASA PARROCCHIALE: Pietro di Domenico da Montepulciano.

S. MARIA DI CASTELNUOVO (EX): Urbani.

Reggio Emilia. CONTI CASSOLI: Costa.

Rheims. MUSÉE DES BEAUX-ARTS: Anguissola, Moroni.

Richmond (Surrey). COOK COLLECTION [For the sake of convenient reference, pictures in the Cook Collection have been listed under their old location. The collection has, in fact, been split up and many paintings are on temporary loan to various museums in Britain]: Anguissola, Balducci, Bernardino di Mariotto, Cesare da Sesto, Ercole da Ferrara, Fei, Giampietrino, Giovenone, Luini, Maineri, Romanino, Ugolino di Nerio.

COOK COLLECTION (EX): Andrea da Salerno, Bernardino di Mariotto, Brescianino, Ceccarelli, Evangelista da Pian di Meleto, Farinati, Francesco di Giorgio, Garofalo, Giovanni Francesco da Rimini, Francesco Morone, Parmigianino, Piero della Francesca.

— (EX?): Giovan Francesco Caroto.

Richmond (Virginia). VIRGINIA MUSEUM OF ART: Andrea di Bartolo, Antonio da Fabriano, Fungai, Giacomo del Pisano, Moroni, Signorelli.

Rieti. MUSEO CIVICO: Antoniazzo Romano, Luca di Tommè.

SEMINARIO: Antoniazzo Romano.

DUOMO: Antoniazzo Romano.

Rimini. PINACOTECA COMUNALE: Perino del Vaga, Riminese Trecento, Giovanni da Rimini, Zaganelli.

PALAZZO DELL'ARENGO: Riminese Trecento.

S. AGOSTINO: Riminese Trecento.

S. FRANCESCO: Piero della Francesca.

SPINA COLLECTION: Riminese Trecento.

Riofreddo (Tivoli). ORATORIO DELL'ANNUNZIATA: Pietro di Domenico da Montepulciano.

Ripatransone (Ascoli): MUSEO CIVICO: Vincenzo Pagani.

Rivarolo Canavese. S. FRANCESCO: Spanzotti.

Rivoli (Turin). MUNICIPIO: Giovenone.

Roccalbegna (Grosseto). PARISH CHURCH: Ambrogio Lorenzetti.

Roccapietra (Valsesia). S. MARTINO: Gaudenzio Ferrari.

MADONNA DI LORETO: Gaudenzio Ferrari.

Rocca S. Angelo or Rocchicciola (Perugia). S. FRANCESCO: Caporali, Lo Spagna.

Rochester (New York). MEMORIAL ART GALLERY: Benaglio, Riminese Trecento.

Rodengo. ABBAZIA: Romanino.

Rodez. MUSÉE DES BEAUX-ARTS: Bartolo di Fredi.

Romagnano (Valsesia). S. SILANO: Lanino.

Romano Lombardo. S. MARIA ASSUNTA: Moroni.

Rome. ACCADEMIA DI S. LUCA: Matteo di Giovanni, Raphael, Romanino.

CAMPIDOGLIO, PALAZZO DEI CONSERVATORI: Pastura.

— PINACOTECA CAPITOLINA: Barnaba da Modena, Cola d'Amatrice, Dosso, Battista Dossi, Francia, Garofalo, Lanino, Macrino d'Alba, Mazzolino, Ortolano, Romanino, Scarsellino, Lo Spagna, 'Ugolino Lorenzetti'.

FARNESINA: Giulio Romano, Peruzzi, Raphael, Sodoma.

GALLERIA BARBERINI (EX): Scarsellino.

GALLERIA BORGHESE: Anguissola, Bernardino de' Conti, Brescianino, Giulio Campi, Cesare da Sesto, Correggio, Costa, Dosso, Battista Dossi, Farinati, Francia, Garofalo, Genga, Giulio Romano, Marco d'Oggiono, Mazzolino, Ortolano, Parmigianino, Perino del Vaga, Perugino, Peruzzi, Raphael, Scarsellino, Sodoma, Solario.

GALLERIA COLONNA: Boccati, Giovan Francesco Caroto, Dosso, Battista Dossi, Luini, Melozzo da Forlì, Niccolò da Foligno, Scarsellino, Zaganelli.

— PRIVATE APARTMENTS: Anguissola, Bernardino di Mariotto, Cola d'Amatrice, Pinturicchio, Stefano da Zevio, Tura.

GALLERIA DORIA PAMPHILJ: Anguissola, Beccafumi, Boccaccino, Dosso, Ferrarese-Bolognese, Fiorenzo di Lorenzo, Garofalo, Giovanni di Paolo, Girolamo da Carpi, Maineri, Mazzolino, Ortolano, Parentino, Parmigianino, Perino del Vaga, Raphael, Romanino, Scarsellino, Torbido.

— PRIVATE APARTMENTS: Mazzolino, Parentino, Sano di Pietro.

GALLERIA NAZIONALE (PALAZZO BARBERINI): Antoniazzo Romano, Aspertini, Beccafumi, Bianchi Ferrari, Brescianino, Butinone, Giulio Campi, Dosso, Francesco di Gentile da Fabriano, Francia, Garofalo, Giolfino, Girolamo di Benvenuto, Giulio Romano, Lorenzo d'Alessandro, Lorenzo da Viterbo, Niccolò da Foligno, Palmezzano, Perugino, Raphael, Riminese Trecento, Giovanni da Rimini, Sano di Pietro, Scarsellino, Sodoma, Solario, Tamagni.

GALLERIA SPADA: Anguissola, Aspertini, Balducci, Bertucci, Fiorenzo di Lorenzo, Palmezzano.

MUSEO DI CASTEL SANT'ANGELO: Dosso, Giampietrino, Girolamo di Benvenuto, Niccolò da Foligno, Perino del Vaga, Pinturicchio, Romanino, Signorelli, Spanzotti.

MUSEO DEL FORO ROMANO (EX-ABBAZIA BENEDETTINA DI S. FRANCESCA ROMANA): Antonio da Viterbo.

MUSEO DI PALAZZO VENEZIA: Benaglio, Bernardino di Mariotto, Bertucci, Farinati, Fiorenzo di Lorenzo, Francesco di Gentile da Fabriano, Garofalo, Giolfino, Girolamo di Giovanni da Camerino, Liberale da Verona, Nanni di Jacopo, Nelli, Niccolò di Segna, Albertino and Martino Piazza, Calisto Piazza, Scarsellino, Simone Martini Follower, Stefano da Zevio.

OPERE RECUPERATE: Altobello Melone, Antoniazzo, Romano.

PALAZZO BALDASSINI: Perino del Vaga.

PALAZZO DELLA CANCELLERIA: Perino del Vaga, Peruzzi.

PALAZZO COLONNA, see under Galleria Colonna, Private Apartments.

PALAZZO MASSIMO ALLE COLONNE: Perino del Vaga.

PALAZZO PATRIZI: Ortolano.

PALAZZO DEI PENITENZIERI: Pinturicchio.

PALAZZO DEL QUIRINALE: Melozzo da Forlì.

Rome. Churches (contd.).

SS. VITO E MODESTO: Antoniazzo Romano.

CONVENTO DI TOR DE' SPECCHI, see S. FRANCESCA ROMANA.

Rome. Private Collections.

ALBERTINI COLLECTION: Giampietrino, Giovanni Agostino da Lodi, Moretto.

MISS ANDERSON: Cesare da Sesto.

SENATORE R. BASTIANELLI: Pietro Lorenzetti.

CONTE BLUMENSTHIL: Ercole da Ferrara.

PRINCIPESSA NICOLETTA BUONCOMPAGNI LUDOVISI: Boccaccino.

PRINCIPE CHIGI: Pinturicchio.

— (EX): Ercole da Ferrara, Giovanni di Paolo, Mazzolino.

BORIS CHRISTOFF: Lorenzo d'Alessandro.

DEL PERO COLLECTION (EX): Girolamo di Giovanni da Camerino.

MARCHESE ALFREDO DUSMET (EX): Costa.

BARONE ALBERTO FASSINI (EX): Ambrosi, Lo Spagna, Taddeo di Bartolo.

FERRONI COLLECTION (EX): Palmezzano.

FINARDI COLLECTION: Civerchio.

GASPARRINI COLLECTION: Dosso.

GERMAN EMBASSY (EX): Cesare Magni.

GRASSI COLLECTION: Bramantino.

JANETTI DEL GRANDE (EX): Bianchi Ferrari.

HELBIG COLLECTION: Segna di Bonaventura.

LAZZARONI (EX): Zenale.

PRINCIPE FABRIZIO MASSIMO (EX): Andrea di Bartolo.

CASTELLI MIGNANELLI COLLECTION: Francesco di Giorgio.

CONTE ALFONSO CASTELLI MIGNANELLI (EX): Sassetta.

CAV. LATTANZIO MARRI MIGNANELLI (EX): Beccafumi.

MARCHESE MISCIATELLI: Cozzarelli, Martino di Bartolomeo da Siena, Sano di Pietro, Sodoma.

NEVIN COLLECTION (EX): Boccati, Vincenzo Pagani, Palmerucci, Sano di Pietro, Zaganelli.

ILO NUNES: Liberale da Verona.

PRINCIPE ODESCALCHI: Gaudenzio Ferrari, Scarsellino.

MARCHESE PATRIZI (EX): Zaganelli.

E. PEDICONI: Scarsellino.

CONTESSA RASPONI SPALLETTI (EX): Pinturicchio.

LORD RENNELL (EX): Giampietrino.

PROF. ODOARDO RUFFINI: Andrea di Bartolo.

SCHIFF COLLECTION (EX): Barnaba da Modena, Duccio Follower, Eusebio da San Giorgio, Giusto de' Menabuoi, Tiberio d'Assisi, Zaganelli, Zoppo.

SENATORE CESARE SILI (EX): Dosso.

SPIRIDON COLLECTION (EX): Bernardino di Mariotto, Defendente Ferrari, Vincenzo Pagani.

STEPANOV COLLECTION (EX): Fiorenzo di Lorenzo.

STERBINI COLLECTION (EX): Pietro di Domenico da Siena, Riminese Trecento.

STROGANOFF COLLECTION (EX): Ercole da Ferrara.

CONTE SUARDI: Bernardino de' Conti.

MARCHESE VISCONTI VENOSTA (EX): Beccafumi, Palmezzano, Albertino and Martino Piazza,

VISCONTI VENOSTA COLLECTION: Bergognone, Costa, Giampietrino, Marco d'Oggiono, Moretto, Neroccio, Ortolano, Pinturicchio, Lo Spagna.

CONTE LEONARDO VITETTI: Balducci, Beccafumi, Dosso, Fei, Palmezzano, Sano di Pietro, Signorelli, Sodoma, Squarcione.

CARDINAL ZELADA (EX): Giovanni da Pisa.

(Environs). MENTANA, FEDERICO ZERI: Anguissola, Dosso, Lanino, Pacchiarotto, Scarsellino.

Rome. Vatican.

BASILICA DI S. PIETRO, ARCHIVIO CAPITOLARE: Master of the Codex of St. George, Simone Martini.

— MUSEO DI S. PIETRO: Antoniazzo Romano, Cavallini.

PALAZZI PONTIFICI, APPARTAMENTO BORGIA: Pastura, Perino del Vaga, Piermatteo da Amelia, Pinturicchio.

— BELVEDERE: Piermatteo da Amelia, Pinturicchio.

— BIBLIOTECA, ARCHIVI: Pinturicchio, Sano di Pietro.

— — SALA DI SISTO IV (FLORERIA APOSTOLICA): Antoniazzo Romano, Melozzo da Forlì.

— CAPPELLA SISTINA: Bartolomeo della Gatta, Perugino, Pinturicchio, Signorelli.

— LOGGE: Raphael.

— MUSEO SACRO: Gentile da Fabriano.

— PAPAL APARTMENTS: Niccolò da Voltri.

— PINACOTECA: Ambrosi, Antoniazzo Romano, Barna da Siena, Bartolo di Fredi, Bartolomeo di Tommaso da Foligno, Bernardino de' Conti, Boccati, Bramante, Cola d'Amatrice, Cossa, Cozzarelli, Defendente Ferrari, Ercole da Ferrara, Eusebio da San Giorgio, Fei, Fiorenzo di Lorenzo, Francesco di Gentile da Fabriano, Garofalo, Genga, Gentile da Fabriano, Ghissi, Giovanni di Paolo, Giovanni Francesco da Rimini, Giulio Romano, Gregorio di Cecco di Luca, Pietro Lorenzetti, Lorenzetti Imitator, Lorenzo d'Alessandro, Luca di Tommè, Margarito, Martino di Bartolomeo da Siena, Master of the Codex of St. George, Master of the Osservanza Triptych, Melozzo da Forlì, Moretto, Nelli, Niccolò di Buonaccorso, Niccolò da Foligno, Nuzi, Pacchia, Vincenzo Pagani, Palmezzano, Pastura, Perugino, Pinturicchio, Raphael, Riminese Trecento, Sano di Pietro, Santi, Sassetta, Scarsellino, Simone Martini, Lo Spagna, Taddeo di Bartolo, Tegliacci, Tiberio d'Assisi, Turino Vanni, Urbani, Lippo Vanni, Vecchietta, Vitale da Bologna.

— STANZE DI RAFFAELLO: Giulio Romano, Perugino, Raphael, Sodoma.

Roncadelle. PARISH CHURCH: Romanino.

Roncola. S. BERNARDINO: Moroni.

Rosazza (Biella). SS. PIETRO E GIORGIO: Defendente Ferrari.

Rosazzo (Udine). BADIA: Torbido.

Rosia (Senese). PIEVE DI S. GIOVANNI BATTISTA: Cozzarelli.

Rossie Priory (Inchture, Perthshire). LORD KINNAIRD: Andrea da Salerno, Pacchiarotto.

Rotterdam. BOYMANS-VAN BEUNINGEN MUSEUM: Arcangelo di Cola, Cozzarelli, Ercole da Ferrara, Fei, Ferrarese, Francesco Napolitano, Maineri, Moroni.

D. G. VAN BEUNINGEN: Defendente Ferrari.

Rouen. MUSÉE DES BEAUX-ARTS: Palmezzano, Perugino.

Rovato. S. MARIA DELL'ANNUNCIATA: Romanino.

Roverchiara (Verona). S. ZENO: Farinati.

Rovetta con Fino, see Fino del Monte.

Sant'Angelo in Colle (Montalcino). S. MICHELE ARCANGELO: Pietro Lorenzetti.

Sant'Ansano in Dofana (Siena). CAPPELLINA DEL MARTIRIO: Pietro Lorenzetti. (Now transferred to Siena, Pinacoteca.)

PARISH CHURCH: Peruzzi.

Sant'Arcangelo di Romagna. COLLEGIATA: Riminese Trecento.

Santa Colomba (Siena). PARISH CHURCH: Niccolò di Segna.

Santhià (Vercelli). S. AGATA: Giovenone.

Santiago de Chile. CARLOS CRUZ COLLECTION: Barnaba da Modena.

São Paulo (Brazil). MUSEU DE ARTE: Francia, Mantegna, Nelli, Perugino.

Sarasota (Florida). RINGLING MUSEUM: Beccafumi, Brusasorci, Ercole da Ferrara, Gaudenzio Ferrari, Lanino, Luini, Mazzolino, Moroni, Palmezzano, Pastura, Calisto Piazza, Sodoma, Zaganelli.

Sarnano (Macerata). S. MARIA DI PIAZZA: Girolamo di Giovanni da Camerino, Lorenzo d'Alessandro, Niccolò da Foligno, Vincenzo Pagani.

Saronno. S. MARIA DEI MIRACOLI: Cesare Magni, Gaudenzio Ferrari, Lanino, Luini.

Sarteano (Val di Chiana). S. FRANCESCO: Pellicciajo.

S. LORENZO: Pacchia.

SS. MARTINO E VITTORIA: Andrea di Niccolò, Beccafumi, Pellicciajo.

Sassari (Sardinia). MUSEO: Martino di Bartolomeo da Siena.

Sassocorvaro. ROCCA: Riminese Trecento.

Sassoferrato. S. FRANCESCO: Riminese Trecento.

Saturnia (Maremma). PARISH CHURCH: Girolamo di Benvenuto.

Savannah (Georgia). TELFAIR ACADEMY: Romanino.

Savona. PINACOTECA: Brea, Foppa, Massone, Niccolò da Voltri, Taddeo di Bartolo.

DUOMO: Brea, Albertino and Martino Piazza.

ORATORIO DI S. MARIA DI CASTELLO: Brea, Foppa.

Schleissheim. GALERIE: Scarsellino.

Schloss Sebenstein. PRINCE LIECHTENSTEIN (EX): Boltraffio, Scarsellino.

Seattle (Washington). MUSEUM OF ART: Bernardino de' Conti, Giampietrino, Giovanni di Paolo, Pietro Lorenzetti, Marco d'Oggiono, Riminese Trecento, Romanino.

Senigallia. CONTE MASTAI FERRETTI: Lanino.

PALAZZO COMUNALE: Perugino.

Seppio (Camerino). S. MARIA: Boccati.

Seriate (Bergamo). S. CRISOGONO: Moroni.

Serrapetrona (Macerata). PARISH CHURCH: Lorenzo d'Alessandro.

— (Environs). CASTEL SAN VENANZIO, PARISH CHURCH: Girolamo di Giovanni da Camerino.

Sestano (Siena). S. BARTOLOMEO: 'Ugolino Lorenzetti'.

Settimo (Pisa). S. BENEDETTO: Martino di Bartolomeo da Siena.

Shenfield (Berkshire). J. HASSON COLLECTION (EX): Perugino.

Siena. PINACOTECA NAZIONALE: Ambrosi, Andrea di Bartolo, Andrea di Niccolò, Anguissola, Balducci, Barna da Siena, Bartolo di Fredi, Beccafumi, Benedetto di Bindo, Benvenuto di Giovanni, Brescianino, Ceccarelli, Cozzarelli, Domenico di Bartolo, Duccio, Duccio Follower, Farinati, Fei, Francesco di Giorgio, Francesco di Giorgio (sculpture), Francesco di Vannuccio, Fungai, Genga, Gera, Giacomo del Pisano, Giovanni di Paolo, Girolamo di Benvenuto, Girolamo da Cremona, Gualtieri di Giovanni da Pisa, Guido da Siena, Ambrogio Lorenzetti, Pietro Lorenzetti, Lorenzetti

Siena (contd.). SOCIETÀ ESECUTORI PIE DISPOSIZIONI (former Confraternita della Madonna sotto le Volte o dei Disciplinati), GALLERIA: Benvenuto di Giovanni, Cozzarelli, Duccio, Martino di Bartolomeo da Siena, Sano di Pietro, Sodoma, Tegliacci.

Siena. Churches, Confraternities, Monasteries.

BATTISTERO: Benvenuto di Giovanni, Vecchietta.

CHIESA DI FONTEGIUSTA: Cozzarelli, Fungai, Girolamo di Benvenuto, Peruzzi.

S. AGOSTINO: Ambrogio Lorenzetti, Matteo di Giovanni, Perugino, Simone Martini, Sodoma.

— COLLEGIO CONVITTO TOLOMEI (former monastery): Ambrogio Lorenzetti.

S. ANDREA: Giovanni di Paolo.

S. ANSANO IN CASTELVECCHIO: Vecchietta.

SANT'ANSANO, ANTICA COMPAGNIA DI: Martino di Bartolomeo.

COMPAGNIA DI S. ANTONIO ABATE (ARCICONFRATERNITA DELLA MISERICORDIA): Beccafumi, Cozzarelli.

S. BARTOLOMEO (ORATORIO DELLA CONTRADA DELL'ISTRICE): Master of Panzano Triptych.

S. BERNARDINO: Beccafumi, Pacchia, Sano di Pietro, Sodoma.

S. BERNARDINO FUORI PORTA CAMOLLIA: Fei.

SANTUARIO CATERINIANO, ORATORIO DELLA CAMERA: Girolamo di Benvenuto.

— ORATORIO SUPERIORE: Fungai.

— S. CATERINA IN FONTEBRANDA (ORATORIO DELLA CONTRADA DELL'OCA): Neroccio, Pacchia, Sodoma, Tamagni.

S. CATERINA DELLA NOTTE (ORATORIO DELLA COMPAGNIA DI), see Spedale di S. Maria della Scala.

CHIESA DELLA CONTRADA DEL BRUCO: Luca di Tommè.

S. CRISTOFORO: Master of Osservanza Triptych, Pacchia, Sano di Pietro.

S. DOMENICO: Beccafumi, Benvenuto di Giovanni, Francesco di Giorgio, Francesco di Vannuccio, Fungai, Pietro Lorenzetti, Matteo di Giovanni, Lippo Memmi, Sano di Pietro, Sodoma, Andrea Vanni, Lippo Vanni.

S. DONATO (FORMER S. MICHELE): Pacchia, Sodoma, Andrea Vanni.

S. EUGENIO A PORTA PISPINI: Matteo di Giovanni.

S. FRANCESCO: Ambrogio Lorenzetti, Pietro Lorenzetti, Martino di Bartolomeo da Siena, Sodoma, Andrea Vanni.

— (FORMER CONVENT), PONTIFICIO SEMINARIO REGIONALE PIO XII: Pietro Lorenzetti.

— — CAPPELLA: Ambrogio Lorenzetti, Lippo Vanni.

SS. GHERARDO E LUDOVICO (nr. S. FRANCESCO): Girolamo di Benvenuto, Taddeo di Bartolo.

S. GIOVANNI DELLA STAFFA (S. GIOVANNI IN PANTANETO): Francesco di Vannuccio.

SS. GIOVANNINO E GENNARO: Giovanni di Paolo, Sodoma.

S. GIROLAMO: Pacchia, Sano di Pietro.

— CLOISTER OF FORMER MONASTERY: Fungai.

S. GIROLAMO IN CAMOLLIA, FORMER MONASTERY, see Casa di Riposo in Campansi.

S. MARGHERITA, REFECTORY OF FORMER MONASTERY (ISTITUTO DEI SORDOMUTI): Fungai.

S. MARIA ASSUNTA (DUOMO): Balducci, Beccafumi, Benedetto di Bindo, Benvenuto di Giovanni, Brescianino, Cozzarelli, Domenico di Bartolo, Duccio, Fei, Francesco di Giorgio (sculpture), Guido da Siena, Matteo di Giovanni, Neroccio (also sculpture), Pinturicchio, Vecchietta, Vecchietta (sculpture).

— CHAPTER HALL: Pacchiarotto, Sano di Pietro.

Siena. Churches, Confraternities, Monasteries (contd.).

SEMINARIO, see S. Francesco.

Siena, Private Collections

BARGAGLI PETRUCCI COLLECTION (EX): Beccafumi.

BICHI RUSPOLI COLLECTION: Sano di Pietro.

CARLO CINUGHI (EX): Sano di Pietro.

GUARINI DEL TAIA COLLECTION: Beccafumi.

GIUSEPPINA LICCIOLI (EX): Matteo di Giovanni.

E. MARTINI HEIRS: Pacchia.

CONTE PICCOLOMINI: Francesco di Giorgio.

CONTE GIUSEPPE PLACIDI (EX): Cozzarelli.

SERGARDI BIRINGUCCI COLLECTION: Neroccio, Sano di Pietro.

CANONICO MANFREDO TARCHI (EX): Matteo di Giovanni.

CONTE TOLOMEI: Matteo di Giovanni.

UGURGERI COLLECTION (EX): Brescianino.

Siena (Environs). BELCARO, BARZELOTTI CAMAIORI COLLECTION: Cozzarelli, Pacchiarotto, Peruzzi.

GRANCIA A CUNA: Luca di Tommè.

LE GROTTE: Fungai.

LECCETO: Lippo Vanni.

S. LEONARDO AL LAGO: Giovanni di Paolo, Lippo Vanni.

MONISTERO DI S. EUGENIO: Benvenuto di Giovanni, Sodoma.

— (EX): Fungai.

OSSERVANZA: Ambrosi, Andrea di Bartolo, Girolamo di Benvenuto, Master of the Osservanza Triptych, Neroccio, Sano di Pietro.

— MUSEO: Benvenuto di Giovanni, Francesco di Giorgio, Girolamo di Benvenuto.

VICOBELLO, CHIGI ZONDADARI BONELLI COLLECTION: Cozzarelli.

Sigillo (Gubbio). S. ANNA (CHIESA DEL CIMITERO): Matteo da Gualdo.

S. MARIA DELLA SCIRCA: Matteo da Gualdo.

Sigmaringen. MUSEUM: Tiberio d'Assisi.

Sinaia (Rumania). CASTLE OF PELES: Signorelli.

Sinalunga (Val di Chiana). MADONNA DELLE NEVI: Benvenuto di Giovanni.

S. BERNARDINO: Benvenuto di Giovanni, Cozzarelli, Sano di Pietro.

S. CROCE: Signorelli.

S. LUCIA: Benvenuto di Giovanni.

COLLEGIATA DI S. MARTINO: Pacchia, Sodoma.

— (Environs). ORATORIO DELLA FRATTA: Sodoma.

Soave (Verona). PARISH CHURCH: Francesco Morone.

S. LORENZO: Farinati.

Soiana (Pisa). PARISH CHURCH: Giovanni di Nicola da Pisa.

Soissons. MUSÉE: Bergognone.

Solarolo Ranieri. PARISH CHURCH: Galeazzo Campi.

Solofra. COLLEGIATA: Andrea da Salerno.

Somerley. EARL OF NORMANTON: Parmigianino.

Sommacampagna. ZENO FORLATI: Liberale da Verona.

Sommariva Perno. SANTUARIO DELLA MADONNA DEL TAVOLETO: Spanzotti.

Soncino (Crema). S. MARIA DELLE GRAZIE: Giulio Campi.

Southam (Gloucestershire). EARL OF ELLENBOROUGH (EX): Garofalo.

Southampton. ART GALLERY: Anguissola, Nuzi.

South Hadley (Massachusetts). MOUNT HOLYOKE COLLEGE: Duccio, Giovanni di Paolo, Guariento, Simone Martini Follower.

   MRS SAMUEL HALE: Duccio Follower.

Sovere (Bergamo). S. MARTINO: Moroni.

Sovicille (Senese). VILLA BUDINI GATTAI: Luca di Tommè.

Spello. S. ANDREA: Pinturicchio.

   ORATORIO DI S. BERNARDINO: Pinturicchio.

   COLLEGIATA DI S. MARIA (or S. MARIA MAGGIORE): Perugino, Pinturicchio.

   — CAPPELLA DEL SEPOLCRO, MUSEO: Niccolò da Foligno.

Spello (Environs). S. GIROLAMO: Mezzastris, Perugino.

Spliska (Island of Brazza or Brac). CASTLE OF CERINEO FAMILY: Bernardino de' Conti.

Spoleto. PALAZZO COMUNALE, PINACOTECA: Giovanni Francesco da Rimini, Niccolò da Foligno, Lo Spagna.

   ARCIVESCOVADO: Giovanni Francesco da Rimini, Matteo da Gualdo.

   S. MARIA ASSUNTA (DUOMO), CAPPELLA EROLI: Pinturicchio.

   S. ANSANO: Lo Spagna.

Spoleto (Environs). CLITUNNO, ORATORIO: Lo Spagna.

Stafford House. DUKE OF SUTHERLAND (EX): Lo Spagna.

Stenico (Val Giudicaria, Trento). CASTELLO: Romanino.

Stimigliano (Val Teverina). S. MARIA IN VESCOVIO: Cavallini Follower.

Stockholm. NATIONAL MUSEUM: Andrea di Bartolo, Cozzarelli, Dosso, Francesco Napolitano, Pacchiarotto, Perugino.

   UNIVERSITY GALLERY: Liberale da Verona, Moretto, Signorelli.

   DR W. A. GREEN (EX): Giovanni di Paolo.

   R. PETRE COLLECTION (EX): Brescianino.

   DR L. TELANDER (EX): Altobello Melone, Pacchia.

Strasbourg. MUSÉE: Beccafumi, Cesare da Sesto, Correggio, Ferrarese, Fungai, Garofalo, Genga, Giulio Romano, Macrino d'Alba, Marco d'Oggiono, Nuzi, Perugino, Riminese Trecento, Sodoma, Spanzotti, Zaganelli.

Stresa Borromeo. ISTITUTO ROSMINI: Defendente Ferrari, Spanzotti.

Stroncone (Terni). S. FRANCESCO: Tiberio d'Assisi.

Stuttgart. STAATSGALERIE: Brusasorci, Giulio Campi, Defendente Ferrari, Farinati, Giampietrino, Domenico Morone.

Subiaco. S. FRANCESCO: Antoniazzo Romano, Tamagni.

Sundorne Castle (Shrewsbury). DOWAGER LADY BURGHLEY (EX): Giampietrino.

Susa. S. GIUSTO (DUOMO): Defendente Ferrari.

Sutton Place (Guildford). J. PAUL GETTY COLLECTION: Pacchia.

Syon House (Middlesex). DUKE OF NORTHUMBERLAND: Garofalo, Giampietrino, Solario.

Szekesfervar (Hungary). BISHOP'S PALACE, CHAPEL: Domenico Morone.

Taggia (Porto Maurizio). S. DOMENICO: Brea, Massone, Parmigianino.

Talamello (Urbino). S. LORENZO: Riminese Trecento.

Taplow Court (Bucks). LORD DESBOROUGH (EX): Luini.

Turin (contd.). FONTANA COLLECTION (EX): Giovanni Agostino da Lodi.
VINCENZO FONTANA (EX): Giovan Francesco Caroto.
ING. GALLO: Marco d'Oggiono.
AVV. RICCARDO GUALINO (EX): Butinone, Dosso, Fungai.
DI ROVASENDA COLLECTION: Luini.
Tuscania (Viterbo). DUOMO: Andrea di Bartolo.
S. MARIA DEL RIPOSO: Pastura, Piermatteo da Amelia.
Tyninghame House (Prestonkirk, East Lothian, Scotland). EARL OF HADDINGTON: Ceccarelli, Dosso.
— (EX): Segna di Bonaventura.

Ubeda (Andalusia). SAN SALVADOR: Sodoma.
Uccle (Brussels). VAN GELDER COLLECTION: Fei, Signorelli.
— (EX): Palmerucci.
Udine. GALLERIA D'ARTE ANTICA: Caporali.
CATTEDRALE: Vitale da Bologna.
CONTE CERNAZAI (EX): Matteo Giovannetti da Viterbo.
Umbertide (Perugia). S. CROCE: Signorelli.
Uopini (Monteriggioni). S. MARCELLINO: Sano di Pietro.
Upton House (Banbury, Oxon.). NATIONAL TRUST: Giovanni di Paolo.
Urbana (Illinois). UNIVERSITY, KRANNERT ART MUSEUM: Neroccio, Ugolino di Nerio.
Urbania. CHIESA DEI MORTI: Pietro da Rimini.
CHIESA DEL CARMINE: Riminese Trecento.
Urbino. GALLERIA NAZIONALE DELLE MARCHE: Andrea di Bartolo, Bartolomeo di Gentile da Urbino, Cola d'Amatrice, Evangelista da Pian di Meleto, Giovanni Francesco da Rimini, Girolamo di Giovanni da Camerino, Lorenzo d'Alessandro, Melozzo da Forlì, Nuzi, Perugino, Piero della Francesca, Riminese Trecento, Giovanni Baronzio da Rimini, Salimbeni, Santi, Signorelli, Viti.
DUOMO: Evangelista da Pian di Meleto.
ARCHIVIO CAPITOLARE DEL DUOMO: Bartolomeo della Gatta.
S. AGOSTINO: Viti.
S. CROCE: Evangelista da Pian di Meleto.
ORATORIO DI S. CROCE: Nelli.
ORATORIO DI S. GHERARDO: Nelli.
ORATORIO DI S. GIOVANNI BATTISTA: Salimbeni.
CASA DI RAFFAELLO: Raphael, Santi.
Urbino (Environs). MADONNA DELL'HOMO or S. MARIA DEL LOMO: Nelli.
Utrecht. ART INSTITUTE: Duccio Follower, Giovanni di Paolo, Master of Città di Castello, Neroccio, Sano di Pietro.
ARCHIEPISCOPAL MUSEUM: Butinone, Guido da Siena, Giovanni da Rimini.
Utrera (Seville). S. MARIA DELLA MESA: Luini.

Vaduz. LIECHTENSTEINSCHE SAMMLUNG: Barnaba da Modena, Bartolomeo di Tommaso da Foligno, Beccafumi, Butinone, Ceccarelli, Costa, Defendente Ferrari, Ferrarese, Francesco di Giorgio (sculpture), Garofalo, Luini, Michele da Verona, Moretto,

Moroni, Palmezzano, Perino del Vaga, Raphael, Riminese Trecento, Taddeo di Bartolo, Zaganelli.

Valcesura (Ferrara). S. MARGHERITA: Garofalo.

Valdagno. CONTE G. MARZOTTO: Riminese Trecento.

Valduggia (Valsesia). S. GIORGIO: Gaudenzio Ferrari, Lanino.

ORATORIO DI S. ROCCO: Gaudenzio Ferrari.

Valencia. MUSEO DE PINTURAS: Antoniazzo Romano, Cavallini, Giampietrino, Pinturicchio.

Valenciennes. Francesco di Gentile da Fabriano.

Vallo di Lucania (Salerno). S. MARIA DELLE GRAZIE: Andrea da Salerno.

Vangadizza (Verona). PARISH CHURCH: Farinati.

Vaprio d'Adda (Milan). VILLA LITTA MELZI: De Predis.

Varallo Sesia (Biella). PINACOTECA: Bernardino de' Conti, Gaudenzio Ferrari, Lanino, Sano di Pietro.

S. GAUDENZIO (COLLEGIATA): Gaudenzio Ferrari.

S. MARIA DELLE GRAZIE: Gaudenzio Ferrari.

Varallo Sesia (Environs). MADONNA DI LORETO: Gaudenzio Ferrari.

SACRO MONTE, CHAPELS ALONG THE ROAD LEADING TO THE CHURCH: Gaudenzio Ferrari.

Varano (Lunigiana). PARISH CHURCH: Puccinelli.

Varese. CARANTANI SCARINI COLLECTION: Moretto.

Velletri. CATTEDRALE, MUSEO CAPITOLARE: Antoniazzo Romano, Gentile da Fabriano.

Venice. ACCADEMIA: Benaglio, Boccaccino, Giovan Francesco Caroto, Fungai, Garofalo, Giovanni Agostino da Lodi, Girolamo dai Libri, Mantegna, Moretto, Francesco Morone, Calisto Piazza, Piero della Francesca, Riminese Trecento, Romanino, Tura.

CA' D'ORO: Andrea di Bartolo, Antoniazzo Romano, Bernardino di Mariotto, Boccaccino, Boccati, Domenico di Bartolo, Farinati, Giovanni Agostino da Lodi, Giovanni di Nicola da Pisa, Girolamo di Benvenuto, Mantegna, Palmezzano, Signorelli, Zaganelli.

MUSEO CORRER: Boccaccino, Brusasorci, Ferrarese, Guariento, Matteo Giovannetti da Viterbo, Francesco Morone, Palmezzano, Parentino, Schiavone, Tura.

PALAZZO DUCALE: Boccaccino, Guariento.

SEMINARIO: Beccafumi.

S. GIORGIO MAGGIORE, FONDAZIONE GIORGIO CINI: Ferrarese-Bolognese.

SS. GIOVANNI E PAOLO: Guariento.

S. GIULIANO: Boccaccino.

S. LIO: Liberale da Verona.

S. MARIA DEL CARMELO (I CARMINI): Francesco di Giorgio (sculpture).

S. MARIA DEI FRARI: Mantegna.

S. MARIA DELLA PIETÀ: Moretto.

S. STEFANO: Giovanni Agostino da Lodi.

S. ZACCARIA: Farinati.

CONTE S. BAROZZI: Parentino.

CONTE VITTORIO CINI: Ambrosi, Arcangelo di Cola da Camerino, Baldassarre d'Este, Bartolomeo di Tommaso da Foligno, Bergognone, Bertucci, Boccati, Giulio Campi, Costa, Dosso, Battista Dossi, Duccio Follower, Ercole da Ferrara, Ferrarese, Ferrarese-Bolognese, Foppa, Francia, Garofalo, Giovanni Francesco da Rimini, Girolamo di Benvenuto, Girolamo di Giovanni da Camerino, Guariento, Master of Osservanza

Triptych, Master of Stratonice, Mazzolino, Niccolò di Segna, Ortolano, Palmezzano, Parentino, Perugino, Riminese Trecento, Sassetta, Scacco, Signorelli, Tura, Vecchietta, Zenale.

CONTE FOSCARI: Michele da Verona.

BARONE RAIMONDO FRANCHETTI (EX): Andrea di Niccolò.

A. FREZZATI (EX): Dosso.

CESARE LAURENTI (EX): Francesco dai Libri (Il Vecchio).

Venice (Environs). Lido. G. BRUINI: Bergognone.

S. LAZZARO DEGLI ARMENI: Giovanni Agostino da Lodi.

S. PIETRO MARTIRE A MURANO: Giovanni Agostino da Lodi.

Venosa (Melfi). SS. TRINITÀ: Roberto di Oderisio da Napoli.

Ventimiglia. CAPPELLA DI S. SECONDO: Barnaba da Modena.

Vercelli. MUSEO BORGOGNA: Brea, Cesare Magni, Defendente Ferrari, Francia, Gaudenzio Ferrari, Giolfino, Giovenone, Lanino, Palmezzano, Sodoma, Spanzotti.

PALAZZO ARCIVESCOVILE: Giovenone, Lanino.

S. ANDREA: Lanino.

S. BERNARDINO: Lanino.

S. CRISTOFORO: Gaudenzio Ferrari, Giovenone, Lanino.

S. FRANCESCO: Giovenone.

S. GIULIANO: Giovenone, Lanino.

S. PAOLO: Lanino.

Verona. MUSEO DI CASTELVECCHIO: Altobello Melone, Badile, Benaglio, Bonsignori, Brusasorci, Giovanni Caroto, Giovan Francesco Caroto, Cavazzola, Civerchio, Farinati, Francesco dai Libri (Il Vecchio), Francia, Giolfino, Giovanni Agostino da Lodi, Girolamo dai Libri, Liberale da Verona, Mantegna, Marco d'Oggiono, Michele da Verona, Moretto, Domenico Morone, Francesco Morone, North-Italian Gothic, Parentino, Perugino, Albertino and Martino Piazza, Calisto Piazza, Pisanello, Solario, Stefano da Zevio, Torbido, Zaganelli.

CASA DEGLI ACOLITI (PIAZZA VESCOVADO): Farinati.

CASE MAZZANTI: Giolfino.

CASA NICOLIS: Farinati.

CASA PARMA LAVEZZOLA: Giolfino.

CASA DI TORELLO SARAINA (VIA DELLA STELLA): Torbido.

CASA VIGNOLA: Giovan Francesco Caroto.

PALAZZO ARCIVESCOVILE: Brusasorci, Giovan Francesco Caroto, Liberale da Verona.

PALAZZO DELLA GRAN GUARDIA: Brusasorci, Farinati, Francesco Morone.

PALAZZO RIDOLFI DA LISCA: Brusasorci.

PALAZZO N. 29 VIA DEL PARADISO: Cavazzola.

PALAZZO N. 320 VIA XX SETTEMBRE: Francesco Morone.

PIAZZA DELL'ERBE, N. 23: Girolamo dai Libri.

PIAZZA DELL'ERBE, N. 27: Liberale da Verona.

PIAZZA DELL'ERBE, N. 36: Giovan Francesco Caroto.

TABERNACLE IN VIA MAZZA: Domenico Morone.

Verona. Churches.

S. ANASTASIA: Altichiero, Bonsignori, Giovan Francesco Caroto, Farinati, Francesco dai Libri (Il Vecchio), Giolfino, Girolamo dai Libri, Liberale da Verona, Michele da Verona,

Francesco Morone, North-Italian Gothic, Pisanello, Stefano da Zevio.

S. BERNARDINO: Badile, Benaglio, Bonsignori, Giovan Francesco Caroto, Cavazzola, Giolfino, Domenico Morone, Francesco Morone.

— CAPPELLA DEI MEDICI O DI S. ANTONIO: Domenico Morone, Francesco Morone.

— OLD LIBRARY: Domenico Morone, Francesco Morone.

— REFECTORY: Francesco Morone.

S. CHIARA: Michele da Verona, Francesco Morone.

S. ELENA: Francesco dai Libri (Il Vecchio).

S. EUFEMIA: Brusasorci, Giovanni Caroto, Giovan Francesco Caroto, Moretto, Stefano da Zevio, Torbido.

S. FERMO MAGGIORE: Brusasorci, Giovan Francesco Caroto, Liberale da Verona, Francesco Morone, Pisanello, Stefano da Zevio, Torbido.

S. GIORGIO IN BRAIDA: Brusasorci, Giovanni Caroto, Giovan Francesco Caroto, Farinati, Girolamo dai Libri, Moretto, Romanino.

S. GIOVANNI IN FONTE: Farinati.

S. GIOVANNI IN VALLE: Brusasorci, North-Italian Gothic.

S. GIROLAMO: Giovan Francesco Caroto.

S. LORENZO: Brusasorci, Francesco dai Libri (Il Vecchio), Liberale da Verona.

MADONNA DI CAMPAGNA: Farinati.

S. MARIA DELLA VITTORIA NUOVA: Michele da Verona.

S. MARIA MATRICOLARE (DUOMO): Giovanni Caroto, Francesco dai Libri (Il Vecchio), Giolfino, Liberale da Verona, Francesco Morone, Torbido.

— BIBLIOTECA CAPITOLARE: Francesco dai Libri (Il Vecchio), Liberale da Verona.

S. MARIA IN ORGANO: Brusasorci, Giovan Francesco Caroto, Cavazzola, Farinati, Giolfino, Giulio Romano, Francesco Morone, Torbido.

S. MARIA DEL PARADISO: Farinati, Liberale da Verona.

S. MARIA DELLA SCALA: Brusasorci, Giovanni Caroto, Giolfino.

SS. NAZARO E CELSO: Badile, Bonsignori, Brusasorci, Cavazzola, Farinati, Francesco dai Libri (Il Vecchio), Girolamo dai Libri.

S. PAOLO (DI CAMPO MARZIO): Bonsignori, Giovanni Caroto, Farinati, Girolamo dai Libri.

S. PIETRO MARTIRE: Brusasorci.

S. PIETRO IN MONASTERO: Farinati.

S. STEFANO (FILIPPINI): Brusasorci, Giovanni Caroto, Farinati, Stefano da Zevio.

S. TOMASO CANTUARIENSE: Farinati, Girolamo dai Libri.

S. TOSCANA: Liberale da Verona.

SS. TRINITÀ: Brusasorci.

S. ZENO: Mantegna, Torbido.

CONVENTO DELLE STIGMATE: Liberale da Verona.

MARCHESE DI CANOSSA: Liberale da Verona.

Verona (Environs). CA' DI DAVID, PARISH CHURCH: Farinati.

SAN GIOVANNI LUPATOTO: Farinati.

BOSCHI S. MARCO: Liberale da Verona.

Versailles. JAMES H. HYDE: Balducci.

Vertine (Senese). PARISH CHURCH: Niccolò di Segna.

Verucchio (Rimini): COLLEGIATA DEI SS. MARTINO E FRANCESCO: Riminese Trecento.

Mantegna, Master of Griselda, Matteo di Giovanni, Lippo Memmi, Neroccio, Nuzi, Perugino, Pisanello, Raphael.

— A. MELLON BRUCE FUND: Ercole da Ferrara.

— ROSENWALD COLLECTION: Tura.

— TIMKEN COLLECTION: Correggio, Moroni.

— WARBURG GIFT: Pietro Lorenzetti, Domenico Morone.

— WIDENER COLLECTION: Benaglio, Benvenuto di Giovanni, De Predis, Mantegna, Moroni, Neroccio, Raphael.

CORCORAN GALLERY: Andrea Vanni.

DUMBARTON OAKS: Francesco di Gentile da Fabriano.

HOWARD UNIVERSITY: Fungai, Giampietrino, Pietro di Domenico da Montepulciano.

NATIONAL COLLECTION OF FINE ARTS, HARRIET LANE JOHNSTON BEQUEST: Luini.

WASHINGTON CATHEDRAL: Andrea da Salerno.

Washington Crossing (Pennsylvania). MRS F. JEWETT MATHER: Sassetta, Spanzotti.

Weimar. GOETHEHAUS: Palmezzano.

Wellesley (Massachusetts). COLLEGE, NORTON SIMON FOUNDATION LOAN: Francia.

Whitby (Yorks). MARQUESS OF NORMANBY: Luini.

Wiesbaden. STÄDTISCHES MUSEUM: Albertino and Martino Piazza, Scarsellino.

VON HENCKELL COLLECTION: Niccolò di Segna, Riminese Trecento.

Wilanow. CASTLE: Battista Dossi.

Williamstown (Massachusetts). STERLING AND FRANCINE CLARK ART INSTITUTE: Bergognone, Cozzarelli, Matteo di Giovanni, Perugino, Piero della Francesca, Signorelli, Ugolino di Nerio.

WILLIAMS COLLEGE, MUSEUM OF ART: Giovanni di Nicola da Pisa.

Winter Park (Florida). ROLLINS COLLEGE, KRESS COLLECTION: Riminese Trecento.

Woburn Abbey (Bedfordshire). DUKE OF BEDFORD: Moroni.

Wolfenbüttel. HERZOG AUGUST BIBLIOTHEK: Girolamo dai Libri.

Worcester (Massachusetts). ART MUSEUM: Andrea di Bartolo, Bernardino de' Conti, Boltraffio, Giulio Campi, Costa, Defendente Ferrari, Dosso, Farinati, Foppa, Francia, Meo da Siena, Moroni, Nelli, Pastura, Raphael, Simone Martini Follower, Sodoma, Solario, Stefano da Zevio.

— (EX): Antoniazzo Romano.

Wrotham Park. EARL OF STRAFFORD (EX): Parmigianino.

Würzburg. UNIVERSITÄT, WAGNER MUSEUM: Bergognone, Bernardino de' Conti.

York. CITY ART GALLERY: Bianchi Ferrari, Bonsignori, Francia, Fungai, Girolamo di Benvenuto, Parmigianino, Scarsellino.

Zagarolo (Lazio). S. LORENZO: Antoniazzo Romano.

Zagreb. ART GALLERY: Aleni, Andrea da Salerno, Antoniazzo Romano, Giulio Campi, Caporali, Defendente Ferrari, Francesco di Gentile da Fabriano, Gualtieri di Giovanni da Pisa, Lorenzo d'Alessandro, Maineri, Pacchiarotto, Palmezzano, Sassetta, Solario.

Zara (Dalmatia). MONASTERY OF S. MARIA: Andrea Vanni.

Zurich. KUNSTHAUS: Francesco Napolitano, Margarito, Nuzi, Riminese Trecento.

LANDOLTHAUS: Brescianino.

TOPIC MIMARA (EX): Lorenzetti Follower.

STEHLI COLLECTION: 'Ugolino Lorenzetti'.

Homeless. Altobello Melone, Ambrosi, Andrea di Bartolo, Andrea di Niccolò, Antoniazzo Romano, Aspertini, Barnaba da Modena, Bartolomeo di Tommaso da Foligno, Beccafumi, Benaglio, Benvenuto di Giovanni del Guasta, Bergognone, Bernardino de' Conti, Bernardino di Mariotto, Bertucci, Boccaccino, Bonfigli, Bonsignori, Bramantino, Brea, Brescianino, Butinone, Giulio Campi, Caporali, Cavazzola, Cecco di Pietro, Civerchio, Cola d'Amatrice, Costa, Cozzarelli, Defendente Ferrari, Dosso, Battista Dossi, Duccio Follower, Ercole da Ferrara, Eusebio da San Giorgio, Fei, Ferrarese, Ferrarese–Bolognese, Foppa, Francesco di Gentile da Fabriano, Francesco dai Libri (Il Vecchio), Fungai, Garofalo, Giovanni di Nicola da Pisa, Giovanni di Paolo, Giovanni Francesco da Rimini, Girolamo di Benvenuto, Giusto de' Menabuoi, Guariento, Liberale da Verona, Pietro Lorenzetti, Lorenzetti Follower, Lorenzo d'Alessandro, Luca di Tommè, Macrino d'Alba, Maineri, Marco d'Oggiono, Martino di Bartolomeo da Siena, Master of Panzano Triptych, Master of Stratonice, Matteo di Giovanni, Lippo Memmi, Ottaviano Nelli, Neroccio, Niccolò di Buonaccorso, Nuzi, Pacchia, Pacchiarotto, Palmerucci, Palmezzano, Parentino, Pastura, Pisanello, Raphael, Riminese Trecento, Romanino, Sano di Pietro, Sassetta, Scacco, Scarsellino, Segna di Bonaventura, Signorelli, Simone Martini, Solario, Taddeo di Bartolo, Tamagni, Traini, Urbani, Andrea Vanni, Lippo Vanni, Zaganelli, Zenale.